paris

FODOR'S TRAVEL PUBLICATIONS
NEW YORK • TORONTO • LONDON • SYDNEY • AUCKLAND

WWW.FODORS.COM

Contents

KEY TO SYMBOLS

- Map reference
- Address
- Telephone number
- Opening times
- Admission prices
- Métro station
- Bus number
- Train station
- Ferry/boat
- Driving directions
- Tourist office
- Tours
- Guidebook
- Restaurant
- Café
- Shop
- Toilets
- Number of rooms
- Parking
- No smoking
- Air conditioning
- Swimming pool
- Gym
- Cross reference
- Other useful information

How to Use this Book

Understanding Paris is an introduction to the city, its geography, economy and people. **Living Paris** gives an insight into the city today, while **The Story of Paris** takes you through its past.

For detailed advice on getting to Paris—and getting around once you are there—turn to **On the Move**. For useful practical information, from weather forecasts to emergency services, turn to **Planning**.

Paris's key attractions are listed alphabetically in **The Sights** and are located on the maps on pages 66–69. The key sightseeing areas are described on pages 70–75 and are circled in blue on the map on the inside front cover.

Turn to **What to Do** for information on shops, entertainment, nightlife, sport, children's activities and festivals and events. Entries are listed by these themes, then alphabetically. Shops are located on the maps on pages 172–175 and theatres on the maps on pages 194–197. The top shopping areas are described on pages 177–181 and circled in green on the map on the inside front cover.

Out and About offers five walks around Paris, a river trip and six excursions that encourage you to explore farther afield.

Eating and Staying gives you selected restaurants and hotels, listed alphabetically. Restaurants are located on the maps on pages 256–259 and hotels on the maps on pages 282–285.

Map references refer to the locator maps within the book or the street atlas at the end. For example, the Tour Eiffel has the grid reference 66 G7, indicating the page on which the map is found (66) and the grid square in which the tower sits (G7). Grid squares remain the same whatever page the map is on.

UNDERSTANDING PARIS

Paris is a seductive capital, legendary for its cuisine, fashion, art collections and architectural beauty. It is a vibrant international city and the heart of France's political, economic, social and cultural life. Although it is thoroughly modern, reminders of the past are vital to the tourism economy, and the government strictly enforces building codes and protects historic monuments. So change comes in smaller ways—in fashions, food styles and shop façades. Parisians are still as willing to take to the streets in protest as they were during the Revolution, although they can also demonstrate a strong conservative, conformist streak. The city is making a concerted effort to help visitors feel welcome and Parisians are friendlier and more helpful than they are sometimes reputed to be.

FINDING YOUR WAY AROUND

Paris has no shortage of must-see sights, but if you spend your visit dashing between the Eiffel Tower, Notre-Dame, the Louvre and Sacré-Cœur you'll miss out on the essence of the city. The secret to glimpsing Paris's heart is to enjoy the humble pleasures as well as the world-famous landmarks. Make time to people-watch in a café in St-Germain-des-Prés, relax in the peaceful Jardin du Palais Royal or shop for cheese at one of the local markets.

The Métro is a good way of getting around, with stops by all the key sights, but to really get to know the layout of the city, you can't beat walking between the *quartiers* (districts). Try wandering from St-Germain-des-Prés, through the Latin Quarter, to the Île de la Cité, or from Bastille to Le Marais and across to the Centre Georges Pompidou.

In addition to its *quartiers*, identified by name, Paris is broken into *arrondissements*, numbered 1 to 20. These spiral out in a clockwise direction from the Louvre. You can usually tell which *arrondissement* your destination is in by looking at the last two digits of the postal code.

Paris is split in two by the curving river Seine, with the northern section called the Right Bank

and the smaller southern part called the Left Bank. Thirty-seven bridges connect the two sides. Northeast of the Latin Quarter, two islands sit in the middle of the Seine: the historic Île de la Cité and the tiny Île St-Louis.

THE ECONOMY

Paris and the rest of the Île-de-France region are the economic powerhouse of France, accounting for 30 per cent of French GDP. The Île de France has a population of 11 million and is home to more than 650,000 companies, while Paris has just over two million residents and 300,000 companies. Tourism is one of its major economic strengths—Paris attracted 27 million visitors in 2006, over a million more than in 2004. Other key sectors are financial services, information technology, digital imaging, fashion, design and creative industries. It is not one of the world's cheapest cities—a 2007 survey of the cost of living in 144 cities ranked Paris as the 13th most expensive. As in many other European countries, France's economic growth is currently sluggish, and reform of state employment and pension laws is high on the agenda for the next five years. Trade unions and worker's groups are already planning stiff opposition to any loss of privileges.

PARIS'S DISTRICTS AT A GLANCE

Latin Quarter (Left Bank, east): Paris's heart of learning since the Middle Ages, packed with churches, medieval alleyways and the beautiful Jardin du Luxembourg.

St-Germain-des-Prés (Left Bank, central): Bordering the Latin Quarter and packed with cafés and bookshops.

Montparnasse (Left Bank, south): Dominated by the giant Tour Montparnasse.

Chaillot (Right Bank, west): Its focal point is the Palais de Chaillot, with its wonderful views across the Seine to the Eiffel Tower.

Champs-Élysées (Right Bank, west-central): Paris's most famous avenue is packed with shops, cinemas and cafés, and crowned by the Arc de Triomphe.

Faubourg St-Honoré (Right Bank, north of Champs-Élysées): The place to head for haute couture.

The flower market, Île de la Cité   Cabaret at Montmartre   Enjoying a drink on the Île St-Louis

Les Halles (Right Bank, central): Once the hub of market life, Les Halles now has a vast modern shopping complex, as well as Paris's most confusing Métro station.

Le Marais (Right Bank, east-central): Trendy cafés, shops and avant-garde art galleries. The Centre Georges Pompidou sits on its western border.

Bastille (Right Bank, east): Once the launch pad of the Revolution, now a fashionable nightspot, close to Le Marais.

Île de la Cité (on the Seine): This hectic island is the birthplace of Paris, and home to Notre-Dame, the Conciergerie and Sainte-Chapelle.

Île St-Louis (on the Seine): Smaller and quieter than its more famous cousin, the Île de la Cité.

Pigalle (Right Bank, south of Montmartre): The red-light district.

Montmartre (Right Bank, far north): This former village, on a hill overlooking the city, has two of Paris's most famous landmarks—Sacré-Cœur and, on the Pigalle border, the Moulin Rouge.

POLITICS

Paris is the undisputed heart of national power, although the government has been making some moves to decentralize and devolve power to the regions. The 2007 national elections were the most keenly contested in recent history, with two charismatic candidates – Ségolène Royal on the left, the first woman to stand for this position, and Nicolas Sarkozy on the right. Sarkozy won by a larger majority than the pundits had predicted, but met with stiff opposition from unions and student bodies during the autumn of 2007 as a series of strikes crippled the country. This battle between the two sides of the political spectrum will dictate the future of France for at least the next decade.

Paris is run by the popular Socialist mayor Bertrand Delanoë, who is working on the greening of the city. He has angered motorists by closing the highway running along the Seine's Right Bank to traffic in the summer, turning part of it into Paris Plage, an urban beach and pleasure park, complete with sand and deck chairs.

LANGUAGE AND SOCIETY

French is spoken by the entire population of France, although the country has some regional dialects. Most children study English, and many Parisians make the effort to speak it to visitors. The French are extremely proud of their language, however, and make a concerted effort to protect it from anglicization by coining French replacements for such words as Walkman (balladeur) and email (mèl).

Paris is a multicultural city, with large communities of people of North African, African, Vietnamese, Chinese and other origins. Like most major cities, it is undergoing gentrification, with families and people on lower incomes pushed out to the suburbs as property prices rise in the central districts.

Crime rates have increased in recent years, but Paris is still a fairly safe city for visitors, as long as they take reasonable precautions to protect their belongings from pickpockets.

LA DÉFENSE

Île de la Grande Jatte

Cimetière de Montmartre

17

Parc Monceau

Mare St-James

ALLÉE DE LONGCHAMP

Ruisseau de Longchamp

Bois de Boulogne

Lac Inférieur

Lac Supérieur

Lac Supérieur

Arc de Triomphe

8

ST-HONORÉ

BOULEVARD HAUSSMANN

Opéra Palais Garnier

AVENUE DES CHAMPS-ÉLYSÉES

CHAILLOT

Grand Palais

Place de la Concorde

RUE DE

Jardin des Tuileries

1

Seine

Palais de Chaillot

QUAI D' ORSAY

Musée Marmottan Monet

16

QUAI BRANLY

Tour Eiffel

Esplanade des Invalides

Musée d'Orsay

Parc du Champs de Mars

Les Invalides

Musée Rodin

ST-DES-

7

BD DE GRENELLE

RUE DE SÈVRES

6

AVENUE DE VERSAILLES

QUAI ANDRÉ CITROËN

RUE DE LA CONVENTION

LECOURBE

RUE

Tour Montparnasse

BOULEVARD MURAT

Parc André Citroën

RUE DE VAUGIRARD

Cimetière du Montparnasse

15

MONTPARNASSE

14

QUAI DU PONT DU JOUR

Parc Suzanne Lenglen

Parc Georges Brassens

BOULEVARD LEFEBVRE

Parc Departemental de l'Île St-Germain

D76

N189

BOULEVARD BRUNE

Île St-Germain

QUAI DE STALINGRAD

BOULEVARD PÉRIPHÉRIQUE

BD

D989

Parc Frederic Pic

D50

D71

AVENUE DE PARIS

D906

AVENUE ARISTIDE BRIAND

N20

D61

Seine

BD DE VERDUN

QUAI DU MARÉCHAL JOFFRE

Seine

D7

BOULEVARD JEAN JAURÈS

RUE MARTRE

D19

BOULEVARD VICTOR HUGO

AV GABRIEL PÉRI

D909

BOULEVARD BESSIÈRES

AVENUE DE CLICHY

BOULEVARD MALESHERBES

D908

BOULEVARD BINEAU

AVENUE CHARLES DE GAULLE

N13

BOULEVARD PÉRIPHÉRIQUE

AVENUE VICTOR HUGO

▬▬	**Motorway (Expressway)**
▬	**National road**
▬	**Regional road**
14	*Arrondissement numbers*
▪	**Atlas section**

0 ——— 1 km
0 ——— 1 mile

AVENUE MICHELET

Cimetière Parisien
de St-Ouen

BOULEVARD

PÉRIPHÉRIQUE

AUTOROUTE DU NORD
E19

AV DU PRÉSIDENT WILSON

N1

Canal St-Denis

D31

D114

AVENUE JEAN JAURÈS

SEINE-ST-DENIS

*Cimetière Parisien
de Pantin-Bobigny*

BOULEVARD NEY

RUE   ORDENER

Canal   de   l'Ourcq

AVENUE JEAN LOLIVE

N3

MONTMARTRE

**Sacré-
Cœur**

18

AVENUE DE FLANDRE

Parc de la
Villette

Bassin
de la Villette

19

Parc de la
Butte Rouge

D117

PIGALLE

9

RUE   LA

BOULEVARD   FAYETTE

10

Canal St-Martin

Parc des
Buttes Chaumont

RUE   DE   BELLEVILLE

Parc de
Belleville

BOULEVARD MORTIER

2

BD DE SÉBASTOPOL

MAGENTA

RÉPUBLIQUE

AV DE LA RÉPUBLIQUE

20

2

*Jardin du
Palais Royal*

**Musée des
Arts Décoratifs**

RIVOLI

3

**Musée d'Art et
d'Histoire du
Judaïsme**

**Musée
Picasso**

**Centre
Georges
Pompidou**

**LES
HALLES**

**Cimetière du
Père-Lachaise**

N302

**Musée du
Louvre**

LE MARAIS

**Musée
Carnavalet**

BOULEVARD   VOLTAIRE

PARIS

**Sainte-
Chapelle**

Conciergerie

*Île de
la Cité*

4

Notre-Dame

**Places des
Vosges**

11

**GERMAIN
PRÉS**

ST-MICHEL

**Musée National
du Moyen Âge**

*Île
St-Louis*

BASTILLE

BOULEVARD

*Jardin du
Luxembourg*

RUE ST-JACQUES

Panthéon

**Institut du
Monde Arabe**

BOULEVARD   DIDEROT

12

**QUARTIER
LATIN**

*Jardin des
Plantes*

La Mosquée

**Muséum
National
d'Histoire
Naturelle**

QUAI D'AUSTERLITZ

5

Parc de
Bercy

BERCY

N6

*Lac
Daumesnil*

BOULEVARD   ARAGO

BD VINCENT AURIOL

QUAI DE BERCY

BOULEVARD PONIATOWSKI

*Île de
Bercy*

*Île de
Reuilly*

*Bois de
Vincennes*

*Parc
Montsouris*

JOURDAN

13

RUE

AVENUE D'ITALIE

AVENUE DE CHOISY

DE

TOLBIAC

BOULEVARD MASSÉNA

Seine

D50B

QUAI DES CARRIÈRES

E50

3

*Parc
Kellerman*

AUTOROUTE DU SOLEIL

E15

D127

AUTOROUTE DU SOLEIL

AVENUE DE VERDUN

D94B

D124

D55

ED3

**VAL-DE-
MARNE**

BEST MUSEUMS AND GALLERIES

Centre Georges Pompidou (▷ 82–86): It's not to everyone's taste, but this eye-catching venue holds a vast collection of modern art.

Musée Carnavalet (▷ 114–115): Paris's history is brought to life with lavish re-creations of period rooms, memorabilia from the Revolution and prehistoric finds.

Musée du Louvre (▷ 118–123): One of the world's most famous art galleries—but you'll have to fight your way through crowds to see the *Mona Lisa*.

Musée National du Moyen Âge—Thermes de Cluny (▷ 128–129): Don't be put off by the mouthful of a title—this 15th-century mansion is home to a fascinating collection of medieval art, religious items and day-to-day objects.

Musée d'Orsay (▷ 130–134): This former station hosts a stunning collection of Impressionist paintings, and a lot more besides.

Musée Picasso (▷ 135): Paintings, sculptures and drawings by the great 20th-century artist, in the beautiful Hôtel Salé.

Musée Rodin (▷ 136): This wins a mention as much for its idyllic surroundings as its art. Auguste Rodin's mesmerizing sculptures are dotted around a soothing garden.

The wonderful station clock at the Musée d'Orsay (above)

Le Penseur (left) takes a pause for thought at the Musée Rodin

BEST LANDMARKS

Arc de Triomphe (▷ 76–79): The focal point for some of France's most prestigious celebrations.

Grande Arche (▷ 94): It's not yet as famous as the other landmarks mentioned here, but this colossal marble-clad arch symbolizes Paris's eye to the future.

Notre-Dame (▷ 137–141): France's most visited religious building, with wonderful views from its towers.

Sacré-Cœur (▷ 154–157): This glistening basilica crowns Montmartre's hill.

Tour Eiffel (▷ 164–169): Test your nerves on the third level, 280m (896ft) above ground.

A lively character from the Stravinsky Fountain, near the Centre Georges Pompidou

The Arc de Triomphe (left), commissioned by Napoleon

BEST VIEWS

All the landmarks mentioned above give unbeatable views, but the following are also worth a photo stop:

Palais de Chaillot (▷ 143): Go to the central terrace for wonderful views across the Seine to the Eiffel Tower.

Panthéon (▷ 144): You can see the Eiffel Tower from the front steps, but for the best panoramas, climb the 206 steps to the circular colonnade.

Parc de la Turlure (▷ 226): A small, out-of-the-way park in Montmartre with lovely views over Paris and an unusual view of the northern side of Sacré-Cœur.

Place de la Concorde (▷ 148): Look northwest along the Champs-Élysées to the Arc de Triomphe, southeast through the Jardin des Tuileries, and southwest across the Seine to the Palais Bourbon.

Pont des Arts (▷ 151): The breathtaking view downriver takes in the whole length of the Louvre along the Right Bank.

Tour Montparnasse (▷ 170): Take the lift to the 59th-floor terrace for vertigo-inducing views across the city.

Le Ciel de Paris restaurant, on the 56th floor of Tour Montparnasse

You can shop for almost anything in Paris

Dining at the Brasserie La Lorraine (above), near the Arc de Triomphe. Les Deux Magots (below) is one of Paris's most famous café-bars

Clubbing

BEST PLACES TO SHOP

Agnès B (▷ 184): Chic Parisian fashion.
Antik Batik (▷ 184): Ethnic-chic.
Fauchon (▷ 187): The best of French food—at a price.
Marché aux Puces de St-Ouen (▷ 107): Browse through this vast flea market and you may strike it lucky and find a worthwhile antique.
Shakespeare and Company (▷ 183): A famous American bookshop alongside the Seine.
Vanessa Bruno (▷ 186): Casual-chic fashion.

BEST PLACES TO STAY

L'Hôtel (▷ 287): Oscar Wilde spent his last days at this deluxe four-star hotel.
Hôtel Duc de St-Simon (▷ 289): In a beautifully decorated 18th-century mansion near the boulevard St-Germain.
Hôtel Square (▷ 292): An urban-chic four-star hotel close to the Eiffel Tower.
Pavillon de la Reine (▷ 293): Louis XIII's wife once lived in this 17th-century residence, on the place des Vosges.
Ritz (▷ 293): The ultimate in elegance and luxury, former guests include Coco Chanel and Ernest Hemingway.
Terrass Hotel (▷ 293): There are stunning views from some of the rooms at this four-star hotel in Montmartre.

BEST PLACES TO EAT

La Coupole (▷ 266): An art deco brasserie once frequented by Pablo Picasso.
Georges (▷ 268): Wonderful views and nouvelle cuisine on the top floor of the Centre Georges Pompidou.
Guy Savoy (▷ 269): A gastronomic temple, close to the Champs-Élysées.
Market (▷ 270): Contemporary venue with a raw bar and fusion food.
La Tour d'Argent (▷ 276): Chic interior, great views and exquisite French cuisine.

BEST CAFÉS AND SALONS DE THÉ

Café Beaubourg (▷ 213): A trendy café near the Centre Georges Pompidou.
Café de Flore (▷ 213): Follow in the footsteps of Jean-Paul Sartre.
Les Deux Magots (▷ 210): Hemingway was a frequent visitor to this café-bar in St-Germain-des-Prés.
Jean-Paul Hévin (▷ 270): Some of Paris's tastiest chocolate.
Muscade (▷ 271): Enjoy traditional afternoon tea in the grounds of the Palais Royal.

BEST BARS AND CLUBS

Les Bains Douches (▷ 213): Dance until 6am at this club.
Café de l'Industrie (▷ 210): A stylish bar in the trendy Bastille area.
Fourmi (▷ 211): This bar, with its retro interior, is popular with arty types.
New Régine's Club (▷ 215): A popular restaurant-club, near the Champs-Élysées.
VIP Room (▷ 215): Popular with the beautiful and the moneyed.

THE BEST OF PARIS

TOP 15 EXPERIENCES

Get a bird's-eye view of Paris at night by climbing the Eiffel Tower (▷ 164–169) or the Arc de Triomphe (▷ 76–79).

Sit in a café in St-Germain-des-Prés and watch the world go by, or find a bench in the animated Jardin du Luxembourg or Jardin des Tuileries.

Take a boat trip along the Seine—it's a cliché but it really is a great way to appreciate the city's major landmarks (▷ 234–235).

Visit place des Vosges (▷ 150) on a Sunday afternoon, when the cafés are packed with Parisians relaxing to the sounds of street musicians.

Take advantage of late-opening nights at the Louvre (Wednesdays and Fridays) and Musée d'Orsay (Thursdays), when there are fewer people.

Indulge in some retail therapy in one of the fashion capitals of the world (▷ 177–181 for some of the top shopping areas).

Stroll along the Champs-Élysées, Paris's most famous avenue.

Take the Métro out to Montmartre for a taste of village life and wonderful views of the city.

Visit Notre-Dame cathedral just before a service is due to start.

Haggle at one of the city's markets (▷ 190–192), where you can buy anything from cheese and olives to furniture and chandeliers.

Leave your Métro *carnet* behind for an afternoon and take a wander—it's the best way to get to know the layout of the city (▷ 224–233 for some suggestions).

Treat yourself to a meal in one of Paris's top restaurants—if your credit card is up to it.

See a performance at the prestigious Opéra Palais Garnier or the striking Opéra Bastille, or experience the glitz of a show at the famous Moulin Rouge.

Escape the city and enjoy some fresher air in the leafy Bois de Vincennes or Bois de Boulogne (▷ 236–237).

Stroll through the elegant 19th-century shopping arcades known as Les Galeries (▷ 93).

(From left to right) paintings of Paris; gazing up at the Eiffel Tower; street musicians in Montmartre

The Moulin Rouge (below)

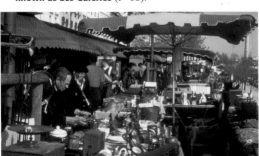

Walking the dog in the Bois de Vincennes (above).
Antiques stands at Bastille (left)

Living Paris

This luxury foodstore (left), in place de la Madeleine, has been selling mustard since 1747

A LA CARTE

Les Bonnes Recettes de la Truffe

An informal lunch in the Jardin du Palais Royal (left). Truffle recipes for a more sophisticated meal (top right)

Food in Paris

A traditional croissant

Since Paris no longer has a monarchy, it would be easy to assume the class system is dead and buried. Wrong. In this city, one is defined by the table one chooses. No one eats for mere sustenance—food is a lifestyle statement, an evening's entertainment and a way of life. At the sharp end, new chefs flit in and out of vogue with the changing of the seasons. Each September's newspaper reviews can determine the fortunes of a fashionable restaurant as surely as a drama critic's pen assures the life or death of a new musical on Broadway.

However, the chic eateries are but the tip of a gastronomic iceberg. Regional restaurants reflect the diversity of French cuisine, with special dishes from Auvergne and Alsace, the Loire and Provence, offering French out-of-towners a taste of home and Parisians a hint of what lies beyond the city. Café culture has an equally wide following, with the smart crowd sipping designer coffees on terraces outside the more fashionable museums and blue-collar Parisians chatting in slang at the zinc counters of their local bars.

Le Train Bleu

High above the 21st-century fleet of TGV high-speed trains at Gare de Lyon nestles a relic from travel's golden age. Le Train Bleu is a belle-époque station brasserie of the type that elsewhere on Europe's flagship railway system has been demolished to make room for high-tech efficiency and cutting-edge design. The restaurant featured in the 1972 film *Travels with My Aunt* and on news broadcasts when President Mitterrand famously entertained Margaret Thatcher there. Ornate mirrors, chandeliers and paintings have been lovingly restored to match the moustachioed waiters, with their starched ankle-length aprons. Service is as unhurried as ever, and it would not be unusual to spend longer over lunch than on the three-hour journey to the south of France.

A mouth-watering dessert (below) from Gérard Mulot's patisserie

Enjoying a meal in the Restaurant du Jour (above).
The elegant Train Bleu (below) is not your average station diner

No ice cream, please, it's summer!

When the best ice-cream store in town is closed, you can be sure that winter is long gone and summer has arrived. One of the great ironies of Paris is that from around mid-July until the end of August, the Maison Berthillon, on the Île St-Louis, shuts up shop, since true Parisians spend the height of summer on the coast. Likewise, the owners have resisted franchising the Berthillon name, so for the remaining months of the year, queues extend round the block as staff take their time preparing delicate scoops of home-made *glaces* and sorbets.

The Star of Stars

In France there's only one measure of culinary success, the Michelin star. Entry into this exclusive club guarantees success, but standards are high and only four restaurants within the Paris *périphérique* meet the exacting criteria. The top rating of three stars is awarded to very few restaurants so the current 'King of the Kitchen' has to be Alain Ducasse. The only chef to have been awarded three Michelin stars for restaurants in three different countries, Ducasse was born in Castelsarrazin in 1956 and received his first Michelin stars at La Terrasse restaurant in Juan-les-Pins in 1984. He is currently executive chef at Plaza Athénée restaurant on avenue Montaigne, and in 2007 he took the helm of the Jules Verne restaurant in the Eiffel Tower.

Celebrated chef
Alain Ducasse

Shut your eyes and enjoy the taste

In the 1990s, when interior decoration began to upstage the food in some of the hippest restaurants, there were mutterings that style was in danger of eclipsing the substance of cuisine. Then, a novel dining concept hit town: eating in pitch darkness. The idea was simple. Visitors would be escorted by blind waiters into a dining room with no light or windows. Deprived of sight, diners relied on other senses to judge the meal. And so a witty assault on food fads evolved into a reappraisal of priorities. You can try the experience for yourself at Dans le Noir (51 rue Quincampoix, 75004; tel 01 42 77 98 04; www.danslenoir.fr), near Centre Georges Pompidou.

Le fast food

After decades of barely concealed hostility, Paris is learning to love *le fast food*, or at any rate *le Marks & Spencer sandwich*. When the Paris branch of this British institution closed in 2001 (to prime ministerial protest), there came an unlikely rescuer, France's most decorated chef, Alain Ducasse, who reinvented the deli sandwich bar with the opening of BE Boulangépicier, his upscale interpretation of the deli. Here, eat-in customers enjoy their meals standing up. What next? Trend-watchers suggest Yatoo Patoo machines—vending machines that offer a full meal—springing up in the unlikeliest corners. The name means Everything Everywhere (*il y a tout partout*)!

Browse in the boutiques in Galerie Vivienne (top, right) or at an exclusive store on the place Vendôme (right)

Style in Paris

Parisian style takes a lot of effort or none at all. It is the expensively coutured mannequin walking her identically attired and tinted dog along the Champs-Élysées. Then again, it is also the scruffy unshaven student with his upturned collar and dangling cigarette, flirting with the pretty girl outside a Métro station.

Paris loves style, in that it celebrates those who are happy with and proud of their own image. Parisian style is as much about lifestyle as the packaging. It is not enough simply to wear the right clothes, you must wear them in the right places, be it a sophisticated bar in the 8th *arrondissement* or a hang-out for poets in the Bastille district. Just as new designers emerge with each fashion week, so up-and-coming streets stake their claim on the consumer map: People shopping for traditional art and antiques choose the galleries by the Louvre and Musée d'Orsay; those on the cutting edge prefer the racier art showrooms around the quai d'Austerlitz; and the truly self-confident set their own trends with finds from the flea markets.

Haute couture for less

Every well-tailored Parisian knows the avenue Matignon, but they may not be so ready to admit familiarity with the rue de la Pompe. After all, it would be folly to confess to having spent a mere fraction of the showroom price on a genuine Moschino or Versace original. Nevertheless, canny good dressers will brave the hordes picking their paths through the racks at the seven Réciproque stores in the road in order to snatch up Lacroix and Dior. Since celebrities rarely wear an outfit again after it has been photographed by the paparazzi, so Réciproque buys them to resell. To deter thieves, Chanel suits have their prized buttons removed, to be sewn back on once the transaction is complete!

Open secrets of the Left Bank

The nearest the art and antiques dealers of the Left Bank get to shouting about their wares is during the Cinq Jours de l'Objet Extraordinaire, in late spring. The Carré Rive Gauche is an association of galleries on the tributaries of the rue du Bac and rue de Lille. For five days in early summer, the dealers choose to flaunt their most prized possessions. Each shop selects one special item to promote. To celebrate this uncharacteristic sharing of buried treasure, red carpets suddenly appear outside and abundant floral displays grace the doorways. In recent years, visitors have been invited to admire Venetian chandeliers long hidden away in a Sicilian palazzo, Egyptian textiles and rare Beauvais tapestries.

Even the buses are telling you to go shopping (below)

Police officers have joined the in-line skating craze

It's a girl thing

No matter how expensive the hotel or how hard you push the credit card, as a casual visitor to Paris you can usually just look on in envy at the assurance of the true society *Parisienne*. But now you have the chance to join the ladies who lunch, women who shop and glamorous patrons of the arts. For a price, women staying at the Hôtel Meurice are paired with a chic local girlfriend for the day and taken out on the town. They can visit Left Bank artists' studios for a private viewing, stop off for a bite to eat and a gossip at the latest see-and-be-seen restaurant, or go shopping with the girls, touring the boutiques of up-and-coming fashion designers.

Choccy couture

Since the opening of the Carrousel du Louvre, the catwalk has rarely been free from the popping of flashbulbs and the scrutiny of the fickle arbiters of style. But between the seasonal prêt-à-porter shows and Paris Fashion Week, there is one event where all the critics agree that every item of clothing is good enough to eat. Edible couture is the highlight of the autumn *Salon du Chocolat*, with a catwalk show combining the talents and skills of the finest chocolatiers with the city's more daring designers. Despite the irony of painting whisper-thin supermodels in calorie-laden treats, the event appeals to those who like their style off the shoulder as much as on the tip of the tongue.

In the fast lane

The Champs-Élysées is packed with traffic even in the small hours, but once a month the famous avenue closes to cars. To benefit, pack your in-line skates. Pari-Roller is the social event of the week, as tens of thousands gather near Montparnasse station on Friday evening. Skaters start to gather at 9.30 and at 10pm the crowd becomes a parade and sets off to explore the city. Strictly for experienced skaters, the route varies each week. Itineraries are posted on the website before the event. Once a month, two hours after the skaters have left the starting point, they turn into place Charles-de-Gaulle for the high-speed descent down the Champs-Élysées.

Catwalk couture by Jean-Charles de Castelbajac and Jean-Paul Gaultier (right)

Contemporary meets classic: the Institut du Monde Arabe (far right) and the Louvre through the glass pyramid (top)

Culture and
Design

The futuristic Géode at Parc de la Villette (above)

For a city that is so proud of its artistic and architectural heritage, Paris is surprisingly open to new and challenging ideas. Somehow, the integration of the classic and the avant-garde is irresistibly successful. One of the most controversial encounters between old and new was I. M. Pei's Pyramid in the courtyard of the Louvre. Some people were appalled at the idea of setting such an uncompromisingly modern structure within the arms of the palace. Yet the brilliant play of light and water not only revived the museum, but focused attention on the beauty of the original building. Likewise, the 1970s Centre Georges Pompidou stands next to the 16th-century church of St-Merri, and, on the Left Bank, the shadows of the 1980s Institut du Monde Arabe mingle with those of Notre-Dame, on the Île de la Cité. The same refreshing attitude marks out the city's cultural life. Where else are you as likely to see a Katharine Hepburn film as an Eddie Murphy flick? As varied a crowd will pack a church for an evening of Vivaldi as will join a jam session by street musicians.

The film that saved the station

When Orson Welles came to Europe to film Franz Kafka's *The Trial*, he saved a Paris landmark from demolition. Having just learned that the production had run out of money and could no longer afford expensive Yugoslav locations, he looked across the river from his room in the Hôtel Meurice and saw two full moons—the twin rose windows of the abandoned Gare d'Orsay. He was inspired to film the rest of the movie inside the imposing railway station, so Orsay became a cathedral and even a court of law. The station had a happier ending than the movie, since filming delayed demolition and gave protesters time to lobby the Ministry of Culture to convert the terminus into one of the world's great museums.

Fashion designer Jean-Paul Gaultier (left).
Music at the Théâtre des Champs-Élysées
(above).
The courtyard at the Palais Royal (below)

Bigger than the big screen

No matter how huge the blockbuster, there is one cinema in Paris that can always be relied upon to upstage the action on screen. Le Grand Rex, on the boulevard Poissonnière, is the last of the world's extravagant picture palaces of the 1930s still operating as a mainstream cinema. A Mediterranean night sky adorns the interior of the spectacular domed building, and an arched art deco stage once hosted lavish shows. You can rent an audioguide for a fabulous high-tech walk backstage, through and above the screen, where you'll face a life-size King Kong that escapes its tethers and terrorizes chorus girls waiting in the wings. Eventually, you'll become the unsuspecting star of a film premiere, performing on the big screen alongside the movie greats.

Monsieur Shakespeare's first night

Shakespeare is big in Paris. His plays pack commercial theatres and the Bois de Boulogne has a garden planted with flowers, herbs and trees mentioned in his works. But one play had to wait until 1999 before receiving its Parisian premiere—the jingoistic *Henry V*, in which English bowmen decimate the French army at the Battle of Agincourt. In fact, outside the village itself, Agincourt remains relatively unknown in France. Director Jean-Louis Benoît risked opening his Avignon festival production in the capital, managing to blame the defeat of the French army on an inept and weak monarchy. The choice of venue was laden with ironies—La Cartoucherie, a former French army arsenal, is in the grounds of the Château de Vincennes, where the victorious Henry V died in 1422.

Redesigning Paris

He was the man who changed the face of café society, with the most influential and much missed Café Costes. Philippe Starck first came to the public's attention when he was commissioned to strip François Mitterrand's presidential apartments at the Élysée Palace of their stuffy imperial furnishings and replace them with the bare minimum. Today, Starck's designs are the sign that you have arrived in a city where style is more important than budget. Nightclubs and bars that have undergone the Philippe Starck treatment are strictly reserved for the beautiful people—the door policy at Les Bains Douches nightclub, which Starck designed in the 1970s, is still strictly observed. Weekenders coming from London can imbibe the Starck chic before reaching town, in Eurostar trains revitalized by the designer.

Summer cinema

Summer is the season of cinema in the open air—and in the most unlikely places. From mid-July until the end of August huge screens are erected on the lawns of the Parc de La Villette for the annual Cinéma en Plein Air. Specializing in original-language movies with French subtitles, this is the big event of the picnic season. For the last fortnight of the event, the entire city takes part in Cinéma au Clair de Lune, a series of moonlight screenings in appropriate locations. Previous festivals have seen *Le Fabuleux Destin d'Amélie Poulain* in the streets of Montmartre, the 1947 version of *Les Misérables* outside Victor Hugo's home on place des Vosges, seafaring yarns on the canal banks and major pastoral idylls in the outlying parks.

**Philippe Starck's juice squeezer (above, inset).
Part of the zany
Stravinsky Fountain
(above, top)**

Filming the 1957 movie *Funny Face* (below), with Audrey Hepburn and Fred Astaire

French actress Juliette Binoche (left), star of *Chocolat* (2000) and *The English Patient* (1996)

Entertainment in Paris

Paris comes with a musical soundtrack. Any place that has inspired so many classic love songs is bound to lure musicians from all corners. On the Métro at all hours, outside packed restaurants at noon and in shop doorways by night, itinerant musicians play popular tunes. The music reaches its crescendo at the *Fête de la Musique* on 21 June, with live bands and orchestras in the main railway stations and huge stages erected in public squares for a night of free concerts.

Music cuts across society, no more so than at the end of the Gay Pride celebrations in June, when party animals of all persuasions dance on the banks of the Seine as the celebrations end with the several-thousand strong dawn chorus of *La Vie en Rose*.

Indoor entertainment ranges from productions at the concert halls and the two opera houses to feathered and sequinned showgirl performances. Between the two extremes is a drama scene as varied as that in the West End or Broadway. Many English-language productions are also staged.

The Moulin Rouge lit up at night

The fabulous Paris of Amélie

Jean-Pierre Jeunet's cinematic vision *Le Fabuleux Destin d'Amélie Poulain* (2001) re-established Paris as a city for smooching. Keen to capture for themselves a hint of the romance, visitors eagerly scout locations from the film's most memorable moments. Much of the movie was shot around Montmartre, where the Métro station and streets are just as bustling and picturesque in real life as on screen. The actual café and shops featured in the film are on rue des Trois Frères. Other key scenes took place at the Gare de l'Est and Gare du Nord, behind which lies Amélie's hideaway, the Canal St-Martin. The funfair, where actress Audrey Tautou and actor Mathieu Kassowitz ride the ghost train, is the Foire du Trône, in the Bois de Vincennes, a fair which takes place every April and May.

The Opéra Palais Garnier (below) was once the largest venue of its kind in the world

Paris's entertainment scene ranges from partying at Club Med World (above) to listening to a brass band in the Jardin du Luxembourg (left, top)—not forgetting the famous Moulin Rouge (left)

Cabaret on the hill

Just as Baz Luhrmann's sensational 2001 film *Moulin Rouge* dazzled audiences, so the sails of the famous red windmill still dominate the entertainment strip between Pigalle and Clichy, at the foot of Montmartre's hill. Yet beyond the glitz of today's touristy Moulin lie many less lavish, but still authentic, cabaret shows. Rue des Martyrs is home to rumbustuous musical entertainment every night. Michou, with his outrageous glasses and sharp suits, still presents Paris's most famous drag revue. Across the road is the rival drag show at Madame Arthur, while more conventional cancan can be seen at the fabulously brash La Nouvelle Eve, at 25 rue Fontaine. For a glimpse of the former haunt of penniless artists, climb Montmartre's hill to Au Lapin Agile, at 22 rue des Saules.

Stars in their natural habitat

The gossip columns will have you believe that movie stars always hang out at places such as the Buddha Bar (▷ 210). In truth, celluloid legends who call Paris home tend to be seen in the streets around their houses and apartments. Icon Catherine Deneuve likes to shop and sip on the Left Bank—not around the postcard vendors of St-Michel, but the quieter streets beyond the boulevard St-Germain. Le Bon Marché is the department store where you are most likely to bump into a French film star doing the weekly shop. Opposite the shop is the Hotel Lutétia, where Miss Deneuve may be seen granting an interview to journalists from *Madame Figaro* or *Marie Claire*.

Dancing by the bridge of songs

Films sell Paris as a place where lovers burst into song and dance at the drop of a shoulder strap. The most danced under, over and on bridge in the city is le Pont Neuf. This was the backdrop for Gene Kelly to sweep Leslie Caron off her feet to the strains of George Gershwin's 'Our Love is Here to Stay' in *An American in Paris* (1951). Woody Allen paid homage to that scene when he re-created the moment, with the help of Goldie Hawn in *Everyone Says I Love You* (1996). The location shared top billing in *Les Amants du Pont Neuf* (1991) and was the spot where Jeanne Moreau dived into the Seine in François Truffaut's *Jules et Jim* (1962). Romance also blossomed here for Audrey Hepburn and Fred Astaire in *Funny Face* (1957).

Of petticoats and safety pins

These days the whirl and blur of bright petticoats of the cancan are as much a part of Paris sightseeing as the Eiffel Tower and Louvre. But it was not always socially acceptable. Banned as licentious, the cancan was performed, without underwear, beyond the city limits by prostitutes when it arrived in Paris in the first half of the 19th century. When dance halls gained respectability, performers were obliged to wear suitable undergarments onstage. Some performers continued to indulge in a little private enterprise by tearing holes in opportune places, and so, at the Moulin Rouge, Monsieur Durocher sat in the wings to check that the girls were properly dressed before going on stage. If he discovered a tear, he would repair it with safety pins.

ENTERTAINMENT IN PARIS 19

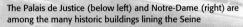

The Palais de Justice (below left) and Notre-Dame (right) are among the many historic buildings lining the Seine

The River Seine

Kindness is its own reward

There is a sign above the door of the rickety American bookstore across the water from Notre-Dame, in the Latin Quarter, that reads 'Be not inhospitable to strangers, lest they be angels in disguise'. Shakespeare and Company is a strange and delightful sanctuary, where new and second-hand volumes stacked on the floor or arranged on shelves are pushed aside to store a blanket here and a sleeping bag there. Visiting writers and artists are welcome to sleep among the paperbacks. When fire ravaged part of the old building, many such strangers worked tirelessly to repay hospitality to angels in disguise.

To say that a river runs through Paris is to do the Seine a disservice. It would be fairer to acknowledge that Paris runs along the river. Originally the entire city was surrounded by the Seine, when the Romans founded Lutetia on the Île de la Cité.

Principal sites are strung along the riverbanks. From early February to early January, a water shuttle—the Batobus—stops at many of them, from the Eiffel Tower in the west, to the Bibliothèque Nationale de France–Site François Mitterrand in the east. Year round, *bateaux mouches* dinner cruises glide past the illuminated buildings and bridges for those who prefer to sightsee from their table. But to discover the true spirit of the riverside and all its contrasts, try to explore the *quais* on foot. There are floating nightclubs by quai François Mauriac on Saturday nights, families strolling along quai de Montebello on Sunday afternoons and the St-Michel *bouquinistes* selling old books and vintage postcards.

Party time

It is the ultimate Parisian dilemma: Do you stay in town and be seen at all the key openings, private views and fashion shows, or get away from the city and indulge in the blend of beach, barbecue and sheer self-indulgence that is a holiday in the sun? Since many Parisians love to travel, but hate to leave home, Paris has a special resort on the banks of the Seine (pictured above). Saving locals the trouble of going to Mauritius and Martinique, Club Med World has the requisite bamboo umbrellas, pitchers of fruit punch and sun-kissed barmen making cocktails. Robbie Williams and Britney Spears have joined locals dancing in the converted Bercy wine warehouse for a one-night holiday.

Paris at sunset (left)

Browsing in the Shakespeare and Company bookshop (below)

A poster in the Galerie Documents, on the rue de Seine (right)

Pegasus guards Pont Alexandre III (below)

Liberty

The allée des Cygnes is the Seine's lesser-known island. By night it is a popular lovers' rendezvous, but what raises eyebrows on the passing pleasure boats is the sight of the Statue of Liberty by the Pont de Grenelle, facing west to New York. This miniature version of Auguste Bartholdi's famous work is a reminder that the original was a gift from France. Paris is dotted with souvenirs of Bartholdi's giant creations, with another incarnation of Liberty's head peeking out from the bushes of the Jardin du Luxembourg. At place Denfert-Rochereau stands Gustave Eiffel's copper copy of Bartholdi's remarkable Lion of Belfort. The original is sculpted into the famous fortifications of the city of Belfort, in eastern France.

When the pool floats again

Long before the Paris Plage idea, citizens of the capital would cool off at Piscine Deligny, a floating swimming pool moored at quai Voltaire. Constructed from the timbers of the *Dorade*, the ship that brought Napoleon's ashes to Paris, the lido welcomed the beautiful people to flaunt perfect tans by day and hosted fabulous soirées for the 'in' crowd until one day in 1993 when one of the pontoons moved and the legendary pool was swallowed up by the Seine in less than an hour. Parisians were in mourning, but not for long. In July 2006 the Piscine Joséphine Baker was opened on the river in front of the Bibliothèque Nationale de France—Site François Mitterand. The complex, built on a huge barge, has more luxuries than its predecessor, including a sauna, whirlpool and solarium.

Down by the riverside

An eclectic collection of boats is moored along the eastern section of the Seine. In the ungainly shadow of the Bibliothèque Nationale de France, the Chinese junk and light-boats become Paris's floating nightclub district, where the young and charmed take to the decks to dance until dawn. Waterside partying is the latest thing. Or is it? Farther along the quaysides, just beyond the Bois de Vincennes, is Joinville-le-Pont, where the Seine meets the River Marne. Here blue-collar Parisians have been dancing at the water's edge for generations. Real *guinguette* bars, where the grandparents of today's party animals romanced by the light of the moon, still have accordionists who play the songs of Edith Piaf and you can dance to the strains of java, tango and the waltz.

The Eiffel Tower at night—the city's ultimate romantic view

There's no getting away from romance, even among the skyscrapers of La Défense district (above)

The Pont des Arts (right) is one of Paris's most romantic bridges

Romance in Paris

Je t'aime

Incurable romantic Frédéric Baron asked visitors to Montmartre to write down 'I love you' in their own language in the 1990s. He collected more than a thousand *billets-doux* (love letters), which were transcribed by calligrapher Claire Kito and transformed into a mural of tiles and broken hearts by artist Daniel Boulogne. This wall, Le Mur des Je t'Aime, stands in the Jean Rictus garden on place des Abbesses. Here, holiday romances are sealed by young lovers sharing their innermost thoughts in languages such as Esperanto, Basque and Navajo. The garden has cult status among lovers and serial wooers alike, and the wall has a website (www.lesjetaime.com), where lovers can perfect their pronunciation in order to melt hearts in situ at dusk.

Blame it on the love songs and movie clichés, but Paris is a city of romance. The legendary tolerance and celebration of passion in a city that blends intimacy and anonymity lends a frisson to any encounter. Couples celebrating a silver wedding still find the buzz of an affair to remember. Romantic locations abound, from the Pont des Arts footbridge across the Seine (good for watching sunsets) to the temple of love perched on top of a cliff in the Parc des Buttes-Chaumont. This is accentuated by the sheer range of restaurants designed for 'sweet nothings' to be whispered across a candlelit table. A literary heritage illuminated by tragic lovers and grand passions also helps to fuel present-day relationships. But Parisian romance is not just about candlelit dinners and sunset-watching on bridges: There is little to match the magic of breakfasting on onion soup in a Les Halles bistro after a night on the town, then walking home hand-in-hand through the flower market.

Outkissing Rodin

Auguste Rodin's *The Kiss* is immortalized in stone in his former home on the rue de Varenne, now the Musée Rodin. Visitors wishing to preserve their own French kiss should make their way past an even more popular museum. A few steps beyond the Centre Georges Pompidou is the tiny passage Molière. Here, artist Brigitte Massoutier will take a life cast of the lips of your loved one and provide you with a permanent reminder of your Parisian passion in plaster or bronze. She made her name through casting babies' hands and feet as Mother's Day gifts. But her workshop has become a magnet to romantics seeking to commemorate *grands amours* with frozen kisses. The studio is open on Friday and Saturday afternoons.

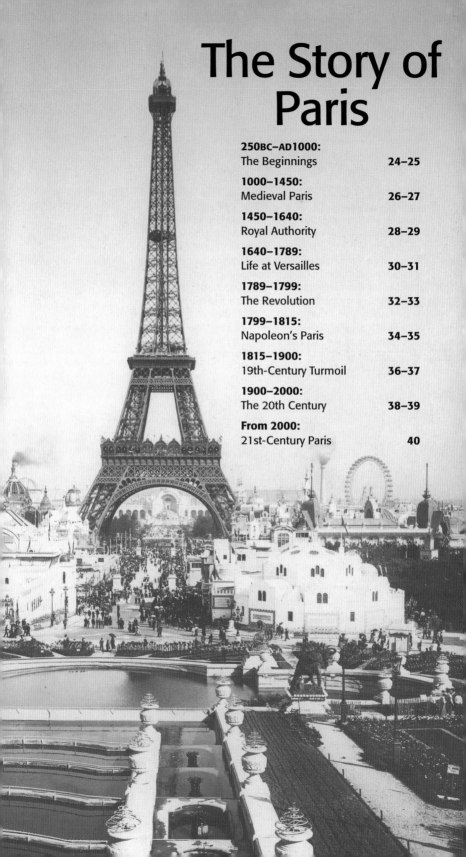

The Story of Paris

The Beginnings
Paris

Paris began on the Île de la Cité, an island in the middle of the river Seine, when a peaceful Celtic tribe known as the Parisii set up camp there in around 250BC. The Romans began moving up from southern France in about 52BC, after making what is now Provence into a colony in 118BC. They sometimes met tough resistance from Celtic tribes, who united under Vercingetorix to confront them. But the Celts were crushed and all the lands from Belgium to the Mediterranean, and from the Atlantic to the Alps, were renamed Gaul by the Romans. The principal Gallic city was Lyon, while Paris, known as Lutetia, remained a northern backwater. With the collapse of Roman rule in the 5th century AD, Germanic tribes invaded from across the Rhine. Chief among those who settled in northern Gaul were the Franks, who based themselves at Paris. They grew immensely powerful and extended the Frankish empire until, under Charlemagne in the 8th century AD, the Franks controlled all of Roman Gaul. In AD987, Hugues Capet, the Count of Paris, was crowned king of France and made Paris his capital.

Lutetia

The Roman town grew, spreading onto the Left Bank of the Seine. It had a theatre, a forum (public square) and a 10,000-seat arena for circuses and popular entertainments such as pitting humans against animals. The Romans also built luxurious public baths, where people met to wash, have a massage, gossip and engage in wrestling contests. On the island, still occupied mainly by Parisii, the Romans built a temple to Jupiter. Then disaster struck. In the 3rd century AD, ferocious warrior tribes from Germany attacked the town and destroyed it before being defeated themselves. The town was triumphantly rebuilt, enlarged, modernized and renamed Paris. The barbarians' fate was to be the latest entertainment in the arena.

These baths (left), in what is now the Latin Quarter, were the hub of social life in Gallo-Roman Paris

Charlemagne enters Paris (below)

Julius Caesar (above) ordered his troops to take Paris in 52BC

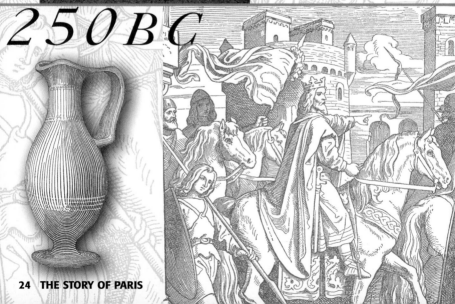

250BC

St. Denis

St. Denis, the patron saint of France, was born in Italy and was one of seven bishops sent by the Pope to convert Gaul to Catholicism in AD250. Denis became the first bishop of Paris and was so good at converting the populace that the Romans had him killed. He was beheaded at Montmartre (Martyr's Hill) and, according to legend, the indefatigable Denis picked up his own head and kept walking. It is more likely that his body was thrown into the Seine and later rescued by followers, who built the Basilica of St-Denis on the spot. And where did the legend come from? St. Denis was always depicted with his head in his hands and in the medieval mind image and reality became one.

St. Geneviève

St. Geneviève, patroness of Paris, was a forceful woman who won through despite the misogyny of the times. She even saved Paris from Attila the Hun. Born in Nanterre in AD422, it is said that St. Germain of Auxerre caught the look in her eye when she was seven and suggested she dedicate her life to God. She did so, eating only twice a week and having frequent visions. The Bishop of Paris appointed Geneviève Mother Superior to the nuns of Paris and her inspiration and energy helped the Parisians when Attila's armies approached the city in AD451. She told the citizens to trust in God and to repent of their sins. When they did, the Huns turned away and galloped on to Châlons-en-Champagne.

Clovis, Chief of the Franks

Geneviève's spiritual powers did not work against the next wave of invaders. With Roman power collapsing, it was impossible for the inhabitants of Paris to fight off warrior tribes like the Franks. With their powerful leader Clovis at their head, the Franks swept into Paris and took control. Clovis based himself in the offices of the expelled Roman governor on the Île de la Cité, and commanded his troops as they fought other tribes for more territory. Geneviève visited Clovis, preached to him, and eventually converted the warrior king to Christianity. A changed man, Clovis built an abbey where in death he and his queen Clotilde could be buried alongside saintly Geneviève.

Charlemagne

The power of the Franks culminated in the rise of a majestic yet simple leader, Charlemagne, or Carolus Magnus (Charles the Great). He was a hero of poetry, song and legend and grandson of Carolus Martel (Charles The Hammer), who had triumphed over the Moorish forces invading from the south. Charlemagne directed an indomitable army into every corner of Gaul and much of Germany and Italy, carving out a vast kingdom. Throughout his dominion, he imposed a devout Christianity and the pursuit of learning. In AD800, the Pope crowned him the first Holy Roman Emperor. Charlemagne the Frank had proved beyond doubt that Gaul was now France.

This bust, decorating the 17th-century Hôtel Libéral Bruant, in Le Marais, harks back to earlier times

Hugues Capet (right), King of France in the 10th century

St. Geneviève (below, left), the patron saint of Paris

The Celtic leader Vercingetorix (below)

AD1000

Medieval Paris

The growing importance of Paris in medieval times had much to do with the city's position on the river Seine. The institutions of church and government stood on the Île de la Cité, while much of the population lived in simple homes on the Left Bank. Many were skilled craftsmen, while others continued to farm the land. Important religious sites, notably at St-Denis and St-Germain, attracted large commercial fairs that brought in thousands of traders and visitors. Everything was dominated by the Church—its beliefs and authority were beyond question. Those who did disagree with the Church risked their lives and at the end of the 12th century, Jews all over France were rounded up and slaughtered. However, the Church was also the chief provider of education and medical care to the poor and was the guiding hand behind the greatest engineering project in medieval Paris: the draining of the marshes of the islands and the Right Bank. When this was done, the city really began to grow.

Notre-Dame

One of the greatest European cathedrals, Notre-Dame dates from 1163 and took almost 200 years to complete. It is a symbol of Paris but was not always treated respectfully. The revolutionaries desecrated it in the 18th century and turned it into a Temple of Reason, even decapitating the statues in the Gallery of Kings. Victor Hugo, romantic creator of a mythic Paris, restored it to the public imagination in 1831 with his novel *Notre-Dame de Paris*. Rebuilding soon followed and, like Quasimodo, the Parisians discovered that 'the cathedral was not only company [for them]…it was the universe, nay, more, it was Nature itself.'

Charles VII (left) liberated Paris from the English in 1437

Notre-Dame (left) remains one of France's most important religious sites

Sainte-Chapelle (below) was built by Louis IX to house holy relics

1000

Queen Isabella, wife of Charles VI, arrives in Paris in the 14th century

Abélard and Héloïse

Peter Abélard, a much admired 12th-century scholar, taught philosophy at the university in Paris. Héloïse, the niece of Canon Fulbert of Notre-Dame, was one of his students. The two fell madly in love and would meet secretly in Héloïse's uncle's house. When Héloïse became pregnant, she fled to Abélard's family home in Brittany and he pledged to marry her. But the enraged Fulbert had Abélard castrated. Héloïse became a nun and Abélard entered a monastery, yet their letters show a torment of love that continued until Abélard's death in 1142. Héloïse lived for another 21 years, and was buried in his grave. The tragic lovers were moved to Père Lachaise cemetery in the 19th century.

Louis IX and the Crown of Thorns

Louis IX was an enthusiastic buyer of holy relics, acquiring the staff of Moses, a portion of the True Cross and Jesus's swaddling clothes. His greatest prize was the Crown of Thorns, which he bought from the Emperor of Constantinople in the 13th century. The emperor was anxious for French aid, and Louis was eager for the prestige this crown would give his own claim to the throne. The crown cost more than three times as much as Sainte-Chapelle, the chapel Louis built to house it. Sainte-Chapelle is famed for its beauty, particularly its towering stained-glass windows. The Crown of Thorns is still in Paris, in Notre-Dame.

The Sorbonne

Robert de Sorbon founded this college of the University of Paris in 1257. The fellows gave free lectures and lived in a closed community, although without religious vows. Robert de Sorbon was a respected professor and preacher, but also a natural administrator. He drew up a list of regulations for the fellows, which included a dress code (no scandalous clothing) and guidelines for returning library books. Even eating and drinking in private rooms were frowned upon. Robert didn't care to have secrets bandied about, so guests, especially women, were discouraged. Robert seemed to know what caused real trouble, however, when he decided that 'No fellow shall have a key to the kitchen'.

King of France and England

Ten-year-old Henry VI of England was crowned King of France in Notre-Dame on 14 December 1431, although true French kings were always crowned in Reims. Joan of Arc wrote a wonderfully rude letter to Henry, warning 'go home…or beware of the Maid and all the damage you will suffer'. She had attempted to expel the English from France in 1429 and to help Charles VII be crowned King of France in Reims. He did not support Joan in her attack on Paris, although she might have taken it if he had. Henry VI did not enjoy his crown for long—by 1453 the French had driven the English from everywhere except the northern port of Calais.

The tragic lovers
Abélard and Héloïse

Henry VI
of England
was crowned
king of France
in 1431

1450

The Sorbonne was founded in the 13th century; its chapel (left) dates from the 17th century

Joan of Arc (below) fought against the English in the early 15th century

Louis IX (right) gained sainthood in 1297, 27 years after his death

Royal Authority

Paris took several decades to recover from the Hundred Years War against England (mid-14th to mid-15th century), the Black Death (1348) and the decadence of the royal court. But by the end of the 15th century, the city had made a fresh start. It eagerly embraced the ideas and the artistic flair of the Italian Renaissance, giving a French character to the new architecture, and was proud of its role as the capital of the reunited French nation. King François I (R.1515–1547) most embodied the new world of the French Renaissance. A devotee of Italian art, he invited Leonardo da Vinci to live at the royal palace in Amboise. The artist accepted, bringing the *Mona Lisa* with him, which the king used as the cornerstone of his art collection. In 1528, François announced his intention to move to the Louvre and commissioned significant rebuilding of the palace. More fine buildings followed under the Protestant Henri IV, crowned king in 1589. He converted to Catholicism in 1593 in a bid to stop the Wars of Religion that swept through France in the latter half of the 16th century. He was assassinated in 1610 and was succeeded by his son, Louis XIII.

François Villon

François Villon, born in 1431, was one of the greatest of French poets, but he has a bitter connection to Paris. He graduated from the University of Paris and was destined for a career in law or the Church, but he became restless and spent time in taverns mixing with thieves. In 1455 he killed a priest in a drunken quarrel. After this, he wandered the country, spending time in and out of prison until he was banished in 1463 and was never heard of again. Villon's poetry is vigorous and haunting, but without self-pity. It is fashionable to view him as the country's first cultural rebel, although he is actually a mystery.

François Villon

François I commissioned a sumptuous rebuilding of the chateau at Fontainebleau (left) in the 16th century

Leonardo da Vinci shows the *Mona Lisa* to François I (below)

1450

This painting, by Rosso de Rossi, is from the Galerie de François I, at Fontainebleau

Fit for a king

Even for a king, François I was larger than life. He adored Renaissance style—he grew up at the Loire chateau of Amboise, probably the first French building redesigned on Italianate lines—and on becoming king he invited Leonardo da Vinci to live at Amboise. François moved ceaselessly from chateau to chateau, and had two more magnificent palaces built, at Fontainebleau and Chambord. Eventually, he decided to move to the Louvre, taking his art collection with him. He ordered the palace to be completely rebuilt, but died soon after work began. He left his mark on many buildings in Paris in the form of the salamander and the letter F, his way of saying 'François was here'.

The Massacre of St. Bartholomew's Day

The brutal murder of thousands of Protestants in Paris on 24 August 1572 is one of the most shocking events in French history. France was riven by wars between Protestants and Catholics but the marriage of King Charles IX's sister, the Catholic Marguerite de Valois, to the Protestant Henri de Navarre (the future Henri IV) was meant to bring the two sides together. The opposite occurred when the king, pressed by his mother, Catherine de Medici, ordered the massacre of Protestant nobles gathered at the Louvre to celebrate the wedding. Three thousand people died in Paris and many more throughout France. Civil war raged throughout the country for more than 20 years.

The Medici Cycle

Between 1622 and 1625, Rubens painted 21 murals on the life of Marie de Medici, Louis XIII's mother, for her palace in Paris. Marie, second wife of Henri IV, was bad-tempered, ugly and dangerous, so Rubens needed all his diplomatic skills to deal with her. The paintings, he explained carefully, are allegories of how one should look rather than how one does look. In immense baroque extravaganzas, a beautiful Marie is shown arriving in France, getting married and governing the country accompanied by a flock of gods. This propaganda has little to do with reality, as even her husband said she was the biggest troublemaker he had ever known, and her son banished her from France. Ironically, she died in Cologne in a house once occupied by Rubens.

L'Académie Française

Cardinal Richelieu, chief minister to Louis XIII, formed the Académie Française in 1635 and it still exists today. There are 40 members and only death creates a vacancy. Each member is presented with a richly decorated sword and is addressed as *monsieur*, which rankles with the women academicians. Richelieu, busy creating a centralized government, wanted the Académie to act as a ministry to legislate on the French language. In 1638 the academicians began work on their dictionary—it took them a long time. One wit, on hearing they had reached the letter F, loudly hoped to live until they got to G. In 1694, a mere 58 years after starting, their dictionary was published and has been updated regularly ever since.

King François I, despotic and capricious, yet also a refined Renaissance gentleman

The brilliant but hypochondriac Richelieu, chief minister to Louis XIII

1640

Catherine de Medici (right), wife of Henri II

François I chose the Louvre (below) as his new home

A scene (above) from the Wars of Religion, which raged for years in France

Life at Versailles

Louis XIII died in 1643, when his son, Louis XIV, was only five years old. The new king's mother, Anne of Austria, and Cardinal Mazarin governed while he was a child, but in 1661 Louis shocked the Court by announcing he would rule on his own. His authority was absolute and his egotism, extravagance and unrealistic expansionism dominated every aspect of life in Paris and the rest of France. He moved the Court to Versailles and adopted a golden sun as his symbol because, in his opinion, he radiated light over the whole nation. While the Sun King's reign represents the apotheosis of French monarchy, his lavish lifestyle and ceaseless wars led to the political isolation of France, financial problems and extreme social injustice. Much of the vitality of the Great King's reign was extinguished long before his death in 1715. The removal of the five-year-old Louis XV (*R.*1715–1774) to the Tuileries palace by the regent launched a renewal for the capital. The Court and nobility returned to Paris to throw themselves into a life devoted to pleasure. Though the Court returned to Versailles in 1724, the palace would never again be the focus of French life. By the middle of the reign of Louis XVI (*R.*1774–1793) and his beautiful, frivolous, unpopular Queen, Marie-Antoinette, the polite reformist mood of the earlier half of the century had turned into a flood of sedition.

This statue of Louis XIV (left) stands at place des Victoires

The building of Versailles

When Louis XIV ordered Versailles to be built in 1661, 30,000 workers were hired. Leading architect Louis Le Vau, interior designer Charles Le Brun and landscape architect André Le Nôtre were commissioned to provide a royal home of unprecedented grandeur, in classical style. The king required vast formal gardens full of statuary and fountains and a sumptuous interior adorned with Europe's finest craftsmanship. Work continued up to Louis XIV's death in 1715, with no expense spared. While draining the grounds, thousands of workers died from marsh fever, but were quickly replaced. Mature trees from all over France were replanted here and a whole new town was built alongside the palace. The Royal Court moved into Versailles in 1671.

1640

A lavish bedroom at Versailles

Behind the throne

Great minds were at work behind the Sun King. At first, Louis XIV's affairs were run by Chief Minister Cardinal Mazarin, who closely followed the footsteps of his predecessor, Cardinal Richelieu. After Mazarin's death in 1661, the King sought advice on all matters of state from Jean-Baptiste Colbert, a brilliant but unassuming politician, son of a cloth merchant. Colbert arranged the downfall of the Superintendant of Finance and took over as finance minister himself. He increased tax revenues, imposed tariffs to protect French commerce, built new canals, revived ailing industries and enabled the navy to protect French merchant shipping. But Colbert's efforts were undermined by the King's continual search for personal glory.

Lady of letters

With the Court tucked away at Versailles, intellectual life in Paris flourished—and women presided over it. In 1676 the writer Madame de Sévigné spent a day at Versailles, gambling, lolling about in boats on the canal and having supper at midnight. But it was not for her. She decided to stay away and wrote the great series of letters to her daughter that give a picture of life in 17th-century Paris. In the 18th century other ladies held literary *salons* where writers Voltaire and Diderot could discuss the *Encyclopédie*, the great intellectual work of the century. This freedom provided the background to the Revolution, as 'the Church, the Law and the Government' was questioned. Versailles was unaware of any of it.

Ce pays ci

Versailles gradually drifted like a balloon away from the vibrancy of Paris. Courtiers called Versailles *ce pays ci* (this country), walked differently, developed their own argot and lived by hundreds of meaningless rules (dukes kneeled on crooked cushions in church, the royal princes on straight ones). The Parisian bourgeoisie visited Versailles but could never be a part of it. So when Jeanne Poisson, a beautiful Parisian bourgeoise, caught Louis XV's eye, direct contact with the king was not officially allowed. The problem was resolved when she was made Marquise de Pompadour. She left Paris for Versailles and became the royal mistress.

The women of Paris speak

The working-class women of Paris were a tough breed, and members of the Court never knew how they would be received when they ventured from Versailles. Madame de Pompadour, a Parisienne herself, found her carriage splattered in mud and Louis XV built a road round the city to avoid their insults, delivered in the slang of the market women and fishwives, *poissard*. This was an anarchic mix of fractured words and chaotic grammar, ideal for ridicule. Marie-Antoinette invited the fishwives of Paris to Versailles in 1777 to teach her friends *poissard* for their amateur dramatics. In 1789 the women sang a *poissard* song inviting the Court to choke on molten gold since they loved it so much.

The 18th-century writer Voltaire

The Princess de Lamballe (left), Marie-Antoinette's closest friend

Madame de Pompadour, mistress to Louis XV

1789

The Court left Paris and moved to Versailles (left) during Louis XIV's reign

Marie-Antoinette, wife of the hapless Louis XVI

The opulent Hall of Mirrors

The Revolution

The Fronde rebellion (1648–1652) had given just a hint of what was to come and anger simmered beneath the surface of life in Paris. The power of the monarchy and the decadent privileges of the aristocracy contrasted sharply with the poverty of working people, and the growing industrial middle class, resentful at their lack of political voice, demanded a proper constitution. The Royal Court continued to enjoy an exceptionally pampered life. The arts flourished, and craftsmen catering to the aristocracy did well. All over Europe, Paris became a byword for luxury and the good life. At the same time, the state sank further into debt and ordinary people further into poverty. To offset the state's huge debts, repressive taxes were imposed. On 14 July 1789, spontaneous crowds (there had been rumblings of something afoot the previous day) converged on Les Invalides to grab the weapons stored there. From there, to the Bastille. The Revolution had started, and would lead France through many years of savage brutality and instability towards a new Republic.

The guillotine

Dr. Joseph-Ignace Guillotin was a deputy of the National Assembly and in 1789 proposed the use of his machine as a democratic means of death. The machine was set up in the place du Carrousel, and on 21 August 1792 was used for the execution of a Royalist general. As the Revolution progressed so did the executions and by 1794, during the *Grande Terreur*, 26 people a day were being guillotined. Those accused of crimes against the state were despatched on an industrial scale. This brought problems of disposal, with blood flowing in the city's gutters and bodies being thrown into mass graves.

Dr. Joseph-Ignace Guillotin's 'philanthropic beheading machine'

1789

The Customs Wall

The attack on the Bastille on 14 July 1789 was preceded on 12 July by an attack on something less well known: the Customs Wall around Paris, built on the order of the Controller-General, Callone. In a desperate effort to raise money for the huge national debt (60 per cent of the budget went to pay the interest), Callone imposed a duty on goods entering and leaving the city. This was collected by private tax collectors who took a large cut for themselves, and were hated by the citizens of Paris for their brutal tactics. The wall was rather beautiful, the work of the chemist Antoine Lavoisier, who was also a tax collector. These well-fed gentlemen had, for once, miscalculated—after the wall came down, they were swiftly executed.

14 July 1789

The Revolution made a slow start. A bread shortage had caused months of angry revolt in Paris and on 12 and 13 July thousands of rioters surged through the city. On the morning of 14 July a group tricked its way into Les Invalides, seized its huge store of weapons and marched to the Bastille, the fortress-prison. The mob liberated the prisoners (all seven of them), decapitated the governor and paraded his head on a pole. This attack heralded a summer of violence and on 5 October thousands of women marched on Versailles to ask King Louis XVI for bread, which he gave them. Joined by their menfolk, they rampaged through the palace and took the King and Queen Marie-Antoinette to house arrest in Paris.

The Marriage of Figaro

Beaumarchais' play *The Marriage of Figaro* was due to open in Paris in 1783, in a theatre owned by the Queen. She was looking forward to seeing it, but Louis XVI, realizing that its unprecedented attacks on the aristocracy were dangerous, stopped the performance and had the play banned, which led to riots in Paris. After some changes the play finally opened in another Paris venue the following year. When Figaro tells his master, 'You only took the trouble to be born… you're an ordinary person' the people of Paris roared with delight, as did the watching nobles, including Marie-Antoinette. An observer noted with amazement how the aristocracy slapped its own face while laughing at the same time.

Festival of the Supreme Being

On 8 June 1794 (20 Prairial Year 2 by the Revolutionary calendar), the Revolution reached a pitch of insanity, and Paris witnessed the Festival of the Supreme Being, as artificial and ridiculous as any royal pageant. Deputies from the Convention marched along clutching wheat sheaves, girls in white distributed flowers, oxen pulled a printing press and a plough on a chariot and blind children sang inspiring songs. In the Champ de Mars, Maximilien Robespierre, one of the Revolution's leaders, set fire to a statue of Atheism, then descended from the top of a cardboard mountain to enthusiastic applause. 'Did the day of Creation…' he asked, 'shine with a light more agreeable?' Seven weeks later he was guillotined.

Being a leader of the Revolution did not protect Robespierre from the guillotine

Louis XVI (left) lost his life to the guillotine in 1793

The Dauphin Louis XVII (right) in prison

Place de la Concorde witnessed the bloody beheadings of more than 1,300 people

Place de la Bastille as it is today (far left) and during the violent Storming of the Bastille in July 1789 (left)

The absurd Festival of the Supreme Being

Napoleon's Paris

Following the bloody days of The Terror, France was ruled by an intermediary government known as the *Directoire* (1795–1799). Problems arose at once—the war against surrounding countries threatened to turn against France and a violent royalism arose that sought to revive the *ancien régime*. An ambitious young Corsican army general emerged who felt able to deal with both issues—Napoleon Bonaparte (1769–1821). Given command of the army in Italy by the *Directoire* in 1796, he rapidly achieved victory. His next step, the invasion of Egypt, proved a mistake, but nevertheless his rise to power was now unstoppable. He became First Consul of the Republic after the 1799 *coup d'état* that overthrew the *Directoire*. To begin with, things looked good and the French border expanded. But in 1812 Napoleon made the fatal error of invading Russia during winter. Ice and snow killed thousands of his soldiers. In 1814 the Russians invaded Paris and Napoleon was exiled to the island of Elba. He made a brief return in 1815, before meeting his final defeat at Waterloo a few months later. He was expelled to the island of St-Helena, where he died in 1821.

A Republican coronation

Napoleon Bonaparte went through swift changes in under ten years—from extreme anti-royalist Jacobin supporter to army general serving the *Directoire*, to crowned head of state. His military successes, ability to restore order and sweeping vision of a modern France inspired the nation. Despite impeccable Republican credentials, in 1804 the military dictator decided he deserved to wear a crown. In an opulent ceremony fit for a king, Napoleon was crowned Emperor in Notre-Dame. The Pope, summoned to Paris for the purpose, gave his blessing. Since no one had authority to place the crown on Napoleon's head, in an act fraught with symbolism he did the job himself, after having first chivalrously crowned his wife Empress Josephine.

A young Napoleon Bonaparte

Empress Josephine's bedroom (left), in the Château de Malmaison

1799

Napoleon departs for exile on the island of St-Helena

Arc de Triomphe

Military triumph was the essence of Napoleon's right to wear a crown. The Emperor kept France in a constant state of belligerency against the rest of Europe, distributing conquered lands among friends and family. Only a year after his coronation, the greatest moment of glory came at Austerlitz, where French troops defeated the might of Austria. At the height of his power, Napoleon ordered a huge Roman-style triumphal arch to be built to commemorate his victories. The Arc de Triomphe was to stand in pride of place at the end of the Champs-Élysées. Construction had barely started when Napoleon's bubble burst. Work on the arch stopped until after his death.

Napoleon's elephant

To obliterate memories of the Revolution, Napoleon commissioned an enormous bronze elephant, 10m (33ft) high, for the site of the demolished Bastille prison. When it was finally built in 1814, the Empire could only afford a plaster elephant, which soon started to disintegrate into a bizarre, broken-down mess. No one seemed to know why it was there, or even why it was an elephant. A concierge was employed to look after the construction, but that didn't help. The elephant appears in the book *Les Misérables* as the home of the young Gavroche. Author Victor Hugo calls it a mysterious and mighty phantom. In 1846 the wretched beast was finally demolished, vanishing from the place de la Bastille as mysteriously as it had appeared.

Bistro! Bistro!

When Russian soldiers occupied Paris in 1814 they liked to visit the small cafés in the city. Unsurprisingly, they got the cold shoulder from their French waiters. *'Bystro! Bystro!'* (Quickly!) shouted the unhappy Cossacks and legend has it that this is the origin of this uniquely French type of restaurant. However, the word didn't enter the language until 1884 and there are other less attractive explanations for it. Bistro could originate from the word *bistre* (dull yellowy brown), meaning a smoky, gloomy place.

The Russians haven't made many notable contributions to French cuisine, so it's nicer to think they've sneaked in a term known for simple, but excellent, food.

The funeral of Napoleon

Napoleon's funeral at Les Invalides on 15 December 1840 was not a jolly affair. Inside, kings, princes and ancient heroes sat for hours in pious boredom. They were surrounded by black and purple drapes fringed with silver, hundreds of glowing candles glittering on marble, military decorations and the Imperial Crown itself. Outside, it was a different story. The day was bitterly cold and so the waiting crowd and the soldiers lining the route had to keep themselves warm somehow. A few people in the stands started to dance, which then spread to the crowds on the streets and then to the soldiers themselves, until a vast, happy round-dance snaked along the funeral route, only to stop when the coffin finally went by.

An older Napoleon, in uniform

Louis XVIII came to the throne in 1814, after Napoleon was exiled

1815

The Arc de Triomphe (left), intended as a celebration of Napoleon's victories

A Russian soldier in 1814 (left)

Napoleon's funeral cortège passes through place de la Concorde (below), in 1840

19th-Century Turmoil

The turbulence of the Napoleonic period, its war-making patriotism, far-reaching social changes and violent politics, continued through the rest of the 19th century. The people of Paris, marked out in the Revolution as more passionately radical than their provincial compatriots, continued to call for equality, democracy and workers' protection. The 1830 Uprising brought the 'citizen king' Louis-Philippe of Orléans to the throne. Yet Parisians seemed to hanker for grandiose, dictatorial leadership along the lines of a Sun King or a Bonaparte. Following the 1848 Revolution that finally did away with the French monarchy, a brief Second Republic gave way to yet another authoritarian, egotistical ruler: Napoleon's nephew, Napoleon III. He used his power to enhance Paris, especially during the transformation overseen by Baron Haussmann, when much of the city was rebuilt. Constant themes of Parisian life still remained, such as the poverty of workers, the lavish hedonism of the rich, and war. During the bloody episode of the Commune, in 1871, Paris even waged war against the rest of France. The century began with war against the Prussians, later saw the Prussians bombard Paris, and ended with another war looming. But for those with money, the mood was increasingly festive in *gay Paris*.

Haussmann's grand design

Napoleon III adored luxury and prestige as much as his uncle had done. He and Empress Eugénie mixed with the crowned heads of Europe and came to exemplify the aristocratic style that Paris had suffered so much in trying to abolish. At the same time, the Emperor, like Bonaparte, had grand plans to improve the look of his capital city and so he commissioned Baron Haussmann to undertake massive urban improvement. Haussmann demolished large areas of the city, including almost everything on the historic Île de la Cité, sweeping away overcrowded and rebellious workers' districts. In their place he constructed wide, straight boulevards radiating from the riverside. The workers were rehoused in new suburbs away from the heart of the city.

Baron Haussmann redesigned much of Paris, including the area around the *Étoile* (left)

1815

The opening of the boulevard du Prince Eugene, by Napoleon III in 1862

The Eiffel Tower (right) was controversial when it opened in 1889

Louis Pasteur (below)

The Petit Palais (right), built for the 1900 Universal Exhibition

The siege of Paris

Thanks to the Emperor and Baron Haussmann, Paris had become the world's most beautiful and modern city. The Emperor had even agreed to improving workers' rights and an enjoyment of life permeated the city. But Napoleon III's pre-emptive declaration of war against Prussia in 1870 came as a blow to the city. Confronting the Prussians, the French suffered an immediate defeat and the country called for Napoleon III to abdicate. Later that year, Prussians surrounded the city and the siege of Paris began. For six winter weeks, nothing was allowed in or out and freezing Paris began to starve, resorting to eating rats, cats and even zoo animals. In January 1871, the bombardment began and France accepted defeat rather than see Paris destroyed.

The Commune

The Prussian war infuriated Parisians, who felt that monarchist elements were to blame. To get away from the Paris mob, the government of the new, conservative National Assembly left the city for Versailles. In Paris, the people took the law into their own hands, establishing an anarchist-socialist Commune to run the city in March 1871, which planned to re-establish the gains of the Revolution. The Communards (*fédérés*) seized National Guard weapons and fought pitched battles in the streets against government troops. During the *Semaine Sanglante* (Bloody Week) of 21 to 28 May, the army ruthlessly regained control. Leading *fédérés* were executed in Père Lachaise cemetery. Around 10,000 Parisians were killed and 40,000 arrested.

A saint in the rue du Bac

In 1830, while revolution rocked Paris, Catherine Laboure, a nun in a convent on the rue du Bac, experienced three visions of the Virgin Mary. Standing on a globe with rays of light shining out, Mary commanded that a medal be struck that would give grace to anyone who wore it. Church authorities approved and the first medal was made in 1832. But illiterate Catherine, who had been a waitress before taking her vows, continued to live out her drab existence at the convent, where she looked after the poultry and was a gatekeeper. She was strangely uninterested in her visions, and her superiors branded her insignificant, cold and apathetic. She died in 1876.

The cancan

Paris was the city of pleasure in the 1890s, with performers dancing the wildly daring cancan at the Moulin Rouge (immortalized in Henri de Toulouse-Lautrec's lithographs). The dance may have started in Brittany in the 16th century, when women performed a similar dance by lifting their dresses and kicking their legs to the ceiling, although the version that came to Paris in the 1820s is probably a bawdy version of the quadrille. Two well-known dancers were Jane Avril and La Goulue. Avril was willowy and elegant, while La Goulue, big and earthy, was known as The Glutton due to her penchant for finishing off the customers' drinks. They both came to a melancholy end, drunk, poor and forgotten, with La Goulue selling matches in a Paris park.

Napoleon III, who ruled from 1852 to 1870

Jules Verne (1828–1905), author of *Around the World in 80 Days*

The writer Victor Hugo (1802–1885)

1900

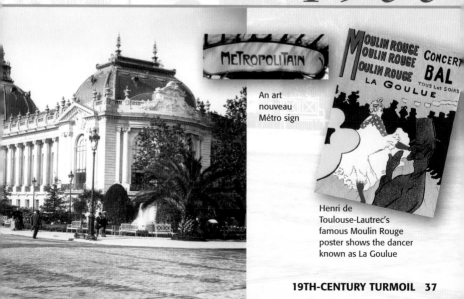

An art nouveau Métro sign

Henri de Toulouse-Lautrec's famous Moulin Rouge poster shows the dancer known as La Goulue

The 20th Century

A savage century came to an end, but a worse one was to come, despite a *fin-de-siècle* atmosphere of frivolity and avant-garde art. The two world wars were the great disaster of the 20th century. In post-war years, the population of Paris grew rapidly, as did its prosperity, and the city itself expanded into new suburbs. Once more the preoccupations of Paris returned to luxury and fashion, sophisticated entertainment, good food and wine, avant-garde art, literature and now also film. A brief interlude of disorder in 1968 was a reminder that Paris had not lost its capacity for revolutionary politics. Nor had it lost its flair for architecture and development on a Napoleonic scale, with magnificent modern buildings and immense rebuilding schemes, like Mitterrand's *Grands Projets*, continuing to make Paris one of the world's greatest cities.

The Rite of Spring

The premiere of the ballet *The Rite of Spring* in May 1913 was a genuine Parisian scandal. Stravinsky's wild music and Nijinsky's even wilder choreography were matched by a riot in the audience. The crowd made so much noise booing that Nijinsky had to stand in the wings shouting out the rhythms for his deafened dancers. The poor aesthetes in the stalls turned on the aristocrats in their boxes. The Comtesse de Pourtalès, tiara askew, shouted that no one had ever dared to make fun of her, when threatened by excitable young men who loved new art. The owner of the venue, Gabriel Astruc, leaned out of his box and screamed at the audience, 'First listen! Then boo!'

A drawing (left) from the front cover of *Art Goût Beauté*, in September 1922

Russian composer Igor Stravinsky (1882–1971), whose ballet *The Rite of Spring* caused uproar when it premiered in Paris in 1913

1900

Armistice talks at the Versailles Conference, 1919

German troops enter Paris in 1940 (above)

The costume worn by ballet dancer Vaslav Nijinsky in the 1912 production of Claude Debussy's *L'Apres Midi d'un Faune*, by the Ballets Russes

City of art and literature

Le Consulat bar, on a street corner in Montmartre, together with À La Bonne Franquette across the road, were haunts of the large crowd of young artists gathering in the city. Such was Paris's reputation in the early years of the century that artists such as Pablo Picasso, Georges Braque and Marc Chagall came to stay or live in the city. Picasso, who moved to Paris in 1904, was one of few who did not derive his inspiration from the people, streets and bars of Montmartre, concentrating on more imaginative imagery and, with Braque, the development of Cubism. Between the wars, many French and foreign writers came to immerse themselves in Paris, among them Gertrude Stein, Ernest Hemingway, Ezra Pound and Henry Miller.

Occupation and liberation

Nazi Germany invaded France in May 1940, and a month later entered Paris. German troops and tanks marched proudly down the Champs-Élysées. Many Parisians fled, and the government departed for Vichy. There was staunch resistance, but also collaboration.

In July 1942, some 13,000 Jews were rounded up and deported to concentration camps. This was the turning point, and the silent majority began to form an underground resistance movement.

Paris's liberation in August 1944 saw thousands of people throng the Champs-Élysées in celebration. Resistance politician Charles de Gaulle swept to power.

May 1968

Paris was caught up in the mood of anti-authoritarianism and liberty that swept the world in 1968. It started as a student sit-in against the regime at the out-of-town University of Nanterre, but a heavy-handed police response changed the mood to anger and confrontation. Action spread to the Sorbonne university, with demonstrators' demands expanding to include sweeping away all that was outdated and repressive in society. A heady air of revolution took hold as millions of discontented factory workers joined the fray. The army was called in but at first could not contain the situation. Yet by mid-June, less than a month later, order had been restored. Workers were unwilling to see the state toppled, but a far-reaching liberalization began to take place.

Mitterrand's *Grands Projets*

On becoming the first Socialist President of the Fifth Republic, François Mitterrand indulged grandiose ambitions to enhance the capital. One of these was the gigantic Grande Arche, in the business district of La Défense, which marks the western end of an imaginary line across the city joining the Arc de Triomphe and the Louvre. The Louvre was enhanced by the glass pyramid, and the Opéra Bastille, a gigantic cultural venue, appeared in the working-class district of Bastille.

Other Mitterrand projects include the transformation of the former river port at Bercy and the building of the Institut du Monde Arabe and the new Bibliothèque Nationale.

General de Gaulle (1890–1970) ruled France briefly after World War II and again from 1958 to 1969

François Mitterrand (1916–96), president from 1981 to 1995

Jacques Chirac (*b.* 1932), president from 1995–2007

2000

The prestigious Opéra Bastille (left)

La Grande Arche (below), finished in time for France's bicentenary celebrations in 1989

21st-Century Paris

Paris is one of the world's most-loved cities, welcoming more than 27 million foreign visitors each year. The capital has a population of just over two million people, including students and temporary workers. In 1851, three per cent of French citizens were Parisian but by 2002 that figure had risen to four per cent. Around 11 million people live in the suburbs and satellite towns of the Île de France, and fast, inexpensive and relatively pleasant rail services bring these out-of-town Parisians into the city to work, shop, dine and be entertained.

Summer heat

Summer 2003 took a tragic turn when hundreds of elderly Paris residents died of hyperthermia and dehydration, as temperatures soared to above 40°C (104°F).

In July, the heatwave was assumed to be nothing more than part of a national hot spell and television news reports advised people leaving town to take plenty of cold drinks and keep children cool. But by mid-August the crisis in Paris had grown, with nine-day waits for funerals, and the government added heatwaves to the list of national emergencies covered by the White Plan. This grants special powers to hospital chiefs and local authorities in the event of terrorist attacks and nuclear accidents.

High-speed TGV trains at the Gare de Lyon

Paris Plage

Paris Plage, the beach by the Seine, has become a summer must-see in Paris. From mid-July to mid-August, when most Parisians desert the city, part of the Right Bank is transformed into a seaside. Palm trees (Parisian-style, in a chic row) sway over 100m (330ft) of imported sand, along with 300 deckchairs, 150 parasols and striped changing tents.

Paris Plage was introduced in summer 2002 and by 2007, 3km (2 miles) of river bank were included in the scheme.

City of protest

Parisians seem to feel it a matter of pride to pour into the streets to express their grievances by rallying, marching and putting up barricades. But while the Left demonstrates on the streets, when it is time to step into the polling booths it is the Right that has consistently won control of Paris.

The election of a Socialist mayor in 2001 meant that for the first time in almost a century the capital was to be ruled by the Left. The new mayor, Bertrand Delanoë, proudly declared 'For the first time since 1909, the forces for progress hold the majority. Paris is still the capital of the movement…a city that will neither conform nor submit.'

Protesters attending a rally in Paris (above)

Paris Plage (below)

Many Parisians voted 'no' in the referendum on the EU Constitution in 2005

2000…

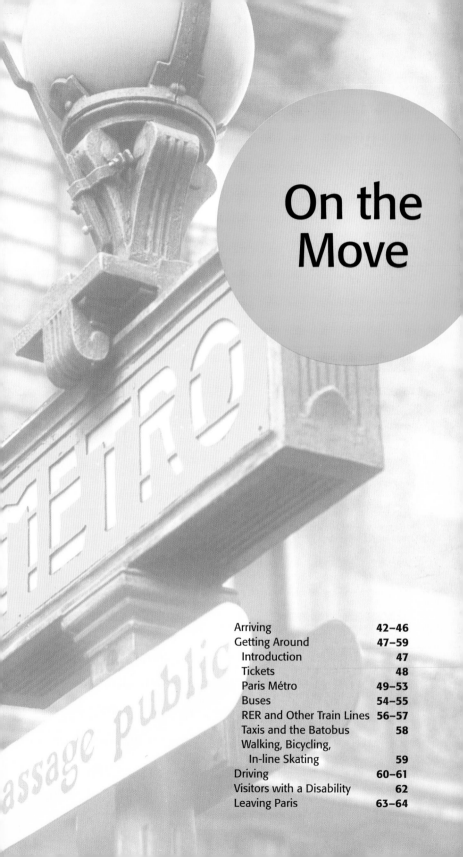

On the Move

ARRIVING

Arriving by Air

You can get flights to Paris from most major European cities and from many other destinations worldwide. Major international carriers use the larger Roissy-Charles de Gaulle Airport, 23km (14 miles) northeast of central Paris. There are good rail and bus links. Orly Airport has domestic flights and some international flights. It is 14km (8.5 miles) south of the city heart, with bus but no direct rail links.

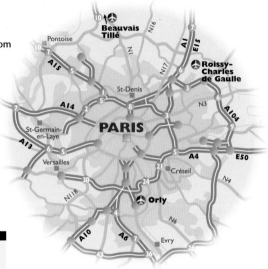

TIPS

● The tourist office on the arrivals level of Orly Ouest is open from 7.30am to 11pm. The office in T1 of Roissy-Charles de Gaulle is closed during restructuring of the terminal.
● When departing from Roissy-Charles de Gaulle make sure you know which terminal you are leaving from, as terminals 1 and 2 are a fair distance apart.
● When departing from any of the airports, you should allow plenty of time for extra security checks.

ROISSY-CHARLES DE GAULLE

Paris's busiest airport has three terminals: T1, T2 and T3 (formerly T9). Terminal 2 is subdivided into 2A, 2B, 2C, 2D and 2F. Airlines operating out of T1 include Aer Lingus, British Midland, KLM, United Airlines and US Airways. T2 serves Air France, American Airlines, British Airways and others. Airlines using T3 include the low-cost easyJet. Terminals do change so always check before setting off.

You'll find information desks, shops, restaurants, banks, bureaux de change, car rental firms and first aid facilities in T1 and T2. For security reasons there are no left luggage facilities. T3 has shops, cafés, a bureau de change and car rental outlets.

The airport has two RER stations—CDG1 for T1 and T3 and CDG2 for T2. Shuttle buses run from the terminals to both stations. You can then take RER line B into Paris. Buses also run to the city (see chart below).

GETTING TO PARIS FROM THE AIRPORT		
AIRPORT	**TAXI**	**RER**
Roissy-Charles de Gaulle (CDG)	Cost: €50–60. Journey time: 30 min–1 hour.	RER line B takes you into the heart of Paris (Gare du Nord, Châtelet or St-Michel). Trains leave every 5–15 min, 5am–0.15am. Cost: €8.20. Journey time: 35 min.
Orly (ORY)	Cost: around €40. Journey time: 15–30 min.	The Orlyval train (Mon–Sat 6am–10.30pm, Sun 7am–11pm) takes you two stops to Antony, where you pick up RER line B. Cost: €9.30. Journey time: 35 min.
Beauvais Tillé (BVA)	Cost: around €130–170. Journey time: 1 hour 20 min.	None.

ORLY

Orly Airport has two terminals—Orly Sud and Orly Ouest. Shuttle buses or the Orlyval train link the two. The airport has shops, restaurants, bureaux de change, car rental firms and medical facilities. There are no direct rail links into Paris, but the Orlyval train takes you two stops to Antony, where you can change to RER line B. The Orlybus runs from the airport to Denfert-Rochereau Métro station; the Air France bus will take you farther into the city, to Les Invalides. Alternatively, take a shuttle bus to Pont de Rungis RER station then RER line C to Gare d'Austerlitz,

Checking the departures board at Roissy-Charles de Gaulle

St-Michel-Notre-Dame or Les Invalides.

BEAUVAIS TILLÉ

Beauvais Tillé is a small airport in Beauvais, north of Paris, in the Oise *département*. It is currently used by low-cost airlines. Facilities include a news vendor, restaurant and car rental desks. A bus connects with incoming flights and takes you to Porte Maillot, on the northwestern edge of Paris. It is also possible to take a taxi, although this is an expensive option.

MÉTRO	BUS		CAR
None.	The Air France bus runs from Terminals 1 and 2 to Montparnasse and Gare de Lyon every 30 min, 7am–9pm. Cost: €14. Journey time: 45 min–1 hour. Another Air France bus runs to the Arc de Triomphe every 15 min, 5.45am–11pm. Cost: €13. Journey time: 45 min–1 hour. The Roissybus runs every 15 min from Terminals 1, 2 and 3 to Opéra, 6am–11pm. Cost: €8.60. Journey time: 50 min.		Take the A1 south to Paris. Journey time: 30 min–1 hour, depending on traffic.
None.	The Air France bus runs from Orly Sud and Ouest to Les Invalides and Gare Montparnasse every 15 min, 6am–11.30pm. Cost: €9. Journey time: 30 min. The Orlybus runs from Orly Sud and Ouest to Denfert-Rochereau Métro station every 15–20 min, 6am–11.30pm. Cost: €6.10. Journey time: 30 min.		Take the A6, then A6A or A6B into Paris. Journey time: 15–40 min, depending on traffic.
None.	Bus to Porte Maillot. Cost: €13. Journey time: around 1 hour 15 min.		Take the N1, A16, N1 then A1. Journey time: 1 hour 20 min.

Arriving by Train

The Channel Tunnel rail link has revolutionized travel between London and Paris, allowing you to reach France's capital from Britain's in less than three hours, without leaving the ground or boarding a boat. The Queen and François Mitterrand, France's president at the time, opened the tunnel in 1994, almost 200 years after the first designs were submitted for an undersea link between England and France. It is the longest undersea tunnel in the world, with 39km (24 miles) of its 50km (31 mile) length under the English Channel.

BOARDING EUROSTAR

● Up to 16 trains per day travel to Paris from London; some stop en route at Ashford International and Ebbsfleet International (UK) and Calais (France). There are also direct trains to Disneyland Resort Paris. The journey time to Paris is 2 hours 15 minutes.

● Trains leave from a dedicated base at St Pancras International Station, which has connections to underground services for central London locations and mainland train services.

● The terminal is a combination of fully refurbished Victorian architecture and a 21st-century glass edifice, incorporating a shopping mall, eateries and the longest champagne bar in Europe.

● Automatic check-in facilities are available for passengers with suitable tickets, otherwise check in at the desks. You must do this at least 30 minutes before your train is due to leave.

● Before you reach the departure lounge you must go through airport-style security checks and passport control. French passport control is actually carried out at St Pancras.

● Once in the departure lounge there are newspaper

Paris is easily reached by train from all parts of Europe

and gift shops, cafés, toilets, internet points and a post box.

● Boarding begins around 20 minutes before departure. Information screens in the lounge tell you where and when to board.

● Each train has 18 carriages (cars) so you could face a long walk along the platform. Trolleys (carts) are available, but you'll need a £1 coin as a deposit.

● Once on board, large cases must be stored on the luggage racks at the end of each carriage, although you can put smaller bags in the racks above your seat.

THE JOURNEY

● A buffet car serves drinks, snacks and light meals. There are toilets and baby-changing facilities on board. The journey through the tunnel takes around 20 minutes and an announcement is made just before you enter.

ARRIVING

● When you arrive at Paris's Gare du Nord station you don't need to go through passport control

● You'll usually pay less for your ticket if you reserve it in advance. It is highly recommended that you do this, since non-reserved seats are limited.

● The train is split into Premium, First and Standard class. Premium and First class give you a meal, extra legroom, a reclining seat and free newspapers. Certain tickets also allow admission to the business lounges in London and at Gare du Nord.

● Remember that you need your passport to travel between Britain and France (see Passports and Visas, ▷ 297).

● The official luggage allowance is two suitcases and one piece of hand luggage. Luggage labels must be marked with your name and seat number.

● Luggage trolleys (carts) are available on the platforms in London and at Gare du Nord, but you need a £1 or €1 coin (refundable). If you have a heavy case a trolley is a good idea as the walk along the platform can be long if your carriage (car) happens to be the last of 18.

again. Watch for pickpockets at the station.

● The covered taxi stand is well signposted. Don't be too depressed by the long queue (line)—it moves fairly quickly. A taxi into the heart of Paris usually costs €10 to €15. There are extra charges for luggage and for travel after 7pm and on Sundays.

Châtelet, then on to the Left Bank (St-Michel-Notre-Dame and Luxembourg). The RER can be a confusing rail system to the uninitiated (▷ 56) so if it's your first time in Paris it may be better to take the Métro or a taxi.

LEAVING PARIS

● The Eurostar terminal is on the first floor of the Gare du Nord. There are a few gift shops and coffee bars, but facilities are not as comprehensive as in London. There is no post box, so rid yourself of any last-minute postcards before you get to the terminal. British officials check passports at the Gare du Nord, immediately after check-in.
● Electronic screens will tell you which of the two boarding points to use and when to board.

FACTS AND FIGURES

● Construction work on the tunnel began in 1987 and was completed in 1991.
● The tunnel is 40m (131ft) below the seabed.
● Trains travel at up to 300kph (186mph).

USEFUL NUMBERS
Eurostar:
From within the UK:
08705 186 186
From outside the UK:
+ 44 1233 617 575
In France: 0892 353 539 (in English)
www.eurostar.com
Lost luggage at St Pancras:
020 7833 1596 (UK number)
Lost luggage at Gare du Nord:
01 55 31 54 54 (French number)

● Each train is 400m (1,312ft) long.
● There are two main tunnels and a service tunnel. This doubles as a safety tunnel and is designed to stay smoke-free in the event of a fire.
● Trains have a driver's carriage at either end, so they can quickly change direction and exit the tunnel if an emergency arises ahead.
● Celebrated French designer Philippe Starck has worked on various Eurostar projects, ranging from new staff uniforms to redesigned business lounges and train interiors.

It is best to reserve tickets ahead

● Gare du Nord is on Métro lines 4 (purple) and 5 (orange). Line 4 (direction Porte d'Orléans) will take you across the river to the Left Bank. If your hotel is on the Right Bank, you can change lines at Gare de l'Est, Strasbourg St-Denis, Réaumur Sébastopol or Châtelet. Line 5 (direction place d'Italie) is handy if you're heading to the Bastille area.
● Gare du Nord is also on three RER lines: D (green), E (mauve) and B (blue). Line B takes you to

The busy Gare du Nord

Arriving by Car or Long-Distance Bus

If you want to drive from the UK to France you can take either the Eurotunnel or a ferry, both of which run to Calais. From here it should take around 3 hours 15 minutes to drive to Paris. Driving to France from countries on mainland Europe is straightforward.

ON THE MOVE

EUROTUNNEL

If you are driving from the UK, you can load your car onto the Shuttle train at Folkestone for the 35-minute journey under the English Channel to Calais/Coquelles. There are up to four departures per hour, 24 hours a day. Reserve ahead.

To reach the Folkestone terminal take the M20 to junction 11A, then follow signs to the Channel Tunnel. French border controls take place in the UK.

You stay with your vehicle during the journey, although you can go to the toilet or walk about within the air-conditioned carriage (car). There is an on-board radio station and staff are available if you need assistance.

To reach Paris from Calais you can take the A16 (E40) in the direction of Dunkerque, then join the A26 (E15). At the junction with the A1, head southbound on the A1 (E15), which takes you to Paris. You will have to pay *autoroute* tolls. See pages 60–61 for more driving information.

Eurotunnel Contact Details

08705 35 35 35 (UK number); www.eurotunnel.com

BY SEA

The cost of crossing to France from England by ferry varies widely according to the time, day and month of travel. Most companies require you to check in at least 30 minutes before departure, although you may need to arrive earlier.

P&O Ferries and **Seafrance** sail from Dover to Calais (journey time: 70 to 90 minutes). Facilities on board the ferries include shops, cafés, bureaux de change and lounges. From Calais, it takes around 3 hours 15 minutes to drive to Paris—for directions, see Eurotunnel.

The **Speedferries** service from Dover to Calais is the fastest sea crossing on this route, with a journey time of 50 minutes. This is a personal vehicle only service, which means that commercial traffic and buses, including motorhomes and caravans, are not permitted.

Brittany Ferries sail from Portsmouth to Caen (journey time: 6 hours). The drive to Paris takes around 2 hours 40 minutes.

P&O Ferries sail from Portsmouth to Le Havre (journey time: 5 hours 30 minutes). The drive to Paris takes around 2 hours 25 minutes.

Ferry Contact Details

Brittany Ferries: 0870 907 6103 (UK); www.brittany-ferries.co.uk
P&O Ferries: 0870 598 0333 (UK); www.poferries.com
Seafrance: 0871 663 2546 (UK); www.seafrance.co.uk
Speedferries: 0871 222 7456 (UK); www.speedferries.com

BY LONG-DISTANCE BUS

Taking the bus from the UK can be a useful option if you're on a tight budget, although the journey from London takes almost eight hours. Eurolines runs from Victoria coach station to Paris up to five times a day, with pick-up points at Canterbury and Dover, in Kent. The Channel crossing is made either by Eurotunnel or ferry. You arrive at the bus terminal in avenue du Général de Gaulle, in Bagnolet, on the eastern edge of Paris.

Reserve your ticket at least 30 days in advance to get the best prices.

Eurolines Contact Details

08705 808080; www.eurolines.co.uk

TIPS

- It is often less expensive to reserve Eurotunnel tickets online than by telephone.
- LPG vehicles cannot use the Eurotunnel.
- Look out for low-cost ferry deals in British newspapers.
- The phone numbers given on this page are UK-based. To call from the US, dial 011 44, then omit the initial zero from the number. To call from mainland Europe, dial 00 44, then omit the zero.

GETTING AROUND

Paris has a comprehensive, efficient and relatively inexpensive transportation network and you should have few problems finding your way around the city. The Métro (underground/subway) is the backbone of the network. Other useful options include buses, riverboats and the suburban RER trains. Finally, don't forget your own two feet—central Paris is compact and walking is a great way to get your bearings.

The Métro is often the quickest way of getting from A to B, and with around 300 stations you're rarely more than five minutes' walk from a line. Trains vary from ultramodern to past-their-best, depending on the line, but services usually run with minimum delays (barring strike action). Once in the station, be prepared for long walks to reach the platform—especially at Châtelet—although you won't need to go down as deep as, say, the London Underground. During rush hour the trains can become uncomfortably crowded and you're unlikely to find a seat. Lines that connect key visitor attractions (such as Line 1) can be crowded all day.

Buses give you the chance to see the city as you travel and their routes are clearly marked at the stops and on the bus. But they are slower than the Métro and can become just as crowded in rush hour.

The Métro, some RER lines and most buses are operated by RATP.

Taxis are useful if you have lots of baggage or if you don't feel comfortable using the Métro at night.

TRAVEL INFORMATION
● You can pick up free Métro maps at every station.
● For 24-hour recorded information in English, Italian, Spanish and German, call 0892 684 114.
● To speak to an advisor (in French only) call 32 46.
● The major stations have information desks, although communication can sometimes be limited if you don't speak French.
● The website www.ratp.fr has lots of helpful information, in

Using the automatic ticket machines can save time

French and English. Click on *Paris Visite* for advice for visitors.
● There are travel information points at the airports.

ON THE MOVE WITH CHILDREN
● Children under the age of four travel free on the Métro, buses and RER.
● Children under the age of 10 receive a 50 per cent reduction on ticket prices.
● Some buses have ramps for pushchairs (and wheelchairs) at the central doors.
● Taking a pushchair on the Métro can be tricky, due to awkward ticket barriers and the many steps to and from platforms.

TICKETS
● The Métro and buses use the same tickets and travel cards (▷ 48). These can also be used on the RER within central Paris.
● The city is divided into fare zones. Most of the key sights are in Zone 1, although the Grande Arche is in Zone 3,

Roissy-Charles de Gaulle airport is in Zone 5 and Orly airport is in Zone 4.
● Buy tickets at Métro stations, on buses (single tickets only) and at some news-stands.
● To save time, use the ticket machines in station concourses. Instructions are given in a choice of languages.
● Most stations have ticket offices, generally open from 5.30am to midnight. If you don't speak French, take a copy of the RER or Métro map with you so you can point to where you want to go if necessary.
● Major credit and debit cards are accepted at stations, although cash is more convenient.
● A single ticket costs €1.50 and covers all Métro stations, RER stations within the heart of Paris and most buses (▷ 48).
● If you are planning to make good use of the Métro and buses during your visit, a *carnet* (book) of ten tickets or a travelcard could be a better option.
● For more information on tickets and travelcards, ▷ 48.

ON THE MOVE

TICKETS

TYPE	PRICE	VALID	EXTRA INFORMATION
Single ticket	€1.50	Tickets are valid on the Métro, the RER (within central Paris) and most buses. You don't have to use them on the day of purchase, but once you have stamped a ticket (by slotting it through the automatic barrier at Métro stations or in the machine on buses) it is valid for 90 minutes.	You can change Métro and RER lines within one journey on the same ticket, but you can't change from the Métro to a bus on the same ticket. t+ tickets, sold by RATP, are valid for bus to bus and bus to tram transfers, but not, currently, tickets sold by bus drivers on vehicles.
Carnet	€11.10 for 10 single tickets	As single tickets, see above.	This is cost-effective if you are planning eight journeys or more.
Mobilis	Zones 1–2: €5.60 Zones 1–3: €7.50 Zones 1–5: €12.50	Valid for one day, within the relevant zones, on the Métro, buses, RER and Transilien services, except airport shuttles Roissybus, Orlybus and Orlyval.	A less expensive option than the one-day Paris Visite card (see below).
Paris Visite, Zones 1–3	1 day: €8.50 2 days: €13.95 3 days: €18.60 5 days: €27.20 Children's passes (4- to 11-year-olds) are roughly half-price	Valid for an unlimited number of journeys on the Métro, bus, RER and Transilien services, within zones 1–3. The ticket is valid from the first occasion you use it.	If you need to travel for one day only or if you are staying within zone 1, the Mobilis pass (see above) is a less expensive option. But with the Paris Visite card you also receive special offers for various sights. Buy the ticket at Paris tourist offices or at stations.
Paris Visite, Zones 1–6	1 day: €17.05 2 days: €27.15 3 days: €38.10 5 days: €46.60	Valid for an unlimited number of journeys on the Métro, bus, RER and Transilien services, within zones 1–5 (including Versailles, Disneyland Resort Paris, and Orly and Roissy–Charles de Gaulle airports).	An expensive option.
La Carte Orange-Coupon Hebdomadaire, Zones 1–2	€15.40	Valid for a week on the Métro, buses and RER within zones 1–2.	The card is officially intended for residents of the Île de France and runs from Monday to Sunday. So the earlier in the week you purchase it, the better the value. You'll need a passport-size photo.
La Carte Orange-Coupon Mensuel, Zones 1–2	€53.50	Valid for a month on the Métro, buses and RER within zones 1–2.	See above.

Paris Métro

Paris's Métro (Métropolitain) system is the lifeblood of the city, carrying around four million passengers each day. The first trains ran in 1900, during the Belle-Époque era. The network has since grown to 16 lines and 211km (131 miles) of track.

The Métro system is efficient, inexpensive and relatively clean. It is the quickest way to travel for most journeys within the city.

Each line is colour-coded and numbered (1–14, 3b and 7b). Stations are identified either by a large M or by the famous art nouveau Métro signs. Steps, or occasionally escalators, lead down into a lobby, where you can buy tickets from either a manned booth or a machine. Larger stations have shops and cafés.

To reach the platforms, validate (composter) your ticket by slotting it into the machine at the automatic barrier, then collect it and keep it with you—inspectors make random checks. You'll often have a fairly long walk to the platform, so follow direction signs carefully. Signs will show the line number and colour. You also need to know the final destination of the train in the direction you wish to travel. Trains are frequent but get crowded during rush hour. An orange *Correspondance* sign on the platform gives directions to connecting lines. Blue signs marked *Sortie* indicate the exits.

UNDERSTANDING THE MÉTRO MAP

The information below will help you understand the Métro map on pages 52–53 and on the inside back cover. Symbols used on the map in this book may differ slightly to the symbols found on the maps posted up at Métro stations.

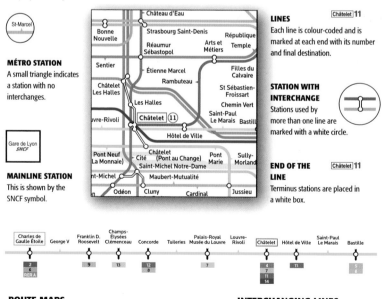

MÉTRO STATION
A small triangle indicates a station with no interchanges.

MAINLINE STATION
This is shown by the SNCF symbol.

LINES   Châtelet 11
Each line is colour-coded and is marked at each end with its number and final destination.

STATION WITH INTERCHANGE
Stations used by more than one line are marked with a white circle.

END OF THE LINE   Châtelet 11
Terminus stations are placed in a white box.

ROUTE MAPS
Route maps are posted up inside each train, allowing you to follow your journey.

INTERCHANGING LINES
On route maps, any connecting lines are marked underneath the station.

HOW TO USE THE MÉTRO

- Trains run from 5.30am to around 12.30am.
- When waiting for the train, stand away from the edge of the platform.

- To open train doors press the button (on newer trains) or lift the handle (on older trains). Most trains on Line 1 have doors that open automatically.
- Let passengers leave the train before you enter.

- A signal sounds when the automatic doors are about to close. Stand clear of the doors.

- Keep your bags close to you and watch out for pickpockets. Don't carry valuables in back pockets or rucksacks.

- Keep hold of your ticket, in case an inspector asks to see it.
- Watch for the gap between the train and the platform as you step onto and off the train.

- If you need to change lines, don't leave the interchange station or you will invalidate your ticket.
- If you find you're going in the wrong direction, come off at the next station and double-back. Follow directions to the correct platform, but stay within the automatic barriers or you'll invalidate your ticket.
- Once you have finished your journey, signs in the station indicate which exit leads to which road.
- As with many large cities, you'll probably come across people begging in Paris's Métro stations.

DID YOU KNOW?
- Hector Guimard's famous art nouveau Métro entrances are at Abbesses and Porte Dauphine.
- Fittingly for a city known for its perfume, Paris's Métro stations are freshened up with a specially created musk and vanilla scent, known as *Madeleine*.
- Look out for Métro stations whose decoration reflects the location. Examples include Bastille, with murals depicting the uprising, and Louvre-Rivoli, with its museum-style displays.
- The newest line, number 14, has glass doors separating the platform and the tracks. On the trains, a PA system announces the station you are approaching.

USEFUL LINES FOR REACHING THE SIGHTS
Line 1 (yellow) runs from east to west across the city, starting at Château de Vincennes and finishing at Grande Arche de la Défense. Key stops include Gare de Lyon, Bastille, Louvre-Rivoli and Concorde. It also runs up the Champs-Élysées—stopping at Champs-Élysées-Clemenceau, Franklin D. Roosevelt, George V and Charles de Gaulle-Étoile—allowing you to hop from one end of the avenue to the other.
Line 4 (light purple) connects the St-Germain-des-Prés district with the Right Bank. It also stops at Gare du Nord, location of the Eurostar terminal.
Line 9 (light green) takes you from the outskirts of the Bois de Boulogne, in the west of the city, up to the popular shopping areas of the Right Bank (Havre-Caumartin for Printemps and Chaussée d'Antin for Galeries Lafayette). It then continues east through République and Nation.
Line 12 (dark green) is useful if you're heading to Montmartre (use the Abbesses stop). It runs from the Left Bank. Useful stations en route include Solférino (for the Musée d'Orsay), Concorde and Madeleine.
Line 14 (purple) is handy if you are staying on the eastern side of the city, within walking distance

HOW TO USE THE MÉTRO

ODÉON

Below is a typical Métro journey from Odéon to Charles de Gaulle-Étoile (the Arc de Triomphe).

● Find a map and note the colours and numbers of the lines you'll need.

● Purchase a single ticket or use one of your *carnet* tickets or a travel pass (▷ 48).

● To reach the platforms, slot your ticket into the automatic barrier and pick it up when it re-emerges.

● Follow signs for Line 4 (light purple) in the direction of Porte de Clignancourt.

● Once at the platform, you shouldn't have too long to wait for a train.

● A route map on board the train allows you to follow your journey.

CHÂTELET

● Get off at Châtelet and follow the orange *Correspondance* signs for Line 1 (yellow), in the direction of La Défense.

● Bear in mind that Châtelet is one of the largest Métro stations, with a long walk between some platforms.

● Board the train, then get off at Charles de Gaulle-Étoile.

● Follow the blue *Sortie* (exit) signs and look for the street exit that you require.

CHARLES DE GAULLE-ÉTOILE

TIPS

● When planning your route, don't confuse Métro lines with the suburban RER lines—both are usually shown on Métro maps. RER lines have letters rather than numbers and will usually flow off the map.

● The RATP website (www.ratp.fr) has a helpful route planner and also gives up-to-date traffic and travel information.

● To estimate your journey time, allow two minutes between each station. Remember that it could take five minutes to walk to the platform (especially in warrens such as Châtelet).

● For recorded travel information in various languages call 0892 684 114.

● To speak to a travel advisor (in French only) call 32 46.

● Cash is more useful than credit cards when paying for tickets.

● Keep hold of your ticket until you have left the station, as you may come across an inspector.

● Street maps of the local areas are posted up in most station lobbies.

ON THE MOVE

of the Gare de Lyon. This ultramodern line is the quickest way to reach the heart of the city, taking you straight to Châtelet with no stops, then on to Pyramides and Madeleine. In the other direction, it runs to Bercy then across the river to the Bibliothèque François Mitterrand.

One of Paris's renowned art nouveau Métro entrances, at Abbesses, in Montmartre

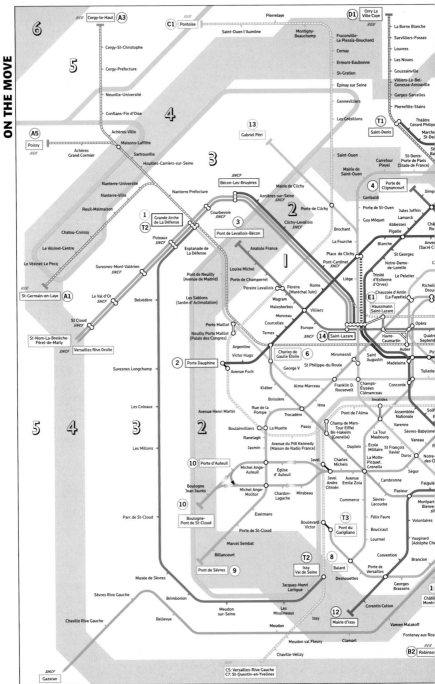

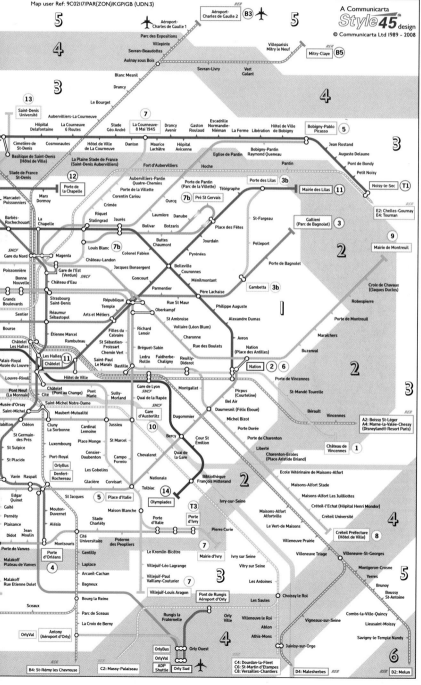

Map user Ref: 9C02117/PAR(ZON)/KGP/GB (UDN.3)

A Communicarta
Style 45 design
© Communicarta Ltd 1989 – 2008

Buses

Paris has a good network of buses, with more than 1,300 vehicles negotiating the city's traffic. Taking the bus is a good idea if you want to see the streets and sights rather than simply passing under them on the Métro, but don't expect to get anywhere quickly—the average speed is less than 13kph (8mph)!

GETTING AROUND BY BUS
● Most buses are painted easy-to-see turquoise and run from 7am to 8.30pm, although some continue until around 12.30am. You're unlikely to have to wait more than 5 or 10 minutes from Monday to Saturday, but services are reduced or, on some routes, non-existent on Sunday.
● The route number is displayed on the front of the bus, along with the final destination.
● Hold out your hand to stop the bus.
● If you need to buy a ticket, have the exact money ready as drivers do not carry much change. You can buy only single tickets on board. For information on travelcards, ▷ 48.
● Enter at the front of the bus and show your travelcard or *carnet* ticket (▷ 48) to the driver. *Carnet* tickets or single tickets must be stamped in the machine next to the driver.
● In rush hour you're unlikely to get a seat. Be prepared for a long and uncomfortable stand.
● If you are unsure of the route, you can track your journey on the route map in the bus.
● Just before your stop, press the red button to alert the driver that you want to get off. You'll see the *arrêt demandé* (stop

UNDERSTANDING BUS STOPS

Bus Numbers
Bus numbers are marked on the stop in the colour in which they appear on the route map. The number is also shown on the front of the bus.

Routes
The route is displayed on a large-scale map and every stop is marked. The stop you are standing at will be highlighted.

Timetables
Information is available about the hours and days each route operates.

Bus Stop Types
● Major bus stops are covered and have a small seat. Minor stops are marked by a pillar showing the bus numbers and routes.
● All bus stops are a distinctive turquoise.
● Major stops will also display a helpful map of the area, as well as the ubiquitous advertising posters.

requested) sign light up.
● Leave by the central doors.
● When planning your return journey, remember that buses do not necessarily follow the same route in both directions, so you may have to find a different bus to take you back.

TICKET OPTIONS
● Buses use the same tickets as the Métro. A t+ ticket allows you to change buses within a 90-minute period, but these must be bought from an RATP kiosk.
● You can buy single tickets on board, but not travelcards or *carnets* of 10 tickets. Have the exact change ready.
● Always stamp single tickets (including *carnet* tickets) in the machine near the driver, but not *Paris Visite*, *Mobilis* or *Carte Orange* passes. Keep your ticket until you have left the bus.

USEFUL ROUTES (OR SECTIONS OF ROUTES) FOR SIGHTSEEING	
ROUTE	**KEY SIGHTS**
27 (southbound)	● Opéra Palais Garnier ● Musée du Louvre ● Pont Neuf ● Pont St-Michel ● Jardin du Luxembourg
29 (eastbound)	● Opéra Palais Garnier ● Bourse ● Place des Victoires ● Centre Georges Pompidou ● Musée Carnavalet ● Place des Vosges ● Bastille
42 (northbound)	● Tour Eiffel ● Rond-Point des Champs-Élysées ● Place de la Concorde ● Place de la Madeleine
69 (westbound)	● Bastille ● Musée du Louvre ● Musée d'Orsay ● Les Invalides ● Champ de Mars
73 (eastbound)	● Arc de Triomphe ● Champs-Élysées ● Place de la Concorde ● Assemblée Nationale ● Musée d'Orsay

FINDING INFORMATION
• The *Grand Plan Lignes et Rues*, available from Métro stations, has a useful bus map.
• www.ratp.fr has bus information in French and English, as well as a handy route planner.
• Call 0892 684 114 for a recorded message in various languages or 32 46 to speak to an advisor (in French).

OTHER SERVICES
Airport buses: ▷ 42–43.
Balabus: The Balabus, aimed at visitors, runs between La Grande Arche and Gare de Lyon, taking in the Right Bank on its eastward journey and the Left Bank on its westward journey. It operates only on Sundays (afternoon to early evening), April to September, and costs between one and three single tickets.
Montmartrobus and funicular: ▷ 108–109.

Noctilien: Night buses link Châtelet with the suburbs from 1am to 5am. Buses are identified by a letter and tickets cost €1.50–3. With waits of up to one hour, you may prefer to take a taxi.
Tour buses: ▷ 248.

Buses are marked with their number and end destination

BUS BUSTER CHART

CHANGE AT OR WALK TO/FROM:
■ Place de la Concorde ■ Châtelet ■ Musée d'Orsay
■ Opéra Palais Garnier ■ Luxembourg ■ Rond-Point des Champs-Élysées
■ Trocadéro w = walk * = walk or take the Montmartrobus to/from Pigalle

Use this chart to find out which buses will take you to your chosen destination. Follow the rows of squares horizontally and vertically from the name of the destinations until they meet. This square contains the number(s) of the bus(es) you'll need to catch. Bus numbers on white squares are direct. Numbers in shaded squares show that you have to change buses or take a bus some of the way and walk the rest. Start out on the first bus listed, then change to the second bus. Look at the key to find out where you must change buses or walk to/from. Note that the bus stop may be a few minutes' walk away from the destination.

Routes are subject to change, and often differ on Sundays, so check an up-to-date timetable or bus map before setting out.

Destinations (diagonal labels, top to bottom): ARC DE TRIOMPHE · BASTILLE · CENTRE GEORGES POMPIDOU · CIMETIÈRE DU PÈRE-LACHAISE · CONCIERGERIE · GRANDE ARCHE · GRAND PALAIS · INVALIDES · JARDIN DU LUXEMBOURG · JARDIN DES TUILERIES · MONTMARTRE · MUSÉE DU LOUVRE · MUSÉE MARMOTTAN · MUSÉE D'ORSAY · NOTRE-DAME · OPÉRA PALAIS GARNIER · PLACE DE LA CONCORDE · PLACE DES VOSGES · QUARTIER LATIN · SACRÉ-CŒUR · TOUR EIFFEL

Chart cell values (each cell shows two bus numbers split by a diagonal):

- BASTILLE: 22/20
- CENTRE GEORGES POMPIDOU: 22/21, 76/29, w
- CIMETIÈRE DU PÈRE-LACHAISE: 73/69, 69, w/69, 69
- CONCIERGERIE: 22/21, 69/w, 47, 69/w
- GRANDE ARCHE: 73, 69/73, 69/73, 69/73, 72/73
- GRAND PALAIS: 73/w, 69/72, w/72, 69/72, w/72, w
- INVALIDES: 92, 69/w, 69, 69/w, 69, 73/28, 93
- JARDIN DU LUXEMBOURG: 73/84, 69/21, w/21, 69/21, 21, 73/84, 72/84, 83
- JARDIN DES TUILERIES: 73, 69/72, w/72, 69/72, w/72, 73/80, 72/80, 93/42, 84
- MONTMARTRE: 73/80, 20/68, w/67*, 69/67*, 67*/w, 73/80, w/80, 93/80, 85, 95
- MUSÉE DU LOUVRE: 73/72, 69/w, w/72, 69/72, 21, 73/72, 72, 69, 21, w, *67
- MUSÉE MARMOTTAN: 30/32, 20/32, 29/32, 21/32, 73/32, w/32, 83/32, 83/32, 42/32, 30/32, 21/32
- MUSÉE D'ORSAY: 73, 69/w, w/69, 69, 73/w, 73, w/73, 69, 84, w, 80/w, 69, 32/63
- NOTRE-DAME: 22/21, w/47, 69/w, w, 73/24, 72/w, w/42, 21, 72, *67/w, 21, 32/22, 69/21, w
- OPÉRA PALAIS GARNIER: 22, 20, w/21, 69/81, w/81, 73/42, 72/42, w/42, 21, w/42, 81, 21, 32/22, 42/42, 21
- PLACE DE LA CONCORDE: 73, 69/72, w/72, 69/72, w, 73, w/72, 83/72, 84, w, 81/42, 72, 32/42, 73/w, 72/42, 42
- PLACE DES VOSGES: 22/29, w/29, w, 69, w/69, 73/69, 72/69, 69, 21/w, 72/69, *67/w, 69, 32/w, 69/21, w/69, 72/69, 69
- QUARTIER LATIN: 22/21, 86/87, 47, 69/21, w/21, 73/24, 72/21, 82/w, w, 24, 85, 21/24, 32/21, 63, w/21, 21/21, 24, 96
- SACRÉ-CŒUR: 73/80, 69/67*, 67*/67*, 67*/67*, w/67*, 73/80, w/80, 93/80, 85, 42/80, w, 67*/w, 32/30*, 73/80, w/67*, 68*/67*, 42/80, 69/67*, 85
- TOUR EIFFEL: 73/42, 69, w/69, 69, 69/w, 73/42, w/42, 93/82, 82, 42, 80/42, 42, 32/w, 69, w/42, 42, 42, w/82, 80/42, 42

RER and Other Train Lines

The RER train network travels through the city en route to the suburbs and can be a good time-saver if you are going from one side of town to the other. For trips farther afield, the Transilien network covers the Île de France region.

RER
The RER (Réseau Express Régional) dates from 1969 and is operated by RATP and SNCF. It serves Disneyland Resort Paris to the east, Roissy-Charles de Gaulle Airport to the north, Versailles to the west and the Orly Airport train link to the south. Trains run underground in central Paris and overground in the suburbs. Bear in mind that the RER can be confusing, so for a short trip you're usually better off using the Métro.

Tickets
● A single Métro ticket is valid for RER journeys in central Paris and you can change lines (including Métro lines) on the same ticket. For journeys farther afield, you'll need to buy a separate ticket valid for the particular destination.
● Travelcards (▷ 48) are valid if they cover all the zones you are going through.

● Keep hold of your ticket as you'll need to slot it through the automatic barrier to exit the station.

Using the RER
● Trains run from around 5.30am to 12.30am.
● The RER has five lines, named A to E. Each line breaks into offshoots, which bear a number after the letter.
● Pick up a *Grand Plan Touristique* or another RER map from the station to identify the

TIPS
● The RATP website (www.ratp.fr) has a helpful route planner, as well as other travel information.
● To speak to an advisor (in French only), call 32 46. To avoid confusion, remember that the French pronounce RER *'air-eu-air'*.
● Few visitors use the RER outside central Paris (unless they are going to Versailles, Disneyland or the airport) so you may feel conspicuous. Be aware that some of the suburbs the RER passes through are somewhat run-down, and the trains and platforms tend to have more graffiti than on the Métro. Outside peak periods, the trains may also be quite empty.
● Trains run fairly frequently in central Paris, but less so in the outlying areas.

WHERE TO GO					
DESTINATION	LINE	STOP	TIME	ZONE	NOTES
Disneyland Resort Paris	A4	Marne-la-Vallée Chessy (Parc Disneyland)	35 min	Zone 5	You can buy passes for Disneyland Resort Paris from some RATP ticket offices, to save time later, although the passes do not include travel.
Versailles	C5	Versailles-Rive Gauche	35 min	Zone 4	Versailles-Rive Gauche is the closest station to the chateau, but you can also travel to Versailles-Chantiers on C7 and C8. Tickets covering train travel and entrance are available (▷ 244).
Roissy-Charles de Gaulle Airport	B3	Aéroport Charles de Gaulle 1 or 2	35 min	Zone 5	Use Charles de Gaulle 1 for Terminal 1 and Terminal 3. Use Charles de Gaulle 2 for Terminal 2.
Orly Airport	B4	Antony	30 min to Antony	Zone 3 (Antony)	From Antony, take the Orlyval train to the airport, which is in Zone 4.
Chantilly	SNCF (Gare du Nord)	Chantilly-Gouvieux	30 min	Outside the zones	The chateau is a 30-min walk from the station.

Signs show which RER lines stop at your station

line and offshoot you need. The RER lines in central Paris are on the Métro map (▷ 52–53).

● Information screens in the foyer should tell you which platform you need; or you could ask at the ticket desk.

● Slot your ticket into the automatic barrier and remember to retrieve it when it emerges.

● An increasing number of platforms have screens with information on arrival times for the next five trains.

● When leaving the train, follow blue *Sortie* signs if it is the end of your journey, or orange *Correspondance* signs if you need to change to another line.

● You'll need to slot your ticket into the automatic barrier to leave the station.

Waiting in line for tickets

TRANSILIEN TRAINS

The Transilien network, operated by SNCF, covers stations all over the Île de France. You are most likely to use these trains if you are taking an excursion to places

TIPS

● SNCF's website (www.sncf.fr) has a useful route planner.

● For information over the phone, call 0891 36 20 20.

● If you are leaving from a mainline station, give yourself plenty of time to buy a ticket and find the correct platform.

● Keep hold of your ticket in case an inspector joins the train.

Paris's mainline stations

such as Fontainebleau (▷ 242–243). Trains leave from mainline stations.

Using Transilien Trains

● Buy tickets from the ticket desk or the machine. Prices vary according to destination. Travelcards are valid if they cover all the zones you travel through.

● Stamp your ticket before boarding, either in the automatic barrier if you pass through one or in the orange machine near the entrance to the platform.

● Timetables are available at the station. Platform numbers are shown on the information boards in the station concourse.

● Check there is a suitably timed train to bring you back into Paris.

Taxis and the Batobus

Taxis are not exorbitantly expensive and can be a relatively stress-free way of getting around. Paris's 14,900 taxis are operated by a variety of companies, but all adhere to the same pricing structure.

USING A TAXI

● The best way to find a taxi is to head to one of the city's 470 taxi stands, marked by a blue *Taxis* sign. You can phone for a taxi but this is more expensive as the meter starts running as soon as the taxi sets off to collect you.
● You can hail a taxi in the street, if you can find one that is free. A white light on the roof indicates the taxi is available. When the light is off, the taxi is busy.
● All taxis are non-smoking.
● Taxi drivers are permitted to refuse a journey if there are more than three people, if you have animals or if it involves taking you outside Paris.
● If you want a receipt, ask for *un reçu*.
● If you have any complaints, contact the Préfecture de Police, Service des Taxis, 36 rue des Morillons, 75015; tel 01 53 73 53 73. Quote the taxi's registration number.

CHARGES

● Prices are regulated and tariffs should be displayed in each taxi. Always check the meter is reset when you enter the taxi. Daytime trips within central Paris should cost under €15.
● Some taxis accept bank cards but it is best to have cash available. It is usual to give a tip of around 10 per cent.
● The three tariffs (A, B and C) are set out in the prices chart (right), along with the surcharges.

TAXI COMPANIES

Taxi companies include:
Alpha Taxis: tel 01 45 85 85 85
Automatic Taxi: tel 0899 65 67 67
Taxis Bleus: tel 0891 701 010; www.taxis-bleus.com
Taxis G7: tel 01 47 39 47 39; www.taxisg7.fr

Taxis can be a convenient way of getting around

THE BATOBUS

The Batobus is a relaxing way to get around, allowing you to hop on and off at eight stops along the Seine. It runs from early February to early January. From early June to early September it runs 10–9.30; ask for times during the rest of the year. Boats leave every 15–30 minutes, stopping at *quais* near the Eiffel Tower, Champs-Élysées, Musée d'Orsay, Louvre, St-Germain-des-Prés, Notre-Dame, Hôtel de Ville and Jardin des Plantes. A one-day pass costs €12, a two-day pass €14 and a five-day pass €17 (half-price for children under 12). You can buy passes at the stops or the tourist office. Tel 0825 050101; www.batobus.com.

TAXI PRICES		
Pickup charge	€2.10 (or €2.80 at mainline stations)	
Tarif A	€0.82 per km	Central Paris 7am–7pm, Mon–Sat.
Tarif B	€1.10 per km	Suburbs 7am–7pm, Mon–Sat. Central Paris 7pm–7am and all day Sun and public hols. Daytime journeys to and from the airports.
Tarif C	€1.33 per km	Suburbs 7pm–7am and all day Sun and public hols. All day, every day outside the suburbs. Night journeys to and from the airports.
Surcharges	You will be charged €2.75 for a fourth passenger, €0.60 for an animal and €1 for each piece of luggage over 5kg. There is a minimum fare of €5.60.	

Walking, Bicycling, In-line Skating

Paris is gradually accepting more eco-friendly ways of getting about. An increasing number of people travel by foot or bicycle—you may well find that some sights can be reached more quickly by either of these methods than by the Métro, with its labyrinthine corridors. Bicyclists need to keep their wits about them, but may find their journeys are quicker than by car or bus. In-line skating is also extremely popular, with up to 12,000 people turning out to the special rides on Friday nights.

WALKING

Métro stations are everywhere and this can make it tempting to hop on a train even for short journeys. But if the weather is good try going on foot instead—it's a great way to get to know the layout of the city. You can easily walk from one district to another and it is far more enjoyable than the Métro.

The down side is the amount of traffic on the busier streets, especially place de la Concorde, Pont Neuf and the roads running alongside the Seine.

BICYCLING

Paris has more than 371km (230 miles) of bicycle tracks and plenty of rental outlets. In 2007 city authorities launched the

---

TIPS

- Be aware that a green-man signal or a striped pedestrian crossing do not necessarily mean cars will stop.
- When crossing roads, British visitors need to remember that traffic drives on the right in France.
- Avoid walking in deserted areas at night.

Velib bike rental initiative (www.velib.paris.fr) to encourage greener transport options. Over 20,000 bikes are available to pick up and drop off at over 1,000 locations around the city. Fees are paid in the form of an access card (current charges are €1 per day, €5 per week or €29 per year) which entitles riders to 30 minutes free use per journey, after which costs are €1 for an additional 30 minutes, €2 for a further 30 minutes and €4 for each additional 30 minutes.

One- and seven-day cards can be bought at rental sites and fees due at the end of the rental period can be paid at automatic machines. Transfers between many major museums and monuments are possible within the initial 30-minute period. The *Paris à Vélo* map, available from the tourist office, town hall or bicycle rental shops, gives details of bicycle routes.

Remember that if a bicycle lane is available, you must use it. You must also wear a helmet and have bicycle lights and a bell. Lock your bicycle well. Bicycles are not allowed on the Métro but are permitted on certain RER lines outside rush hour. A good option if you're keen to bicycle is to take a tour run by Paris à Vélo C'est Sympa or Roue Libre.

Useful Contacts
Paris à Vélo C'est Sympa
Bicycle tours during the day and night. Bicycle rental. Tours leave from 22 rue Alphonse Baudin 75011, and reservation is compulsory.
Tel 01 48 87 60 01
www.parisvelosympa.com

Roue Libre
Bicycle rental and guided bicycle tours, run by RATP.
1 Passage Mondétour (Forum des Halles), 75001
Tel 0810 441 534

IN-LINE SKATING

In-line skating is popular in Paris, helped by the Pari-Roller rides on Friday evening, which can attract up to 12,000 participants. You need to be an experienced skater to take part in this three-hour ride and you must check your insurance cover. The skate departs from outside the Gare

On your skates—it's environmentally friendly and fun

Montparnasse at 10pm (in good weather only).

An easier ride, run by Rollers et Coquillages, leaves from Nomades store, Bastille, on Sunday at 2.30pm.

If you want to skate on your own, remember that by law you must stay off the roads. You are not allowed to skate along the Champs-Élysées walkways or wear skates on the Métro, buses or RER.

Useful Contacts
Pari-Roller
Friday-night ride leaves from Gare Montparnasse at 10pm, weather permitting.
www.pari-roller.com

Nomades
Skate rental.
37 boulevard Bourdon, 75004
Tel 01 44 54 07 44
www.nomadeshop.com

Rollers et Coquillages
Sunday afternoon skate.
Tel 01 44 54 94 42
www.rollers-coquillages.org

DRIVING

Driving in Paris

ON THE MOVE

The best advice for driving in Paris is to avoid it! You'll face heavy traffic, tricky and expensive parking and confusing one-way systems. In addition, petrol (gas) stations can be hard to find. It is far better to use the Métro or buses, or take a taxi. However, if you do decide to drive, here are some tips.

TIPS
- The speed limit in central Paris is 50kph (31mph). On the ring road (périphérique) the limit is 80kph (49mph).
- Don't park or stop on any of the axes rouges (key routes through the city).
- In built-up areas, give way to traffic approaching from the right (priorité à droite), unless signs advise you otherwise.
- Don't use the bus lanes.
- Try to avoid driving during rush hour, weekdays from around 7am to 9.30am and 4.30pm to 7.30pm.
- The city's roads are least congested in August, when many Parisians escape to the coast. But August is also when most road repairs take place.

FINDING YOUR WAY
- Paris's complex network of frequently narrow streets can be very confusing. Always plan your route in advance.
- Useful maps include Plan de Paris par Arrondissement, published by Grafocarte, and Paris par Arrondissement, by Editions L'Indispensable.

LOCAL DRIVING CUSTOMS
- You may find the concept of lanes is not taken too seriously, nor are red traffic lights—but don't be tempted to follow suit as you can be fined €90 for ignoring a red light or stop sign.
- Parisian drivers can be aggressive.
- Cars move fast when they can.
- Watch for delivery vehicles that may block you in by double parking.

PARKING
On-Street Parking
- Charges usually apply from 9am to 7pm, Monday to Saturday. Sundays and holidays are generally free, but always check before parking your car on the street.
- You can park for up to two hours.
- Parking meters accept special cards (buy these from some cafés or tobacconists).
- Hourly rates vary from under €1 to over €2.

Parking Areas
- You'll usually find underground parking areas in shopping complexes, near large department stores, in business districts and in certain tourist areas. Look for the 'P' sign.
- Prices vary, and charges can be by the hour, day, weekend, month or year.
- For more information on parking areas for cars or motorcycles, buy the 288-page guide Parkings de Paris, which lists more than 200 parking areas, above and below ground, and gives prices. It also contains street maps, and maps of the Métro, RER and bus routes. It costs €15 and can be bought at the Paris Tourist Office, bookshops or from Editions Com 3000, 21 rue Lamartine, 75009 (tel 01 45 26 59 74; www.parkingsdeparis.com).

Parking on the Outskirts
- To save parking charges, some people park in the suburbs and take the Métro, RER or bus into central Paris.

You'll need to pay at the meter to park on many streets in Paris

- Stick to one of the safer areas like Maison-Lafitte, Neuilly, St-Cloud or Levallois-Perret (for advice on visiting areas outside the périphérique, ▷ 305).
- It is possible to park for free at some supermarkets—but don't stay overnight.

Towing Away
- If your car isn't where you left it, contact the local police station or the police headquarters (tel 01 53 71 53 71) for details of the car pound.

General Driving Hints

A car is useful if you want to take an excursion out of Paris, or move on to a second destination in France. A good system of *autoroutes* links Paris with the main cities: The A1 leads to the north, the A13 to Normandy and the northwest, the A4 to the east, the A10 to the west and southwest, and the A6 to the Alps and the Riviera. The French drive on the right.

PLANNING

● You must have at least third-party motor insurance to drive in France. But fully comprehensive cover is strongly advised as third party in France covers less than in some countries.

● If driving your own car, display an international sticker near the rear registration plate.

● Adjust headlights of left-hand drive vehicles for driving on the right in France.

RENTING A CAR

● ▷ 299.

ROADS

● The *autoroute* is the French counterpart of the British motorway or American expressway and is marked by an 'A' on maps and road signs. A few sections around key cities are free of charge, but tolls are charged on the rest *(autoroutes à péage)*. Always have cash available as foreign credit cards may not be accepted.

● In France, a highway or trunk road is called a *Route Nationale* (N).

● The next level down is the *Route Départementale* (D), although these roads can still be wide and fast. There are also quieter country roads.

THE LAW

● Always carry a passport or national ID card, a valid driving licence, the vehicle's registration document and a certificate of motor insurance.

● The minimum age to drive in France is 18.

● In built-up areas, vehicles should give way to traffic coming from the right *(Priorité à droite)*, unless signs advise otherwise. At roundabouts (traffic circles) with signs saying *Cédez le passage* or *Vous n'avez pas la priorité*, traffic

already on the roundabout has priority. On roundabouts without these signs, traffic entering has priority. A priority road can also be shown by a white diamond-shaped sign with a yellow diamond within it. A black line through the diamond indicates the end of priority.

CÉDEZ LE PASSAGE

A red-bordered triangle with a black cross on a white back-ground, with the words *passage protégé*, also shows priority.

● You must wear a seatbelt. Children under 10 must travel in the back, with a booster seat, except for babies under nine months with a specially adapted rear-facing front seat (but not in cars with airbags).

● Do not overtake where there is a solid single central line.

● Don't drive after drinking alcohol. There are harsh penalties in place for offenders.

● Always stop at stop signs.

ROAD SIGNS

Allumez vos phares Switch on your lights.
Cédez le passage Give way (yield).
Chantier Roadworks.
Péage Toll.
Priorité à droite/gauche Priority to the right/left.
Rappel Reminder (continue with the previous instruction).
Route barrée Road closed.
Sens interdit No entry.
Sens unique One way.
Serrez à droite/gauche Keep to the right/left.
Stationnement interdit No parking.
Travaux Roadworks.

EQUIPMENT

● Carry a red warning triangle in case of breakdown.
● Have a spare-bulb kit to hand.

FUEL

● Fuel comes as unleaded *(sans plomb*, 95 and 98 octane), lead replacement petrol *(LRP* or *supercarburant)*, diesel *(gasoil* or *gazole)* and LPG.

● Many petrol (gas) stations close on Sundays and at 6pm the rest of the week.

● Prices are high at filling stations on *autoroutes*.

● Filling stations can be far apart in rural areas, so never let your tank get too low.

CAR BREAKDOWN

● Make sure you have adequate breakdown cover.
● If you break down on an *autoroute* or the Paris *périphérique*, you must call the police or the official breakdown service for that area. There are emergency telephones on the roadside.

SPEED LIMITS	
Urban roads	50kph (31mph)
Outside built-up areas	90kph (56mph); 80kph (49mph) in wet weather
Dual carriageways (divided highways) and non-toll *autoroutes*	110kph (68mph); 100kph (62mph) in wet weather
Toll *autoroutes*	130kph (80mph); 110kph (68mph) in wet weather

Visiting drivers who have held a licence for fewer than two years are not allowed to exceed the wet-weather limits, even in good weather.

VISITORS WITH A DISABILITY

Facilities are gradually improving for visitors with a disability. All renovated and newly constructed buildings are now well equipped and some buses and certain RER stations are accessible to wheelchair users. But if you have reduced mobility you're still likely to encounter challenges in getting around Paris—kerbs (curbs) can be high, ramps are few and elevators are sometimes too small.

ON THE MOVE

ARRIVING

By Air Both Roissy-Charles de Gaulle and Orly airports are well equipped for people with disabilities. Shuttle buses between terminals have ramps for wheelchair users, as well as voice announcements for the visually impaired. The terminals have adapted toilets, low-level telephones and reserved parking spaces. For more information, download the *Guide Pratique Roissy* or the *Guide Pratique Orly Sud et Ouest* from the Aéroports de Paris website, www.adp.fr, or order a copy online. Operators that offer specialist transportation from the airports into Paris include AiHROP (01 41 29 01 29; www.aihrop.com) and ATAGH (01 40 05 12 15); in addition, G7 HORIZON (01 47 39 00 91) has a fleet of specially adapted taxis. Reserve them in advance. The Orlyval train (▷ 42–43) is accessible to wheelchairs.
By Train The modern design of the Eurostar trains and terminals makes them wheelchair-friendly. Passengers using a wheelchair can also benefit from discounted tickets.

GETTING AROUND

Paris's main way of getting around—the Métro—is virtually inaccessible to wheelchair users because of its countless steps, warren of passageways and inflexible automatic barriers. The exception is Line 14, which also has voice announcements as the train draws in, for passengers with visual impairments. Certain RER stations on lines A and B have elevators to the platforms, although some can be operated only by a member of staff (press the *Appel* button for assistance). RATP's Mission Accessibilité (tel 01 49 28 18 84) publishes a

Guide Pratique listing the RER stations that are accessible to wheelchair users. Even when a station is listed as accessible, wheelchair users are still likely to need assistance to board the train. Most ticket offices have induction loops for people with hearing impairments.

Buses can be a useful way of getting around, as some have ramps, including routes 20, 21, 24, 26, 27, 30, 38, 39, 53, 60, 62, 80, 88, 91, 92, 94, 95 and 96. The 29, 31, 43, 54, 63, 64, 81, PC1, PC2, PC3 and NOI buses, including routes 26, 63, 80, 84, 91, 92, 94 and 96, are fitted with voice announcements of the next stop for passengers with visual impairments.

For information on accessible bus routes, look up the website of the operator RATP (www.ratp.fr) or pick up the map *Grand Plan Lignes et Rues—2* from stations.

RATP runs an accompaniment service (Les Compagnons du Voyage) to assist people with reduced mobility. You have to reserve in advance and a fee is charged (tel 01 53 11 11 12).

The UK-based Access Project publishes a helpful book giving detailed information on going to Paris, accommodation, sights and getting around (£10 donation; see below for contact details).

USEFUL ORGANIZATIONS

Access Project
www.accessproject-phsp.org/paris/about.htm
39 Bradley Gardens, West Ealing, London, W13 8HE, UK
Detailed advice on getting around.

Les Compagnons du Voyage
Tel 01 53 11 11 12
An accompaniment service on the Métro, RER and buses.

Holiday Care Service
www.holidaycare.org.uk
Tel 0845 124 9971 (UK)
Travel and holiday information for people with disabilities. The organization produces an information pack on France (£5).

Infomobi
www.infomobi.com
Tel 0810 646464
Information about buses, the Métro and RER trains in the Île de France for people with disabilities.

Mobile en Ville
www.mobile-en-ville.asso.fr
Tel 0682 917216
A website packed with information on disability access and related issues.

Mobility International USA
www.miusa.org
Promotes international travel and exchange schemes for people with disabilities.

Paris Tourist Office
www.parisinfo.com
Tel 0892 683000
Useful information about wheelchair access in museums, on buses, the RER and at airports.

RATP Mission Accessibilité
E mail:
mission.accessibilite@ratp.fr
163 bis avenue du Clichy, Impasse Chalabre, Paris 75017
Tel 0810 646464
Set up by the bus and Métro operator RATP to work for improved access for people with disabilities.

Society for Accessible Travel and Hospitality (SATH)
www.sath.org
A US-based organization offering advice for visitors with disabilities and promoting awareness of their travel requirements.

LEAVING PARIS

France has a comprehensive rail network and moving between cities and other European countries is relatively simple. The network, run by SNCF, is made up of *Grandes Lignes* (long-distance lines) and *Lignes Régionales* (regional lines). The *Grandes Lignes* have the regular Corail trains and the faster TGV trains, which can travel at speeds of up to 357kph (221mph). The *Lignes Régionales* have TER trains *(Trains Express Régionaux)*, called Transilien trains in Paris. Paris has six mainline stations, each serving different regions in France and the rest of Europe. There are good connections with the Métro and buses (and RER in some cases).

TICKETS
● Most trains have first and second classes, both of which are perfectly acceptable.
● Fares are split into blue and white (Corail) or normal and peak (TGV). Reduced-rate fares are generally available for normal travel on mainline routes, excluding couchette services.
● Ticket prices vary according to the level of comfort (first or second class; called Comfort Level 1 and Comfort Level 2 on Thalys) and departure time. First class fares are roughly 50 per cent more expensive than second class.
● You can buy tickets at the stations, at SNCF offices around the city and through some travel agents. Tickets for TGV trains must be reserved. You can do this up to a few minutes before departure, although in peak season it is best to book well in advance. Couchettes must be booked at least 75 minutes before the train leaves its first station.
● Make sure you stamp your ticket in one of the orange machines on the platforms before you start your journey. You'll risk a fine if you forget to do this.
● If you are under 26, you can get a 25 per cent discount (called *Découverte 12–25*) on train travel. Seniors also receive discounts (called *Découverte Senior*).
● Other discounts include *Découverte Séjour* (for a round trip), *Découverte à 2* (for two to nine persons) and *Prem's* fares (second class only; available online); special conditions apply to all three.

TGV trains travel across France

● A variety of rail passes are available, which allow travel either within France only, or within France and certain other countries, or within the whole of Europe. You should buy these before you enter France, either through travel agents or Rail Europe (▷ 64).

CATERING SERVICE
● Catering facilities—ranging from sandwiches and salads to hot meals—are available on most TGV and Corail services, but at a price.
● A benefit of first class is that you can have food served at your seat during meal times on most TGV trains. You'll need to reserve in advance, except on TGV *Méditerranée* trains.
● You can reserve meals when you purchase your train ticket. Ticket machines dispense meal vouchers.
● Hot and cold drinks, sandwiches and snacks are served on most trains.
● Overnight trains (and some day services) have vending machines dispensing hot and cold drinks and sweets (candy).

FASTEST JOURNEY TIMES FROM PARIS (APPROXIMATE)
Amsterdam
4 hours 10 min
Bordeaux
3 hours
Brussels
1 hour 20 min
Lille
1 hour
Marseille
3 hours

OVERNIGHT TRAINS
● Most overnight trains offer either reclining seats, couchette berths or a sleeper car.
● Reclining seats are available only in second class. You can adjust the head and foot rests.
● In first class, couchettes are in four-berth compartments; in second class they are in six-berth compartments.
● Sleeper car compartments are for up to two people in first class and up to three people in second class.
● Trains travel to cities in France and to other European countries.

STATION ASSISTANCE

● Larger stations have an information kiosk, which is usually easy to find.
● If you need assistance, look for a member of the station staff, identifiable by their red waistcoats.
● You'll need a €1 deposit to use the luggage trolleys (carts).
● Porters are on hand to help with your luggage in main stations. They wear red jackets and black or navy caps.

LEFT LUGGAGE

● Some stations have a left-luggage office or coin-operated lockers. Electronic locks issue a printed ticket with a code number. You'll need to keep this ticket for when you return to collect your items.
● Don't store valuables in lockers.
● Security concerns mean that left-luggage facilities are not always available.

A packed departures board (right).
The chart (below) indicates the key destinations served by mainline stations in Paris

UNDERSTANDING RAILWAY TIMETABLES

● You can pick up free timetables *(horaires)* at stations.
● SNCF timetables are usually published twice a year—the summer one lasts from mid-June/early July to mid-December and the winter one from mid-December to mid-June/early July.
● There are two styles of timetable: one for the *Grandes Lignes*, covering high-speed TGV and other mainline services, and another for the regional TER trains.
● Be prepared to decipher French railway terminology. On *Grandes Lignes* timetables, two rows of boxed numbers at the top refer to the *numéro de train* (train number) and to the *notes à consulter* (footnotes). In TER timetables, the train number is not listed.
● Footnotes at the bottom explain when a particular train runs *(circule)*. *Tous les jours* means it runs every day; *sauf dimanche et fêtes* means it doesn't run on Sundays and holidays. *Jusqu'au*, followed by a date, indicates the service runs only up until that date.

USEFUL CONTACTS

Rail Europe
Sells a variety of European rail passes.
www.raileurope.com
(for US visitors)
www.raileurope.co.uk
(for UK visitors)

SNCF
www.sncf.com Tel 3635
www.voyages-sncf.com
www.tgv.com
Tel 0033 892 353535 (from outside France)

Thalys
www.thalys.com
Tel 0892 353 536
Trains to cities in northern Europe.

MAINLINE STATION INFORMATION					
STATION	**MAJOR DESTINATIONS**	**MAJOR TRAIN OPERATOR**	**CONNECTIONS: MÉTRO**	**RER**	**TOURIST DESTINATIONS INCLUDE**
Gare d'Austerlitz	Central and southwest France, Spain, Portugal	CORAIL Trainhôtel Elipsos	Lines 5, 10	Line C	Poitiers, Limoges, Madrid, Barcelona, the Alps
Gare de l'Est	Eastern France, Germany, Luxembourg, Switzerland, Austria, Eastern Europe	CORAIL	Lines 4, 5, 7	None	Strasbourg
Gare de Lyon	Southeast France, Switzerland, Italy	TGV	Lines 1, 14	Lines A, D	Lyon, Nice, Grenoble, Milan, Florence, Geneva, Marseille
Gare Montparnasse	Western and southern France, Spain	TGV	Lines 4, 6, 12, 13	None	Brest, Quimper, Nantes, Toulouse, Bordeaux, Biarritz
Gare du Nord	Northern France, UK, Germany, Holland, Belgium, Scandinavia	TGV, Thalys, Eurostar	Lines 4, 5	Lines B, D, E	Brussels, London, Amsterdam, Lille
Gare St-Lazare	Northwest France	CORAIL	Lines 3, 12, 13	Line E	Normandy
TGV services also leave from Aéroport Charles-de-Gaulle TGV and Marne-La-Vallée Disneyland Resort Paris.					

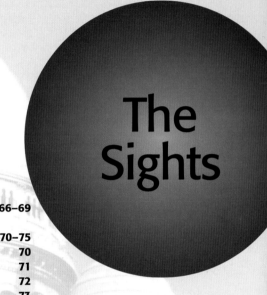

This section is divided into two parts: Sightseeing Areas guides you to the best things to see in six districts of Paris (circled in blue on the map inside the front cover); the A–Z of Sights is an alphabetical listing of places to visit across the city, located on the maps on pages 66–69.

The Sights

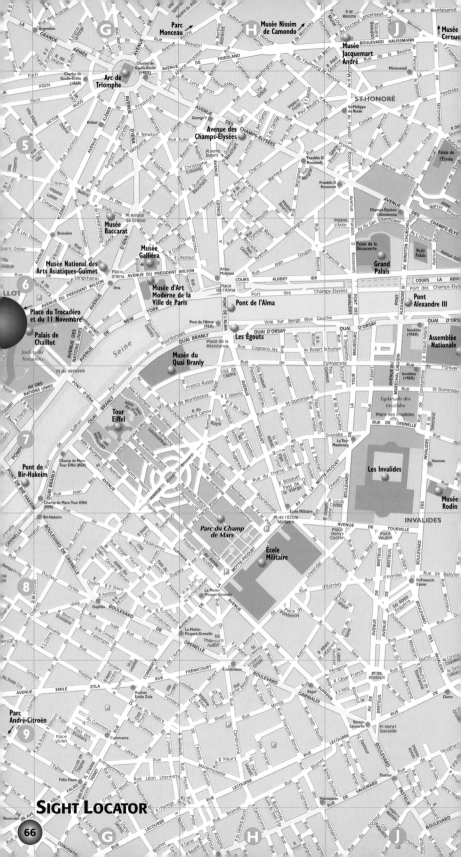

G
H
J

Parc
Monceau

Musée Nissim
de Camondo

↑ Musée
Cernus...

Musée
Jacquemart
André

BOULEVARD   HAUSSMANN

Arc de
Triomphe

ST-HONORÉ

5

Avenue des
Champs-Elysées

Palais de
l'Élysée

Musée
Baccarat

Musée
Galliéra

Musée National des
Arts Asiatiques-Guimet

Grand
Palais

6

Musée d'Art
Moderne de la
Ville de Paris

Place du Trocadéro
et du 11 Novembre

Pont de l'Alma

Pont
Alexandre III

Palais de
Chaillot

Les Égouts

Assemblée
Nationale

Musée du
Quai Branly

7

Tour
Eiffel

Les Invalides

Pont de
Bir-Hakeim

Musée
Rodin

INVALIDES

Parc du Champ
de Mars

École
Militaire

8

Parc
André-Citroën

9

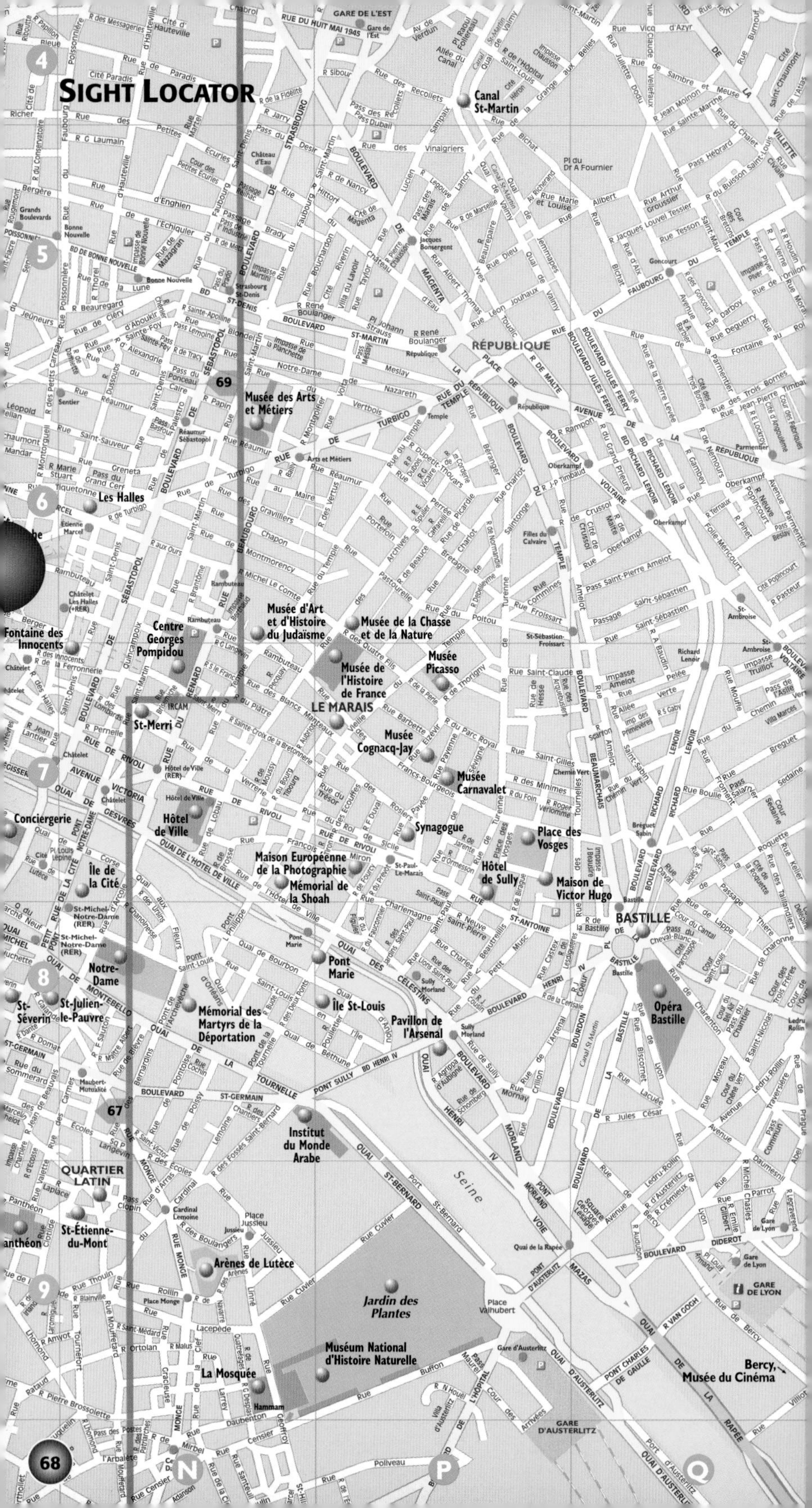
Sight Locator
Gare de l'Est
Canal St-Martin
République
Musée des Arts et Métiers
Les Halles
Fontaine des Innocents
Centre Georges Pompidou
Musée d'Art et d'Histoire du Judaïsme
Musée de la Chasse et de la Nature
Musée de l'Histoire de France
Musée Picasso
Le Marais
St-Merri
Musée Cognacq-Jay
Musée Carnavalet
Hôtel de Ville
Conciergerie
Synagogue
Place des Vosges
Maison Européenne de la Photographie
Mémorial de la Shoah
Hôtel de Sully
Maison de Victor Hugo
Île de la Cité
Bastille
Notre-Dame
Pont Marie
St-Séverin
St-Julien-le-Pauvre
Mémorial des Martyrs de la Déportation
Île St-Louis
Pavillon de l'Arsenal
Opéra Bastille
Institut du Monde Arabe
Seine
Quartier Latin
St-Étienne-du-Mont
Panthéon
Arènes de Lutèce
Jardin des Plantes
Muséum National d'Histoire Naturelle
La Mosquée
Hammam
Gare de Lyon
Gare d'Austerlitz
Bercy, Musée du Cinéma
4
5
6
7
8
9
N
P
Q
67
69

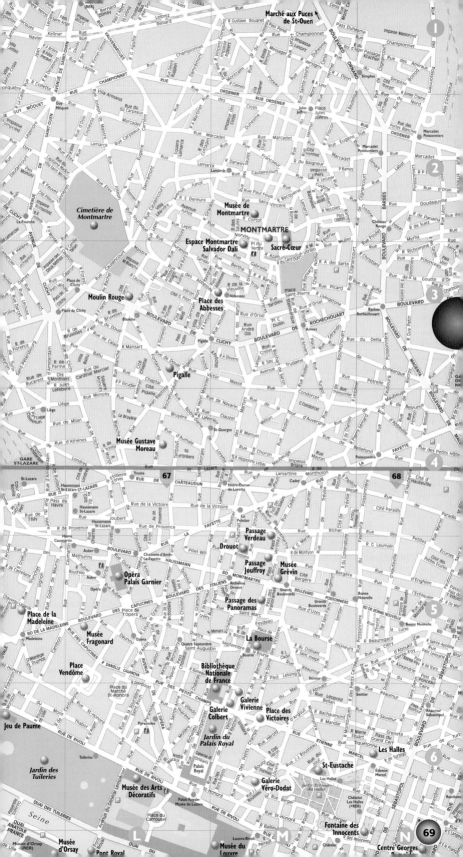

Le Marais

HOW TO GET THERE

Place des Vosges
🚇 St-Paul, Bastille
🚌 29
Centre Georges Pompidou
🚇 Rambuteau, Hôtel de Ville
🚌 29, 38, 47, 75

This district, on the Right Bank, is sandwiched between Les Halles and Bastille and is packed with museums, elegant mansions and quirky shops. The wacky Centre Georges Pompidou sits on its western border.

THE SIGHTS

The Marais gives you a taste of pre-Revolution Paris, when aristocrats vied to create the most elegant mansions and courtyards. Many of these ornate 17th- and 18th-century buildings remain and you can wander around those that have been converted into museums. The district is home to Paris's oldest

The elegant place des Vosges is Paris's oldest square

square, place des Vosges, a leafy haven that takes you by surprise as you stumble upon it from the surrounding bustling streets. It is bordered by smart boutiques and cafés. You'll also find a lively Jewish quarter in the streets around the rue des Rosiers, in addition to stylish boutiques.

The Marais was originally marshland (*marais* means marsh). In the Middle Ages, the northern part was under the rule of the Knights Templar. By the 17th century, aristocrats were moving into the area and building their sumptuous mansions. For more information, ▷ 107.

THE MAIN SIGHTS

Even if you're not a particular fan of museums, try to visit one or two in the Marais, if only to see the interiors of these beautiful mansions. Save time to explore the fashionable shops and to relax in a café in the place des Vosges. To round off the day, a visit to the Centre Georges Pompidou will bring you sharply back to the 21st century.

Centre Georges Pompidou
One of the largest collections of modern art in the world, housed in a suitably spectacular 1970s building that famously has its insides on the outside (▷ 82–86).

Musée Carnavalet
Adjacent 16th- and 17th-century mansions contain a fascinating collection of memorabilia relating to the history of Paris, including plenty from the Revolutionary and Napoleonic eras (▷ 114–115).

Musée Picasso
A must for Picasso fans, with more than 200 paintings, 160 sculptures and numerous drawings, set in the beautiful 17th-century Hôtel Salé (▷ 135).

Place des Vosges
A calming, historic square, inaugurated in 1612 as the place Royale (▷ 150).

OTHER PLACES TO VISIT
Other museums include the **Musée Cognacq-Jay** (▷ 113), the **Musée d'Art et d'Histoire**

du Judaïsme (▷ 112), the **Maison de Victor Hugo** (▷ 106), and the **Musée de la Chasse et de la Nature** (▷ 113). Paris's grand town hall, the **Hôtel de Ville**, stands on the southwestern border (▷ 95).

The eccentric Stravinsky Fountain, outside the Pompidou

WHERE TO EAT
The Centre Georges Pompidou has a first-floor café as well as **Georges** restaurant (▷ 268) on the sixth floor, where you can enjoy great city views. For a drink in a (relatively) tranquil, picturesque setting you can't beat the place des Vosges.

Piccolo Teatro
Vegetarian cuisine with influences from across the world (▷ 273).

Trésor
This chic Italian restaurant is blessed with one of the finest terraces in the city (▷ 276).

Montmartre

HOW TO GET THERE

🚇 Anvers, Abbesses, Blanche, Lamarck-Caulaincourt take you to the outskirts
🚌 Montmartrobus; buses 30, 31, 54, 68, 74, 80, 85 have stops on the outskirts

This hilltop village, to the north of the Right Bank, has two of Paris's most famous symbols: Sacré-Cœur and the Moulin Rouge. Parisians call it *La Butte* (the mound).

Montmartre is a world apart from Paris, despite lying well within the city's boundary. It has managed to retain the atmosphere of its late-19th-century heyday, when artists such as Henri de Toulouse-Lautrec were frequent visitors to its decadent dance halls. Away from the tourist honeypots of Sacré-Cœur and place du Tertre, quiet, cobbled streets take you back hundreds of years—Montmartre's oldest

The entrance to the Espace Montmartre—Salvador Dalí

building dates from the mid-17th century. Wander through these back streets and alleyways to see romantic tree-lined steps, squares, gardens and individually designed houses. There is even a small vineyard, tucked away on the rue des Saules.

Back on the tourist trail, there are wonderful views over Paris from the front steps of Sacré-Cœur. At nearby place du Tertre a bevy of street artists are waiting to paint your portrait or draw your caricature, should you wish.

For more information, ▷ 108–109. For a walk around Montmartre, ▷ 226–227.

THE MAIN SIGHTS

Sacré-Cœur is the big draw for most visitors, but make sure you also explore Montmartre's quieter back streets. If you want to save your legs, the Petit Train de Montmartre (Promotrain) and the Montmartrain tour the area. The Musée de Montmartre will fill you in on the history.

Cimetière de Montmartre
Visit the graves of composer Hector Berlioz and artists Edgar Degas and Jean-Baptiste Greuze (▷ 87).

Espace Montmartre—Salvador Dalí
The biggest Dalí collection in France (▷ 92).

Moulin Rouge
Paris's most famous cabaret venue still hosts glittering shows (▷ 111).

Musée de Montmartre
Montmartre's oldest building is a fitting venue for this museum (▷ 126).

Sacré-Cœur
A stunning basilica crowning Montmartre's hill (▷ 154–157).

OTHER PLACES TO VISIT
At **place des Abbesses** (▷ 145) you can admire one of Paris's few remaining art nouveau Métro entrances. Wander past the vineyard on rue des Saules on the first Saturday in October and you'll see the grapes being harvested. The **Bateau-Lavoir studio,** where Pablo Picasso and

Georges Braque conceived Cubism, once stood on place Émile-Goudeau, although it has been replaced with a concrete structure. Finally, if Sacré-Cœur is teeming with visitors, go to the quieter church

Sacré-Cœur looks best against a clear blue sky

of **St-Pierre-de-Montmartre,** nearby to the west.

WHERE TO EAT
Restaurants on place du Tertre can be rather pricey. For a light bite, there are cafés at place des Abbesses.

Au Pied du Sacré-Cœur
The food at this stylish restaurant ranges from the traditional to the more innovative (▷ 261).

Rose Bakery
Rose Bakery offers excellent sandwiches, soups, salads and pastries, all made using organic ingredients (▷ 274).

THE SIGHTS

Champs-Élysées

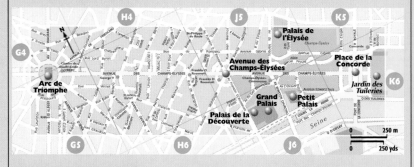

THE SIGHTS

HOW TO GET THERE

Arc de Triomphe
Ⓜ Charles de Gaulle–Étoile
🚌 22, 30, 31, 52, 73, 92

Place de la Concorde
Ⓜ Concorde
🚌 24, 42, 72, 73, 84, 94

Paris's most celebrated avenue sweeps majestically from the Arc de Triomphe to the historic place de la Concorde. It is over 2km

sprinkled between the 8th and adjoining 17th *arrondissements*.

The Champs-Élysées dates from the early 17th century, when Marie de Medici, wife of Henri IV, turned the area into a fashionable driveway. Landscape designer André Le Nôtre added his mark later that century, planting alleys of trees as an extension to the Tuileries gardens.

For more information, ▷ 76–79.

THE MAIN SIGHTS

The Arc de Triomphe is the must-see sight, but the Grand Palais, southeast of the Rond-Point des Champs-Élysées, is also worth visiting. At the eastern end of the avenue, place de la Concorde is brimming with history (and cars).

Arc de Triomphe
Napoleon's grand arch, and the focal point for the city's most famous street (▷ 76–79).

Champs-Élysées
Elegant, historic—and packed with people and traffic (▷ 76–79).

Grand Palais
Prestigious art shows in a magnificent art nouveau palace (▷ 95).

Jardin des Tuileries
Gardens next to place de la Concorde (▷ 105).

Palais de la Découverte
A science museum with a planetarium (▷ 95).

Place de la Concorde
The site of 1,300 grisly beheadings during the Revolution (▷ 148).

OTHER PLACES TO VISIT
The **Petit Palais** (▷ 95), which has undergone a period of extensive renovation, houses the fine Musée des Beaux-Arts de la Ville (Municipal Museum of Fine Arts). It sits opposite the Grand Palais. Just north of the Champs-Élysées, on the rue du Faubourg St-Honoré, the **Palais de l'Élysée** is the official home of the French President.

The Arc de Triomphe towers over the cars

(1.2 miles) long and 71m (232ft) wide.

This broad, tree-lined avenue bustles with activity. By day the wide walkways are packed with people visiting the shops, cafés and the *pièce de résistance*, the Arc de Triomphe. By night it is the turn of the clubs, cinemas and restaurants, either on the avenue itself or in the nearby streets. Many of Paris's luxury hotels and exclusive nightclubs cluster around the Champs-Élysées and nearby avenue Montaigne and Faubourg St-Honoré, and the temples of top chefs are generously

The magnificent lobby of the Palais de la Découverte

WHERE TO EAT

There are plenty of restaurants and cafés along the Champs-Élysées, mainly at the Arc de Triomphe end. Some charge a premium for the location so you may prefer to venture into the side streets. The Grand Palais and Palais de la Découverte both have cafés and the Jardin des Tuileries has open-air cafés.

Asian
A tea room and Asian restaurant (▷ 261).

Bistro Romain
Italian cuisine at this chain restaurant (▷ 263).

Around the Louvre

HOW TO GET THERE

Musée du Louvre

🚇 Palais-Royal/Musée du Louvre

🚌 21, 27, 39, 48, 67, 69, 72, 74, 75, 76, 81, 85, 95

Forum des Halles

🚇 Les Halles

🚌 29, 38, 47

🚈 Châtelet–Les Halles

Linked with royalty for centuries, the section of the Right Bank around the Louvre is known for its grandeur. The Louvre has a commanding position next to the Seine, with the Jardin des Tuileries to its west and the Palais Royal to its north.

In its former life as a royal palace, the Louvre bestowed a certain amount of regal status on the surrounding area. Gradually other royal buildings sprang up around it, including the Tuileries Palace (destroyed by fire in 1871) and

Relaxing by the pond in the Jardin des Tuileries

the Palais Royal. St-Germain-l'Auxerrois became the royal family's parish church. By contrast, nearby Les Halles was the market district, colonized by traders in the 12th century.

Now, art not royalty draws people to the Louvre, while the tranquil gardens of the Palais Royal offer the chance to escape the noise of the city. Farther north are the imposing Banque de France and Bibliothèque Nationale de France, as well as the circular, stately place des Victoires, with its smart shops. Les Halles lost some of its vitality when the covered market was dismantled in 1969. The

jarringly modern shopping mall, the Forum des Halles, stands in its place, although nearby streets such as the cobbled rue Montorgueil give you a taste of the past.

THE MAIN SIGHTS

The Louvre is the main attraction by far, clocking around 30,000 visitors each day. The Musée des Arts Décoratifs is also worth a visit. When you tire of art galleries, the Jardin des Tuileries and Jardin du Palais Royal are good places to relax. In Les Halles, the Forum des Halles may or may not be to your taste, and the area can be rather seedy at night. But don't miss the vast church of St-Eustache, based on Notre-Dame.

Jardin du Palais Royal

A peaceful, secluded garden surrounded by 18th-century arcades (▷ 104).

Jardin des Tuileries

Stately riverside gardens offering some excellent photo opportunities (▷ 105).

Musée des Arts Décoratifs

Decorative arts (▷ 111).

Musée du Louvre

Home to the *Mona Lisa* and thousands of other world-class works of art (▷ 118–123).

St-Eustache

Paris's second-largest church (▷ 161).

St-Germain-l'Auxerrois

Parish church to royalty (▷ 162).

OTHER PLACES TO VISIT

Pont des Arts (▷ 151) is Paris's most romantic bridge, while the **Pont Neuf** (▷ 151) is the oldest. You can shop in the elegant **place des Victoires**

The vast church of St-Eustache

(▷ 149) or the 19th-century malls of **Galerie Vivienne** and **Galerie Colbert** (▷ 93). If the Louvre and the Musée des Arts Décoratifs have not satisfied your appetite for culture, visit the **Jeu de Paume** (▷ 106) and the **Orangerie** (▷ 142), in the Jardin des Tuileries.

WHERE TO EAT

Le Bar à Soupes
▷ 262.

Grand Colbert
▷ 269.

Muscade
▷ 271.

THE SIGHTS

The Islands and the Quartier Latin

HOW TO GET THERE

Notre-Dame
- Cité, St-Michel, Châtelet
- 21, 24, 38, 47, 85, 96
- RER lines B, C St-Michel

Musée National du Moyen Âge–Thermes de Cluny
- Cluny–La Sorbonne
- 21, 27, 38, 63, 85, 86, 87, 96
- RER lines B, C St-Michel

Happily floating midstream in the Seine, the Île de la Cité and the Île St-Louis are as different in character as the two banks they separate. To their south, the Latin Quarter takes you back to medieval times.

The Île de la Cité is where Paris began, when a Celtic tribe known as the Parisii arrived in around 250BC. The Romans moved in 200 years later and set up the town of Lutetia. The island's

The Île St-Louis is more relaxed than the nearby Île de la Cité

prominence continued into the Middle Ages, with the building of a royal palace—now the Palais de Justice and Conciergerie—and Notre-Dame. Today the island is a hectic but attractive focal point for visitors (▷ 96–97). By contrast, the smaller Île St-Louis is refreshingly peaceful, with a far shorter history (▷ 98).

Five bridges link the Île de la Cité with the Latin Quarter, Paris's intellectual heart (▷ 152–153). The Sorbonne university was founded here in the 13th century and the district takes its name from the language once spoken by the students.

THE MAIN SIGHTS

Notre-Dame is the must-see sight on the Île de la Cité. The best way to appreciate the Latin Quarter is simply to wander through its medieval streets (see the walk, ▷ 228–229). Sights worth visiting en route include the Musée National du Moyen Âge, the mighty Panthéon and the Jardin du Luxembourg. Highlights on the Île St-Louis are the view of Notre-Dame and the legendary ice cream (▷ 98).

Conciergerie
A notorious prison during the Revolution (▷ 89–91).

Jardin du Luxembourg
Parkland in the heart of the city (▷ 102–103).

Musée National du Moyen Âge–Thermes de Cluny
Objects from the Middle Ages, in one of the city's oldest mansions (▷ 128–129).

Notre-Dame
A Paris landmark (▷ 137–141).

Panthéon
A vast neoclassical mausoleum (▷ 144).

Sainte-Chapelle
Stunning stained glass (▷ 158–160).

OTHER PLACES TO VISIT
Churches include St-Séverin (▷ 162–163), St-Étienne-du-Mont (▷ 161) and one of the city's oldest, St-Julien-le-Pauvre

(▷ 162). You can admire the outside of La Sorbonne (▷ 163), and glimpse the impressive courtyard, although the building is not open to the public. If you want to relax, try square René Viviani (▷ 152).

Work started on Notre-Dame in the 12th century

WHERE TO EAT

There are plenty of cafés and restaurants, although you may find some rather touristy. The nearby St-Germain-des-Prés district is known for its cafés.

Le Bar à Huîtres
33 rue St-Jacques
Tel 01 44 07 27 37
Open: daily noon–1am
Tasty seafood platters and shellfish.

Mon Vieil Ami
69 rue St-Louis-en-l'Île, Île St-Louis
Tel 01 40 46 01 35
Open: Wed–Sun 12–2, 7–11
Antoine Westermann's trendy restaurant.

THE SIGHTS

Around La Tour Eiffel

| HOW TO GET THERE |

Eiffel Tower
🚇 Bir-Hakeim
🚌 42, 69, 82, 87
🚆 RER line C, Champ de Mars/ Tour Eiffel

Palais de Chaillot
🚇 Trocadéro
🚌 22, 30, 32, 63, 72, 82

The Eiffel Tower stands on the banks of the Seine, at the edge of the stately 7th *arrondissement*. There are wonderful views of the monument from the terrace of the Palais de Chaillot, across the river in the wealthy 16th *arrondissement*.

As well as boosting morale, Paris's Universal Exhibitions left several new landmarks on the horizon, including the Palais de Chaillot (1937) and the Eiffel Tower (1889). Although the tower attracted two million

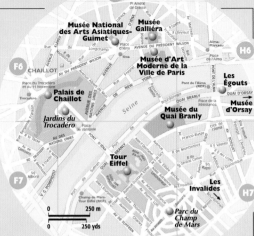

The Eiffel Tower is particularly impressive at night

visitors in its first year, it was not without its critics, including the writers Guy de Maupassant and Émile Zola. But it soon became *the* symbol of Paris and visitors from across the world still come to admire its soaring structure and enjoy the vertigo-inducing views from the top. The tower is backed by the lawns of the Champ de Mars (Field of Mars), where the Romans fought the Celtic Parisii tribe in 52BC. The area was landscaped in the mid-18th century, and the imposing École Militaire (Military Academy) was built at its southern end. Napoleon enrolled here, at the age of 15.

THE MAIN SIGHTS

No prizes for guessing the key attraction—the Eiffel Tower pulls in around six million visitors each year. Across the Seine, the Palais de Chaillot contains a maritime museum and an anthropological museum. Three other museums cluster near the place d'Iéna, farther west.

Musée d'Art Moderne de la Ville de Paris
A fine collection of modern art plus blockbuster exhibitions (▷ 112).

Musée National des Arts Asiatiques-Guimet
An intriguing collection of Oriental antiquities (▷ 126).

Palais de Chaillot
This curved, colonnaded palace has two museums, a theatre and great views of the Eiffel Tower (▷ 143).

Tour Eiffel
The ultimate symbol of Paris, originally conceived as a temporary structure (▷ 164–169).

OTHER PLACES TO VISIT
The **Musée Galliéra** hosts temporary exhibitions of urban fashion (▷ 116). On the Left Bank, the **Musée du Quai Branly**, which opened in 2006 (▷ 126). For a museum with a (rather smelly) difference, visit Paris's sewers, **Les Égouts**, at place de la Résistance (▷ 92). For a break, you can relax by the fountains of the **Jardins du Trocadéro** (▷ 149), in front of the Palais de Chaillot.

| FARTHER AFIELD |

Les Invalides, to the east of the Eiffel Tower, shelters the tomb of Napoleon in its golden-domed church (▷ 99–101). The **Musée d'Orsay** (▷ 130–134) is farther east.

Looking at the Palais de Chaillot from the Jardins du Trocadéro

| WHERE TO EAT |

The Eiffel Tower has a snack bar, as well as the **Altitude 95 restaurant** and the prestigious **Jules Verne restaurant** (book well in advance).

Fakhr El Dine
This Lebanese restaurant has been pulling in the locals for nearly two decades (▷ 267).

Le Sept Quinze
29 avenue de Lowendal
Tel 01 43 06 23 06
Open: Mon–Fri 12–2.30, 8–11, Sat 8pm–11pm. Closed three weeks in Aug
A welcoming bistro near the École Militaire.

Arc de Triomphe and Champs-Élysées

Paris's most famous avenue, crowned by the mighty Arc de Triomphe.

The Champs-Élysées at night

Shields commemorating battles decorate the crown of the Arc; visitors on the viewing platform above appear tiny in comparison

SEEING THE ARC DE TRIOMPHE AND CHAMPS-ÉLYSÉES

The wide, leafy Champs-Élysées is a focal point for the French nation, witness to momentous events such as De Gaulle's triumphal liberation march in 1944 and the soccer World Cup celebrations in 1998. Despite the avenue's glamorous reputation, be prepared also for streams of traffic, swarms of busy people and rather brash cinemas, car showrooms and chainstores. If the Arc de Triomphe is your main goal, take the Métro to Charles-de-Gaulle-Étoile, which drops you just outside. However, if you don't mind a 20-minute stroll, a good place to begin is two-thirds of the way down, at Métro Champs-Élysées-Clemenceau. Leave the Métro station and take a look at the imposing Grand Palais on avenue Winston Churchill (▷ 95), then walk towards place Charles-de-Gaulle, with the Arc de Triomphe looming up majestically in front of you. You'll see greenery as far as the Rond-Point des Champs-Élysées, at which point the commercial side of the avenue takes over. At the top, use the underpass to cross to the Arc, where you can climb the 284 steps to the roof. The views are stunning. Once back down, you could get a bite to eat at one of the nearby cafés or hop on the Métro and travel the four stops to Concorde to see the start of the avenue. This is guarded by copies of the Marly Horses—the originals are in the Louvre.

AVENUE des CHAMPS ELYSEES 8eme

RATINGS	
Historic interest	● ● ● ●
Photo stops	● ● ● ●
Shopping	● ● ●
Walkability	● ● ●

TIPS

● It takes at least 30 minutes to walk from one end of the Champs-Élysées to the other. You may prefer to take the Métro—Line 1 (yellow) runs the length of the avenue.
● Most cafés and restaurants are at the Arc de Triomphe end, although you may find better value in establishments in the side streets.
● The best time for photos from the top of the arch is just after it opens, when the light is clearer, or just before sunset.

HIGHLIGHTS

ARC DE TRIOMPHE

Napoleon conceived the Arc de Triomphe as a symbol of his military might—two centuries on, the colossal monument is still an image of national pride. It plays a central role in many of France's key commemorations, including VE Day (8 May), Bastille Day (14 July) and Remembrance Day (11 November). Within its grounds are the

The Arc de Triomphe (left) is a place of remembrance as well as a visitor attraction

Arc de Triomphe

✚ 66 G5 • place Charles-de-Gaulle, 75008

☎ 01 55 37 73 77

🕐 Apr–end Sep daily 10am–11pm; rest of year daily 10am–10.30pm. Closed 1 Jan, 1 May, 8 May, 14 July pm, 11 Nov pm, 25 Dec

🎫 Free to wander around the base. Rooftop: adult €7, under 18 free

🚇 Charles de Gaulle–Étoile

🚌 22, 30, 31, 52, 73, 92

🚆 RER line A, Charles de Gaulle–Étoile

🎁 Giftshop 🅿 €8

Tomb of the Unknown Soldier, installed in 1920 after World War I, and a poignant Memorial Flame, added three years later.

There are wonderful views from the rooftop, 50m (164ft) above street level. From here you can admire Haussmann's web-like street design and look along the Grand Axis (see panel, ▷ 79) towards place de la Concorde in one direction and the Grande Arche in the other. At night the city shimmers with lights. There is a small shop and museum on the way up. Back at ground level, save some time to admire the magnificent sculpted façade, the work of three different artists. Don't miss the fearsome winged figure of Liberty on François Rude's sculpture *La Marseillaise*, calling the French to defend their nation (northeastern pillar, facing the Champs-Élysées). On the southeast pillar Napoleon is depicted as a victorious Roman emperor. The 30 shields studding the crown of the arch each bear the name of a Revolutionary or Imperial victory.

The tree-lined Champs-Élysées is always packed with people

There are stunning views from the top of the Arc—if you can face the climb

Flowers adorn the Tomb of the Unknown Soldier

📣 For information on guided tours call Centre de Monuments Nationaux on 01 44 54 19 30

🎭

❓ There is a ceremony at the Tomb of the Unknown Soldier daily at 6.30pm

www.monumentsnationaux.fr
In French and English. Click on *Visit the Monuments* to see the Arc de Triomphe

Avenue des Champs-Élysées

✚ 66 H5 • 75008

🚇 Charles de Gaulle–Étoile, Georges V, Franklin D. Roosevelt, Champs-Élysées-Clemenceau

🚌 32, 42, 73 and others

🚆 Charles de Gaulle–Étoile

🍴 🛍 Wide selection

🏬 Plenty of shops

Twelve streets radiate from the Arc de Triomphe

AVENUE DES CHAMPS-ÉLYSÉES

This famous avenue is packed with cinemas, shops, cafés and car showrooms, and bustling with life. Although it is high on most visitors' itineraries, you are as likely to see Parisians going about their business as camera-snapping sightseers. The tree-lined avenue is over 2km (1.2 miles) long and 71m (232ft) wide, stretching between two of the city's most illustrious monuments—the Arc de Triomphe and the Egyptian obelisk in place de la Concorde. A short detour will lead you to other key buildings, including the Grand Palais (▷ 95) and the Palais de l'Élysée, official residence of the French president.

The French come here to celebrate, whether it be winning the soccer World Cup or welcoming home participants in the Tour de France cycle race. The avenue has hosted some of France's most prestigious processions, including the funeral of writer Victor Hugo in 1885, General de Gaulle's liberation march in 1944 and the bicentenary celebrations of the French Revolution in 1989. Catch it on 14 July (Bastille Day) when most of the French army rolls past. Another good time to visit is during the Christmas illuminations.

BACKGROUND

The Champs-Élysées dates back to 1616, when Marie de Medici turned the area into a fashionable driveway. Then, landscape designer André Le Nôtre (of Versailles fame) added alleys of

GRAND AXIS

The Arc de Triomphe is a key element of the *Grand Axis* that runs in an imaginary straight line across the city from the Louvre's Arc de Triomphe du Carrousel to the Grande Arche at La Défense (▷ 92). To emphasize the progression along this route, the Grande Arche is twice as tall as the Arc de Triomphe, which in turn is twice as tall as the Arc de Triomphe du Carrousel.

An eye-catching shop window

ÉTOILE

The Arc de Triomphe's traffic-ridden roundabout is still known as the *Étoile* (star), despite an official name-change to place Charles-de-Gaulle. The *Étoile* label comes from the 12 avenues that radiate from it like the tips of a star, a layout designed by Baron Haussmann in the 19th century. It may look impressive from the roof of the Arc de Triomphe but at ground level it seems to have resulted in all the cars in the capital converging on this one point!

trees and gardens, prompting its current name, Elysian Fields. Walkways and fountains were installed in 1824 and the avenue became crowded with cafés, restaurants and a smart clientele. Napoleon Bonaparte commissioned the Arc de Triomphe in 1806, demanding an awesome memorial to the French army. In 1810 a wooden, life-size model was installed to celebrate the emperor's marriage to Marie-Louise, but the real thing was not ready until 1836, 15 years after his death. Various architects and sculptors worked on the monument, inspired by Rome's Arch of Titus and Arch of Septimius Severus. The arch's symbolic role was confirmed after World War I, when parades of victorious troops marched through.

AVENUE DES CHAMPS-ÉLYSÉES MAP

Boules is a popular pastime at the Arènes de Lutèce

ARÈNES DE LUTÈCE

➕ 68 N9 • Entrances at rue des Arènes, rue de Navarre and 47 rue Monge, 75005 🕙 Daily 9am–9.30pm in summer, 8–5.30 in winter 💷 Free 🚇 Cardinal Lemoine, Jussieu 🚌 47, 67, 89 ❓ Best avoided after dark

This Gallo-Roman arena dates from the end of the second century AD and takes its name from the Roman name for Paris, Lutetia. It was destroyed in AD280, rediscovered in 1869, and restored in the early 20th century. Today, the arena ruins and the gardens are popular with students, boules-players, walkers and picnickers.

ASSEMBLÉE NATIONALE (PALAIS BOURBON)

➕ 66 J6 • Palais Bourbon, 33 quai d'Orsay, 75007 ☎ 01 40 63 64 80 🕙 Guided tours on Mon, Fri and Sat, unless the Assembly is sitting, by appointment only. Telephone and ask for the member of parliament in charge of relations between France and your country. Admission to public debates is also by prior appointment. 💷 Free 🚇 Assemblée Nationale 🚌 24, 63, 73, 83, 84, 94 🚇 RER line C, Invalides www.assemblee-nationale.fr

The 18th-century Palais Bourbon sits on the banks of the Seine and is home to the French National Assembly, the lower house of the French Parliament. Its 577 members debate in the Chamber and have offices nearby. The palace, with its imposing neoclassical façade, was built for Louis XIV's daughter, Louise-Françoise de Bourbon. Its political role began in 1798, when the Council of the Five Hundred met there. **Don't miss** The library ceiling (1838–1847), by Eugène Delacroix, depicts the history of civilization.

BASTILLE

See where the dramatic Storming of the Bastille took place—then enjoy a drink at one of the trendy cafés.

➕ 68 Q8 • Place de la Bastille and surrounding area, 75004/75011/75012 🚇 Bastille 🚌 20, 29, 65, 69, 76, 86, 87, 91 🍴 A good selection of cafés and restaurants (▷ 254)

RATINGS		
Historic interest	● ● ●
Photo stops	● ● ●
Shopping	● ● ●

Frenetic place de la Bastille, now bustling with street cafés and traffic, witnessed one of the pivotal events in France's history. Where in-line skaters and pedestrians now jostle for space, a Revolutionary mob stormed the Bastille prison in 1789 in a violent riot that signalled the start of the French Revolution.

The Bastille was built in 1380 as a fortress guarding the eastern entrance to Paris. It later became a jail for political prisoners, including the Marquis de Sade and Voltaire. Nothing remains of the building, although paving stones now mark its outline. A visual reminder of Paris's turbulent past is the Colonne de Juillet (July Column), which stands 50m (164ft) tall on place de la Bastille's busy roundabout. It was constructed in 1840 to commemorate victims of another revolt, the 1830 uprising, and is topped by the winged *Spirit of Liberty*.

Bastille has been spruced up and is now a lively nightspot, with a wide choice of restaurants and bars. During the day you can shop in the hectic streets that radiate from the Colonne de Juillet. There is also a marina, art galleries and the ultramodern Opéra Bastille (▷ 142). Walk down the rue de Lyon and you'll come to the Viaduc des Arts, an old railway viaduct converted into craft workshops and showrooms (9–129 avenue Daumesnil).

Don't miss To escape the noise and traffic of the Bastille, head down rue St-Antoine, then turn right into the peaceful rue de Birague. Here, browse in shops selling paintings, rugs and ceramics, then walk back in time through an archway to the tranquil place des Vosges (▷ 150).

The Spirit of Liberty watches over the busy place de la Bastille

The strikingly contemporary Palais Omnisports, at Bercy

Les Catacombes—not for the faint-hearted

BERCY

🏠 68 off Q11 • Bercy, 75012 🚇 Bercy
🚌 24, 62, 87

Bercy spreads east from Gare de Lyon through a maze of new apartment and office blocks. Once known for its wine warehouses, it is undergoing intensive development. The most likely reason you'll come here is to see a rock concert or sporting event in the grass-walled Palais Omnisports (www.bercy.fr). Also of interest is the curvilinear former American Cultural Center, designed by Frank Gehry and recently relaunched as the Musée du Cinéma (▷ 113). The freshly landscaped Parc de Bercy relieves the concrete jungle. At the far end, wine warehouses have been converted into the boutiques, bars and restaurants of Bercy Village (www.bercyvillage.com).

BIBLIOTHÈQUE NATIONALE DE FRANCE– SITE FRANÇOIS MITTERRAND

🏠 332 Q11 • quai François-Mauriac, 75013 ☎ 01 53 79 82 22; guided visits 01 53 79 49 49 🕐 Upper Garden reading rooms: Tue–Sat 10–8, Sun 1–7 👤 Adult one-day pass: €3.30; under 18s not admitted to reading room 🚇 Bibliothèque François-Mitterrand 🚌 62, 89 🚉 Bibliothèque François-Mitterrand 🚏 🏬 Bookshop/giftshop
www.bnf.fr

Around 12 million books and innumerable documents belong to the national library, so it's not surprising that it was forced to find additional premises towards the end of the 20th century. The new library, with its glass corner towers designed like four open books, stands on the eastern edge of the Left Bank. The public has access to books, the internet and an excellent audiovisual section of videos, CDs and DVDs.

BIBLIOTHÈQUE NATIONALE DE FRANCE– SITE RICHELIEU

🏠 67 M6 • 58 rue de Richelieu, 75002 ☎ 01 53 79 82 26; guided visits 01 53 79 86 87 🕐 Library: Mon–Fri 9–6, Sat 10–5; Galerie Mansart, Galerie Mazarine and Crypte: Tue–Sat 10–7, Sun 12–7 (during exhibitions only) 👤 Adult €3.30 for one-day pass; €7 for three-day pass 🚇 Bourse 🚌 20, 29, 39, 48, 67, 74, 85 🚏 Guided visits first Tue of month
www.bnf.fr

This former palace has been the base for France's national library since the early 18th century. It is close to the Louvre and Palais Royal and was once home to Cardinal Mazarin, Louis XIII's First Minister. In 1996 part of its collection moved to the new François-Mitterrand site (see this page), creating space to focus on manuscripts, maps, music, prints, photos and coins. Reading room access is reserved for those who prove a genuine research need, but you can see temporary exhibitions in the Galerie Mansart (devoted to photography), Galerie Mazarine and the Crypte. **Don't miss** The Galerie Mazarine has a wonderful painted ceiling.

LA BOURSE

🏠 67 M5 • Palais de la Bourse, rue Vivienne, 75002 ☎ 01 49 27 55 55 🕐 Guided tours between 9am and 4.30pm, Mon–Fri. Reserve ahead 👤 Adult €8.50, child €5.50 🚇 Bourse 🚌 20, 29, 39, 74, 85
www.euronext.com

Paris's money-spinning hub is in the Palais de la Bourse. Designed by architect Alexandre Brongniart, this neoclassical Napoleonic creation was built between 1808 and 1826. In 1902 and 1907 two wings were added, giving the building the shape of a cross. Watch the action from the public gallery, and learn about the

importance of the stock exchange in France's economy with the help of audiovisual presentations.

CANAL ST-MARTIN

🏠 68 P4–5 • Canal St-Martin 🚇 République, Jaurès, Jacques Bonsergent, Goncourt 🚌 26, 46, 75 🚢 Several companies offer boat trips including Canauxrama (▷ 248)

The Canal St-Martin, in the eastern part of the city, makes a peaceful alternative to a boat trip along the Seine. You can also stroll along the tree-lined canal paths. The canal, which opened in 1825, is around 5km (3 miles) long and passes through nine locks and two swing bridges. It is spanned by many picturesque curved metal footbridges. The canal featured in the 2001 film *Le Fabuleux Destin d'Amélie Poulain* and in Marcel Carné's 1938 film *Hôtel du Nord*.

LES CATACOMBES

🏠 330 L11 • 1 place Denfert-Rochereau, 75014 ☎ 01 43 22 47 63 🕐 Tue–Sun 10–5 👤 Adult €7, under 14 free 🚇 Denfert-Rochereau 🚌 38, 68 ❓ Not recommended for young children (or the faint-hearted!)

This labyrinth of tunnels—the world's largest repository of human bones—is the resting place of more than six million Parisians. The inscription above the entrance reads 'Stop! Here is the empire of death!' Skulls and bones are arranged along the walls of these recesses, 20m (65ft) beneath the city. The tunnels were created in Roman times as quarries. Bones were transferred here from overcrowded cemeteries in 1785. During World War II the catacombs were used by the Resistance as a secret meeting place. Be prepared for lots of stairs and take a torch.

Centre Georges Pompidou

**Paris's wackiest building, with one of the largest collections of
modern art in the world.
Around six million visitors each year come to see works by Pablo Picasso,
Andy Warhol, Jackson Pollock and many others.**

*You can see as far as Sacré-
Cœur from the top floor*

*Learn more at the bookstore
about the art you've just seen*

*Walkways are on the exterior,
thanks to the inside-out design*

RATINGS	
Cultural interest	● ● ● ● ●
Good for kids	● ● ●
Photo stops (exterior and views)	● ● ●

PANORAMA

Don't miss the view over Paris
from the top floor. Landmarks
you can spot include Sacré-
Cœur, the Eiffel Tower,
Notre-Dame and the Panthéon.

*One of the eccentric characters
of the Stravinsky Fountain (right)*

*Le Défenseur du Temps—not
your typical clock*

SEEING THE CENTRE GEORGES POMPIDOU

You'll either love or hate the brazen design of the Centre
Georges Pompidou and you may well feel the same about the
contemporary art it displays. The venue has sparked controversy
since it opened in 1977, gracing the historic heart of Paris with
an incongruously modern building that resembles a giant
air-conditioning system. The main entrance, off the lively place
Georges-Pompidou, takes you to level zero, where you can pick
up a plan of the building and buy museum and exhibition tickets.
If you want to visit both the Musée National d'Art Moderne and
the temporary exhibitions, an all-gallery pass may be your best
ticket option. To reach the museum, take the escalator to the
entrance on level four, where you can rent an audioguide. Once
inside the museum you may prefer to head straight to level five,
which covers the first half of the 20th century, before returning to
level four to tackle works from the 1960s to the present day.
Temporary exhibitions are on levels one and six. If you need a
break from the galleries, you can get a bite to eat in the café on
level one or browse in the bookshop on level zero or the
boutique on level one.

HIGHLIGHTS

MUSÉE NATIONAL D'ART MODERNE

Where the Musée d'Orsay (▷ 130–134) leaves off, the Museum of
Modern Art takes over, featuring works from 1905 to the present
day. Up to 2,000 pieces from the 50,000-strong collection are
on display at any one time and range from Cubism by Georges
Braque and Picasso to Pop Art by Andy Warhol and video art by
Korean artist Nam June Paik. The approach to the museum is
almost as unusual as the art it contains. You step onto an escalator
inside a giant transparent tube that runs up the outside of
the building. This takes you to the fourth floor, which covers
1960 to the present day, including works by the French New
Realists, photographers, architects and video artists. There
are also rooms dedicated to graphic art and new media.
Pieces on display change each autumn (fall). For a chronological
overview, start on the fifth floor, tame in comparison, which takes you

back to the first half of the 20th century. The displays here change each spring and include works by Henri Matisse, Picasso, Braque, Juan Gris and Pollock. On both floors, glass walls flood the interior with natural light and give wonderful views.

TEMPORARY EXHIBITIONS AND OTHER ATTRACTIONS

Temporary exhibitions, on the first and sixth floors, are as much a draw as the Musée National d'Art Moderne. Recent themes have ranged from 'Hitchcock and Art' to the designer Philippe Starck. Other attractions on site include children's activities, two cinemas, dance and drama productions and a library. Nearby, at 1 place Igor Stravinsky, the experimental music venue IRCAM (Institut de Recherche et Coordination Acoustique Musique) stages concerts, workshops and lectures. On the other side of the Pompidou, on rue Rambuteau, the Atelier Brancusi is a reconstruction of Romanian sculptor Constantin Brancusi's workshop. Brancusi moved to Paris in 1904 and his studio has been re-created as he left it when he died in 1957.

OUTDOORS

On a sunny day, the square outside comes alive with jugglers, mime artists, fire-eaters and musicians. Don't miss the surreal Stravinsky Fountain round the corner in place Igor Stravinsky. The zany

The controversial exterior of the Centre Georges Pompidou

BASICS

Centre Georges Pompidou
⊞ 68 N7 • place Georges-Pompidou, 75004
☎ 01 44 78 12 33
🕔 Centre Georges Pompidou: Wed–Mon 11–10. Musée National d'Art Moderne and exhibitions: Wed–Mon 11–9 (last ticket 8), Thu until 11 for some exhibitions (last ticket 10). Closed 1 May. Library: Mon–Fri 12–10, Sat–Sun 11–10
💶 Adult all-gallery pass €10. Musée National d'Art Moderne; free first Sun of month. Exhibitions: prices vary (under 13 free)
Ⓜ Rambuteau, Hôtel de Ville
🚌 29, 38, 47, 75
🚆 Châtelet-Les-Halles
📀 €12 (French, English, German, Italian, Spanish, Japanese)
🎧 Audioguide
🍴 Georges restaurant on 6th floor, with good views; tel 01 44 78 47 99
☕ On first floor
📖 Bookshops on levels 0, 4, 6; boutique on 1; post office on 0
🚻

www.centrepompidou.fr
In French, with some information in English; includes photos of some of the works, details of events and exhibitions, and practical information

IRCAM
1 place Igor Stravinsky
☎ 01 44 78 48 43
🕔 Pick up a brochure or check the website for concert details
www.ircam.fr

Atelier Brancusi
55 rue Rambuteau
🕔 Wed–Mon 2–6
💶 Joint ticket with Musée National d'Art Moderne and Children's Gallery: adult €7, under 18 free; free first Sun of month

characters, which squirt water at anyone who dares walk past, are each named after a work by the Russian composer. Finally, look out for Paris's newest public clock in rue Brantôme, the vicious-looking brass-and-steel *Le Défenseur du Temps* (The Defender of Time). The defender fights beasts, representing earth, water and air, on the hour but can be seen at his most ferocious at noon, 6pm and 10pm.

BACKGROUND

The Centre Georges Pompidou was the inspiration of Georges Pompidou, president of France from 1969 until his death in 1974. His vision was a venue where people could enjoy contemporary film, drama, dance, music and visual art. The outlandish complex took five years to build and was a controversial addition to Beaubourg, a run-down district of 18th- and 19th-century town houses. Designers Renzo Piano and Richard Rogers turned the building inside out by placing its 'guts' (all the piping) on the outside. This piping was coded with different shades of paint, with yellow for electrics, blue for air-conditioning, green for water and red for the elevators. Pompidou did not live to see the opening in 1977, but his vision for the arts venue proved sagacious—it was soon attracting 22,000 visitors a day, rivalling the Louvre in popularity. It closed for two years for renovation work in the autumn of 1997, reopening just in time for the new millennium.

The spacious lobby buzzes with people throughout the day

● If you're a traditionalist when it comes to art, let yourself in (relatively) gently to the Museum of Modern Art by starting with the fifth floor (1905–1960) before tackling the more bemusing fourth floor (1960 to today).

● The museum's late opening hours allow you to enjoy a visit after an early evening meal (last ticket sold at 8pm; museum closes at 9pm).

● You may hear local people referring to the Centre Georges Pompidou as Beaubourg.

● The official guidebook has photos and information about 150 of the most important exhibits and is worth buying before you visit the Museum of Modern Art.

● If your mind is spinning from a day of modern art, you may enjoy a calming concert at the nearby church of St-Merri (▷ 162), on Saturdays at 9pm and Sundays at 4pm.

MODERN ART FOR THE UNINITIATED—AN EXPLANATION OF SOME OF THE MOVEMENTS OF MODERN ART

Abstract Expressionism: This movement stemmed from the US and had two main subdivisions—Action Painting and Colour Field Painting. Action Painting focused on the act of painting, rather than the finished piece of art. The most famous artist of this genre was Jackson Pollock, who used sticks and syringes to drip paint onto the canvas, forming abstract shapes.

Arte Povera: Literally 'poor art', Arte Povera is an Italian-based genre that involves the use of cheap, everyday materials to create sculptures or art installations. Artists include Mario Merz and Giuseppe Penone.

Cubism: Created by Picasso, Braque, Fernand Léger and Gris in the early 20th century, Cubism was, in part, a backlash against Impressionism. People and objects are fragmented and portrayed using geometric shapes.

Fauvism: Uses bold blocks of pure colour, seen in the works of Matisse.

Fluxus: A movement launched in the 1960s. Rejected classic ideas of what a work of art is and focused on fluidity, chance and everyday objects and events. Artists include Ben and Joseph Beuys.

Minimalism: The emphasis is on simplicity and repetition, such as the works of Donald Judd and Brice Marden.

New Realism: New Realists used everyday objects in their works, which would sometimes be smashed or burned as a statement against society or fine art. Arman's collection of gas masks, entitled *Home, Sweet Home,* is an example of the genre.

Pop Art: An artistic take on popular culture and advertising. One of the most famous Pop Art pieces is Andy Warhol's *Marilyn Monroe* silkscreen. Other artists include Claes Oldenburg, Roy Lichtenstein and David Hockney.

Surrealism: A rejection of logic and realism for a surreal dream world. This movement was popular in the 1920s and 1930s, with artists such as René Magritte and Salvador Dalí.

Video Art: Experimenting with video footage as art, for example in the work of Nam June Paik.

Napoleon trained to be an army officer at the imposing École Militaire

One of the many intriguing graves at Montparnasse Cemetery

CHAMP DE MARS AND ÉCOLE MILITAIRE

Champ de Mars
⊞ 66 H8 • Champ de Mars, 75007
☎ Mairie de Paris information: 3975
🕐 Always open 🎟 Free 🚇 École Militaire 🚌 42, 69, 80, 82, 87 🚆 RER line C, Champ de Mars-Tour Eiffel

École Militaire
⊞ 66 H8 • 1 place Joffre, 75007
🕐 Visits by written application only
🚇 École Militaire 🚌 28, 80, 82, 87, 92

The green lawns of the Champ de Mars stretch out in a rectangular design between the Eiffel Tower and the imposing 18th-century École Militaire. It was on this site that Roman invaders battled it out with the Parisii in 52BC to win supremacy over the area, and the Parisians later beat off the Vikings.

The Champ de Mars was laid out in 1765 as an army parade ground. Its name, Field of Mars, refers to the Roman god of war. Over the years it has witnessed national celebrations, parades, international exhibitions, horse races and even ballooning experiments by the intrepid Montgolfier brothers. Today it is popular with families, joggers and visitors strolling in the shadow of the Eiffel Tower.

The colonnaded and domed École Militaire dominates the opposite end of the Champ de Mars. It was commissioned in 1751 by Louis XV and his mistress, Madame de Pompadour, who wanted somewhere to train impoverished young gentlemen. Architect Jacques-Ange Gabriel, who also worked on the place de la Concorde and Versailles's Petit Trianon, was responsible for the design. Work finished in 1773 and a new tax on playing cards and the lottery financed the grooming of France's military cadets, including none other

than Napoleon Bonaparte. He entered the academy in 1784, aged 15.

CIMETIÈRE DE MONTMARTRE

⊞ 69 L2 • 20 avenue Rachel, 75018
☎ 01 53 42 36 30 🕐 Mid-Mar to mid-Oct Mon–Sat 8–6, Sun 9–6; rest of year Mon–Sat 8.30–5.30, Sun 9–5.30 (last entry 15 min before closing) 🎟 Free
🚇 Place de Clichy/Blanche
🚌 30, 54, 74, 80, 95
www.paris.fr

Montmartre's cemetery is packed with graves of the famous, including composers Hector Berlioz and Jacques Offenbach, writers Henri Stendhal and Alexandre Dumas, and artists Edgar Degas and Jean-Baptiste Greuze. The imposing tomb of Émile Zola is close to the flower-filled roundabout near the main entrance, although the writer's remains were moved to the Panthéon (▷ 144) in 1906. The cemetery, created in 1798, also holds the grave of Louise Weber, the Moulin Rouge dancer known as La Goulue, who appeared in paintings by Toulouse-Lautrec. Jazz fans may want to find the tomb of the saxophone inventor, Adolphe Sax.

A noticeboard at the main entrance gives times and dates of guided visits.

CIMETIÈRE DU MONTPARNASSE

⊞ 330 K10 • 3 boulevard Edgar Quinet, 75014 ☎ 01 44 10 86 50 🕐 Mid-Mar to early Nov Mon–Fri 8–6, Sat 8.30–6, Sun 9–6; rest of year Mon–Fri 8–5.30, Sat 8.30–5.30, Sun 9–5.30 🎟 Free
🚇 Edgar Quinet, Raspail, Montparnasse-Bienvenüe 🚌 28, 68

Montparnasse Cemetery opened in 1824 and is the final resting place of many notable former residents of the area. Here you can pay homage to an array of illustrious writers, composers, musicians, artists and sculptors, including Jean-Paul Sartre, Simone de Beauvoir, Charles Baudelaire, Guy de Maupassant, Constantin Brancusi, Camille Saint-Saëns, Ossip Zadkine and Auguste Bartholdi, father of the Statue of Liberty. Also buried here are car manufacturer André Citroën and Prime Minister Pierre Laval, who was executed for treason after World War II following his open collaboration with the Germans.

Adorning a tomb in the northeastern corner of the cemetery is Brancusi's charmingly childlike sculpture The Kiss—supposedly a response to Rodin's famous work of the same name.

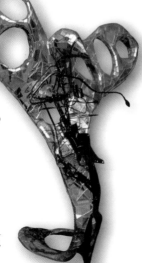
This striking statue decorates a grave at Montparnasse Cemetery

THE SIGHTS

The cobbled avenues of leafy Père-Lachaise Cemetery

CIMETIÈRE DU PÈRE-LACHAISE

One of the most famous burial grounds in the world.

You can visit the graves of luminaries such as Frédéric Chopin, Marcel Proust and Oscar Wilde at this vast cemetery, on the eastern edge of the city. Père-Lachaise covers 44ha (108 acres) on the slopes of Ménilmontant and contains around 70,000 tombs. Tree-lined, cobbled paths are bordered by ornate tombstones and mausoleums. Far from gloomy, it is a great place for a peaceful walk on a sunny day.

ENGLISH ORIGINS

The cemetery is named after Louis XIV's confessor, Père La Chaise, who once owned the land here. It was designed by Brongniart in 1803 to echo an English-style garden. At first, the cemetery was not popular, but once the graves of writers Molière and Jean de La Fontaine and the tragic lovers Abélard and Héloïse had been transferred here—precisely to encourage other Parisians to follow suit—it soon became the most fashionable place to be buried in Paris.

RESTING PLACE OF THE FAMOUS

Père-Lachaise has become a place of pilgrimage—among the famous people buried here are composers Frédéric Chopin and Georges Bizet, Paris town planner Baron Haussmann, artists Amedeo Modigliani and Eugène Delacroix, singers Edith Piaf and Maria Callas, writers Marcel Proust, Honoré de Balzac and Oscar Wilde, actresses Simone Signoret and Sarah Bernhardt, actor Yves Montand and dancer Isadora Duncan. One of the most visited graves is that of Jim Morrison, lead singer of The Doors, who died in Paris in 1971 at the age of 27, probably from a drugs overdose. Fans still leave cigarette stubs, flowers and beads as a mark of respect. In August 2003, French actress Marie Trintignant was buried in the cemetery.

MEMORIALS

The Mur des Fédérés, in the eastern corner of the cemetery, marks the site of the Communards' tragic last stand in 1871, when the 147 survivors of the Commune were lined up against the wall and executed by a government firing squad. They were buried where they fell, in a communal grave. There are also poignant memorials to the victims of Nazi concentration camps and to the Resistance fighters killed in World War II.

RATINGS

Historic interest	●●●●
Photo stops	●●
Value for money	FREE

BASICS

➕ 327 S6 • boulevard de Ménilmontant, 75020 ☎ 01 55 25 82 10

🕐 Mid-Mar to early Nov Mon–Fri 8–6, Sat 8.30–6, Sun 9–6; rest of year Mon–Fri 8–5.30, Sat 8.30–5.30, Sun 9–5.30; last entry 15 min before closing

💵 Free

🚇 Père Lachaise, Gambetta

🚌 61, 69

🚶 Guided tours in English Jul, Aug Sat 3pm (€6)

👫

❓ You can buy a map from the news vendors or florists near the main entrances (avenue Père Lachaise and boulevard de Ménilmontant). You can also obtain a map from the cemetery office by the Père Lachaise entrance

TIPS

• Try to avoid visiting on very windy days as there is a danger of falling branches.
• The cemetery is huge and maps are dotted about, but if you are keen to visit particular graves get obtain your own map beforehand (see above) to help you find your way.

The tomb of 19th-century journalist Victor Noir (above)

Conciergerie

The horrors of the French Revolution linger on in this dimly lit Gothic palace,
where prisoners spent their final days before being led to the guillotine.
The eerie complex also contains Europe's oldest surviving medieval hall, and
the kitchens once used to cook food for royalty.

SEEING THE CONCIERGERIE

Sailing past the Conciergerie's floodlit towers on an evening boat
cruise, it is hard to imagine the fear that lurked within its walls
during the five centuries it served as a prison. But step inside the
gloomy main hall and the sense of oppression is palpable.

The entrance is on the boulevard du Palais, near the gateway to
the Palais de Justice. If you also want to visit Sainte-Chapelle
(▷ 158–160) you can buy a joint ticket. Pick up a plan at the
entrance as signage inside isn't particularly clear. The first three
rooms on your tour—the Salle des Gens d'Armes, the medieval
kitchens and the Salle des Gardes—date from the Middle Ages,
when the Conciergerie was a royal palace. To learn more about its
gruesome role during the Revolution head for the Galerie des
Prisonniers, off the southwestern corner of the main hall. Here
you'll also find a reconstruction of Marie-Antoinette's cell.

HIGHLIGHTS

GOTHIC HALLS

On entry you are immediately plunged into semi-darkness in a vast
Gothic chamber said to be Europe's oldest surviving medieval hall.
Subtle uplighting adds to the eerie atmosphere of the Salle des Gens
d'Armes, 63m (206ft) long and 8.5m (28ft) high. The hall dates from
the 14th century, when it formed the lower floor of the Grand'Salle.

*Dramatic lighting and Gothic
turrets at the eerie Conciergerie*

RATINGS	
Historic interest	● ● ● ●
Photo stops (from the Seine)	● ● ●

Sculptures of Law and Justice flank the clock on the Tour de l'Horloge

The king's staff ate here, up to 2,000 at a time, while royal banquets and marriage celebrations were held upstairs. Later, the hall was divided into separate storerooms, but was restored in the 19th century by Viollet-le-Duc. A spiral staircase leads up to the kitchens, where four walk-in fireplaces, each big enough to roast a couple of sheep, indicate the scale of medieval appetites. From the kitchens walk back into the Salles des Gens d'Armes and up to the Salle des Gardes, in the northeastern corner. This Gothic hall sat underneath the Grand'Chambre, where the Revolutionary Court delivered death sentences like parking tickets to its unfortunate victims.

RE-CREATIONS OF THE REVOLUTION

The Galerie des Prisonniers was once the prison's most animated crossroads, where lawyers, visitors and inmates met. Here you'll find re-creations of the clerk's and concierge's offices, as well as the Salle de Toilette, where barbers cut off prisoners' hair before execution. There is also a poignant reconstruction of Marie-Antoinette's cell. The spartan furnishings (not original), torn wallpaper and stifling gaze of the prison guard paint a sorry picture of the queen's last days. Upstairs in the Room of the Sentenced, wall panels list the 2,780 people guillotined between March 1793 and May 1795. Farther along the eerie upstairs corridor, re-created cells give you a glimpse of the prisoners' harsh living conditions. The first cell, with no beds or lamp, was for the poorest prisoners, the *pailleux* (*paille* means straw). Prisoners with money shared a *chambre à la pistole*, with the relative luxury of beds and chairs. Finally, the famous or the very wealthy were granted their own cell, complete with a desk, bed, lamp and books.

BASICS

🔲 67 M7 • 2 boulevard du Palais, Île de la Cité, 75001

☎ 01 53 40 60 97

🕐 Mar–end Oct daily 9.30–6; Nov–end Feb daily 9–5. Closed 1 Jan, 1 May, 25 Dec

💶 Adult €6.50 (€9.50 for combined ticket with Sainte-Chapelle), under 18 free (bring passport to prove age)

🚇 Cité, Châtelet

🚌 21, 24, 27, 38, 58, 81, 85

🚆 RER line B, C St-Michel-Notre-Dame

📀 Daily guided tours in French, English, Italian. No audioguides

📖 €7

📚 Bookshop

👫

www.monuments-nationaux.fr
In French and English; easy to navigate, with lots of photos and historical information

TIPS

● If you intend to visit Sainte-Chapelle as well, go to the Conciergerie first and buy a joint ticket, to avoid the long queues at Sainte-Chapelle. However, try to get to Sainte-Chapelle before lunchtime, as it is generally more crowded in the afternoon.

● The Conciergerie's main halls are empty of furniture, making it harder to imagine the events that once took place here. Come prepared to work your imagination.

● On the Seine side of the building, take a look at the Tour de l'Horloge, site of Paris's first public clock, commissioned in 1370. The present clock dates from the 16th century and has sculptures of Law and Justice.

The Salle des Gens d'Armes (above) is said to be Europe's oldest surviving medieval hall

THE CHAPEL

At the end of the upper corridor, stairs take you down to the Chapelle des Girondins, named after the 21 condemned Girondins (left-wing members of the 1791 Legislative Assembly) who sat around a banqueting table here on the night before their execution. Leading off this room, the Chapelle Expiatoire stands on the site of Marie-Antoinette's actual cell. The chapel was commissioned by Louis XVIII to commemorate members of the royal family killed during the Revolution. The silver pattern on the walls represents tears.

BACKGROUND

The Conciergerie is notorious for its role as a prison, but it began as a palace, part of a royal complex including Sainte-Chapelle and the Palais de Justice. The oldest parts of the Conciergerie date from the early 14th century, although a fortress probably stood on the western part of the Île de la Cité as far back as Roman times. In the late 14th century, Charles V chose to live elsewhere and its role changed to a law court and prison, with occasional use for royal functions. It was at this time that it gained its name, from the concierge who oversaw the site. During the Revolution, the prison housed more than 4,000 inmates, up to 600 at a time. Conditions were crowded and disease was rife. Prisoners had nothing to do but wait in the dungeon-like interior for the often inevitable death sentence and the terrifying journey through the city to the guillotine. After the Revolution, the Conciergerie continued as a prison until 1914. It now offers visitors a chilling reminder of the darker side of Paris's history.

The shape of things to come? Office blocks at La Défense

The entrance to Espace Montmartre–Salvador Dalí

Luxury treats at Ladurée, in the rue Royale, near Faubourg St-Honoré

THE SIGHTS

LA DÉFENSE

⊞ 333 B2 • 92044 ⬡ Grande Arche de La Défense ▣ 73 🚇 RER line A, La Défense ⬧ A selection

You couldn't find a starker contrast with Paris's historic core than this high-rise business district on the city's western edge.. In addition to office blocks, you'll find Les Quatre Temps shopping complex and the CNIT building (Centre of New Industries and Technologies), looking like an upturned shell. **Don't miss** The main draw for visitors is the imposing Grande Arche (▷ 94), which rises 110m (360ft) above the enormous pedestrian-only square called Le Parvis. Stand on the white marble steps of this 300,000-tonne giant and the people wandering across the vast square seem utterly dwarfed by skyscrapers.

DROUOT

⊞ 69 M5 • 9 rue Drouot, 75009 ☎ 01 48 00 20 20 ⬡ Sep–end Jul Mon–Sat 11–6, Sun times vary ⬧ Free ⬡ Richelieu-Drouot, Le Peletier ▣ 20, 39, 42, 48, 67, 74, 85 www.drouot.fr

Paris's leading auctioneers was founded in the 19th century and takes its name from the Comte de Drouot, Napoleon's aide-de-camp. There are 16 auction rooms and the auctions, in French, usually begin at 2pm. Viewing is from 11 to 6 the day before the sale and 11 to noon on the day of the sale. You'll find details on the website and in *La Gazette de l'Hôtel Drouot*, published weekly.

LES ÉGOUTS

⊞ 66 H6 • place de la Résistance (Pont de l'Alma). Entrance opposite 93 quai d'Orsay, 75007 ☎ 01 53 68 27 81 ⬡ May–end Sep Sat–Wed 11–5; rest of year Sat–Wed 11–4. Closed 2 weeks in mid-Jan ⬧ Adult €4.10, child €3.30, under 5 free ⬡ Alma-Marceau ▣ 42, 63, 80, 92 🚇 RER line C, Pont-de-l'Alma www.paris.fr

Paris's sewers are a surprisingly popular visitor attraction. A worker guides you through part of the city's 2,100km (1,302 mile) subterranean network and shows you an audiovisual presentation. The sewers were built by Baron Haussmann in the latter part of the 19th century, and during World War II the Germans used some sections as offices. They have even made it onto the stage, featuring in the hit musicals *Les Misérables* and *Phantom of the Opera*.

ESPACE MONTMARTRE–SALVADOR DALÍ

⊞ 69 M3 • 11 rue Poulbot (off place du Tertre), 75018 ☎ 01 42 64 40 10 ⬡ Daily 10–6 ⬧ Adult €10, child €6, under 8 free. Audioguide €2 ⬡ Abbesses ▣ 50, 80, Montmartrobus www.daliparis.com

This surreal museum displays more than 300 weird and wonderful works by the Catalan artist Salvador Dalí (1904–1989), who came to live in Paris in the late 1920s. The disconcerting black-walled interior is a fitting backdrop for the sculptures and illustrations, which form the biggest Dalí collection in France.

LES FAUBOURGS

Faubourg St-Honoré
⊞ 66 J5 • Around rue du Faubourg St-Honoré ⬡ St-Philippe du Roule, Miromesnil, Ternes ▣ 43, 52, 93

Faubourg St-Antoine
⊞ 68 off Q8 • Around rue du Faubourg St-Antoine ⬡ Bastille, Ledru Rollin, Faidherbe Chaligny, Nation ▣ 76, 86 🚇 RER line A, Nation

Faubourg St-Germain
⊞ 67 K8 • West of St-Germain-des-Prés, including rue de Varenne ⬡ Varenne ▣ 69, 87 🚇 RER line C, Invalides

Faubourg Montmartre
⊞ 69 M4–5 • Around rue du Faubourg Montmartre ⬡ Grands Boulevards, Le Peletier ▣ 48, 67, 74, 85

The *faubourgs* (fake boroughs) were Paris's first suburbs and for years the title had derogatory connotations. Now, far from being second-class, many have become highly sought-after areas. One of the oldest is the Right Bank's Faubourg St-Honoré, stretching along the road of the same name. Now a hub of Parisian wealth, it is packed with designer boutiques and is home to the Palais de l'Élysée, the French president's official residence.

Faubourg St-Antoine, which runs east from Bastille to the place de la Nation, was once an explosive district full of rebels. Now more peaceful in spirit, its identity remains linked with the crafts of its former artisans.

To find the real atmosphere of the *faubourgs* look in the area between Faubourg Montmartre and Faubourg Poissonière. From the *grands boulevards*, the Faubourg Montmartre winds uphill towards Pigalle and Montmartre, carrying in its wake a lively string of bars and inexpensive restaurants.

South of the river, Faubourg St-Germain was meadowland in medieval times, evolving into a bourgeois district in the 18th century. Many of the mansions are now foreign embassies and government offices.

But even today *faubourg* can have a pejorative ring, with the comment 'he was born in the *faubourgs*' implying an unsophisticated background.

The Fondation Cartier specializes in contemporary art exhibitions

FONDATION CARTIER

🔲 330 L10 • 261 boulevard Raspail, 75014 ☎ 01 42 18 56 50 🕐 Tue 10–10, Wed–Sun 10–8 💷 Adult €7.50, child (11–24) €5.50, under 10 free 🚇 Raspail 🚌 38, 68, 91 ❓ Nomadic Nights held on certain Thursdays at 8.30pm (advance booking necessary) www.fondation.cartier.fr

The Fondation Cartier has been an avid promoter of contemporary art since it was founded in 1984. In 1994 it moved to central Paris, to the striking steel and glass building designed by architect Jean Nouvel. The light, spacious interior is the perfect setting for the permanent and temporary exhibitions of French and international art. Vast glass windows open onto a garden and small amphitheatre created by artist Lothar Baumgarten.

FONTAINE DES INNOCENTS

🔲 67 N6/7 • square des Innocents, near Forum des Halles, 75001 🚇 Châtelet, Les Halles 🚌 38, 47 (and all buses going along rue de Rivoli) 🚉 Châtelet- Les-Halles 🍴 Plenty in Les Halles ❓ Don't visit the fountain alone at night

Water has gushed from this superb Renaissance fountain since the mid-16th century, although the fountain has not always stood on this spot in Les Halles. It was originally on the corner of the rue St-Denis but was moved to its current position in the late 18th century to replace a cemetery that had run out of soil. The cemetery's two million skeletons were transferred to the Catacombes (▷ 81). After the move, the fountain gained a fourth side, carved by Augustin Pajou. The original three-sided cascade was designed by Pierre Lescot and sculpted by Jean Goujon.

LES GALERIES

These elegant covered passageways, with glass skylights and decorative floors, were the stylish shopping malls of early 19th-century Paris.

Galerie Vivienne 🔲 67 M6 • 4 rue des Petits-Champs/6 rue Vivienne/5 rue de la Banque, 75002 🚇 Bourse Galerie Colbert 🔲 67 M6 • 6 rue des Petits-Champs, 75002 🚇 Bourse Passage des Panoramas 🔲 69 M5 • 11 boulevard Montmartre/10 rue St-Marc, 75002 🚇 Grands Boulevards Galerie Véro-Dodat 🔲 67 M6 • 19 rue Jean-Jacques Rousseau, 75001 🚇 Palais-Royal–Musée du Louvre Passage Jouffroy 🔲 69 M5 • 10 boulevard Montmartre, 75009 🚇 Grands Boulevards Passage Verdeau 🔲 69 M5 • 31 bis rue du Faubourg-Montmartre, 75009 🚇 Le Peletier http://parisinconnu.com/passages (in French only)

RATINGS			
Historic interest	●	●	●
Specialist shopping	●	●	● ●
Value for money			FREE

TIPS

● The *galeries* are an ideal place to visit on a rainy day. Browse in the boutiques, window shop or simply enjoy the ornate architecture, glass roofs and decorative floors.
● If your feet are aching, relax in a café under the skylights and let the surroundings waft you back to 19th-century Paris.

Between the late 18th and early 19th century a network of *galeries* was built on the Right Bank. Fewer than 30 of the original 140 passages survive. Many have been restored; others are dusty reminders of a bygone age. Elegant Galerie Vivienne, built in 1823, is perhaps the most fashionable, with its ornate cast-iron gates, high glass roofs, chandeliers and mosaic floors. It is home to Legrand—one of Paris's best wine-merchants—a toy shop, a bookshop established in 1826, stylish boutiques and a chic *salon de thé* with tables spilling out under the lofty skylights.

Parallel to it is the much-restored Galerie Colbert, dating from 1826 and now an annex of the Bibliothèque Nationale. It has interesting shops and a sophisticated brasserie, the Grand Colbert. Exhibitions are sometimes held in its galleries and auditorium. The Passage des Panoramas, built in 1800, is today a hive of specialist shops with eateries that include a tea room and an Italian trattoria.

The picturesque 1826 Galerie Véro-Dodat is named after two butchers and was one of the first streets in Paris to be illuminated by gas. Today its black-and-white tiled floor, window boxes and carved wooden mouldings make a shadowy, harmonious setting for an old-world restaurant, antiques shops and galleries. Passages Jouffroy and Verdeau are also worth visiting.

Vivienne (top) is one of Paris's most fashionable galeries

The Grande Arche (above) towers 110m (360ft) over La Défense. One of the business district's contemporary art installations (left)

BASICS

➕ 333 A2 • 1 parvis de la Défense, 92044
☎ 01 49 07 27 55
🕐 Apr–end Sep daily 10–8; Oct–end Mar daily 10–7; last entry 30 min before closing
💶 Adult €9, child (6–17) €7.50
🚇 Grande Arche de la Défense
🚌 73
🚆 RER line A, La Défense
📘 €6
🍴 Restaurant on top floor, but no view
📖 Small bookshop/giftshop on top floor
🚻

www.grandearche.com
In French and English; information on exhibitions and photos of the views

TIPS

● The best view of the Arc de Triomphe is not from the roof of the Grande Arche but from the top of the 54 marble steps leading up to the elevators.
● To experience the bustle of business-focused La Défense, visit on a weekday.

GRANDE ARCHE

Paris's most striking modern monument.

The Grande Arche is best admired from below, looking up into the vast chasm that is greater than the height of Notre-Dame and the width of the Champs-Élysées. The futuristic monument-cum-office block was designed as a symbolic western gateway to Paris and focal point of the new business district, La Défense (▷ 92). Work finished in 1989, in time for the bicentenary of the French Revolution.

TEST YOUR NERVES

Standing below the Grande Arche is an unnerving experience, as you look up at 300,000 tonnes of concrete, marble-cladding and glass rising 110m (360ft) above the ground. But if you think that's daunting, wait until you take the glass elevator that climbs up the cavity of the arch on what looks disconcertingly like a piece of scaffolding. When you reach the top, you might wonder if the hair-raising ride was worth it. The elevator deposits you in a closed-in area lacking the walls of windows you would expect from such a lofty position. To see the view you have to walk outside, up some steps onto a viewing platform. The panorama is partly obscured by wire fencing and the office blocks of La Défense. If you climb only one of Paris's tall buildings, the Grande Arche is probably not the one to choose. But if you have already seen the view from the Eiffel Tower and the Arc de Triomphe, the Grande Arche offers a new perspective on the city. On a clear day you can see along part of Paris's *Grand Axis* (▷ 79), towards the Arc de Triomphe. Farther to the right is a quirky view of the Eiffel Tower, with the Tour Montparnasse lined up directly behind it—at first glance it looks as if the Eiffel Tower is surrounded by scaffolding. Back inside, there is a restaurant and temporary art exhibitions.

LONG-AWAITED

The Grande Arche was the culmination of many unsuccessful attempts to find a nucleus for La Défense in the 1970s. The design, by Danish architect Johan Otto von Spreckelsen, was finally chosen in 1983 and the venture became one of President Mitterrand's *Grand Projets* (▷ 39).

Gleaming statues guard the roof of the Hôtel de Ville

LES HALLES

⊞ 68 N6 • 75001 (the area bordered by rue Beaubourg, rue du Louvre, rue Réaumur and rue de Rivoli) ⊛ Les Halles 🚌 29, 38, 47 🚆 Châtelet-Les-Halles 🍴 Au Pied de Cochon, 6 rue Coquillère ❓ Les Halles can be seedy at night, especially along rue St-Denis www.forum-des-halles.com

'The belly of Paris' (so said the writer Émile Zola) is a curious mixture of old and new, picturesque and seedy. It started life as a food market in the 12th century and continued this role until 1969, when the superb 1860s pavilions were demolished. A decade later they were replaced by the garish Forum des Halles, a vast underground shopping mall. You can also visit the church of St-Eustache (▷ 161) and the Fontaine des Innocents (▷ 93). **Don't miss** The atmosphere of Les Halles in years gone by remains in the surrounding streets, including the cobbled rue Montorgueil.

HÔTEL DE VILLE

⊞ 68 N7 • place de l'Hôtel de Ville, 75004 ☎ 01 42 76 40 40 🕐 Weekly guided tours in French, by appointment only; call 01 42 76 54 04 at least 7 days in advance 🎟 Free guided tours ⊛ Hôtel de Ville 🚌 38, 47, 58, 67, 70, 72, 74, 75, 96 www.paris.fr

The imposing town hall, built in neo-Renaissance style in the late 19th century, is home to Paris's city council. Its predecessor was destroyed in the 1871 uprising. **Don't miss** The place de l'Hôtel de Ville is a pedestrian-only haven in the middle of a mammoth traffic jam. Fountains at either end drown out some of the noise and it's a pleasant spot to admire the 136 statues of historical characters that decorate the town hall's façades.

GRAND PALAIS

An eye-catching exhibition hall hosting major art shows and a science museum.

Grand Palais
⊞ 66 J6 • avenue Winston-Churchill, 75008 (entrance on avenue du Général Eisenhower) ☎ 01 44 13 17 17; reservations 0892 684694 🕐 Thu–Mon 10–8, Wed 10–10 💶 Depends on exhibition ⊛ Champs-Élysées-Clemenceau 🚌 42, 73, 83, 93 📷 Depends on exhibition 📱 Audioguides available 🛍 📚 Bookshop 🚻 www.rmn.fr/galeriesnationalesdugrandpalais

Palais de la Découverte
⊞ 66 J6 • avenue Franklin D. Roosevelt, 75008 ☎ 01 56 43 20 21 🕐 Tue–Sat 9.30–6, Sun 10–7 💶 Adult €7, child (5–18) €4.50, €3.50 extra for Planetarium ⊛ Champs-Élysées-Clemenceau 🚌 28, 42, 72, 73, 83, 93 🛍 📚 🚻 www.palais-decouverte.fr

Petit Palais
⊞ 66 J6 • avenue Winston Churchill, 75008 ☎ 01 53 43 40 00 🕐 Tue–Sat 10–6 🎟 Free ⊛ Champs-Élysées-Clemenceau 🚌 28, 42, 72, 73, 83, 93

RATINGS			
Cultural interest	●	●	● ●
Historic interest	●	●	●
Photo stops (exterior)	●	●	●

TIPS
● It is best to book in advance for exhibitions at the Grand Palais, especially if you want to visit in the morning. Reserve tickets by telephone or via www.fnac.com
● The exhibits in the Palais de la Découverte may be of limited interest to children who do not speak French.
● Even if you don't want to visit the science museum, take a peek at its foyer, with mosaic floor and glass-domed ceiling.

The Grand Palais, with its soaring glass and iron domes, occupies a commanding position between the Seine and the Champs-Élysées. It was built for the 1900 Universal Exhibition, along with the nearby Pont Alexandre III and Petit Palais. The aim was to form a prestigious axis running from the golden-domed Les Invalides to the Champs-Élysées. The colossal building is a striking mix of art nouveau and neoclassical and it is well worth walking around the outside before venturing inside to see the high-profile exhibitions.

The Palais is home to the Musée des Beaux-Arts de la Ville, offering an eclectic collection of mainly 19th-century paintings. On the western side, the Palais de la Découverte is a hands-on science museum aimed primarily at children, with a Planetarium. Topics range from climate change to the workings of the human heart.

Across the road is the Petit Palais, the focus of a recent €264 million restoration. In the grounds outside you will see the statue of a rather stern-looking Winston Churchill.
Don't miss There are wonderful friezes on the eastern and western façades of the Grand Palais.

Île de la Cité

**The historical heart of Paris, packed with must-see sights and offering wonderful views of the Seine.
Key attractions include the Gothic Conciergerie, the glistening Sainte-Chapelle and the stately Notre-Dame cathedral.**

*The western tip of the Île de la Cité, joined to the Right and Left banks by the Pont Neuf (above).
Inside the Mémorial des Martyrs de la Déportation (top)*

RATINGS

Good for kids	● ● ●
Historic interest	● ● ● ● ●
Photo stops	● ● ● ● ●

BASICS

✚ 68 N7 • Île de la Cité, 75001 and 75004
Ⓒ Cité (also Pont Neuf, St-Michel, Châtelet, Hôtel de Ville)
🚌 21, 24, 27, 38, 47, 58, 70, 85, 96
🚇 RER line B, C, St-Michel-Notre-Dame
🍽 On Île de la Cité, the nearby Île St-Louis and in the Latin Quarter
🏨 A selection

The ornate gates of the Palais de Justice

SEEING THE ÎLE DE LA CITÉ

The Paris story began on the Île de la Cité more than 2,000 years ago. Today it is still a key part of the city, packed with visitors, traffic and fabulous architecture. The island sits in the middle of the Seine like a tug, towing the smaller Île St-Louis behind it. One of the best ways to appreciate its beautiful architecture is by boat, taking one of the trips that start from below the Pont Neuf, Paris's oldest bridge. From the water you'll see the elegant Notre-Dame rising high above the banks, and the stern façade of the Conciergerie, once Paris's most notorious prison. In the evening, lighting gives the island an almost magical glow. On foot, the Île de la Cité's charms may be harder to appreciate at first, thanks to the heavy traffic, frequent police sirens and seemingly impenetrable stream of tourists. But persevere and you'll be rewarded with some of Paris's key sights.

HIGHLIGHTS

KEY MONUMENTS

The Île de la Cité shelters three of Paris's most historic buildings—Notre-Dame (▷ 137–141), the Conciergerie (▷ 89–91) and Sainte-Chapelle (▷ 158–160). The most famous is Notre-Dame cathedral, but it is worth fitting all three into your visit. The eerie Gothic halls of the Conciergerie contrast wonderfully with the brightness of nearby Sainte-Chapelle, which in turn seems less intimate than Notre-Dame, despite its smaller size.

THE QUIETER SIDE

When you have ticked off the key sights, there are quieter squares where you can relax and enjoy the views. The grassy square Jean XXIII is a good spot to sit and admire Notre-Dame, while square de l'Île de France, at the island's eastern tip, gives lovely views of the Seine and the Île St-Louis (▷ 98). It is also home to the Mémorial des Martyrs de la Déportation (▷ 107).

Don't miss The flower market in place Louis Lépine (▷ 191) sells anything from delicate blooms to trees.

BACKGROUND

A Celtic tribe called the Parisii settled here in around 250BC. The Romans arrived 200 years later, building the town of Lutetia, which expanded onto the Left Bank. They built a governor's palace and fortress on the western side of the Île de la Cité. In AD508 the king of the Franks made the island his capital, and in the Middle Ages it again became a seat of political power, gaining a royal palace (now the Palais de Justice and Conciergerie). Much of the island was cleared in the 19th century during Baron Haussmann's re-drawing of Paris. Today, it is no longer a political power base, but it retains the Palais de Justice (the Law Courts) and the Préfecture de Police. The island is also the official heart of the city—distances from Paris to the rest of France are measured from the bronze star in the square in front of Notre-Dame.

A dazzling display at the flower market

Strolling past the Patrick Allain florist on rue St-Louis-en-l'Île

ÎLE ST-LOUIS

🗺 68 P8 • Île St-Louis, 75004 🚇 Pont Marie, Sully Morland 🚌 67, 86, 87
🍴 A selection

This leafy island sits discreetly behind the more conspicuous Île de la Cité. Visitors pack its main road, the narrow rue St-Louis-en-l'Île, to browse in the shops and sample the famous ice cream at Maison Berthillon (closed Mon, Tue and Aug). Architect Louis Le Vau designed many of the elegant town houses on the tiny island in the 17th century. He was so pleased with the result he decided to live there himself. **Don't miss** You'll get wonderful views of Notre-Dame from the western tip of the island.

INSTITUT DE FRANCE

🗺 67 L7 • 23 quai de Conti, 75006
☎ 01 44 41 44 41 🕐 Entry by guided tour only: Sat, Sun, public hols at 3; advance booking obligatory, tel: 01 44 41 45 32 🎫 Adult €3.10 🚇 Pont Neuf, Odéon, Louvre-Rivoli 🚌 24, 27, 58, 70 www.institut-de-france.fr

The Institut de France, with its striking cupola, has a prime position on the Left Bank. The building was designed in 1663 by Louis Le Vau and financed by Cardinal Mazarin, who wanted a college for provincial students. The college closed in 1790 and in 1805 Napoleon transferred the Institut de France to the building. The Institut, founded in 1795, aims to protect the arts, literature and the sciences and is made up of five Académies: Inscriptions et Belles-Lettres, Sciences, Beaux-Arts, Sciences Morales et Politiques and the prestigious Française. The Académie Française, founded in 1635, is limited to 40 members. Its rule over the standards of the French language is still very real and is embodied in the *Dictionnaire de la Langue Française.*

INSTITUT DU MONDE ARABE

A must for anyone interested in the history of the Arabic-Islamic world and for fans of contemporary architecture.

🗺 68 N8 • 1 rue des Fossés-St-Bernard, 75005 ☎ 01 40 51 38 38
🕐 Tue–Sun 10–6. Library: Tue–Sat 1–8 🎫 Adult €7, child €5, under 12 free 🚇 Jussieu, Cardinal Lemoine, Sully Morland 🚌 24, 63, 67, 86, 87, 89 🚏 Guided tours (in French): Sat–Sun 3pm. Tours last 1 hr 30 min, €5 (over entrance price)
🍴 Le Ziryab panoramic restaurant (9th floor) 🍴 Café Littéraire (ground floor) and Le Moucharabieh cafeteria (9th floor)
🛍 Shop (ground floor) selling books, CDs, ceramics and gifts 🚹

RATINGS			
Cultural interest	●	●	● ●
Historic interest	●	●	●
Photo stops (exterior and views)	●	●	●

www.imarabe.org (in French, packed with information on the museum, library, exhibitions and events at the Institute; also information on Arab countries)

In 1974, France and 19 Arab countries decided to create the Institut du Monde Arabe (the Arab World Institute). The foundation document was signed in 1980 and the institute opened on the Left Bank in 1987. The stunning aluminium-and-glass building was dreamed up by a group of architects—Jean Nouvel, Pierre Soria, Gilbert Lezenes and Architecture Studio. Its design combines modern materials with the spirit of traditional Arab architecture. The southern façade consists of 240 identical metal light-sensitive screens, adjusted every hour, which electronically filter the sunlight as it enters the building. Their design is taken from carved wooden screens called *moucharabiehs,* used in buildings from Morocco to southeast Asia. The high-speed transparent lifts alone make a visit worthwhile, so let them take you to the ninth floor, where you can admire the river views from the terrace or eat in the elegant restaurant.

The entrance to the museum is on the seventh floor and the displays move chronologically to the sixth and fourth floors, with over 600 items on view. From Spain to India and from prehistoric times to the 19th century, the ceramics, bronzes, ivories, astrolabes, calligraphy, tapestries, textiles and carpets of this collection reflect the brilliance of the Arabic-Islamic civilization. There are also temporary exhibitions, including displays of photography and contemporary art.

The institute is more than a museum. It houses a facility for Arab language and civilization, a cinema, an auditorium, a library of more than 50,000 books, research facilities and an audiovisual venue, and it publishes two magazines. Events include lectures, music, dance and drama performances, creative workshops and educational activities.

Metal screens filter the sunlight at the Institut du Monde Arabe

Les Invalides

**Learn more about Napoleon Bonaparte and his military campaigns in the absorbing army museum.
Then see the emperor's tomb in the stunning, golden-domed Église du Dôme.**

The imposing façade of Les Invalides, 195m (640ft) in length

The Church of the Dome, resting place of Napoleon

SEEING LES INVALIDES

On entering the stately grounds of Les Invalides you'll be following in the footsteps of many a military hero, including General de Gaulle and Winston Churchill. The august building started life as a hospital for wounded soldiers but now houses an army museum. The adjacent Église du Dôme shelters Napoleon's tomb. Unless you are a particular devotee of war history, you may be tempted to skip the Army Museum and head straight to Napoleon's tomb. Don't. The museum is one of the largest of its kind in the world and among the extensive collections of weapons, armour, flags, uniforms and paintings are some real gems. The museum is split into three wings—east, south and west. The west wing has reopened after a comprehensive renovation. For the poignant World War II exhibition head to the south wing; to see the Musée des Plans-Reliefs, with its huge scale models of French towns, go to the fourth floor of the east wing. The entrance to the Église du Dôme is at the front of the church, on the south side of the complex.

HIGHLIGHTS

REMINDERS OF NAPOLEON

As you would expect, Napoleon Bonaparte features prominently in the Musée de l'Armée and you can see his frock coat, hat, coronation saddle and even his actual horse, Vizir (not for the squeamish). There is a re-creation of the room where he died in exile on the island of St-Helena and a variety of paintings, including Paul Delaroche's portrait of the emperor looking unusually undignified just before his abdication in Fontainebleau in 1814.

WORLD WAR II EXHIBITION

Don't miss the World War II exhibition, which moves chronologically through the war years over three floors of the south wing. The evocative, sometimes chilling, displays use film footage, photos and day-to-day objects to convey the horrors of the war and the bravery of those who fought against Hitler. Exhibits include a BBC microphone, French Resistance equipment and a cheerful red, white and blue dress worn during the French Liberation celebrations.

RATINGS	
Good for kids	● ● ●
Historic interest	● ● ● ●
Photo stops (exterior)	● ● ●

BASICS

✚ 66 J7 • Hôtel National des Invalides, 129 rue de Grenelle, 75007

☎ 01 44 42 38 77

🕐 Apr–end Sep daily 10–6 (Église du Dôme mid-Jun to mid-Sep also 6–7pm); rest of year daily 10–5. Closed 1 Jan, 1 May, 1 Nov, 25 Dec and 1st Mon of each month

💷 Adult €8 (with audioguide), under 18 free

Ⓜ La-Tour-Maubourg, Invalides, Varenne

🚌 28, 63, 69, 82, 83, 93

🚆 RER line C, Invalides

Ⓖ Guided tours available

📙 €7

🍴 Selling salads, pizza and sandwiches

🏬 Giftshop/bookshop

♿

www.invalides.org

In French and English; lots of practical and historical information

TIPS

● The best way to appreciate the grandeur of Les Invalides is to approach the site from the Pont Alexandre III (▷ 151).
● The Army Museum is busiest between 11am and 1pm.
● As an antidote to Les Invalides's war focus, unwind in the nearby gardens of the Musée Rodin (▷ 136).

THE COUR D'HONNEUR

It is worth spending a few minutes admiring the architecture of this central courtyard. The arcades that surround it were thriving thoroughfares during Les Invalides's heyday in the late 17th and early 18th centuries. During this time the site was a mini-town, home to around 1,500 soldiers. At times demand for places was so high that only soldiers with 20 years' service were admitted. On arrival they were measured for their blue uniform and black hat, and issued with a comb, knife and wooden spoon. They were not allowed tobacco or to leave the site without permission, and punishments for wrongdoing included being placed on a water-only diet. There was a hospital on site, staffed by almost 40 nurses. From the courtyard, look up to the first floor and you'll see the small grey doors that led to the dormitories. The soldiers ate in dining halls surrounded by paintings of battle. Today Les Invalides is still home to around 100 war veterans.

ÉGLISE DU DÔME

The golden dome of this church rises 107m (350ft) above the ground, a glistening monument to two of France's most influential and charismatic rulers: Louis XIV and Napoleon. The emperor's tomb sits in a grandiose crypt directly below the dome. He died in exile on the island of St-Helena in 1821 but his remains were brought back to France in 1840. It took another 21 years to create his mausoleum and the task was not without controversy as it involved excavating part of the church. Napoleon's remains are encased in six coffins, inside a red porphyry sarcophagus, set on an immense granite base. The 12 statues guarding the tomb represent his military campaigns. Behind the Église du Dôme stands the Soldier's Church, reached from the Cour d'Honneur. It was originally designed by Jules Hardouin-Mansart as part of a vast church with two separate entrances, one for the king (on the south side of what is now the Église du Dôme) and one for soldiers (on the north side of the Soldier's Church). In time, the two churches became separate entities, known respectively as the Église du Dôme and St-Louis-des-Invalides.

Looking across the Cour d'Honneur to the golden dome of the Église du Dôme (far left)

Napoleon's tomb (left, inset), in the crypt of the Église du Dôme

BACKGROUND

Pompous, severe and authoritarian, Les Invalides was actually built to house wounded and elderly soldiers. Louis XIV was thinking of others for once when he commissioned Libéral Bruant to design the imposing building, with its 195m (640ft) façade. The first soldiers arrived in 1674 and were welcomed by the king himself. It took another 32 years before the gold-encrusted Église du Dôme was completed. Bruant's design for the church never got off the ground and in 1676 the king approved new plans by Versailles architect Jules Hardouin-Mansart. The church, dedicated to St. Louis, was finally completed in 1706. Its inauguration was a grand affair, attended by Louis XIV.

Les Invalides looks no less commanding at night

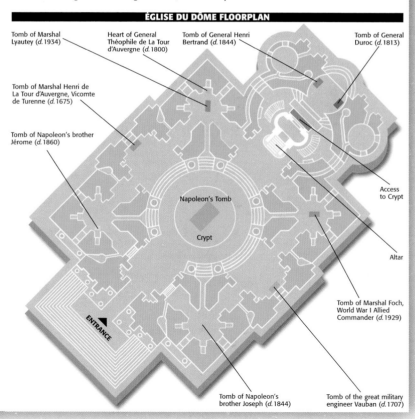

ÉGLISE DU DÔME FLOORPLAN

Tomb of Marshal Lyautey (d.1934)

Heart of General Théophile de La Tour d'Auvergne (d.1800)

Tomb of General Henri Bertrand (d.1844)

Tomb of General Duroc (d.1813)

Tomb of Marshal Henri de La Tour d'Auvergne, Vicomte de Turenne (d.1675)

Tomb of Napoleon's brother Jérome (d.1860)

Napoleon's Tomb

Crypt

Access to Crypt

Altar

ENTRANCE

Tomb of Marshal Foch, World War I Allied Commander (d.1929)

Tomb of Napoleon's brother Joseph (d.1844)

Tomb of the great military engineer Vauban (d.1707)

Jardin du Luxembourg

One of Paris's most popular parks, with a boating pond, children's activities, fabulous flower displays and an Italianate palace. A great place to escape the bustle of the nearby Latin Quarter and St-Germain-des-Prés.

A donkey ride is just one of the children's activities available…

…sailing model boats on the pond is another

The French Senate meets in the Palais du Luxembourg

RATINGS	
Good for kids	●●●●
Photo stops	●●●
Value for money	FREE
Walkability	●●●●

Birds prefer the statues to the green metal chairs!

SEEING THE JARDIN DU LUXEMBOURG

The Jardin du Luxembourg, 24ha (60 acres), forms an attractive southern boundary to St-Germain-des-Prés and the Latin Quarter. Here, students come to relax after lectures and visitors find some breathing space between sightseeing. There are entrances all around the park and wide paths lead to the main attractions, including the octagonal pond and the Théâtre du Luxembourg. Plenty of seats and refreshments are available. The Palais du Luxembourg, home of the French Senate, is on the northern edge. Book ahead for guided tours.

HIGHLIGHTS

RELAXING IN SCENIC SURROUNDINGS

The park contains some of the most beautiful public flower displays in Paris and is landscaped in an appealing mixture of French, English and Italian styles. The focal point is a large octagonal pond, elegantly encircled by stone urns and statues of French queens and other notable women. In good weather the park is full of Parisians sunbathing, playing either *boules* or chess, or jogging along the shady paths. Other attractions include tennis courts, a bandstand and even a bee-keeping school. The Musée du Luxembourg, in the former orangery, stages temporary exhibitions. Despite the crowds, the park is a welcome respite from the hectic Paris streets. But there is no forgetting you are in the heart of the city—the Eiffel Tower and Tour Montparnasse loom on the horizon.

PALAIS DU LUXEMBOURG

The Italianate Palais du Luxembourg is a reminder of the park's Florentine origins and is now home to the French Senate. It was commissioned by Marie de Medici in the 17th century and during the Revolution was commandeered as a prison.

ACTIVITIES FOR CHILDREN

Children are well catered for, with pony rides (during French school holidays only), puppet shows in the Théâtre du Luxembourg (Wednesday, Saturday and Sunday from 2pm) and the usual swings and slides. They can also try their hand at being skippers by renting remote-control model yachts to sail on the pond.

STATUES

The Fontaine Médicis is a popular romantic spot to the east of the Palais du Luxembourg. The grotto was commissioned by Marie de Medici in the 17th century and sculptures include allegorical characters representing the rivers Seine and Rhône, as well as the queen's coats of arms. Later, a sculpture showing the angry Polyphemus preparing to throw a rock at the innocent lovers Acis and Galatea was added. At the western end of the park you can see a miniature Statue of Liberty.

BACKGROUND

Bored with the Louvre, Marie de Medici commissioned the gardens and palace in 1615, hoping for a reminder of her native Florence. She bought the land from Duke François of Luxembourg (hence the park's name) and asked architect Salomon de Brosse to use the Pitti Palace as inspiration. Work finished in the mid-1620s but Marie, widow of Henri IV, did not have long to enjoy her creation. She was exiled from France by the powerful Cardinal Richelieu and died penniless in Cologne. A petition of 12,000 signatures failed to save parts of the gardens from Baron Haussmann's development plans in the mid-19th century, but the remaining greenery continued to be a refuge for artists, writers and philosophers, including Ernest Hemingway, Victor Hugo and Jean-Paul Sartre.

Feeding the birds

BASICS

🚇 67 L9 • rue de Vaugirard/rue de Médicis/boulevard St-Michel, 75006

☎ Park: 01 42 34 23 89. Senate: 01 42 34 20 00. Musée du Luxembourg 01 42 34 25 95

🕐 Times vary depending on season; generally dawn–dusk

💶 Free

Ⓜ Odéon

🚌 38, 63, 70, 82, 83, 84, 85, 86, 87, 89, 96

🚉 RER line B, Luxembourg

🚶 Guided tours of the Palais du Luxembourg on the first Sat of each month. To book a place call 01 44 54 19 49. To sit in on a Senate debate call 01 42 34 20 00

🍴 Open-air cafés, kiosk restaurant

🥤 Kiosk

❓ An oak tree dedicated to the victims of 9/11 has been planted near the Statue of Liberty

🚻

www.senat.fr

In French, English, German and Spanish, with historical information and photos

The surprisingly contemporary fountain in the Cour d'Honneur (above). Strolling through the arcades (left)

JARDIN DU PALAIS ROYAL

An oasis of calm only a few steps (and a million miles) from the bustle of the city.

This tranquil garden is the perfect place to recharge your batteries after a visit to the Louvre. The flower-filled enclave is separated from the 21st century by a cordon of handsome 18th-century arcades. These shelter traditional *salons de thé* and quirky shops selling anything from art, jewellery and clothes to pipes, silverware and model soldiers. In good weather the gardens are full of Parisians resting, reading and playing *boules*. The flower beds are vibrant, and a central statue and refreshing fountain add to the elegant calm. Children come to roller-skate around the rather incongruous grey-and-white striped mini-columns in the Cour d'Honneur, a controversial 1986 addition by artist Daniel Buren. The courtyard's sleek water features blend more easily with the rest of the garden.

THE PALACE

The Palais Royal was commissioned by Louis XIII's advisor, Cardinal Richelieu, in the 17th century and was originally called the Palais-Cardinal. Molière and his troupe of actors used to perform in the Théâtre du Petit Cardinal, which once stood at the southern corner of the palace. It was here in 1673 that the illustrious playwright fell ill, ironically during a production of *Le Malade Imaginaire* (The Hypochondriac). He died a few hours later. The nearby Comédie Française still stages his plays today. Louis XIV spent part of his childhood in the Palais Royal and authors Colette and Jean Cocteau lived within the grounds. Now the building houses the French Ministry of Culture and is not open to the public.

UPRISING

The arcades and apartments surrounding the palace garden were constructed in the 18th century. Only a few years later, on 12 July 1789, Camille Desmoulins made a passionate speech in the garden that sparked the uprising and the storming of the Bastille two days later (▷ 33).

RATINGS

Good for kids	●●●
Photo stops	●●●
Specialist shopping	●●●
Value for money	FREE

BASICS

✚ 67 M6 • place du Palais-Royal, 75001 (entrance to the gardens is through an arch to the left of the Palais Royal)

🕐 Jun–end Aug daily 7am–11pm; Apr–end May daily 7am–10.15pm; Sep daily 7am–9.30pm; Oct–end Mar daily 7.30am–8.30pm

💷 Free

🚇 Palais Royal/Musée du Louvre

🚌 21, 48, 67, 69, 72, 81

🍴 Restaurants and tea rooms around the outside, including Muscade tea room (▷ 271)

🏬 Plenty of small shops in the arcades

There are plenty of seats by the pond if you feel like taking a break

JARDIN DES TUILERIES

A chic park offering great views of Paris's most famous landmarks.

Dominated at one end by the hectic place de la Concorde and at the other by the mighty Louvre, this is not one of those parks that lets you forget you're in the heart of the city. But what the elegant, French-style grounds lack in seclusion they make up for in photo opportunities, with marvellous views of the Louvre, Eiffel Tower, Arc de Triomphe, Musée d'Orsay and Egyptian obelisk. The park, once considered the best-kept in Europe, runs alongside the Seine.

ART AND NATURE
The grandest way to enter is through the gilded gates at the Concorde end. This brings you to the first of two large ponds, balanced at either end of the park—ideal for relaxing with a book. Two art galleries stand on terraces either side of this first pond, the Jeu de Paume (▷ 106) and the Orangerie (▷ 142). Look out for Henry Moore's *Reclining Figure* (1951), which sits on the steps leading up to the Orangerie. Follow the wide central avenue towards the Louvre and the gravel of the western half of the park gradually gives way to grass and well-tended flower beds. You'll pass allegorical statues, open-air cafés and children's playgrounds. All around people are relaxing. At the other end of the park, the neoclassical Arc du Carrousel acts as a symbolic gateway to the Louvre and is also the first arch in Paris's *Grand Axis*, the imaginary straight line linking the Louvre, the Arc de Triomphe and the Grande Arche.

ITALIAN ORIGINS
The park was the inspiration of Catherine de Medici, who wanted an Italian-style garden to complement the Tuileries Palace, built in 1564. Lavish balls, concerts and fireworks ensured her garden became a key social venue. The park as we know it today dates from 1649, when Louis XIV asked his preferred landscape gardener, André Le Nôtre, to redesign it in the formal French style. He added the central avenue, as well as two raised walkways running along either side, and the garden soon became a fashionable promenading area. The palace went up in smoke at the hands of the Communards in 1871 but the garden survived. After years of neglect and pollution in the 20th century, it received a makeover in time for the start of the 21st century.

RATINGS	
Good for kids	●●●●
Photo stops	●●●
Value for money	FREE
Walkability	●●●●

BASICS
✚ 67 K6 • place de la Concorde, 75001
☎ 01 40 20 90 43
🕐 Apr–end Sep daily 7am–9pm; rest of year daily 7.30–7
✋ Free
Ⓜ Tuileries, Concorde
🚌 24, 68, 72, 73, 84, 94
💶 €7
☕ Open-air cafés
📖 Bookshop at Concorde end
👫
❓ No dogs allowed

TIPS
● Children can rent model yachts to sail on the pond at the Louvre end of the park.
● Free guided tours take place during the summer months. For more information see the noticeboards or call 01 49 96 19 33.

A sculpture of Balzac by Auguste Rodin

You'll find both modern and traditional tapestries at Gobelins

The house where Victor Hugo once lived is now a museum

THE SIGHTS

JEU DE PAUME

✚ 67 K6 • 1 place de la Concorde, 75008 ☎ 01 47 03 12 50 🕐 Tue–Fri 12–7, Sat–Sun 10–7, also Tue 7–9 💷 €8 🚇 Concord 🚌 24, 42, 52, 72, 73, 84, 94 🛇 ❓ Closed between temporary exhibitions; programme available on 01 47 03 12 52 (recorded information) www.jeudepaume.org

The illustrious Jeu de Paume started life as an indoor tennis court, metamorphosed into a world-famous art gallery, then lost its prize exhibits to the Musée d'Orsay. It is now part of the Centre National de la Photographie. It combines its efforts with the Site Sully, housed in the 17th-century Hôtel de Sully in Le Marais, to present the art of photography from the 19th to the 21st centuries through temporary exhibitions.

The airy, neoclassical Jeu de Paume, idyllically located in the Jardin des Tuileries (▷ 105), was commissioned by Napoleon III as an indoor court for *réal* (royal) tennis, played with the *paume* (palm) of the hand. When lawn tennis took over in popularity the court was used for art exhibitions and after World War II it became one of the world's finest Impressionist museums, until the exodus of its rich collection to the Musée d'Orsay in 1986.

MAISON DE BALZAC

✚ 321 F7 • 47 rue Raynouard, 75016 ☎ 01 55 74 41 80 🕐 Tue–Sun 10–6 💷 Free (except temporary exhibitions) 🚇 Passy, La Muette 🚌 32, 50, 70, 72 www.paris.fr

The writer Honoré de Balzac (1799–1850) lived in this pretty house on the Passy hillside from 1840 until 1847. Pursued by debtors, he lay low here using a false identity. It was also here, in a creative flow that often lasted all night, that Balzac penned some of the masterpieces of *La Comédie Humaine, La Cousine Bette* and *Le Cousin Pons*. The house is now an intimate museum dedicated to his life and works. Many original editions, illustrations and manuscripts are on show and there is a library devoted to his works. You can also visit temporary exhibitions.

MAISON EUROPÉENNE DE LA PHOTOGRAPHIE

✚ 68 P7 • 5–7 rue de Fourcy, 75004 ☎ 01 44 78 75 00 🕐 Wed–Sun 11–8 (last entry 7.30; closed during changeover of exhibitions) 💷 Adult €6, child €3, under 8 free; free to all Wed 5–8 🚇 St-Paul 🚌 67, 69, 76, 96 🛇 In basement www.mep-fr.org

The Maison Européenne de la Photographie is a stylish venue for dynamic exhibitions of contemporary photography. The galleries spread over five floors of the 18th-century Hôtel Hénault de Cantobre, as well as in a new wing, which opened in 1996. A 100-seat auditorium screens films related to the exhibitions, and there is also a library and video-viewing facilities.

MAISON DE VICTOR HUGO

✚ 68 P7 • 6 place des Vosges, 75004 ☎ 01 42 72 10 16 🕐 Tue–Sun 10–6 💷 Permanent collections free. Temporary exhibitions: adult €8, under 14 free 🚇 Bastille, St-Paul 🚌 20, 29, 65, 69, 96 www.paris.fr

The quirky Maison de Victor Hugo conjures up a vivid impression of literary life in 19th-century Paris. It is in the Hôtel de Rohan-Guéménée, where Victor Hugo lived from 1832 to 1848 with his wife and four children. He wrote part of his world-famous novel *Les Misérables* here, and met with fellow writers such as Alexandre Dumas and Alphonse de Lamartine.

As you climb the stone steps to the upper floors you'll see a series of old posters advertising various theatrical productions of *Les Misérables*.

In the permanent exhibition on the second floor, the rooms are laid out to echo the interiors of Hugo's various homes, including one on the Channel Island of Guernsey, where he spent time in self-imposed political exile. Memorabilia include a bust of Hugo by Auguste Rodin and furniture from actress Juliette Drouet's room in Guernsey, some of it carved and decorated by Hugo. There is also a reconstruction of the room where Hugo died in 1885.

Temporary exhibitions are staged on the first floor and there is a library on the third floor, although access to this is by appointment only.

Don't miss The luxurious wallpaper alone makes a visit to the permanent exhibitions on the second floor worthwhile. The *salon chinois* (Chinese room) is also striking.

MANUFACTURE DES GOBELINS

✚ 331 N11 • 42 avenue des Gobelins, 75013 ☎ 01 40 13 46 46 🕐 Visit by guided tour only (in French): Tue–Thu at 2 and 3. Arrive 10 min before the start of the tour 💷 Adult €10, child €7, under 7 free 🚇 Les Gobelins 🚌 27, 47, 83, 91

Originally a dyeworks set up by the Gobelin brothers in the 15th century, the Manufacture des Gobelins attracted the attention of Colbert, Louis XIV's astute minister, and by 1662 it had become the royal tapestry factory. It rapidly expanded to

One of the many interesting shops in the Marais district

Browsing in the Marché aux Puces de St-Ouen

include furniture and carpet workshops. Much of the interior decoration of Versailles was woven, carved or inlaid here.

Today you see the centuries-old looms clicking away, worked by expert weavers. The 90-minute guided tour also takes in some of the workshops of the famous Beauvais tapestry and Savonnerie carpet factories.

LE MARAIS

➕ 68 P7 • Le Marais 🅶 St-Paul, Rambuteau, Hôtel de Ville, Bastille 🚌 29, 69, 75, 76, 96

Stretching west to east between Les Halles and the Bastille and north to south from the place de la République to the Seine, the Marais district has a beguiling combination of history, ornate architecture and trendy chic boutiques, bars, restaurants and galleries. The area was once an expanse of low-lying marshland, hence its name *marais* (marsh). Now it is home to cobblestone courtyards, medieval streets, beautiful mansions, a bustling Jewish quarter, and the oldest square in Paris—place des Vosges (▷ 150).

During the 17th century, aristocrats competed here to build the most elegant mansion. The area subsequently fell into neglect until, in 1962, Culture Minister-cum-writer André Malraux pointed out the historic value of numerous crumbling monuments, and a restoration scheme began.

Today it is impossible to wander through the Marais without stumbling across architectural masterpieces, even if you can only admire them from their courtyards. Many of these mansions (called *hôtels*) now house museums, including the Musée Picasso (▷ 135), the Musée Carnavalet (▷ 114–115) and the Musée

d'Art et d'Histoire du Judaïsme (▷ 112).

Don't miss Enjoy a leisurely drink in the place des Vosges.

MARCHÉ AUX PUCES DE ST-OUEN

➕ 69 off M1 • Porte de Clignancourt, 75018 (from the Métro station turn right onto avenue de la Porte de Clignancourt, past the tacky unofficial stands. Walk under the flyover and the market is on your left) ☎ 0892 705 765 🕐 Sat–Mon 9–7 (some stands open earlier) 🎟 Free 🅶 Porte de Clignancourt 🚌 56, 85 🍴 Cafés and restaurants on rue des Rosiers ❓ Beware of pickpockets www.parispuces.com

Pick up a piece of bygone Paris—or a cheap imitation—at what claims to be the world's largest antiques market, spread over 7ha (17 acres) north of Montmartre, just beyond the *périphérique*. Even if you have no intention of buying, you'll find an Aladdin's Cave of fascinating objects, ranging from Louis XV mirrors and luxurious 19th-century chandeliers to weird and wacky 1970s furniture.

Don't be put off by the cluster of tacky stands along the approach to the market. Walk swiftly past them, under the flyover, then decide which of the 13 official markets you'll tackle first. There are around 2,000 shops and stalls to choose from. Watch out for pickpockets and remember that prices fluctuate according to the weather, so be prepared to haggle. Sunday afternoons are particularly busy. If you prefer breathing space, arrive early.

MÉMORIAL DES MARTYRS DE LA DÉPORTATION

➕ 68 N8 • square de l'Île de France, Île de la Cité, 75004 ☎ 01 46 33 87 56 🕐 Daily 10–12, 2–7 (2–5 in winter)

🎟 Free 🅶 Cité 🚌 24, 47 🅶 St-Michel Notre-Dame 🍴 Plenty on Île de la Cité

This haunting monument commemorates the 200,000 French people who died in concentration camps during the Holocaust. The roof of the memorial sits in a peaceful grassy square on the eastern tip of the Île de la Cité, from where you can enjoy views of the river and the Île St-Louis.

By contrast, walk down the narrow staircase into the shadowy crypt and you are limited to mere glimpses of the Seine through iron bars, a chilling reminder of the incarceration experienced by the prisoners. A long, dark tunnel leading from the crypt is studded by 200,000 fragments of shining glass, one for each person who died. A light at the end symbolizes hope. This is no ordinary, lifeless monument—it gives an unsettling reminder of the horrors of World War II.

MÉMORIAL DE LA SHOAH

➕ 68 N7 • 17 rue Geoffroy-l'Asnier, 75004 ☎ 01 42 77 44 72 🕐 Sun–Fri 10–6 (also Museum Thu 6–10, Salle des Noms Thu 6–7.30) 🎟 Museum, crypt, multimedia centre and reading room: free; exhibition: €5 🅶 St-Paul, Pont Marie 🚌 67, 69, 76, 96 www.memorialdelashoah.org

Inaugurated in January 2005 for the 60th anniversary of the liberation of Auschwitz, the Mémorial houses the tomb of the unknown Jewish martyr (in the crypt), the Mur des Noms bearing the names of the 76,000 Jews deported from France, and a museum relating the fate of the Jewish people during World War II. This comprehensive information and research centre is the largest of its kind in Europe.

Montmartre

A village within a city, with cobbled streets, quirky museums, stunning views and the mighty Sacré-Cœur basilica. Follow in the footsteps of artists Toulouse-Lautrec, Pierre-Auguste Renoir and Pablo Picasso...and a headless saint.

For the price of a Métro ticket, the funicular (above) will save you a lengthy climb up to Sacré-Cœur

A traditional merry-go-round (right inset)

RATINGS

Good for kids	● ● ●
Historic interest	● ● ● ●
Photo stops	● ● ● ● ●

BASICS

✚ 69 M2 • 75018
🔘 Anvers, Abbesses, Blanche, Lamarck
🚌 Montmartrobus; 30, 31, 54, 68, 74, 80, 85 have stops around the edge of Montmartre
🍴 La Maison Rose, rue de l'Abreuvoir; tel 01 42 57 66 75 (open 12–3, 7–11; closed Wed lunch and Tue and Thu dinner). There are plenty of restaurants and cafés in the area, many of them very touristy
🎫 A selection

www.montmartrenet.com
In French and English; packed with history, practical information and photos

SEEING MONTMARTRE

The hilltop village of Montmartre, to the north of the city core, has a split personality. There are teeming tourist traps, including place du Tertre and the front steps of Sacré-Cœur, but venture a few minutes off the beaten track and you'll find quiet cobbled streets, white-washed cottages and all the atmosphere of a small village. The Métro will take you to the outskirts of the district, but to reach the key sights you'll have to either walk or take the Montmartrobus, which runs a circular route from place Pigalle, past Sacré-Cœur, and north to the Métro station Jules Joffrin. You can avoid the daunting walk up the steps to Sacré-Cœur by taking the funicular from square Willette (costing one Métro ticket each way).

HIGHLIGHTS

TOURIST MONTMARTRE

Montmartre is crowned by the Basilique du Sacré-Cœur (▷ 154–157), a dazzling white neo-Byzantine creation whose domes and turrets look stunning against a blue sky. There are sweeping views over Paris from its front steps. The nearby place du Tertre (literally 'Hillock Square') is Paris's highest point and swarms with visitors and street artists. The restaurant La Mère Catherine, at number 6, was founded in 1793 and was said to have given rise to the name *bistro*. Legend has it that in 1814, Russian troops, who had become regulars at the restaurant, would shout *bystro* (quickly) to hurry along their food (▷ 35). You can sometimes try Montmartre's own wine here, made from grapes grown in the area's only remaining vineyard, on rue des Saules.

VILLAGE MONTMARTRE

Place du Tertre is tourist Montmartre at its peak, but only a few minutes' walk away are quieter streets, including rue de l'Abreuvoir, rue des Saules and rue Girardon. Make sure you save some time to wander through this less showy side of Montmartre (see walk, ▷ 226–227), where you'll find cobblestones, romantic tree-lined steps and even two windmills. It's hard to remember you're still in France's capital. At 22 rue des Saules is the tiny but legendary cabaret venue Au Lapin Agile, once frequented by Picasso and still providing entertainment. Nearby, at 12 rue Cortot, is the Musée de Montmartre (▷ 126), where you can learn more about the history of the area. A short walk away, off rue Lepic, is one of Montmartre's two remaining windmills, the Moulin de la Galette, built in 1622 and formerly known as Le Moulin du Blute-fin. Legend claims that one of its millers, Pierre-Charles Debray, was strung up on its sails in 1814 for trying to stop the invading Cossacks, although it is more likely he was killed by a stray bullet. Later in the 19th century the Debray family converted the mill into a popular open-air dance hall, providing inspiration for many artists, including Renoir and Vincent Van Gogh. Nearby is the Moulin Radet, now part of a restaurant called Moulin de la Galette.

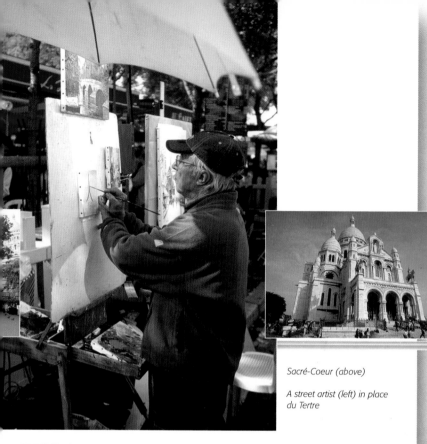

Sacré-Coeur (above)

A street artist (left) in place du Tertre

ARTISTS' MONTMARTRE

Montmartre earned an almost mythical status at the end of the 19th century, thanks to its community of artists and its raunchy nightlife. Toulouse-Lautrec immortalized scenes of dancing girls at the world-famous cabaret venue Moulin Rouge (▷ 111), while Renoir captured the exuberance of a ball at the Moulin de la Galette. Twentieth-century artists who converged on Montmartre included Picasso and Georges Braque, who gave birth to Cubism in the Bateau-Lavoir studios, on place Emile-Goudeau. The original timber building burned down in 1970 and was replaced by a concrete studio, now closed to the public. To view some 20th-century art head for the surreal Espace Montmartre—Salvador Dalí (▷ 92).

BACKGROUND

Montmartre started life as a place of worship, a far cry from its later hedonistic reputation. The Romans built a temple to Mercury here, naming the hill Mons Mercurii. It was later called Mont des Martyrs, following the murder of Paris's first bishop, St. Denis, in the 3rd century AD. He was said to have picked up his head and taken it to a nearby fountain to wash away the blood, before collapsing (see his statue in square Suzanne-Buisson). Montmartre's religious connection was renewed in the 12th century, when Louis VI founded a Benedictine Abbey there. With monks around, the area was soon filled with vineyards. By the end of the 17th century around 30 windmills stood on the hill and Montmartre prospered with the production of wine, flour and gypsum (plaster of Paris) for the city below. Gypsum quarrying stopped in the early 19th century because the hill was in danger of collapsing. Montmartre became known for its decadent cabarets at the end of the 19th century. Nowadays the district is no longer the hub of Paris's nightlife, but visitors still come to La Butte (the mound) for a taste of its Bohemian past.

TIPS

● Le Petit Train de Montmartre (Promotrain) offers a 40-minute tour of Montmartre's main sights, starting from place Blanche and including a stop at place du Tertre (10–6; until midnight at weekends and during July and August; adult €5.50, child €3.50). The Montmartrain runs a similar circuit.
● Montmartre's cemetery (▷ 87) is well worth a visit to search out the graves of Hector Berlioz, Jacques Offenbach, Émile Zola and other composers and writers.

Café culture still reigns in Montparnasse

LA MOSQUÉE

A gem of 20th-century European Islamic architecture, with exquisitely carved arcades and a magnificent minaret, 33m (108ft) high.

68 N9 • La Mosquée: place du Puits-de-l'Ermite, 75005; Hammam: 39 rue Geoffroy St-Hilaire ☎ La Mosquée: 01 45 35 97 33; Hammam: 01 43 31 38 20 🕐 La Mosquée: guided tours in French: Sat–Thu 9–12, 2–6. Hammam: Men: Tue 2–9, Sun 10–9. Women: Mon, Wed, Thu, Sat 10–9, Fri 2–9 💶 La Mosquée: adult €3, child €2, under 7 free. Hammam: prices vary for different treatments 🚇 Jussieu, Place Monge, Censier-Daubenton 🚌 47, 67, 89 🍴 Restaurant: 39 rue Geoffroy St-Hilaire 🫖 *Salon de Thé:* 39 rue Geoffroy St-Hilaire 📚 Small bookshop at La Mosquée; a souk at 39 rue Geoffroy St-Hilaire sells ceramics, jewellery, bags, postcards, lampshades and other items 🛁 In the Hammam www.la-mosquee.com (in French and English, includes practical information about the Hammam)

RATINGS	
Cultural interest	●●●
Historic interest	●●●
Specialist shopping (souk)	●●●

The splendid Paris Mosque is one of the Left Bank's most pleasant surprises, with its impressive square minaret and ornate decoration. It was built between 1922 and 1926, with French funds, to commemorate North African military support during World War I.

Faithful to ornate Hispano-Moorish architecture, its roofs are green tiled, its fountains are pink marbled and its doors are exquisitely carved. The grand patio was inspired by the Alhambra in Granada, Spain, and has decorative mosaics and fine cedar and eucalyptus woodwork. The finely carved arcades are also decorated with intricate mosaics. A spiritual base for Paris's Muslim community, the prayer room is exceptional for its ornamentation and fine carpets. The courtyard garden is a symbol of Muslim paradise. The Mosque is also home to a library and an Islamic teaching facility.

The rest of the Mosque complex is accessible from rue Geoffroy St-Hilaire and includes a restaurant, a *salon de thé* and the Hammam (Turkish baths). The Hammam is the perfect escape from the bustle of city life. Seated around a marble fountain, let your mind drift to exotic shores. Later, you can sit at an outdoor table in the pretty courtyard of the *salon de thé*, sipping mint tea and eating couscous. There is also a shop, reminiscent of a small souk, crammed with an array of distinctive items.

Mosaics decorate the arcades at La Mosquée

MONTPARNASSE

329 K10 • Montparnasse 🚇 Montparnasse-Bienvenüe, Vavin, Edgar Quinet 🚌 28, 58, 82, 88, 89, 91, 92, 94, 95, 96

Montparnasse was a popular district with artists and writers in the early 20th century, attracting the likes of Amedeo Modigliani, Marc Chagall and Ernest Hemingway. Legendary meeting places (including La Coupole, ▷ 266) still exist, haunted by shadows of literary and artistic giants from the 1920s and 1930s.

Although Montparnasse's main boulevards have lost some of their charm, sacrificed to the whims of consumerism, the area's many theatres, cafés, cinemas and cabarets remain lively.

Tour Montparnasse (▷ 170) looms over the district and you get wonderful views from the public gallery on the 56th floor. The tower, 209m (685ft) high, was built in the early 1970s as part of a huge urban development project. Across a windy esplanade is the Gare Montparnasse, one of the most confusing stations in Paris.

Years of hectic redevelopment in Montparnasse have replaced atmospheric narrow streets with uninspiring apartment blocks. Some corners are worth seeking out, however, such as 18 rue Antoine Bourdelle, where you can visit the Musée Bourdelle (Tue–Sun 10–6). The museum focuses on the sculptor Émile-Antoine Bourdelle (1861–1929), a former pupil of Auguste Rodin, who once lived and worked in this picturesque house.

Also worth a visit is the Cimetière du Montparnasse (▷ 87) where many notable former residents are buried, including Jean-Paul Sartre, Simone de Beauvoir and Guy de Maupassant.

A windmill in name only—the world-famous Moulin Rouge

MOULIN ROUGE

➕ 69 L3 • 82 boulevard de Clichy, 75018 ☎ 01 53 09 82 82 🕐 Shows nightly at 9pm and 11pm; dinner at 7pm ✋ Dinner and show €135–€165; show only €85–€95 🚇 Blanche 🚌 30, 54, 68, 74 www.moulin-rouge.com

The Moulin Rouge is the famous symbol of Montmartre. Its decadent, pleasure-seeking reputation was initially fuelled by Toulouse-Lautrec's posters and more recently by the 2001 film *Moulin Rouge*, starring Nicole Kidman and Ewan McGregor. The 'Red Windmill' was never actually a windmill but was launched as a cabaret venue in 1889. It soon became known for its saucy shows, featuring scantily clad cancan girls who entertained an audience from all walks of life. Over the years many stars have made guest appearances, including Edith Piaf, Frank Sinatra, Liza Minnelli and Elton John. You can still see lively shows here (at a price), complete with the famous *cancaneuses* dancers.

MUSÉE DES ARTS ET MÉTIERS

➕ 68 N6 • 60 rue Réaumur, 75003 ☎ 01 53 01 82 00 🕐 Tue–Sun 10–6 (also Thu 6pm–9.30pm). ✋ Adult €6.50, under 18 free 🚇 Arts et Métiers, Réaumur-Sébastopol 🚌 20, 38, 39, 47 📷 www.arts-et-metiers.net/

Art meets science at this quirky museum, with a fascinating collection of early scientific machinery, vintage cars and mechanical toys. You can see a primitive calculating machine invented by Blaise Pascal, one of Thomas Edison's phonographs and a mechanical toy created for Marie-Antoinette. A Formula 1 racing car sits incongruously in the former chapel.

MUSÉE DES ARTS DÉCORATIFS

A remarkable collection of decorative arts from the Middle Ages to the present day.

➕ 67 L6 • 107 rue de Rivoli, 75001 ☎ 01 44 55 57 50 🕐 Tue–Fri 11–6 (Thu 6–9), Sat–Sun 10–6. Closed public hols ✋ Adult €8, under 18 free; €16.50 for all four museums 🚇 Palais-Royal/Musée du Louvre, Tuileries 🚌 21, 27, 39, 48, 69, 72, 81, 95 ☎ Phone in advance for details of guided tours: 01 44 55 59 26 📖 Bookshop and giftshop 🚻 www.ucad.fr

RATINGS			
Cultural interest	●	●	● ●
Historic interest	●	●	●

The Union Centrale des Arts Décoratifs (UCAD) was founded at the end of the 19th century by a group of industrialists whose aim was to display beauty in function. Today UCAD is composed of a decorative arts library, three schools and four museums. Three of the museums, including the Musée des Arts Décoratifs, are housed in the Pavillon de Marsan and Rohan wing of the Louvre.

The Musée des Arts Décoratifs has more than 150,000 items covering almost every aspect of the decorative arts, from ceramics, glass and embroidery to wood and metalwork. Collections include the Middle Ages and Renaissance, art nouveau, art deco, modern and contemporary, and a further five specialist departments: glass, toys, drawings, wallpaper and a dazzling display of 1,200 items of jewellery from the Middle Ages to today.

The art nouveau collection includes several pieces of furniture by Emile Gallé, one of the masters of the genre. The Middle Ages and Renaissance galleries contain a rich collection reflecting religious art and domestic life from the 13th to 16th centuries. The Galerie des Retables contains a fine collection of European altarpieces carved in wood and stone. Tapestries are on display in the Salle de la Vie Rurale dans la Tapisserie. The Salle du Maître de la Madeleine contains medieval sculptures and paintings, and the Cabinet de Travail, a delightful period room, is decorated with refined marquetry panelling. The Salle des Vitraux contains French and Italian furniture, Flemish tapestries, 16th-century stained glass and objets d'art.

The final museum is the Musée Nissim de Camondo, the grand collection of objets d'art amassed by the Comte de Camondo during the late 18th century, housed in an early 19th-century family home (▷ 126).

A tapestry from the museum's medieval collection (above)

Explore modern art and design

MUSÉE D'ART ET D'HISTOIRE DU JUDAÏSME

Discover the rich cultural heritage of the Jewish community in France and beyond.

🔲 68 N6 • Hôtel de St-Aignan, 71 rue du Temple, 75003 ☎ 01 53 01 86 60 🕐 Mon–Fri 11–6, Sun 10–6. Closed Sat 💳 Adult €6.80, under 18 free 🚇 Rambuteau, Hôtel de Ville 🚌 29, 38, 47, 75 🎧 Audioguide included in the entry price 🍴 Café 📖 Substantial bookshop ♿
www.mahj.org (in French only; see photos of the collections and find out about temporary exhibitions)

RATINGS	
Cultural interest	●●●○
Historic interest	●●●○
Specialist shopping (books)	●●●○

This museum vividly illustrates the development of Jewish culture from the Middle Ages to the present day, in France and farther afield. It also highlights the contribution members of the Jewish community have made to European life and art. The main focus is on French Jews, although you can also see items from the rest of Europe, as well as North Africa.

An audioguide, included in the entry price, directs you chronologically through the museum. Themes include the Middle Ages, the Emancipation of the Jews after the French Revolution, intellectual and artistic achievements in the 19th century, and the tragedies and triumphs of the modern era. Medieval exhibits include a rare Hanukkah lamp, dating from before the expulsion of the Jews in the 14th century. Later items include a vivid Jewish marriage contract from 1752 and a 19th-century Algerian wedding outfit. Artists represented include Marc Chagall and Amedeo Modigliani. The archives of the Dreyfus Affair contain around three thousand letters, photographs, books and official documents relating to the case of French Jewish army captain, Alfred Dreyfus, who was falsely convicted of passing secrets to the Germans in 1894.

The museum opened in 1998 in the Hôtel de St-Aignan, a restored 17th-century mansion named after an early owner, the Duc de St-Aignan. The mansion became home to Jewish immigrants from Eastern Europe in the 19th century, and during World War II its residents were arrested by the Germans and sent to concentration camps. Their memory is kept alive by an art installation by Christian Boltanski, called *Les habitants de l'Hôtel de Saint-Aignan en 1939* (1998).

An ironwork detail at the 17th-century Hôtel de St-Aignan

THE SIGHTS

MUSÉE D'ART MODERNE DE LA VILLE DE PARIS

🔲 66 G6 • 11 avenue du Président Wilson, 75016 ☎ 01 53 67 40 00 🕐 Tue–Sun 10–6; temporary exhibitions also Fri–Sat 6–8 💳 Free. Temporary exhibitions: adult €5, under 13 free 🚇 Iéna, Alma-Marceau 🚌 32, 42, 72, 80, 82, 92
www.paris.fr

Temporary exhibitions of outstanding quality help keep this modern-art museum within an international sphere. The collection covers Fauvism, Cubism, Surrealism, Abstraction and Nouveau Réalisme. *La Danse* (1932), a mural by Henri Matisse, hangs in a room entirely devoted to the artist.

Next door to the museum, the Palais de Tokyo houses the Centre d'Art Contemporain (▷ 198).
Don't miss Raoul Dufy's 1937 mural *La Fée Electricité* is a staggering 60m (197ft) by 10m (33ft).

MUSÉE BACCARAT

🔲 66 G5 • 11 place des États-Unis, 75016 ☎ 01 40 22 11 00 🕐 Mon and Wed–Sat 10–6.30. 💳 Adult €2.50 🚇 Boissière, Kléber 🚌 22, 30, 32, 82 📷 Guided tours available in French, English, German and Japanese 📖 Giftshop
www.baccarat.fr

Baccarat began making windowpanes, mirrors and goblets in the village of Baccarat, in Lorraine, in 1764. The company fired up its first crystal kiln in 1816, and since then prestigious clients have included Louis XVIII, Tsar Nicholas II of Russia and Napoleon III. The operation moved to Paris in 1831. The museum displays around 5,000 examples of Baccarat's work.
Don't miss Look for items made for the many World's Fairs attended by Baccarat.

The Cernuschi Museum

Canaletto's View of the Canal of Santa Chiara

MUSÉE CARNAVALET

See pages 114–115.

MUSÉE CERNUSCHI

✠ 66 off J4 • 7 avenue Vélasquez, 75008 ☎ 01 53 96 21 50 🕒 Tue–Sun 10–6 🖐 Free (except temporary exhibitions) 🚇 Monceau, Villiers 🚌 30, 94 www.paris.fr

Banker Henri Cernuschi went on an 18-month world tour in the 1870s and came back with an enchanting assortment of ancient art from China and Japan. On his death in 1896 he left the collection to the city, along with his neoclassical mansion next to Parc Monceau (▷ 145).

Since then, further items have been added, including the prized eighth-century painting *Chevaux et Palefrenier (Horses and Groom)*. Ancient statuettes, jade objects and pottery are all on display, as well as contemporary Chinese paintings. The approach to the museum is attractive, whether through the picturesque Parc de Monceau or the beautiful gilded gates that lead into avenue Vélasquez from the boulevard Malesherbes.

MUSÉE DE LA CHASSE ET DE LA NATURE

✠ 68 P6 • 60 rue des Archives, 75003 ☎ 01 53 01 92 40 🕒 Tue–Sun 11–6. 🖐 Adult €6, under 18 free 🚇 Rambuteau 🚌 29, 75 www.chassenature.org

Housed in two beautifully restored mansions – the Hôtel de Guénégard and the Hôtel de Mongelas – in the heart of the Marais district, the Museum of Hunting and Nature is packed with stuffed animals, hunting weapons, paintings and decorative arts. It may not be to everyone's taste, but it gives an insight into an activity pursued since time immemorial. The collection of hunting weapons spans prehistory to the 19th century. Some displays are dedicated to big-game hunting, with souvenirs of the museum's founder, François Sommer. There are also hunting-related paintings, including works by François Desportes (court artist at Versailles), Jean-Baptiste-Siméon Chardin, Carle Vernet and a joint canvas created by Rubens and Jan Brueghel (the Elder).

MUSÉE DU CINÉMA

✠ 68 off Q9 • 51 rue de Bercy, 75012 ☎ 01 71 19 33 33 🕒 Visit the website for opening times 🚇 Bercy 🚌 24, 62, 87 www.51ruedebercy.com

This new cinema museum is in the former American Cultural Center, a striking curved building created by architect Frank Gehry. The site includes the Henri Langlois Cinema Museum, four cinemas, the Cinémathèque Française, a film library, an exhibition room, a bookshop and a restaurant.

MUSÉE COGNACQ-JAY

✠ 68 P7 • Hôtel Donon, 8 rue Elzévir, 75003 ☎ 01 40 27 07 21 🕒 Tue–Sun 10–6. Garden open mid-May to mid-Sep (in good weather) 10–12.15, 4–5.35 🖐 Free 🚇 St-Paul 🚌 29, 69, 76, 96 www.paris.fr

The Musée Cognacq-Jay is a discreet, unassuming museum whose charm far exceeds its small size. Part of its appeal is the setting, in an elegant mansion furnished in 18th-century style. Narrow corridors and stairways lead to intimate chandeliered rooms, packed with paintings, porcelain, sculpture and objets d'art. The collection was put together in the early 20th century by Ernest Cognacq and his wife Louise Jay, founders of La Samaritaine department store. Their busts are displayed near the reception.

In 1990 the collection was transferred to the 16th-century Hôtel Donon, in the Marais district. Works by Rembrandt, Jean Honoré Fragonard and Giovanni Battista Tiepolo are among the pieces on display. There is also a garden (open in the summer only) and a small bookshop.

If you can read French, information cards placed at key points around the museum will fill you in on the collection. If not, just enjoy the refined atmosphere—a taste of the life led by wealthy Parisians in the 18th century.

Don't miss The Venetian scenes by Canaletto are impressive.

MUSÉE EDITH PIAF

✠ 327 R6 • 5 rue Crespin du Gast, 75011 ☎ 01 43 55 52 72 🕒 Visit by appointment only: Oct–end May, Jul, Aug Mon–Wed 1–6, Thu 9–12 🖐 Free (donations appreciated) 🚇 Ménilmontant 🚌 96

Edith Piaf, the Little Sparrow, was born Edith Giovanna Gassion in 1915. Brought up in the working-class east end of Paris, she began her career as a singer in local bars and cafés. Although she achieved international acclaim in the 1930s, appearing in many plays and films, she is best remembered for songs such as *La vie en rose* and *Non, je ne regrette rien*.

This small museum is crammed with Piaf memorabilia, including posters, letters, photographs, dresses and shoes. A visit is worthwhile if only to hear her original records playing in the background as you look around. Nearby is the Cimetière du Père-Lachaise (▷ 88) where you can visit her grave—thousands of people attended her funeral here in 1963.

THE SIGHTS

Musée Carnavalet

**Immerse yourself in the turbulent history of Paris.
See prison keys from the Revolution, Napoleon Bonaparte's picnic case
and lavish furniture from the reign of Louis XV.**

Ivy-clad arcades

The museum is housed in two elegant mansions (far right)

TIPS
● Staff shortages mean some rooms are closed at times.
● Explanation panels are in French only, so you may like to buy the guidebook before you begin your tour.

GALLERY GUIDE
HÔTEL CARNAVALET
Ground floor: Middle Ages to 16th century. Also Grand Salon de l'Hôtel d'Uzès.
1st floor: 17th and 18th centuries (to end of Louis XVI's reign).

HÔTEL LE PELETIER DE ST-FARGEAU
Ground floor: 19th century, from Napoleon I to 1848.
1st floor: 19th and 20th centuries (from Napoleon III).
2nd floor: the Revolution.

ORANGERIE
Paris's beginnings, from prehistory to Roman times.

SEEING THE MUSÉE CARNAVALET

Step into these adjoining mansions and you'll be setting off on an intriguing journey through Paris-past. Paintings, memorabilia and sumptuous re-creations of period rooms evoke the spirit of the city in previous eras, including the French Revolution and the reign of Napoleon I. The emphasis is on conveying an atmosphere rather than listing historical facts, so if you're expecting a detailed account of each era you may be disappointed. But if you want a taste of the high life during Louis XV's rule or a glimpse of the terrors of the Revolution, this is the place to come. The museum is housed in two mansions—the Hôtel Carnavalet and the adjoining Hôtel Le Peletier de St-Fargeau. Use the main entrance on rue de Sévigné, rather than the entrance on rue des Francs-Bourgeois. This takes you into the Hôtel Carnavalet. There is an information desk here where you can ask for a plan of the museum (in English). Be sure to do this—you'll have little hope of making sense of the layout of the site without it. To reach the Hôtel Le Peletier de St-Fargeau, walk across the *galerie* on the first floor.

HIGHLIGHTS

THE REVOLUTION
The museum has a poignant collection of memorabilia from the French Revolution on the second floor of the Hôtel Le Peletier de St-Fargeau. You can see a set of keys from the Bastille prison, comic strips by Le Sueur and furniture used by the royal family while they were in prison. Paintings include works by Hubert Robert, who was imprisoned during the Revolution, and a portrait of the Revolutionary leader Robespierre, who later fell victim to the guillotine himself. A collection of fans, plates, clocks and furniture show that Revolutionary slogans infiltrated even household goods.

HOW THE OTHER HALF LIVED
A world away from the horrors of the Revolution, the lavish tastes of Paris's richer residents through the years are brought to life by vivid re-creations of their rooms. On the ground floor of the Hôtel Carnavalet, the Grand Salon de l'Hôtel d'Uzès evokes the opulence of pre-Revolution days, with a profusion of gold, mirrors and chandeliers. Architect Claude-Nicolas Ledoux designed the original room in 1767. On the first floor, rooms 21 to 23 are dedicated to the mansion's most famous resident, Madame de Sévigné, and include two portraits of her. Rooms 27 to 48 depict Paris during the reign of Louis XV (1715–1774). Literary and theatrical life is illustrated in room 47, with brightly painted wooden statuettes from the Théâtre Séraphin. The reign of Louis XVI (1774–1793) is covered in rooms 49 to 64. Don't miss the charming Boudoir Circulaire in room 51 and the stunning wallpaper throughout the first floor, made at the Gobelins workshops (▷ 106) and based on 18th-century designs.

19TH- AND 20TH-CENTURY DISPLAYS

Highlights from the Napoleonic era include the Emperor's 110-piece picnic case and his death mask (on the ground floor of the Hôtel Le Peletier de St-Fargeau). Reconstructions on the first floor of the Hôtel Le Peletier de St-Fargeau include the elegant art nouveau interior of the famous jewellers, Fouquet (1900), and Madame Wendel's 1920s Queen-of-Sheba ballroom. Also worth seeing is the re-creation of Marcel Proust's room, soundproofed with cork to protect the reclusive writer from unwanted noise.

BACKGROUND

The building is a piece of history in itself—an ornate mansion built in the 1540s for the president of the Paris *parlement*, Jacques des Ligneris. Architect François Mansart put his stamp on the site in 1660, when he added a new wing. Shortly after, the celebrated lady of letters, Madame de Sévigné, moved in.
The idea for a museum of Parisian history originally came from Baron Haussmann, the man responsible for reshaping the city in the 19th century (▷ 36). The Hôtel Carnavalet was chosen and the museum opened in 1880. More than a century later, in 1989, the collections were able to expand into the adjoining Hôtel Le Peletier de St-Fargeau.

BASICS
✚ 68 P7 • 23 rue de Sévigné, 75003 (also an entrance on rue des Francs-Bourgeois)
☎ 01 44 59 58 58
🕐 Tue–Sun 10–6
💷 Free (except temporary exhibitions)
Ⓜ St-Paul
🚌 29, 69, 76, 96
🔊 Guided tours in French and occasionally in English at various times; information: 01 44 59 58 31
💶 €9
📖 Bookshop with a comprehensive selection of history-related titles
🚻

www.paris.fr/musees/musee_carnavalet
In French but photos of the collections and a museum plan are easily accessible

The bedroom at the Musée Gustave Moreau

Come face to face with fashion designer Jean-Paul Gaultier and the opera singer Maria Callas at the Musée Grévin

MUSÉE FRAGONARD

🗺 67 L5 • Musée du Parfum: 9 rue Scribe, 75009. Théâtre-Musée des Capucines: 39 boulevard des Capucines, 75002 ☎ Musée du Parfum: 01 47 42 04 56. Théâtre-Musée des Capucines: 01 42 60 37 14 🕐 Mon–Sat 9–6 (Musée du Parfum also open mid-Mar to mid-Oct Sun 9.30–4) 🎟 Free 🚇 Opéra 🚌 21, 27, 42, 68
www.fragonard.com

This museum tells the story of perfume-making over 3,000 years, from Ancient Egyptian times to the present day. It is split into two parts, in two buildings near the Opéra Palais Garnier. The Musée du Parfum is in a 19th-century town house in rue Scribe, and the Théâtre-Musée des Capucines is in an attractive theatre dating from 1895. Both are home to fascinating collections of perfumery paraphernalia, from bottles and burners to paintings and photographs. There are displays explaining how perfume is made, including an overview of the raw materials. At the Musée des Capucines a miniature factory with 19th-century copper-distilling equipment demonstrates extraction methods.
    Fragonard has been creating perfumes since 1926 and uses a mixture of traditional and modern techniques. Products are on sale at factory prices in the gift shops.

MUSÉE GALLIÉRA– MUSÉE DE LA MODE DE LA VILLE DE PARIS

🗺 66 G6 • Palais Galliéra, 10 avenue Pierre ler de Serbie, 75016 ☎ 01 56 52 86 00 🕐 Tue–Sun 10–6 (during exhibitions only). 🎟 Ticket prices vary, under 14 free 🚇 Iéna 🚌 32, 63, 72, 92 🚉 RER line C, Pont de l'Alma 🎧 Audioguide is included in entry ticket
www.paris.fr

Urban fashion from the 18th century to the present day is the theme of the temporary exhibitions held here, which draw from a collection of 80,000 objects. Dresses by Jean-Paul Gaultier, outfits worn by Marlene Dietrich and ball gowns from the 19th century are among the items that have appeared here.

MUSÉE GRÉVIN

🗺 69 M5 • 10 boulevard Montmartre, 75009 ☎ 01 47 70 85 05 🕐 Daily 10-7 (last entry 1 hour before closing) 🎟 Adult €18, child (6–14) €10.50, under 6 free 🚇 Grands Boulevards 🚌 20, 39, 48, 74, 85 ❓ You can buy tickets in advance at FNAC, Carrefour, Auchan, Virgin Megastore and the tourist office
www.grevin.com

If you are hoping to spot a celebrity or two while in Paris, why not cheat a little and visit this waxwork museum? Here you can mingle with Sean Connery, Julia Roberts and Bruce Willis at a cocktail party, join George W. Bush, Queen Elizabeth II and Vladimir Putin in the Élysée Palace and watch Auguste Rodin and Salvador Dalí at work in their studios. You'll find the ubiquitous Elvis Presley and Marilyn Monroe among the 300 waxwork models, and even Lara Croft.
    When you've had enough of 21st-century glitz, step back in time to Paris's turbulent past. The French Revolution is re-created with plenty of blood and gore, and you can also witness the assassination of Henri IV and meet Napoleon and Louis XIV.
    The Musée Grévin (also known simply as Grévin) is the Parisian answer to Madame Tussaud's and was launched in 1882 by cartoonist and sculptor Alfred Grévin and journalist Arthur Meyer. Since 2001, a group of journalists known as

the Académie Grévin has met twice a year to decide which famous faces should be immortalized in wax. Recent additions include the French philosopher Bernard-Henri Lévy, US senator Hillary Clinton and singer Céline Dion.

MUSÉE GUSTAVE MOREAU

🗺 69 L4 • 14 rue de la Rochefoucauld, 75009 ☎ 01 48 74 38 50 🕐 Wed–Mon 10–12.45, 2–5.15 🎟 Adult €5, under 18 free, free to all on 1st Sun of month 🚇 Trinité 📖 Bookshop
www.musee-moreau.fr

This studio-museum, on the edge of Pigalle, offers an intriguing view of how a late-19th-century artist lived. On the lower floors you'll find the studios of the Symbolist painter Gustave Moreau (1826–1898), teacher to Henri Matisse. Upstairs is a reconstruction of his private apartment, where you can see the kind of paintings, objects and furniture he chose to surround himself with. Paintings gracing his walls include works by Edgar Degas and Théodore Chassériau.
    It was Moreau himself who wanted his house to be preserved for posterity as a museum. His wish has been accomplished and the museum now displays around 800 of his own evocative paintings and drawings, many of them with biblical or mythological themes.

MUSÉE DE L'HISTOIRE DE FRANCE (HÔTEL DE SOUBISE)

🗺 68 P7 • Hôtel de Soubise, 60 rue des Francs-Bourgeois, Hôtel de Rohan, 87 rue Vieille du Temple, 75003 ☎ 01 40 27 60 96 🕐 Mon and Wed–Fri 10–12.30, 2–5.30, Sat–Sun 2–5.30 🎟 Adult €5, under 18 free 🚇 Rambuteau, Hôtel de Ville 🚌 29, 75, 96 📖 Giftshop/bookshop

| Musée Jacquemart André, in a splendid 19th-century mansion | The 18th-century Hôtel de Soubise, fit for a princess |

The star attraction of the Museum of French History is its sumptuous setting. The Hôtel de Soubise, in the Marais district (▷ 107), was built by Delamair in the early 18th century for the Princesse de Soubise at the same time as the Hôtel de Rohan on rue Vieille du Temple, intended for her son, the future Cardinal de Rohan.

Delamair incorporated into his design the 14th-century double-towered entrance on the rue des Archives, a remnant of a medieval manor originally on the site.

The Prince's Apartment (*Appartement du Prince*), on the ground floor, is lavishly decorated by painters including Carle Van Loo and François Boucher. The artistry continues upstairs in the Princess's Apartment (*Appartement de la Princesse*).

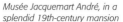

The history museum, housed in both mansions, is document-based and so probably not of great interest to non-French speakers. It draws on the National Archives for its exhibitions, a rich store that includes letters written by Charlemagne and Joan of Arc, the wills of Louis XIV and Napoleon I, and the last correspondence of Marie-Antoinette before her execution.

MUSÉE JACQUEMART ANDRÉ

✚ 66 J4 • 158 boulevard Haussmann, 75008 ☎ 01 45 62 11 59 🕐 Tue–Sun 10–6, Mon 10–9.30 💶 Adult €9.50, child €7, under 7 free 🍴 Daily 10–6 Ⓜ St-Philippe-du-Roule, Miromesnil 🚌 22, 28, 43, 52, 80, 83, 84, 93 🚉 RER line A, Charles-de-Gaulle-Étoile www.musee-jacquemart-andre.com

Banker Edouard André and his painter wife Nélie Jacquemart were keen collectors of European art and amassed an impressive private collection of European masterpieces. In 1875 they built a stately mansion to display their acquisitions, complete with a ballroom, picture gallery and ornate swirling staircase. Nélie outlived her husband, but when she died she respected his wish to donate the mansion and its contents to the Institut de France. It opened as a museum in 1913.

More than 90 years on you can wander through the elegant picture gallery, music room, grand salon and other parts of the mansion where paintings, sculptures and tapestries are displayed. The collection includes paintings and sculptures by Italian artists (including

Canaletto, Botticelli and Della Robbia), Flemish and Dutch masters (Van Dyck, Rembrandt and Hals) and French artists (Boucher, David and Fragonard). As well as the permanent collection, the museum hosts popular temporary exhibitions.

An audioguide, in a choice of six languages, is included in the entry price.

Don't miss The former dining room (now the café) has a ceiling painted by Giovanni Battista Tiepolo. The walls are decorated with 17th-century tapestries from Brussels.

MUSÉE DU LOUVRE

See pages 118–123.

MUSÉE MARMOTTAN MONET

See pages 124–125.

MUSÉE DE LA MONNAIE

✚ 67 M7 • Hôtel de la Monnaie, 11 quai de Conti, 75006 ☎ 01 40 46 55 35 🕐 Tue–Fri 11–5.30, Sat–Sun 12–5.30 💶 Adult €8, under 16 free, free to all on 1st Sun of month Ⓜ Pont Neuf, Odéon 🚌 27, 58, 70 🎧 Audioguide included in entry price. Guided tour of the workshops (advance booking): Wed and Fri 2.15pm, €3 (free for under 16) 🏪 The shop sells coin collections, books, historical medals, posters. The Paris Mint shop, at 2 rue Guénégaud (Mon–Sat 10–6), sells a variety of items produced in its workshops www.monnaiedeparis.fr

Elegant Hôtel de la Monnaie, on the Left Bank alongside the Seine, housed the workshops of the Paris Mint from the 18th century until 1973. Today the workshops produce commemorative coins and medals. The *hôtel* is also home to a coin and medal museum, dating back to the 19th century. Here you can learn about the development of minting techniques.

Musée du Louvre

**One of the world's largest museums.
Legendary works of art include the *Mona Lisa, Venus de Milo* and
a 4,000-year-old Egyptian sphinx.**

The museum entrance

Illustrated papyrus from the
Egyptian collection

A ticket allows same-day re-entry
to the museum

SEEING THE MUSÉE DU LOUVRE

The Louvre is one of the most famous art galleries in the world
and it covers a vast period, from around 7,000BC to 1848. There
is no way you'll be able to see all 35,000 works on display in one
visit, so you need to be selective. If you don't know where to
begin, consider taking one of the *Visite-Découverte* guided tours.
The free museum plan, available from the information desk, also
highlights the key works.

The main entrance is through I. M. Pei's striking glass pyramid
in the middle of the large Napoleon Courtyard. From here
escalators take you down to the gleaming marble underground
foyer, with its cloakroom, information desk and entrances to the
museum's three wings: Richelieu, Sully and Denon. If you already
have a ticket or a museum pass, you can enter through the
passage Richelieu, off the rue de Rivoli, where the wait is usually
shorter. Other access points are through the Carrousel du Louvre
shopping area and the Porte des Lions (closed on Fridays). When
it's time for a break, the museum has a choice of cafés and
restaurants. Alternatively, you can leave the site and find a café
nearby, as your ticket allows re-entry on the same day.

RATINGS	
Cultural interest	●●●●
Historic interest	●●●●
Shopping (art books)	●●●●

HIGHLIGHTS

MONA LISA

When Leonardo da Vinci set up his easel in Florence in the early
16th century to paint the *Mona Lisa*, little did he know he was
creating what was to become one of the world's most famous works
of art. The diminutive painting, only 77cm (30in) tall and 53cm
(20in) wide, is on the first floor of the Denon wing, surrounded by
bullet-proof glass and a constant crowd of admirers. The identity of
the woman is not known for certain, although she is believed to be
the wife of Francesco del Giocondo, hence the portrait's other name,
La Gioconda. Da Vinci painted the work between 1503 and 1506.
François I obtained the painting soon after its completion. It has since
spent time in Versailles and in the former Tuileries Palace and has
even hung in Napoleon's bedroom. In 1911 an Italian stole the
portrait, wanting to return it to its native Florence. It was recovered
two years later, after a police hunt that won it worldwide fame.

I. M. Pei's pyramid theme
continues inside (left)

BASICS

67 M7 • 99 rue de Rivoli, 75001

☎ 01 40 20 50 50. Information in
French and English: 01 40 20 53 17.
Auditorium: 01 40 20 55 55

🕐 Thu, Sat–Mon 9–6, Wed
9am–9.45pm, Fri 9am–10pm (last entry
45 min before closing). Some rooms
closed in rotation

💳 Adult €9 (€6 after 6pm on Wed and
Fri), under 18 free. Temporary
exhibitions in the Hall Napoléon €9
Tickets are valid all day, so re-entry is
allowed. Tickets combining entrance
and rail travel are available at railway
stations. The museum is free on the 1st
Sun of each month and 14 July (except
for exhibitions in the Hall Napoléon)

🚇 Palais Royal/Musée du Louvre

🚌 21, 24, 27, 39, 48, 68, 69, 72, 76,
81, 95

🚉 Châtelet-Les-Halles

🎧 Various guided tours are available in
English and French, including the *Visite-
Découverte* (Discovery Visit) in English
at 11, 2 and 3.45 (11.30 only on Sun;
not 1st Sun of month) and in French at
11.30. Audioguides are available in
French, English, German, Spanish,
Italian and Japanese. Pick them up from
the entrances to the three wings of the
museum (€5). Special tours are
available for those with reduced
mobility. There is also a sculpture
gallery for those with visual impairments. Ask at the information desk
for a leaflet about disability access

📚 Range of guidebooks. Free leaflet
available at information desk

🍴 Cafés and restaurants

📖 Large bookshop

♿

www.louvre.fr
In French, English, Spanish and Japanese;
see the works and take a virtual tour

The Puget Courtyard (right)

*You can see part of the Louvre's
medieval base on the lower level*

VENUS DE MILO AND *THE WINGED VICTORY OF SAMOTHRACE*

The eternally serene *Venus de Milo* (ground floor, Sully) is the most
famous of the Louvre's Greek antiquities. She was discovered on the
island of Melos in 1820. As Aphrodite, the goddess of love, she
portrays the Greek image of perfect beauty. The marble statue was
created around 100BC, during Greece's Hellenistic period, although
its simple style harks back to Classical Greek sculpture.

Among the other Greek antiquities, don't miss the *Winged Victory
of Samothrace* (first-floor landing, Denon), soaring 3m (9.8ft) high.
The statue was sculpted in 190BC to celebrate a maritime victory and
shows the goddess Victory, as if on the prow of a boat. The fluid style
of the carving gives the impression the sea wind is blowing through
her dress and wings. The sculpture had to be painstakingly
reassembled from 300 pieces found on the island of Samothrace
in 1863.

ETRUSCAN AND ROMAN ART

While Ancient Greek civilization was thriving, the Etruscans were
carving out their own civilization in northern Italy. Highlights of their art
include a charming terracotta sarcophagus (c530BC) showing a
husband and wife reclining on wineskins (ground floor, Denon). Both
wear the contented smiles that are a common feature of Etruscan
sculpture. The Louvre's collection of Roman art (ground floor, Denon)
includes mosaics, sculpture, plates, vases and sarcophagi.

THE EGYPTIAN COLLECTION

You get a captivating glimpse of life at the time of the pharaohs, as
much as 5,000 years ago, in the Egyptian rooms. The collection is the
largest of its kind outside Egypt, containing 55,000 items, around
5,000 of which are on show. There are commanding sphinxes and
statues of the all-powerful pharaohs, but just as fascinating are the
smaller, everyday items, including mirrors, combs, necklaces and
intricately carved spoons for applying cosmetics. Don't miss the pink
granite Grand Sphinx, part pharaoh, part lion, that once protected the
corridors of a holy shrine (ground floor, Sully). Its exact age is
unknown, but stylistic details suggest it could be more than 4,600
years old.

The collections are presented thematically on the ground floor of the
Sully wing, where topics include fishing, funerals and writing. On the first
floor the displays are chronological, starting with prehistory, tracing the
rule of the pharaohs and ending just before the arrival of the Romans in
333BC. To see how Egyptian culture developed under Roman rule you
can continue your tour on the lower floor of the Denon wing.

FRENCH HISTORICAL/ALLEGORICAL PAINTINGS

These vast paintings, on the first floor of the Denon wing, draw you
into the action not simply through their immense size but also in the
vivid detail. Some of the subjects would have seemed uncomfortably
contemporary when the paintings were first unveiled. Théodore
Géricault's *The Raft of the Medusa* (1819) portrays a controversial
French shipwreck that took place near Senegal three years earlier.
Only 15 of the 150-strong crew survived, clinging to
a hastily constructed raft, and there were rumours of
cannibalism and treachery. Early viewers of the
paintings were shocked by the realism of the
corpses.

Dead bodies also appear in Eugène Delacroix's
Liberty Leading the People (1830), although the
presence of the allegorical figure Liberty brings a
sense of triumph to the destruction and chaos. The
painting depicts the uprising of 1830.

Jacques-Louis David's neoclassical painting
The Coronation of Napoleon I seems rather cold
when set against the passion of Delacroix and
Géricault's works. Almost 10m (33ft) wide, it was
commissioned by the Emperor himself, and
completed in 1807.

TIPS

● Don't miss the Galerie d'Apollon (Denon, 1st floor) reopened at the end of 2004. Commissioned by Louis XIV, it inspired the Hall of Mirrors at Versailles and was embellished for 200 years by artists from Le Brun to Delacroix. It now displays the Crown Jewels.

● The entrance fee is reduced to €6 after 6pm on Wednesday and Friday.

● To avoid long waits for tickets, use a *Paris Museum Pass* (▷ 307) or prebook your ticket by phone, internet, FNAC (01 41 57 32 28; small commission charged) or at certain department stores. This allows you to use the passage Richelieu entrance.

● You can view many of the Louvre's paintings and other exhibits on the website, allowing you to decide before your visit where to focus your attention.

● Staff shortages mean that not all the rooms are open every day. If there are particular things you want to see, check the website for the schedule of closures.

● The entrance ticket is valid on the same day for the collections and temporary exhibitions of the Musée National Eugène Delacroix (▷ 126).

OTHER HIGHLIGHTS

● *The Lacemaker* by Jan Vermeer (1670–71; Richelieu, 2nd floor)
● *Dying Slave* by Michelangelo (1513–15; Denon, ground floor)
● *The Marly Horses* by Coustou (1743–45; Richelieu, Cour Marly)
● Cour Khorsabad (Richelieu, ground floor)
● *The Wedding Feast at Cana* by Veronese (1562–63; Denon, first floor)
● Medieval fortifications (lower ground floor)

Old meets new in the architecture of the Napoleon Courtyard (above right)

In this cross section of the Louvre, Sully wing is behind you

BACKGROUND

The building dates back to the 14th century, when Charles V transformed Philippe-Auguste's 12th-century fortress into a medieval castle. Nearly two centuries later, the wily Renaissance king François I instigated considerable rebuilding, and also

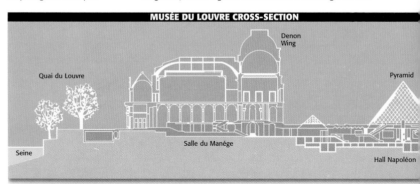

MUSÉE DU LOUVRE CROSS-SECTION

Denon Wing

Quai du Louvre

Pyramid

Salle du Manège

Seine

Hall Napoléon

GALLERY GUIDE

The Louvre operates a useful system of colour-coding on its maps. The departments are:

Egyptian Antiquities (green): The main collection is on the ground and first floor of Sully. Roman and Coptic Egypt are on the lower floor of Denon.

Greek, Etruscan and Roman Antiquities (blue): First and ground floor of Sully, ground floor of Denon. Pre-Classical Greece is on Denon's lower floor.

Oriental Antiquities (yellow) and Arts of Islam (dark green): Arts of Islam are on the lower ground floor of Richelieu. The Cour Khorsabad is on the ground floor of Richelieu, and Antique Iran and Levant are on the ground floor of Sully.

Paintings (red): Paintings from France, Flanders, Holland and Germany are on the second floor of Richelieu and Sully; large French paintings are on the first floor of Denon. Italian and Spanish paintings are on the first floor of Denon; English on the first floor of Sully.

Drawings and Prints (pink): French drawings are on the second floor of Sully; German, Flemish and Dutch on the second floor of Richelieu; Italian on the first floor of Denon.

Objets d'Art (mauve): First floor of Richelieu, Denon and Sully.

Sculptures (beige): French sculptures are on the ground and lower ground floors of Richelieu. Italian sculptures are on the ground and lower ground floors of Denon.

History of the Louvre (brown): Remains of the medieval fortress are on Sully's lower ground floor.

Arts of Africa, Asia, Oceania and the Americas (white): Denon ground floor (on loan from the Musée du Quai Branly, ▷ 126).

launched the Louvre's art collection, bringing the *Mona Lisa* and its creator, Leonardo da Vinci, to France. Various kings carried out improvements to the building, until Louis XIV moved the court to Versailles in the 17th century. During the Revolution, an art museum opened to the public in the Grand Galerie.

Napoleon celebrated his marriage to Marie-Louise in the Louvre in 1810, and lived in the nearby Tuileries Palace, which has since burned down. He immediately set about creating a central courtyard dominated by the Arc du Carrousel, building a new wing and adding floors. His numerous victories overseas, and the subsequent looting, added significantly to the Louvre's stock. The latest improvements, in the 1980s and 1990s, saw the creation of I. M. Pei's stunning glass pyramid, as well as extensive renovations to the museum's galleries.

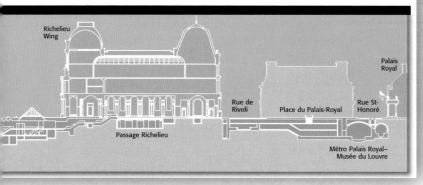

Richelieu Wing

Palais Royal

Rue de Rivoli

Place du Palais-Royal

Rue St-Honoré

Passage Richelieu

Métro Palais Royal–Musée du Louvre

THE SIGHTS

Musée Marmottan Monet

The world's largest collection of paintings by Claude Monet, in an
intimate town house.
You can also see medieval manuscripts, Napoleonic furniture and paintings
by Monet's contemporaries.

Monet's Impression—soleil levant,
*which gave Impressionism its
name*

RATINGS	
Cultural interest	●●●●
Historic interest	●●●

*This 'illuminated' letter R depicts
St. Catherine of Alexandria*

SEEING THE MUSÉE MARMOTTAN MONET

It's a bit of a trek out to this museum in the leafy 16th
arrondissement but you'll be rewarded with a feast of famous
paintings by Monet and his contemporaries. The intimate setting
in a discreetly elegant 19th-century town house makes a pleasant
change from Paris's larger, more impersonal museums. And if the
Impressionist works fail to satisfy your appetite, there are also
paintings and furniture from the Napoleonic period, as well as
more than 300 illustrated pages from medieval and Renaissance
manuscripts. It's a curious but compelling combination.

The walk to the museum from La Muette Métro station is well
signed and takes you through the pleasant Jardins du Ranelagh.
There is no café at the museum, so you may wish to bring your
own refreshments to have in the park on the way back.

HIGHLIGHTS

MONET

Without a doubt, the main draw for visitors is the Monet collection,
built up over the last 50 years through donations from the artist's son,
Michel, and various other collectors. Many of the 60 paintings on
display are in the purpose-built basement gallery—remarkably light
and airy considering its underground location. Clouds of irises, wisteria
and water lilies fill many of the frames, inspired by the artist's 43
years at Giverny. Various views of the Thames are also on display,
including *Londres: Le Parlement, Reflets sur la Tamise* (1899–1901).
Monet worked on almost 100 paintings of the river during a visit to
London at the turn of the 20th century. The gallery has a selection of
works from the *Rouen Cathedral* series, created during two visits to
Rouen in 1892 and 1893. Don't miss the influential *Impression—
soleil levant* (c1873), which gave the Impressionist movement its
name. The masterpiece depicts the port at Le Havre and focuses on
one of Monet's preferred themes—the play of light on water. It is the
only painting behind glass, after it was stolen in 1985 and recovered
five years later in Corsica.

OTHER IMPRESSIONISTS

The Impressionist collection, on the upper floor, includes works by Edgar Degas, Gustave Caillebotte, Camille Pissarro, Berthe Morisot and Pierre-Auguste Renoir. Look for Renoir's beguiling *Claude Monet lisant* (Claude Monet reading; 1872). Monet was particularly fond of this portrait, painted by his friend, and kept it until his death.

THE EMPIRE COLLECTION

Highlights from the Empire period include the Geographical Clock (1813) on the ground floor, originally made for Napoleon and later altered by Louis XVIII.

THE ILLUMINATIONS

The museum has around 300 medieval and Renaissance illustrated pages, collectively known as the Illuminations, on the ground floor. These were amassed by art dealer Georges Wildenstein and were donated to the museum by his son in 1980. Many of the pages come from French and Italian religious manuscripts and are vividly illustrated with saints and biblical characters. Others are from Books of Hours, compilations of prayers and religious sayings. Some show scenes from feudal life in the 15th century.

BACKGROUND

The Marmottan Museum did not start life as a showcase for Monet's work. It takes its name from art historian Paul Marmottan, who left his house and collection of Empire paintings and furniture to the nation in 1932. The collection, built up by both Paul and his father Jules, also includes paintings from the Flemish, Italian and German primitives. It wasn't until later that various donors added the Impressionist works that have now become the museum's main attraction.

Monet was born in Paris in 1840 and died in Giverny 86 years later. During his life he drew inspiration from his travels around France, as well as those to London, Norway, Holland and Italy. But it was in the gardens of Giverny, his home from 1883 until his death, that he produced some of his most famous works. You can see family portraits near the steps to the basement gallery.

BASICS

✚ 321 off E7 • 2 rue Louis-Boilly, 75016
☎ 01 44 96 50 33
🕐 Tue–Sun 10–5.30 (last entry 5). Closed Mon, 1 Jan, 1 May, 25 Dec
💷 Adult €8, child €4.50, under 8 free
🚇 La Muette (then a 10-min walk; follow signs from the station)
🚌 22, 32, 52
🚆 RER line C, Boulainvilliers
📖 €7.50
🏬 Giftshop/bookshop
🚻

www.marmottan.com
In French and English; a comprehensive website showing the major works and giving news and practical information about the museum

TIPS

• Look out for the amusing *Le Havre* caricatures (c1858), on the first floor, markedly different in style to Monet's later, more famous paintings.
• The museum lets you see some of Monet's most famous works in a refreshingly tranquil setting. But if you are in Paris for only a few days you may find it easier to see the Impressionist collection in the more central Musée d'Orsay (▷ 130–134).
• If you have time, you may like to combine a trip to the Musée Marmottan Monet with a visit to the Musée National des Arts Asiatiques-Guimet (▷ 126) or the Musée Galliéra (▷ 116), a few stops back on Métro line 9, at Iéna.

GALLERY GUIDE

LOWER FLOOR
Monet collection.

GROUND FLOOR
The Illuminations, the Primitives, the Empire Collection and the bookshop.

UPPER FLOOR
Other Impressionist works and temporary exhibitions.

The museum has a collection of elegant furniture

THE SIGHTS

Two Cranes on the Edge of a Pond, *from the Musée Guimet*

Paintings in the Musée National Eugène Delacroix, in the former home of the artist

THE SIGHTS

MUSÉE DE MONTMARTRE

✚ 69 M2 • 12 rue Cortot, 75018
☎ 01 49 25 89 37 🕐 Wed–Sun 11–6
💳 Adult €7, child €5.50, under 10
free 🚇 Lamarck 🚌 Montmartrobus;
80

Montmartre's history is arguably the most enchanting of all Paris's districts, with its walking beheaded saint, prosperous windmills and infamous nightlife. You can find out more at the unassuming Musée de Montmartre, in a delightful 17th-century mansion that once belonged to Rose de Rosimond, a member of Molière's stage troupe. The house, behind Montmartre's one remaining vineyard, later welcomed the painter Pierre-Auguste Renoir.

MUSÉE NATIONAL DES ARTS ASIATIQUES-GUIMET

✚ 66 G6 • 6 place d'Iéna, 75016
☎ 01 56 52 53 00 🕐 Wed–Mon 10–6
💳 Museum only: adult €6.50.
Museum and temporary exhibitions: adult €8.50, under 18 free. Temporary exhibitions only: adult €7, under 18 free, free to all on 1st Sun of month
🚇 Iéna, Boissière 🚌 22, 30, 32, 63, 82
🎧 Free audioguides (lasting around 90 min) are available in several languages. For information on guided tours, see the schedule at the entrance
www.museeguimet.fr

This museum, which opened in 1889, has a remarkable display of Oriental antiquities, built up by industrialist Émile Guimet (1836–1918). Around 45,000 items are on display, including sculptures, carvings, paintings and other objects from Korea, China, Japan, Tibet, Afghanistan, Thailand, Pakistan and India.

The stunning collection of Khmer art (6th to 19th centuries) includes serene stone buddhas and Hindu gods. The museum also has richly painted Tibetan and Nepalese *tankas* (portable paintings). The Indian department includes bronze deities from southern India, and Moghul and Rajput miniatures. The rich Chinese department has a vast ceramics collection.

Japanese religious art is represented in the museum annexe, the Buddhist Pantheon at 19 avenue d'Iéna (open Wed–Mon 9.45–5.45).

MUSÉE NATIONAL EUGÈNE DELACROIX

✚ 67 L7 • 6 rue de Furstemberg, 75006 ☎ 01 44 41 86 50
🕐 Wed–Mon 9.30–5 (last entry 4.30)
💳 Adult €5, under 18 free, free to all 1st Sun of month 🚇 St-Germain-des-Prés, Mabillon 🚌 39, 63, 95
www.musee-delacroix.fr

Romantic painter Eugène Delacroix (1798–1863) spent the last six years of his life in this apartment. His living quarters and studio are now a small museum. On display are his paintings, drawings, pastels, sketches, furniture and personal documents. You can see many of his major works in the Louvre (▷ 118–123) and the Musée d'Orsay (▷ 130–134).

MUSÉE NATIONAL DU MOYEN ÂGE–THERMES DE CLUNY

See pages 128–129.

MUSÉE NISSIM DE CAMONDO

✚ 66 off H4 • 63 rue de Monceau, 75008 ☎ 01 53 89 06 50
🕐 Wed–Sun 10–5.30 💳 Adult €8, under 18 free 🚇 Villiers, Monceau
🚌 30, 84, 94
www.ucad.fr

The elegance of the furniture and ornaments on display in this stylish town house hides a tragic family story. Moïse de Camondo left his house and collection to the State on his death in 1935, stipulating that it should be named in memory of his son, Nissim, who was killed in action during World War I. Fewer than 10 years after Moïse's death, his daughter and her family were killed at Auschwitz.

The mansion is laid out as an 18th-century home and contains Moïse's tasteful collection of decorative arts, mainly from the second half of the 18th century. Vases once owned by Marie-Antoinette are among the items on display. You can also see a silver dinner service made for Empress Catherine II of Russia.

Despite its 18th-century furnishings, the mansion was built in the early 20th century to designs inspired by Versailles's Petit Trianon.

MUSÉE D'ORSAY

See pages 130–134.

MUSÉE PICASSO

See page 135.

MUSÉE DU QUAI BRANLY

✚ 66 G7 • 29–37 quai Branly, 75007 (east of the junction with avenue de la Bourdonnais) ☎ 01 56 61 70 00
🕐 Tue–Wed, Sun 11–7, Thu–Sat 11–9
💳 Adult €8.50, under 18 free 🚇 Pont de l'Alma 🚌 42, 63, 72, 80, 92
🚊 Champ de Mars-Tour Eiffel
www.quaibranly.fr

The cultural heritage of Africa, Asia, Oceania and the Americas is the focus of this new museum, near the Eiffel Tower. Themes range from African musical instruments to the relationship between man and the natural world.

The permanent collection is supplemented by a strong series of temporary exhibitions plus lecture, dance, theatre and musical performances.

Tree-lined avenue in the Jardin des Plantes (above).
A greenhouse shimmers in the sunlight (right)

MUSÉUM NATIONAL D'HISTOIRE NATURELLE AND JARDIN DES PLANTES

These beautifully laid out gardens contain several natural history museums, tropical greenhouses and one of the oldest zoos in the world.

The Jardin des Plantes is one of the city's prettiest parks and an ideal place for a stroll. Its wide tree-lined avenue, flanked by museums on one side and gardens on the other, is especially picturesque in autumn (fall) when the leaves are changing hue. Paths lead off to the gardens with flowers, statues and a great view of the striking Grande Galerie de l'Évolution (see below). The Jardin des Plantes was founded in 1626 by two of Louis XIII's physicians as the royal garden of medicinal plants. It opened to the public in 1640 and was extended by the naturalist Buffon in the 18th century.

MUSÉUM NATIONAL D'HISTOIRE NATURELLE

The Natural History Museum is made up of several separate galleries within the Jardin des Plantes. The highlight is the Grande Galerie de l'Évolution, in a mammoth glass-roofed structure built in 1889 and renovated in the early 1990s. Contemporary displays cover themes ranging from evolution and the diversity of the living world to endangered and extinct species. The Galerie de Paléontologie, which opened in 1898, has fossils dating back millions of years. The Galerie d'Anatomie Comparée focuses on the classification of more than 1,000 vertebrates, while the Galerie de Minéralogie and Géologie displays gems, precious minerals and giant crystals.

PLANTS AND ANIMALS

Tropical greenhouses (closed until 2008), including a winter garden and a Mexican greenhouse, shelter thousands of plant species. The Alpine garden is home to more than 2,000 species from mountainous regions including the Alps, Corsica and the Himalayas. The Ménagerie opened in 1794 and houses around 1,100 mammals, birds and reptiles, in addition to a Microzoo for insects and spiders.

RATINGS	
Good for kids	●●●●●
Historic interest	●●●
Photo stops	●●●

BASICS

✚ 68 P9 ☎ 01 40 79 56 01; 01 40 79 30 00 (recorded information)
🚇 Gare d'Austerlitz , Jussieu, Place Monge 🚌 24, 57, 61, 63, 67, 89, 91
🎁 Gift and bookshops 🔲 👬
www.mnhn.fr (mainly in French)

Jardin des Plantes
57 rue Cuvier, 75005 🕐 Daily dawn–dusk 🎟 Free
Grande Galerie de l'Évolution
36 rue Geoffroy St-Hilaire, 75005
🕐 Wed–Mon 10–6. Closed 1 May
🎟 Adult €8, child (4–13) €6, under 4 free
Galeries de Paléontologie et d'Anatomie Comparée
57 rue Cuvier, 75005 🕐 Wed–Mon 10–5. Closed 1 May 🎟 Adult €6, child (4–13) €4, under 4 free
Galerie de Minéralogie & Géologie
36 rue Geoffroy St-Hilaire, 75005
🕐 Wed–Mon 10–5. Closed 1 May
🎟 Adult €6, child €4, under 4 free
Les Serres (tropicales)
57 rue Cuvier, 75005
🕐 The tropical greenhouses are closed until 2008
Ménagerie (Zoo)
57 rue Cuvier, 75005
🕐 Daily 9–6
🎟 Adult €7, child €5, under 4 free

Musée National du Moyen Âge—Thermes de Cluny

A collection of medieval tapestries, altarpieces and statues that takes you back to the days of courtly love and feudal living.

Sight, *from the 15th-century* Lady and the Unicorn *series*

Take a close-up look at some vivid stained glass

Carvings on the exterior of the 15th-century mansion

RATINGS	
Cultural interest	● ● ● ●
Historic interest	● ● ● ●
Photo stops (exterior)	● ● ●

BASICS
✚ 67 M8 • 6 place Paul-Painlevé, rue du Sommerard, 75005
☎ 01 53 73 78 16; 01 53 73 78 00
🕐 Wed–Mon 9.15–5.45
💶 Adult €7.50 (Sun €5.50), under 18 free, free to all on 1st Sun of month
Ⓜ Cluny-La Sorbonne
🚌 21, 27, 38, 63, 85, 86, 87, 96
🚇 RER line B, C, St-Michel
🎧 Guided tours available in English. Audioguide €1
📷 €19.50
🏬 Bookshop/giftshop
♿

www.musee-moyenage.fr
Main website in French only; boutique in French and English. See photos, read background information, browse the boutique, or find out about concerts, guided tours and family activities

SEEING THE MUSÉE NATIONAL DU MOYEN ÂGE–THERMES DE CLUNY

The Cluny Museum offers an intriguing glimpse into medieval life. Animated tapestries, dazzling necklaces, headless statues and religious paraphernalia are among the 23,000 exhibits, displayed in an intimate Gothic mansion in the Latin Quarter. What makes the collection so compelling is that you get a close-up view of objects that you usually admire only from a distance. Vivid stained-glass windows you would normally crane your neck to see are suddenly down at eye level, while altarpieces created to sit imposingly at the far end of a church are right in front of you. The detail is exceptional.

Entrance to the museum is through a splendid Gothic courtyard, whose gargoyles and turrets put you in the mood for the exhibits inside. Pick up a free plan at the ticket desk, then start your tour by walking through the bookshop to room 2. From here it is easy to find your way around as you simply follow the numerical order of the rooms, 2 to 12 on the lower floor and 13 to 23 on the upper floor. After your visit, you can take a break in the medieval gardens, whose entrance is on the corner of boulevards St-Michel and St-Germain.

HIGHLIGHTS

TAPESTRIES

Vivid tapestries paint an enchanting, if idealized, picture of medieval life. Walking, bathing and reading are among the everyday activities portrayed in the 16th-century series *La Vie Seigneuriale* (Manorial Life; room 4). The floral background, known as *mille fleurs,* was a popular artistic device at the time. Don't miss the 16th-century *Les Vendanges* (room 12), created in the southern Netherlands and portraying a busy grape harvest. The six allegorical tapestries of *La Dame à la Licorne* (The Lady and the Unicorn; room 13) were woven in silk and wool in the 15th century in the Netherlands. Each of the first five tapestries shows a lady acting out one of the five senses. In the enigmatic sixth piece, *À mon seul désir (To my only desire)*, she returns the necklace she has been wearing to its box, symbolizing, it is thought, a refusal to give in to worldly passions.

THE HEADS OF NOTRE-DAME

The concert hall (room 8) displays a surreal collection of heads that were knocked off statues on the west front of Notre-Dame by zealous Revolutionaries who thought they represented French kings. In fact, the statues, dating from the 13th century, were of biblical characters. Historians assumed the heads had been destroyed, until they were unearthed in a bank vault in 1977.

GALLO-ROMAN BATHS

The museum is on the site of Paris's most ancient Gallo-Roman baths, the ruins of which can still be seen. In the second century AD bathers would progress through three stone chambers offering different water temperatures—warm in the *tepidarium,* hot in the *caldarium* and cold in the *frigidarium.* Much of the vast *frigidarium* still remains and has been incorporated into the lower floor of the museum (room 9). It is an imposing chamber, with walls 2m (6ft) thick, rising 15m (49ft) high. In one corner stands Paris's oldest sculpture, the recently renovated *Pilier des Nautes* (AD30). A network of Roman vaults leads off from the *frigidarium.* Outside, you can see the ruins of the Roman gymnasium from the boulevard St-Germain.

BACKGROUND

The turreted Hôtel de Cluny, one of Paris's oldest mansions, was built at the end of the 15th century as a pied-à-terre for a wealthy order of Benedictine monks from Cluny, in Burgundy. Illustrious residents included Mary Tudor, sister of Henry VIII, who was widowed at age 16 after a three-month marriage to Louis XII, and James V of Scotland. In the early 19th century the art collector Alexandre du Sommerard bought the property—it is his rich finds that form the basis of the museum today.

The museum is housed in one of the city's oldest mansions (above)

Musée d'Orsay

**A vast collection of world-famous Impressionist paintings joins other art from the mid-19th century to early 20th century.
Housed in a magnificent Industrial Age train terminus, with a soaring glass and iron roof and wonderful station clock.**

The soaring roof allows plenty of light into the museum

End of an Arabesque, by Edgar Degas (1877)

The elegant exterior of the former train station

TIPS

● A *Paris Museum Pass* (▷ 307) gives you free entrance and allows you to skip the queues.
● Tuesday, Saturday and Sunday are the museum's busiest days. Thursday evening is the quietest time to visit.
● To see Monet's paintings in a more tranquil setting, visit the Musée Marmottan Monet (▷ 124–125).
● The Musée d'Orsay is closed on Monday, unlike the Louvre and Centre Georges Pompidou, which close on Tuesday.
● Entrance is free to teachers, art students and professional artists.
● The café on the upper floor gives you a stunning (and slightly surreal) view of Paris through the glass of the huge station clock. If the wait for a table is daunting, try the self-service cafeteria just above it. There is also a lavish restaurant on the middle level.

Children learning about Carpeaux's La Danse *(right)*

SEEING THE MUSÉE D'ORSAY

The Musée d'Orsay's collection spans 1848 to 1914, a crucial period in Western art that witnessed such giants as Claude Monet, Pierre-Auguste Renoir and Paul Cézanne. Chronologically, the museum fits neatly between the Louvre and the Centre Georges Pompidou. Most people come to see the breathtaking Impressionist collection, which includes Monet's *Houses of Parliament,* Vincent van Gogh's *The Church at Auvers-sur-Oise* and Renoir's *Ball at the Moulin de la Galette.* But Impressionism forms less than a third of the vast display, which also includes sculpture, Symbolist and historical paintings, photography and art nouveau furniture. The building is an attraction in itself, with its vast main hall, lavish ballroom and wonderful station clocks.

In recent years, queues for the museum have stretched far along the Seine. Improvements to the museum's entrance area have recently been completed, but it's still too early to say whether the problem has been solved. To see the works chronologically, start with the lower level, then take the escalators to the upper level, before finishing on the middle level.

HIGHLIGHTS

MONET

The Impressionist and post-Impressionist collections (upper level) are a real treat, with airy galleries filled with row upon row of legendary works by Renoir, Edgar Degas, Monet, Edouard Manet, Van Gogh and others. Monet, one of the father figures of Impressionism, is well represented, with works such as *Régate à Argenteuil* (c1872), *Nymphéas Bleus* (c1916–19) and *La Gare St-Lazare* (1877). There are five paintings from the 28-strong *Cathédrales de Rouen* series, painted between 1892 and 1894. Monet rented a studio opposite the cathedral to allow him to paint the building in different lights and weather conditions. More from the series can be seen at the Musée Marmottan Monet (▷ 124–125).

RENOIR

Renoir's cheerful *Le Bal du Moulin de la Galette* (1876; upper level) portrays Montmartre when it was the hub of Paris's nightlife. Renoir

Marking time—the surreal station clock

painted it while actually at the open-air dance hall, on the site of the Galette windmill (▷ 108). Notice the play of light and shade on the dancers, a key Impressionist theme, and the way the dancers seem almost to merge with their surroundings. Like many artists of the time, Renoir had studios in Montmartre and was a regular at the Moulin de la Galette.

VAN GOGH

Van Gogh is among the most prominently displayed post-Impressionists (upper floor), with masterpieces including the vivid *La Chambre à Arles* (1889), the sinisterly swirling *L'Église d'Auvers-sur-Oise* (1890) and the relaxed *La Sieste* (1889–90). His turquoise self-portrait of 1889 was painted in the same year he admitted himself to a psychiatric hospital in St-Rémy-de-Provence. It is one of the last of the artist's 40 self-portraits and shows him as pale and gaunt. Van Gogh suffered from severe depression and hallucinations and a year after painting this portrait he killed himself.

Van Gogh's L'Église d'Auvers-sur-Oise *(1890)*

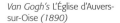

SCULPTURE ON THE LOWER LEVEL

Even if your sole reason for visiting the museum is the Impressionist collection on the upper level, don't leave without wandering through the central aisle on the lower floor. This is the best place to catch the atmosphere of the building—part museum, part Belle-Époque train station—with its ornate clock, magnificent glass roof and contrastingly solid stone-clad floor and walls. In addition to allowing you to admire the building, the central aisle is also a gallery for 19th-century neoclassical sculpture. Near the east end, look out for Jean-Baptiste Carpeaux's *La Danse* (1869), formerly part of the façade of the Opéra Palais Garnier (▷ 142) and controversial when it was first unveiled because of the detail in the nude figures. Also worth spotting, in the entrance hall, is François Rude's ferocious bust *Génie de la Patrie* (1836), moulded from a larger bas relief on the Arc de Triomphe.

HIGHLIGHTS ON THE MIDDLE LEVEL

The middle level brings you up to just before World War I. Here you can see examples of Naturalism (Jules Dalou, Fernand Cormon), Symbolism (Edward Burne-Jones and Arnold Böcklin) and the Nabis school. Most striking here are Auguste Rodin's sculptures (including the powerful *Balzac*) and those of his followers Camille Claudel, Medardo Rosso, Émile-Antoine Bourdelle and the rounded forms of Aristide Maillol. This floor also displays some superb applied arts, concentrating on art nouveau furniture and objects, including creations by Charles Rennie Mackintosh (room 27, between floors, at the east end of the museum).

THE BALLROOM

Don't miss the lavish Salles des Fêtes (room 51), tucked away at the end of the middle level. The extravagantly chandeliered and mirrored room was originally part of the station's hotel and served both as a reception room and venue for special events. In 1958 General de Gaulle declared his return to government here to a gathering of reporters.

Part of the museum's extensive sculpture collection (below, left)

An art nouveau dining room designed by Alexandre Charpentier (below, middle)

Learning from the masters, in the Impressionist gallery (below)

BACKGROUND

The imposing Orsay station and its accompanying hotel were constructed along the banks of the Seine in just two years, in time for the Exposition Universelle in 1900. Victor Laloux designed the soaring glass and iron roof, together with the wildly ornate belle-époque restaurant and ballroom; all still intact. The station boasted all modern facilities, including elevators and underground tracks. But in 1939 the advent of longer electric trains forced it to close for long-distance travel (it was still used for suburban trains). During the war it became a mail depot, then a reception venue for freed prisoners of war. Later, various films were shot here, including Orson Welles' *The Trial*. Public protest saved the station from demolition, and final approval was given to turn it into a museum in 1977. Italian architect Gae Aulenti masterminded the conversion of the interior, encasing both the walls and floors with stone, and President François Mitterrand opened the museum in December 1986.

The central sculpture aisle, with its ornate station clock

THE SIGHTS

GALLERY GUIDE

If you opt for a chronological visit, look at the sculpture and paintings on the lower level then take the escalator at the end of the hall straight to the upper level, leaving the middle level for the end (rooms are numbered accordingly).

KEY

- **Architecture**
- **Decorative Arts**
- **Painting**
- **Photography**
- **Sculpture**
- **Temporary Exhibitions**

LOWER LEVEL

Central Aisle: Sculpture, including Carpeaux's *Ugolin* (1860) and Louis-Antoine Barye's *Seated Lion* (1847).
Side galleries: Pre-Impressionist paintings, including works by Eugène Delacroix and Gustave Courbet.
Also historical paintings and early works by Monet, Renoir and Manet.

MIDDLE LEVEL

Ballroom
Side galleries: Symbolism, Naturalism and the Nabis school. Also decorative arts.
Seine Terrace (mezzanine): Sculpture, including Camille Claudel's *Middle Age* (1899–1903).
Lille Terrace (mezzanine): Sculpture, including François Pompon's *Polar Bear* (1922–23).
Rodin Terrace: Sculpture by Rodin, including *Gates of Hell* (1880–1917) and *Balzac* (1897).
Restaurant

UPPER LEVEL

Galleries: Impressionist and post-Impressionist paintings; sculpture by Degas, Renoir and Paul Gauguin.
Café des Hauteurs.

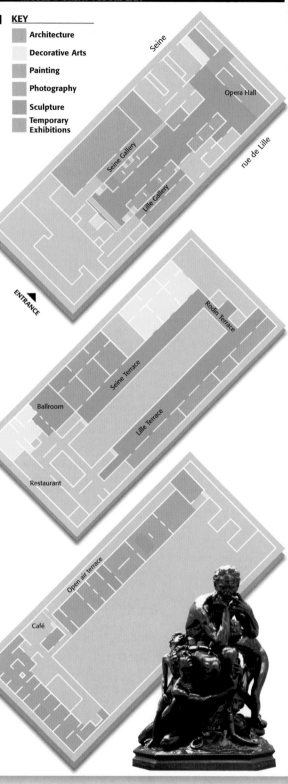

Seine

Opera Hall

rue de Lille

Seine Gallery

Lille Gallery

ENTRANCE

Rodin Terrace

Seine Terrace

Ballroom

Lille Terrace

Restaurant

Open air terrace

Café

The Picasso Museum has more than 200 paintings by the artist

MUSÉE PICASSO

An outstanding collection of works by Pablo Picasso—a must for anyone interested in 20th-century art.

The grand opening of this museum in 1985 put an end to 11 years of wrangling over the death duties of Pablo Picasso (1881–1973). Thanks to a law allowing payment of these duties in the form of works of art, the French State received one quarter of Picasso's collection from his heirs. The collection, including 203 paintings, 158 sculptures, 16 collages and more than 1,500 drawings and prints, was extended further after the death of Picasso's wife in 1990. Also on display is Picasso's personal collection of works by his mentors and contemporaries, including Paul Cézanne, Pierre-Auguste Renoir, Joan Miró, Georges Braque and Henri Matisse.

THE WORKS

The art is arranged chronologically, from Picasso's early 1900s Blue and Pink periods, through his years of Cubist experimentation with Georges Braque, to the 1930s and beyond. Look out for the *Trois Femmes à la Fontaine* (1921) at the top of the staircase to the left, and the sculpture of *La Guenon et Son Petit* (*the Baboon with Young;* 1951) in room 18, whose head is made from two toy cars.

Other highlights are his *Self-Portrait* (1901) in room 1, *The Goat* (1950) in room 16, *The Bathers* (1918) and *Two Women Running on the Beach* (1922) in room 6, and the tragic yet moving *Seated Old Man* (1970–71) in room 20. The collection captures the freshness and inventiveness that ran through the core of Picasso's long and creative life.

MANSION SETTING

The museum is in the Hôtel Salé, a beautiful 17th-century mansion in the Marais district. After changing hands several times the mansion was acquired by the Ville de Paris in 1962, and in 1976 architect Roland Simounet began work to convert the interior to the Musée Picasso. The chandeliers and furniture were designed by Diego Giacometti and extensive, and expensive, renovation work was needed before the museum opened to the public. A small room dedicated to the history of the Hôtel Salé displays black-and-white photographs and information on the building and its occupants over the years.

RATINGS	
Cultural interest	● ● ● ●
Historic interest	● ● ●

BASICS

✚ 68 P7 • Hôtel Salé, 5 rue de Thorigny, 75003

☎ 01 42 71 25 21

🕐 Apr–end Sep Wed–Mon 9.30–6; rest of year Wed–Mon 9.30–5.30; last entry 45 min before closing. Closed 1 Jan, 25 Dec

💶 Adult €6.30, 18–25 €4.50, under 18 free; free to all on 1st Sun of month

🚇 St-Paul, Chemin Vert, St-Sébastien Froissart

🚌 29, 69, 75, 96

📣 Guided tours Sep–end Jun Mon and Fri 2.30 (€6.30)

🎧 €3

☕ Garden café, mid-Apr to mid-Oct

📖 Bookshop and giftshop

♿

www.musee-picasso.fr (in French)

TIPS

● Even for those who are not ardent Picasso fans, the museum is still worth a visit to admire the interior of the magnificent Hôtel Salé.
● Wall plaques in each of the rooms give detailed information (in English) about the works on display.

Strolling past The Walking Man *(1900–1907)*

RATINGS

Cultural interest	●●●●
Good for kids (garden)	●●●
Photo stops (garden)	●●●
Value for money (garden)	●●●●

BASICS

✚ 66 J7 • 77 rue de Varenne, 75007
☎ 01 44 18 61 10
🕐 Apr–end Sep Tue–Sun 9.30–5.45
(gardens stay open until 6.45); rest of
year Tue–Sun 9.30–4.45
💷 Adult €6, under 18 free, free to all
on 1st Sun of month. Garden only: €1
🚇 Varenne
🚌 69, 82, 87, 92
🚆 RER line C, Invalides
🎧 Audioguides €4. Guided tours once
a week 🔊 €9.50 ☕ Garden café
📖 Bookshop/giftshop
🚻 In the gardens

www.musee-rodin.fr
In French and English, with photos of
Rodin and his works

TIPS

● The garden-only ticket lets
you view some of Rodin's
most important works for only
€1; children should enjoy the
play area.
● If the Rodin Museum whets
your appetite for open-air
sculpture, try the Musée de la
Sculpture en Plein Air, on quai
St-Bernard, which has around
40 avant-garde works. (Visit
during the day only.)
● There are few information
boards in the garden, so rent
an audioguide or pick up a free
leaflet from the Hôtel Biron.

MUSÉE RODIN

**In this museum's soothing gardens, hidden in the heart of the
city, you can wander past Auguste Rodin's world-famous
sculptures or relax among the roses.**

The Musée Rodin's open-air gallery, spread over 3ha (7 acres) of
beautiful garden, makes a great escape from more strenuous
sightseeing. After a stroll through the grounds, you can see more
of Rodin's works in the Hôtel Biron, the airy 18th-century mansion
where he once lived.

THE GARDEN

Don't miss the brooding bronze *Le Penseur* (*The Thinker*;
1880–1904), thought to represent the Italian poet Dante and
originally placed outside the Panthéon, or the gruesome doorway
La Porte de l'Enfer (*The Gates of Hell*; 1880–1917), inspired by
Dante's *Divine Comedy*. *Les Bourgeois de Calais* (*The Burghers of
Calais*; 1884–89) depicts six burghers who gave up their lives to
save their townsfolk during a siege by the English in the 14th century,
while *Balzac* (1891–98) is a rather unflattering portrayal of the
writer in his dressing gown.

THE HÔTEL BIRON

Inside the elegant mansion, you can follow Rodin's artistic evolution
chronologically, from his early academic sketches and paintings to his
vigorous watercolours. The highlight is the passionate white marble
Le Baiser (*The Kiss*; 1882–98), one of Rodin's best-known pieces.
There are also works by the artist's contemporaries, including Camille
Claudel, Pierre-Auguste Renoir, Vincent Van Gogh and Claude Monet.

THE ARTIST

Rodin was born in Paris in 1840 and showed an early aptitude for
drawing. In 1857 he applied to study sculpture at the École des
Beaux-Arts but was rejected because tutors felt his style was old-
fashioned. Most of his famous pieces date from the latter half of his
life. In 1908 Rodin moved into the ground floor of the rococo Hôtel
Biron (1730), where other residents included Jean Cocteau, Henri
Matisse and Isadora Duncan. In 1916 he welcomed a decision to turn
the mansion into a museum of his work, but he died in 1917, two
years before the plans became reality.

Notre-Dame

This beautiful Gothic cathedral is one of France's most visited religious sites. Climb the towers for wonderful views over the city or take a boat trip to admire the famous flying buttresses.

Take a closer look at the gargoyles—if you can face the climb

A postcard stand in the bustling square in front of the cathedral

Sunset over Notre-Dame

SEEING NOTRE-DAME

Notre-Dame anchors the Île de la Cité with its powerful presence and more than 850 years of history. The cathedral is as famous a symbol of Paris as the Eiffel Tower and around 10 million people enter its doors each year. Despite this, it retains an inspiring sense of calm.

Entry is through the huge doorways of the west façade, in the touristy place du Parvis Notre-Dame. You can buy a guidebook at the bookstand just inside the cathedral, before wandering around the dimly lit interior. There are fewer crowds in the early morning, when the cathedral is also at its brightest. If you're not in a hurry, you may like to visit the Treasury, reached from the south side of the choir. The entrance to the crypt is outside, on place du Parvis Notre-Dame.

Keep some time for strolling around the outside of Notre-Dame to admire the architecture, including the buttresses. One of the best views of the exterior is from the Seine, on a boat trip that circles the Île de la Cité. Finally, if your legs will agree to it, there are wonderful views from the top of the towers. Queues are shortest in the morning, Tuesday to Friday.

HIGHLIGHTS

WEST FAÇADE

The symmetrical west façade, dominated by Notre-Dame's towers, appears rather heavy and angular compared with the elegant curves and spires you see from the eastern side. But it is packed with sculptures, originally painted and intended as a Bible for the illiterate. The 28 large statues lined up between the doors and the windows form the Gallery of the Kings. Although the figures represent biblical characters, revolutionary zealots mistook them for French kings and beheaded them. The statues you see today are 19th-century replicas, but you can see some of the original heads at the Musée National du Moyen Âge (▷ 128–129). Below the Gallery of the Kings, the left portal is dedicated to the Virgin Mary, the central portal shows the Last Judgement and the right portal, dedicated to St. Anne, shows Mary holding the infant Jesus, while Louis VII and Bishop Sully kneel in worship.

TIPS

● Try to visit just before a service to experience the palpable sense of anticipation as lights are gradually turned on and people gather to worship.

● Instead of paying tourist prices in the nearby cafés and restaurants, enjoy a picnic in the grassy square Jean XXIII, on the southern side of the cathedral.

TOWERS

It's a tough climb, but it is worth tackling the towers, 69m (226ft) high, for the views over Paris and a closer look at the gargoyles. You'll be following the fictional footsteps of Notre-Dame's bell ringer, Quasimodo. Two-thirds of the way up (and a mere 285 steps) is the gargoyle parapet known as the Galerie des Chimères, where you can enjoy views across the Latin Quarter to the Tour Montparnasse, as well as along the Seine and across the Île de la Cité to Sainte-Chapelle. This is a great place to photograph the quirky gargoyles, added in the 19th century by Viollet-le-Duc (see background, ▷ 140). A wooden staircase in the South Tower leads to the 13-tonne Emmanuel bell, recast in 1686 and evoking memories of a tormented Quasimodo. A separate spiral staircase leads up to the top of the South Tower (another 115 steps), where the panoramic views

BASICS

Cathedral

✚ 68 N8 • place du Parvis Notre-Dame, 75004

☎ 01 42 34 56 10

🕐 Daily 8–6.45. Closed on some religious feast days

🎟 Free

🚇 Cité, St-Michel, Châtelet

🚌 21, 38, 47, 58, 70, 72, 74, 81, 82, 85, 96

🚆 RER lines B, C, St-Michel

📖 A wide choice in many languages

🎧 Guided tours: in French, Mon–Fri 2

Notre-Dame—a symbol of Paris   The vibrant south rose window   Prayer candles

take in Sacré-Cœur to the north, the Arc de Triomphe to the west, the modern Bibliothèque Nationale to the east and the Panthéon to the south. At the top, take a moment to consider how the view must have changed since the towers were completed in 1245.

THE WINDOWS

Notre-Dame has stunning stained glass and it is hard to imagine how the cathedral must have looked in the 18th century, when officials replaced many of the medieval windows with clear glass to let in more light. Much of the current stained glass dates from the 19th and 20th centuries. The south rose window, 13m (42ft) in diameter, is especially glorious when the sun shines through, adding extra vibrancy to the purple hues. Christ stands in the heart of the window, encircled by angels, apostles, martyrs and scenes from the New Testament. Opposite, the middle of the north rose window shows Mary holding a young Jesus. Old Testament prophets, priests and kings fill the rest of the window, one of the cathedral's few originals.

CHOIR SCREEN, ALTAR AND NOTRE-DAME DE PARIS

Don't miss the cathedral's intricately carved and painted 14th-century choir screen, restored in the 1960s. Its enchanting depictions of gospel scenes include the Wise Men bringing their gifts to baby Jesus, Jesus riding into Jerusalem on a donkey, and the Last Supper.

The modern bronze high altar in the middle of the cathedral was consecrated in 1989. It depicts gospel writers Matthew, Mark, Luke and John and Old Testament prophets Isaiah, Ezekiel, Daniel and Jeremiah.

Nearby you can see the most famous of Notre-Dame's 37 statues of the Virgin Mary. Known as Notre-Dame de Paris, it dates from the 14th century and was installed in the cathedral in the 19th century.

CHAPELS

The cathedral is lined with small chapels, added during the 13th and 14th centuries and dedicated to saints. Guilds used to meet in these chapels and each May Day they would donate a painting to the cathedral. Some of these works of art remain on display today, including pieces by 17th-century artists Charles Le Brun and Eustache Le Sueur.

and 3, Sat 2.30; in English, Wed–Thu at 2, Sat at 2.30. Extra tours in English in August

🍴 Plenty on Île de la Cité and in the nearby Latin Quarter

📖 Small bookshop in the cathedral. Larger bookshop/giftshop halfway up the tower

❓ Organ recitals at 4.30 on Sun

Towers

✉ Rue du Cloître Notre-Dame (entrance is on the northwestern corner of the cathedral) ☎ 01 53 10 07 00

🕐 Jul–end Aug Mon–Fri 9–6.30, Sat–Sun 9am–11pm; Apr–end Jun, Sep daily 10–6.30; rest of year daily 10–5.30; last entry 45 min before closing

🎟 Adult €7.50, under 18 free

Treasury

✉ Entrance is within the cathedral, on the southern side near the choir

🕐 Mon–Fri 9.30–6, Sat 9.30–6.30, Sun 1.30–6.30

🎟 Adult €2.50, child €1

Crypt

✉ 1 place du Parvis Notre-Dame

☎ 01 55 42 50 10

🕐 Tue–Sun 10–6

🎟 Adult €3.30, child €2.20

www.notredamedeparis.fr
In French and English

The portal of the Last Judgement (left), on the west façade

THE SIGHTS

FACTS AND FIGURES

● The cathedral is 128m (420ft) long and its transept is 48m (157ft) wide.

● The spire is 90m (295ft) high. The towers are 69m (226ft) high.

● More than 1,300 oak trees were felled to make the cathedral's wooden frame.

● The organ dates from the early 18th century and has 7,800 pipes.

TREASURY AND CRYPT

Notre-Dame's Trésor holds medieval manuscripts, religious paraphernalia and relics, including the Crown of Thorns, bought for an exorbitant amount by Louis IX (▷ 160). It's not a vital part of the Notre-Dame experience, but the gold and jewel-encrusted items give an insight into the wealth and power wielded by the Church over the years. The cathedral's crypt is often overlooked by visitors, perhaps because the entrance is outside, on the opposite side of the place du Parvis Notre-Dame. Down here you'll see Roman foundations and archaeological finds.

BACKGROUND

In the 12th century, Bishop Maurice de Sully decided that Paris needed its own cathedral. Pope Alexander III laid the foundation stone in 1163 and the choir was constructed in just under 20 years. Guilds of carpenters, stone-carvers, iron forgers and glass craftsmen worked on the grand project but it took almost 200 years to complete, finishing in 1345. For years Notre-Dame doubled as a meeting place for trade unions and a dormitory for the homeless. Its cathedral school was renowned throughout Europe. But by the time Napoleon was crowned in the cathedral in 1804 it was in a state of disrepair. Victor Hugo, author of *The Hunchback of Notre-Dame*, campaigned for its restoration, concerned at the absence of countless statues (toppled during the Revolution), the lack of stained glass and the amputation of the spire in 1787. His ranting met with some success. The statues in the Gallery of Kings were eventually reproduced and a 90m (295ft) spire was erected. Viollet-le-Duc oversaw the restoration in the mid-19th century. His work included replacing some of the clear-glass windows with stained glass and modestly adding a statue of himself among the Apostles. It wasn't until after World War II that the rest of the windows were replaced. Today, Notre-Dame remains an important place of worship, as well as one of Paris's top visitor attractions.

The striking silhouette of
Notre-Dame at sunset (above)

The vast interior (left)

NOTRE-DAME FLOORPLAN

Porte Rouge

High altar

Louis XIV

Pietà

Portail du
Cloître

North rose
window

Louis XIII

Choir stalls

Entrance
to tower

Notre-Dame
de Paris

Portail de
St-Étienne

ENTRANCE

Portail de
la Vierge

Portail de
Jugement Dernier

Portail de
Sainte-Anne

South rose
window

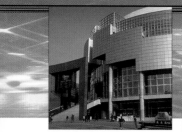

The strikingly modern Opéra Bastille

OPÉRA BASTILLE

🔲 68 Q8 • place de la Bastille (box office: 120 rue de Lyon), 75012 ☎ 01 40 01 19 70 (information); 0892 899 090 (reservations) 🕐 Box office: Mon–Sat 10–6.30 🎫 Guided tours: adult €11, child (under 19) €6; call for details 🚇 Bastille 🚌 20, 29, 69, 76 www.operadeparis.fr

The geometric marble façade of this modern opera house dominates place de la Bastille (▷ 80), and the 2,700-seat auditorium hosts prestigious productions (▷ 202). The imposing building made its presence felt even before it was constructed. The project, championed by President Mitterrand in the early 1980s, ran into controversy when a design by a relatively unknown architect, Carlos Ott, was selected from more than 700 entries. The opera house attracted further criticism for its ungainly volume and its cost, but it was ready to open for the bicentenary of the French Revolution in 1989.

ORANGERIE

🔲 67 K6 • Jardin des Tuileries, 75001 ☎ 01 44 77 80 07 🕐 Wed–Thu, Sat–Mon 12.30–7, Fri 12.30–9 🎫 Adult €6.50, under 18 free 🚇 Concorde 🚌 24, 42, 52, 72, 73, 84, 94

The stately Orangerie started life as a greenhouse but is now an art gallery housing eight of Monet's world-famous *Water Lily* paintings. It was constructed in 1852, in Second Empire style, to overwinter orange trees from the Jardin des Tuileries (▷ 105). It became an art gallery in the early 20th century, and now shelters the Walter-Guillaume collection of around 140 Impressionist and 20th-century paintings. Artists represented include Pierre-Auguste Renoir, Paul Cézanne and Pablo Picasso.

OPÉRA PALAIS GARNIER

This architectural masterpiece, designed by Charles Garnier, was the largest theatre in the world when it opened in 1875.

🔲 67 L5 • place de l'Opéra, 75009 ☎ 01 41 10 08 10. Box office: 08 92 89 90 90. Museum: 01 40 01 22 63 🕐 Daily 10–6, 10–1 during matinee performances. Closed 1 Jan, 1 May

RATINGS			
Cultural interest	●	●	● ●
Historic interest	●	●	●
Photo stops (exterior)	●	●	●

and when there is a matinée performance/special event. The auditorium is closed during rehearsals and shows 🎫 Adult €8, child (10–19) €4, under 10 free 🚇 Opéra 🚌 20, 21, 22, 27, 29, 42, 52, 53, 66, 68, 81, 95 🎫 Guided tours last 1 hr 30 min and cost €11 (child €6); in French Wed, Sat, Sun at 11.30 and 3.30; in English Wed, Sat, Sun at 11.30 and 2.30. Telephone in advance. 📷 €7 🎁 Gift shop 🚻
www.operadeparis.fr (an informative site, in French, with some English pages, including practical information, history, events calendar and photo gallery)

The sumptuous Opéra Palais Garnier was commissioned by Napoleon III and inaugurated in 1875. Charles Garnier beat more than 170 hopefuls in a competition to design the prestigious building. Work finished 15 years after the official acceptance of his riotous design.

The opera house was for a time the largest theatre in the world (11,000sq m/118,404sq ft), a fittingly lavish epitaph to the architecture of the Second Empire. The stage can accommodate up to 450 performers and the opulent auditorium holds around 2,200 spectators under a domed ceiling painted by Marc Chagall in 1964. The Italianate, horseshoe-shaped auditorium has red and gold décor and a huge crystal chandelier.

The decorative façade has been likened to a huge ornamental wedding cake. Look out for Carrier-Belleuse's provocative lamp-bearing statues and the copy of Jean-Baptiste Carpeaux's sculpted group *La Danse* to the right of the front arcade (the 1869 original is now in the Musée d'Orsay). A small library-museum presents the history of the Opéra and includes paintings, photographs and operatic memorabilia. Temporary exhibitions are held throughout the year. Many operatic performances are today staged at the Opéra Bastille (see left). The Opéra Palais Garnier is almost exclusively devoted to ballet (▷ 202).

Don't miss The splendid marble and gilt Grand Staircase and the baroque Grand Foyer are highlights inside.

Charles Garnier's lavish opera house, crowned by a statue of Apollo

A model ship on display at the Musée National de la Marine

PALAIS DE CHAILLOT

From the terrace of the elegant Palais de Chaillot there is a breathtaking view across the Seine to the Eiffel Tower.

The colonnaded Palais de Chaillot was built for the *Exposition Universelle* of 1937 and offers stunning views of the Eiffel Tower, and the Champ de Mars beyond. Its curved wings are dotted with gleaming bronze statues and the wide terraces, overlooking the fountains of the Jardins du Trocadéro, bustle with street artists, souvenir sellers, food kiosks and visitors admiring the Eiffel Tower. The palace currently houses two museums and the Théâtre National de Chaillot (tel 01 53 65 30 00; www.theatre-chaillot.fr), which sits beneath the terrace, between the two wings.

MUSEUMS

The Musée National de la Marine and the Musée de l'Homme are in the palace's west wing. The Musée National de la Marine is one of the largest maritime museums in the world and was founded by Charles X in 1827. It focuses on French naval history from the 18th century to the present day and displays paintings, naval instruments and a vast array of model ships. There is also a workshop where you can watch the models being restored. The Musée de l'Homme has collections of anthropology and prehistory illustrating the evolution of the human species, the growth of the world's population and the similarities and diversity of mankind. The ethnological collections were transferred to the Musée du Quai Branly, which opened in 2006 (▷ 126).

THE EAST WING

The east wing of the *palais* was renovated following a fire in 1997 and forms part of a prestigious development, the Cité de l'Architecture et du Patrimoine, the national repository of architectural excellence and the École de Chaillot restoration school. The Musée des Monuments Français is the principal visitor attraction, its galleries filled with excellent casts and reproductions of monumental stone architecture found on cathedrals and châteaux around the country. These were made during the late 19th and early 20th centuries, in the years after Viollet-le-Duc reignited interest in medieval French architecture. Because many of the originals were later lost in the two world wars, these copies now form an important historical archive.

RATINGS

Good for kids	● ● ●
Historic interest	● ● ●
Photo stops (views)	● ● ● ●

BASICS

✚ 66 F6 • 17 place du Trocadéro et du 11 Novembre, 75016

🚇 Trocadéro

🚌 22, 30, 32, 63, 72, 82

Musée National de la Marine
☎ 01 53 65 69 69
🕐 Wed–Mon 10–6 (last entry 5.15). Closed 1 Jan, 1 May and 25 Dec
💶 Adult (museum + exhibition + audioguide) €9, child (6–18) €5, under 6 free
🎧 Audioguides (French, English; included in the entrance fee)
📖 Bookshop/gift shop
🚹🚺
www.musee-marine.fr

Musée de l'Homme
☎ 01 44 05 72 72
🕐 Wed–Fri and Mon 9.45–5.15, Sat–Sun 10–6.30 (last entry 30 min before closing)
💶 Adult €7, child €5
🍴 Café-restaurant place du Trocadéro
📖 Bookshop/gift shop
🚹🚺
www.mnhn.fr

Musée des Monuments Français
☎ 01 58 51 52 00
🕐 Mon, Wed, Fri noon–8, Thu noon–10, Sat–Sun 11–7. Closed Tue and 1 Jan
💶 Adult €7, child €5
📖 Bookshop/gift shop
🚹🚺

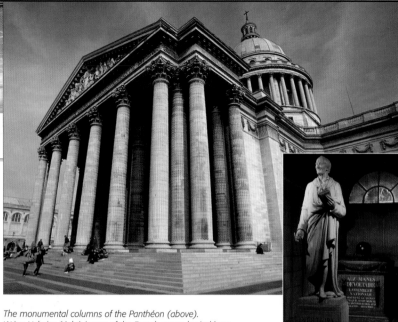

The monumental columns of the Panthéon (above).
Writer Voltaire (right) is one of the French greats buried here

RATINGS	
Historic interest	● ● ●
Photo stops (exterior and views)	● ● ●

BASICS

✚ 67 M9 • place du Panthéon, 75005
☎ 01 44 32 18 00
🕐 Apr–end Sep daily 10–6.30; rest of year daily 10–6; last entrance 45 min before closing
🎟 Adult €7.50, under 18 free
Ⓜ Cardinal Lemoine
🚍 21, 27, 84, 85, 89
🚆 RER B, Luxembourg
🚖 €7
🎧 Guided tours in French. Ring ahead for other languages
📖 Small bookshop/giftshop
♿ Near crypt

www.monuments-nationaux.fr
In French and English

TIPS

● See the noticeboard outside the Panthéon for times for the guided tours up to the dome's circular colonnade.
● If you don't feel like climbing to the colonnade, you can still enjoy views of the Eiffel Tower from the top of the Panthéon's steps.

PANTHÉON

Originally a basilica, this striking monument is now the final resting place of some of France's greatest citizens.

The neoclassical grandeur of the Panthéon is an arresting sight after you have wandered through the warren-like streets of the Latin Quarter to reach it. This colossal mausoleum contains the tombs of many illustrious citizens, including writers Victor Hugo, Émile Zola and Voltaire, scientists Marie and Pierre Curie, Braille inventor Louis Braille, and World War II Resistance martyr Jean Moulin. To be 'pantheonized' is one of the greatest accolades in France and arguments still ignite periodically about who merits a re-burial here.

GIVING THANKS

The monument was commissioned by Louis XV as a basilica dedicated to St. Geneviève, patron saint of Paris, in thanks for his recovery from gout. The king laid the foundation stone in 1764 and work finished in 1790, by which time the original architect, Jacques Germain Soufflot, had died. Only a year later, in 1791, the Revolutionaries seized the building, bricking up the windows and changing its function to a secular Temple of Fame.

VISITING THE PANTHÉON

You enter the building through an imposing peristyle, based on the grandiose frontage of Rome's Pantheon. The sculpted pediment portrays France's heroes receiving their rewards. Inside the vast, cross-shaped chamber the atmosphere feels austere. Religious heroes are prominent in many of the paintings in the naves, including St. Geneviève (western nave and choir), the beheaded St. Denis (western nave), Joan of Arc (northern nave) and St. Louis (northern nave). The Revolution also features in paintings and sculptures. Look up into the dome—the scientist Foucault hung a pendulum here in 1851 to prove the earth rotates. To climb to the colonnade beneath the dome, 35m (115ft) high, you must take a guided tour—and tackle 206 steps. Downstairs in the huge, shadowy crypt you can see the tombs of Voltaire, Victor Hugo, Émile Zola, Marie Curie and others.

5ᵉ Arr!
PLACE DU PANTHÉON

The Parc Monceau, a few Métro stops from the Arc de Triomphe

The magnificent art nouveau Métro entrance at place des Abbesses

PARC ANDRÉ-CITROËN

66 off F9 • rue Balard, rue Leblanc, quai André-Citroën, 75015 ☎ Mairie de Paris information 3975 🕐 Mon–Fri 8–dusk, Sat–Sun 9–dusk 🎟 Free 🚇 Balard, Javel 🚌 42, 88 🚈 RER line C, Boulevard Victor www.paris.fr

As the name suggests, this futuristic park replaced a vast Citroën car factory in the southwest of Paris. Nearly 14ha (35 acres) of ultramodern landscaping lead down to the Seine, burying embankment traffic in their wake. Specialist gardens are colour-coded and you'll find zany experimentation with metal and water. Even the customary Orangery has had the postmodern treatment, evolving into two gigantic high-tech glasshouses. The park opened in 1992, following Citroën's decision to move its factory out of Paris in the 1970s.

PARC MONCEAU

66 off H4 • boulevard de Courcelles, 75008 ☎ Mairie de Paris information 3975 🕐 Apr–end Sep daily 7am–10pm; rest of year daily 7am–8pm 🎟 Free 🚇 Monceau 🚌 30, 84, 94 🖥 www.paris.fr

It's worth taking a trip out to this timeless park, northeast of the Arc de Triomphe, with its fake ruins, tree-shaded pond and magnificent wrought-iron gates. The weekend is best, when the park buzzes with joggers, families and residents of the classy surrounding area. From the Métro station, with its art nouveau entrance, you enter the park through tall, gilded wrought-iron gates. Inside, there's a pond bordered with fake Roman columns, a pyramid, a rotunda, various statues and plenty of trees and flowers. For children there are donkey rides, swings and a merry-go-round. The park

was landscaped in the English style by Thomas Blaikie in 1783 and became a public park in 1861. Nearby attractions include the Musée Cernuschi (▷ 113) and the Musée Nissim de Camondo (▷ 126).

PARC MONTSOURIS

330 off L11 • boulevard Jourdan/ avenue Reille, 75014 ☎ Mairie de Paris information 3975 🕐 Apr–end Oct daily 8am–8.30 or 9.30pm; rest of year daily 8am–5.30 or 6pm 🎟 Free 🚇 Porte d'Orléans 🚌 21, 88 🚈 RER line B, Cité Universitaire

Parc Montsouris, in the south of the city, is a vast English-style park, laid out in 1878. The site was originally a granite quarry and was once dotted with windmills. Now paths twist up gentle slopes among a large variety of trees and plants. There are also play areas and a lake with a waterfall. The park is home to a meteorological observatory. The nearby artists' studios were once inhabited by luminaries such as Georges Braque and Salvador Dalí.

PARC DE LA VILLETTE

See pages 146–147.

PAVILLON DE L'ARSENAL

68 P8 • 21 boulevard Morland, 75004 ☎ 01 42 76 33 97 🕐 Tue–Sat 10.30–6.30, Sun 11–7 🎟 Free 🚇 Sully Morland 🚌 67, 86, 87 www.pavillon-arsenal.com

If you want to learn more about how Paris has evolved as a city, this architectural and town-planning information site is worth a visit. At ground level, a permanent exhibition uses drawings, models, documents and photographs to explain the development projects that have shaped the city. There is also a huge scale model, a bookshop and a seating area where you can read newspapers, including

foreign titles. The upper floors of the skylit venue host temporary exhibitions.

The iron-and-glass building was constructed in 1879, near an area where gunpowder was made, hence the name.

PIGALLE

69 L3 • south of Montmartre 75009/75018 🚇 Pigalle 🚌 30, 54, 67; Montmartrobus

The name Pigalle is synonymous with the blatant sex trade that has flourished there for decades. There are sleazy bars, sex shops and peep shows in the boulevard Rochechouart and surrounding streets. In the 19th century, the painters Pierre-Auguste Renoir and Henri de Toulouse-Lautrec were frequent visitors, scouting around place Pigalle looking for models among the dancers.

PLACE DES ABBESSES

69 M3 • place des Abbesses, Montmartre, 75018 🚇 Abbesses 🚌 Montmartrobus 🍴 A selection

Place des Abbesses is less touristy than place du Tertre, farther up the Montmartre hill, so makes a quieter coffee stop.

The square has a magnificent art nouveau Métro entrance, that leads into Paris's deepest station, 40m (131ft) below ground. The church of St-Jean-de-Montmartre (1904) picks up on the art nouveau theme, with decorative windows that enliven the rather ugly red-brick cladding. This conspicuous brickwork earned it the nickname St-Jean-des-Briques. The square takes its name from the abbey that once stood on the site. A mischievous legend claims that Henri de Navarre, who later became King Henri IV, had a fling with the abbess in 1590.
Don't miss Seek out the Mur des Je t'Aime (▷ 22).

Parc de la Villette

**One of the world's largest scientific and cultural sites.
This urban park combines arts and sciences with nature.**

THE SIGHTS

BASICS

Cité des Sciences et de l'Industrie
✚ 320 S1 • 30 avenue Corentin-Cariou, 75019 ☎ 01 40 05 80 00 (recorded information)
🕐 Explora exhibitions: Tue–Sat 10–6, Sun 10–7. Planetarium: Tue–Sun, shows every hour from 11–5 (except 1pm). Aquarium: Tue–Sat 10–6, Sun 10–7. Géode: Tue–Sat 10.30–8.30, Sun 10.30–7.30 (times vary Mon and public hols). Argonaute: Tue–Fri 10.30–5.30, Sat–Sun 10–6.30. Cinaxe: Tue–Sun, shows every 15 min from 11–1 and 2–5 (times vary on public hols)
💶 Explora exhibitions: adult €8, child €6, under 7 free. Planetarium: adult €3 (plus admission to Explora), under 7 free. Cité des Enfants: €6 per person for a 90-min session. Aquarium: free. Géode: €11, child €9.50. Argonaute: €3. Cinaxe: €5.40, child €4.80
🚇 Porte de la Villette
🚌 75, 152, PC2, PC3
🚤 Canauxrama organizes canal trips to the Parc de la Villette, ▷ 248
🎧 Explora exhibitions: Audioguides (€3.80) available in several languages, including English. Géode: Headsets, in English, available free from the information point
📖 Guidebook €7
🍴 Le Hublot, level -2
🛍 Several 🏬 Gift shop/bookshop
❓ Children under 3 are not admitted to the Géode, L'Argonaute, Cinaxe, Planetarium and Cité des Enfants
www.cite-sciences.fr
www.lageode.fr

Cité de la Musique
✚ 320 S2 • 221 avenue Jean-Jaurès, 75019
☎ 01 44 84 44 84 (information and reservations)
🕐 Tue–Sat 12–6, Sun 10–6 (concert times vary)
💶 Museum: adult €6.50, under 18 free
🚇 Porte de Pantin
🚌 75, PC2, PC3
🍴 Café de la Musique
🏬 Bookshop and gift shop
www.cite-musique.fr

SEEING THE PARC DE LA VILLETTE

The ultramodern Parc de la Villette catapults you into a futuristic world. Its innovatively landscaped 55ha (135 acres) have a range of cultural and leisure activities, including a science museum, music complex, hemispheric cinema, exhibition venue and concert hall.

The park is northeast of the city's heart and is easily reached by Métro. For the Cité des Sciences et de l'Industrie take line 7 to Porte de la Villette. For the Cité de la Musique take line 5 to Porte de Pantin. A covered walkway runs the length of the park, linking the two attractions. The walk takes around 15 minutes. The reception desks in the Cité des Sciences et de l'Industrie have information in several languages. You can also pick up a schedule (Le Programme) of the shows, films and presentations here. Reserve shows, films and activities as soon as you arrive at the Cité des Sciences et de l'Industrie because they are very popular.

HIGHLIGHTS

CITÉ DES SCIENCES ET DE L'INDUSTRIE
This giant, futuristic science and technology venue is packed with high-tech, hands-on displays, in addition to shows, audiovisual presentations, optical illusions and interactive experiments. The Explora exhibitions, on levels 1 and 2, cover five main themes: The Universe; Water and the Earth; Challenges of the Living World; Industry; and Communication. There is a planetarium on level 2 and the excellent Cité des Enfants on level 0. Here games and fun experiments encourage children to learn. The Louis-Lumière cinema, on level 0, shows 3D films, and the Aquarium, on level -2, has more than 200 species of marine life from Mediterranean waters. The Cité des Sciences et de l'Industrie also has a Médiathèque (a multimedia library), a health village (offering information), a cyber-base and the Cité des Métiers (providing careers guidance).

LA GÉODE, L'ARGONAUTE AND LE CINAXE
Just south of the Cité des Sciences, across the moat, stands the space-age Géode cinema. This gigantic sphere measures 36m (118ft) in diameter. The exterior is covered with curved triangles of polished steel creating a spectacular distorted mirrored effect. Inside, you can see films on a 1,000sq-m (10,764sq-ft) hemispheric screen—the images are 10 times larger than in a normal cinema. Next to the Géode you can explore the Argonaute, a military submarine that was launched in 1957 and served in the Toulon submarine squadron for 24 years. On the western side of the Cité des Sciences stands the 56-seater Cinaxe—one of the biggest simulator cinemas in the world. The high-tech simulator moves in synchronization with the film. 3-D glasses add to the excitement of this bumpy ride.

CITÉ DE LA MUSIQUE
The highlight here is the Musée de la Musique, a fascinating music museum displaying around 900 musical instruments, dating from the Renaissance to the present day. As you walk around, an infrared audioguide plays the music of the instruments in front of you.

Paintings, sculptures and beautiful models of concert halls are also displayed. Concerts are staged in the amphitheatre, with its baroque organ. The Cité also contains research facilities, a media library, music and dance information rooms and the Conservatoire National Supérieur de Musique de Paris.

BACKGROUND

Parc de la Villette was created in the 1980s, designed by architect Bernard Tschumi. He transformed the former abattoir into landscaped grounds containing water features, themed gardens, children's playgrounds, cultural sites, cafés and events venues. The site straddles the Canal de l'Ourcq and is decorated with red metal follies. The city abattoirs stood here from 1867 until 1974 and their cattle hall was transformed into La Grande Halle, now used for trade fairs and concerts. The Cité des

CONCERTS

On the eastern edge of the park, a 6,000-seat venue called Zénith stages pop and rock concerts. Music events are also held in the 15,000-seat Grande Halle.

Sciences et de l'Industrie opened in 1986, on the same day that Halley's Comet passed near the earth. Its concrete, steel and glass building, surrounded by a moat, was designed by Adrien Fainsilber. The Cité de la Musique, designed by Christian de Portzamparc, is one of the newer arrivals at the park. It opened in 1995.

The Cité des Sciences et de l'Industrie (above, left).
Enjoying a drink in the Café de la Musique (above, middle).
You never know what you might find at Parc de la Villette (above)

PARC DE LA VILLETTE

One of the fountains in the place de la Concorde (above).
Hieroglyphics on the obelisk, Paris's oldest monument (left)

PLACE DE LA CONCORDE

**Paris's largest square is home to the city's oldest monument.
It also played a gruesome role during the Revolution.**

RATINGS

Historic interest	●●●○
Photo stops	●●●○

BASICS

✚ 67 K6 • place de la Concorde, 75008
🎟 Free
🚇 Concorde
🚌 24, 42, 72, 73, 84, 94
🚻 In the nearby Jardin des Tuileries

TIPS

● Use the pedestrian crossing when walking to the middle of the square—but be careful, as the traffic does not always stop when it should.
● Take time to appreciate the wonderful views from the heart of the square, especially up the Champs-Élysées.

Hectic place de la Concorde was once an area of swampland but now buzzes with people and traffic. It sits on the intersection of two principal axes and standing in the middle you get four dramatic views. To the west is the Champs-Élysées, leading to the Arc de Triomphe, and to the east you can look past the ornate gates of the Jardin des Tuileries down towards the Louvre. North along the rue Royale is La Madeleine church and to the south, across the Pont de la Concorde, is the colonnaded Palais Bourbon, home to the Assemblée Nationale.

ROYAL DESIGN

The square was designed by Jacques-Ange Gabriel and laid out between 1755 and 1775 to accommodate an equestrian statue of the reigning king, Louis XV. Gabriel designed the two properties flanking the rue Royale—the Hôtel Crillon and the Hôtel de la Marine— in addition to the stone pedestals in each corner of the octagonal square. These are topped with female statues each representing a major French city—Lille, Strasbourg, Lyon, Marseille, Bordeaux, Nantes, Brest and Rouen.

HORRORS OF THE REVOLUTION

The square was originally called place Louis XV but was renamed place de la Révolution during the Revolution. The statue of Louis XV was removed and the guillotine erected in its stead. Between 1793 and 1795 more than 1,300 people were beheaded here, including Louis XVI and his queen, Marie-Antoinette. With the cooling of revolutionary passions in 1795, the square was renamed the place de la Concorde, in the hope of a less troubled future. Soon after, Guillaume I Coustou's magnificent *Chevaux de Marly* (1743–45) were added to the entrance of the Champs-Élysées. The ones you see today are replicas—the originals are now in the Louvre.

EGYPTIAN OBELISK

In 1833 Mohammed Ali, Viceroy of Egypt, presented King Louis-Philippe with a 230-tonne, pink granite obelisk, 23m (75ft) high. It is around 3,300 years old, engraved with hieroglyphics, and was once used to measure the sun's shadow at the Temple of Thebes.

Place de la Madeleine is the place to go for luxury food

Gold statues adorn the Palais de Chaillot, on place du Trocadéro

Shopping in place Vendôme

PLACE DE LA MADELEINE

✚ 67 K5 • place de la Madeleine, 75008 🔲 Madeleine
🚌 24, 42, 52, 84, 94

The colossal church of La Madeleine (open daily 9–7) dominates this square. It is supported by 52 enormous Corinthian pillars and resembles a Greek temple. The triangular pediment bears a sculpted frieze of the Last Judgement. Construction began in 1764, but did not finish until 1842. The church has had a varied career, narrowly avoiding being transformed into a railway station, stock exchange, bank and yet another temple to Napoleon. It is now a popular venue for society weddings and funerals and has seen the coffins of notables such as Frédéric Chopin and Marlene Dietrich.

After you have climbed the steps to the main entrance, turn around to admire the view down the rue Royale to the obelisk in the place de la Concorde (▷ 148), across the river to the Palais Bourbon (▷ 80) and beyond to the golden cupola of Les Invalides (▷ 99–101).
Don't miss Food connoisseurs should visit Fauchon, the exclusive foodstore synonymous with the best of French food. There are plenty of other food shops and restaurants on the square, as well as a small flower market.

PLACE DU TROCADÉRO ET DU 11 NOVEMBRE

✚ 321 F6 • place du Trocadéro et du 11 Novembre, 75016 🔲 Trocadéro
🚌 22, 30, 32, 63

Semicircular place du Trocadéro et du 11 Novembre faces the monumental wings of the Palais de Chaillot (▷ 143), the fountains of the Jardins du Trocadéro and, across the Seine, the Eiffel Tower. Six avenues radiate from it and an equestrian statue of World War I Allied Commander Marshal Foch stands at its heart.

The square was named after an Andalusian fort occupied by the French in 1823 and was given its present shape in 1858, when a first palace was built. This palace was replaced with the Palais de Chaillot, built for the 1937 Universal Exhibition. There are plenty of cafés and restaurants in the area.

PLACE VENDÔME

✚ 67 L5 • place Vendôme, 75001
🔲 Opéra, Tuileries 🚌 21, 27, 29, 68, 72, 81, 95
www.paris.fr

Stately place Vendôme is the supreme symbol of Parisian chic. You'll need a hefty bank balance to venture into its exclusive jewellery stores, and its hotel, the Ritz, is among the most prestigious in the world. Noted residents of the square have included Frédéric Chopin, who died at number 12, and Anton Mesmer, founder of the theory of mesmerism, who held experiments at number 16. Marcel Proust, Ernest Hemingway and Coco Chanel were guests at the Ritz, and Diana, Princess of Wales, dined there before her fateful car journey across Paris in August 1997.

Louis XIV commissioned the classical square in 1685, choosing Versailles architect Jules Hardouin-Mansart, who had impressed him with his design for place des Victoires (see right). The focal point was an equestrian statue of the king, but this fell victim to the mob during the Revolution. In 1810 it was replaced by a 44m (144ft) bronze column, based on Trajan's column in Rome, but this was pulled to the ground during another revolution, the Paris Commune of 1871. It was rebuilt and now supports a Caesar-like statue of Napoleon. The bronze for the column came from canons captured at the Battle of Austerlitz.

The square's turbulent past has caused its name to be changed frequently over the years, with titles including place des Conquêtes, place Louis le Grand, place des Piques and place Internationale.

Keep an eye out for traffic while admiring the square—despite the cobbles, it is not pedestrian-only.

PLACE DES VICTOIRES

✚ 67 M6 • place des Victoires, 75002
🔲 Bourse, Sentier 🚌 29
www.paris.fr

Elegant, circular place des Victoires is tucked quietly at the end of the busy shopping street, rue Étienne Marcel. Its curved mansions house the chic boutiques of Kenzo, Cacharel and other leading fashion names. The square was laid out in 1685 by the architect Jules Hardouin-Mansart, who also worked on Versailles. It was commissioned by the Maréchal de la Feuillade to celebrate the victories of the Sun King, Louis XIV. A statue of the king was destroyed during the Revolution and later replaced by an equestrian sculpture by Bosio.
Don't miss Look down rue Catinat to see the imposing Banque de France.

Napoleon tops the column in place Vendôme

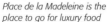

THE SIGHTS

Tranquil place des Vosges (above).
A carving on one of the elegant buildings lining the square (left)

PLACE DES VOSGES

Paris's oldest square is the perfect place to while away a few hours, relaxing in an outdoor café or enjoying the fountains.

Picturesque place des Vosges is steeped in history and only minutes away from the busy, modern Bastille district. It is a great example of the Paris phenomenon where you can be on a traffic-filled road teeming with people one minute, and in a quiet grassy square the next, seemingly miles from 21st-century bustle. Here you can browse in the boutiques, antiques shops and art galleries in the arcades surrounding the square or sip hot chocolate in one of the cafés.

PLACE ROYALE
A royal palace originally stood on this site but was demolished in the 16th century by Catherine de Medici when her husband, Henri II, was killed in a tournament here. Later, Henri IV commissioned the symmetrical place Royale, one of the first examples of town planning in Paris. The square was inaugurated in 1612, amid spectacular celebrations. In 1800, it was renamed place des Vosges in tribute to the first French *département* to pay its new taxes.

SYMMETRY
The square's harmonious form is created by 36 red brick- and stone-faced houses, nine on each side, with arcaded ground floors and steep pitched roofs. These striking buildings surround a formal garden containing fountains, trees, gravel paths, a children's play area, ornate lampposts and a statue of Louis XIII. The north and south façades of the square retain a royal touch, as each has a larger, central house, respectively the Pavillon de la Reine (Queen's pavilion) and the Pavillon du Roi (King's pavilion). The Pavillon de la Reine is now a four-star hotel (▷ 293).

FAMOUS RESIDENTS
Many famous characters have inhabited the square's mansions and apartments. Princesses, duchesses, official mistresses, Cardinal Richelieu, the Duc de Sully, writer Alphonse Daudet and, more recently, the painter Francis Bacon and the architect Richard Rogers have all gazed out at its perfect symmetry. Another French author, Victor Hugo, penned many a manuscript at number six, his home from 1832 to 1848, and now a museum (▷ 106).

RATINGS
Historic interest	●●●○
Photo stops	●●○

BASICS
✚ 68 P7 • place des Vosges, 75004
🚇 Bastille, St-Paul, Chemin Vert
🚌 29, 96

TIPS
● Sunday afternoon is a good time to see the square, as this is when Parisians come for a stroll, to the accompaniment of outdoor musicians.
● To find out more about Paris life during the place des Vosges's heyday, visit the nearby Musée Carnavalet (▷ 114–115).

A winged Pegasus shimmers on top of the Pont Alexandre III

The Pont des Arts, linking the Louvre with the Institut de France

The Pont Neuf, Paris's oldest bridge

PONT ALEXANDRE III

✚ 66 J6 • cours La Reine/quai d'Orsay
Ⓜ Invalides, Champs-Élysées-Clémenceau 🚌 63, 83, 93
Ⓡ RER line C, Invalides

Four gilded bronze Pegasus figures watch over this wildly ornate bridge, which sparkles in the setting sun. The bridge forms a link between Les Invalides (▷ 99–101) on the Left Bank and the Grand Palais and Petit Palais (▷ 95) on the Right, its glory marred only by the stream of traffic.

Symbolic of the optimism of the Belle Époque, it was built for the 1900 *Exposition Universelle* and dedicated to a new alliance between Russia and France. The foundation stone was laid by Tsar Nicholas II, son of Alexander III, and the façade bears the coats of arms of both Paris and Russia. The bridge is crammed with elaborate decoration by more than 15 artists.

PONT DE L'ALMA

✚ 66 H6 • place de l'Alma/place de la Résistance Ⓜ Alma-Marceau
🚌 42, 63, 72, 80, 92 Ⓡ RER line C, Pont de l'Alma

The first Pont de l'Alma was built in 1856 to commemorate a victory over the Russians by the Franco-British alliance in the Crimean War. The bridge developed subsidence and was replaced in 1974. The underpass running along the Seine here is where the fatal car crash involving Diana, Princess of Wales, happened in August 1997. The Liberty Flame, placed near the entrance in 1987 by the *International Herald Tribune* as a symbol of American and French friendship, has become a memorial to the People's Princess.

Don't miss A statue of a Zouave soldier from the original bridge is now a high-water marker.

PONT DES ARTS

✚ 67 L7 • quai du Louvre/quai de Conti Ⓜ Louvre-Rivoli 🚌 24, 27, 39, 69, 72

This is one of Paris's most romantic bridges and is also a popular place for street performances and impromptu parties. Also known as the Passerelle (footbridge) des Arts, it links the Louvre (hence its name) with the Institut de France, and was rebuilt in 1984 with seven steel arches. Napoleon commissioned the original cast-iron bridge, Paris's first. It had nine arches and was completed in 1804.

PONT DE BIR-HAKEIM

✚ 66 F7 • quai Branly
Ⓜ Bir-Hakeim, Passy 🚌 72

The Pont de Bir-Hakeim was built between 1903 and 1905, replacing a 19th-century footbridge. The two-tiered art nouveau bridge has a walkway, roadway and a viaduct for the Métro. It is made up of two unequal metal structures on either side of the allée des Cygnes. Trains rattle across the top level, which is supported by cast-iron pillars. Originally called the Passy Viaduct, the bridge was renamed the Pont de Bir-Hakeim in 1949, in memory of the victory of General Koenig in Libya in 1942.

PONT MARIE

✚ 68 P8 • quai des Célestins/Île St-Louis Ⓜ Pont Marie 🚌 67

This stone bridge, linking the Île St-Louis with the Right Bank, had a controversial beginning. Île St-Louis property developer Christophe Marie first suggested the bridge in 1605, but objections from officials at Notre-Dame delayed completion until 1635. Disaster struck in the spring thaw of 1658. The bridge

was top-heavy with tall houses (all the more *écus* for the developer) and a powerful flood caused two arches, along with the homes, shops and occupants they supported, to topple into the Seine. The bridge was subsequently rebuilt—without any new houses.

PONT NEUF

✚ 67 M7 • Île de la Cité Ⓜ Pont Neuf 🚌 24, 27, 58, 70

Ironically, the New Bridge is actually Paris's oldest surviving bridge, dating from 1604. It was Henri II's idea, in 1556, in order to ease his journey between the Louvre Palace and the abbey of St-Germain-des-Prés. The bridge opened almost half a century later, when the flamboyant Henri IV inaugurated it by galloping across on his charger. His equestrian statue still stands there, although it is a replacement of the original, which was melted down during the Revolution. For years this was the site of a permanent funfair. In 1985, the land-artist Christo ceremoniously wrapped the entire bridge.

PONT ROYAL

✚ 67 L7 • quai des Tuileries/quai Voltaire Ⓜ Palais Royal 🚌 24, 68, 69, 72 Ⓡ RER line C, Musée d'Orsay

The Pont Royal was a gift from Louis XIV, replacing a wooden bridge that had been destroyed by fire. The king chose one of his most prized architects, Jules Hardouin-Mansart, to design the graceful stone structure, and the bridge was in place by 1689. Nobles used it to travel from the exclusive Faubourg St-Germain district to the Tuileries Palace. In the 18th century, the bridge became the site of major Parisian festivities and fireworks. The hydrographic scales on each end pillar show high-water levels.

THE SIGHTS

Quartier Latin

Mingle with students in this historic district, with its Roman ruins, medieval alleyways and abundance of cafés. Other attractions include a medieval museum, a 12th-century church and the soothing Luxembourg Garden.

St. Michael slays a dragon in the bustling square bearing his name

Browsing through the street stalls on the boulevard St-Michel

Enjoying a café-break—a popular pastime in the Latin Quarter

RATINGS

Historic interest	●●●○
Photo stops	●●●○
Shopping	●●○○
Walkability	●●○○

BASICS

✚ 68 N9 • Left Bank between Carrefour de l'Odéon and Jardin des Plantes, 75005

🚇 St-Michel, Cluny La Sorbonne, Odéon, Maubert-Mutualité, Cardinal Lemoine

🚌 21, 24, 27, 38, 63, 84, 85, 86, 87, 89

🚆 RER line B, C, St-Michel-Notre-Dame, Luxembourg

🍴 Selection of restaurants and cafés (▷ 254)

🏬 Clothes stores and bookshops

TIPS

● For a stroll through the Latin Quarter ▷ 228–229.
● You could while away an hour or so browsing in the English-language bookshop Shakespeare and Company (▷ 183). Or head for the Gothic courtyard of the Musée National du Moyen Âge (▷ 128–129) to admire the turrets and gargoyles.

The renowned bookstore Shakespeare and Company (top right)

SEEING THE LATIN QUARTER

The Latin Quarter is an essential part of the Paris experience. Its picturesque narrow side streets take you back to the Middle Ages, while the presence of many students gives the area a refreshing vibrancy. No other district of Paris claims so many bookshops or colleges, and there is also a host of historic churches, cinemas, jazz clubs and restaurants. You'll find a relaxed and youthful atmosphere compared to the frenetic, business-focused Right Bank. Here, the cliché of students and artists lingering for hours in cafés is actually true.

Your first taste of the Latin Quarter is likely to be the chaotic place St-Michel, with its imposing fountain symbolizing St. Michael slaying the dragon. From here there are views of Notre-Dame (▷ 137–141) on the nearby Île de la Cité. The busy boulevard St-Michel (or *Boul Mich* to students) runs from place St-Michel along the length of the district and teems with students, visitors and magazine kiosks. Unless you want to browse in its clothes stores and bookshops, it is best to venture onto the picturesque side streets.

HIGHLIGHTS

WANDERING IN MEDIEVAL STREETS

The area to the east of place St-Michel is a warren of winding, historic alleyways, redolent of the Middle Ages. You'll find small specialist shops in the streets off the *quais* and Greek restaurants in rue de la Huchette and rue de la Harpe. It is worth seeking out the small 12th-century church of St-Julien-le-Pauvre (▷ 162) and the beautiful stained-glass windows of St-Séverin (▷ 162–163). The tranquil square René Viviani, off the quai de Montebello, is home to what is said to be Paris's oldest tree, planted in the early 17th century.

LITERARY LIFE

Farther south, in the area around the Sorbonne, you can plunge into the heart of academia and probably find a café once frequented by Latin Quarter intelligentsia such as Paul Verlaine or Jean-Paul Sartre. This is also where you'll find the Panthéon (▷ 144), final resting place of France's scientific, literary and political heroes.

Crossing the Pont des Arts

RIVE DROITE

✉ • North of the Seine

The Right Bank (Rive Droite) is by far the larger of Paris's two parts and so is harder to define than the southern Left Bank (Rive Gauche). Kings built their palaces here, Baron Haussmann created his wide arteries and every ruler left at least one monument. The area boasts the Musée du Louvre, the outlandish Centre Georges Pompidou and two prestigious opera houses. Cushioning the grandeur are newer, burgeoning districts, including Bercy and La Villette, and spruced up older ones, such as the Marais. The Right Bank also contains the city's banking and business heart. In the far north is the former hilltop village of Montmartre.

RIVE GAUCHE

✉ • South of the Seine

The Seine curves gently round the southern part of the city, known as the Left Bank, which is significantly smaller than the Right Bank. Despite this, many Left Bank residents claim they hardly ever cross the Seine; they have their Roman ruins, galleries, literary cafés and colleges in the Latin Quarter and St-Germain. France's rulers sit in the Palais Bourbon and Palais du Luxembourg, and the 7th arrondissement is packed with stately residential avenues. Many of the landmarks that make up Paris's skyline are here: the Eiffel Tower, Les Invalides and the tall shadow of Tour Montparnasse. The four glass towers of the new national library, the Bibliothèque François Mitterrand, crown a huge redevelopment project in the 13th arrondissement, which is also the starting point for Paris's newest Métro line (14).

GALLO-ROMAN BATHS

On the corner of boulevards St-Michel and St-Germain are the remains of the Gallo-Roman baths. The vast stone chamber that housed the Frigidarium (cold bath) is now part of the Musée National du Moyen Âge (▷ 128–129).

GREEN LUNG

On the Latin Quarter's southern boundary, the flower-filled Jardin du Luxembourg (▷ 102–103) is the perfect place to rest your aching feet after a day exploring the streets.

BACKGROUND

The Latin Quarter owes its scholarly, literary and artistic reputation to the founding of the Sorbonne university in the 13th century (▷ 163) in an area known as the Montagne Ste-Geneviève. An animated crowd of European students soon flocked here, turning the university into a Catholic city-within-a-city. Other colleges grew up around it and the area gained the name Latin Quarter, after the language used by the students for everyday conversation. In the 15th century the introduction of printing presses made the rue St-Jacques France's publishing headquarters. Later, the district acquired a reputation for undisciplined and bohemian inhabitants, making it fertile soil for the Revolution. In May 1968, its rebellious streak re-emerged when students took to the streets (▷ 39).

Sacré-Cœur

●

A gleaming white neo-Byzantine basilica, where you'll get wonderful views over Paris. Its stunning golden mosaic, inside, is one of the largest of its kind and its bell is one of the heaviest in the world.

Panoramic views over Paris (above)

SEEING SACRÉ-CŒUR

The mighty Sacré-Cœur basilica is one of Paris's most prominent landmarks, shimmering at the top of Montmartre's hill. Its eastern-inspired dome is the second-highest point in Paris and the views from the top stretch up to 50km (31 miles). This sweeping panorama is the main attraction for its many visitors, who gather in hordes on the front steps. But walk inside the hushed interior, especially during Mass, and it is an altogether more spiritual experience.

The basilica is not the most accessible place, sitting north of central Paris, without an adjoining Métro station. Take the Métro to Anvers or Abbesses, then walk to square Willette, where a funicular (or flight of steep steps for the energetic) takes you the final way up the hill. Enter the basilica from the front doors on place du Parvis du Sacré-Cœur. If Mass is in progress, you may find your movements restricted, but otherwise you are free to roam. To climb to the dome or visit the crypt, leave the basilica and turn right, to a side door on the west of the building. Tickets for the dome are issued from a machine here.

HIGHLIGHTS

PANORAMA

The views from Sacré-Cœur make the trip out here worthwhile even if you don't want to visit the basilica itself. Try to choose a clear day, when you'll see farther across the city and when the contrast between the glistening white domes of the basilica and the blue sky behind is at its most dramatic. If you are short of time, the view from the front terrace should keep your camera satisfied. Among the landmarks you can see are Notre-Dame, the gold dome of Les Invalides, and Tour Montparnasse. For striking views of the Eiffel Tower, head round the corner into rue Azaïs.

If you have the time (and energy), it is worth climbing the dome. The entrance, shared with the crypt, is on the western side of the basilica, in rue du Cardinal Guibert. A steep spiral staircase leads to the colonnade, where you'll have a vertigo-inducing view down into the basilica, as well as out across Paris. The bronze statue you see just

Sacré-Cœur during a service (left)

TIPS

● Sacré-Cœur is a 10-minute walk from Abbesses or Anvers Métro stations. Or you could take the Montmartrobus to the base of the funicular.
● The funicular costs one Métro ticket each way—you'll probably consider it worthwhile when you see how many steps lead up to the basilica!
● Try to visit just before a service takes place (times are posted on the website). The basilica can seem rather sombre otherwise.

If you don't use the funicular, it's a long climb up to the basilica (below)

• Sacré-Cœur's hilltop location makes its bell tower and dome the second-highest points in Paris, after the Eiffel Tower. The bell tower is 84m (275.5ft) tall, 67cm (26in) higher than the dome.

• The basilica was originally designed by Paul Abadie, a pupil of Viollet-le-Duc, although six more architects were called in over the 39-year building project.

• The unstable ground under the basilica meant that pillars had to be sunk 33m (108ft) into the ground.

• The Savoyarde bell plays a C, while the four smaller bells—Félicité, Louise, Elisabeth and Nicole—play C, D, G and E.

in front of the colonnade shows St. Michael killing a demon. Behind the dome stands the main bell tower, which houses one of the world's largest bells, the 19-tonne La Savoyarde.

The basilica itself is best viewed from below, in place St-Pierre, where the turrets and towers rise up majestically into the sky, seeming to bridge the gap between earth and heaven. To find some more unusual views, wander around the back of the basilica (▷ 226–227).

MOSAIC

Inside the basilica, the vast golden mosaic that hovers over the choir is a striking focal point. It is one of the largest of its kind, covering 475sq m (5,145sq ft), and was created by Olivier Merson between 1900 and 1922. Christ stands in the middle, with outstretched arms and a golden heart. Immediately surrounding him, the Virgin Mary, Joan of Arc, St. Michael, the Pope and a figure representing France look up in reverence.

Farther to the left, the characters in the lower row represent the earthly church, while above you can see members of the heavenly church, including St. Peter and St. Paul. To the right, the lower row portrays the builders of Sacré-Cœur, while above them are French saints, including St. Louis and St. Geneviève. God the Father and the Holy Spirit are represented on the ceiling, and the Latin inscription below the mosaic reads 'To the most holy Heart of Jesus, France, fervent, penitent and grateful'.

SCULPTURES

Joan of Arc and St. Louis guard the entrance to the basilica, on horseback in sculpted bronze. A stone statue of Christ stands high above them, in an arched recess. Gospel stories are portrayed on the bronze doors. Inside, look for the statue of *Our Lady of Peace*, in the Virgin Chapel, by Georges Serraz. Other sculptures include a silver statue of Christ, *Le Sacré-Coeur*, by Eugène Benet, and a silver *Virgin and Child* by Paul Brunet. Further statues can be seen in the crypt, including archbishop Cardinal Guibert, who approved the building of the basilica in 1872, and a *Pietà* by Jules Coutan.

BACKGROUND

Sacré-Cœur was commissioned as atonement for the deaths of 58,000 people during the Franco-Prussian war of 1870–71 and the bloody events of the Commune (▷ 37). Money was donated from across France and the first stone was laid in 1875. Various problems hampered the building work, including unstable ground on a hill full of gypsum quarries, and the basilica was not ready until 1914. Then World War I intervened, and Parisians had to wait until 1919 for the consecration. The stained-glass windows were destroyed by bombs in 1944. Despite its setbacks—and the constant stream of visitors—the basilica has not lost its focus as a place of worship. More than 130 years after the vow to build Sacré-Cœur, priests still work in relays to maintain constant prayer for forgiveness for the horrors of war.

BASICS
✚ 69 M2 • place du Parvis du Sacré-Cœur
☎ 01 53 41 89 00
🕐 Basilica: daily 6am–10.30pm. Dome and crypt: daily 9–5.45 (also 5.30–7 in summer)
💶 Basilica: free. Dome: adult/child €5
Ⓜ Anvers/Abbesses, then walk to funicular
🚌 Montmartrobus
💶 €5 (in French, English, German, Spanish and Italian)
🍴 Cafés and restaurants in Montmartre (▷ 254)
📖 Small bookshop/giftshop
❓ There is a lift at 35 rue du Chevalier de la Barre to help people with disabilities gain access to the basilica

www.sacre-coeur-montmartre.com
In French, with some pages in English; find out more about the history and life of the basilica

The basilica looks most striking when viewed from below

Sainte-Chapelle

Stunning stained-glass windows turn this 13th-century royal chapel into a shimmering jewel, hidden within the Palais de Justice complex. It was here that St. Louis brought his holy relics in the 13th century.

SEEING SAINTE-CHAPELLE

It's not quite heaven, but the celestial rays of blue, red and golden light streaming through the windows of Sainte-Chapelle certainly seem out of this world. The only downside is the crowds, which, as with Rome's Sistine Chapel, can detract from what should be an awe-inspiring experience.

You reach the chapel through a shared entrance with the Palais de Justice, on the boulevard du Palais, where your bags will be screened. From here, walk round to the main entrance of the chapel. The wait for tickets can be long, but you can avoid this if you have a *Paris Museum Pass* (▷ 307) or a joint ticket with the Conciergerie (▷ 89–91). The entrance leads you first into the lower chapel, where there is a small giftshop. A steep spiral staircase takes you to the upper chapel.

HIGHLIGHTS

THE WINDOWS

When you step into the upper chapel you are immediately hit by colour coming at you from all directions, not only from the glorious windows but also from the patterned floor, the golden columns and the painted lower walls. Fifteen windows, up to 15m (49ft) tall, and a glorious rose window depict more than 1,100 biblical scenes, from the Creation to the Apocalypse. Two-thirds of the windows are 13th-century originals, the oldest stained glass in Paris. The panels tell key biblical stories, starting with Genesis in the window on the left as you enter and working clockwise round the chapel to the Apocalypse in the rose window. The only non-biblical theme is in the final window, which tells how the holy relics came to Paris.

CARVINGS

Although the windows are undoubtedly the highlight of the upper chapel, take time to notice other features, such as the incredible detail of the sculpted golden foliage on the column capitals (including oak leaves, holly, thistle and hops) and the statues of the apostles, which appear to be supporting the pillars (an allusion to their role as pillars of the Christian faith). Some are 19th-century copies—the originals are in the Musée National du Moyen Âge (▷ 128–129).

RATINGS

Cultural interest	● ● ●
Historic interest	● ● ● ●

BASICS

✚ 67 M7 • 4 boulevard du Palais, Île de la Cité, 75001

☎ 01 53 40 60 97

🕔 Mar–end Oct daily 9.30–6 (last entry 5.30); rest of year daily 9–5. Closed 1 Jan, 1 May, 25 Dec

💶 Adult €6.50, under 18 free. Joint ticket with Conciergerie €9.50

🚇 Cité, Châtelet

🚌 21, 24, 27, 38, 85, 96

🚆 RER line B, C, St-Michel-Notre-Dame

📷 Guided tours by appointment only; tel 01 53 40 60 93

📖 €7

🎁 Small gift shop in lower chapel

🏠 Off the Cour de la Sainte-Chapelle, in the Palais de Justice complex

www.monuments-nationaux.fr
In French and English

Louis IX demanded a grand setting to display his holy relics— he certainly got that with the glorious Sainte-Chapelle (left)

- The upper chapel can become extremely crowded. The quietest times to visit are Tuesday to Friday morning.
- You can buy a joint ticket for the Conciergerie (▷ 89–91) and Sainte-Chapelle. Buy this at the Conciergerie, where the queues are often shorter.
- To help decipher the windows in the upper chapel, pick up an information card from the stand by the exit.
- Try to visit when the sun is shining, to experience the windows at their iridescent best. Sunset is the best time to see the rose window, although the chapel is likely to be crowded then.
- If you have binoculars, bring them with you to help you see the higher windows.
- For details of the candlelit concerts held in the chapel ask the ticket office or tourist information office.

THE LOWER CHAPEL

Before reaching the brilliance of the upper chapel, you walk through the dark lower chapel, originally used by palace staff and dedicated to the Virgin Mary. Its blue, red and gold ceiling is decorated with fleurs-de-lys, symbol of the French monarchy, while some of the pillars bear Castilian towers, from the coat of arms of Louis IX's mother. The paintwork dates from the mid-19th century, when attempts were made to reproduce the medieval style. This followed damage caused during the Revolution, when the chapel was used as a flour warehouse.

BACKGROUND

Sainte-Chapelle was commissioned by Louis IX (St. Louis) in the 13th century to house holy relics and to promote the king's authority as a divinely appointed leader. It was constructed in the royal palace complex (now the Palais de Justice) in less than six years. The architect is not known for certain, although it was possibly Pierre de Montreuil, who also worked on Notre-Dame. He made clever use of discreet pillars to support the 670sq m (7,169sq ft) of stained glass without the need for walls. The relics were displayed on a wooden-canopied platform that you can still see today in front of the altar. They included what was reputed to be the Crown of Thorns, pieces of the Cross and drops of Christ's blood. Louis IX was so eager to take possession of these objects that he paid the Emperor of Constantinople 135,000 *livres* for the Crown of Thorns alone—more than three times the building costs of the chapel. The Crown of Thorns is now kept in Notre-Dame's Treasury. The other relics, along with the silver- and copper-plated reliquary in which they sat, were melted down during the Revolution.

After the Revolution the chapel was used as an archive for court documents. It was restored in the mid-19th century, when its fifth (and current) spire was constructed, rising 75m (245ft) above the ground.

UPPER CHAPEL FLOORPLAN

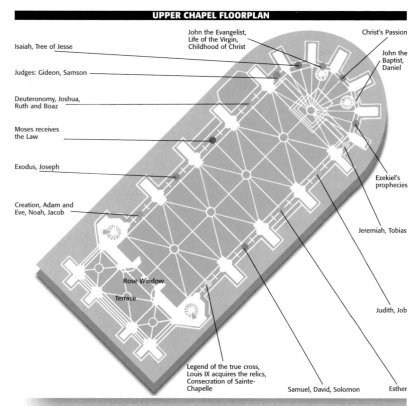

Isaiah, Tree of Jesse

John the Evangelist, Life of the Virgin, Childhood of Christ

Christ's Passion

John the Baptist, Daniel

Judges: Gideon, Samson

Deuteronomy, Joshua, Ruth and Boaz

Moses receives the Law

Exodus, Joseph

Ezekiel's prophecies

Creation, Adam and Eve, Noah, Jacob

Jeremiah, Tobias

Rose Window

Terrace

Judith, Job

Legend of the true cross, Louis IX acquires the relics, Consecration of Sainte-Chapelle

Samuel, David, Solomon

Esther

Henri de Miller's curious sculpture L'Écoute, *outside St-Eustache*

ST-ÉTIENNE-DU-MONT

✚ 68 N9 • place Ste-Geneviève, 75005 ☎ 01 43 54 11 79 🕒 Mon 2.30–7, Tue–Sat 8.45–7.30, Sun 8.45–12, 2.30–7.30 🎟 Free 🚇 Cardinal Lemoine 🚌 84, 89

As you approach St-Étienne-du-Mont from place du Panthéon the church seems dwarfed by its mighty companion. But the closer you get, the more it steals your attention with its intricately carved façade and delicate bell tower.

Work started in 1492, replacing a smaller chapel that was part of the abbey of Ste-Geneviève. It continued until 1626, which explains the bizarre architectural mix of Gothic, Renaissance and Classical. Paris's archbishop was assassinated in the church in 1857. **Don't miss** The delicately fretted rood screen is a highlight.

ST-EUSTACHE

✚ 67 M6 • 2 impasse St-Eustache, 75001 ☎ 01 42 36 31 05 🕒 Mon–Fri 9.30–7, Sat 10–7, Sun 9–7.15 🎟 Free 🚇 Les Halles 🚌 29, 67, 74, 85 🚆 RER lines A, B, D, Châtelet-Les-Halles www.st-eustache.org

Paris's second-largest church stands in the busy Les Halles district (▷ 95), next to the incongruously modern Forum des Halles. The Gothic structure is second in size only to Notre-Dame, on which it is based. Building work started in 1532 and continued for more than 100 years. Since then, the church has played a prominent role, hosting Louis XIV's first communion, Cardinal Richelieu's baptism and the premières of Liszt's *Grand Mass* and Berlioz's *Te Deum*.

The church's musical reputation continues today, with regular concerts, including organ recitals on Sundays from 5.30pm to 6pm.

ST-GERMAIN-DES-PRÉS

A charming district with narrow lanes, chic boutiques, the oldest church in Paris and an abundance of cafés, restaurants, antiques shops and art galleries.

✚ 67 L7 • 75006 🚇 St-Germain-des-Prés, Odéon, St-Sulpice, Mabillon 🚌 39, 63, 70, 86, 87, 95, 96

RATINGS	
Historic interest	● ● ● ○
Shopping	● ● ● ○

St-Germain-des-Prés, in the heart of the Left Bank, is eternally magnetic to visitors and residents alike, with a more leisurely pace than on the other side of the river. At its core is the Église St-Germain-des-Prés (▷ 162), the oldest church in Paris, dating from the 11th century. Its picturesque bell tower is symbolic of the area. Nearby, in the tranquil rue de Furstemberg, is the Musée National Eugène Delacroix (▷ 126).

The pulse of the district is along the boulevard St-Germain, running west from the Latin Quarter to join the government buildings and bourgeois mansions of the 7th *arrondissement*. Lively cafés on this boulevard—the rendezvous of the literary élite—include the illustrious Café de Flore—once frequented by Jean-Paul Sartre—Brasserie Lipp and Café Les Deux Magots, a former haunt of Ernest Hemingway.

South of the boulevard, the streets widen and the atmosphere changes. From the church of St-Sulpice (▷ 163) to the pretty Jardin du Luxembourg (▷ 102–103), through the shopping streets of rue Bonaparte, rue de Sèvres and rue de Grenelle, this is the St-Germain of fashion boutiques and publishing houses. Trendy bars replace crowded cafés, and furniture shops line the boulevard Raspail leading to the crossroads of Sèvres-Babylone, home of Paris's first department store, Le Bon Marché. North of the boulevard, towards the Seine, remains an arty area, packed with small cinemas, art galleries, antiques shops, the École Nationale Supérieure des Beaux-Arts and the Hôtel de la Monnaie (▷ 117). **Don't miss** The green stalls of *les bouquinistes* (the booksellers) line the banks of the Seine.

Enjoying a drink at Les Deux Magots, in front of the church of St-Germain-des-Prés

The church of St-Germain-l'Auxerrois, near the Louvre

St-Julien-le-Pauvre is one of the oldest churches in Paris…

…but not quite as old as St-Germain-des-Prés

ST-GERMAIN-L'AUXERROIS

🚇 67 M7 • place du Louvre, 75001 ☎ 01 42 60 13 96 🕐 Daily 8–5. No visits during services (Mass: Mon–Sat 8.20, 12.15, 6.30; Sun 10, 11.15, 5.30, 9.15) 🎫 Free 🚇 Louvre-Rivoli, Pont Neuf 🚌 21, 67, 69, 74, 85

Kings from the nearby Louvre palace used St-Germain-l'Auxerrois as their parish church until the Revolution and you can still see the royal pew, near the pulpit. Other highlights include the beautiful stained-glass windows, the carved choir screen and the 18th-century organ, moved from Sainte-Chapelle in 1791. The site's religious connections date back to AD500, when an oratory was built here. In later years it was used to hastily baptize children whose lives were in danger from floods. The current church was built between the 13th and 16th centuries but lost its religious role during the Revolution and became, for a time, a police station, town hall, barn and printers' workshop. Viollet-le-Duc restored the building in the 19th century.

The church's bell (1529) notoriously signalled the onset of the bloody St. Bartholomew's Day Massacre in 1572 (▷ 29). **Don't miss** The church is a pleasant place for a stop after a visit to the Louvre. You can sit on benches on the grassy area outside and admire the Louvre's façade.

ST-GERMAIN-DES-PRÉS (ÉGLISE)

🚇 67 L8 • 3 place St-Germain-des-Prés, 75006 ☎ 01 55 42 81 33 🕐 Daily 9–7 🎫 Free 🚇 St-Germain-des-Prés 🚌 39, 63, 86, 95 www.eglise-sgp.org

The Église St-Germain-des-Prés is the oldest church in Paris and lies at the heart of the district that bears its name (▷ 161). The Merovingian king Childebert I founded an abbey here in the sixth century. The current church was consecrated by Pope Alexander III in 1163, although its bell tower dates from the previous century. The mix of Romanesque and Gothic styles is the result of many additions over the years. The structure was badly damaged during the Revolution and only one of the three original towers remains. The massive 12th-century flying buttresses are still intact. During the 19th century, the church underwent various restorations, and the murals in the nave and choir, by Flandrin, date from this period.
Don't miss The tomb of the philosopher René Descartes (1596–1650) lies in the St-Benoît side chapel.

ST-JULIEN-LE-PAUVRE

🚇 67 M8 • 79 rue Galande, 75005 ☎ 01 43 54 52 16 (for concert information call 01 42 28 43 85) 🕐 Daily 9.30–1, 3–8 🎫 Free 🚇 St-Michel 🚌 24, 47 🚊 RER lines B, C, St-Michel-Notre-Dame

This small church, one of the oldest in Paris, is tucked away in a quiet corner of the Latin Quarter, near the tranquil square René Viviani (▷ 152). It dates from the 12th century and is said to stand on the site of a Merovingian burial ground. In the late Middle Ages the church had strong ties with the nearby university and elections for the rectors took place within its walls. During the Revolution it became a salt store, then in 1889 it was given to the Melkite Church (Greek-Catholic).

Inside the low-ceilinged building are various religious paintings and sculptures, although subdued lighting makes it hard to appreciate them fully. There is also an iconostasis (an Orthodox rood screen where icons hang) dating from around 1900. The church hosts classical music concerts.

ST-MERRI

🚇 68 N7 • 78 rue St-Martin, 75004 ☎ For concert information: 01 42 71 40 75 🕐 Daily 3–7 🎫 Free 🚇 Hôtel de Ville 🚌 38, 47 🚊 RER lines A, B, D, Châtelet-Les-Halles

St-Merri, a short walk from the Centre Georges Pompidou, is named after the Right Bank's patron saint. The 16th-century church is a superb example of Flamboyant Gothic. It contains Paris's oldest bell, made in 1331 and a remnant from the medieval chapel that once stood on the site. Inside, the stained-glass windows feature Joseph in Egypt, St. Nicholas of Myre, St. Agnès and the Paris merchant Étienne Marcel.

The *Carnaval des Animaux* composer Camille Saint-Saëns was organist here in the 1850s. Today, you can enjoy free concerts on Saturdays at 9pm and Sundays at 4pm.
Don't miss The ornate pulpit was carved in 1753 by the sculptor P. A. Slodtz, one of two brothers who worked on the church in the 18th century.

ST-SÉVERIN

🚇 67 M8 • 1 rue des Prêtres St-Séverin, 75005 ☎ 01 42 34 93 50 🕐 Mon–Sat 11–7, Sun 9–8.30 🎫 Free 🚇 St-Michel 🚌 21, 24, 27, 38, 47, 85 🚊 RER lines B, C, St-Michel-Notre-Dame ❓ There is a ramp for wheelchair users at the back of the church, off rue St-Jacques www.saint-severin.com

This beautiful church, in the Latin Quarter, would probably attract more visitors were it not for the grander Notre-Dame a

Gargoyles decorate the church of St-Séverin

The fountain in place St-Sulpice

S for Sorbonne

THE SIGHTS

few minutes' walk across the river (▷ 137). As it is, the Gothic St-Séverin remains a well-kept secret, but its beautiful stained glass makes it worth seeking out.

The church dates from the 13th century, although a fire led to much of it being rebuilt in the 15th century. Highlights include the Chapelle du St-Esprit, the double ambulatory and the palm-tree vaulting. The church originally took its name from a sixth-century hermit called Séverin the Solitary, although its allegiance later changed to a fifth-century Swiss abbot of the same name, whose statue now stands outside.

Ask at the church office for the information leaflet (in English), which gives a plan of the building and details about its key features.
Don't miss Among the historic panes of stained glass it is refreshing to see some contemporary designs, installed in 1970, at the top end of the church. The vibrant windows, designed by Jean Bazaine, represent the Seven Sacraments.

ST-SULPICE

✚ 67 L8 • place St-Sulpice, 75006
☎ 01 46 33 21 78 ⏰ Daily 7.30–7.30
🎟 Free 🚇 St-Sulpice 🚌 58, 63, 70, 86, 87, 95, 96

St-Sulpice is a masterpiece of classical architecture. It took six architects and 134 years to build the enormous church, 119m (390ft) long and 57m (187ft) wide. Work finished in 1780. The imposing façade is flanked by two asymmetrical towers; the south tower, still unfinished, is 5m (16ft) shorter than the north. One of the architects who worked on the towers was Jean-François Chalgrin.

St-Sulpice is home to one of the world's largest church organs, but has many other treasures, including 17th-century stained-glass windows, paintings by Carle Van Loo and carvings and statues by sculptors Edme Bouchardon, Jean-Baptiste Pigalle, the Slodtz brothers and Louis-Simon Boizot.

The opulently carved and gilded pulpit was designed in 1788 by Charles de Wailly. Paintings by 17 renowned artists were commissioned to hang in the transept and the chapels in the 19th century.

Look out for the astronomical gnomon (sundial) in the form of a bronze meridian line stretching from the south to the north transept. At noon on the winter solstice the image of the sun is reflected onto a white marble obelisk while at noon on the summer solstice the light falls onto a marble plaque in the south transept—a fine testament to France's 19th-century scientific spirit.
Don't miss Murals by Eugène Delacroix are in the Chapelle des Anges, the first chapel on the right.

LA SORBONNE

✚ 67 M8 • 42 rue des Écoles, 75005
☎ 01 40 46 22 11 ⏰ Closed to the public (guided tours are available for groups but you must telephone in advance for a reservation: 01 40 46 23 49) 🚇 Cluny La Sorbonne 🚌 21, 27, 38, 63, 85, 86, 87 🚇 RER B, C, Cluny La Sorbonne
www.Sorbonne.fr

La Sorbonne is the symbol of France's great spirit of learning. The university dates from the 13th century, when Robert de Sorbon, chaplain to St. Louis, set up a college to house poorer theology students. For centuries the university maintained an independent attitude to the state,

recognizing the English Henry V as King of France, condemning Joan of Arc and fiercely opposing the 18th-century philosophers. This continued into the 20th century, with the student revolt of 1968 (▷ 39).

Cardinal Richelieu was responsible for rebuilding the dilapidated college in the 17th century, although Lemercier's domed chapel, where the Cardinal now lies, is all that remains. Today's amphitheatres and endless corridors date from the 19th century.

The premises are now used by four separate universities—Paris Sorbonne, Sorbonne Nouvelle, Panthéon-Sorbonne and René Descartes.

Occasional exhibitions are held in the Chapelle de la Sorbonne and you can catch something of the college atmosphere in the student-filled place de la Sorbonne.
Don't miss Although the university is closed to the general public, you can sneak a glimpse of the imposing courtyard off the rue de la Sorbonne.

SYNAGOGUE

✚ 68 P7 • 10 rue Pavée, 75004
☎ 01 48 87 21 54 ⏰ Visits by request only. Telephone Sun–Thu between 10 and 4 🎟 Free 🚇 St-Paul 🚌 69, 76, 96

The synagogue lies in the heart of the Marais district's Jewish quarter (▷ 107). It was built in 1913 to designs by architect Hector Guimard, best remembered for his fanlighted Métro entrances. Guimard was one of the leading lights in the French art nouveau movement and was prolific between 1895 and 1910. He continued to work until 1930 but, distressed by the rise of Fascism, he emigrated with his Jewish wife to the United States, where he died in 1942.

ST-GERMAIN-L'AUXERROIS–SYNAGOGUE 163

Tour Eiffel

**The Eiffel Tower is the symbol of Paris and one of the world's
most famous monuments.
From the top, there are breathtaking views across the city and beyond.**

*Across the Champ de Mars to
the Tour Montparnasse*

*The Eiffel Tower looks
stunning at night*

It's a long way up!

RATINGS	
Good for kids	●●●
Historic interest	●●●
Photo stops	●●●●●

TIPS

● To skip the wait for the lifts,
walk up the stairs to
level one, then catch the
lift to level two. The climb isn't
too daunting.
● The wait for the lift is
generally shorter at night.
● Pushchairs are allowed up
the tower only if they are
collapsible.
● If you want to dine at the
elegant Jules Verne restaurant
book well ahead.

SEEING LA TOUR EIFFEL

Whether you see it as a 'hollow candlestick' or an elegant
emblem of Paris, you can't ignore the Eiffel Tower. Its sleek iron
silhouette, rising up 324m (1,063ft), finds its way into many of
the city's best views.

Around six million people visit the Iron Lady each year, so be
prepared for a long wait (and the indefatigable attentions
of trinket salesmen). Before you buy a ticket, you'll need to
decide whether you want to go as far as level one (57m/187ft),
level two (120m/394ft) or level three (280m/918ft), and
whether you'll take the elevator or brave the stairs (to levels one
and two only). The price will vary accordingly. The stairs are at
the south pillar. The two-level elevators, with room for 80 people,
are in the north, west and east pillars, although only one or two
are operational at any one time. These take you as far as levels
one and two, then you face another wait for a second, smaller
elevator that takes you on the three-minute journey to level
three. The plush Jules Verne restaurant, on level two, has a
separate elevator at the south pillar.

HIGHLIGHTS

THE VIEW

The view is the reason you climb the Eiffel Tower, whether it's for the
magnificent sweep across the city or to test your nerves peering down
120m (394ft) through the glass window on the floor of level two. The
tower was the world's tallest building for 40 years, and from the
gallery on level three you can see up to 75km (46 miles) on a clear
day. If you can't face the vertigo-inducing top level, the views are just
as impressive on level two, where you can see the city in more detail.
There is also a viewing gallery on level one, with information boards.
Sights to look out for include the Arc de Triomphe (north), the
elegantly colonnaded wings of the Palais de Chaillot (northwest),
the gardens of the Champ de Mars (southeast), with the Tour
Montparnasse farther back, and the golden dome of Les Invalides
(east). The views are often at their best in the run up to sunset, when
the light is kinder to cameras. At night a totally different picture
unfolds, as hundreds of thousands of lights sketch out the city.

*A few of the 18,000 metal
sections and 2.5 million rivets
holding together the tower (right)*

There are great views of the Eiffel Tower from the Palais de Chaillot and the place du Trocadéro, across the Seine

THE LIGHTS

Make sure you catch a glimpse of the tower at night, even if you want to reserve your actual visit for daylight. A staggering 10,000 light bulbs contribute to the glittering spectacle. More than 350 spotlights illuminate the latticework, topped by a rotating beacon that can be seen up to 80km (50 miles) away. One of the best ways to appreciate the shimmering display is on a boat trip (▷ 234–235), when the tower takes you by surprise as you turn the corner at the Pont de l'Alma. On foot, the views from the Palais de Chaillot (▷ 143) are memorable.

The tower was originally lit by gas, before electricity was introduced in time for the Universal Exhibition in 1900. In 1925, car manufacturer André Citroën bankrolled a dramatic display of lights advertising his company. The current 350,000-watt system was inaugurated on New Year's Eve 1985. It replaced an unpopular system that beamed light onto the tower from more than 1,000 spotlights on the Champ de Mars, dazzling visitors inside. The rotating beacon was added in 1999. Special displays were staged for the centenary of the tower in 1989 and for the countdown to 2000. Now, for ten minutes every hour from nightfall to 2am, 20,000 extra bulbs add a magical shimmer to the golden lighting of the tower.

THE ANTICS

The Eiffel Tower has inspired more than its fair share of eccentric behaviour. In 1912 a would-be Icarus plunged to his death when his cape failed to act as wings as he had hoped. In 1928 a watchmaker tried out an innovative new design for a parachute but, once again, it failed to open and he rapidly met his maker. A bicyclist who pedalled down the steps to win a bet in 1923 was more successful, although he was arrested when he reached the bottom. Mountaineers have scaled the tower, pilots have tried to fly through its pillars and in 1909

the Comte de Lambert circled 100m (328ft) above it in a flying machine. More recently, in 1984 a British couple survived an unofficial parachute jump from level three and in 1989 Philippe Petit walked a tightrope strung up between the tower and the Palais de Chaillot.

Humans are not the only ones involved in antics at the tower. While animals are usually banned, in 1948 a circus elephant was allowed to walk up the stairs!

OTHER ATTRACTIONS
On level three, a panoramic photo helps you to identify monuments on the skyline. You can also discover the distance from the tower of various capital cities (none of them within sight!). Once you have soaked up the view, you can learn more about the history of the tower from the short film shown at Cineiffel (level one). Other attractions on the first floor include the Observatory, where you can monitor the tower's sway, and the Feroscope, focusing on all things iron. You can also see the original hydraulic elevator pump and a piece of the original spiral staircase, as used by Monsieur Eiffel himself. If you want to boast of your whereabouts to your friends back home, you can have your postcards franked with *Tour Eiffel* at the post office (open 10–7).

BACKGROUND

CONTROVERSIAL BEGINNINGS
Slammed as a 'hollow chandelier' and 'tower of Babel' when it was built in 1889, the Eiffel Tower went on to become the emblem of Paris. Gustave Eiffel took only two years to complete the unconventional monument, finishing just in time for the 1889 Universal Exhibition. At the peak of the construction work, the tower grew 30m (98ft) a month. Despite this breakneck

➕ 66 G7 • quai Branly, Champ de
Mars, 75007

☎ 01 44 11 23 23

🕐 Mid-Jun to end Aug daily 9am–
midnight; rest of year daily 9.30am–
11pm (stairs close at 6.30); last entry
30 min before closing

🛗 By elevator: Adult/child over 12
€4.50 (level one), €7.80 (level two),
€11.50 (level three); child (3-11) €2.30
(level one), €4.30 (level two), €6.30
(level three). By stairs: Over 25 €4,
under 25 €3.10, under 3 free.

🚇 Bir-Hakeim

🚌 42, 69, 72, 82, 87

🚆 RER line C, Champ de Mars–Tour Eiffel

🍽 Altitude 95 on level one, Jules Verne
on level two

🍴 Snack bars on ground floor, level
one and level two

📻 Centre des Monuments Nationaux
leads occasional guided tours (tel 01 44
54 19 33)

📖 In a variety of languages

🎁 Gift shops on levels one and two.
Post office on level one

🚻

❓ Wheelchair access to first and
second levels only. Classical music
concerts are organized by the
Association Musique et Patrimoine
(tel 01 42 50 96 18)
www.ampconcerts.com

www.tour-eiffel.fr (in French and English)

LEVEL ONE
Cineiffel, Observatory, Feroscope,
gift shop, post office, viewing
gallery, Altitude 95 restaurant,
snack bar, hydraulic elevator
pump, part of the original
spiral staircase.

LEVEL TWO
Jules Verne restaurant, glass-floor
viewing window, gift shops,
viewing gallery, snack bar.

LEVEL THREE
Viewing gallery, panoramic
photo, reconstruction of Gustave
Eiffel's office.

*The north pillar of the tower
(above right)*

*Looking across the fountain-filled
Jardins du Trocadéro to the Eiffel
Tower (left)*

operation, when the opening day came, Gustave Eiffel and a
gaggle of officials still had to walk up the 1,665 steps to the top
because the elevators weren't working. The tower is a feat of
engineering, weighing more than 10,000 tonnes and made up of
18,000 iron parts. No one knew then that it would become the
symbol of Paris—it was due to be demolished after 20 years. By
the time its allotted two decades were up it had as many fans as
opponents. It was eventually saved simply for its broadcasting
antennae. Its growing popularity vindicated the opinions of
literary and artistic allies such as Guillaume Apollinaire, Raoul
Dufy, Maurice Utrillo and Camille Pissarro. The objections of Paul
Verlaine, Émile Zola and Guy de Maupassant were relegated to
history. For 40 years the tower basked in the glory of being the
highest structure in the world until New York's Chrysler Building
usurped the title. It gained another 20m (66ft) in 1957 when
television antennae were added. Famous visitors have included
Thomas Edison, King George VI and his wife Queen Elizabeth
(later to become the Queen Mother), and the Shah of Persia.

TOWERING FIGURE
Gustave Eiffel beat more than 100 other entrants in the
competition to design a focal point, 300m (984ft) high, for the
1889 Universal Exhibition. The resulting tower is the ultimate
symbol of his skill and imagination, but the 'magician of iron' has
left hundreds of other constructions all over the world. Born in
1832 in Burgundy, he was already working on Bordeaux bridge
at the age of 26. Bridges soon became his area of expertise: Iron
and the hydraulic methods he used for installing their supports
helped to build his reputation. Factories, churches, a synagogue
(rue des Tournelles), shops (Le Bon Marché), banks and, over a
period of 18 years, 31 railway viaducts and 17 major bridges all
came within his creative sphere. Egypt, Peru, Portugal, Hungary
and Bolivia all have their Eiffel monuments. He even designed
the frame for New York's Statue of Liberty. Eiffel kept an office
in his most famous tower until his death. You can see a
reconstruction of the room, complete with waxwork figures,
on level 3. A bust of the engineer, by Bourdelle, stands near
the north pillar. He died in 1923, at the age of 91.

THE SIGHTS

Viewing the Eiffel Tower from the 59th-floor terrace (above). The Tour Montparnasse from below (left)

RATINGS

Photo stops ● ● ● ○

BASICS

✠ 67 K9 • 33 avenue du Maine, 75015
☎ 01 45 38 52 56
🕐 Apr–end Sep daily 9.30am–11.30pm; rest of year Sun–Thu 9.30am–10.30pm, Fri, Sat 9.30am–11pm; last elevator up 30 min before closing
🎫 Adult €9.50, child (5–14) €4
Ⓜ Montparnasse-Bienvenüe
🚌 28, 82, 89, 92, 94, 95, 96
🚉 Gare Montparnasse
📖 €2.50
🍴 Bar on the 56th floor
📷
🚻

www.tourmontparnasse56.com
In English, French and German, with practical and historical information

TIPS

● The 59th-floor open-air terrace is closed on very windy days.
● If you're short on time, don't stop to watch the film—enjoy the amazing views instead.
● The guidebook has photographs of different viewpoints. Major landmarks are identified, with a short accompanying description.

TOUR MONTPARNASSE

An enormous tower with panoramic views across Paris and beyond.

The Tour Montparnasse dominates the Paris skyline, rising 209m (685ft) over the Montparnasse district. For awe-inspiring views of the city let the ear-popping lift whizz you up to the enclosed, air-conditioned viewing gallery on the 56th floor, in just 38 seconds. From here you can spot many of Paris's major attractions, including the Eiffel Tower, Les Invalides, the Arc de Triomphe, Sacré-Cœur, the Louvre, Musée d'Orsay, Centre Georges Pompidou, St-Germain-des-Prés, Église St-Sulpice, Notre-Dame and the Panthéon. A mini-cinema projects a 20-minute film by Albert Lamorisse showing aerial views of Paris. There are also temporary exhibitions and displays. Farther up, the 59th floor is the highest open-air terrace in Paris—and not for the faint-hearted. You can see up to 40km (25 miles) on a clear day.

OFFICE BLOCK

The tower has 58 floors, each covering an area of almost 2,000sq m (21,528sq ft). There is also a 59th-floor terrace. Offices occupy 52 floors, with a workforce of around 5,000 people. Only two floors are open to the public—the 56th floor and the 59th-floor terrace. The tower is 62m (203ft) long, 32m (105ft) wide and weighs 120,000 tonnes. Its foundations reach a depth of 70m (230ft). It has a concrete core with a steel structure. The façades are predominantly glass, aluminium and bronze.

AN EYESORE?

The Tour Montparnasse was built between 1969 and 1973, as part of a huge urban development project to modernize Montparnasse. It was designed by architects Beaudouin, Cassan, De Marien and Saubot and stands on the site of the old railway station—the Métro runs directly underneath it. The tower has always been highly controversial. President Georges Pompidou, who authorized its construction, took a helicopter tour to observe the completed job and is reported to have said to his urban planners, 'That's enough, we stop right there'. It is still considered an eyesore by many Parisians, and remains one of the capital's least-liked buildings, despite the spectacular views it offers.

This chapter gives information on things to do in Paris other than sightseeing.
Shops and entertainment venues are located on the maps at the beginning of each section.

What to Do

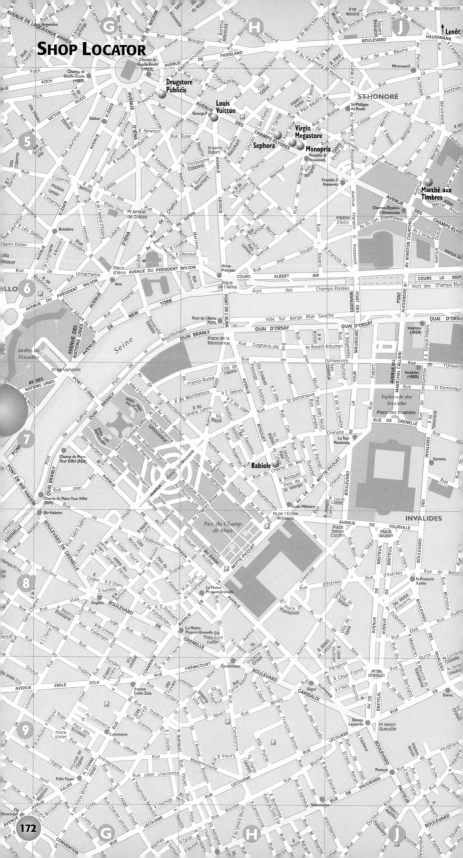

Shop Locator

Shop Locator

MONTMARTRE

PIGALLE

Judith Lacroix

GARE ST-LAZARE

Le Printemps

Galeries Lafayette

Du Pareil au Même

Gien Boutique

Fauchon

Ventilo

Lavinia

Daum

Chanel

Jamin Puech

Vanessa Bruno

WHSmith

Iki Mezura

Colette

Lagerfeld Gallery

IKKS

Bill Tornade

Kiliwatch

Salons du Palais Royal Shiseido

Agnès B

La Droguerie

Barbara Bui

Jardin des Tuileries

Why!

Xuly Bët

Agatha

Cité de la Femme - Etam

Biche de Bère

Zara

La Samaritaine

LES HALLES

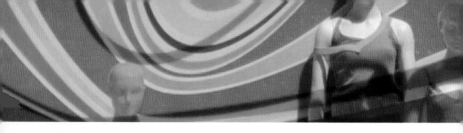

SHOPPING

When it comes to shopping, Paris has it all: fine department stores, quirky and super-chic boutiques, inexpensive chain stores, big and small flea markets, and everything in-between.

FASHION

Clothing, of course, is the thing to buy in Paris, still the world's fashion capital in spite of serious competition from London, New York and Milan. All the top-name designers have boutiques in the city, concentrated on Faubourg St-Honoré and avenue Montaigne and in St-Germain-des-Prés. For those on a tighter budget, *dépôt-vente* (second-hand) shops sell Madame's

There are plenty of elegant shoe boutiques to choose from

(and occasionally Monsieur's) designer cast-offs from last year's collections, often at very reasonable prices. The rue d'Alésia is lined with stock shops selling labels at discounts of up to 70 per cent. La Vallée Outlet Shopping Village, outside Paris, sells designer clothing at discounts of up to 60 per cent (take the RER line A4 to Val d'Europe, 45 minutes from Paris). Designer corners can be found in the three top department stores: the exclusive Left Bank Le Bon Marché and the huge Right Bank stores Galeries Lafayette and Printemps. The BHV department store is less

expensive and not as chic. It is famous for its fully stocked DIY basement. High-street chain stores are concentrated in Forum des Halles and on the Champs-Élysées, rue de Rivoli and boulevard St-Michel, while one-off boutiques are clustered in Le Marais and St-Germain-des-Prés, with a scattering of more youthful, offbeat shops along the Canal St-Martin, in Montmartre near Métro Abbesses and on and around rue Oberkampf.
If shoes are your thing, head directly for rue du Cherche-Midi and rue de Grenelle, in the 6th and 7th *arrondissements* respectively, for the top names in shoe designs.

PERFUME

Paris is also perfume capital of the world. All the department stores sell the major names in fragrances and every district has a perfumery.

FOOD

There is plenty of choice for food lovers, from foie gras to fine wine and champagne, in shops such as Hédiard and Fauchon in place de la Madeleine, the Grande Épicerie de Paris next to Le Bon Marché department store, and Lafayette Gourmet in Galeries Lafayette. Many *boulangeries* make their own chocolate (look for the word *chocolatier*) and special chocolate shops abound, but you can also get bars of high-quality chocolate (70 per cent or higher cocoa content) in any supermarket.

ANTIQUES AND BOOKS

For antiques and second-hand bargain hunters, the Marché aux Puces de St-Ouen (▷ 107) is a virtual city of antiques and

bric-a-brac, while smaller markets at Porte de Montreuil and Porte de Vanves may also offer bargains. Roving flea markets (*brocantes*), often set up in the streets at weekends, are always fun to browse through. Fine antiques shops are clustered around quai Voltaire and rue de Beaune in the 7th *arrondissement* and in the Louvre des Antiquaires, where some 250 vendors sell their wares, across rue de Rivoli from the museum. For rare books, wander through the 5th and 6th *arrondissements* and along the *quais* of the Seine, lined with booksellers' stalls.

Head to Poilâne for magnificent French bread

PRACTICALITIES

Stores are generally open from 9 or 10am to 7 or 7.30pm. Most stores close on Sunday, although many of the boutiques in the Marais are open on Sunday afternoon. Small boutiques may close on Monday morning and every lunchtime. Most stores accept major credit cards. Always say *bonjour* and *au revoir* to sales staff. If they offer unwanted assistance, say *Je regarde* ('just looking').

SHOPPING AREAS

The following five pages highlight areas in Paris that are particularly good for shopping.

Faubourg St-Honoré

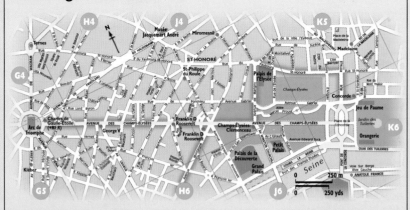

Ⓜ Concorde

No self-respecting fashionista would miss rue du Faubourg St-Honoré and avenue Montaigne, where most of the well-known couture houses and some of the less-famous

Lanvin—one of many designer names in Faubourg St-Honoré

ones have shops. Those on a tighter budget can stroll down the Champs-Élysées, where there are a number of high street chain shops (see chain store guide, ▷ 190–191) in addition to pricier boutiques.

RUE DU FAUBOURG ST-HONORÉ

Unless you're just browsing, make sure your credit card limits are high or you have a large wad of cash in your Gucci handbag for this exclusive district.

From Concorde Métro station, walk along rue Royale, where you'll find Gucci's sleek, modern store (No. 21). Turn onto the rue du Faubourg St-Honoré, where the parade of designer names includes Prada (No. 6), Lanvin (Nos. 15–22), Hermès (No. 24), Valentino (No. 27), Givenchy (No. 28), Yves Saint Laurent Rive Gauche (No. 38), Chloé (No. 54), Christian Lacroix (No. 73), Valentino (No. 27), Gianfranco Ferre (No. 23), Dolce & Gabbana (No. 3) and Sonia Rykiel (No. 70). You'll also find top jewellers like Cartier (No. 17) and Chopard (No. 72).

AVENUE MONTAIGNE

If your credit card isn't maxed out yet, when you reach place Beauvau, turn left onto the tree-lined avenue de Marigny and cross the Champs-Élysées to the wide, beautiful avenue Montaigne, where names such as Dior (flagship store, No. 30), Ungaro (No. 2), Chanel (No. 42) and Nina Ricci (No. 39) have set up shop in elegant style.

AVENUE DES CHAMPS-ÉLYSÉES

The shops, cinemas, car showrooms and cafés on this world-famous avenue are between Métro stations Franklin D. Roosevelt and Charles de Gaulle-Étoile. The avenue's renovation by the City of Paris, which endowed it with wider walkways and double rows of trees, has attracted new retailers and given it a new lease of life. The main attractions include a Virgin Megastore (No. 52), in a magnificent former bank complete with a grand staircase and stainless steel vault (part of the bookshop); popular fragrance seller Sephora's flagship store (No. 70); and FNAC (No. 74), the French version of Virgin Megastore. The galleries along the avenue are mini-shopping malls housing various boutiques.

You will enjoy window-shopping on the Champs-Élysées

LADURÉE
75 avenue des Champs-Élysées, 75008
Tel 01 40 75 08 75
www.laduree.fr
Open daily 7.30am–12.30am
Ladurée is famous for its unusual macaroons, with varieties such as rose, lime-basil and apricot-ginger, but all its desserts, sandwiches, hot dishes and chocolates are delicious. You can enjoy tea in its refined setting or buy goodies to take away. (It's near Métro Franklin D. Roosevelt.)

Le Marais

WHAT TO DO

HOW TO GET THERE

🚇 St Paul-Le Marais

This historic quarter, with its narrow streets and 17th- and 18th-century town houses, is a haven for small, one-off boutiques and one of the few areas where you can be sure to find many shops open on a Sunday afternoon. It is also the city's gay quarter and a hub for the Jewish community, which is concentrated on the rue des Rosiers, where Jewish bakeries, restaurants and shops mingle with trendy clothing boutiques such as L'Eclaireur (No. 3 ter), purveyor of avant-garde designer labels.

RUE DU ROI DE SICILE

From St Paul-Le Marais Métro station, take rue Pavée to rue du Roi de Sicile and turn left.

Chocoholics should head for the rue Vieille-du-Temple

Alternatives (No. 18) is one of the few *dépôt-vente* (second-hand) shops that caters for both men and women—it offers names such as Helmut Lang and Comme des Garçons. The trendier-than-thou Noir Kennedy boutique (No. 22) sells the latest fashions from Delphine Murat and Fake London Genius.

RUE VIEILLE DU TEMPLE

Take a right onto rue Vieille-du-Temple. Stop at Mosavitra (No. 23) to gaze at the handmade stained glass created by Claudia Gauthier (shop by appointment only; tel 06 08 17 30 19). If you need chocolate to keep you

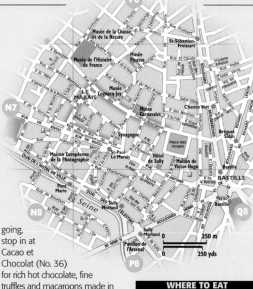

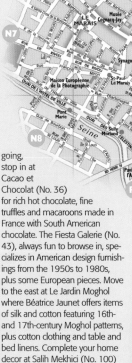

going, stop in at Cacao et Chocolat (No. 36) for rich hot chocolate, fine truffles and macaroons made in France with South American chocolate. The Fiesta Galerie (No. 43), always fun to browse in, specializes in American design furnishings from the 1950s to 1980s, plus some European pieces. Move to the east at Le Jardin Moghol where Béatrice Jaunet offers items of silk and cotton featuring 16th- and 17th-century Moghol patterns, plus cotton clothing and table and bed linens. Complete your home decor at Salih Mekhici (No. 100) with one of his award-winning lamps.

RUE DES FRANCS-BOURGEOIS

Take another right onto the boutique-packed rue des Francs-Bourgeois. On the corner is Issey Miyake's minimalist A.POC shop (No. 47), featuring his simple designs in original fabrics. Next to it is Art du Bureau, selling handsome designer office accessories, watches and handbags, followed by Muji (No. 47), with its inexpensive clothing for men and women, as well as homewares and office supplies in the shop next door. La Chaise Longue (No. 20) is a great place to pick up gifts for yourself or others, with many of its homewares and accessories based on 1950s designs. For wearable women's clothing with an exotic touch, go to Abou d'Abi Bazar (No. 10). Autour du Monde Home offers stylish furnishings and accessories for the home, as well as bright women's clothing.

WHERE TO EAT

L'ÉTOILE MANQUANTE

34 rue Vieille du Temple, 75004
Tel 01 42 72 48 34; www.cafeine.com
Open daily 9am–2am
An attractive modern café

Window-shopping in the rue des Francs-Bourgeois

serving light meals such as salads, soups, sandwiches and charcuterie or cheese platters between noon and 1.30am. Hot dishes are also offered at lunchtime. For dessert, try Christian Constant's delicious ice cream. Check out the starlit, stainless-steel toilets.

COUDE FOU

12 rue du Bourg-Tibourg, 75004
Tel 01 42 77 15 16
Open Mon–Sat 11–10.30, Sun 7pm–10.30pm
A busy little restaurant decorated with rustic murals of farm life. The traditional French food is hearty and tasty.

Around Opéra

HOW TO GET THERE
Ⓜ Chaussée d'Antin-La Fayette
Ⓜ Auber

The main shopping attractions near Paris's beautifully restored 19th-century Opéra Palais Garnier are the two major department stores, Galeries Lafayette and Printemps. In one or the other, you'll find everything imaginable in terms of clothing, accessories, shoes, perfumes and cosmetics, home furnishings and household linen. A short walk away is place de la Madeleine, with all you need to satisfy your cravings for luxury foods.

BOULEVARD HAUSSMANN

When you step out of the Chaussée d'Antin-La Fayette Métro station, you'll be right in front of Galeries Lafayette

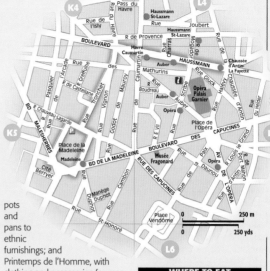

The impressive glass dome and balconies at Galeries Lafayette

(No. 40). The Magasin Coupole (named after its enormous stained-glass dome) sells everything but menswear, which is next door in Lafayette Homme—also the home of the first-floor Lafayette Gourmet food hall. Walkways on the first and second floors of the Magasin Coupole lead to the second and third floors of Lafayette Homme.

Down the street at No. 64 is Galeries Lafayette's main competitor, Printemps, which has three buildings: Printemps de la Mode, with eight floors of women's and children's fashions; Printemps de la Maison, selling everything for the home, from

pots and pans to ethnic furnishings; and Printemps de l'Homme, with clothing and accessories for men. For a panoramic view of Paris and a close look at the art nouveau cupola, take the elevator to the ninth floor of Printemps de la Maison. Both department stores have cafés and restaurants, personal shopper services and regular fashion shows.

The streets around the two stores are inhabited mostly by chain stores such as Gap France, H&M and C&A.

RUE TRONCHET AND PLACE DE LA MADELEINE

The shop-lined rue Tronchet has outlets such as Jacadi (No. 17; appealing but expensive childrenswear) and La Bagagerie (No. 12; luggage and handbags). It takes you to place de la Madeleine, where a number of stores offer gourmet foods. The famous Fauchon (No. 26) has a pastry shop, a gourmet grocery store with foods from around the world and a tea room. On the other side of the square is Hédiard (No. 21), with similar offerings of exotic foods and its own restaurant. The flagship store of the Nicolas wine chain (No. 31) has a huge cellar stocked with everything from the priciest to the most inexpensive bottles. Other gourmet goodies can be found at the Caviar Kaspia boutique and restaurant (No. 17) and Maison de la Truffe (No. 19), which specializes in truffles and foie gras. For something crystal to serve them in, go to Baccarat (No. 11).

WHERE TO EAT
LAFAYETTE GOURMET
40 boulevard Haussmann, 75009
Tel 01 42 82 34 56
Open Mon–Sat 9.30–8.30, Thu 9.30–9
What could be more chic than

Shopping in place de la Madeleine, southwest of Opéra

eating lunch in the middle of a gourmet supermarket? Choose the food stand that appeals to you and find a chair. The fruit and vegetable stand has salads, quiches, vegetable soup and freshly squeezed juices. Other counters offer Italian food, cheese dishes, grilled meats and fresh fish.

L'ECLUSE
15 place de la Madeleine, 75008
Tel 01 42 65 34 69
www.leclusebaravin.com
Open daily 8.30am–1am
This chain of six wine bars is reliable for its tasty meals, fine wines and friendly service.

WHAT TO DO

Palais Royal/Les Halles

HOW TO GET THERE
🚇 Palais-Royal-Musée du Louvre

The Forum des Halles is an underground shopping mall marked by a mirrored, above-ground architectural eyesore. It's a good option if you're looking for chain stores, but it's not particularly Parisian. The Carrousel du Louvre is a classier underground mall with museum boutiques, a nature-themed store and a branch of Virgin Megastore. If you want to see Paris while you shop, go to the beautiful Jardin du Palais Royal, Galerie Vivienne and place des Victoires, all of which are worth visiting in their own right, as well as for shopping.

JARDIN DU PALAIS ROYAL
Enter the Palais Royal from the rue St-Honoré side, have a look

A wacky window display at Jean-Paul Gaultier

at Daniel Buren's interestingly incongruous striped columns, then continue into the main courtyard, where you can rest in the garden or shop in the surrounding arcades. Among the more interesting shops are Didier Ludot's three boutiques selling vintage haute couture by such fashion legends as Chanel, Dior and Balenciaga (No. 20 galerie de Montpensier), accessories (No. 24) and, on the eastern side, nothing but little black dresses—all vintage—and fur coats (No. 125 galerie de Valois). Nearby, is the Salons du Palais Royal Shiseido boutique (No. 142), with its dimly lit mauve

interior, selling the fragrance creations of Serge Lutens. You'll also find art galleries and unusual shops such as Drapeaux de France (1 place Colette), with a huge collection of toy soldiers.

GALERIE VIVIENNE
Leave the Palais Royal from the galerie de Beaujolais side and walk up rue Vivienne. Start a visit to the Galerie Vivienne at Jean-Paul Gaultier (No. 6) for a look at the designer's ready-to-wear and couture clothes in a chic, spacious boutique. From here wander into the elegant passageways of the early 19th-century gallery (which connects with the parallel Galerie Colbert) to browse in a series of interesting shops. Librairie D F Jousseaume (No. 45) has stacks of old and rare books. La Marelle (No. 21) is an excellent *dépôt-vente* (second-hand clothing shop) with designer labels for women and children. Legrand Filles et Fils (1 rue de la Banque), a purveyor of fine wine, wine-related books and utensils, and gourmet foods, also has a wine bar and holds regular tastings.

PLACE DES VICTOIRES
Exit the Galerie Vivienne onto rue des Petits Champs (which becomes rue de la Feuillade), turn left and walk the short distance to the stately 17th-century place des Victoires, a circular 'square' created by Louis XIV. Here you'll find the boutiques of Kenzo (No. 3), Thierry Mugler (No. 8), Esprit de

Corps (No. 9) and Victoire (No. 10). To continue your shopping, walk down either the rue Croix des Petits Champs back towards rue de Rivoli or down rue Étienne Marcel to the newly trendy rue Tiquetonne.

Take a break in the beautiful 19th-century Galerie Vivienne

WHERE TO EAT
A PRIORI THÉ
35–37 galerie Vivienne, 75002
Tel 01 42 97 48 75
Open Mon–Fri 9–6, Sat 9–6.30, Sun 12.30–6.30
Tea room serving hot dishes and salads at lunchtime and delicious desserts at teatime. Brunch on Sunday.

RESTAURANT DU PALAIS ROYAL
43 rue de Valois, 75001
Tel 01 40 20 00 27
Open Mon–Sat 12.30–2.30, 7–10
A handsome restaurant, with outdoor tables in the Palais Royal garden in warm weather.

WHAT TO DO

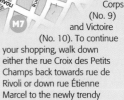

St-Germain-des-Prés

HOW TO GET THERE

🚇 St-Germain-des-Prés

Once the domain of small boutiques, art galleries and antiques shops, St-Germain-des-Prés has been transformed over the past decade by the arrival of designer boutiques. Smart as it is, the area hasn't yet replaced the Faubourg St-Honoré as the city's couture hub and retains much of its historical and some of its bohemian charm.

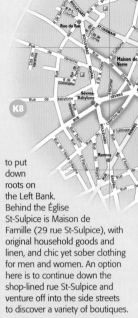

RUE BONAPARTE

Admire the gracious tower of the Église St-Germain-des-Prés as you come out of the St-Germain-des-Prés Métro station. Across the street is the Louis Vuitton store (6 place St-Germain-des-Prés), with its famous trunks and more modern travel wares. Head south down rue Bonaparte. You

Designer labels, such as Prada, are abundant in Paris

can't miss the Emporio Armani store, complete with an Italian restaurant, on the corner of boulevard St-Germain. Back on rue Bonaparte, you'll pass the boutiques of Zapa (No. 55), Georges Rech (No. 54), Max Mara (corner of rue du Four), Jas Ventilo (No. 59) and Cacharel (No. 64). Stop in at Pierre Hermé (No. 72), the smartest patisserie in town, for exquisite pastries, macaroons or chocolates, but be prepared to wait, especially on weekends. Move on to Yves Saint-Laurent Rive Gauche (6 place St-Sulpice) across the street, the first big-name designer boutique

to put down roots on the Left Bank. Behind the Église St-Sulpice is Maison de Famille (29 rue St-Sulpice), with original household goods and linen, and chic yet sober clothing for men and women. An option here is to continue down the shop-lined rue St-Sulpice and venture off into the side streets to discover a variety of boutiques.

RUE DU CHERCHE-MIDI

From place St-Sulpice, take rue du Vieux-Colombier (passing more shops, including Agnès B at No. 6) to rue du Cherche-Midi, where one stylish shoe shop follows another, among them Robert Clergerie (No. 5), with everything from strappy high-heeled sandals to fur-covered slip-ons with toes as sharp as daggers. Take a right at place Alphonse Deville and a left down rue de Sèvres to browse in Le Bon Marché (No. 24), Paris's oldest and most elegant department store. Alternatively, go right along rue de Sèvres and then left down rue de Grenelle.

RUE DE GRENELLE

Here you'll find even smarter shoe shops, including Stephane Kélian (No. 13 bis) and Patrick Cox (No. 21), as well as designer labels Sonia Rykiel (Nos. 4 and 6), Prada (No. 5), Miu Miu (No. 16) and Max Mara (No. 9). For something a little different, check out the 'barbaric' furniture designs at En Attendant les Barbares (No. 35) and the designer perfumes at Editions de Parfums Frédéric Malle (No. 37).

WHERE TO EAT

CAFÉ DE FLORE

172 boulevard St-Germain, 75006
Tel 01 45 48 55 26
www.cafe-de-flore.com
Open daily 7.30am–1.30am

Relax at an outdoor table at the Café de Flore

You can't get more Parisian than the Flore, still popular with French and international celebrities despite the tourist invasion. Prices are steep for café food (club sandwiches, omelettes and salads), but the art deco interior, professional service from white-aproned waiters, and bustling Left Bank ambience make it worth it.

LE PETIT ST-BENOÎT

4 rue St-Benoît, 75006
Tel 01 42 60 27 92
Open Mon–Sat 12–2.30, 7–10.30
Simple, hearty French dishes at this Left Bank institution.

WHAT TO DO

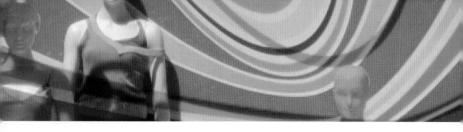

Shopping Directory

This selection of shops, arranged by theme, includes some of Paris's countless fashion boutiques, specialist food shops, markets, department stores, antiques shops and bookstores.

- ▷ 172–175 for shopping locator maps
- ▷ 190–191 for chain stores
- ▷ 298 for clothing sizes

- ▷ 172–175 for shopping locator maps
- ▷ 190–191 for chain stores
- ▷ 298 for clothing sizes

ANTIQUES

DÉPÔT VENTE DE PARIS
Map 174 off Q8
81 rue de Lagny, 75020
Tel 0890 711777
www.depotventedeparis.com
This is France's biggest second-hand shop, with more than 1,000 pieces of furniture and nearly 100,000 items. There are some direct imports from Asia (eight arrivals per year).
🕐 Mon–Sat 10–7, Sun 3–7
🚇 Nation

GALERIE CAPTIER
Map 173 L7
33 rue de Beaune, 75007
Tel 01 42 61 00 57
The antique Chinese furniture (17th to 19th century) and old Japanese screens here have been chosen by owners Bernard and Sylvie Captier, who regularly travel to Asia to search out exotic and refined works of art.
🕐 Tue–Sat 10.30–7, Mon 2.30–7
🚇 Rue du Bac

LA GALERIE SCANDINAVE
Map 173 L8
31 rue de Tournon, 75006
Tel 01 43 26 25 32
www.lagaleriescandinave.com
This Left-Bank gallery, located in an elegant 17th-century mansion, specializes in Scandinavian design from 1950 to 1970. There are chairs, sofas, tables, desks but also light fittings, ceramics and glassware, all original items by famous and lesser-known designers such as Arne Jacobsen, Kaare Klint, Poul Henningsen, Grete Jalk and Ilmari Tapiovaara.
🕐 Tue–Sat 11–8 🚇 Odéon

GALERIE YVES GASTOU
Map 173 L7
12 rue Bonaparte, 75006
Tel 01 53 73 00 10
www.galerieyvesgastou.com
The gallery specializes in furniture, sculpture and objects from the 1940s to the 1970s. Designers represented include Jacques Adnet, Marc du Plantier, Paul

A taste of the Orient at Galerie Captier

Dupré-Lafon and Gilbert Poillerat.
🕐 Tue–Sat 11–7
🚇 St-Germain-des-Prés

SALLE RASPAIL
Map 173 L10
224 boulevard Raspail, 75014
Tel 01 56 54 11 90
This second-hand shop stocks antiques from the 18th, 19th and 20th centuries. The selection is wide enough to have some funky 1970s pieces sitting next to a chest of drawers from the 19th century. It's likely that everyone will be tempted by something, all the more because

only quality pieces are displayed here.
🕐 Tue–Fri 11–8, Sat 11–7 🚇 Raspail

XXO
Map 174 off Q8
78 rue de la Fraternité, 93200
Romainville
Tel 01 48 18 08 88
www.xxo.com
XXO stands for Extra Extra Original, and the furniture purchased, sold and rented out is indeed quite original. Exclusively distributing 1950s to 1980s furniture, this shop has classics such as Colombo chairs and lip-shaped sofas. Many of its rentals are to the movie industry.
🕐 Mon–Fri 9–6.30, Sat 1.30–6.30
🚗 A few minutes' drive from Porte de Bagnolet

BOOKS

ARTAZART
Map 174 P5
83 quai de Valmy, 75010
Tel 01 40 40 24 00
www.artazart.com
This bookshop on the banks of the Canal St-Martin specializes in visual arts, including design, architecture, photography and fashion. A small gallery welcomes work by up-and-coming artists. The friendly and well-informed staff may even offer you coffee.
🕐 Mon–Fri 10.30–7.30, Sat–Sun 2–8
🚇 Jacques Bonsergent or République

GIBERT JOSEPH
Map 173 M8
26 boulevard St-Michel, 75006
Tel 01 44 41 88 88
You'll find an impressive range of books here, covering nearly every subject, from travel to maths via religion! Look out for used books, which are usually in pristine condition but come at a discounted price. This shop is very popular with students from the nearby Sorbonne university.
🕐 Mon–Sat 10–7.30 🚇 St-Michel

WHAT TO DO

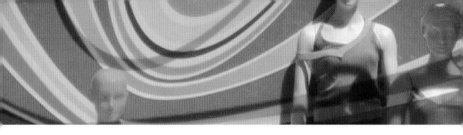

LA HUNE

Map 173 L8
170 boulevard St-Germain, 75006
Tel 01 45 48 35 85
This is the haunt of the literary crowd, as is prestigious Café de Flore, nearby. There is little in the fields of poetry and art that you won't find here. Book signings and literary evenings in the presence of eminent writers are organized regularly.
Mon–Sat 10am–midnight, Sun 11–8
St-Germain-des-Prés

LIBRAIRIE ULYSSE

Map 174 P8
26 rue St-Louis en l'Ile, 75004
Tel 01 43 25 17 35
www.ulysse.fr
The books (both new and used), maps and magazines here span almost every country in the world. The shop is also a congenial venue for people exchanging stories, souvenirs and tips, and planning further adventures.
Tue–Fri 2–8 Sully Morland

SHAKESPEARE AND COMPANY

Map 173 M8
37 rue de la Bûcherie, 75005
Tel 01 43 25 40 93
www.shakespeareco.org
An American bookstore, Shakespeare and Company (▷ 20) is named after the famous bookshop started by Sylvia Beach in the 1920s. This place is special, with its old floor tiles, little well full of coins and floor-to-ceiling shelves. The stock includes both new and used books. There is a small library upstairs, where books can be browsed. This 'wonderland of books' hosts regular readings and book signings.
Daily noon–midnight
St-Michel

TASCHEN

Map 173 M8
2 rue de Buci, 75006
Tel 01 40 51 79 22
www.taschen.com
This art bookshop is itself a work of art: Its interior was designed by Philippe Starck (there are tawny tones, and a large screen at the back shows silent films). Publications by this successful German publishing house include books on photography, popular culture, design, painting, eroticism and architecture.
Mon–Thu 11–8, Sat 11am–midnight Odéon

Browse in elegant surroundings at Taschen

WH SMITH

Map 173 K6
248 rue de Rivoli, 75001
Tel 01 44 77 88 99
www.whsmith.fr
This is a piece of England in the heart of Paris. France's biggest English bookseller stocks just as many English books and newspapers as its sister stores across the Channel. British daily papers are available on the day of publication.
Mon–Sat 9–7.30, Sun 1–7.30
Tuileries

DEPARTMENT STORES

BHV (BAZAR DE L'HÔTEL DE VILLE)

Map 174 N7
14 rue du Temple, 75001
Tel 01 42 74 90 00
www.bhv.fr
The City Hall Bazaar has been operating since 1856 and is incredibly well stocked. Clothes, furniture, home goods—just about everything you could possibly need or think of has been gathered under one roof.
Mon–Tue, Thu–Sat 9.30–7.30, Wed 9.30–9 Hôtel de Ville

LE BON MARCHÉ

Map 173 K8
24 rue de Sèvres, 75007
Tel 01 44 39 80 00
www.lebonmarche.fr
You'll find the classiest brands and goods in this Left-Bank store. The modernist interior adds to the elegant atmosphere. Don't miss the beauty centre, appropriately named 'Théâtre de la Beauté', on the ground floor, and the food hall, La Grande Epicerie, in an adjoining building, stocking delicacies from all over the world.
Mon–Wed, Fri 9.30–7, Thu 10–9, Sat 9.30–8 Sèvres-Babylone, Vaneau

CITÉ DE LA FEMME—ETAM

Map 173 M7
67–73 rue de Rivoli, 75001
Tel 01 44 76 73 73
This store, housed on seven floors, offers the full range of Etam clothing (including lingerie, Tammy collection for teenagers and Maternité collection for pregnant women). There are also some home goods, a restaurant with a beautiful view of the bustling rue de Rivoli, and even a crèche (open Wednesday, Saturday and public holidays).
Mon–Wed, Fri–Sat 10–8, Thu 10–9
Châtelet

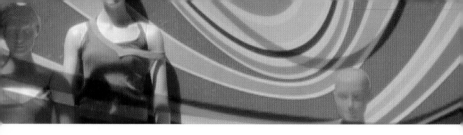

GALERIES LAFAYETTE

Map 175 L5
40 boulevard Haussmann, 75009
Tel 01 42 82 34 56
www.galerieslafayette.com
Inaugurated in 1912, the main building of this grand old department store has an impressive stained-glass dome, balconies and gilded balustrades. It is a luxurious setting for the hundreds of brands stocked here, including fashion and beauty items, accessories, home goods and fine foods.
🕐 Mon–Wed, Fri–Sat 9.30–7.30, Thu 9.30–9 🚇 Chaussée d'Antin

MONOPRIX

Map 172 H5
52 avenue des Champs-Élysées, 75008
Tel 01 53 77 65 65
www.monoprix.fr
Monoprix offers all the conveniences the urban crowd is looking for. There is food, cosmetics and fashion, as well as facilities such as photocopying and a photo booth. This branch of Monoprix stays open late.
🕐 Mon–Sat 9am–midnight
🚇 Franklin D. Roosevelt

LE PRINTEMPS

Map 175 L4
64 boulevard Haussmann, 75009
Tel 01 42 82 50 00
www.printemps.com
Since 1865 it has been this store's ambition to be the most modern of its time. Under its main building's impressive stained-glass cupola, there are six floors of women's fashion and Europe's largest perfume department. There is also a men's store, and a department dedicated to home decoration.
🕐 Mon–Wed, Fri–Sat 9.35–7, Thu 9.35am–10pm 🚇 Havre-Caumartin

AGNÈS B

Map 175 M6
6 rue du Jour, 75001
Tel 01 45 08 56 56
www.agnesb.fr
Sober yet trendy, Agnès B's fashion is the epitome of young Parisian chic. Sharply cut clothes with original details are her signature, and her little waistcoat with press studs is a classic. She has three shops on rue du Jour packed with clothing for women, men and children. The designer is also worth celebrating for her artistic engagement—she sponsors many budding creators.

Shop in splendour at Galeries Lafayette

🕐 Mon–Sat 10–7.30
🚇 Les Halles

ANTIK BATIK

Map 174 P7
18 rue de Turenne, 75004
Tel 01 44 78 02 00
Come here for the finest of ethnic chic: embroidered blouses made of cotton or silk, long batik-printed stoles, a collection of bags that look as if they were bought at a souk, and which offer the perfect finishing touch. There is even some sexy lingerie, with sheer fabrics and little sequins.
🕐 Tue–Sat 11–7, Sun–Mon 2–7
🚇 Hôtel de Ville

ANTOINE ET LILI

Map 174 P4
95 quai de Valmy, 75010
Tel 01 40 37 41 55
www.antoineetlili.com
Knick-knacks from all over the world, oriental beauty products and vivid outfits in luxurious fabrics: This is hippie-chic kingdom. There are two shops here—one for clothes, another for gifts—and also a small restaurant.
🕐 Tue–Fri 11–8, Sat 10–8, Sun 9–2, 3–6, Mon 11–7 🚇 Jacques Bonsergent, Gare de l'Est

BARBARA BUI

Map 175 N6
23 rue Étienne Marcel, 75001
Tel 01 40 26 43 65
www.barbarabui.com
The lines are sleek, original and often have a sexy twist, but are never provocative. You'll find tailored jackets, fitted tops, tight trousers and an impressive range of high-heeled shoes. The collection is aimed at the urban woman and is classy, modern and feminine.
🕐 Daily 10.30–7.30
🚇 Étienne Marcel

BILL TORNADE

Map 175 M6
44 rue Étienne Marcel, 75002
Tel 01 42 33 66 47
www.billtornade.com
Bill Tornade sells beautiful fabrics, 1960s-style jackets, pinstripe suits and fine Italian leather shoes. Some outfits are part of a limited edition, for a rather exclusive touch.
🕐 Mon–Sat 11–7.30
🚇 Étienne Marcel

CHANEL

Map 173 K5
31 rue Cambon, 75001
Tel 01 42 86 28 00
www.chanel.com
The tweed suit and the little black dress, Coco Chanel's signature outfits, keep on being re-invented by Karl Lagerfeld, head of this

WHAT TO DO

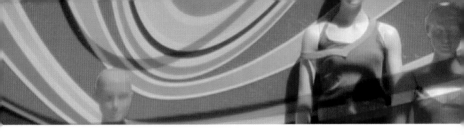

fashion house since 1984. Classy, sexy and feminine, Chanel's designs, enhanced by exclusive perfumes, embody Parisian elegance.
Ⓒ Mon–Sat 10–7 Ⓜ Madeleine

COLETTE
Map 173 L6
213 rue St-Honoré, 75001
Tel 01 55 35 33 90
www.colette.fr
Exclusive shopping par excellence! Come here for cutting-edge design from one of the industry's rising names, or for imported beauty products that are difficult to find elsewhere. A glance at the press box will ensure you keep abreast of the trends. The water bar downstairs offers more than a hundred different brands of bottled water.
Ⓒ Mon–Sat 11–7 Ⓜ Tuileries, Pyramides

COMME DES GARÇONS
Map 173 K5
54 rue du Faubourg St-Honoré, 75008
Tel 01 53 30 27 27
Japanese designer Rei Kawakubo's approach to fashion is almost architectural. Her asymmetrical cuts produce sleek lines and one of her outfits can remodel a body. The collection caters to those looking for something unique, modern and with a couture accent. Comme des Garçons's perfume is also sold here.
Ⓒ Mon–Sat 11–7 Ⓜ Madeleine, Concorde

IKKS
Map 175 M6
3 rue d'Argout, 75002
Tel 01 40 28 18 38
www.ikks.com
IKKS is one of the new must-have brands of cool streetwear for kids, youths and adults. Casual styling in denim and cotton for just about any occasion modern life can throw at you.
Ⓒ Mon–Sat 10–7 Ⓜ Étienne Marcel

ISABEL MARANT
Map 174 Q8
16 rue de Charonne, 75011
Tel 01 49 29 71 55
www.isabelmarant.fr
Now a regular on the catwalk, Isabel Marant has updated Parisian elegance by giving it a bit of a bohemian bourgeois twist. Silk paisley shirts, big woollen wrap-over tops: This is casual chic at its best.
Ⓒ Mon–Sat 10.30–7.30 Ⓜ Bastille

JUDITH LACROIX
Map 175 L4
3 rue Henri Monnier, 75009
Tel 01 48 78 22 37
www.judithlacroix.com

Chanel is a safe bet for iconic Parisian fashion

This young designer originally made a name for herself with her successful children's range—notably using a fabric that resembled a page from a child's homework book. After her work was distributed at leading outlets such as Barneys in New York, she opened her own boutique in 2002 and extended her range to include womenswear.
Ⓒ Mon–Sat 10–7
Ⓜ St-Georges

KILIWATCH
Map 175 M6
64 rue Tiquetone, 75002
Tel 01 42 21 17 37
Kiliwatch offers the very best in retro gear that's carefully chosen for its classic styling, then cleaned and pressed before being put on sale. Every garment is very good quality, so the vintage Hawaiian shirts and bright 1970s skirts often come at a price. A line of new denim outfits completes the collection. Be sure to check the press box which displays the sharpest fashion and design reviews.
Ⓒ Tue–Fri 11–7, Sat 11–7.30, Mon 2–7
Ⓜ Étienne Marcel

LAGERFELD GALLERY
Map 175 M5
12 rue Vivienne, 75002
Tel 01 44 50 22 22
This art gallery-cum-boutique is where designer Karl Lagerfeld of Chanel fame sells his own brand of women's ready-to-wear fashions. Lagerfeld added touches of vivid colour to his 2007–2008 catwalk show.
Ⓒ Tue–Sat 11–6.30
Ⓜ Bourse

MARITHÉ + FRANÇOIS GIRBAUD
Map 173 K8
8 rue Babylone, 75007
Tel 01 45 48 78 86
www.girbaud.com
Come here for designer streetwear in innovative fabrics and lines. The jeans collection, the signature of the brand, is particularly futuristic and the store design is striking and modernist.
Ⓒ Tue–Sat 10–7, Mon 11–9
Ⓜ Sèvres-Babylone

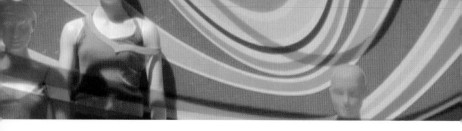

DU PAREIL AU MÊME
Map 173 K5
15 rue des Mathurins, 75008
Tel 01 42 66 93 80
www.dpam.fr
This is one of a chain of boutiques selling colourful, creative, trendy, high-quality and affordable clothing for children from birth to early teens.
🕐 Mon–Sat 10–7 🚇 Havre Caumartin

SONIA RYKIEL
Map 173 L8
175 boulevard St-Germain, 75006
Tel 01 49 54 60 60
www.soniarykiel.com
This is the designer's main ready-to-wear boutique: sexy, fluid clothes and lingerie with suitable accessories (such as bags in colourful shining leather decorated with medals, and huge hats).
🕐 Mon–Sat 10.30–7
🚇 St-Germain-des-Prés

VANESSA BRUNO
Map 173 L6
12 rue Castiglione, 75001
Tel 01 42 61 44 60
This French designer's feminine creations spice up classicism with a modern twist; check out the sequined canvas shopping bag or satin knickerbockers. Old also meets new in the shop's interior, with wooden floorboards, lofty pillars and a succession of bare and lacquered walls. Vanessa Bruno's other boutique is on the shop-lined rue St-Sulpice (No. 25, tel 01 43 54 41 04) in the smart and trendy St-Germain-des-Prés district.
🕐 Mon–Sat 10.30–7.30 🚇 Tuileries

XULY BËT
Map 174 N6
1 rue Pierre-Lescot, 75001
Tel 01 42 33 50 40
Malian designer Lamine Kouyate adds an ethnic twist to glamour. His creations show the influence of his native Africa (distinctive, patterned fabrics), but the sexy cuts are

more reminiscent of a daring couture designer such as Versace. There are some beautiful tight-fitting dresses, often with red stitching. Alongside the clothes is a collection of objects for the home, handmade in Africa.
🕐 Daily 11–2, 3–7 🚇 Les Halles

ZARA
Map 173 M7
88 rue de Rivoli, 75001
Tel 01 44 54 20 42
www.zara.com
The Emporio Armani-inspired collection (neutral tones and sleek lines for a casual chic look) offers unbeatable value for money. Alongside this

Rose-lovers' heaven at Au Nom de la Rose

main range there are funkier clothes for teenagers and children and a smaller collection for men.
🕐 Mon–Sat 10–8 🚇 Châtelet

| FLORISTS |
AU NOM DE LA ROSE
Map 173 L8
4 rue de Tournon, 75006
Tel 01 46 34 10 64
www.aunomdelarose.fr
Only one kind of flower is sold here—the rose. There are numerous varieties and hues, for some truly original bouquets. This was the first Au Nom de la Rose shop, established in 1991. There are now around 20 in France.

🕐 Daily 9–9 (closed Sun in summer)
🚇 Odéon

| FOOD AND DRINK |
ANDROUËT
Map 174 N9
Rue Mouffetard, 75005
Tel 01 45 87 85 05
www.androuet.com
France is famous for producing more than 350 different types of cheese, and Androuët stocks over 200 of them, serving discerning Parisian clients since 1909. All the cheeses are made with unpasteurised milk and the staff offer excellent advice on storing and serving.
🕐 Tue–Fri 9.30–1, 4–7.30, Sat 9.30–7.30, Sun 9.30–1.30 🚇 Censier Daubenton

BARTHÉLÉMY (STÉ)
Map 173 K7
51 rue de Grenelle, 75007
Tel 01 42 22 82 24
Established in 1904, this is a cheese-lover's paradise, selling Brie, Mont d'Or (from Jura), Roquefort and much more. The old-fashioned shop supplies both the Élysée Palace and Matignon, home to France's president and prime minister respectively.
🕐 Tue–Sat 8–1, 4–7.30
🚇 Rue du Bac

DRUGSTORE PUBLICIS
Map 172 G5
133 avenue des Champs-Élysées, 75008
Tel 01 44 43 79 00
www.publicisdrugstore.com
This is a night owl's paradise. When other shops have closed, you can come here for newspapers, tobacco and alcohol, cosmetics, pharmaceutical products and much more—but you'll pay quite a premium. There is also a restaurant for light meals, including salads and *croques*.
🕐 Mon–Fri 8am–2am, Sat–Sun 10am–2am 🚇 Charles de Gaulle-Étoile, George V

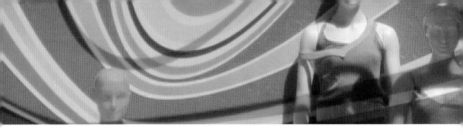

FAUCHON
Map 173 K5
26 place de la Madeleine, 75008
Tel 01 70 39 38 00
www.fauchon.fr
This is the tastiest (and possibly most expensive) delicatessen in Paris. Foie gras, fine condiments, great wines: The very best of French cuisine has been available here since 1886. And not only French: Beluga caviar, the best vintages of the finest spirits from all over the world, and many more exotic delicacies can also be found. There is also a tea room.
🕙 Mon–Sat 8am–9pm
🚇 Madeleine

LAVINIA
Map 173 K5
3–5 boulevard de la Madeleine, 75001
Tel 01 42 97 20 20
www.lavinia.es (in Spanish)
You'll find more than 5,000 wines and 1,000 spirits spread over three floors here. There is also wine paraphernalia, books, a bar and a restaurant where you can buy the finest French wines by the glass.
🕙 Mon–Fri 10–8, Sat 9–8
🚇 Madeleine

LENÔTRE
Map 172 off J4
15 boulevard de Coucelles, 75008
Tel 01 45 63 87 63
www.lenotre.fr
Lenôtre has long been famous for its fine foods and pastries, but the launch of the *macarré*, a bright and surprisingly square-shaped macaroon, has made it even more fashionable. Unusual varieties include chocolate-cherry and aniseed-blackcurrant.
🕙 Daily 9–9 🚇 Villiers

MARIAGE FRÈRES
Map 174 N7
30 rue du Bourg-Tibourg, 75004
Tel 01 42 72 28 11
www.mariagefreres.com
Founded in 1854, this tea house is a Parisian institution. It stocks hundreds of teas from all over the world, including some exclusive house blends. If you are passionate about tea, sample some here or take a new discovery home. China and tea-based delicacies are also for sale: The *matcha* tea-scented salt is a must. The Tea Museum displays rare objects from the 17th century onwards (including tea-caddies and teapots); a selection of copies is on sale.
🕙 Daily 10.30–7.30 🚇 Hôtel de Ville

OLIVIERS & CO
Map 174 P7
47 rue Vieille du Temple, 75004
Tel 01 42 74 38 40
www.oliviers-co.com

Fauchon has supplied the finest food in Paris for over a century

Dedicated to olive oil, Oliviers & Co stocks vintages from all over the Mediterranean, plus many products in which it is a core ingredient (tapenade, olive-oil biscuits). The company produces a range of organic cosmetics said to be high in anti-oxidants. It also stocks spices, olive-wood bowls and utensils.
🕙 Daily 11–8 🚇 Hôtel de Ville

PIERRE HERMÉ
Map 173 L8
72 rue Bonaparte, 75006
Tel 01 43 54 47 77
Couture pastries? Chef Pierre Hermé works in association with a designer so his creations are as visually exciting as they are tasty. His gold-leaf ornamented chocolate cake is legendary. Be prepared for a wait at his small boutique, more like a jeweller's shop than a patisserie, but remember, satisfaction is at the other end of the line.
🕙 Tue–Sun 9–7
🚇 St-Sulpice, Mabillon

POILÂNE
Map 173 L8
8 rue du Cherche-Midi, 75006
Tel 01 45 48 42 59
www.poilane.fr
What is often regarded as the best French bread is still baked here from secret family recipes, guarded by the Poilânes since the 1930s. The country nut-and-raisin bread is a must, but other delicacies include the traditional baguette, croissant and rye loaf.
🕙 Mon–Sat 7.15am–8.15pm
🚇 Sèvres-Babylone, St-Sulpice

DE VINIS ILLUSTRIBUS
Map 174 N9
48 rue de la Montagne Ste-Geneviève, 75005
Tel 01 43 36 12 12
www.devinis.fr
This exceptional wine store sells rare vintages from the early 1900s to the present day, along with everyday wines and all the oenophile paraphernalia, such as quality glasses and carafes. The staff offer excellent advice and the cavernous old wine cellars are wonderful. A well-worn staircase leads down to the stone cellars dating from 1636, where the oldest vintages are stored.
🕙 Tue–Sat 11–8 🚇 Maubert Mutualité

WHAT TO DO

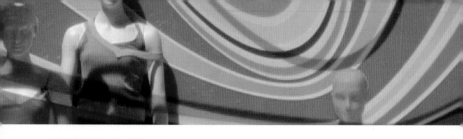

WHAT TO DO

GIFTS

ANNE MAISONNEUVE
Map 173 L9
112 boulevard Raspail, 75006
Tel 01 42 22 42 70
www.annemaisonneuve.com
This shop will make you want to travel. Every visit is relaxing—you are soothed by the sound of Zen fountains and intoxicated by the smell of fragrant wood. Anne Maisonneuve has brought back beautiful wooden bowls, sea-grass mats and jewellery from Indonesia and the Philippines. She also designs her own pieces, including original greetings cards.
Ⓒ Mon–Sat 11–8 Ⓜ Notre-Dame des-Champs, Vavin, St-Placide

BABIOLE
Map 172 H7
22 rue du Champ de Mars, 75007
Tel 01 47 53 03 26
www.babiole.com
This is a truly fun shop specializing in Eiffel Tower souvenirs, plus other Paris themed items. It has everything from miniature towers and T-shirts to fine bone china with a tower motif.
Ⓒ Daily 9–7.30 Ⓜ École Militaire

DAUM
Map 173 L5
4 rue de la Paix, 75002
Tel 01 42 61 25 25
www.daum.com
Daum have been producing glass and crystal objets d'art and jewellery since the era of art nouveau using the *pâte de verre* technique. The ornate styles and colours hark back to the beginnings of modernism.
Ⓒ Mon–Sat 9–7 Ⓜ Opéra

DOM CHRISTIAN KOBAN
Map 174 N7
21 rue Ste-Croix de la Bretonnerie, 75004
Tel 01 42 71 08 00
www.dom-shop.com
Designer Christian Koban caters to the urban home, at more than affordable prices.

Trendy objects and pieces of furniture offer sleek lines, but with a funky twist. The shop also has some truly kitsch but amusing trinkets.
Ⓒ Mon–Sat 11–8, Sun 2–8 Ⓜ Hôtel de Ville

LES FÉES D'HERBE
Map 174 off Q8
23 rue Faidherbe, 75011
Tel 01 43 70 14 76
Les Fées d'Herbe ('the grass fairies') is a play on the street name, Faidherbe. The shop stocks paper dragonflies, exotic artificial flowers and distinctive china, as well as real plants, including herbs for

Fashionable domestic design at Dom Christian Koban

the kitchen and beautiful rare orchids.
Ⓒ Tue–Sat 10–8 Ⓜ Faidherbe Chaligny

WHY?
Map 175 N6
93 rue Rambuteau, 75001
Tel 01 40 26 39 56
www.why.fr
This is one of several Why shops in Paris where pigs really do fly. Expect the most unusual, the funniest and definitely the kitschest items (including zebra-print fur wallets and pink inflatable ottomans). Here, you'll find things you'd never thought of buying and may never

need, but they are sure to make you laugh.
Ⓒ Daily 11–8 Ⓜ Les Halles

HEALTH AND BEAUTY

MAÎTRE PARFUMEUR ET GANTIER
Map 173 K7
84 bis rue de Grenelle, 75007
Tel 01 45 44 61 57
www.maitre-parfumeur-et-gantier.com
This exclusive boutique is inspired by the 17th-century perfume 'salons' where creators used to welcome their elegant clientele. Besides fragrances for men and women, there are scented objects and candles for the home as well as fine leather gloves.
Ⓒ Mon–Sat 10.30–6 Ⓜ Rue du Bac

L'OCCITANE
Map 173 K7
90 rue du Bac, 75007
Tel 01 42 22 55 28
www.loccitane.fr
The essence of Provence is captured here in perfumed bath oils, shower gels, shampoos, olive-oil based creams for the face and body, and fragrances. There are perfumes for the home, scented candles and herbal incenses such as fig tree and sandalwood.
Ⓒ Mon–Thu 11–7.30, Fri–Sat 10.30–7.30 Ⓜ Rue du Bac, Sèvres-Babylone

PATYKA
Map 174 N7
14 rue Rambuteau, 75003
Tel 01 40 29 49 49
In this *patyka* (pharmacy in Hungarian) you'll find natural beauty products devised according to ancient French and Hungarian recipes. Their *huile absolue* (absolute oil) is a must: This concentrate of essential oils is almost a panacea. The products come in pretty glass bottles.
Ⓒ Daily 12–8 Ⓜ Rambuteau

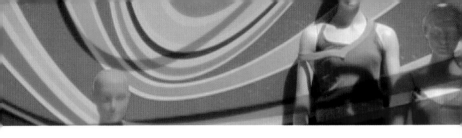

SALONS DU PALAIS ROYAL SHISEIDO
Map 173 M6
142 Galerie de Valois, 75001
Tel 01 49 27 09 09
www.salons-shiseido.com
Everything here is special: the nearby Palais Royal, the prune and lilac theme that imitates a *Directoire*-period boudoir, and, of course, perfumes created by Serge Luytens—a world exclusive—presented in crystal bottles engraved on request with the name of your choice. You'll also find the full range of Shiseido beauty products.
🕐 Mon–Sat 10–7 🚇 Louvre-Rivoli, Palais Royal-Musée du Louvre

SEPHORA
Map 172 H5
70 avenue des Champs-Élysées, 75008
Tel 01 53 93 22 50
www.sephora.fr
This well-stocked perfumery has a slightly futuristic interior, with sleek lines and shiny black and red surfaces. Fragrances, displayed in alphabetical order, come with a description of their core ingredients and the moods they evoke. A full range of cosmetics is available, including some brands hard to find elsewhere in France.
🕐 Sun–Thu 10am–midnight, Fri–Sat 10am–1am 🚇 Franklin D. Roosevelt

HOME AND GARDEN

THE CONRAN SHOP
Map 173 K8
117 rue du Bac, 75007
Tel 01 42 84 10 01
www.conran.com
English designer Sir Terence Conran is a hit with the Parisian crowd. Fine materials, a post-1970s influence, and sometimes an ethnic twist give Conran's furniture a modern elegance. Bathroom, kitchen and garden accessories complete the range. Fine foods from all over the world are also sold in this fine building, designed by Gustave Eiffel.

🕐 Tue–Sat 10–7, Mon 12–7
🚇 Sèvres-Babylone

LA DROGUERIE
Map 175 M6
9 rue du Jour, 75001
Tel 01 45 08 93 27
www.ladroguerie.com
Beads, buttons, ribbons and wool are invitations to let your imagination fly. This shop sells everything you'll need to make your own jewellery, knit or customize your home.
🕐 Tue–Sat 10.30–6.45, Mon 2–6.45
🚇 Les Halles

Unleash your creative potential at La Droguerie

GIEN BOUTIQUE
Map 173 K5
18 rue de l'Arcade, 75008
Tel 01 42 66 52 32
www.gien.com
This traditional faïence dinnerware manufacturer from central France pays homage to the capital in one of its latest collections entitled 'Joli Paris', a real feast for the eyes.
🕐 Tue–Fri 10.30–7, Sat 11–6.30
🚇 Madeleine

NATURE ET DECOUVERTES
Map 174 off Q9
8–10 cour St-Émilion, 75012
Tel 01 53 33 82 40
www.natureetdecouvertes.com

This chain celebrates the richness of nature. Garden furniture and accessories are available alongside natural products (gems, incense) and instruments to better appreciate nature (telescopes, microscopes, barometers). There are also educational games, CDs, candles and some inspiring books.
🕐 Mon–Fri 11–9, Sat–Sun 10–9
🚇 Cour St-Émilion

RÉSONANCES
Map 174 off Q9
13 cour St-Émilion, 75012
Tel 01 44 73 82 82
Every object here is evocative of a particular atmosphere: Pure wax and old ceramics may remind you of your grandma's home, while the bright vases should suit any modern interior. The shop is part of Bercy Village, a pedestrianized street where outlets offer the latest trends.
🕐 Daily 11–9 🚇 Cour St-Émilion

VIADUC DES ARTS
Map 174 Q8
1–29 avenue Daumesnil, 75012
Tel 01 44 75 80 66
www.viaduc-des-arts.com
Around 50 artists have a home here under the old 1859 railway arches, an area which has been beautifully gentrified over the last few years. Cabinetmakers, porcelain artists, Zen designers, blown glass, tapestries, bronze lighting, and terracotta tiles are just some of the artisans and objects found here. This is an excellent place to browse for something special.
🕐 Individual galleries vary, core hours Tue–Sat 10–4 🚇 Ledru Rollin

JEWELLERY

AGATHA
Map 173 L6
Galerie Commerciale du Carrousel du Louvre, 99 rue de Rivoli 75001
Tel 01 42 96 03 09
www.agatha.fr
Agatha offers classic jewellery at very fair prices, specializing

WHAT TO DO

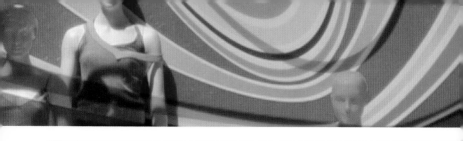

CHAIN STORES

NAME	Menswear	Womenswear	For children	Shoes	Cosmetics and toiletries	Sports equipment and clothing	Accessories	Household items	Books, music and DVDs	Perfume	CONTACT NUMBER
Alain Manoukian	✔	✔		✔			✔				0810 66 56 65
André			✔	✔			✔				01 53 26 28 28
Bata			✔	✔			✔				01 42 33 07 54
The Body Shop					✔		✔			✔	01 53 05 51 51
Caroll		✔		✔			✔				0810 304030
Celio	✔						✔				01 43 42 31 68
Courir			✔	✔			✔				01 45 62 50 77
Du Pareil au Même			✔	✔			✔				01 42 36 07 57
Etam		✔					✔				01 55 90 70 70
FNAC									✔		0825 02 00 20
Foot Locker			✔	✔		✔	✔				01 42 33 03 33
Gap	✔	✔	✔	✔			✔			✔	01 44 88 28 28
Go Sport	✔	✔	✔	✔		✔	✔				01 43 14 32 82
H&M	✔	✔	✔				✔				01 53 20 71 00
Kookaï		✔					✔				01 40 26 59 11
Mango		✔		✔			✔				01 53 30 82 70
Marionnaud										✔	01 40 75 23 06
Minelli				✔			✔				01 53 35 86 10
Monoprix	✔	✔	✔	✔	✔		✔	✔		✔	01 55 20 70 00
Morgan		✔					✔				01 43 59 83 72
Naf Naf	✔	✔	✔	✔			✔				01 48 13 88 88
Pimkie		✔	✔	✔			✔				01 44 27 06 02
Promod		✔		✔			✔				01 53 53 02 30
Virgin Megastore									✔		01 49 53 50 00
Zara	✔	✔		✔			✔				01 55 78 88 88

in semi-precious stones, and silver- and gold-plated materials. The regularly changing collection of watches, pendants, rings and bracelets often features the brand's mascot, a fox terrier.
🕐 Mon–Sat 10–7 🚇 Châtelet

BICHE DE BÈRE
Map 174 N7
15 rue des Innocents, 75001
Tel 01 40 28 94 47
www.biche-de-bere.com
Nelly Biche de Bère, who trained as an industrial designer, creates original, easy-to-wear jewellery. Gold- or silver-plated materials often have a hammered appearance and simple geometrical shapes.
🕐 Mon–Sat 11–7.30 🚇 Châtelet

GALERIE ELSA VANIER
Map 173 L7
7 rue du Pré aux Clercs, 75007
Tel 01 47 03 05 00
www.elsa-vanier.fr
This small gallery stocks the modern jewellery collections of over 50 designers, with many one-of-a-kind items. There are also regular exhibitions where you can meet the gold- and silversmiths themselves. Bespoke items can also be ordered.
🕐 Tue, Thu–Sat 11.30–7, Wed by appointment only
🚇 Rue du Bac

MARKETS
MARCHÉ D'ALIGRE
Map 174 off Q8
Place d'Aligre, 75012
This is one of Paris's liveliest

markets. Many restaurants send staff here to shop for fresh fruit and vegetables, fish and meat. Some merchants sell by auction, and everyone joyfully jostles everybody else—a truly Parisian experience.
🕐 Tue–Sun 6.30–1 🚇 Ledru-Rollin, Faidherbe Chaligny

MARCHÉ DU BOULEVARD RASPAIL
Map 173 K8
Boulevard Raspail, 75006
Organically grown fruit and vegetables are sold here, as well as organic honey, bread and wine. Another organic market is held on boulevard des Batignolles on Saturday mornings.
🕐 Tue, Fri, Sun 9–1 🚇 Rennes

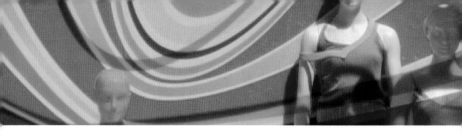

Paris, like any other Western European capital, has its fair share of chain stores as well as its individual boutiques. Branches of the stores in the chart below can be found across the city. There are also individual listings for Etam (▷ 183), Monoprix (▷ 184), Virgin Megastore (▷ 192) and Zara (▷ 186).

NUMBER OF SHOPS	DESCRIPTION	WEBSITE
5	Stylish clothes and accessories for women and men.	www.alain-manoukian.com
15	Footwear for men, women and children.	www.andre.fr
6	Smart and sporty shoes and boots for men, women and children.	www.bata.com
9	Make-up and skin and body products for men and women.	www.thebodyshop.com
8	Elegant clothes and accessories for women.	www.caroll.com
18	Popular clothing and accessories for men.	www.celio.com
10	Sports footwear and accessories (watches and bags) for the whole family.	www.courir.com
21	Clothes, toys, pushchairs (strollers) and equipment for babies/children.	www.dpam.com
19	Inexpensive fashion, lingerie and accessories for women.	www.etam.com
9	Books, music, DVDs, computer equipment and concert tickets.	www.fnac.com
3	Sports shoes and sporty accessories such as sunglasses, watches and bags.	www.footlocker.com
8	Everyday clothes and accessories for the whole family.	www.gap.com
7	Sports clothing, shoes, equipment and accessories for all.	www.gosport.fr
9	A must for fashion lovers on a budget. High fashion at rock-bottom prices.	www.hm.com
15	Fashion and accessories for women.	www.kookai.com
4	Fashion and accessories for women.	www.mango.es
25	Perfume store with branches all over the city.	www.marionnaud.com
12	Funky shoes and boots.	www.vivarte.fr
25	Department store selling food, household items, clothes and cosmetics.	www.monoprix.fr
3	Fashion for women.	www.morgandetoi.com
11	Clothes for women and children (Naf Naf) and men (Chevignon).	www.nafnaf.com
8	Clothes and accessories at rock-bottom prices for women and girls.	www.pimkie.fr
17	Reasonably priced clothes for women.	www.promod.com
6	DVDs, videos, books, CDs, posters, computer games and concert tickets.	www.virginmegastore.fr
26	Stylish clothes and accessories for men, women and children.	www.zara.com

MARCHÉ DE LA CRÉATION
Map 173 K9
Boulevard Edgar Quinet, 75014
www.marchecreation.com
Some 100 artists and craftsmen exhibit and sell their creations–paintings, engravings, sculpture, ceramics and painted silks–in this district traditionally popular with artists. There is a similar event near Bastille (Sat 9–7).
🕐 Sun 10am–nightfall (in summer the market closes around 9pm; in winter around 5pm) 🚇 Edgar-Quinet

MARCHÉ AUX FLEURS
Map 174 N7
Place Louis Lépine, Île de la Cité, 75004
This market has a lovely setting on the Île de la Cité, close to Notre-Dame. You'll find a wide selection of plants and flowers displayed near the banks of the river or in greenhouses, with a couple of specialist stands (such as orchids or herb gardens).
🕐 Mon–Sat 8–7.30; bird market, Sun 8–7 🚇 Cité

MARCHÉ AUX PUCES DE ST-OUEN
See Sights, ▷ 107.

MARCHÉ AUX TIMBRES
Map 172 J5
On the corner of avenue de Marigny and avenue Gabriel, 75008
Stamp lovers, professionals and amateurs alike, meet every week in this fashionable area, a stone's throw from the Elysée Palace.
🕐 Thu, Sat–Sun 9–7
🚇 Champs-Élysées-Clemenceau

MARCHÉ RÉUNION
Map 174 Q8
Place de la Réunion, 75020
Fruit and vegetables are available here at rock-bottom prices. Come near to closing time for the best deals. After noon, everything is sold by auction, in French and in Arabic, and the market starts to resemble a souk. Fish, flowers and bread are also on offer.
🕐 Thu, Sun 8–2 🚇 Alexandre Dumas

MARCHÉ SAINT-GERMAIN
Map 173 L8
Within the square formed by rue Mabillon, rue Clément, rue Félibien and rue Lobineau
A market has been held here since the 13th century. This covered market was

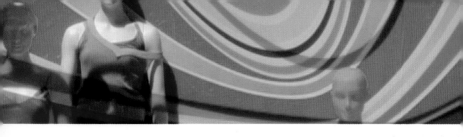

remodelled between 1985 and 1995. Besides being a traditional fresh-food market, it offers a wide choice of ready-to-wear brands such as Gap.
🕐 Tue–Sat 8.30–1, 4–7.30, Sun 8.30–1 🚇 Mabillon, St-Germain-des-Prés

MUSIC

VIRGIN MEGASTORE
Map 172 H5
52–60 avenue des Champs-Elysées, 75008
Tel 01 49 53 50 00
www.virginmegastore.fr
This megastore, surrounded by bars and cinemas, stays open late, so you can pop in and sample the latest CDs, DVDs and books before a film or after a drink. There is also a café-restaurant upstairs.
🕐 Mon–Sat 10am–midnight, Sun noon–midnight
🚇 Franklin D. Roosevelt

SHOES AND ACCESSORIES

IKI MEZURA
Map 173 L6
318 rue St-Honoré, 75001
Tel 01 40 20 47 37
www.iki-mezura.com
Here, the shoes are constantly re-invented. In winter, high-heeled boots appear in interesting materials such as fake crocodile leather, while in summer, stilettos may be adorned with pearl butterflies. The workmanship and finish are always impeccable.
🕐 Tue–Sat 10.30–7, Sun–Mon 2.30–7 🚇 St-Paul

JAMIN PUECH
Map 175 N4
61 rue d'Hauteville, 75010
Tel 01 40 22 08 32
www.jamin-puech.com
Beaded or embroidered, ornamented with little leather flowers or golden chains: Each bag offers precious and unique details, and is quite simply a work of art. Jamin Puech has brought jewellery to leather craft and is now one of Paris's fashion-scene darlings.
🕐 Tue–Fri 10–7, Mon, Sat 11–7 🚇 Poissonnière, Bonne Nouvelle

JEAN-CLAUDE MONDERER
Map 174 P7
22 rue des Francs-Bourgeois, 75004
Tel 01 48 04 51 41
On the picturesque rue des Francs-Bourgeois, this shop is for men and women who love elegant, original footwear. Fine materials, remarkable finishing and interesting designs are Monderer's trademarks.
🕐 Tue–Sat 10.30–7.30, Sun 2–7, Mon 10.30–7 🚇 St-Paul

LOLLIPOPS
Map 173 L8
40 rue du Dragon, 75006
Tel 01 42 22 09 29
www.lollipops.fr
Bags, scarves, hats and some

Head to Louis Vuitton for the finest in chic accessories

jewellery form this chic but playful collection, with its interesting use of materials such as wool, suede and velvet. Products are displayed by colour, so it is easy to find matching pieces.
🕐 Wed–Fri 10.30–7, Sat 10.30–7.30, Mon 12–7, Tue 11–7 🚇 St-Sulpice

LOUIS VUITTON
Map 172 H5
101 avenue des Champs-Élysées, 75008
Tel 0810 810010
www.vuitton.com
The beige and brown chequered pattern and the interlaced LV initials are the house's signature and a

symbol of chic par excellence. You'll find coordinated leather goods, from suitcases to key rings via wallets, but also some high-quality clothes with classy finishing touches.
🕐 Mon–Sat 10–8, Sun 11–1, 2–7 🚇 George V

MEPHISTO
Map 173 off L10
116 avenue du Général Leclerc, 75014
Tel 01 45 40 74 75
www.mephistoparis-sud.com
This vast shop specializes in the famous Mephisto brand of fine leather walking shoes, sandals and golf shoes for men and women, with shock absorbers in the soles and heels.
🕐 Tue–Sat 10–7, Mon 11–7 🚇 Alesia

VENTILO
Map 173 K5
13 boulevard Madeleine, 75001
Tel 01 42 60 46 40
The ethnic chic attitude promoted by this fashion label has been extended to accessories. In this former Hungarian grocery store, with a Chinese-inspired interior, you'll find shoes, embroidered scarves and hand-painted bags, as well as candles and incense.
🕐 Tue–Sat 10.30–2, 3–7, Sun 1–7 🚇 Madeleine

SPORTING GOODS

AU VIEUX CAMPEUR
Map 173 M8
48 rue des Écoles, 75005
Tel 01 53 10 48 48
www.auvieuxcampeur.fr
No fewer than 22 adjoining boutiques cover a range of sports goods, including winter sports, mountain climbing and scuba-diving. The professional staff offer advice, and you can try out some of the equipment, for example on their indoor rock-climbing wall.
🕐 Mon, Tue, Wed, Fri 11–7.30, Thu 11–9, Sat 10–7.30 🚇 Maubert Mutualité

WHAT TO DO

ENTERTAINMENT

Paris has a rich heritage in the performing arts, ranging from the classics through to avant-garde, at venues from small clubs to huge auditoriums. To find out what's on, check magazines such as *Pariscope* and *L'Officiel des Spectacles*.

THEATRE

The founding of the Comédie Française (www.comedie-francaise.fr) in 1680 kick-started a national love of the theatre, and Paris now offers a wealth of classical, avant-garde and foreign-language plays. French theatre tends to be rather intellectual—the Comédie Française (▷ 206) still concentrates on the classics. Many theatres are closed from mid-July to September.

Paris is one of Europe's leading jazz venues

DANCE

Modern and contemporary dance is an active force within French arts. Leading the way is the Centre Georges Pompidou (▷ 82–86).

CLASSICAL MUSIC

Paris has no world-renowned orchestra, and live classical music has less of a high profile here than in some European capitals. However, several ensembles, such as the Orchestre de Paris (www.orchestredeparis.com), have an annual schedule. Versailles' *Grandes Eaux Musicales* (▷ 246) are also

popular. Churches often host reasonably priced classical music concerts—look for posters on the noticeboards.

JAZZ

Paris's plethora of small clubs, including New Morning (▷ 205), cater to an army of aficionados. Jazz festivals include the Autumn Festival du Jazz, and Paris Jazz in the Bois de Vincennes.

BALLET AND OPERA

The ornate Opéra Palais Garnier (▷ 202) and Opéra Bastille (▷ 202) lead the field. The Opéra Bastille opened in 1989 and is a striking example of modern architecture. Reserve well in advance.

CINEMAS

The French are renewing their interest in home-grown films, but you should always be able to find an English-language movie if you want to—your best bet is one of the multiplex cinemas. Look for the symbol 'VO' *(version originale)*, which shows that a non-French film is being shown in its original language. For something more Parisian in character, try one of the many art-house cinemas.

CABARET

Paris's world-famous cabaret venues tend to attract tourists rather than locals. Many offer a joint dinner-and-show ticket and you can unload a small fortune on the sometimes exorbitantly priced drinks.

BOOKING TICKETS

Most theatre box offices sell tickets to their own performances and will accept

phone bookings with payment by credit card. If you are calling from abroad, be aware that box offices often have '089' premium-rate numbers. It may be less expensive to use the venue's general administration number, then ask to be put through to the box office *(bureau de location)*. FNAC stores (www.fnac.com) are ticket agents. For rock/pop/jazz concerts try Virgin Megastore (www.virginmega.fr), or for multi-venue arts festivals try the tourist office. The Kiosque Théâtre sells cut-price tickets for the day of the performance for most Paris

The Opéra Palais Garnier is an architectural masterpiece

theatres. There are outlets at 15 place de la Madeleine and at Gare Montparnasse. Matinée performances are often less expensive than evening shows, and tickets for that day's performances (if available) are also sold at a discount.

DRESS CODE

Evening theatre, operatic and orchestral performances require smart but not necessarily formal clothing, although you can dress to the hilt if you want to. For other types of performance, casual clothing is perfectly acceptable.

Entertainment Locator

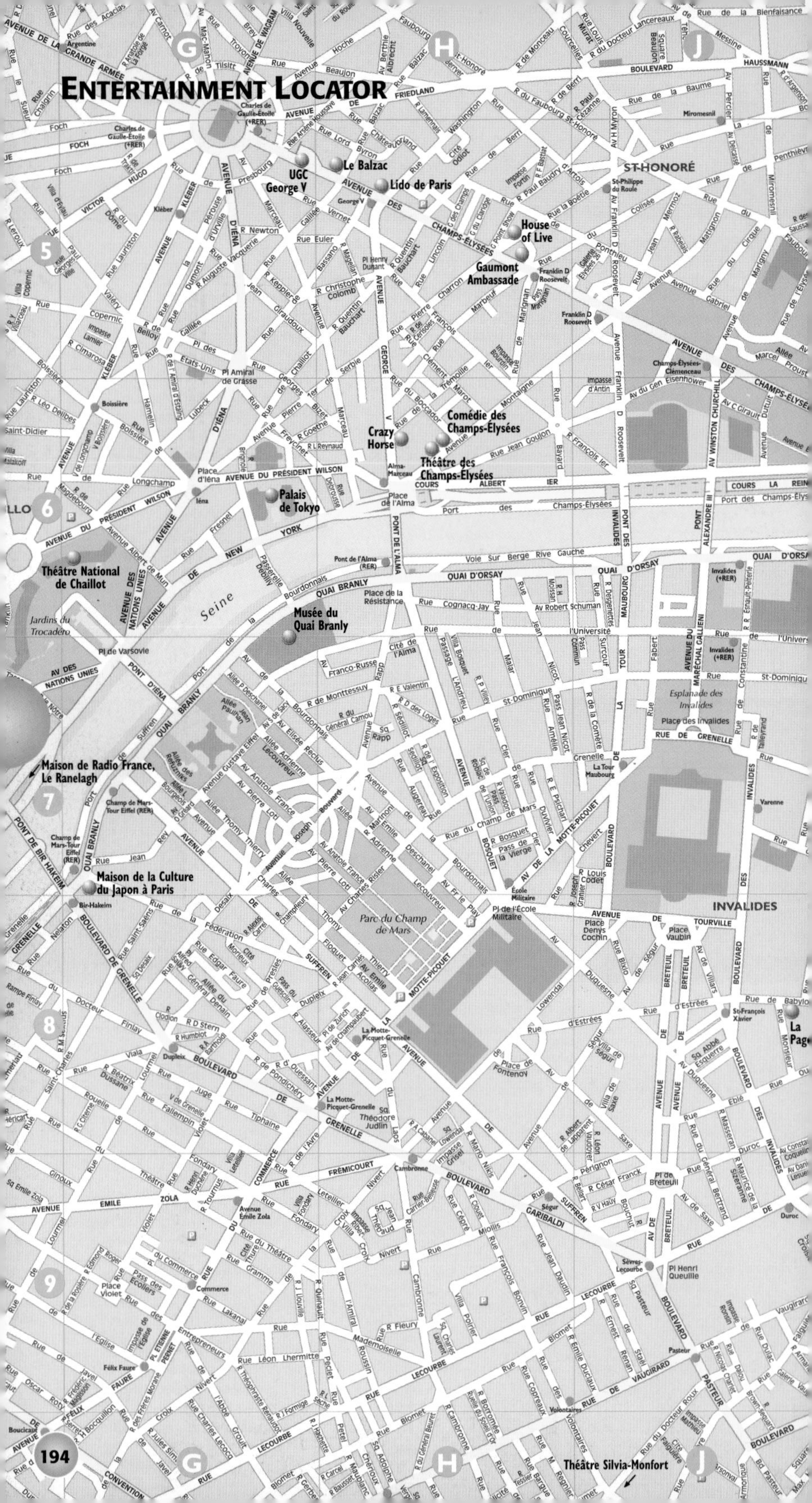

UGC George V
Le Balzac
Lido de Paris
House of Live
Gaumont Ambassade
Comédie des Champs-Elysées
Crazy Horse
Théâtre des Champs-Elysées
Palais de Tokyo
Théâtre National de Chaillot
Musée du Quai Branly
Maison de Radio France, Le Ranelagh
Maison de la Culture du Japon à Paris
Théâtre Silvia-Monfort
La Pagode
ST-HONORÉ
INVALIDES
Seine
Parc du Champ de Mars
Esplanade des Invalides

ENTERTAINMENT LOCATOR

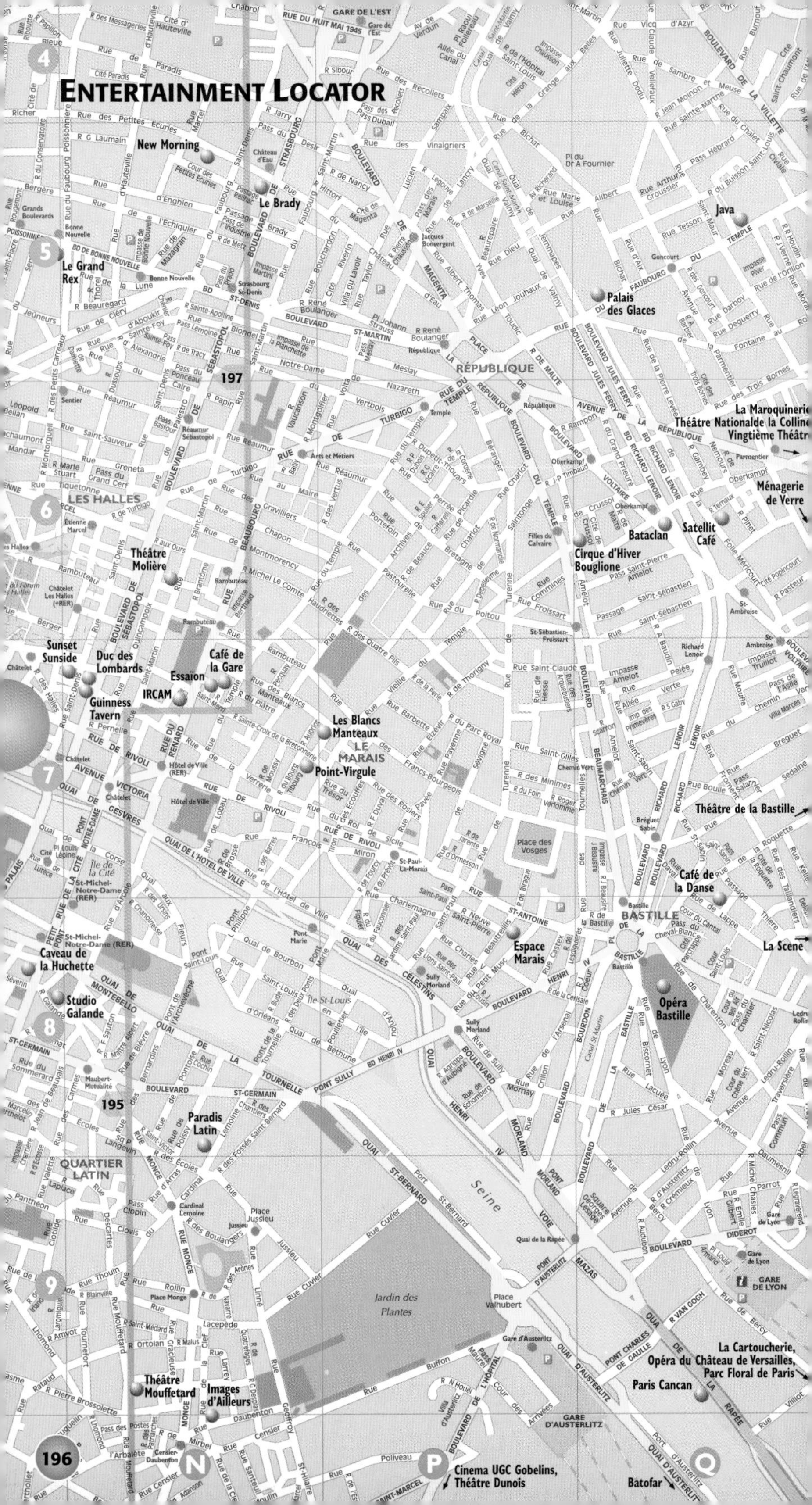

New Morning

Le Brady

Java

Le Grand Rex

Palais des Glaces

197

La Maroquinerie
Théâtre Nationalde la Colline
Vingtième Théâtre

Ménagerie
de Verre

LES HALLES

Théâtre
Molière

Satellit
Café

Bataclan

Cirque d'Hiver
Bouglione

Sunset
Sunside

Duc des
Lombards

Essaion

Café de
la Gare

Guinness
Tavern

IRCAM

Les Blancs
Manteaux

LE
MARAIS

Point-Virgule

Théâtre de la Bastille

Café de
la Danse

Caveau de
la Huchette

Hôtel de Ville

BASTILLE

La Scène

Studio
Galande

195

Espace
Marais

Opéra
Bastille

Paradis
Latin

QUARTIER
LATIN

Seine

Jardin des
Plantes

GARE
DE LYON

La Cartoucherie,
Opéra du Château de Versailles,
Parc Floral de Paris

Théâtre
Mouffetard

Images
d'Ailleurs

Paris Cancan

GARE
D'AUSTERLITZ

196

N

P Cinema UGC Gobelins,
Théâtre Dunois

Batofar

Q

ARTS VENUES

BATACLAN
Map 196 Q6
50 boulevard Voltaire, 75011
Tel 01 43 14 00 30
www.le-bataclan.com
A varied schedule of modern music and traditional Latin rhythms, plus folklore, orchestral performances and rock.
🕐 On performance nights from 7.30 or 8pm 🎫 Varies 🚇 Oberkampf

ESPACE MARAIS
Map 196 P8
22 rue Beautreillis, 75004
Tel 01 48 04 91 55
www.theatreespacemarais.com
This small theatre, occupying the left wing of a 17th-century mansion where Baudelaire once lived and Cézanne had his studio, has a contemporary interior and a central stage. Its varied programme includes dance and music as well as plays.
🕐 Varies 🎫 €24–€34 🚇 Bastille

GLAZ'ART
Map 197 off N3
7–15 avenue de la Porte de la Villette, 75019
Tel 01 40 36 55 65
www.glazart.com
Named after a group of pro-art activists and located in a refurbished bus station, this experimental café has avant-garde performances (including concerts, exhibitions and video projections) in a decadent, arty atmosphere.
🕐 Sun–Fri 8.30pm–2am, Sat 10pm–5am 🎫 Around €10 🚇 Porte de la Villette

LA MAROQUINERIE
Map 196 off Q6
23 rue Boyer, 75020
Tel 01 40 33 35 05
www.lamaroquinerie.fr
Once a fine leather shop (as its name indicates), La Maroquinerie is a springboard for new talent. It has an eclectic, audacious and ever-changing schedule, with literary conversations,

techno music concerts, drama and more.
🕐 Mon–Sat 11am–1am 🎫 €15–€17 🚇 Gambetta

MUSÉE DU QUAI BRANLY
Map 194 G6/7
29–37 quai Branly, 75007
Tel 01 56 61 70 00
www.quaibranly.fr
This new museum and cultural venue offers a diverse series of performances from Africa, the Pacific region and the Far East, including martial arts displays, marionette and shadow plays, and traditional song and dance.
🕐 Varies 🎫 Varies 🚇 Champ de Mars-Tour Eiffel

Au Lapin Agile is a Montmartre institution

PALAIS DE TOKYO
Map 194 G6
13 avenue du Président Wilson, 75016
Tel 01 47 23 54 01
www.palaisdetokyo.com
Dedicated to contemporary art, this venue is attempting to revive the spirit of Andy Warhol's factory. Contrasting with its chic surroundings, this large space, with its exposed concrete, hosts temporary exhibitions, concerts, film projections and debates.
🕐 Tue–Sun noon–midnight 🎫 Gallery: €6 🚇 Iéna, Trocadéro

LA SCÈNE
Map 196 off Q8
2 bis rue des Taillandiers, 75011
Tel 01 48 06 50 70
www.la-scene.com
This concert venue and its adjoining restaurant are in an old warehouse. There is a lounge bar upstairs, where the concerts can be seen (but not heard). Electro and acoustic music features, sometimes accompanied by video projections.
🕐 Varies 🎫 Between €10 and €16 🚇 Ledru-Rollin

THÉÂTRE MOLIÈRE–MAISON DE LA POÉSIE
Map 196 N6
157 rue St-Martin, 75003
Tel 01 44 54 53 00
www.maisondelapoesie-moliere.com
The Molière theatre, dating from 1791, is home to the 'House of Poetry', where activities include readings, sometimes with music or dance. Festivals explore the literature of other countries.
🕐 Varies 🎫 €5–€20 🚇 Rambuteau

CABARET

AU LAPIN AGILE
Map 197 M2
22 rue des Saules, 75018
01 46 06 85 87
www.au-lapin-agile.com
This Montmartre cabaret has been a meeting place for artists for nearly 150 years. On the walls, many souvenirs tell of this glorious past. French singers and poets perform here Tuesday to Sunday in a cordial but intimate atmosphere.
🕐 Show: Tue–Sun 9pm–2am 🎫 Show and drink: €24 🚇 Lamarck-Caulaincourt

LA BELLE ÉPOQUE
Map 195 L5
36 rue des Petits-Champs, 75002
Tel 01 42 96 33 33
www.belleepoqueparis.com
The truly sparkling show *La Vie est Belle* (Life is Beautiful) includes the cancan, which the audience is then invited to

WHAT TO DO

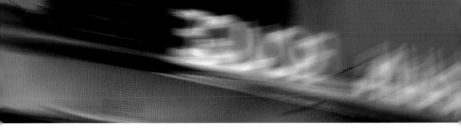

dance. Fine French cuisine is served during the show.
🎭 Show: daily 9pm 🍽 Show and dinner: €70–€100 🚇 Pyramides

CARROUSEL DE PARIS
Map 197 L3
40 rue Fontaine, 75009
Tel 01 42 82 09 16
www.carrouseldeparis.fr
After a diverse show—French cancan, comedians, magic tricks and much more—it is your turn to come onto the dance floor. One of the few cabarets/clubs.
🎭 Show: daily 8.30pm 🍽 Show and dinner: €49 🚇 Blanche

CRAZY HORSE
Map 194 H6
12 avenue George V, 75008
Tel 01 47 23 32 32
www.lecrazyhorseparis.com
This Parisian institution was established in 1951. Its *Taboo* show presents dancers who, as a result of lighting effects, appear to be almost nude. Dinner is served during the show.
🎭 Show: Sun–Fri 8.30pm, 11pm, Sat 7.30pm, 9.45pm, 11.50pm
🍽 Show and dinner: €135
🚇 Alma-Marceau, George V

FOLIES-BERGÈRE
Map 197 M4
32 rue Richer, 75009
Tel 01 44 79 98 60
www.foliesbergere.com
The legendary Folies-Bergère opened in 1869 and became famous for its risqué shows. It now hosts Broadway-style musicals, variety shows, and concerts. Dinner is served before or after the show.
🎭 Show: Tue–Sun 7pm 🍽 Show and dinner: €127–€132 🚇 Cadet, Grands Boulevards

LIDO DE PARIS
Map 194 H5
116 bis avenue des Champs-Élysées, 75008
Tel 01 40 76 56 10
www.lido.fr
A prestigious address for this cabaret, which offers a

titillating show, with scantily dressed dancers and magic tricks, and some fine French cuisine, under the direction of chef Paul Bocuse.
🎭 Show: daily 7.30pm 🍽 Show: €80–€100. Show and dinner: €140–€200 🚇 George V

MADAME ARTHUR
Map 197 M3
75 bis rue des Martyrs, 75018
Tel 01 42 54 15 92
Impersonators of both sexes play famous French singers, including Sheila and Sylvie Vartan. A bit of cancan spices up your dinner, with dancing until the early hours after the show.

The Moulin Rouge stands out on the boulevard de Clichy

🎭 Show: daily 9pm 🍽 €47 (weekends and holidays €63) 🚇 Pigalle

MOULIN ROUGE
Map 197 L3
82 boulevard de Clichy, 75018
Tel 01 53 09 82 82
www.moulin-rouge.fr
The 'Red Windmill' opened in 1889 and became even more of a Parisian institution after the release of the eponymous movie in 2001 (▷ 111). Fine food is served in the magnificent building while you watch the titillating *Féerie* show.
🎭 Shows: daily 9pm, 11pm
🍽 Show: €89–€99. Show and dinner: €145–€175 🚇 Blanche

OPÉRA COMIQUE
See Classical Music, Dance and Opera, ▷ 202.

PARADIS LATIN
Map 196 N8
28 rue Cardinal Lemoine, 75005
Tel 01 43 25 28 28
www.paradis-latin.com
Built by Gustave Eiffel at the same time as his tower, this cabaret flourished until Montmartre robbed it of the limelight in the early 20th century, but found a new lease of life in the late 1970s. Its show *Paradis d'Amour* is dedicated to love in the true French cabaret tradition.
🎭 Wed–Mon 8pm; show at 9.30pm
🍽 Show: €82. Show and dinner: €117–€170 🚇 Cardinal-Lemoine

PARIS CANCAN
Map 196 Q9
Port de la Rapée, 75012
Tel 01 45 85 07 43
www.pariscancan.net
This cruise-dinner-show on the theme of Paris and French cancan takes you back to Toulouse-Lautrec's Paris while you glide past immortal landmarks and enjoy a gourmet dinner on the *Alizé*'s panoramic deck. There is dancing after the show.
🎭 Thu–Fri 7.45pm; other days: ask
🍽 Cruise, dinner and show: €119 🚇 Gare de Lyon

CINEMAS
LE BALZAC
Map 194 H5
1 rue Balzac, 75008
Tel 01 45 61 10 60
www.cinemabalzac.com
Le Balzac is famous for its screenings of American independent films (shown in the original language) and for the debates that often follow. The biggest of the three screens often has photography exhibitions. There is also a bar on site.
🎭 Daily 2–10 🍽 Adult €9, child €7
🚇 George V, Charles de Gaulle-Étoile

LE BRADY

Map 196 N5
39 boulevard de Strasbourg, 75010
Tel 01 47 70 08 86
Here you can see a mix of action movies, cult classics and B-movies.
Daily 1.30–10 Adult €7, child €5 Château d'Eau

LE CHAMPO

Map 195 M8
51 rue des Écoles, 75005
Tel 01 43 54 51 60
Come here for cult classics. Numerous retrospectives explore the work of directors such as the Marx Brothers and Jacques Tati. Films are shown in their original language.
Daily 1.50–10 Adult €7, child €5.50 St-Michel, Odéon, Cluny-La Sorbonne

CINÉMA DES CINÉASTES

Map 197 K3
7 avenue de Clichy, 75017
Tel 01 53 42 40 20
In a former cabaret venue designed by Gustave Eiffel, this three-screen complex shows avant-garde films, usually in their original language. Bar-restaurant on site.
Daily 1.30–10.30 Adult €7.70, child €6 Place de Clichy

CINEMA UGC GOBELINS

Map 196 off P9
66 bis avenue Gobelins, 75013
Tel 0892 70 00 00
All the latest French and Hollywood hits are screened at this multiplex close to the Manufacture des Gobelins. English-language films are dubbed.
Daily 9am–10pm Adult €9.80, child €5.90 Les Gobelins

L'ENTREPÔT

Map 195 off K10
7–9 rue Francis de Pressensé, 75014
Tel 01 45 40 07 50
A cinema that film buffs dream of: Cult movies and art films, from all periods and parts of the world, are screened in

their original language. There are many themed retrospectives. There is a bar-restaurant on site.
Daily 2–10 Adult €7, child €4 Pernety

FORUM DES IMAGES

Map 195 M6
Porte St-Eustache, Forum des Halles, 75001
Tel 01 44 76 63 00
www.forumdesimages.net
This complex offers four different screenings daily of films (some in their original language) illustrating various themes as well as retrospectives about Paris. There are also children's

One of Paris's many cinemas

afternoons, and a wide selection of films about Paris which can be viewed on individual screens.
Tue–Sun 1–9 (Tue until 10) Day pass: adult €9, child €5 Les Halles

GAUMONT AMBASSADE

Map 194 H5
50 avenue des Champs-Élysées, 75008
Tel 0892 696696 ext. 120
www.gaumont.com
This prestigiously sited seven-screen cinema has a varied schedule: from mass-market productions to art films via some premières. All are shown in their original language.

Daily 12–10 Adult €9.80, child €6.90 Franklin D. Roosevelt

LA GÉODE

Map 197 off N3
26 avenue Corentin-Cariou, 75019
Tel 01 39 17 10 00
www.cite-sciences.fr
La Géode is at the Parc de la Villette (▷ 146–147). A gigantic hemispheric screen and an auditorium with digital stereo sound really take you into the movie. No recent releases are screened as only films specially adapted to this technology can be shown.
Daily 10.30–9.30 Adult €9, child €7 Porte de la Villette

LE GRAND REX

Map 197 M5
1 boulevard Poissonnière, 75002
Tel 01 42 36 83 93
Paris's last grand old cinema, founded in 1936, has a lavish auditorium and one of Europe's largest screens. Mass-market productions dominate the bill. Some films are shown in their original language.
Daily 10–7 Adult €8, child €4.90 Bonne Nouvelle

IMAGES D'AILLEURS

Map 196 N9
21 rue de la Clef, 75005
Tel 01 45 87 18 09
As its name 'Pictures from Elsewhere' suggests, this cinema shows films and documentaries from around the world in their original language, sometimes followed by debates. There are also films for children, some of them in their original language.
Fri–Mon 2–10
Adult €5.50, child (under 12) €4.90 Censier-Daubenton

MK2 PARNASSE

Map 195 L9
11 rue Jules-Chaplain, 75006
Tel 0892 698484 ext. 494
www.mk2.com
Minutes from Tour Montparnasse, this small

cinema is an eminent member of the MK2 chain, which puts the emphasis on independent films. There are many themed weeks and retrospectives, and all films are in their original shown language.
🎬 Daily 1.30–10 🎟 Adult €8, child €5.90 🚇 Vavin

LA PAGODE
Map 194 J8
57 rue de Babylone, 75007
Tel 01 45 55 48 48
Housed in a Chinese pagoda, this cinema has two screens and the larger one has lavish surroundings. Cult classics and recent arty releases fill the schedule. Films are shown in their original language. There is a small tea room on site.
🎬 Daily 2–10 🎟 Adult €8, child €6.50 🚇 St-François-Xavier

PARIS STORY
Map 197 L5
11 bis rue Scribe, 75009
Tel 01 42 66 62 06
www.paris-story.com
This thrilling 45-minute multimedia show on a giant screen illustrates Paris's history over the past 2,000 years. It's brought to life by Victor Hugo himself to music by Lully, Berlioz, Gounod, Saint-Saëns and others. There is also an exhibition on the architectural styles of Paris's monuments.
🎬 Daily 9–7 on the hour; available in 12 languages through headsets 🎟 Adult €10, child €6 🚇 Opéra

STUDIO GALANDE
Map 195 M8
42 rue Galande, 75005
Tel 01 43 54 72 71
www.studiogalande.fr
Cult movie The Rocky Horror Picture Show is shown here every Friday and Saturday evening–come dressed up if you like. The rest of the week screenings vary from art films to cartoons.
🎬 Daily 2–10.30. Open only to over 12s 🎟 Adult €7.70, child €6 🚇 St-Michel, Maubert Mutualité

UGC CINÉ FORUM LES HALLES
Map 195 M6
7 place de la Rotonde, 75001
Tel 0892 700 000 ext. 11
www.ugc.fr
Films are shown in their original language at this 19-screen complex. Look out for the jumbo-sized pictures of stars of the silver screen in the hall.
🎬 Daily 9am–10.30pm 🎟 Adult €9.80, child €5.90 🚇 Châtelet-Les Halles

UGC GEORGE V
Map 194 G5
146 avenue des Champs-Élysées, 75008
Tel 0892 700 000
www.ugc.fr

Catch a film in a unique setting at La Pagode

Of all the cinemas on the Champs-Élysées, this is probably the one offering the largest choice. Foreign films are shown in their original language.
🎬 Daily 10am–10.30pm 🎟 Adult €9.80, child €5.90 🚇 Charles de Gaulle-Étoile

CIRCUS
CIRQUE D'HIVER BOUGLIONE
Map 196 Q6
110 rue Amelot, 75011
Tel 01 47 00 28 81
www.cirquehiver.com
This lavishly decorated 19th-century arena has been home to the Bouglione family circus since 1934. Alongside

traditional performances by trapeze artists, clowns and wild animals, concerts are sometimes held here.
🎬 Varies 🎟 €21.50–€40.50 🚇 Oberkampf, Filles du Calvaire

CLASSICAL MUSIC, DANCE AND OPERA

AUDITORIUM DU LOUVRE
Map 195 L6
Le Louvre, 75001 (entrance by the Pyramid)
Tel 01 40 20 55 00
www.louvre.fr
This 420-seat auditorium has an impressive setting beneath the Louvre's Pyramid. The excellent and varied schedule includes sacred music, film themes and recitals.
🎬 Concerts: Wed 8pm, Thu 12.30pm 🎟 €30 (8pm), €10 (lunchtime) 🚇 Louvre-Rivoli

CENTRE NATIONAL DE LA DANSE
Map 197 off N3
1 rue Victor-Hugo, 93507 Pantin
Tel 01 41 83 27 27
www.cnd.fr
The National Dance Centre puts on shows here and at other venues. There are also debates, lectures and films on many aspects of dance, as well as professional workshops.
🎬 Varies 🎟 Varies 🚇 Hoche

CITÉ DE LA MUSIQUE
Map 197 off N3
221 avenue Jean-Jaurès, 75019
Tel 01 44 84 44 84
www.cite-musique.fr
This postmodern building at the Parc de la Villette (▷ 146–147) hosts a wide range of opera, jazz, classical and world music concerts.
🎬 Varies 🎟 Varies 🚇 Porte de Pantin

WHAT TO DO

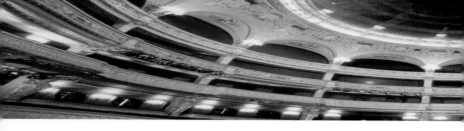

ÉGLISE DE LA MADELEINE

Map 195 K5
Place de la Madeleine, 75008
Tel 01 44 51 69 00
www.eglise-lamadeleine.com
This neoclassical church, dating from 1842, hosts free organ recitals at least two Sundays a month. Chamber music, symphony orchestras and vocal performances complete its schedule.
🕐 Free organ recitals: some Sun 4pm. Times of other performances vary
💶 Varies 🚇 Madeleine

MAISON DE LA CULTURE DU JAPON À PARIS

Map 194 G7
101 bis quai Branly, 75015
Tel 01 44 37 95 00
www.mcjp.asso.fr
This modern, open-plan, glass and steel building showcases Japanese culture. Some dance performances, both modern and traditional, are staged. The modular auditorium can hold up to 300 people.
🕐 Varies 💶 Varies 🚇 Bir-Hakeim

MAISON DE RADIO FRANCE

Map 194 off F7
116 avenue du Président-Kennedy, 75016
Tel 01 56 40 15 16
www.radio-france.fr
Top-notch symphony orchestras, jazz concerts and operas are all presented here, either as live broadcasts or pre-recorded for subsequent broadcasts.
🕐 Varies 💶 Free (or small charge) 🚊 Kennedy Radio France

MÉNAGERIE DE VERRE

Map 196 off Q6
12 rue Léchevin, 75011
Tel 01 43 38 33 44
The glass roof and concrete walls distinguish this venue. You can see modern dance performances and festivals combining video, dance and visual arts. Credit cards are not accepted.
🕐 Performance: daily 8.30pm
💶 €13 🚇 Parmentier

MUSÉE NATIONAL DU MOYEN ÂGE–THERMES DE CLUNY

Map 195 M8
6 place Paul-Painlevé, 75005
Tel 01 53 73 78 16
www.musee-moyenage.fr
This medieval mansion is home to a museum dedicated to the Middle Ages (▷ 128–129), but it also hosts classical and chamber music concerts. It's a unique setting.
🕐 Performances: Fri 12.30pm, Sat 4pm and occasional evenings at 7pm
💶 Free with admission to museum (€7.50). Evening performances €16
🚇 Cluny–La Sorbonne

The Opéra Comique was originally built in 1780

OPÉRA BASTILLE

Map 196 Q8
120 rue de Lyon, 75012
Tel 0892 899 090
www.operadeparis.fr
This massive modern auditorium, with its 2,700 seats, opened in 1989, amid much controversy (▷ 142). Operas and symphony orchestras benefit from its exceptional acoustics, and there is also some ballet.
🕐 Varies 💶 €7–€160 🚇 Bastille

OPÉRA DU CHÂTEAU DE VERSAILLES-OPÉRA ROYAL

Map 196 off Q9
Château de Versailles, RP 834, 78008
Tel 01 39 20 16 20

www.chateauversailles.fr
The auditorium at the Château de Versailles was originally built for Louis XVI's wedding, and opened in 1770. Ballet, opera and drama are all performed here, in an impressive setting, surrounded by statues, trompe l'oeil marble and a painted ceiling.
🕐 Varies 💶 Varies 🚊 Versailles Rive Droite, Versailles Rive Gauche, Versailles Chantier

OPÉRA COMIQUE

Map 197 M5
5 rue Favart, 75002
Tel 0825 01 01 23
www.opera-comique.com
The lavish interior here has frescoes on the ceiling and gilded mouldings. Music aficionados will appreciate the eclectic mix of events, from symphony orchestras to variety shows, via operettas.
🕐 Varies 💶 Varies 🚇 Richelieu-Drouot

OPÉRA PALAIS GARNIER

Map 197 L5
Place de l'Opéra, 75009
Tel 0892 899 090
www.operadeparis.fr
This architectural masterpiece was built during the 19th century by Charles Garnier (▷ 142). It provides a lavish, prestigious setting for visiting ballet and opera companies, and orchestras.
🕐 Varies 💶 €7–€160 🚇 Opéra

PARC FLORAL DE PARIS

Map 196 off Q9
Esplanade du Château de Vincennes, 75012
Tel 01 49 57 24 84
www.parcfloraldeparis.com
This beautiful park, with hundreds of plant species, hosts an annual jazz festival from June to July and a classical music festival during August and September. See top-class performances in this exceptional open-air setting. Credit cards are not accepted.
🕐 Varies 💶 Varies 🚇 Château de Vincennes

WHAT TO DO

THÉÂTRE DE LA BASTILLE
Map 196 off Q7
76 rue de la Roquette, 75011
Tel 01 43 57 42 14
www.theatre-bastille.com
Formerly a cinema, this venue
shows avant-garde plays and
dance performances. Keen on
hosting new talent, it also
welcomes big names such
as German choreographer
Pina Bausch.
⊙ Performances: Tue–Sat 7.30pm,
9pm, Sun 5pm 🖐 €20 🚇 Bastille

THÉÂTRE DES CHAMPS-ÉLYSÉES
Map 194 H6
15 avenue Montaigne, 75008
Tel 01 49 52 50 50
www.theatrechampselysees.fr
This grand auditorium, with
red velvet seats and balconies,
hosts performances of opera,
ballet, classical and chamber
music, as well as some jazz
and solo variety singers.
⊙ Performances: almost daily at
around 7.30–8pm 🖐 Varies
🚇 Franklin D. Roosevelt, Alma-Marceau

THÉÂTRE DE LA CITÉ INTERNATIONALE
Map 195 off L10
21 boulevard Jourdan, 75014
Tel 01 43 13 50 50
Paris's International Halls of
Residence are home to this
imposing complex of three
auditoriums (with 500, 280
and 150 seats), created in
1968. Dance performances
and contemporary plays form
most of the schedule.
⊙ Performances: Mon–Tue and
Thu–Sat evening, Sun afternoon
🖐 €21 🚇 Porte d'Orléans
🚊 Cité Universitaire

THÉÂTRE MUSICAL PARIS CHÂTELET
Map 195 M7
2 rue Edouard Colonne, 75001
Tel 01 40 28 28 40
www.chatelet-theatre.com
Built in 1862, this venue is
famed for its grandeur, with
candelabra and gilded
mouldings. It attracts

an audience of classical music
lovers who like to dress up
for the orchestra, concerts,
ballet and opera staged here.
⊙ Performance: daily (concerts 8pm/
opera 7.30pm) 🖐 €20–€23
🚇 Châtelet

THÉÂTRE LE RANELAGH
See Theatre, ▷ 208.

THÉÂTRE SILVIA–MONFORT
See Theatre, ▷ 208.

THÉÂTRE DE LA VILLE
See Theatre, ▷ 208.

THÉÂTRE DE LA VILLE–SALLE DES ABBESSES
See Theatre, ▷ 208.

*La Balle au Bond has fine
acoustics and beautiful views*

COMEDY
LES BLANCS MANTEAUX
Map 196 P7
15 rue des Blancs Manteaux, 75004
Tel 01 48 87 15 84
www.blancsmanteaux.fr
This café-theatre, in a 17th-century mansion, stages
one-man comedy shows and
sketches. *Plateaux d'Humour*
(Humour Platters), which
present budding talent, are on
Wednesdays.
⊙ Show: daily 8 or 9.30pm 🖐 €16
🚇 Hôtel de Ville

CAFÉ D'EDGAR–THÉÂTRE D'EDGAR
Map 195 K9
58 boulevard Edgar Quinet, 75014
Tel 01 42 79 97 97
www.edgar.fr
This was a pioneer of the café-theatre style launched in the
1970s. It still offers small-production comedy acts that
appeal to a wide audience, and
is a springboard for new talent.
⊙ Performance: varies 🖐 Varies
🚇 Edgar Quinet

CAFÉ DE LA GARE
Map 196 N7
41 rue du Temple, 75004
Tel 01 42 78 52 51
Well-hidden in a listed court-yard, this venue perpetuates the
tradition of the café-theatre.
Actor Gerard Depardieu made
his debut here.
⊙ Every evening, times vary
🖐 Around €23 🚇 Hôtel de Ville

GUICHET MONTPARNASSE
Map 195 K10
15 rue du Maine, 75014
Tel 01 43 27 88 61
www.guichetmontparnasse.com
This small auditorium (50
seats) stages lively comedy
shows, often involving
promising young actors.
⊙ Shows: Wed–Sat 7pm, 8.30pm or
10pm 🖐 €18 🚇 Montparnasse-Bienvenüe

PALAIS DES GLACES
Map 196 Q5
37 rue du Faubourg du Temple, 75010
Tel 01 42 02 27 17
www.palaisdesglaces.com
This theatre, with its two
auditoriums, occupies an old
cinema. There are comedy acts
of all kinds, but one-man
shows dominate the bill.
⊙ Show: Tue–Sat evening
🖐 €17–€30 🚇 République

POINT-VIRGULE
Map 196 N7
7 rue Ste-Croix de la Bretonnerie, 75004
Tel 01 42 78 67 03
www.lepointvirgule.com
See all sorts of comedy acts
at this venue, renowned for

its Humour Festival in September. Credit cards are not accepted.
🎭 Shows: daily 8pm, 9.15pm, 10.30pm 💶 €17 🚇 Hôtel de Ville

THÉÂTRE DES DEUX ANES
See Theatre, ▷ 207.

THÉÂTRE DE LA MICHODIÈRE
See Theatre, ▷ 207.

LA BALLE AU BOND
Map 195 L7
Facing 3 quai Malaquais, 75006 (Apr–end Sep); facing 55 quai de la Tournelle, 75005 (Oct–end Mar)
Latin Quarter and St-Germain-des-Prés
Tel 01 40 46 85 12
www.laballeaubond.fr
Moored on the banks of the Seine, this barge hosts all kinds of concerts, including rock, blues and French song.
🎭 Concert: daily around 9pm 💶 €8; drink compulsory (from €5)
🚇 Pont Neuf (location 1), Maubert Mutualité (location 2)

BATOFAR
Map 196 off Q10
Port de la Gare, 75013
Tel 01 53 60 17 30
www.batofar.org
This lightship is moored between Bercy and Tolbiac bridge, on the banks of quai de la Gare, and hosts some of the best techno and house music DJs. Its mixed schedule also includes experimental video nights. There is a restaurant on board and a bar on the deck.
🎭 Sun–Thu 8pm–3am, Fri–Sat 8pm–dawn 💶 €5–€8
🚇 Quai de la Gare, Bibliothèque François Mitterrand

LA BOULE NOIRE
Map 197 M3
120 boulevard Rochechouart, 75018
Tel 01 49 25 81 75
www.laboule-noire.fr
Plenty of famous names have played at this diminutive venue in the heart of Pigalle, including Franz Ferdinand, Jamie Cullum, Metallica and

The Dandy Warhols. It's an eclectic mix but a popular one.
🎭 Varies 💶 Varies 🚇 Pigalle

CABARET SAUVAGE
Map 197 off N3
Parc de la Villette, 75019
Tel 01 42 09 01 09
www.cabaretsauvage.com
Modern architecture (glass, red and silver steel) is the setting for this 'cabaret', where you can listen to world music, electronica, R & B and more. There is a jovial ball on Sundays.
🎭 Show: daily around 8.30pm (but very flexible). Sunday ball: 6pm
💶 Varies 🚇 Porte de la Villette

Take in a gig at the Élysée Montmartre

CAFÉ DE LA DANSE
Map 196 Q8
5 passage Louis-Philippe, 75011
Tel 01 47 00 57 59
www.chez.com/cafedeladanse
There's an intimate feel to this 500-seat auditorium, with its small platform and exposed brick walls. Pop, rock and world music dominate the bill, with some drama and dance. There is a small bar on site. Credit cards are not accepted.
🎭 Performance: daily around 8.30pm 💶 Around €20 🚇 Bastille

CAVEAU DE LA HUCHETTE
Map 195 M8
5 rue de la Huchette, 75005
Tel 01 43 26 65 05
www.caveaudelahuchette.fr
Minutes from the Sorbonne, this popular, two-floor club has hosted famous jazz musicians.
🎭 Performance: daily 9.30pm
💶 €11–€13 🚇 St-Michel, Cluny–La Sorbonne

LA CIGALE
Map 197 M3
120 boulevard de Rochechouart, 75018
Tel 01 49 25 81 75
www.lacigale.fr
This grand former theatre, dating from 1887, has been modernized with a striking black and red theme. It now hosts musicals, rock and pop, and music festivals.
🎭 Varies 💶 Varies 🚇 Anvers, Pigalle

CITÉ DE LA MUSIQUE
See Classical Music, Dance and Opera, ▷ 201.

LE DIVAN DU MONDE
Map 197 M3
75 rue des Martyrs, 75018
Tel 01 42 52 02 46
www.divandumonde.com
This small, inviting concert hall runs theme nights, with an emphasis on world music. It also welcomes new talent. There are lively Saturday evenings with names like Groovy People Party.
🎭 Performance: varies 💶 €10 upwards 🚇 Pigalle

DUC DES LOMBARDS
Map 196 N7
42 rue des Lombards, 75001
Tel 01 42 33 22 88
A Parisian institution, the most prestigious jazz musicians have regularly performed at this intimate club. Their performances have culminated in memorable jam sessions.
🎭 Performance: Mon–Sat 9pm
💶 €19–€25 🚇 Châtelet

ÉLYSÉE MONTMARTRE
Map 197 M3
72 boulevard Rochechouart, 75018
Tel 01 44 92 45 47
www.enroutepourleelysee.com
Over a century old, this
establishment has retained its
original interior and is now
host to some of the best
pop-rock concerts. It is
also famous for its ball and
techno nights.
Varies About €15 Anvers

GUINNESS TAVERN
Map 196 N7
31 bis rue des Lombards, 75001
Tel 01 42 33 26 45
Live rock music is played here
every day of the year from the
great classics of the 1970s to
contemporary tunes, in a
convivial wooden interior.
The draught Guinness helps to
warm the atmosphere.
Concert: daily 10pm Free
Châtelet

HOUSE OF LIVE
Map 194 H5
124 rue de la Boétie, 75008
Tel 01 42 25 18 06
You can enjoy free rock and
blues concerts at this café/bar,
close to the Champs-Élysées.
Concert: 10.30pm Free
George V

IRCAM
Map 196 N7
1 place Igor-Stravinsky, 75004
Tel 01 44 78 48 43
www.ircam.fr
Founded in 1975 by
composer Pierre Boulez, this
institute brings together
musicians and research
scientists for a thorough
exploration of the subject of
music. It is affiliated to the
Centre Georges Pompidou,
where some performances
are held.
Varies Varies Rambuteau,
Hôtel de Ville, Châtelet

JAVA
Map 196 Q5
105 rue du Faubourg du Temple, 75010
Tel 01 42 02 20 52
Latino bands often play at
this concert hall. Salsa
and other Latino strains,
orchestrated by talented DJs,
keep you dancing until the
early hours. Formerly a
cabaret, the venue has been
swinging since 1920 and saw
famous French singer Edith
Piaf make her debut.
Concerts: 8.30pm Varies
Goncourt

MAISON DE RADIO FRANCE
See Classical Music, Dance and
Opera, ▷ 202.

*The Centre Georges Pompidou,
venue for some IRCAM events*

NEW MORNING
Map 196 N5
7–9 rue des Petites Écuries, 75010
Tel 01 45 23 51 41
www.newmorning.com
This famous club has
welcomed the world's most
prestigious jazz musicians over
the years. Bossa nova and
salsa are also played here.
Concert: 9pm (days vary)
Around €25 Château d'Eau

LE PETIT JOURNAL
MONTPARNASSE
Map 195 K10
13 rue du Commandant-Mouchotte,
75014
Tel 01 43 21 56 70
www.lepetitjournal-montparnasse.com

This club, offering quality jazz
and cuisine, has hosted some
of France's best-loved jazz
musicians. It is sister venue to
the Petit Journal on the Latin
Quarter's boulevard St-Michel.
Concert: Mon–Sat 10pm €16
Montparnasse-Bienvenüe

SATELLIT CAFÉ
Map 196 Q6
44 rue de la Folie-Méricourt, 75011
Tel 01 47 00 48 87
www.satellit-cafe.com
This self-proclaimed Parisian
ambassador of world
music, which can hold up to
250 people, has a varied
schedule including Latino,
blues, African, Balkan and
Mediterranean strains.
Concert: Tue–Sat 9pm
Around €10 Oberkampf,
St Ambroise

SUNSET SUNSIDE
Map 196 N7
60 rue des Lombards, 75001
Tel 01 40 26 46 60
www.sunset-sunside.com
Young European talent
frequently heats up this little
cellar during frenzied,
memorable jam sessions.
This is a place for jazz-lovers
who like to wander off the
beaten track.
Concerts: daily 9pm, 10pm
(sometimes closed Mon) €20
Châtelet

THÉÂTRE DES CHAMPS-
ELYSÉES
See Classical Music, Dance and
Opera, ▷ 203.

LE ZÉNITH
Map 197 off N4
Parc de la Villette
Tel 0890 71 02 07
www.lezenith.com
One of the city's premier
venues since 1984, Zenith
featured Elton John in the
autumn of 2007. The prototype
hexagonal lightweight building
has been copied in towns and
cities around France.
Varies Varies Porte de Pantin

THEATRE

ATHÉNÉE THÉÂTRE LOUIS-JOUVET
Map 195 L5
24 rue Caumartin, 75009
Tel 01 53 05 19 19
www.athenee-theatre.com
Built in 1896 and now a listed building, this magnificent venue has a 700-seat auditorium. It stages the classics of drama, opera and chamber music.
Performances: Sep–end Jun Tue–Sat evening, Sun matinée
€10–€36 Havre-Caumartin

BOUFFES DU NORD
Map 197 off N3
37 bis boulevard de la Chapelle, 75010
Tel 01 46 07 34 50
www.bouffesdunord.com
World-famous producer Peter Brook has been managing this venue since 1974 and he continues to direct some of the drama productions here. There are also occasional classical music concerts.
Performances: Tue–Fri 8.30pm, Sat 3.30 and 8.30pm €12–€24
La Chapelle

LA CARTOUCHERIE
Map 196 off Q9
Route du Champ-de-Manoeuvre, 75012
Tel 01 43 74 87 63
www.theatre-du-soleil.fr
At the heart of the Bois de Vincennes, in a former cartridge depot (cartoucherie), you'll find several playhouses: Aquarium, Soleil (Sun), Tempête (Tempest), Chaudron (Cauldron) and Épée de Bois (Wooden Sword). They all host contemporary, avant-garde plays.
Performances: Tue–Sat evening, Sun afternoon From €18
Château de Vincennes (then free shuttle, bus number 112 or walk)

CASINO DE PARIS
Map 197 L4
16 rue de Clichy, 75009
Tel 01 49 95 22 22
www.casinodeparis.fr
You won't find any slot machines here. Concerts,

musicals and plays are on the bill at this legendary venue, which played host to Joséphine Baker in the 1920s.
Performances: Mon–Sat 8 or 8.30pm, Sun 4 or 5pm €18–€60
Trinité d'Estienne d'Orves

COMÉDIE DES CHAMPS-ÉLYSÉES
Map 194 H6
15 avenue Montaigne, 75008
Tel 01 53 23 99 19
www.comediedeschampselysees.com
Set amid luxury shops, this elegant art nouveau venue, with 631 seats, hosts various theatrical productions, including comedy and drama. There are also occasional

The Comédie des Champs-Élysées hosts a range of productions

variety shows. (Not to be mistaken with the Théâtre des Champs-Élysées, at the same address.)
Varies Varies Alma-Marceau, Franklin D. Roosevelt

COMÉDIE FRANÇAISE/SALLE RICHELIEU
Map 195 L6
2 rue de Richelieu, 75001
Tel 01 44 58 15 15
www.comedie-francaise.fr
The Comédie Française is France's most prestigious troupe of actors, established by Molière in 1680. Today, the repertoire is made up of the classics, including works by Shakespeare and Molière.

Performance: daily 8.30pm, some matinées on Sat–Sun €12–€35
Palais Royal–Musée du Louvre

COMÉDIE FRANÇAISE/THÉÂTRE DU VIEUX-COLOMBIER
Map 195 L8
21 rue du Vieux-Colombier, 75006
Tel 01 44 39 87 00
www.comedie-francaise.fr
This 330-seat venue with a modern design was established in 1913. It is associated with the Comédie Française (see above), who interpret contemporary plays here.
Performances: Tue–Sat evening, Sun afternoon €27
St-Sulpice

ESSAÏON
Map 196 N7
6 rue Pierre-au-Lard, 75004
Tel 01 42 78 46 42
www.essaion.com
This 12th-century cellar is now home to two auditoriums: Genet (100 seats) and Beckett (70 seats). It stages small productions by living, French-speaking writers, and some musicals.
Performances: Tue–Sat at 8, 8.30 or 9.30pm Around €15
Rambuteau, Hôtel de Ville

HÉBERTOT
Map 197 off K3
78 bis boulevard des Batignolles, 75017
Tel 01 43 87 23 23
Built in 1830, this venue takes its name from Jacques Hébertot, who was manager here from 1940 to 1973. Quality classics and contemporary plays are on the schedule.
Performances: Tue–Sat 7pm or 9pm €15–€40 Villiers, Rome

LUCERNAIRE/CENTRE NATIONAL D'ART ET D'ESSAI
Map 195 L9
53 rue Notre-Dame-des-Champs, 75006
Tel 01 45 44 57 34
www.lucernaire.fr
This complex has three cinemas, a drama school, art

WHAT TO DO

gallery, bar, restaurant and two theatres. The 'Black' and 'Red' auditoriums, with 130 seats each, stage performances of the classics and quality contemporary plays.
🎭 Performances: Tue–Sat evening 🎫 €20–€30 🚇 Vavin, Notre-Dame des-Champs

THÉÂTRE DE L'ATELIER
Map 197 M3
Place Charles Dullin, 75018
Tel 01 46 06 49 24
www.theatre-atelier.com
The descendant of the Théâtre de Montmartre, which was established here in 1822, this venue dates from 1922. It focuses on well-known works.
🎭 Performances: Tue–Sat 7 or 9pm, Sun 3 or 6pm 🎫 €7–€38 🚇 Anvers

THÉÂTRE DE LA CITÉ INTERNATIONALE
See Classical Music, Dance and Opera, ▷ 203.

THÉÂTRE DES DEUX ANES
Map 197 L3
100 boulevard de Clichy, 75018
Tel 01 46 06 10 26
www.2anes.com
Since 1922, the Théâtre des Deux Anes (Theatre of the Two Donkeys) has remained true to its motto: 'to bray and let laugh'. Its satirical comedies, frequently mocking the French political scene, are sure to entertain.
🎭 Performances: Tue–Fri 8.30pm 🎫 €35–€39 🚇 Blanche

THÉÂTRE DUNOIS
Map 196 off P10
108 rue du Chevaleret, 75013
Tel 01 45 84 72 00
www.theatredunois.org
This theatre, established in 1987, caters specifically to a young audience. There are puppet shows, adaptations of children's books and some choreography—magical and poetic.
🎭 Performances: Wed, Sat, Sun afternoon 🎫 €16, under 15 €6.50 🚇 Chevaleret

THÉÂTRE FONTAINE
Map 197 L3
10 rue Fontaine, 75009
Tel 01 48 74 74 40
This 650-seat former dance hall stages high-quality acts. Contemporary plays and enduring classics are interpreted by well-known actors.
🎭 Performances: Tue–Fri 9pm, Sat 6pm, 9pm 🎫 €16–€32 🚇 Blanche, St-Georges, Pigalle

THÉÂTRE DE LA HUCHETTE
Map 195 M8
23 rue de la Huchette, 75005
Tel 01 43 26 38 99
www.theatrehuchette.com
Two of Ionesco's masterpieces,

The Théâtre National de Chaillot has an elegant setting

La Cantatrice Chauve (The Bald Soprano) and *La Leçon* (The Lesson), have been performed here six days a week for over 50 years. This small venue, in the Latin Quarter, is a Parisian Institution.
🎭 Varies 🎫 €19 for one performance, €29 for both 🚇 St-Michel

THÉÂTRE DE LA MICHODIÈRE
Map 197 L5
4 bis rue de la Michodière, 75002
Tel 01 47 42 95 22
Since its opening in 1925, this theatre has been true to the formula that secured its success: top-quality comedies interpreted by the best actors—Arletty in the 1930s, Roland

Giraud nowadays.
🎭 Performances: Tue–Fri 8.30pm, Sat 5pm, 8.30pm, Sun 3pm 🎫 €8–€44 🚇 Quatre Septembre

THÉÂTRE MOGADOR
Map 197 L4
25 rue de Mogador, 75009
Tel 01 53 32 32 32
www.mogodor.net
Classical music concerts, musicals and operettas make up the majority of the shows at this 1,700-seat auditorium. Comedy and dance are also on the bill.
🎭 Performances: Tue, Fri, Sat evening, Wed, Sat, Sun afternoon 🎫 €25–€95 🚇 Trinité d'Estienne d'Orves

THÉÂTRE MOLIÈRE–MAISON DE LA POÉSIE
See Arts Venues, ▷ 198.

THÉÂTRE MOUFFETARD
Map 196 N9
73 rue Mouffetard, 75005
Tel 01 43 31 11 99
www.theatremouffetard.com
This theatre aims to appeal to all tastes and all ages with plays by classic and contemporary authors, shows sparkling with music and humour, and lively puppet shows for the benefit of their young public.
🎭 Tue–Sat 7 or 9pm; children's show Wed 2.15pm, Sat 3pm and school holidays, Sun 3pm sometimes 🎫 Evening: €16–€22; afternoon: €8 🚇 Place Monge

THÉÂTRE NATIONAL DE CHAILLOT
Map 194 G6
1 place du Trocadéro, 75016
Tel 01 53 65 30 00
www.theatre-chaillot.fr
This theatre, in the imposing Palais de Chaillot, stages productions of all kinds, from top-quality contemporary works to classics.
🎭 Performances: Tue–Sat 8.30pm, Sun 3pm 🎫 €27–€33 🚇 Trocadéro

THÉÂTRE NATIONAL DE LA COLLINE
Map 196 off Q6
15 rue Malte-Brun, 75020
Tel 01 44 62 52 00
www.colline.fr
Housed in a modern building, this is the first national theatre exclusively dedicated to performing the work of contemporary playwrights. There are two auditoriums: the Grand Théâtre (760 seats) and the Petit Théâtre (200 seats).
🎭 Performances: Tue–Sat evening, Sun afternoon 💷 €27 🚇 Gambetta

THÉÂTRE DE NESLE
Map 195 M7
8 rue de Nesle, 75006
Tel 01 46 34 61 04
This vaulted basement, in a 17th-century mansion, hosts American plays produced in English, as well as top-notch French plays and performances specially put on for children (including puppet shows and shadow theatre).
🎭 Performances: Tue–Sat evening, Wed and Sat afternoon 💷 €6–€15 🚇 Odéon, Pont Neuf

THÉÂTRE DU NORD-OUEST
Map 197 M5
13 rue du Faubourg-Montmartre, 75009
Tel 01 47 70 32 75
www.theatredunordouest.com
Edith Piaf performed here in the 1930s, when this venue was a cabaret. It has been a theatre, with two auditoriums, since 1997, and the classics on the bill are re-interpreted by young companies.
🎭 Varies 💷 €20 🚇 Grands Boulevards

THÉÂTRE DU PALAIS ROYAL
Map 195 L6
38 rue Montpensier, 75001
Tel 01 42 97 40 00
www.theatrepalaisroyal.com
This elegant theatre, with its red velvet seats and gilded panels, is wonderfully located within the gardens of the Palais Royal and was built in 1783. Plays and comedy acts dominate the schedule but some classical music can also be enjoyed here.
🎭 Performances: Tue–Fri 8.30pm, Sat 9pm, Sun 3.30pm 💷 Varies 🚇 Bourse, Palais Royal-Musée du Louvre

THÉÂTRE LE RANELAGH
Map 194 off F7
5 rue des Vignes, 75016
Tel 01 42 88 64 44
www.theatre-ranelagh.com
This 340-seat venue, built in 1890, has a somewhat rococo interior with carved wood panels and a lacunar ceiling. The high-quality, varied schedule includes

Check out the posters for the latest shows

classics, contemporary plays and opera.
🎭 Performances: Tue–Sat evening, Sun afternoon 💷 €23 and €30 🚇 La Muette

THÉÂTRE SILVIA-MONFORT
Map 194 off J10
106 rue Brancion, 75015
Tel 01 56 08 33 88
www.silviamonfort.com
The comedienne Silvia Monfort was given this theatre by the city of Paris and went on to produce excellent plays, dance shows and concerts which continues today.
🎭 Performances: Tue, Thu–Sat 8.30pm, Wed 8pm 💷 €15–€26 🚇 Porte de Vanves

THÉÂTRE DE LA VILLE
Map 195 M7
2 place du Châtelet, 75004
Tel 01 42 74 22 77
www.theatredelaville-paris.com
Forever associated with Sarah Bernhardt, who used to play here at the beginning of the 20th century, this grand theatre (1,000 seats) hosts plays and modern dance. In September 2007, 37-year-old Emmanuel Demarcy-Mota, director of the theatre of comedy and drama in Reims, succeeded Gérard Violette as director, and was charged with bringing theatre to a new, younger audience.
🎭 Performances: Mon–Fri 8.30pm, Sat 5pm, 8.30pm 💷 €16–€26 🚇 Châtelet

THÉÂTRE DE LA VILLE–SALLE DES ABBESSES
Map 197 L3
31 rue des Abbesses, 75018
Tel 01 42 74 22 77
www.theatredelaville-paris.com
This auditorium offers the same type of productions as its sister venue, the Théâtre de la Ville (see above): contemporary plays and dance performances.
🎭 Performances: Tue–Sat 8.30pm, Sun 3pm 💷 €16–€26 🚇 Abbesses

VINGTIÈME THÉÂTRE
Map 196 off Q6
7 rue des Platrières, 75020
Tel 01 43 66 01 13
www.vingtiemetheatre.com
This unpretentious venue stages dance, comedy, French song and more. Conferences and debates on pertinent themes are sometimes held alongside the performances.
🎭 Performances: Tue–Fri evening, Sat matinée and evening 💷 €22 🚇 Ménilmontant

WHAT TO DO

NIGHTLIFE

Loyalties change rapidly in Paris but the listings in magazines such as *Pariscope* and *L'Officiel des Spectacles* should help keep you up to date with the places to be seen. The action doesn't start until after midnight at most clubs, and usually continues until dawn on Fridays and Saturdays. You'll often have to pay an entrance fee, and dress well to get past the bouncers. If clubbing isn't your scene, there are thousands of bars across the city, ranging from small and friendly to fiery Latino or trendy-chic.

BARS

L'ATELIER RENAULT
53 avenue des Champs-Élysées, 75008
Tel 0811 88 28 11
www.atelier-renault.com
The Renault car showroom also has a bar, restaurant and trend laboratory, with exhibitions, events and fashion shows. The place has been

There are bars in Paris catering for every taste

transformed into a massive loft, worlds away from a regular car dealer.
🕙 Sun–Thu 10.30pm–12.30am, Fri–Sat 10.30pm–2.30am
🚇 Franklin D. Roosevelt

BAR FLEUR'S
3 rue des Tournelles, 75004
Tel 01 42 71 04 51
Probably the most unusual bar in the city, Bar Fleur's mixes a champagne and vodka/tequila bar with a florist shop. The decor is ultra-cool, with a vast range of fizz and distillates to try.
🕙 Daily 7pm–2am 🚇 Bastille

BAR HEMINGWAY
Hôtel Ritz, 15 place Vendôme, 75001
Tel 01 43 16 33 65
www.ritzparis.com
Within the Ritz hotel, this bar pays tribute to the celebrated writer. Papa himself used to enjoy the elegant atmosphere, where old malts, champagne and cigars are de rigueur.
🕙 Mon–Sat 6.30pm–2am
🚇 Opéra, Madeleine

BARFLY
49–51 avenue George-V, 75008
Tel 01 53 67 84 60
This bright bar used to be a newspaper depot. It is popular with the show business crowd, who come here for a drink or for the innovative fusion food.
🕙 Daily noon–2am 🚇 George V

BARRAMUNDI
3 rue Taitbout, 75009
Tel 01 47 70 21 21
www.barramundi.fr
India meets Africa for the style, and chill-out world music spices up the atmosphere. This place is a hit with the fashion crowd, who come here for a drink in the bar or fusion food in the restaurant.
🕙 Mon–Fri 12–3.30, 6.30–2, Sat 7pm–5am 🚇 Richelieu-Drouot

BA-TA-CLAN CAFÉ
50 boulevard Voltaire, 75011
Tel 01 49 23 96 33
Named after the eponymous adjoining concert hall, this bar welcomes the same trendy clientele. The interior has ochre walls and rattan furniture.
🕙 Daily 7am–2am 🚇 Oberkampf

BELLE HORTENSE
31 rue Vieille-du-Temple, 75004
Tel 01 48 04 71 60
www.cafeine.com
Wine and literature are combined here. If the first should be consumed with moderation, no restrictions apply when it comes to the second. The shelves are full of enticing books.
🕙 Daily 5pm–2am 🚇 Hôtel de Ville

BOCA CHICA
58 rue de Charonne, 75011
Tel 01 43 57 93 13
www.labocachica.com
A fiesta mood reigns at this fully spiced-up tapas bar with its bright stools, long steel bar

Many bars provide an intimate atmosphere

and funky lighting. Come here for a drink or a bite to eat, and enjoy the lively Latino rhythms.
🕙 Sun–Thu 10am–2am, Fri–Sat 10am–5am 🚇 Ledru-Rollin

BOTTLE SHOP
5 rue Trousseau, 75011
Tel 01 43 14 28 04
This unpretentious but trendy café-bar in the lively Bastille area has a small terrace outside, a wooden interior and a convivial atmosphere. Brunch is served on Sundays.
🕙 Daily 11.30am–2am
🚇 Ledru-Rollin

BUDDHA BAR
8 rue Boissy d'Anglas, 75008
Tel 01 53 05 90 00
www.buddha-bar.com
Trendy bar and restaurant where you go to spot celebrities as much as to listen to the music and admire the amazing décor. As a result the place is crowded and the service can be indifferent, unless you are famous.
🕐 Bar and restaurant: Mon–Fri from noon, Sat–Sun from 4pm 🚇 Concorde

CAFÉ DES ANGES
66 rue de la Roquette, 75011
Tel 01 47 00 00 63
The small terrace consists of just one row of bistro tables, but it's perfect for people-watching. The retro interior has wooden tables, a mosaic-tiled floor, a long bar and a lively atmosphere.
🕐 Daily 8am–2am 🚇 Bastille

CAFÉ CHARBON
109 rue Oberkampf, 75011
Tel 01 43 57 55 13
A former coal merchant's, dating from 1890, this café-bar is full of character, with large mirrors and frescoes on the walls. One of the trendiest of rue Oberkampf's many bars, it is packed in the evenings.
🕐 Daily 9am–2am 🚇 Rue St-Maur

CAFÉ DE L'INDUSTRIE
16 rue St-Sabin, 75011
Tel 01 47 00 13 53
Two facing corner locations, a wooden interior, punctuated by exotic curios and pictures of actors, marks this modern bistro. It's very popular with the Bastille area's trendy crowd.
🕐 Sun–Fri 10am–2am
🚇 Bréguet Sabin, Bastille

CAFÉ NOIR
65 rue Montmartre, 75002
Tel 01 40 39 07 36
Between Les Halles and the Bourse, Café Noir is gaining a reputation with the young and beautiful crowd. The terrace is a great place for warm summer evenings.
🕐 Daily 10am–2am 🚇 Sentier

CAFÉ RUC
159 rue St-Honoré, 75001
Tel 01 42 60 97 54
A smart interior—red velvet, columns and indirect lighting—coupled with a prestigious address on a street famous for its couture shops, make this place a hit with the fashion crowd.
🕐 Daily 8am–2.30am 🚇 Palais Royal-Musée du Louvre

CANNIBALE CAFÉ
93 rue Jean-Pierre Timbaud, 75011
Tel 01 49 29 95 59
The retro interior includes a long bar, moleskin wall-seats and large mirrors. It's a convivial venue, which has its

Les Deux-Magots is the perfect place for a philosophical interlude

regulars but also warmly welcomes anyone passing through.
🕐 Daily 8am–2am 🚇 Couronnes

CASEY'S BAR
120 rue Montmartre, 75002
Tel 01 40 13 01 62
This is an Irish pub in the traditional style, with all the latest sporting events enjoyed with noisy enthusiasm, and traditional pub games including darts and pool. There are a couple of tables outside where you can enjoy the fresh air.
🕐 Daily noon–4am 🚇 Sentier

CHAO BA CAFÉ
22 boulevard de Clichy, 75018
Tel 01 46 06 72 90
This is an island of exoticism in the middle of Paris's red-light district. Rattan furniture, bamboo, indirect lighting and chill-out music take you on a visual and aural journey. There's a DJ at weekends.
🕐 Sun–Thu 8.30am–2am, Fri–Sat 8.30am–5am 🚇 Pigalle

CORCORAN'S
28 rue St-André des Arts, 75006
Tel 01 40 46 97 46
This venue takes you to Dublin, with Guinness on tap and old Irish adverts on the walls. Good pub food, including fish and chips and stews, is served at lunchtime.
🕐 Sun–Wed 11am–3.30am, Thu 11am–4.30am, Fri–Sat 11am–5.30am 🚇 St-Michel

CUBANA CAFÉ
45 rue Vavin, 75006
Tel 01 40 46 80 81
www.cubanacafe.com
Revolutionary Cuba at the heart of chic Paris—this evocation of La Havana comes complete with posters, pictures and slogans on the walls, and cigars and rum-based cocktails on the menu.
🕐 Sun–Thu 10am–3am, Fri–Sat 10am–5am 🚇 Vavin

DE LA VILLE CAFÉ
36 boulevard Bonne-Nouvelle, 75010
Tel 01 48 24 48 09
The monumental staircase, stained glass and wrought-iron work give this café a theatrical touch. Lounge music is provided by good DJs.
🕐 Daily 11am–2am
🚇 Bonne Nouvelle

LES DEUX-MAGOTS
6 place St-Germain-des-Prés, 75006
Tel 01 45 48 55 25
www.lesdeuxmagots.fr
A hub for philosophers and artists in the 1950s, and popular with Hemingway, this establishment has kept some of its literary feel thanks to the

proximity of La Hune bookshop. A Parisian institution.
🕐 Daily 7.30am–1am
Ⓜ St-Germain des-Prés

LES EDITEURS
4 carrefour de l'Odéon, 75006
Tel 01 43 26 67 76
www.lesediteurs.fr
Les Editeurs is frequented by the literary crowd. The warm, wooden interior, comfortable red velvet armchairs and subdued lighting make the perfect setting for reading—you're invited to pick up a book from the in-house library. Readings, signings and exhibitions regularly take place and the café is the venue of famous literary awards, including the Prix des Éditeurs.
🕐 Daily 8am–2am Ⓜ Odéon

L'ENDROIT
67 place du Docteur-Félix-Lobligeois, 75017
Tel 01 42 29 50 00
The stylish modern interior has long, black leather wall-seats, indirect lighting and a massive semi-circular bar. The good vibes, with ambient techno and trip hop, suit its trendy clientele.
🕐 Daily noon–2am Ⓜ Rome

LES ÉTAGES
35 rue Vieille-du-Temple, 75004
Tel 01 42 78 72 00
This building has a budget-chic style, with used armchairs and sofas that must have had a glorious past. Imaginative cocktails are served in the lively downstairs bar; you'll find a more intimate mood in the rooms upstairs.
🕐 Daily 3.30pm–2am
Ⓜ Hôtel de Ville

L'ÉTOILE MANQUANTE
34 rue Vieille-du-Temple, 75004
Tel 01 42 72 48 34
www.cafeine.com
This café, full of interesting artwork, is an invitation to daydream. Look up at the pop art sky-like ceiling and don't forget to check out the

toilets, with their abundance of steel and video screens.
🕐 Daily 9am–2am Ⓜ Hôtel de Ville

FAVELA CHIC
18 rue du Faubourg-du-Temple, 75011
Tel 01 40 03 02 66
www.favelachic.com
Sexy-sounding cocktails (the *caipirinha* is a must) and world music spun by DJs are on the bill at this hot Brazilian bar. Some South American food is also available.
🕐 Mon–Fri noon–2am, Sat 7.30–4am
🎟 Free entry (most of the time)
Ⓜ République

Perfect cocktails are on offer at Harry's New York Bar

FOOTSIE
10–12 rue Daunou, 75002
Tel 01 42 60 07 20
Close to Paris's stock market, this bar, named after London's stock index, operates according to the same principle: The drink prices fluctuate according to supply and demand.
🕐 Mon–Thu 12–3, 6–2, Fri–Sat 12–3, 6–4 Ⓜ Opéra

FOURMI
74 rue des Martyrs, 75018
Tel 01 42 64 70 35
Named 'La Fourmi' (the Ant) in reference to La Fontaine's fable, this convivial venue—popular with the arty crowd—has a beautiful retro style with

a large bar, small wooden tables and ochre walls. The concert hall La Cigale (▷ 204) is nearby.
🕐 Mon–Thu 8am–2am, Fri–Sat 8am–4am, Sun 10am–2am
Ⓜ Pigalle

THE FROG & ROSBIF
116 rue St-Denis, 75002
Tel 01 42 36 34 73
www.frogpubs.com
As the name suggests, the Frog & Rosbif is an English pub in Les Halles and one of four Frog pubs in the capital. The company brews its own English-style beer in six varieties. Sports coverage for those that want it, and wi-fi for others.
🕐 Daily noon–2am Ⓜ Étienne Marcel

FUMOIR
6 rue de l'Amiral-de-Coligny, 75001
Tel 01 42 92 00 24
Relax in voluptuous calm—sink into one of the deep armchairs and browse the international newspapers. You can also indulge in a cigar if you wish.
🕐 Daily 11am–2am Ⓜ Louvre-Rivoli

HARRY'S NEW YORK BAR
5 rue Daunou, 75002
Tel 01 42 61 71 14
www.harrys-bar.fr
Hundreds of cocktails are on offer here, perfectly mastered by highly professional barmen. The chic interior combines wood with red moleskin.
🕐 Daily 10am–4am Ⓜ Opéra

HAVANITA
11 rue de Lappe, 75011
Tel 01 43 55 96 42
Club armchairs, palm trees and fans make up the interior; rum-based cocktails and cigars the menu. This little piece of Cuba is on a pedestrianized street where bars are legion.
🕐 Daily 4pm–2am Ⓜ Bastille

KLEIN HOLLAND
36 rue du Roi de Sicile, 75004
Tel 01 42 71 43 13
This is the haunt of the Dutch in Paris, who gather here when

WHAT TO DO

their national soccer team is playing. The beer is inexpensive and there is a pub atmosphere.
🕐 Daily 5pm–2am 🚇 Hôtel de Ville

LIZARD LOUNGE
18 rue du Bourg-Tibourg, 75004
Tel 01 42 72 81 34
www.cheapblonde.com
This lively pub has a wooden interior and beer on tap. Concerts take place in the basement. Not surprisingly, it is a hit with the Brits.
🕐 Daily noon–2am 🚇 Hôtel de Ville

OPA
9 rue Biscornet, 75012
Tel 01 49 28 12 90
Good sounds, with electronica but also 1980s classics, and late opening, make this two-level loft the perfect stop before a night out clubbing.
🕐 Sep–end Jun Tue–Thu 8pm–2am, Fri–Sat 8pm–6am; Jul–end Aug nightly 9.30pm–6am 🎟 Free 🚇 Bastille

O'SULLIVANS BY THE MILL
92 boulevard de Clichy, 75018
Tel 01 42 23 00 30
www.osullivans-pubs.com
Rubbing shoulders with the famed Moulin Rouge, O'Sullivans is a huge venue serving Irish stout and great food, plus it has several large plasma screens to keep sports fans in their seats and a dance floor for those who'd rather groove to the latest sounds.
🕐 Mon–Thu noon–5am, Fri–Sun noon–6am 🚇 Blanche

LE PETIT FER À CHEVAL
30 rue Vieille-du-Temple, 75004
Tel 01 42 72 47 47
www.cafeine.com
Named after its horseshoe-shaped bar, where you can order a coffee or a glass of wine, this venue has a small terrace and retro dining room serving bistro food.
🕐 Daily 9am–2am 🚇 Hôtel de Ville

LES PHILOSOPHES
28 rue Vieille-du-Temple, 75004
Tel 01 42 72 47 47
www.cafeine.com

This café has a smart bistro interior and lots of artwork on the walls. The main attraction, however, is its lovely outside terrace overlooking a quiet, picturesque cul-de-sac. Live piano music.
🕐 Daily 9am–2am 🚇 Hôtel de Ville

LE PISTON PÉLICAN
Rue de Bagnolet, 75020
Tel 01 43 70 35 00
This unpretentious yet trendy bar has an exceptionally convivial atmosphere. It is Bistro-style, with a large bar, old prints, lots of wood and a tiny terrace.
🕐 Mon–Fri 8am–2am, Sat–Sun 10am–2am 🚇 Alexandre Dumas

A fine choice of beverages at Lizard Lounge

RÉSERVOIR
16 rue de la Forge-Royale, 75011
Tel 01 43 56 39 60
www.reservoirclub.com
The luxurious yet funky style mixes leopard print, red velvet, wrought iron and interesting light fixtures. Besides the place's *je ne sais quoi*, it's the lively atmosphere and occasional concerts that draw the trendy crowd.
🕐 Tue–Sat 8pm–late into the night; Sun–Mon invitations only
🚇 Ledru-Rollin

RHUMERIE
166 boulevard St-Germain, 75006
Tel 01 43 54 28 94
www.larhumerie.com

The perennial colonial interior of this venue is the key to its appeal. Punch, palms and rattan furniture let you forget that the sun isn't always there. And when it is, a cocktail on the terrace is a must.
🕐 Daily 9am–2am 🚇 Mabillon

SANZ SANS
49 rue du Faubourg St-Antoine, 75011
Tel 01 44 75 78 78
www.sanzsans.com
Gold and red velvet give a classy touch to this trendy bar, where good DJs, playing techno and R & B, regularly spice up the atmosphere. Restaurant upstairs.
🕐 Tue–Sat 9am–5am, Sun 6pm–5am, Mon 9am–2am 🚇 Bastille

SCHERKHAN
144 rue Oberkampf, 75011
Tel 01 43 57 29 34
Deep sofas, chill-out music and an imposing stuffed tiger set the atmosphere. A warm welcome awaits you at this address in bar-packed rue Oberkampf.
🕐 Daily 5pm–2am 🚇 Ménilmontant

STOLLY'S
16 rue Cloche-Perce, 75004
Tel 01 42 76 06 76
www.cheapblonde.com
This tiny bar in the Marais made its appearance in 1991. Crowds still venture here to enjoy the cocktails, including the signature Cheap Blond, and the terrace, which is great for summer evenings.
🕐 Daily 4.30pm–2am 🚇 St-Paul

LES TROIS MAILLETS
56 rue Galande, 75005
Tel 01 43 54 00 79
It's said that the cellars of this bar played no small part in the Resistance against the German occupation during World War II. Today it's a lively drinking and music venue with occasional live cabaret.
🕐 Daily noon–4am 🚇 St-Michel

CAFÉS

APPAREMENT CAFÉ
18 rue des Coutures-St-Gervais, 75003
Tel 01 48 87 12 22
A café that feels like home. Comfortable armchairs surround coffee tables and there is a library, plus board games—it's also possible to have something to eat here.
◉ Mon–Fri noon–2am, Sat 4pm–2am, Sun 12.30–midnight ◙ St-Paul, Fille du Calvaire

CAFÉ DE L'ATELIER
95 boulevard du Montparnasse, 75014
Tel 01 45 44 98 81
This café welcomes you round the clock for a drink or a snack, inside or on its terrace (heated when necessary). It is a young and trendy spot in a district otherwise home to timeless venues such as the brasserie La Coupole (▷ 266).
◉ Daily 24 hours ◙ Vavin

CAFÉ BEAUBOURG
43 rue St-Merri, 75004
Tel 01 48 87 63 96
This modern, stylish café-restaurant has a terrace spilling out onto the piazza Beaubourg. It is one of the best spots in Paris for people-watching and is a good place to stop after visiting the nearby Centre Georges Pompidou. The simple recipes are perfectly mastered.
◉ Sun–Thu 8am–1am, Fri–Sat 8am–2am ◙ Rambuteau

CAFÉ DE FLORE
172 boulevard St-Germain, 75006
Tel 01 45 48 55 26
Once the haunt of celebrated writers and philosophers (Jean-Paul Sartre used to be a regular), this café still welcomes customers all day long, for a snack or a drink in elegant surroundings.
◉ Daily 7.30am–1.30am
◙ St-Germain-des-Prés

CAFÉ DE LA MAIRIE
8 place St-Sulpice, 75006
Tel 01 43 26 67 82
Spilling onto a picturesque square, the terrace of this café is the perfect spot to appreciate the French way of life. Snacks are available. Credit cards are not accepted.
◉ Mon–Fri 7am–2am, Sat 8am–2am
◙ St-Sulpice, Mabillon

CHAISE AU PLAFOND
10 rue du Trésor, 75004
Tel 01 42 76 03 22
www.cafeine.com
Nestled in a quiet cul-de-sac, this café has a very pleasant terrace that is heated when necessary. The beautiful

People-watching in chic surroundings at Café Beaubourg

wooden interior has amusing details (have a look into the bathroom peepholes). Good standard bistro food is served.
◉ Daily 9am–2am ◙ St-Paul, Hôtel de Ville

DANDY'S CAFÉ
9 rue Nicolas Flamel, 75004
Tel 01 42 74 45 82
Formerly named Onix café, this chic and trendy spot is near the Centre Georges Pompidou and close to the gay district. You'll find good music and vibes in the evening.
◉ Daily 3pm–2am
◙ Châtelet

LOU PASCALOU
14 rue des Panoyaux, 75020
Ménilmontant
Tel 01 46 36 78 10
You're guaranteed to receive a warm welcome at this unpretentious yet arty little café. Sit on the delightful terrace and sample one of the best mint teas in Paris.
◉ Daily 9am–2am ◙ Ménilmontant

LE MABILLON
164 boulevard St-Germain, 75006
Tel 01 43 26 62 93
Near the Sorbonne, Le Mabillon is popular with students and trendy 20-somethings who appreciate the café's red velvet interior and electric atmosphere.
◉ Daily 7.30am–6am ◙ Mabillon, St-Germain-des-Prés

NO STRESS CAFÉ
2 place Gustave-Toudouze, 75009
Tel 01 48 78 00 27
As its name suggests, this trendy café located in the peaceful Nouvelle-Athènes district, just south of Pigalle, extends a relaxed yet lively welcome; tables spill onto the tiny square as soon as the sun comes out.
◉ Daily 11.30am–1.30am; Dec–end Mar closed Mon
◙ St-Georges

PAUSE CAFÉ BASTILLE
41 rue de Charonne, 75011
Tel 01 48 06 80 33
High ceilings, ancient tiled floors and a welcoming U-shaped bar create a beautiful interior for this hip café-restaurant. The terrace is pleasant on spring and summer days.
◉ Mon–Sat 7.45am–2am, Sun 9–8
◙ Bastille, Ledru-Rollin

CLUBS

LES BAINS DOUCHES
7 rue du Bourg-l'Abbé, 75003
Tel 01 48 87 01 80
www.lesbainsdouches.net
Once a favourite with celebrities, this club lost some of its attraction with the departure of the Guettas,

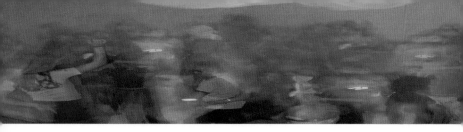

its former owners and true king and queen of Paris nightlife. It's a good place to groove to the sound of disco though. Enjoy a meal in the upstairs restaurant while you wait for the dancing to start.

🕐 Daily 11.30pm–6am
💶 €20; sometimes €15 before 1am
Ⓜ Étienne Marcel

LE BARON

6 avenue Marceau, 75008
Tel 01 47 20 04 01
www.clublebaron.com
Part of a brasserie/club complex, Le Baron is a cool venue with a range of live performances from artists from around the globe and guest DJs.

🕐 Daily 11pm–6am 💶 Varies
Ⓜ Étoile

DUPLEX

2 bis avenue Foch, 75016
Tel 01 45 00 45 00
www.leduplex.fr
Near the Champs-Élysées, this is a club for well-to-do 20-somethings. Smart gear is de rigueur. A bowling alley and some dance, house and techno beats spice up the action.

🕐 Tue–Sun 11.30pm–6am 💶 Fri–Sat €20, Sun, Tue–Thu €15 (includes one drink) Ⓜ Charles de Gaulle-Étoile

L'ÉTOILE

12 rue de Presbourg, 75016
Tel 01 45 00 78 70
www.letoileparis.com
Dressing smartly should grant you the right to enter this temple of chic and trendy Parisian nightlife. Disco, dance and techno are played, the setting is beautiful and the terrace has a superb view of the Arc de Triomphe.

🕐 Mon–Sat 11pm–5am 💶 Free
Ⓜ Charles de Gaulle-Étoile

FOLIE'S PIGALLE

11 place Pigalle, 75009
Tel 01 48 78 55 25
www.folies-pigalle.com
A nightclub emblematic of Paris's red-light district and a

favourite haunt of the gay community. A young crowd moves to the sound of house in a highly charged atmosphere. On Sundays the rhythms are more varied.

🕐 Mon–Thu midnight–6am, Fri–Sat noon–6am, Sun 6pm–6am 💶 €20
Ⓜ Pigalle

LE FREQUENCE CAFÉ

56 rue Notre Dame de Lorette, 75009
Tel 01 42 82 95 06
www.frequencecafe.com
An eclectic mix of bright prink walls, massive mirrors and red plastic chairs makes the interior of Le Frequence Café unforgettable. Have a meal before joining the DJ for

The action hots up after midnight at most clubs

dancing or one of several theme nights.

🕐 Tue–Sun 9pm–2am 💶 Menus from €26, entry to nightclub included Ⓜ St-Georges

LE GIBUS

18 rue du Faubourg-du-Temple, 75011
Tel 01 47 00 78 88
www.gibus.fr
Once a temple of underground culture, this club has become a true ravers' heaven. Hard beats keep the mid-20s straight and gay crowd dancing until the early hours. Trance on Wednesdays and Fridays, house on Saturdays.

🕐 Wed, Fri–Sat midnight–7am 💶 €15
Ⓜ République

LA LOCO

90 boulevard de Clichy, 75018
Tel 01 53 41 88 89
www.laloco.com
Three dance floors, with a beautiful steel design, offer pop and electronica, house club and gay club. There are 'Revenge' evenings on Saturday with live show, and concerts most evenings from 6.30pm.

🕐 Mon–Wed, Sun 11pm–5am, Thu–Sat 11pm–6am 💶 Mon–Thu €12 without drink, €14 with drink. Free entry for women before 1am. Fri–Sat before 1am €10 without drink, €13 with drink; after 1am €16 without drink, €20 with drink Ⓜ Blanche

LOUNGE BAR DU ZEBRA SQUARE

3 place Clément-Ader, 75016
Tel 01 44 14 91 91
The intimate surroundings suit the somewhat older clientele (35-plus), comfortably seated on Chesterfield sofas, listening to the music. This is part of a complex that includes the Hôtel Square (▷ 292) and the Zebra Square restaurant.

🕐 Mon–Sat 8pm–4am
💶 Free Ⓜ Passy, Ranelagh

MADAM

128 rue la Boëtie, 75008
Tel 01 53 76 02 11
www.madam.fr
Electric reds and purples are subdued by low lighting around the many booths at MadaM, which stays open well after other club DJs have headed home to bed. The 'After Work' session on Thursday evenings encourages an early start to the weekend.

🕐 Free, except Thu after work €12 with drinks and bar snacks 💶 Thu 7.30pm–8.30am; Fri–Sat midnight–8.30am Ⓜ St-Philippe du Roule or Franklin D. Roosevelt

LE MEMPHIS

3 impasse de Bonne-Nouvelle, 75010
Tel 01 45 23 34 47
www.le-memphis.fr
Run by the same family for three generations, this disco

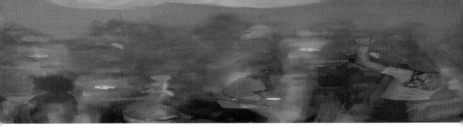

has become an institution, reputed for keeping up with the latest sound and lighting innovations. 'Memphis Fever' night on Thursday has the best 80s music.

🕐 Wed–Thu, Sun 11.30pm–5.45am, Fri–Sat 11.30pm–6.30am 💷 Women: Wed–Thu €5, Fri €8, Sat €16. Men: Wed–Thu €11, Fri–Sat €18 🚇 Bonne-Nouvelle

MOLOKO
26 rue Fontaine, 75009
Tel 01 48 74 50 26
In Paris's red-light district, this club has an eclectic range of music, from R & B to salsa. There is a dance floor downstairs and a lounge bar upstairs.

🕐 Daily 11pm–7am 💷 Free 🚇 Blanche

NEW RÉGINE'S CLUB
49–51 rue Ponthieu, 75008
Tel 01 43 59 21 13
The club may claim to be new, but Régine has been at the heart of the city's social scene forever. The restaurant-club draws a clientele of elegant 40-somethings, but it's the younger crowd who usually occupy the dance floor. The entertainment on offer is different every night but Thursday and Saturday evenings are particularly popular.

🕐 Tue–Sun 11pm–5am 💷 Free 🚇 Franklin D. Roosevelt

LE NOUVEAU CASINO
109 rue Oberkampf, 75011
Tel 01 43 57 57 40
www.nouveaucasino.net
It didn't take long for this club to develop a regular clientele after opening in 2001. Excellent DJs, a beautiful interior (lots of steel and vivid hues) and a great location are the keys to its success.

🕐 Thu–Sat midnight–6am; concerts most nights at 7.30 or 8pm 💷 Around €15 🚇 Parmentier, Ménilmontant, Rue St-Maur

QUEEN
102 avenue des Champs-Élysées, 75008
Tel 0892 70 73 30
www.queen.fr
This trendy club has a prestigious address and attracts a straight as well as gay crowd. House and garage music is mixed by international DJs. Themes and atmospheres vary each day of the week.

🕐 Daily midnight–7am 💷 €15 Mon, €10 Tue–Thu and Sun, €20 Fri–Sat 🚇 George V

REX CLUB
5 boulevard Poissonnière, 75002
Tel 01 42 36 10 96
www.rexclub.com

Cutting-edge design at the highly popular Le Nouveau Casino

The best international DJs have come here to spin—including Carl Cox and Daft Punk. For an attentive 20-something crowd of house/techno connoisseurs, this is the place to go.

🕐 Wed–Sat 11.30pm–5am 💷 €10–€14 🚇 Bonne Nouvelle

LE TRIPTYQUE
142 rue Montmartre, 75001
Tel 01 40 28 05 55
www.letriptyque.com
Former printing works turned into a temple of contemporary music with a wide range of styles. Concerts of jazz, electro-jazz and rock-funk in the early evening; house music later on.

Mixed 20- to 30-something crowd.

🕐 Concerts: Tue–Sun from 8pm; Disco: Thu–Sun midnight–6am 💷 Concerts: varies; disco: Thu €3–€5, Fri–Sat €10–€12, Sun €5 🚇 Bourse

VIP ROOM
76 avenue des Champs-Élysées, 75008
Tel 01 58 36 46 00
www.viproom.fr
A clientele of VIPs do enjoy this club, which has a superb baroque interior (red velvet, leopard print, candelabra). Be ready for selective entry: the beautiful or the seriously rich.

🕐 Tue–Sun 11.30pm–5am 💷 Free 🚇 Franklin D. Roosevelt

LE VOGUE
25 boulevard Poissonnière, 75002
Tel 01 40 26 28 30
A mainly gay crowd moves to the sound of house and techno from midnight to the early morning in this rather trendy place close to the fashionable Opéra district.

🕐 Wed–Sat midnight–7am 💷 From €12 🚇 Grands Boulevards

WAGG
62 rue Mazarine, 75006
Tel 01 55 42 22 01
www.wagg.fr
A smaller dance floor (up to 350 people) gives this venue its welcoming atmosphere. The house and dance music draws a trendy mid-20s to mid-30s crowd to the heart of St-Germain-des-Prés.

🕐 Wed–Sun 11.30pm–5am 💷 Fri–Sat €12 , Thu, Sun €10, Wed free 🚇 St-Germain-des-Prés, Odéon

ZED CLUB
2 rue des Anglais, 75005
Tel 01 43 54 93 78
This disco is for those who prefer a varied mix of rock 'n' roll, jazz, swing and salsa (no techno or rap); 60s to 90s music on Friday and Saturday.

🕐 Fri–Sat 11pm–5.30am, Thu 10.30pm–3am 💷 Thu €10 ; Fri–Sat €18 🚇 Maubert-Mutualité, Saint-Michel

SPORTS AND ACTIVITIES

Highlights of the Parisian sporting calendar include the Roland Garros International Tennis Grand Slam tournament (late May to early June), the final leg of the Tour de France bicycle race in July (▷ 222) and the Prix de l'Arc de Triomphe horse race in October. There are also many rugby and soccer internationals. The Paris St-Germain soccer team play at the Parc des Princes, although France's international soccer and rugby matches are held at the Stade de France (tel 01 55 93 00 00; ticketline 0892 700 900; www.stadefrance.fr).

Participatory sports are not high on most people's agenda during a visit to Paris, but if you want to sweat off some calories head to the Bois de Boulogne (▷ 236) and Bois de Vincennes (▷ 237) for bicycling, jogging or boating. There are also gyms and swimming pools dotted around the city. For golf, contact the Fédération Française de Golf (tel 01 41 49 77 00). Boules, or pétanque, is a less strenuous option and is popular in parks and grassy squares.

▷ 222, ▷ 236, ▷ 237

Pétanque is played in open spaces throughout the city

AQUA PARK
AQUABOULEVARD
4–6 rue Louis Armand, 75015
Tel 01 40 60 10 00
www.aquaboulevard.com
The main attraction here is the aquapark with several giant slides, whirlpools, geysers, Jacuzzi, a waterfall, and vast indoor and outdoor 'shore' areas. The quality of the water is checked several times a day and there are pool attendants. In addition, there are seven tennis courts, six squash courts as well as several restaurants and shops. Fitness and dance classes are also on offer.

🕐 Mon–Thu 9am–11pm, Fri 9am–midnight, Sat 8am–midnight, Sun 8am–11pm 🎟 Entry to aquapark: €20, €10 child (3–11) 🚇 Balard, Porte de Versailles

BICYCLING
PARIS À VÉLO C'EST SYMPA
22 rue Alphonse-Baudin, 75011
Tel 01 48 87 60 01
www.parisvelosympa.com
A bicycle ride is a great way to discover Paris. Various guided tours are available in French and English: Heart of Paris, Paris at Dawn and Unusual Paris. Unaccompanied bicycle and tandem rental is also available.

🕐 Tours: May–Sep Fri, Sun, Mon 10am, Sat 10am, 8.30pm; Apr, Oct Fri–Mon 10am; Nov–Mar Sat–Sun 10am 🎟 €34 for a 3-hour ride 🚇 Richard-Lenoir

BILLIARDS
CERCLE CLICHY-MONTMARTRE
84 rue de Clichy, 75009
Tel 01 48 78 32 85
www.academie-billard.com
Occupying a former brasserie built in 1880, this billiard hall has a lot of character. Play American and French billiards, snooker and pool.

🕐 Daily 11am–6.30am 🎟 Around €10 per hour 🚇 Place de Clichy

BOWLING
BOWLING DE MONTPARNASSE
25 rue du Commandant-Mouchotte, 75014
Tel 01 43 21 61 32
This venue has 16 bowling lanes, pool billiards and some video games. Every Friday and Saturday night you can bowl in the dark, with the lanes illuminated by fluorescent lighting.

🕐 Sun–Thu 10am–2am, Fri 10am–4am, Sat 10am–5am 🎟 €4.30–€5.80 per game, per person 🚇 Montparnasse-Bienvenüe

Cycling is a popular way of keeping fit

DANCE
CENTRE DE DANSE DU MARAIS
41 rue du Temple, 75004
Tel 0892 686870
www.parisdanse.com
A picturesque courtyard is home to this music school, restaurant (The Studio), café-theatre (Café de la Gare) and dance school, where you can take all sorts of classes: ballet, rock, flamenco, salsa, tango, African, tap-dancing and more.

🕐 Varies according to classes 🎟 €16–€20 per 90-min class 🚇 Rambuteau, Hôtel de Ville

DANCENTER PARIS

6 impasse Lévis, 75017
Tel 01 43 80 90 23
www.cours-de-danse.com
All partner dances are taught
here: rock, salsa, boogie-
woogie, bebop, West Coast
swing, Latino, samba, and
much more. Enjoy the rock
party on Friday and salsa on
Saturday.
🕐 Mon–Thu 6.30–9.30, Sat 1–4
💶 Varies according to class; 1-hour trial
session €15 🚇 Villiers

FLYING

AÉROCLUB PARIS NORD

Aérodrome de Persan Beaumont,
95340 Bernes-sur-Oise
Tel 01 30 34 70 02 36
www.aeroclub.parisnord.free.fr
Flying lessons for all levels. An
interesting option for beginners
(FIP) offers 3 hours of flying
time, half of it in the co-pilot's
seat.
🕐 Depends on booking and weather
💶 FIP: €270 (3 lessons)
🚗 N1 north then 2nd right after the
bridge over the Oise and left at the 5th
roundabout.

GOLF

GOLF DU BOIS DE BOULOGNE

Hippodrome d'Auteuil, 75016
Tel 01 44 30 70 00
www.golfduboisdeboulogne.com
Paris's largest golf course,
within a race track, includes an
area where you can practise
your swing, a putting green
and a crazy-golf area with
small greens interspersed with
bunkers and watercourses.
🕐 Oct–Apr daily 8–8; May–Sep
Mon–Sat 8am–9pm, Sun 8–8 (closed
on race days) 💶 No membership
required. €4 per bucket of balls, €5 per
half-hour of crazy golf, 30-min lesson
€25 🚇 Porte d'Auteuil

HELICOPTER TOURS

PARIS HÉLICOPTÈRE

Zone Aviation Affaires, Aéroport, 93350
Le Bourget
Tel 01 48 35 90 44
www.paris-helicoptere.fr
Want to see all of Paris's main
sights in less than 30 minutes?

Take a monument-spotting
tour over Paris. Longer tours
are also available, for a bird's-
eye view of the Château de
Versailles and farther afield.
🕐 Every Sunday afternoon (reserve
ahead) 💶 Around €130 for a 25-min
tour 🚗 Le Bourget 🚌 152 (Musée de
l'Air stop)

HORSE-RIDING

HARAS DES HAUTES FONTAINES

Rue Maria-Valla, 77111 Solers
Tel 01 64 06 74 21
www.haras-de-solers.com
This equestrian centre, in
the leafy outskirts of Paris,
organizes classes, competitions
and rides in the nearby forest

*France Montgolfières offers a
unique perspective on the region*

on a regular basis. A pony club
welcomes children over three.
🕐 Varies 💶 Around €20 per hour
🚗 Gare de Gretz
🚌 Take the D319 direction Provins

HOT-AIR BALLOON TOURS

FRANCE MONTGOLFIÈRES

24 rue Nationale, Montrichard, 41400
Tel 0810 00 01 53
www.franceballoons.com
A hot-air balloon tour enables
you to see Paris's surroundings
as you soar above villages,
chateaux, rivers and forests.
You can also go to Burgundy
and the Loire. Some trips
include a hotel stay.
🕐 Tours from mid-Mar to end Nov;
book ahead 💶 Mon–Fri €185, Sat–Sun

€225 for 3.5-hour tour 🚇 Père
Lachaise

MONTGOLFIÈRES AVENTURES

6 place de la Madeleine, 75008
Tel 01 40 47 61 04
www.montgolfieres-aventures.fr
Enjoy breathtaking views of the
Loire chateaux, the Périgord
or Paris's surroundings.
Champagne and a first-flight
certificate are awarded upon
landing.
🕐 All year long; book ahead
💶 €220–€250 per person
🚇 Madeleine

IN-LINE SKATING

RANDONNÉE EN ROLLERS

Meet in front of Nomades: 37
boulevard Bourdon, 75004
Tel 01 44 54 07 44
In partnership with Nomades
sports store, the Rollers and
Coquillages Society organizes
mass in-line skating through
Paris every Sunday afternoon.
The 3-hour circuit changes
regularly.
🕐 Sun 2.30pm 💶 Free 🚇 Bastille

KARTING

KART'IN

23 rue du Puits Dixme, 94320 Thiais
Tel 01 49 79 79 79
www.kart-in.fr
The racing circuit here is
regularly modified, so it never
becomes routine. Times are
displayed on a big screen to
maximize the thrill. You can
watch the races from the
restaurant alongside the track.
There's a second circuit at
Porte de la Villette.
🕐 Tue–Thu 7pm–1am, Fri
8.30pm–2am, Sat 3pm–2am, Sun
3pm–8pm 💶 Around €20 for 10 min

MARTIAL ARTS

ÉCOLE D'ARTS MARTIAUX ERIC PARISET

21 boulevard Richard-Lenoir, 75011
Tel 01 47 00 34 38
www.jujitsuericpariset.com
Ju-jitsu is the main focus here,
but judo and *atemi-waza* are
also taught. The school is
famous for its numerous books
and videos on the subject, and

Eric Pariset himself takes most of the classes.
🎯 Varies 🎟 Private lesson with Eric Pariset €50 (no membership required) 🚇 Bréguet-Sabin

ENJOY BY FKC
36 rue de Nantes, 75019
Tel 01 40 35 05 05
www.enjoy-fkc.com
Founded by a full-contact expert, this fitness venue offers a wide range of martial arts lessons including kick-boxing, kung fu and tae kwon do. Fitness classes and a sauna are also available.
🎯 Mon–Fri 9am–10pm, Sat 9–7, Sun 9–1 🎟 €20 per day, around €40–€60 per month on an annual basis 🚇 Corentin Cariou

FALUN GONG
Jardin du Luxembourg, 75006
Similar to t'ai chi, Falun Gong consists of a series of exercises aimed at combatting anxiety and increasing vitality. The charming surroundings of the Luxembourg Garden are an added bonus. Meet next to Marie de Medici statue.
🎯 Sat–Sun 9.30am–11am 🎟 Free 🚊 Luxembourg

PAINTBALL
100% LOISIRS
6 place Léon Deubel, 75016
Tel 01 45 27 87 04
www.paintballidf.com
This shop stocks paintball equipment and arranges paintball parties. These take place east of Paris, near Disneyland Resort, in 28ha (70 acres) of woods divided into themed areas.
🎯 Full day 11–5 🎟 €35 per day 🚇 Porte de St-Cloud

PELOTA
FRONTON CHIQUITO DE CAMBO
8 quai St-Éxupéry, 75016
Tel 01 40 50 09 25
www.ligue-idf-pelotebasque.com
A convivial pelota school, where it's possible to play indoors and out. The indoor court boasts terraces and,

surprisingly, a glass wall onto which the ball is thrown. There is a bar on the premises.
🎯 Daily 7am–midnight 🎟 €28 per hour 🚇 Porte de St-Cloud

SOCCER
PARC DES PRINCES
24 rue du Commandant-Guilbaud, 75016
Tel 0825 07 32 75 (closed Fri and public hols)
www.psg.fr
Inaugurated in 1972, the park has been home to Paris-St-Germain (PSG) soccer club since 1990. Within its boundaries you'll also find the Musée National du Sport (National Sport Museum; tel 01 40 71 45 48), a shop

Some of the city's tennis courts are conveniently central

with PSG merchandise and a restaurant, the 70.
🎟 Varies; guided tours of stadium €6 🚇 Porte d'Auteuil, Porte de St-Cloud

SPORTS CLUBS
CLUB MONTMARTROIS
50 rue Duhesme, 75018
Tel 01 42 54 49 88
www.club-montmartrois.fr
Among the 30 activities on offer are fitness, cardio-training, yoga, stretching and dance. There is a steam room (women only) and sauna (one for men, one for women).
🎯 Mon–Fri 8am–9.30pm, Sat 8.30–7, Sun 9–5.30 🎟 Day membership €15 🚇 Lamarck-Caulaincourt

CLUB QUARTIER LATIN
19 rue Pontoise, 75005
Tel 01 55 42 77 88
www.clubquartierlatin.com
No membership is required and late opening and a whole array of classes and equipment (aquagym, cardio-training, squash and sauna) are on offer. This club is popular with both visitors and local students.
🎯 Mon–Fri 9am–midnight, Sat–Sun 9.30–7 🎟 €20 per day 🚇 Cardinal Lemoine

SPORTS COMPLEX
CENTRE T.E.P. DAVOUT
134 boulevard Davout, 75020
Tel 01 43 61 39 26
This complex contains two tennis courts, an area for playing boules, a roller park, two concrete courts where you can play handball or volleyball, and a running track.
🎯 Mon–Fri 8am–10pm, Sat 8–8, Sun 8–6 🎟 Free use of equipment (except tennis courts: €7 per hour) 🚇 Porte de Montreuil, Porte de Bagnolet 🚌 57, 76

SPORTS PARK
PARC DE BELLEVILLE
Rue des Couronnes, 75020
Created in 1998, this park has a terraced layout and offers wonderful views of Paris. A walkers' and joggers' paradise, it also has basketball courts and soccer pitches.
🎯 Daily 6am–dusk 🎟 Free 🚇 Couronnes, Belleville

SQUASH
SQUASH FRONT DE SEINE
21 rue Gaston-de-Caillavet, 75015
Tel 01 45 75 35 37
Here you'll find eight courts, a sauna and a bar where you can reconcile yourself with your opponent after a fierce game. Free initiation is on Mondays by appointment. Classes are also available.
🎯 Mon–Fri 9am–11pm, Sat–Sun 9–8 🎟 €13 per person per half-hour 🚇 Charles Michels

SQUASH MONTMARTRE
14 rue Achille Martinet, 75018
Tel 01 42 55 38 30
www.slot-montmartre.com
Facilities at this friendly squash club include four courts, a gym, sauna, solarium, clubhouse and restaurant.
🕐 Mon–Fri 10am–10.30pm, Sat–Sun 10–7 💶 €10 for 30 min, €14 for 45 min 🚇 Lamarck-Caulaincourt

STADIUMS
STADE PIERRE DE COUBERTIN
82 avenue Georges-Lafont, 75016
Tel 01 45 27 79 12
Built for the 1937 International Exhibition, destroyed during World War II and rebuilt in 1946, this 4,500-seat stadium now hosts all sorts of competitions, ranging from fencing and French boxing to handball and dance.
💶 Varies 🚇 Porte de St-Cloud

STADE ROLAND-GARROS
2 avenue Gordon-Bennett, 75016
Tel 01 47 43 48 00
www.rolandgarros.fr
This stadium is home to the eponymous tennis tournament (▷ 222) and has 24 courts. Inaugurated in 2003, the Tenniseum is a tennis museum with a comprehensive multimedia section in French and English.
🕐 Museum: Mar–end Oct Tue–Sun 10–6 except during the tournament; rest of the year Wed, Fri–Sat 10–6 💶 Varies; Museum: €7.50 (under 18 €4) 🚇 Porte d'Auteuil

SWIMMING
PISCINE DE LA BUTTE AUX CAILLES
5 place Paul Verlaine, 75013
Tel 01 45 89 60 05
This pool has lots of character, with Italian tiles and a vaulted roof. The indoor pool is open all year; the outdoor pool during summer.
🕐 Tue 7–8.30, 11.30–1.30, 4.30–7; Wed 7–7; Thu, Fri 7–8.30, 11–6.30; Sat 7–8.30, 10–6.30; Sun 8–6 (longer hours during school hols) 💶 €3 🚇 Place d'Italie

PISCINE GEORGES-VALLEREY
148 avenue Gambetta, 75020
Tel 01 40 31 15 20
Built in 1924 for the Olympic Games and renovated in 1989, this vast pool has a sunroof (open when weather permits), a 1,500-seat terrace and a cafeteria. It was here during the Games that Johnny Weissmuller (later star of the Hollywood *Tarzan* films) broke the 400m record. You can see competitions here or come for a swim yourself. Credit cards are not accepted.
🕐 Mon 11.45–1.30, 5–7; Tue, Thu 11.45–1.30, 5–10; Wed 5–10; Fri 11.45–5; Sat–Sun 9–5 💶 €4 entrance 🚇 Porte des Lilas

Paris has some excellent pools for cooling off

PISCINE JEAN TARIS
16 rue Thuin, 75005
Tel 01 55 42 81 90
This pool's main attractions are its location, in the Latin Quarter near the Panthéon, and the view: The large windows face a leafy garden. There is one big pool and a smaller one for children. Credit cards are not accepted.
🕐 Tue, Thu 7–8.30; Wed 7–8.30, 11.30–6; Fri 7–8.30, 11.30–1.30, 5–8; Sat 7–6; Sun 8–6 💶 €4 🚇 Cardinal Lemoine

PISCINE JOSÉPHINE BAKER
Quai François Mauriac, 75013
Tel 01 56 61 96 50
Paris rejoiced when this new pool complex was moored on the banks of the Seine. The vast pool is complemented by a gym and spa.
🕐 Mon 7–8.30, 1–3, 5–9; Tue noon–5, 7–midnight; Wed 7–8.30, 1–9; Thu noon–3, 5–9; Fri 7–8.30, 1–5, 9–midnight; Sat–Sun 10–8 💶 Term time: €2.60, school holidays €5 🚇 Bibliothèque National de France – François Mitterand

PISCINE MUNICIPALE DE REUILLY
13 rue Hénard, 75012
Tel 01 40 02 08 08
With its large windows, this modern pool is bright and airy. A solarium, two main pools and a smaller one for children are on site. Credit cards are not accepted.
🕐 Mon 12–1, Tue, Fri 7–8, 12–1, Wed 6–8, 12–4.45; Thu 12–1, 4–10; Sat 9.30–6; Sun 8–6 💶 €3 🚇 Montgallet

TENNIS
TENNIS DU LUXEMBOURG
Jardin du Luxembourg, 75006
Tel 01 43 25 79 18
The setting for these six fine courts, the lack of a membership fee and competitive rates mean it can be difficult to get a booking.
🕐 Daily 8.30–4.30, till 9.30 in summer 💶 €3.50 per half-hour, €6.50 per hour 🚇 Luxembourg

YOGA
CENTRE SIVANANDA DE YOGA VEDANTA
123 boulevard de Sébastopol, 75002
Tel 01 40 26 77 49
www.sivananda.org/paris
Run by Vedanta monks, true to ancestral Indian tradition, this venue offers an holistic approach to yoga with relaxation classes, but also an introduction to the philosophy of yoga and positive thinking.
🕐 Daily 11–8 💶 €115 for 10 sessions or €15 per session 🚇 Réaumur Sébastopol

WHAT TO DO

HEALTH AND BEAUTY

If you feel like unwinding away from Paris's busy streets, there are a number of ways you can indulge yourself.

AQUARELLE INSTITUT
9 rue St-Didier, 75016
Tel 01 45 53 09 09
www.aquarelle-institut.fr
Located in the Trocadéro area, this salon offers face and body treatments, manicures and massages using different techniques (including reflexology and body and face shiatsu) in a relaxing atmosphere.
🕐 Tue–Wed, Fri 10–7, Thu 10–9, Sat 10–1, Mon 2–7 💆 Face treatments €60–€72, body treatments €50, manicure €24–€30, massages €55–€70, face and body treatment +

Treat yourself to a massage after a hard day's sightseeing

manicure + make-up €152.50
Ⓜ Boissière

BASTIEN GONZALEZ
Hotel Le Bristol Day Spa, 108 rue de Faubourg St-Honoré, 75008
Tel 01 42 66 24 22
www.bastiengonzalez.com
Pedicurist to the stars, Bastien Gonzalez has a unique approach to feet and can make toenails shine for up to three months without the aid of varnish. There are also Bastien Gonzalez facilities at two other salons in the city (see website).
🕐 By appointment 💆 €130 Ⓜ St-Philippe du Roule

INSTITUTE DE BEAUTÉ LES PORTES DE BACOPA
45 avenue George V, 75008
Tel 01 40 73 40 73
www.lesportesdebacopa.com
This spa concentrates on facials and skin problems, including redness and pigment problems, as well as more mainstream massage and treatments. The speciality involves being wrapped in lots of chocolate, none of it for eating.
🕐 Mon–Fri 10–8, Sat 10–7
💆 Chocolate wrap €140 Ⓜ George V

INSTITUT LANCÔME
29 rue du Faubourg St-Honoré, 75008
Tel 01 42 65 30 74
www.lancome.com
Fully personalized treatments, including facials, masks and massages for men and women. Relaxing and energizing programmes are conceived in collaboration with the International Music Therapy Centre.
🕐 Mon–Sat 10–7 💆 Face treatments €85–€115, body treatments around €90 Ⓜ Concorde, Madeleine

INDRAJIT GARAI
10 place de Clichy, 75009
Tel 01 48 78 21 39
Indrajit Garai offers state-of-the-art Ayurvedic Indian massages. Having worked in Spain and London, he has set up this practice at his Parisian home. He collaborates with physiotherapists for a therapeutic approach. Credit cards are not accepted.
🕐 By appointment only 💆 Varies Ⓜ Place de Clichy

VILLA THALGO
218–220 rue du Faubourg St-Honoré, 75008
Tel 01 45 62 00 20
www.thalgo.fr

This high-class institute brings thalassotherapy to the heart of Paris. The 7-hour session includes bodyscrub, seaweed wrap, balneotherapy, jet shower, aquagym and massages. Shorter treatments are also available. Both women and men are welcome.
🕐 Mon, Tue, Thu 8.30–8.30, Wed, Fri 8.30–7, Sat 9–7 💆 60-min treatment around €75, 30-min €40
Ⓜ Ternes, Charles de Gaulle-Étoile

HAMMAM DE LA MOSQUÉE DE PARIS
See page 110.

The Institut Lancôme offers a range of treatments

RASA YOGA RIVE GAUCHE
21 rue St-Jacques, 75005
Tel 01 43 54 14 59
www.rasa-yogarivegauche.com
Well-established spa concentrating on yoga for wellness and balance (including sessions for children), plus massage.
🕐 Mon, Wed, Fri 7am–9.30pm, Tue, Thu 10–9.30, Sat 10–4.30, Sun 11–6.30
💆 Yoga class €20, 1-hour massage €70 Ⓜ Cluny-La Sorbonne

CHILDREN'S PARIS

Many of the city's museums and galleries arrange children's activities (often on Wednesday or Saturday) and provide worksheets. Entry is often free to under-18s. Parks such as the Jardin du Luxembourg have amusements for youngsters, including puppet shows, model yachts and playgrounds. Outside the city limits, there are the popular Disneyland Resort Paris (▷ 240–241) and Parc Astérix.

(▷ 240–241)

BALLOONING

LE BALLON DE PARIS
Parc André Citroën, rue de la Montagne de la Fage, 75015
Tel 01 44 26 20 00
www.aeroparis.com
The largest balloon in the world rises 150m (490ft) up into the air over Paris, offering exhilarating views of the city.
🕐 9am–park closure, every 30 mins (weather permitting) 💶 Mon–Fri Adult

Hard at play at the Cité des Sciences et de l'Industrie

€10, child (12–17) €9, child (3–11) €5; Sat–Sun adult €12, child (12–17) €10, child (3–11) €6 🚇 Javel

FARMS AND WILDLIFE PARKS

FERME OUVERTE DE GALLY
Route de l'aérodrome, 78000 St-Cyr-l'École
Tel 01 30 14 60 60
www.gally.com
At this working farm, children can get close to all sorts of animals. They can also take part in activities such as apple pressing and honey collection.
🕐 Farm: Mon, Tue, Thu, Fri 4–5.30, Wed 10–12.30, 2–6, Sat–Sun 10–6.30. Garden: daily 9.30–7 💶 Farm: adult €3.80, child (3–12) €2.90. €2 per child

for each activity 🚇 St-Cyr 🚗 A13 exit 6 take direction Bailly Noisy le Roi exit St-Cyr-l'École

PARC ZOOLOGIQUE DE PARIS
See page 237.

PARC ZOOLOGIQUE DE THOIRY
Château de Thoiry, 78770 Thoiry
Tel 01 34 87 40 67
www.thoiry.tm.fr
At this safari park you drive past animals from zebras and tigers to flamingoes. Part of it can be seen on foot.
🕐 Daily 10–6 (until 5 in winter) 💶 Zoo: adult €22.90, child (3–12) €15.90 🚗 A13 direction Versailles, exit Bois d'Arcy direction Dreux. Take N12 exit Pontchartrain then D11 to Thoiry

MUSEUMS

CITÉ DES SCIENCES ET DE L'INDUSTRIE
See pages 146–147.

MUSÉE GRÉVIN
See page 116.

MUSÉUM NATIONAL D'HISTOIRE NATURELLE
See page 127.

PARKS AND GARDENS

JARDIN D'ACCLIMATATION
Main entry: boulevard des Sablons, Bois de Boulogne, 75016
Tel 01 40 67 90 82
www.jardindacclimatation.fr
With its ponds and tree-lined alleys, this 'garden within a wood' is a walker's paradise. Activities for children include mini-golf, playgrounds, bowling, wildlife discovery, theatre and sports. A trip on the little train is a good introduction.
🕐 Daily 10–7 (until 6 in winter) 💶 Adult €2.50, children (under 3) free 🚇 Les Sablons

PARC FLORAL
See page 237.

THEATRE

THÉÂTRE MOUFFETARD
See page 207.

THEME PARKS

AQUABOULEVARD
See page 216.

CLUB MED WORLD
39 Cour St-Émilion, 75012
Tel 0810 810 410 or 01 44 68 70 09
www.clubmedworld.fr
This place offers activities on three main themes: travel (with a travel agency on site), tastes (with food from all over the world) and talents (circus,

Thrills and spills with Astérix, Obélix and friends

dance, rock-climbing lessons).
🕐 Tue–Thu 11am–2am, Fri–Sat 11am–6am, Sun 11am–8pm 💶 Varies 🚇 Cour St-Émilion

DISNEYLAND RESORT PARIS
See pages 240–241.

PARC ASTÉRIX
A1 Paris–Lille Highway, 60128 Plailly
Tel 03 44 62 31 31
www.parcasterix.fr
Characters from the famous Astérix books await you with shows and attractions.
🕐 Apr to mid-Jul, Sep–early Nov generally Mon–Fri 10–6, Sat, Sun 9.30–7 💶 Adult €35, child (3–11) €25, under 3 free 🚇 Roissy-Pôle

FESTIVALS AND EVENTS

See page 307 for the dates of France's 11 national holidays.

JANUARY

FÊTE DES ROIS
6 January
Epiphany is celebrated with a special almond cake called a *galette des rois*.

CHINESE NEW YEAR
Late January/early February
Celebrated between the avenue d'Ivry and avenue de Choisy.
🚇 Tolbiac

APRIL

MARATHON INTERNATIONAL DE PARIS
First Sunday in April
Tel 01 41 33 15 68

Paris's marathon attracts more than 30,000 runners

www.parismarathon.com
Paris's marathon starts on the Champs-Élysées and finishes just behind the Arc de Triomphe.
🚇 Charles de Gaulle–Étoile

MAY

FOIRE DE PARIS
Paris Expo, Porte de Versailles, 75015
Tel 01 49 09 60 00
www.foiredeparis.fr
Garden, home and leisure are the themes of this fair.
🚇 Porte de Versailles

LABOUR DAY
1 May
Processions through the streets.

PRINTEMPS DES RUES
Tel 01 47 97 36 06
www.leprintempsdesrues.com
A weekend of outdoor events, at various locations, with a different theme each year.

MAY–JUNE

ROLAND-GARROS
Stade Roland Garros, 2 avenue Gordon-Bennett, 75016
Tel 01 47 43 48 00
www.rolandgarros.com
The prestigious French Tennis Open lasts two weeks.
🚇 Porte d'Auteuil

JUNE

FÊTE DE LA MUSIQUE
21 June
Tel 01 40 03 94 70
www.fetedelamusique.culture.fr
Free concerts are held all over the city, with everything from classical to techno.

JUNE–JULY

FOIRE ST-GERMAIN
In and around place St-Sulpice
Tel 01 43 29 61 04
www.foiresaintgermain.org
This village fair dates back to the 12th century.
🚇 St-Sulpice

JULY

BASTILLE DAY
14 July
Fireworks and fire station bells on 13 July, followed by a military parade down the Champs-Élysées on 14 July.

TOUR DE FRANCE
Tel 01 41 33 14 00
www.letour.fr
This famous bicycle race finishes on the Champs-Élysées.

JULY–AUGUST

PARIS QUARTIER D'ÉTÉ
Tel 01 44 94 98 00
www.quartierdete.com
Drama, music and dance in open spaces all over the city.

FESTIVAL DE CINÉMA EN PLEIN AIR
Parc de la Villette, 75019
Tel 01 40 03 75 75
www.villette.com
Open-air film festival.
🚇 Porte de la Villette, Porte de Pantin

SEPTEMBER–DECEMBER

FESTIVAL D'AUTOMNE
Mid-September to December
Tel 01 53 45 17 17
www.festival-automne.com
Avant-garde cultural festival, at various venues.

OCTOBER

FIAC (FOIRE INTERNATIONAL D'ART CONTEMPORAIN)
5 days in October

Fireworks are an essential part of Bastille Day celebrations

Grand Palais du Louvre
Tel 01 47 56 64 21
www.fiacparis.com
A vast modern-art fair.
🚇 Louvre

NUIT BLANCHE
Tel 3975 (Mairie de Paris information)
Concerts and other events take place in unusual venues across the city through the night.

NOVEMBER

BEAUJOLAIS NOUVEAU
Third Thursday in November
Bars spill out into the street as the new Beaujolais arrives.

Paris is best explored on foot and this section describes five walks that take in key parts of the city. The locations of the walks are marked by a red star on the map on the inside front cover of the book. This section also gives suggestions for excursions farther afield and details of a river trip.

Out and About

LE MARAIS

The Marais is one of the prettiest districts in central Paris, home to elaborate mansions (known as *hôtels*), medieval streets, huge doorways with ornate handles, pretty gardens and squares, a bustling Jewish quarter and the oldest square in Paris, the place des Vosges.

THE WALK

Distance: 3km (2 miles)

Allow: 2 hours

Start/end at St Paul-Le Marais Métro station

How to get there: 🚇 St Paul-Le Marais 🚌 69, 76, 96

Leave St Paul-Le Marais Métro station and head east along rue St-Antoine, passing the impressive façade of the church of St-Paul-St-Louis (1627–1641) on the right. At No. 62, on your left, is the **❶** Hôtel de Sully.

This magnificent 17th-century mansion was once home to Henri IV's chief minister, the Duc de Sully. Today it houses the headquarters of the Centre des Monuments Nationaux.

Turn left into the peaceful rue de Birague which leads to the **❷** place des Vosges (▷ 150).

This picturesque square was commissioned by Henri IV and completed in 1612. During the 17th century it was home to significant figures such as Cardinal Richelieu, Louis XIII's hypochondriac minister, and the playwright Molière. In the 19th century writer Victor Hugo moved in. His house, number 6, is now a museum (▷ 106).

Continue around the square, walking under the arcades, past restaurants, galleries and shops. Look into the garden entrance of number 28, the Pavillon de la Reine, now a hotel (▷ 293). If you feel like a drink, stop at one of the cafés with its tables spread out under the arcades.

Leave the square by rue des Francs-Bourgeois. On your right is the **❸** Musée Carnavalet (▷ 114–115), built in 1548 and later home to the writer Madame de Sévigné. As you walk past you can see the beautiful courtyard and gardens.

The Musée Carnavalet, in two adjoining mansions, focuses on the story of Paris, from prehistory to the 20th century. The Revolution, Napoleon Bonaparte and art nouveau interiors are among its themes.

Turn right into rue Payenne. The gardens on the right and courtyards on the left are in typical 17th-century Marais style. Notice the elaborate wooden gates of the Hôtel de Châtillon, on your left, at number 13.

Follow rue du Parc Royal to the left, walk around place de Thorigny and then turn right into rue de Thorigny, to reach the Hôtel Salé, built in 1656, and now home to the **❹** Musée Picasso (▷ 135).

Here you can see a vast collection of Picasso's works—more than 250 paintings, 160 sculptures and 1,500 drawings. There are also pieces by his contemporaries, notably Paul Cézanne, Joan Miró, Georges Braque and Henri Matisse.

Turn left along rue Debelleyme, passing some contemporary art galleries, and then left again down rue Vieille du Temple. On the left you will see the lovely gardens of the Musée Picasso.

Halfway down on your right at number 87, you pass the carved

gates of the Hôtel de Rohan and, on the corner of rue des Francs-Bourgeois, the picturesque turret (1510) of the Maison de Jean Hérouët.

Turn right here, past more elegant mansions and the Crédit Municipal (municipal pawnshop) at number 55 on your left. On the right is the courtyard of the **❺** Hôtel de Soubise.

This mansion was constructed between 1705 and 1708 and is now home to the National Archives and the Musée de l'Histoire de France (▷ 116–117).

Turn left into rue des Archives and take the next left into rue des Blancs Manteaux. This brings you back to rue Vieille du Temple. Turn right and after a short walk turn left to follow **❻** rue des Rosiers.

This bustling street is the hub of the Jewish district, full of specialist shops as far as rue Pavée. Chic boutiques and trendy furniture stores trade alongside traditional Jewish fast-food stalls, cafés and bookshops.

Turn right into rue Pavée. On the left you'll pass the synagogue, designed by Hector Guimard (▷ 163). Continue south to return to St Paul-Le Marais Métro station.

OUT AND ABOUT

WHEN TO GO

During the day, when the shops and museums are open.

WHERE TO EAT

The place des Vosges has plenty of cafés. Ma Bourgogne, at number 19, and L'Ambrosie, at number 9, both have outdoor tables under the arcades.

The cloisters of the Église des Billettes, in rue des Archives

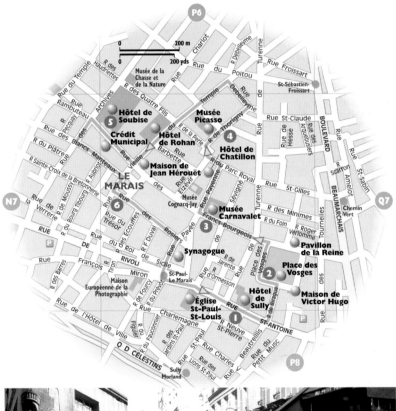

OUT AND ABOUT

A bustling street scene in Le Marais (above).
The brightly painted L'Oiseau Bariolé bar (left).
Classic elegance at the Hôtel de Soubise (far left)

MONTMARTRE

There is so much more to Montmartre than the towering Sacré-Cœur basilica, impressive though this is. This walk shows you the lesser-known side of Paris's hilltop village, with its picturesque cottages, cobbled streets and panoramic views.

THE WALK

Distance: 3km (2 miles)	
Allow: 2 hours	
Start at place Blanche	
End at place des Abbesses	
How to get there: 🚇 Blanche 🚌 30, 54, 68, 74	

Starting from place Blanche, walk west along boulevard de Clichy, past the ❶ Moulin Rouge on your right.

When the Moulin Rouge (▷ 111) first opened its doors in 1889, its vivacious cancan dancers were an immediate hit. The venue still stages cabaret shows, now aimed at visitors.

Turn right into avenue Rachel and carry on to the entrance of the ❷ Cimetière de Montmartre (▷ 87).

Here you can seek out the tombs of the writer Stendhal, composer Hector Berlioz and saxophone inventor Adolphe Sax.

Leave the cemetery at avenue Rachel and walk up the steps on the right to rue Caulaincourt (a flyover). Turn right onto this road and walk to the junction with rue Joseph de Maistre. Turn right and after a few minutes, turn very sharp left up rue Lepic. Van Gogh lived at number 54 of this winding road from 1886 to 1888.
  Follow the curve until you come to the junction with rue Tholozé. Look up to the left, past the green arch, to the ❸ Moulin de la Galette. Farther along the road, on the corner with rue Girardon, is the Moulin Radet.

The Moulin de la Galette (literally the 'biscuit windmill') became a dance hall in the 19th century and was the inspiration behind Pierre-Auguste Renoir's painting Le Bal du Moulin de la Galette (1876). The

windmill is now privately owned. The Moulin Radet now forms part of a restaurant, confusingly called the Moulin de la Galette.

Turn left into rue Girardon, cross avenue Junot and enter the pleasant ❹ square Suzanne-Buisson, on the left.

The square is named after a World War II resistance heroine. The macabre statue here is of the 3rd-century bishop St. Denis, who was beheaded by the Romans. Legend has it that he picked up his head and washed off the blood in a fountain on this spot.

Facing the statue, turn right and leave the square into place Casadesus, in rue Simon Dereure. Turn right into the allée des Brouillards. Renoir lived in one of the houses on the left in the 1890s. The 18th-century mansion on the right was once a dance hall and a shelter for homeless artists.
  Continue to place Dalida, named after the singer and actress who died in 1987, then walk up the cobbled rue de l'Abreuvoir. Formerly a country lane, the road takes its name from the watering trough (l'abreuvoir) that once stood at number 15. Number 14 attracted many of Montmartre's artists when it was the Café de l'Abreuvoir, while number 12 was home to Camille Pissarro from 1888 to 1892. If you're feeling hungry, stop for lunch at La Maison Rose (The Pink House).
  Turn left after La Maison Rose and walk down the steep cobbled rue des Saules to the legendary cabaret spot, Au Lapin Agile (▷ 198). Turn right (east) along rue St-Vincent, past Montmartre's vineyard on your right. Cross rue du Mont Cenis, once home to Hector Berlioz (number 22), and walk uphill to rue de la Bonne. This leads into the hidden-away ❺ Parc de la Turlure.

This tranquil park, well off the tourist trail, gives you magnificent views over Paris, as well as an unusual perspective on Sacré-Cœur.

Wander up through the park, then exit onto rue du Chevalier de la Barre. Continue along rue du Cardinal Guibert to the entrance to ❻ Sacré-Cœur, on place du Parvis du Sacré-Cœur.

The neo-Byzantine basilica of Sacré-Cœur (▷ 154–157) was commissioned as atonement after the Franco-Prussian war (1870–1871). Building work took nearly 45 years.

Leave Sacré-Cœur and turn right along rue Azaïs, with its stunning views over the city. Turn right up rue St-Eleuthère to ❼ St-Pierre-de-Montmartre.

Humbler than its grand companion, this peaceful church was originally part of the 12th-century Benedictine abbey of Montmartre.

Enter the touristy place du Tertre (▷ 108) and leave by the gift-shop strewn rue Norvins. Turn second left, through place Jean-Baptiste Clément. Turn right into rue Ravignan, and continue round to the left into the tree-shaded ❽ place Émile Goudeau.

On the right of this square, look for the Bateau Lavoir, where Pablo Picasso, Juan Gris and Georges Braque had studios and where Cubism was born. The original ramshackle wooden building burned down in 1970, but has since been rebuilt.

To leave the square, walk down a small flight of steps and continue down rue Ravignan until you reach rue des Abbesses. Turn left here to ❾ place des Abbesses (▷ 145).

OUT AND ABOUT

Before stopping for a drink at place des Abbesses, take a look at the art nouveau Métro entrance and the unusual façade of the church of St-Jean-l'Evangeliste-de-Montmartre (1904), nicknamed St-Jean-des-Briques for its profusion of red bricks.

The Moulin de la Galette restaurant, crowned by the Moulin Radet

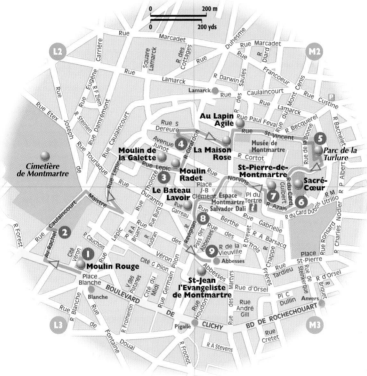

There is a village look about the buildings in Montmartre

Picturesque tree-lined steps

WHEN TO GO
It is best to follow this walk during the day, as parts of Montmartre can be seedy at night.

WHERE TO EAT
Try La Maison Rose or one of the cafés around place des Abbesses.

TIP
For another stunning view of Sacré-Cœur, head from place des Abbesses down rue Yvonne Le Tac to the base of the funicular.

QUARTIER LATIN

This walk takes you beyond the swarming boulevard St-Michel to the quiet cobbled alleyways, peaceful gardens, historic churches and laid-back cafés of the Latin Quarter.

THE WALK	
Distance: 2.5km (1.5 miles)	
Allow: 1 hour 30 minutes	
Start/end at place St-Michel	
How to get there: 🚇 St-Michel	
🚌 21, 24, 27, 38, 85, 96 🚆 RER line C, St-Michel-Notre-Dame	

Start at place St-Michel and walk across to the ❶ Fontaine St-Michel.

The sculpture symbolizes St. Michael slaying a dragon. Place St-Michel is the main gateway to the Latin Quarter from the Île de la Cité. Numerous visitors, students and Parisians pass through here every day.

Cross boulevard St-Michel and walk down the medieval rue de la Huchette. Cross over rue de Petit Pont. Turn left, then immediately right into rue de la Bûcherie, with its views of Notre-Dame. Continue to ❷ square René Viviani.

This is a pleasant place to sit for a few moments, admiring the flowers and enjoying the gurgle of running water from the fountain. The acacia here is said to be one of the oldest trees in Paris, dating from the early 17th century.

Leave the square near the partly Gothic church of ❸ St-Julien-le-Pauvre (▷ 162).

This small, low-ceilinged church is one of the oldest in Paris, dating from the 12th century. You may find its sculptures and paintings hard to make out in the subdued lighting.

From the church, follow the road round to rue St-Jacques. Cross rue St-Jacques and walk down rue St-Séverin, alongside the church of ❹ St-Séverin (▷ 162–163).

The church dates from the 13th century, although much of it had to be rebuilt in the 15th

century after a fire. To visit, turn left into rue des Prêtres St-Séverin. Don't miss the vivid stained-glass windows at the far end, installed in 1970 and representing the Seven Sacraments.

Continue along rue St-Séverin to medieval rue de la Harpe, which, to the left, leads to boulevard St-Germain. Cross the boulevard to the medieval garden of the Musée National du Moyen Âge—Thermes de Cluny. Turn right up the boulevard, then left onto ❺ boulevard St-Michel.

This traffic-thundering road, with its clothes stores, book-shops and newsstands, is the Latin Quarter's main artery.

Walk up boulevard St-Michel, then turn right onto rue de l'École de Médecine. Turn left onto rue André Dubois, then up the steps to reach ❻ rue Monsieur le Prince. Turn left onto this road.

Rue Monsieur le Prince closely follows the line of Paris's old city wall, built by King Philippe-Auguste, who reigned in the late 12th and early 13th

centuries. Today it has shops and inexpensive restaurants, including the bistro Polidor at number 41, which was launched in 1845.

Just before Polidor, turn right into rue Racine, then walk along to place de l'Odéon, dominated by the 18th-century Odéon Théâtre de l'Europe. Wander down the rue de l'Odéon, with its unusual shops, to reach ❼ Carrefour de l'Odéon.

If you feel like a rest, you can stop for a coffee in one of the cafés here.

Continue to boulevard St-Germain. Cross the boulevard and walk down ❽ rue de l'Ancienne Comédie.

On your right you'll pass Paris's oldest café, Le Procope, founded in 1686 and now a restaurant (▷ 274).

At the Buci crossroads turn sharp right onto rue St-André des Arts. This leads back to place St-Michel. You could have a drink in one of the nearby cafés or cross the Pont St-Michel to explore the Île de la Cité.

OUT AND ABOUT

WHEN TO GO

Daytime is best for this walk, when the shops and churches are open.

WHERE TO EAT

There is a choice of cafés on Carrefour de l'Odéon, or Pizza Milano at place St-Michel.

NEARBY ATTRACTIONS

The Latin Quarter has plenty to occupy you, including the Musée National du Moyen Âge–Thermes de Cluny (▷ 128–129), the stately Panthéon (▷ 144) and the refreshing Jardin du Luxembourg (▷ 102–103). You can while away a few hours in some of the many cafés or shop for clothes along boulevard St-Michel (pictured right).

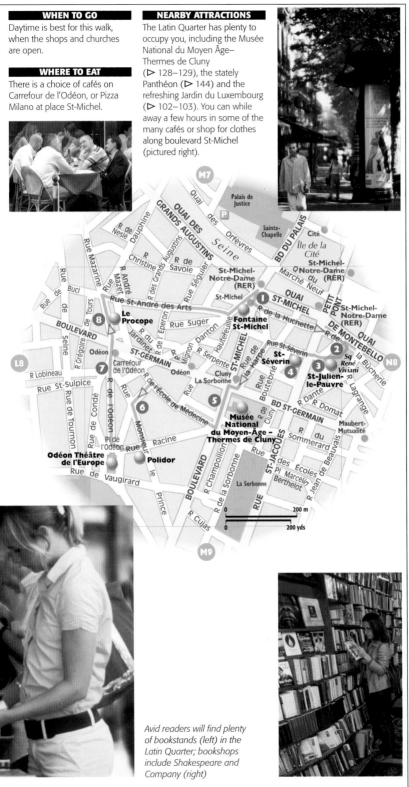

Avid readers will find plenty of bookstands (left) in the Latin Quarter; bookshops include Shakespeare and Company (right)

RIVE DROITE

A relaxing walk that combines restful gardens with chic shops.

THE WALK	
Distance: 3.5km (2 miles)	
Allow: 2 hours	
Start/end at place de la Concorde	
How to get there: 🚇 Concorde	
🚌 24, 42, 72, 73, 84, 94	

Carefully cross the stream of traffic flowing through ❶ place de la Concorde to take a look at the obelisk in the heart of this historic square (▷ 148).

Place de la Concorde was designed in the mid-18th century as a regal setting for an equestrian statue of Louis XV. The square, originally named after the king, was promptly re-titled place de la Révolution when the guillotine arrived. Louis XVI and Marie-Antoinette were among the 1,300 people executed here. The pink granite obelisk came to Paris from Luxor, Egypt, in the 1830s and is around 3,300 years old.

Cross to the ornate gates of the ❷ Jardin des Tuileries and stroll through this vibrant public garden (▷ 105).

The Tuileries is one of the oldest public gardens in Paris and offers fabulous views of the Louvre, the Eiffel Tower, place de la Concorde and the Arc de Triomphe. Parisians come here to relax by the two large ponds when the sun comes out, or stroll along the terraces on either side of the park.

At the end of the park, turn left to reach rue de Rivoli. Turn right onto rue de Rivoli and walk alongside the ❸ Louvre (▷ 118–123).

Many of France's rulers have left their mark on the Louvre, including Charles V, François I and Napoleon. The original medieval fortress was transformed into a castle in the 14th century, then became a royal palace, before assuming its present role as one of the most prestigious museums in the world.

Cross rue de Rivoli into place du Palais Royal. From here, cross rue St-Honoré and bear left, towards the Comédie Française. Enter the ❹ Jardin du Palais Royal through a discreet arch on the left of the palace.

This garden (▷ 104) is only moments from the traffic and crowds of rue de Rivoli but a million miles away in atmosphere. You enter through a courtyard decorated with curious grey-and-white striped mini-columns, designed by the artist Daniel Buren in 1986. The garden, with its vivid flowerbeds, is surrounded by elegant 18th-century arcades with individual shops.

Walk to the end of the garden and leave on the left side, past the historic restaurant Le Grand Véfour—look through the window at the lovely painted ceiling. This brings you to rue de Beaujolais. Turn right onto here, left up rue Vivienne, followed by a left turn onto rue des Petits Champs. You'll pass the ❺ Bibliothèque Nationale de France (▷ 81) as you walk along this road.

This building was once the palace of 17th-century prime minister Cardinal Mazarin, but has housed France's national library since the 18th century. By the 1990s the mammoth collection had outgrown the site and in 1996 an additional library (▷ 81) opened in the 13th *arrondissement*, named after former president François Mitterrand.

Continue until you reach avenue de l'Opéra. Cross the avenue and walk up towards the ❻ opera house (▷ 142).

The sumptuous Opéra Palais Garnier was designed by Charles Garnier and opened in 1875. It is an extravagance of marble, gold and sculpture and was once the largest opera house in the world.

Just before place de l'Opéra, turn left down rue de la Paix, brimming with elegant jewellery shops. This leads to the even more exclusive ❼ place Vendôme (▷ 149).

You'll need a hefty bank balance to go shopping in this supreme symbol of Parisian chic, with its jewellery shops and world-famous Ritz Hotel. Be careful of the traffic—the cobbles give the false impression that the square is pedestrian-only.

Cross the square and walk down rue de Castiglione, with its elegant shopping arcades. Turn right onto rue de Rivoli, which returns you to place de la Concorde. Back in the square, don't miss the view down the Champs-Élysées to the Arc de Triomphe.

The Palais Royal courtyard

WHEN TO GO

The best time to do this walk is during the day, when the shops are open and the Jardin des Tuileries is at its best. If you decide to take an evening stroll, avoid the Jardin des Tuileries and walk up rue de Rivoli instead.

WHERE TO EAT

For a meal try the chic but traditional brasserie Le Grand Colbert, at 4 rue Vivienne, near the Jardin du Palais Royal (▷ 269). For tea and cake visit the chic Muscade tea room, within the *jardin* grounds, at 36 rue Montpensier/67 galerie Montpensier (May–end Aug Tue–Sun 10–11.30, 3–6; rest of year 10–11.30, 3–8).

The obelisk in place de la Concorde (above) once stood at the Temple of Luxor.
Reading in the Jardin des Tuileries (below)

The imposing entrance to the Bibliothèque National de France (above).
Elegant place Vendôme (below)

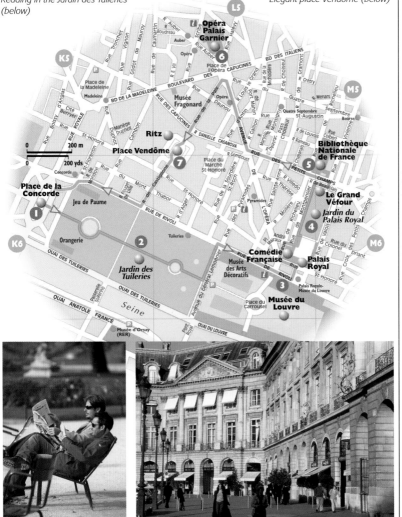

OUT AND ABOUT

ST-GERMAIN-DES-PRÉS

...lk takes you through the picturesque lanes of St-Germain-des-Prés, along the
...Left Bank of the Seine and around the beautiful Jardin du Luxembourg.

THE WALK

Distance: 3km (2 miles)
Allow: 2 hours 30 minutes
Start at St-Sulpice Métro station
End at St-Germain-des-Prés Métro station
How to get there: 🚇 St-Sulpice
🚌 63, 70, 84, 86, 87, 96

Leave St-Sulpice Métro station and walk east along rue du Vieux Colombier to place St-Sulpice. Straight ahead, across the square, is the immense ❶ Église St-Sulpice (▷ 163).

St-Sulpice church displays a mixture of architectural styles and dominates the square and its elaborate fountain. It took 134 years and six architects to build the church and even now the south tower remains unfinished. Treasures inside include murals by Eugène Delacroix, an extravagant pulpit and one of the world's largest organs.

From the main entrance of the church, head south down rue Férou. At the end, cross over rue de Vaugirard and turn right. Almost immediately on your left is an entrance to the ❷ Jardin du Luxembourg (▷ 102–103).

The landscaped Jardin du Luxembourg, commissioned by Marie de Medici in the early 17th century, is one of the most popular parks in Paris. The Palais du Luxembourg, within its grounds, is now home to the French Senate.

Leave the gardens by the northern exit, to the right of the Palais du Luxembourg. Cross the road and head north along rue Rotrou. Pass the neoclassical Odéon Théâtre de l'Europe on the right. When you reach place de l'Odéon turn around to admire the theatre's colonnaded façade.
    Walk across the square and carry on up rue de l'Odéon to the crossroads, carrefour de l'Odéon. Continue north a short distance until you reach

boulevard St-Germain. Cross over, turn right and then almost immediately left into the ❸ cour du Commerce St-André.

This narrow cobblestone passage was built in 1776 on the site of a tennis court. It became a hive of revolutionary activity, with Jean-Paul Marat printing his pamphlet at number 8, the anatomy professor Dr. Guillotin perfecting his 'philanthropic beheading machine' at number 9 and revolutionary leader Georges Danton living at number 20.

Turn left into rue St-André des Arts and almost immediately right at the carrefour de Buci into rue Dauphine. Walk to the end of this bustling street and you arrive at the Pont Neuf, the oldest bridge in Paris. Turn left, before the bridge, onto quai de Conti. On your left is the neoclassic façade of the ❹ Hôtel de la Monnaie.

The workshops of the Paris Mint were here from the 18th century. The *hôtel* now houses the Musée de la Monnaie (▷ 117), a coin and medal museum. Around 2,000 coins and hundreds of medals and tokens are on display, as well as prints, documents and engravings. The museum also shows the development of minting techniques.

Cross over the road to walk along the edge of the Seine. Next to the Hôtel de la Monnaie, on the left, you'll see the splendid dome of the Institut de France (▷ 98), home of the Académie Française. Notice the beautiful Pont des Arts footbridge, composed of seven steel arches, spanning the river to the Louvre. As you walk along you'll see ❺ the *bouquinistes* (booksellers) lining the banks of the Seine.

Their green bookstalls, selling second-hand books, postcards and prints, have a history

dating back 300 years. In the early days, the booksellers used to transport their goods in wheelbarrows across the river to sell them on the banks of the Seine.

Head south down rue Bonaparte. On your right you'll pass the most celebrated fine art school in Paris, the École Nationale Supérieure des Beaux-Arts. Turn left into rue Jacob and then right into rue de Furstemberg. At number 6, in the corner of a charming little square, you'll find the ❻ Musée National Eugène Delacroix (▷ 126).

The artist Eugène Delacroix lived in St-Germain-des-Prés for the last six years of his life, from 1857 to 1863. His apartment has been converted into a museum, where you can see some of his paintings and sketches, in addition to his personal possessions.

Head left down rue de l'Abbaye. Continue to head east on rue de Bourbon le Chateau. When you reach rue de Buci, home to one of Paris's most popular markets (closed Mondays), turn right. Turn right again and walk along boulevard St-Germain, passing the southern side of the ❼ Église St-Germain-des-Prés (▷ 162) on your right. Continue until you come to place St-Germain-des-Prés; turn right into the square, where you'll find the entrance to the church.

The Église St-Germain-des-Prés dates from the 11th century and is the oldest church in Paris. Damaged during the Revolution, the church was restored in the 19th century. The huge 12th-century flying buttresses of the choir are still intact.

The walk ends at St-Germain-des-Prés Métro station, on boulevard St-Germain, on the southern side of the church.

OUT AND ABOUT

Browsing in the rue de Buci (right).
Elegant Le Bon Marché department store (below)

Jardin du Luxembourg   0   200 m
                        0   200 yds

Jean-Paul Sartre was once a regular at the Café de Flore

PLACE
SARTRE – BEAUVOIR
JEAN–PAUL SARTRE
1905 – 1980
SIMONE DE BEAUVOIR
1908 – 1986
PHILOSOPHES ET ÉCRIVAINS

OUT AND ABOUT

WHEN TO GO
It is best to do this walk during the day, when the museums, gardens and churches are open. The market in the rue de Buci is closed on Mondays.

WHERE TO EAT
Two of the city's most famous cafés are on the boulevard St-Germain, at the end of the walk. Les Deux Magots is at number 170 and Café de Flore is at number 172. There are also plenty of other cafés and restaurants along the route.

ALONG THE SEINE

A river cruise along the Seine is a great way to view some of Paris's key sights from a different perspective. It is also ideal if you are short on time—in just over an hour you can see many of the famous landmarks.

THE RIVER TRIP

Distance: 11km (7 miles)

Allow: Just over 1 hour

Start/end at square du Vert-Galant, Pont Neuf

How to get there: 🚇 Pont Neuf
🚌 24, 27, 58, 67, 70, 72, 74, 75.
From the Métro station walk over the Pont Neuf bridge. Just over halfway across, on the right, is a sign for the Vedettes du Pont Neuf. Go down the steps to the square du Vert-Galant, on the Île de la Cité, and turn right. The boarding platform is straight ahead.

The boat leaves from the pretty square du Vert-Galant and heads west. The first bridge you pass under is the pedestrian-only Pont des Arts. This was originally built in 1804 but replaced in 1984. It is one of the most romantic bridges in Paris and is also a popular meeting place for artists. On the Right Bank you can see the ❶ Musée du Louvre (▷ 118–123).

The Louvre, one of the largest museums in the world, was once the residence of the kings and queens of France. It now houses an outstanding collection of art, from ancient times to the 19th century.

After passing under the Pont du Carrousel and the Pont Royal you'll see the façade of the ❷ Musée d'Orsay (▷ 130–134) on the Left Bank.

The museum, in the former Orsay railway station, displays fine and applied arts from

Relaxing on steps leading down to the river (right).
Ornate Pont Alexandre III (below)

1848 to 1914. It has one of the best Impressionist collections in the world.

The next two bridges are the Passerelle de Solférino, spanning the river between the Jardin des Tuileries and the Musée d'Orsay, and the Pont de la Concorde, built with stones from the Bastille prison, which was destroyed during the French Revolution. On the Left Bank is the home of the Assemblée Nationale, the 18th-century Palais Bourbon (▷ 80), and on the Right Bank is ❸ place de la Concorde (▷ 148).

Place de la Concorde, laid out between 1755 and 1775, is the largest square in Paris. At its heart stands the city's oldest monument, an Egyptian obelisk 23m (75ft) high and around 3,300 years old.

The boat passes under the ornate Pont Alexandre III, built for the 1900 Exposition Universelle and dedicated to the Franco-Russian alliance. On the Right Bank you can see the Grand Palais and Petit Palais (▷ 95) and on the Left Bank, in the

distance, is ❹ Les Invalides (▷ 99–101).

Here you'll find the Musée de l'Armée, with fascinating displays of military art and equipment. Napoleon's tomb is in the Église du Dôme.

After passing under the Pont des Invalides, the Pont de l'Alma and the Passerelle Debilly, the boat rounds a bend and you are greeted by a spectacular view of the ❺ Eiffel Tower (▷ 164–169) on the Left Bank.

The tower, symbol of Paris, was constructed between 1887 and 1889, is 324m (1,063ft) high and has more than six million visitors each year. The views from the top are breathtaking.

The Pont d'Iéna spans the river between the Eiffel Tower on the Left Bank and the Jardins du Trocadéro on the Right Bank. The boat passes under this bridge before turning and heading back in the opposite direction to the Île de la Cité. As you sail along look out for the houseboats and brightly painted restaurant-barges

OUT AND ABOUT

G5 · H5

F6

Pont de l'Alma

Palais de Chaillot

Jardins du Trocadéro

Musée du Quai Branly

Pont d'Iéna

F7

❺ Tour Eiffel

Parc du Champ de Mars

École Militaire

F8

0   500 m
0   500 yds

G9 · H9

moored along the banks of the Seine. You'll see the grand cupola of the Institut de France on the right before you pass under the southern side of the **6** Pont Neuf.

The 'new bridge' is actually the oldest in Paris, dating from the 17th century. It was the first bridge across the Seine to be built without houses on it.

The next two bridges are the Pont St-Michel, leading to the Latin Quarter and the Sorbonne university (▷ 163), and the Petit Pont, the smallest bridge in Paris. On the Île de la Cité you can see the beautiful **7** Cathedral of Notre-Dame (▷ 137–141).

Notre-Dame was constructed between the 12th and 14th centuries and is a masterpiece of Gothic architecture. Notice its impressive flying buttresses and its spire, 96m (315ft) high.

Several bridges farther along the river, to your right, lies the Institut du Monde Arabe (▷ 98) and the outdoor sculptures of the Musée de la Sculpture en Plein Air. The boat now turns to circle around the picturesque Île St-Louis (▷ 98). After three more bridges, including the romantic Pont Marie, you can see Paris's town hall, the Hôtel de Ville (▷ 95), on the Right Bank.

As the boat sails back along the other side of the Île de la Cité (and under another three bridges), you'll pass the city's oldest hospital, the Hôtel-Dieu, and the **8** Conciergerie (▷ 89–91).

Originally part of a royal palace, the Conciergerie later became a prison. More than 2,600 people held here during the Revolution were sent to the guillotine, including Queen Marie-Antoinette. Look out for the 16th-century clock, the Tour de l'Horloge, on the façade of the Conciergerie.

The boat passes back under the Pont Neuf and the cruise ends where it began.

BASICS

☎ 01 46 33 98 38

🕐 Mar–end Oct daily 10.30, 11.15, 12 and every half-hour from 1.30 to 7, then 8, 9, 9.30, 10 and 10.30; rest of year Mon–Thu 10.30, 11.15, 12, 2, 2.45, 3.30, 4.15, 5, 5.45, 6.30, 8 and 10, Fri–Sun 10.30, 11.15, 12 and every half-hour from 2 to 6.30, then 8, 9, 9.30, 10 and 10.30. Times may vary

💷 Adult €11, child (4–12) €6, under 4 free

📖 Pick up a free route map from the boarding platform www.vedettesdupontneuf.com

WHEN TO GO

Evening is a great time to go on this trip, when the monuments are lit up. Day or night, try to go

Several companies offer boat trips along the Seine, including Bateaux Parisiens (above)

when the weather is good so you can sit on deck and get the best views.

WHERE TO EAT

There is a small bar on the boarding platform and vending machines on the boat.

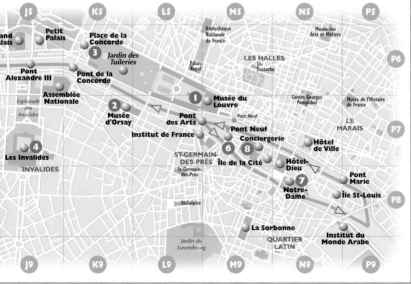

OUT AND ABOUT

Even if you have only a few days in Paris, it can be worth venturing out of the city to see what the rest of the Île-de-France has to offer. The opulent palaces of Versailles and Fontainebleau, the art galleries of the Château de Chantilly or the woods of the Bois de Boulogne and Bois de Vincennes all make a pleasant day trip. If you have children in tow, you could take them to Disneyland Resort Paris, only a short train ride away.

1. EXCURSION

BOIS DE BOULOGNE

The Bois de Boulogne is Paris's western lung, with 845ha (2,090 acres) of parkland, lakes, flower gardens, waterfalls and follies.

BASICS

Parc de Bagatelle
✉ Route de Sèvres à Neuilly
☎ 39 75
🕐 Daily, hours vary according to time of year. Jul–end Aug 9.30–8
🎟 Adult €3, child (7–25) €1.50, under 7 free
🚇 Pont de Neuilly, then bus 43 or 93; Porte Maillot, then bus 244

Jardin d'Acclimatation
✉ Boulevard des Sablons
☎ 01 40 67 90 82
🕐 Jun–end Sep daily 10–7; rest of year daily 10–6
🎟 Adult and child over 3 €2.50, under 3 free
🚇 Les Sablons
www.jardindacclimatation.fr

Jardin Shakespeare
✉ Pré-Catelan
🕐 Daily, hours vary
🚇 Porte Maillot, then bus 244

Jardin des Serres d'Auteuil
✉ 3 avenue de la Porte d'Auteuil
☎ 39 75
🕐 Daily 10–5 (until 6 in summer)
🎟 Adult €1, child 50c
🚇 Porte d'Auteuil

GREEN SPACE

The Bois de Boulogne lies just outside the *périphérique* and draws joggers, bicyclists and people who want to escape the city for an hour or two. There are cafés and restaurants, two lakes linked by waterfalls, follies, winding paths, an open-air theatre, two racecourses and more than 140,000 trees.

A highlight is the Parc de Bagatelle, on the northwestern edge. Its small chateau, built in 1775, looks out over a romantic park laid out by landscape gardener Thomas Blaike. There are more than 700 types of roses.

Farther north, the Jardin d'Acclimatation is good for children, with playgrounds, mini-golf, puppet shows, a toy train and the 'Explor@dome'.

Moving south, the Jardin Shakespeare has an open-air theatre staging productions in French and English, as well as a garden laid out with flowers, herbs and trees mentioned in Shakespeare's plays and sonnets.

In the Jardin des Serres d'Auteuil, in the south, 19th-century greenhouses shelter tropical plants. A short walk away is Roland-Garros, home of the French Tennis Open.

BACKGROUND

Like the Bois de Vincennes on the eastern side of the city (▷ 237), the Bois de Boulogne was used for hunting in medieval times, before becoming an aristocratic leisure ground in the 18th century. Napoleon III and his town planner Baron Haussmann were responsible for the park's current layout.

The Bois de Boulogne is great for bicycling

BOIS DE VINCENNES

The Bois de Vincennes forms the perfect antidote to hectic city life. Only a Métro ride from central Paris, it has three lakes, a historic castle, a beautiful floral park and one of France's largest zoos. On a sunny day, you may find it hard to drag yourself back to the city.

BASICS

Château de Vincennes
✉ Avenue de Paris, 94300 Vincennes
☎ 01 48 08 31 20
🕐 May–end Aug daily 10–12, 1–6; rest of year daily 10–12, 1–5.
💷 Grounds: free. 45-min tour: €4.60 (under 18 free); 75-min tour €6.10 (under 18 free). Château: €7.50 (under 18 free)
www.monuments-nationaux.fr (French and English)

Parc Zoologique de Paris
✉ 53 avenue de St-Maurice, 75012
☎ 01 44 75 20 00
🕐 Mon–Sat 9–6, Sun 9–6.30
🚻 🍴
💷 €5 (under 4 free)
www.mnhn.fr (click on *parc zoologique* to reach the zoo)

Parc Floral
✉ Off Esplanade du Château
☎ Mairie de Paris information 3975
🕐 9.30–8 in summer; 9.30–5 in winter
💷 Adult €5, child €2.50
☕ Two cafés, open daily in summer, Wed, Sat–Sun in winter
www.parcfloraldeparis.com

HOW TO GET THERE

The **Bois de Vincennes** is 6km (4 miles) east of central Paris

Métro: Château de Vincennes for the chateau and the Parc Floral; Porte Dorée for the Parc Zoologique de Paris

Bus: 46, 56, 115, 118, 124, 318, 325 for the chateau; 46, 112 for the Parc Floral; 46, 86, 325 for the Parc Zoologique

CHÂTEAU DE VINCENNES
The Château de Vincennes has led a far from quiet life, despite its peaceful surroundings. Louis XIV spent his honeymoon within these walls, Winston Churchill attended a war conference in the underground chambers and the Germans executed prisoners in the courtyards during the Occupation of Paris.

Today, you can wander around the grounds and try to piece together the range of architectural styles, from the 14th-century medieval keep to the 17th-century classical Pavillon du Roi and Pavillon de la Reine and the 19th-century Pavillon des Armes. The keep has been restored, and you can take a guided tour around Charles V's study and the chapel, based on Paris's Sainte-Chapelle. Inside you can see Paris's second-oldest bell, the 700kg (1,540 lb) Vincennes bell, commissioned for the keep by Charles V in 1369. Whole sections of the chapel's windows were destroyed during the storms of 1999, although the stunning Rose Window survived unharmed.

PARC ZOOLOGIQUE DE PARIS
Giraffes, penguins and pandas are not usually on the visitor's itinerary in Paris, but if you feel like a change from museums and monuments this could fit the bill. The zoo, part of the Muséum National d'Histoire Naturelle (▷ 127), is home to around 1,200 animals. A highlight is the *Grand Rocher* (literally 'big rock'), a man-made mini-mountain, 65m (213ft) high, with goats careering up and down its slopes. You can take a lift to the top of the rock to enjoy an unusual view of Paris.

PARC FLORAL
The floral gardens are a lovely place to wander after a visit to the nearby Château de Vincennes. The flower displays are exceptional and attractions for children include mini-golf, quad-biking and the Théâtre pour Enfants (certain days only). The park has a striking dahlia garden, an iris garden, medicinal plants, a Valley of Flowers, and forests of rhododendrons and azaleas. It also houses France's national collection of camellias and geraniums. A jazz festival gets the park jiving from early June to the end of July and classical music concerts are held in August and September.

BACKGROUND
The Bois de Vincennes was a rich royal hunting ground in the 12th century, sectioned off by one of Philippe-Auguste's walls. By Louis XV's reign it had become a popular promenading area and in the 19th century Baron Haussmann landscaped it for the working-class population of eastern Paris. The woods suffered serious damage in the storms of 1999.

TIPS
● If your French is not very strong, think twice before embarking on the Château de Vincennes tour. Much of the route covers grounds in which you can wander freely anyway.
● The zoo is most crowded on Wednesday afternoons and at weekends.
● The zoo is due for renovation in the near future—check opening hours before going.

A leafy street near the Château de Vincennes

OUT AND ABOUT

CHANTILLY

This fairytale Renaissance chateau, surrounded by a moat, sits in beautiful parkland and is home to an outstanding art collection.

BASICS

Château de Chantilly—Musée Condé

✉ BP 70243, 60631 Chantilly

☎ 03 44 27 31 80

🕒 Museum and park: mid-Mar to early Nov Wed–Mon 10–6 (park Jul–end Aug daily until 8pm); rest of year Wed–Mon 10.30–5

💶 Museum and park: adult €9, under 18 free. Park: adult €5, under 18 free

🚌 Guided tours need to be booked in advance; audioguides €2

🎧 Several to choose from; prices vary

🎁 Giftshop

❓ The Small Apartments can be visited by guided tour only. Buy tickets from the giftshop

www.chateaudechantilly.com (French, English; includes historical information and details of activities, events and temporary exhibitions)

Musée Vivant du Cheval

✉ Grandes Écuries, BP 60242, 60631 Chantilly

☎ 03 44 57 40 40; tourist office 03 44 67 37 37

🕒 Apr–end Oct Mon, Wed–Fri 10.30–6.30, Sat, Sun and public hols 10.30–7 (also open May, Jun Tue 10.30–5.30); rest of year Mon, Wed–Fri 2–6, Sat, Sun and public hols 10.30–6.30. Last admission 1 hour before closing

💶 Adult €9, child (4–17) €7

❓ Equestrian demonstrations (lasting 30 min) take place at 11.30, 3.30 and 5.30 (3.30 only weekdays in winter). Pass Domaine de Chantilly (admission to both attractions and park): adult €16, child (4–17) €7

www.musee-vivant-du-cheval.fr (plenty of information in English, including details of shows, events and demonstrations)

HOW TO GET THERE

Chantilly is 40km (25 miles) north of Paris

By train: Gare du Nord to Chantilly-Gouvieux (30 min). It takes around 30 min to walk from the train station to the chateau. There are occasional buses or you can get a taxi from outside the station (around €6)

By car: Take the autoroute du Nord (A1) and leave on the Survilliers-St-Witz exit. Alternatively take the N16 or N17

OVERVIEW

The Château de Chantilly is one of the most picturesque castles in the region. It is surrounded by attractive parkland, with the forest of Chantilly beyond, and contains a magnificent art collection.

The town of Chantilly is one of the leading training venues in Europe for racehorses and is home to a world-famous racecourse and the Musée Vivant du Cheval horse museum.

Chantilly has two culinary claims to fame—the delicious whipped and sweetened cream known as *crème chantilly* and the 17th-century master chef Vatel. He met a tragic end in 1671, when he committed suicide because he didn't have enough fish to feed the visiting Louis XIV and his courtiers.

CHÂTEAU DE CHANTILLY

Chantilly was founded by a Roman named Cantilius but it was the famous head of the French army, High Constable Anne de Montmorency, who played a key role in developing the site in the 16th century. He decided to transform the medieval castle into a Renaissance chateau, and added the Petit Château, which still survives today.

Chantilly passed into the hands of the powerful Condé family in the mid-17th century and the prince, known as the Grand Condé, called in Versailles landscape architect André Le Nôtre to create the Grand Canal, lakes, waterfalls, ornamental ponds and a maze. The chateau became a popular venue for festivals and other gatherings, and literati who attended included Jean de La Fontaine and Molière.

During the Revolution much of the Grand Château was pillaged and destroyed and the building was used as a prison. In around 1830 Henri d'Orléans, Duke of Aumale, inherited the property, then commissioned Honoré Daumet to carry out a major restoration in 1875. In 1886 the duke gave Chantilly to

A winged statue on the Island of Love, in the English Garden

The Château de Chantilly dates from the 14th to 19th centuries

the Institut de France, stipulating that his art collections should be preserved and the chateau must open to the public. The Musée Condé opened in April 1898, less than a year after his death.

MUSÉE CONDÉ

The art and furnishings on display here date from the Renaissance to the 19th century. The picture galleries have works by French, Italian, Dutch, English, Flemish and Spanish painters, in addition to 18th-century Chantilly porcelain and 19th-century Chantilly lace. Look out for works by Raphael, Jean Fouquet, Fra Angelico, Eugène Delacroix and Camille Corot. In a skylit room called The Tribune there are masterpieces by Antoine Watteau, Eugène Delacroix and Jean Auguste Dominique Ingres. The Psyche Gallery has 42 stunning 16th-century grisaille stained-glass windows and The Sanctuary exhibits Raphael's *Trois Grâces* (1500–1505) and 40 miniatures by Jean Fouquet (1445). The library has a vast collection of rare and important books—don't miss a reproduction of the illuminated medieval manuscript *Très Riches Heures du Duc de Berry* (15th century). The chapel has beautiful stained-glass windows from Ecouen, and the word *L'Espérance* (Hope) decorates the ceiling.

Tours of the Large Apartments take in the Prince's Bedchamber, the Music Room and the Great Condé Victory Gallery. The sumptuously furnished Small

Apartments of the Duke and Duchess of Aumale (guided tours only) were decorated in the 19th century with wood panels, marquetry furniture, brocade drapes and family portraits. The Small Monkey Gallery, painted in the 18th century, is covered in decorative panels with monkey motifs.

THE PARK

The grounds cover around 115ha (276 acres) and are ideal for strolling. Attractions include the Grand Canal, the waterfall, the 18th-century Anglo-Chinese garden, Le Nôtre's 17th-century French gardens, the Maison de Sylvie and the romantic English Garden with its Island of Love, Swan Lake, Temple of Venus and Beauvais waterfall. There is also the Enghien Castle, a children's play area, a kangaroo enclosure and Le Hameau (the Hamlet), built in 1774 for the Prince of Condé.

In the spring and summer you can sail along the moats and canals in an electric boat, take a nostalgic trip in a horse-drawn carriage or go for a ride on a little train.

MUSÉE VIVANT DU CHEVAL

The stables (Grandes Écuries), with their striking façade, were built for Louis-Henri, Duke of Bourbon, in the 18th century. According to legend, he believed he would be reincarnated as a horse after his death. The stables, 186m (610ft) long, were intended to accommodate

240 horses and more than 400 hounds for stag and boar hunts. Today they are devoted to the Living Horse Museum. Created in 1982 by Yves Bienaimé, this internationally renowned museum is considered the biggest and most beautiful of its kind. You can see horses of different breeds, equestrian exhibits, works of art and riding demonstrations.

TIPS
● There are information cards in several languages in each room of the Musée Condé.
● Holders of a *Paris Museum Pass* (▷ 307) receive free entry to the Musée Condé.

WHERE TO EAT
Château de Chantilly: La Capitainerie restaurant and tea room (open all year; closed Tue and evenings; tel 03 44 57 15 89).

The Hamlet: Les Goûters Champêtres restaurant, serving regional dishes (mid-Mar to mid-Nov; tel 03 44 57 46 21).

Park: La Courtille, in the English Garden, offering snacks, drinks and ice creams (Mar to mid-Nov; tel 03 44 57 46 21).

OUT AND ABOUT

DISNEYLAND® RESORT PARIS

Experience the magic of Disneyland—a must for kids of all ages.

OUT AND ABOUT

✉ BP 100, Marne-la-Vallée, 77777 Cedex 4

☎ 01 60 30 60 30

🎢 **Disneyland® Park:** mid-Jul to end Aug daily 9am–11pm; Sep–late Oct Mon–Fri 10–8, Sat–Sun 9–8; late Oct–early Nov daily 9–8; early Nov to mid-Dec Mon–Fri 10–8, Sat–Sun 9–8; mid-Dec to end Dec daily 9–8 (31 Dec 9am–1am); Jan to mid-Jul Mon–Fri 10–8, Sat–Sun 9–8; school holidays 9–8
Walt Disney Studios® Park: early Apr–end Aug daily 9–6; Sep–late Oct Mon–Fri 10–6, Sat–Sun 9–6; late Oct–early Nov daily 9–6; early Nov to mid-Dec Mon–Fri 10–6, Sat–Sun 9–6; mid-Dec to end Dec daily 9–6; Jan–end Mar Mon–Fri 10–6, Sat–Sun 9–6

🎟 1-day ticket (valid for either Disneyland Park or Walt Disney Studios Park): adult €46, child (3–11) €38, under 3 free.
3-day Disney Parks Hopper Ticket (valid for both theme parks): adult €128, child (3–11) €105, under 3 free. Prices may vary according to season

🏬 Shops and boutiques sell a huge range of items, including clothes, toys, books, ornaments and postcards

🅿 €8 per day; free if you are staying at a Disneyland Resort Paris hotel

❓ Height and age restrictions apply to some of the rides
www.disneylandparis.com
(packed with information in several languages, with entertainment schedules and details about hotels and restaurants. You can also book tickets)

Disneyland Resort Paris is 32km (20 miles) east of Paris

By train: RER line A runs from Châtelet-les-Halles and Gare de Lyon to Marne-la-Vallée/Chessy (around 40 min). The station is 100m (320 ft) from the entrances to both Disneyland Park and Walt Disney Studios Park

By car: take the A4 motorway (Autoroute de l'Est), in the direction of Metz/Nancy. Leave at exit 14, to Parcs Disneyland

You never know who you may bump into (inset, top right). It wouldn't be Disney without those famous ears (inset, right). Sleeping Beauty Castle (right)

OVERVIEW

Disneyland Resort Paris attracts millions of visitors to its two Parks—Disneyland Park and Walt Disney Studios Park. The resort, in the Marne-la-Vallée countryside east of Paris, opened in 1992 to a blaze of publicity. It was Disney's fourth Park, following in the footsteps of California, Florida and Tokyo. The Walt Disney Studios Park opened in 2002. Other attractions include the Disney® Village entertainment complex, seven hotels and a 27-hole golf course.

DISNEYLAND® PARK

You can visit five different 'lands' at the 56ha (140-acre) Disneyland Park, each with its own themed rides, restaurants and shops.

Main Street, USA takes you back in time with its nostalgic scenes from an American town at the turn of the 19th century. Seasonal parades bring scenes from Disney's animated films to life, with dancers and, of course, the famous Disney characters (see the website for dates and times).

Fantasyland, especially popular with younger children, includes Sleeping Beauty Castle, the 'It's a Small World' ride and the enchanting Pays de Contes de Fées canal cruise.

Adventureland boasts the swashbuckling Pirates of the Caribbean, Adventure Isle and the high-speed Indiana Jones and the Temple of Peril ride.

Frontierland, with its canyons, gold mines and rivers, offers two thrill-seeker attractions—the Big Thunder Mountain runaway train and the ghostly Phantom Manor.

Discoveryland was inspired by Jules Verne's visions of the

Swashbuckling activities at Adventureland

future, and the Mystery of the Nautilus ride is based on the film *20,000 Leagues Under the Sea*. Reaching top speeds of 68kph (43mph), the Space Mountain: Mission 2 roller coaster is not for the faint-hearted. The spectacular Star Tours flight simulator whisks visitors onto an interplanetary journey.

WALT DISNEY STUDIOS® PARK

The Walt Disney Studios Park is based on the concept of the popular Disney–MGM Studios in Florida. It is divided into four zones, each aiming to create the atmosphere of a real film studio. The 33m (105ft) water tower, crowned with Mickey's instantly recognizable black ears, dominates the Front Lot. Studio 1 in this zone gives an insight into what goes on behind the scenes in the world of cinema. In Animation Courtyard you can watch the Animagique 3D animated show in a 1,100-seat venue. Or, let yourself be whirled away on the Flying Carpets over Agrabah ride. The Production Courtyard offers the thrilling Catastrophe Canyon ride, while in the Backlot you can experience the excitement of the Rock 'n' Roller Coaster Starring Aerosmith and the fantastic Moteurs…Action Stunt Show Spectacular® featuring cars, motorbikes and jet skis.

DISNEY® VILLAGE

The entertainment complex Disney Village sits between both Disney® Parks and the Disney® hotels. The Village, open until the early hours, is bustling with themed restaurants, bars, shops, street artists and multi-screen cinemas. You could end the day with the popular dinner-spectacular Buffalo Bill's Wild West Show or dance the night away at Hurricanes nightclub.

TIPS

● Disneyland Resort Paris is easily accessible from Paris and makes a terrific day trip.
● Look for the information areas (City Hall in Disneyland Park and Studio Services in Walt Disney Studios Park), which provide entertainment schedules, maps and general information.
● The free FASTPASS system is available on some of the more popular rides in Disneyland Park, reducing waiting time.

WHERE TO EAT

There are dozens of restaurants to choose from and the cuisine ranges from French, Italian and English to Bavarian, Mexican and, of course, American. There are waiter-service and self-service restaurants as well as an array of snack bars. Booking in advance is recommended for the popular sit-down restaurants.

All photography © Disney

FONTAINEBLEAU

The Château de Fontainebleau rivals Versailles in grandeur and historic interest but has the bonus of fewer crowds. It is steeped in regal and imperial resplendence, with 1,900 opulent rooms and exquisite landscaped gardens.

OUT AND ABOUT

BASICS

✉ Château de Fontainebleau, Fontainebleau, 77300

☎ 01 60 71 50 70/60

🕐 Renaissance Rooms, Sovereign's State Apartments and Napoleon I's Imperial Apartment: Jun–end Sep Wed–Mon 9.30–6; rest of year Wed–Mon 9.30–5. Last admission 1 hour before closing.
Small Apartments and Napoleon I Museum: guided tour only.
Chinese Museum: times vary.
Gardens: May–end Sep daily 9–7; Oct daily 9–6; Nov–end Feb daily 9–5; Mar–end Apr daily 9–6

💷 Adult €8, under 18 free, free to wander in the grounds.
Small Apartments and Napoleon I Museum adult €12.50, under 14 free

🚌 See the noticeboard at the ticket desk for times. Audioguides are in French, English, Italian and Japanese, and cost €1 in addition to the admission charge

ℹ 4 rue Royale (next to the Château de Fontainebleau bus stop); tel 01 60 74 99 99
www.musee-chateau-fontainebleau.fr (in French only, but easy to navigate if you have a basic knowledge of the language. If not, click on *Visite virtuelle* for photos of the highlights)

HOW TO GET THERE

By train: Gare de Lyon to Fontainebleau-Avon, roughly every hour, on the Transilien line (around 45 min). From Fontainebleau-Avon station the A/B bus takes you to the chateau in around 15 min
By car: take the A6 motorway from the Porte d'Orléans and leave at the Fontainebleau exit

OVERVIEW

Fontainebleau has witnessed some momentous events in French history, including the birth of Louis XIII in 1601 and Napoleon signing his deed of abdication in 1814. The site was popular with royalty as far back as the 12th century, when kings went hunting in the 17,000ha (40,800 acres) of forest. The keep in the Oval Courtyard is the only remnant of a medieval castle dating from these times.

The pivotal period for Fontainebleau was the 16th century, when François I commissioned a sumptuous royal residence, enticed by the hunting opportunities. He employed the cream of Italy's artists and craftsmen to decorate the palace's interior and laid out the garden with lakes and canals.

A century later, the gardens were re-landscaped by André Le Nôtre, the man responsible for Versailles's stately parterres. Subsequent rulers put their stamp on the palace with numerous modifications, including Napoleon, who chose it as a suitably majestic base and had it completely refurnished in 1804.

RENAISSANCE ROOMS

François I wanted Fontainebleau to be packed with prestigious art and this is reflected in the lavish decoration of Les Salles Renaissance.

The highlight is the Salle de Bal, the ceremonial ballroom, which hosted many a glittering occasion. The dazzling 30m (98ft) hall is decorated with wood panels and frescoes illustrating mythological and hunting themes. Vast windows bathe the room in light and give lovely views over the Oval Courtyard on one side and the Grand Parterre on the other. An imposing fireplace by Philibert Delorme stands at the far end. Pre-recorded Renaissance music helps you imagine the festivities once enjoyed here. In the Galerie François I you can see frescoes painted by the Florentine artist Rosso, a disciple of Michelangelo. For years they lay hidden behind other paintings and were rediscovered only in the 20th century.

SOVEREIGN'S STATE APARTMENTS

Les Grands Appartements des Souverains are even more opulent than the Renaissance Rooms. Hardly an inch of space on the walls or ceilings has escaped intricate decoration. Don't miss the huge tapestries in the Salon François I and in the next-door Tapestry Room, created at the Gobelins factory. The ornate bed in the Empress's Bedchamber was made for Marie-Antoinette, although she never actually slept in it.

Napoleon Bonaparte converted the former king's bedchamber into a Salle du Trône (throne room) in 1808. The preposterously extravagant room is a decorative mixture of Louis XIII, XIV and XV styles.

NAPOLEON I'S IMPERIAL APARTMENT

These rooms offer a fascinating insight into some of the more personal aspects of Napoleon's life, although they are not his private apartments (Small Apartments)—they can be seen

The exuberant Galerie François I dates from the 16th century

You can go rowing on the Carp Pond in summer

by guided tour only. His ceremonial bedchamber is suitably lavish, while the Petite Chambre à Coucher de l'Empereur is more humble, with a camp bed. This room doubled as Napoleon's study, as you can see from the large desk. The Salon Particulier de l'Empereur witnessed a key moment in France's history on 6 April 1814, when Napoleon signed his abdication papers at its round table.

THE GROUNDS

Fontainebleau's grounds are stunning and in good weather you should allow at least an hour to wander through them. For a self-guided walk (8km/5 miles), pick up the *circuit découverte* leaflet at the information desk.

A good place to start is the stately Cour du Cheval Blanc (Courtyard of the White Horse), at the entrance to the chateau. Napoleon bid farewell to his Imperial Guard at the horseshoe staircase here in 1814, before his exile on the island of Elba. The courtyard is also known as the Cour des Adieux in his memory.

To the right of the courtyard (as you face the chateau) is the Jardin Anglais (English Garden), dating from the early 19th century. To the left is the Jardin de Diane. From here, a pleasant stroll around the chateau leads to the elegant Grand Parterre, with its square central pond. Beyond is the 1.2km (0.75 mile) canal, created in 1606 by Henri IV. Be sure to continue round to the vast Carp Pond, separating the Jardin Anglais from the Grand Parterre and formerly used for water tournaments. In calm weather the reflections on the water are wonderful.

TIPS

● Gare de Lyon is a large station and finding the correct platform for Fontainebleau can be confusing. It helps to know that the lettered platforms are in the main concourse area, while the numbered platforms are at the end of platform A. For a timetable of trains to Fontainebleau-Avon, ask at the ticket desk that deals with RER and Métro trains.
● Combined rail and entrance tickets are available.
● Holders of a *Paris Museum Pass* (▷ 307) receive free entry to the castle.

WHERE TO EAT

There is no café, so bring your own refreshments. Picnics are allowed in the park, but not the gardens. There are cafés and restaurants in the town.

The chateau, beautifully mirrored in the Carp Pond

OUT AND ABOUT

VERSAILLES

Versailles is France's ultimate royal palace, an opulent monument to the super-ego of the Sun King, Louis XIV. More like a town than a chateau, it was the seat of French power for more than 100 years and kept members of the royal family safely cushioned from their subjects in Paris—until the invasion of the bloodthirsty Revolutionary mob. Now the invaders are visitors, who come to see the lavish State Apartments and majestic, fountain-filled formal gardens.

BASICS

✉ Versailles, 78000

☎ 01 30 83 78 00

⏰ State Apartments: Apr–end Oct Tue–Sun 9–6.30; rest of year Tue–Sun 9–5.30. Grand and Petit Trianon: Apr–end Oct daily 12–6.30; rest of year daily 12–5.30. Gardens: daily 9–6. Fountains play: late Apr–end Sep Sat–Sun 11–12, 3.30–5 (also other occasional days). Park: daily 8 or 9–dusk. On public hols phone ahead to check opening times

🚌 See Getting Your Bearings, below

🍴 La Flottille (tel 01 39 51 41 58) and La Petite Venise (tel 01 39 53 25 69)

☕ Café in the Cour de la Chapelle. Two snack bars in the grounds

🎧 Guided tours are available. Book at 9am. Audioguides for the State Apartments (€4.50) come in 8 languages. You need to leave a passport, credit card or driving licence as a deposit

♿ Entrance H is for visitors with disabilities. There is an elevator to the State Apartments

🚻 Keep some coins available for the toilets

www.chateauversailles.fr (in French, English and Spanish; practical information, historical background and photos. You can also check when the fountains are playing)

HOW TO GET THERE

By train: RER line C takes 30 min to Versailles Rive-Gauche, followed by a 10-min walk to the palace. A mainline train from Gare Montparnasse takes 15 min to Versailles Chantiers, followed by a 20-min walk. The mainline train from Gare St-Lazare takes 25 min to Versailles Rive-Droite, followed by a 15-min walk

By car: take autoroute A13 to the Versailles-Château exit, then follow signs

GETTING YOUR BEARINGS

● Many people expect to be immediately overawed by the grandeur of Versailles, but instead, your first impression could well be confusion. The palace has a bewildering number of entrances and ticket options, and when you finally start the tour you'll find very few of the rooms have information boards.

It's a good idea to rent an audioguide before you start.

● It's ambitious to try to see everything in one visit, but if that's your aim consider buying a *passeport* at the station in Paris Apr–end Oct Mon–Fri €20, Sat–Sun €25; Nov–end Mar €16. This covers train travel to Versailles Rive-Gauche or Versailles Chantiers and entry into the Château, gardens and the Grand Trianon. The *passeport* includes free entry to the Domaine de Marie-Antoinette between April and the end of October and access to the Grands Eaux Musicales on week-ends and public holidays from April to the end of September.

● For a less hectic day limit yourself to the Château (€13.50; 3 Apr–end Oct €10 after 4pm; Nov–2 Apr €10 after 3pm, audioguide included) and its immediate gardens (free or €10 when fountain show is on). With this ticket you can enjoy all the public areas of the vast building, including the Grands Appartements, the Hall of Mirrors and the Queen's Apartments, along with the Chambre de Roi and the Petits Appartements.

● If you still have the energy, you can then enjoy the Domaine de

Marie-Antoinette (3 Apr–end Oct €9, after 5pm €5; Nov–2 Apr €5), the parts of the grounds loved by the doomed queen, including the Grand Trianon and Petit Trianon. These are a 25-minute stroll away, or take the mini train (adult €5.50, child (11–18) €3.50, under 11 free).

• A *Paris Museum Pass* (▷ 307) gives free access to the Grands Appartements, the Grand Trianon and Petit Trianon.

• Entrance to Versailles is free for under-18s, and for everyone on the first Sunday of the month (October to end March).

KING'S STATE APARTMENT
The Appartement du Roi, part of the Grands Appartements, is a sumptuous shrine to the power

The Latona Fountain (right), with the Grand Canal in the distance. The Treaty of Versailles, ending World War I, was ratified in the lavish Hall of Mirrors (below)

and grandeur of Louis XIV. The ceilings are painted with scenes of thunderous gods and the walls are richly clad with marble and gilded bronze. Each room is dedicated to an Olympian deity symbolizing a royal virtue or duty. The sun god Apollo, closely linked to the cult of the Sun King (Louis XIV), gives his name to the throne room. The ceiling painting in the Hercules Drawing Room depicts 142 characters.

HALL OF MIRRORS

The Galerie des Glaces, also part of the Grands Appartements, bathes you in a sea of chandeliers, natural light and opulence. More than 350 mirrors catch the light pouring in through the huge arched windows, which in turn give spectacular views of the gardens and canal. The hall, 73m (240ft) long, was designed by Jules Hardouin-Mansart and completed in 1686. Since then it has served as a venue for royal wedding celebrations, a place for greeting foreign dignitaries and even a corridor. The Treaty of Versailles was ratified here in 1919. The omnipresent Louis XIV is depicted in the ceiling paint-ings by Charles Le Brun, showing episodes from the king's reign.

QUEEN'S APARTMENT

The Appartement de la Reine runs parallel to the King's State Apartment, with the Hall of Mirrors forming a lavish corridor

between the two. In the Queen's Bedchamber the Queen suffered the ordeal of giving birth in public, to prove royal heirs were genuine. Marie-Antoinette was the last queen to occupy the room and portraits of her family decorate the walls. The exuberant feather-canopied bed is a copy. A poignant portrait of the queen with three of her children hangs in the Antechamber of the Grand Couvert. The empty crib refers to her youngest daughter, Sophie, who died before the portrait was painted.

FOUNTAINS

Versailles's fountains are famous and it is a pity that on most days they remain still. To catch them in full flow, visit during one of the *Grandes Eaux Musicales*. It comes as no surprise that Louis XIV's most-loved deity, the sun god Apollo, plays a prominent role. The Apollo Fountain, guarding the entrance to the Grand Canal, shows the sun god rising out of the water on a chariot, symbolizing the rise of the Sun King's reign. Closer to the chateau, the Latona Fountain depicts Apollo's mother asking Jupiter to turn the Lycian peasants into frogs. Don't miss the Neptune Fountain, past the North Parterre.

THE GROUNDS

Versailles has the largest palace grounds in Europe (100ha/

The Marble Courtyard

247 acres), which were tamed by André Le Nôtre into a geometry so perfect that even nature seemed to obey the Sun King's commands. Louis XIV sailed a flotilla of ships on the 1.6km (1 mile) Grand Canal—today, you can rent rowing boats.

Parc de
Versailles

Part of Le Hameau, a rustic hamlet built for Marie-Antoinette

put a severe strain on France's finances but the palace remained the seat of power until 1789, when a revolutionary mob seized Louis XVI and forced him back to Paris.

TIPS

● The busiest days are Tuesday and Sunday, as well as holiday weekends. The palace is closed on Mondays.
● A pre-purchased ticket (a *Paris Museum Pass* or a combined rail/palace *passeport*) allows you to avoid some of the queues.
● Be prepared for lots of waiting in line—for a ticket, for an audioguide and for the toilets.

WHERE TO EAT

There is plenty of choice on site, with two restaurants, a café and two snack bars. On a summer Sunday it is best to book ahead for the restaurants. Alternatively, you can bring a picnic to eat in the park.

BACKGROUND

Versailles had relatively humble beginnings, as a hunting lodge for Louis XIII. In 1661, Louis XIV decided to move his court to the deserted swamp, 20km (12.5 miles) southwest of Paris, an astute way of isolating the nobility and his ministers while keeping an eye on his not-too-distant capital. He brought in the greatest architects of the day, Louis Le Vau and Jules Hardouin-Mansart, and building work continued right up to his death in 1715. A town soon sprang up to accommodate the court, and the smaller palaces of the Grand Trianon and the Petit Trianon were later created as royal love nests. The building project

VERSAILLES

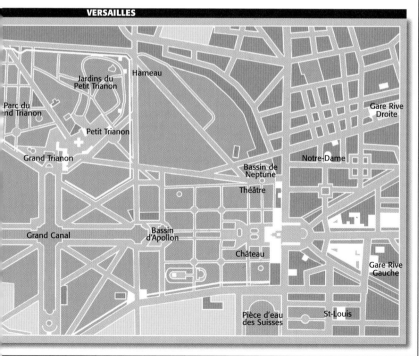

Hameau
Jardins du Petit Trianon
Parc du ~nd Trianon
Gare Rive Droite
Petit Trianon
Grand Trianon
Notre-Dame
Bassin de Neptune
Théâtre
Grand Canal
Bassin d'Apollon
Château
Gare Rive Gauche
Pièce d'eau des Suisses
St-Louis

No visit to Paris is complete without a boat trip down the Seine (▷ 234–235).
Bus tours can also be worthwhile if you want a quick and comfortable introduction to the city.
Alternatively, to really get under the skin of a *quartier*, try a walking tour.

BICYCLE TOURS
See page 59.

BOAT TRIPS
BATEAUX MOUCHES
Tel 01 40 76 99 99; 01 42 25 96 10 (reservations)
www.bateaux-mouches.fr
Board at the Pont de l'Alma for a boat trip down the Seine in a glass-roofed boat. The tour lasts 1 hour 10 minutes. Dinner cruises are available.
Sailings: Apr–end Sep daily 10.15am–11pm every 20–30 min; Oct–end May daily 10.15, 11, 12.15, 2.30, 4, 5, 6, 7, 8, 9
Adult €9, child (4–12) €4, under 4 free

BATEAUX PARISIENS
Tel 0825 01 01 01
www.bateauxparisiens.com
Take a 1-hour cruise along the Seine in a glass-topped boat. Audioguides are available in 12 languages. You can also opt for a dinner cruise. Board near the Eiffel Tower.
Apr–end Oct daily 10am–10.30pm every 30 min (except 1.30 and 7.30); rest of year daily 10–10 every hour
Adult €10, child €5, under 3 free

CANAUXRAMA
Tel 01 42 39 15 00
www.canauxrama.com
Take a trip along the picturesque Canal St-Martin, the waterway that featured in the 2001 film *Le Fabuleux Destin d'Amélie Poulain*. The trip, lasting 2 hours 30 minutes, starts at Port de l'Arsenal, at Bastille, and takes you up to Parc de la Villette. Book ahead.
Daily 9.45, 2.30 (in summer boats also leave from La Villette at 9.45, 2.45)
Mon–Fri adult €15, child (6–12) €8, under 6 free; Sat, Sun €15 to all

VEDETTES DU PONT NEUF
Tel 01 46 33 98 38
www.pontneuf.net
Cruises along the Seine, starting from the Pont Neuf. The trip lasts 1 hour and takes you up to the Eiffel Tower, and back down round the Île de la Cité.
▷ 235
Adult €11, child (4–12) €6, under 4 free

BUS TOURS
LES CARS ROUGES
Tel 01 53 95 39 53
www.carsrouges.com
See the major sights from an open-top, double-decker bus, hopping on and off when you like at any of the nine stops. Commentary is available in French and English. The circuit lasts 2 hours 15 minutes.
Daily 9.30am–early evening every 10–20 min
2-day pass: adult €22, child (4–12) €11, under 4 free

CITYRAMA TOUR
2 rue des Pyramides
Tel 01 44 55 61 00
www.pariscityrama.com
Cityrama offers a 1.5-hour city tour on a double-decker bus, with recorded commentary in 13 languages. Other excursions include Paris by Night, Versailles and Giverny.
Tours: daily 10, 11.30 and 2.30
City tour: adult €18, under 12 free

L'OPEN TOUR
Tel 01 42 66 56 56
www.pariscityrama.com
Hop-on, hop-off open-top double-decker buses run four circuits—the Paris Grand Tour, Montmartre Grands Boulevards, Montparnasse/St-Germain and Bastille/Bercy. There is recorded commentary in French and English.
Apr–end Oct daily every 10–15 min, first bus 9.20am, last round trip 6pm; rest of year daily every 25–30 min, first bus 9.45, last round trip 4pm
One-day pass: adult €26, child (4–11) €13, under 4 free; two-day pass: adult €29, child (4–11) €13, under 4 free

PARIS VISION
214 rue de Rivoli, 75001
Tel 01 42 60 30 01
www.parisvision.com
Paris Vision offer tours by bus and minibus. These range from the 2-hour Paris Express Tour around the city, with recorded commentary, to trips out to Versailles, Giverny and Chartres.
Discovery Tour: daily 9, 12 and 3
Discovery tour: adult €20, child (4–11) free

WALKING TOURS
PARIS À PIED
41 rue des Prairies, 75020
Tel 0879 091365
www.parisapied.fr
Choose from 14 3-hour walking tours (in French) through Paris's varied districts or ask for an itinerary tailored to your wishes (estimate on request).
Adult €20, under 15 €10; reservations required

PARIS WALKS
Tel 01 48 09 21 40
www.paris-walks.com
Take a 2-hour walking tour through the city, with English commentary. Themes range from Hemingway's Paris to the French Revolution.
Call ahead for times and places, or visit the website
Adult €10, child €5

OUT AND ABOUT

Eating and Staying

EATING OUT IN PARIS

Paris is often described as the capital of gastronomy so a meal out has to live up to a big reputation. France claims to have invented haute cuisine, and the standard it sets for its best restaurants— the Michelin rosette—is famed throughout the world as the epitome of gastronomic excellence.

Top chefs such as Alain Senderens and Guy Savoy dictate the food fads of tomorrow. Alain Ducasse even has an out-of-town cooking school where you can learn his fusion-food techniques, while the Cordon Bleu school in central Paris teaches the rules of classic cuisine. If your budget isn't up to the crème-de-la-crème of Paris's restaurants, there are hundreds of less expensive choices, from regional French cuisine to North African, Lebanese or Japanese. Be prepared to take time over your meal—good food is a way of life for many Parisians and meals are something to be enjoyed, rather than rushed.

RESTAURANTS
Restaurants have higher prices than brasseries or bistros but will often provide a refined setting, elegant cuisine and a good wine list. For a special treat, look for multi-starred Michelin chefs such as Alain Ducasse and Guy Savoy. Dress smartly and book in advance. The *menu dégustation*, only found in the finest restaurants, is a prix-fixe menu offering a sample of the finest dishes accompanied by a selection of appropriate wines.

BRASSERIES AND BISTROS
Brasseries are lively but informal restaurants that open long hours. Some have wonderful 19th-century settings. Popular dishes include *steak-frites* and *choucroute* (sauerkraut). Bistros are often small, family-run restaurants serving traditional cuisine, with a limited choice of wines. A new breed of bistros is now springing up, launched by some of Paris's top chefs as satellite venues to their flagship restaurants.

CAFÉS, BARS AND SALONS DE THÉ
Cafés and bars serve coffee, tea (not particularly recommended in Paris), soft drinks, alcohol and snacks. Most open from around 9am (some

earlier) until well into the evening and many have outdoor seating, perfect for people-watching. *Salons de thé* (tea rooms) open from noon until late-evening and some are in grand settings (such as Ladurée, ▷ 271).

CUTTING COSTS
If you are on a budget, have your main meal at lunchtime, when most restaurants serve a *menu du jour,* or daily menu, of two or three courses with a glass of wine for around 50 per cent of the cost in the evening. Most restaurants will offer prix-fixe meals in the evening with three, four or more courses, the best of which is the *menu gastronomique.*

OPENING TIMES
Most restaurants and bistros keep strict serving times. Restaurants open at 12, close at 2.30, then reopen at 7.30. Most Parisians take an hour for lunch and either eat in the staff canteen or in a local bistro. The evening meal is the most important meal of the day and is usually taken *en famille* between 8 and 9pm. Restaurants stop taking orders between 10 and 11pm. If you want to eat later, try a brasserie or some of the venues in Les Halles area. Some restaurants close on weekends and many close during August.

ETIQUETTE
Most restaurants include service in the price of dishes. This is indicated by *service compris* or *s.c.* If the service is exceptional you can leave a tip. Elegant dressing is part of French life and you should dress up to enjoy the experience that is a top-class French restaurant. While few restaurants have a strict dress code, most Parisians dress well when they dine out. Address staff as *Monsieur* and *Mademoiselle.* By law, restaurants and cafés must be no-smoking.

EATING

REGIONAL FRENCH

The advantage of dining in Paris is that you can eat the great regional dishes without leaving town. Below is a quick guide to French regional cuisine. For the names of individual dishes, see the Menu Reader, ▷ 252–253. For restaurants serving regional French cuisine, see Restaurants by Cuisine, ▷ 255.

Petit Chèvre Chaud, made with goats' cheese

The Mediterranean

The sultry climate of Languedoc-Roussillon and Provence encourages wonderful fresh produce. The staples of dishes à la provençale include wild herbs, virgin olive oil and garlic. *Ratatouille*—tomatoes, onions, courgettes (zucchini) and aubergines (eggplants) cooked slowly in garlic and olive oil—epitomizes the cuisine of the region. In days gone by meat was tough (raised on the poor sun-shrivelled grasslands of the upper hills) and cooked slowly in casseroles such as *daubes* or *estouffades* to bring out the taste. The most famous is *cassoulet*, a slow-cooked dish of sausages and duck or goose with haricot beans.

The Pyrenees and the southwest

The cuisine of the southwest offers some of the quintessential French luxury foods—truffles (a fungus), cèpes (a form of mushroom) and foie gras (goose or duck liver). Unlike in the southeast, goose fat is the base of most dishes, the most famed of which is *confit d'oie* (preserved goose cooked in its own fat). Seasonal crops of walnuts and prunes are particularly prized, as is air-dried ham from Bayonne. Some of France's finest wines come from this region, including the *grand crus* of Bordeaux. Cognac produces the most exquisite French brandies.

Brittany and Normandy

Brittany still looks to the sea for its culinary inspiration with excellent oysters, shellfish and fresh fish. The dish lobster à l'Armoricaine was invented in the Côtes-d'Armor. Lambs raised on the salt flats of the coastal plains around the Baie du Mont-St-Michel and the Cotentin Peninsula are said to have a hint of salt in their meat. Normandy's cuisine concentrates on two main products—pork and apples. Every morsel of the pig is used—even the intestines are transformed into delicious andouilles (sausages). Apples don't form the accompaniment to pork but are turned into excellent cider and calvados (apple brandy). Pancakes are the predominant desserts of the region and Normandy produces one of the country's finest cheeses, Camembert.

Camembert cheese, from Normandy

Alsace-Lorraine

Alsace-Lorraine, in the northeast, has bounced between France and Germany for centuries and dishes like *choucroute* (pickled cabbage with sausage, smoked ham and pork) or *cervelas* (sausage) salad are popular, accompanied by wines such as Riesling and Gewürztraminer. Quiche Lorraine was invented here. Munster is a soft fermented cheese from the Vosges mountains, often with added cumin.

Jura and the Alps

Until recently these mountain areas had to be self-sufficient in winter and prepared foods accordingly. They still have an excellent reputation for *charcuterie* (dried and prepared meats) and jams. Gratin and fondues are traditional winter dishes.

Burgundy and the northern Rhône

Praised by the French as the birthplace of cuisine during the Middle Ages, Burgundy matches its top-notch wines with sublime dishes such as *boeuf bourguignon* (beef in red wine), *coq au vin* (male chicken in red wine sauce) and surprisingly delicious *escargots* (snails).

VEGETARIAN

Traditional French dishes are usually meat or fish based, but some restaurants specialize in non-meat dishes (▷ 255).

WORLD

Paris has a vast selection of restaurants serving non-French cuisine, ranging from Italian and Belgian to Japanese, Chinese and Thai. North African dishes are popular and couscous restaurants can be found in every *quartier*. Couscous is wheat grain (coarse semolina) steamed over broth and then heaped in a moist, buttery pile and topped with fresh vegetable stew. This comes with your choice of meat—the best bet is usually *brochettes d'agneau* (lamb kebabs) or *méchoui* (roast lamb). The other mainstay of Moroccan, Algerian and Tunisian cuisine is the *tagine*. Baked in a clay dish, *tagine* is a meat stew (lamb or chicken) with added olives, almonds, prunes and preserved lemons. You can find Chinese restaurants all over the city, especially in Chinatown in the 13th *arrondissement*. For kosher restaurants, try the Jewish quarter in Le Marais.

HAUTE CUISINE

Haute cuisine is top-quality cooking practised by chefs such as Guy Savoy and Alain Ducasse. In recent years it has been influenced by nouvelle cuisine, leading to lighter dishes.

EATING

THE MEDITERRANEAN

...à la languedocienne: with tomatoes, aubergines, cèpes (a type of mushroom) and garlic.

... à la niçoise: with olive oil, garlic, tomatoes, onion and herbs, plus olives, capers, anchovies and tarragon.

... à la provençale: with olive oil, garlic, tomatoes, onion and herbs.

Bouillabaisse: fish stew served with *aïoli* (garlic mayonnaise) or *rouille* (chilli and garlic mayonnaise).

BRITTANY, NORMANDY AND THE LOIRE

Agneau de prés-salés: lamb from animals raised on the salt marshes.

Beurre blanc: butter whipped with white wine vinegar and shallots.

Châteaubriand: a thick cut of tenderloin steak for two people with shallot, herb and white wine sauce.

Coquille St-Jacques: scallop served hot in its shell in a cream sauce topped with melted cheese or toasted breadcrumbs.

Cotriade: fish stew.

Brandade de morue: paste of salt cod mixed with milk, garlic and olive oil.

Cargolade: stew of snails in wine.

Cassoulet: a thick stew of haricot beans and garlic with duck or goose and pork sausage.

Daube: meat stewed in wine.

Foie gras à la toulousaine: goose liver in pastry.

Pistou: sauce comprising ground garlic, basil and cheese bound with olive oil.

Ratatouille: tomatoes, onions, courgettes (zucchini) and aubergines (eggplants) slow-cooked in garlic and olive oil.

Salade niçoise: tomatoes, French beans, anchovies, olives, peppers and boiled eggs.

Soupe de poisson: a soup of puréed mixed fish.

THE PYRENEES AND THE SOUTHWEST

...à la basquaise: meat served with Bayonne ham, cèpes and potatoes.

...à la bordelaise: with red wine sauce accompanied by mixed vegetables.

...à la landaise: dishes cooked in goose fat with garlic.

...à la périgourdine: accompanied by a truffle or foie gras sauce, or stuffed with truffles or foie gras.

Confit de canard: pieces of duck that are salted, cooked and then preserved in their own fat.

Foie gras: the enlarged liver of maize-fed geese or ducks, cooked and served either whole or in slices hot or cold.

Lièvre à la royale: hare boned and stuffed with bacon cooked in wine and served with a truffle sauce.

Magret de canard: boned duck breast, grilled or fried.

Crêpes and galettes: pancakes with either sweet or non-sweet fillings.

Far: a thick, sweet tart with prunes, similar to a flan.

Homard à l'armoricaine: lobster served flambéed in a cream and wine sauce.

Moules marinières: mussels in a white wine, shallot and parsley sauce.

Noisette de porc aux pruneaux: loin of pork with prunes.

Plat (assiette or plateau) de fruits de mer: seafood platter consisting of mixed crayfish (*langouste*), oysters (*huîtres*), prawns/shrimps (*crevettes*), mussels (*moules*), crab (*crabes*) and whelks (*bulots*), served on ice.

Sauce normande: made with cider and cream.

Tarte tatin: upside-down apple tart.

THE NORTH AND ALSACE-LORRAINE

Bäeckeoffe: mixed meat cooked in wine with potatoes and onions.

Carbonnade flamande: beef slow-cooked in beer and spices.

Chou rouge à flamande: red cabbage cooked with apples in vinegar and sugar.

Choucroute garnie: pickled cabbage cooked in wine with pork, sausage and smoked ham, served with boiled potatoes.

Jambon en croûte: ham in a pastry case.

Quiche Lorraine: egg custard tart with bacon, onion and herbs.

Salade de cervelas: cold sausage in vinaigrette sauce.

Waterzooi: a soup originating from Belgium, made of a vegetable and cream stew, with either chicken or freshwater fish.

EATING

BURGUNDY AND THE NORTHERN RHÔNE
Andouille: tripe and pork sausage served cold.
Andouillette: tripe and pork sausage
  served hot, usually grilled.
Boeuf bourguignon: beef slow cooked with
  onions and mushrooms in red wine.
Boudin: black pudding/blood sausage.
Coq au vin: male chicken with mushrooms
  and onions stewed in red wine (traditionally
  Chambertin).
Escargots à la bourguignonne: snails in
  garlic and parsley butter.
Jambon persillé: ham and parsley in jelly
  served cold in slices.

SAUCES
…à la meunière: a method of serving fish,
  fried in butter then served with butter,
  lemon juice and parsley.
Béarnaise: egg-yolk, vinegar, butter, white
  wine, shallots and tarragon.
Béchamel: a classic sauce of flour, butter and
  milk. Often a base of other sauces such as
  Mornay, with cheese.
Chasseur: hunter's style, with wine,
  mushrooms, shallots and herbs.
Demi-glace: brown sauce of stock with sherry
  or Madeira wine.
Diane: cream and pepper sauce.

Pommes à la lyonnaise: fried sliced potatoes
  and onions.
Poulet de Bresse: chicken from Bourg en
  Bresse (considered the best in France).
Poulet (or jau) au sang: chicken in a blood-
  thickened sauce.
Quenelles de brochet: individual fish
  mousses with cream sauce.
Saladier à la lyonnaise: cooked sheep's feet
  and pig's trotters, ox tongue and calf's head
  served with vinaigrette dressing.

JURA AND THE ALPS
Diots: pork sausages.
Fondue: two different types: *au fromage*,
  cubes of bread dipped into molten cheese
  mixed with wine (and sometimes kirsch); or
  bourguignonne: cubes of meat cooked in
  oil, then dipped into sauces.
Gratin dauphinois: sliced potatoes baked in
  milk with nutmeg.
Gratin savoyard: sliced potatoes with cheese
  cooked in stock.

CORSICA
Aziminu: a type of *bouillabaisse* (see
  The Mediterranean).
Brocciu: a sheep's cheese found only on
  Corsica.
Fiadone: cheesecake with lemon.
Fritelles de brocciu: fried doughnuts of
  cheese and chestnut flour.
Oursins: sea urchins, a local delicacy.
Piverunta: lamb stew with bell peppers.
Raffia: a skewer of roasted lamb offal.
Sanglier: wild or semi-wild pig.
Tianu di fave: pork stew with haricot beans.

HOW TO ORDER STEAK
The French taste is for meat to be lightly
cooked. Lamb will automatically come rare
(unless you demand otherwise). If you order
steak, you will be asked how you would like it
cooked. The options are as follows:
Bleu: blue, the rarest steak, served warm on
  the outside but uncooked and cool in
  the middle.
Saignant: bloody, or rare, the steak is cooked
  until it starts to bleed and is warm in
  the middle.
À point: literally 'at the
  point'. The meat is
  cooked until it just
  stops bleeding. Many
  restaurants serve steak *à
  point* with some blood in
  the middle. Those who
  want a warm pink
  middle but no
  visible blood
  could try asking
  for steak *plus à
  point*. It's not an
  official French
  term, but good
  restaurants should
  oblige.
Bien cuit: 'well
  cooked', served
  with only a narrow
  pink middle. If you
  want no pink to
  remain, ask for it
  bien bien cuit,
  although your
  waiter may not
  be able to hide
  his disdain!

Restaurants are listed alphabetically on pages 260–278.

Auteuil
L'Auberge du Mouton Blanc
La Gare
La Grande Cascade
Tsé

Bastille
Le Bar à Soupes
Barrio Latino
Bistrot l'Oulette

L'Envue
Farnesina
Goumard
Ladurée
Maxim's
Toraya

Grands Boulevards
L'Accolade
Brasserie Flo
Le Grand Café
Hard Rock Café
Pomze
La Taverne

Trésor
Vin des Pyrénées

Montmartre
Au Pied du Sacré-Cœur
L'Oriental
Rose Bakery
Le Virage Lepic

Montparnasse
Bistrot d'Hubert
Le Ciel de Paris
La Coupole

Bistrot du Peintre
Blue Elephant
Bofinger
Chez Paul
Les Grandes Marches
Hippopotamus
Le Train Bleu

Belleville/Père Lachaise
La Mère Lachaise

Bercy
Chai Numéro 33

Champs-Élysées
6 New York
L'Alsace
L'Appart
Asian
L'Avenue
Bistro Romain
Les Bouchons de François Clerc
Chiberta
Dragons Élysées
Fermette Marbeuf 1900
Findi
Guy Savoy
Laurent
Market
Pierre Gagnaire
Poona Lounge
Relais Plaza
Spicy Restaurant
Spoon Food and Wine
Taillevent
Toi

Champ du Mars
L'Amaryllis
Le Violon d'Ingres

Concorde
Buddha Bar

Grenelle
L'Ami Jean
Benkay

Les Halles
Ambassade Auvergne
Au Pied de Cochon
Chez Vong
Georges
Joe Allen
Palmiers du Sinaï
Le Pharamond

Île St-Louis
Nos Ancêtres Les Gaulois

Invalides
La Ferme St-Simon
La Fontaine du Mars
Thoumieux

Latin Quarter
Bouillon Racine
Mavrommatis
Le Pré Verre
Le Reminet
La Rôtisserie du Beaujolais
La Tour d'Argent
La Truffière

Louvre/Palais Royal
Café Marly
Grand Colbert
Jean-Paul Hévin
Muscade

Le Marais
404
Le Colimaçon
F&B
Le Pamphlet
Piccolo Teatro

Mouffetard
Marty

Nation
Khun Akorn

République
Chez Jenny
Chez Prune

St-Germain-des-Prés
Alcazar
Au Relais Louis XIII
Barroco
Boulangerie Paul
Café Cassette
Coffee Parisien
Le Comptoir
Jacques Cagna
Le Paradis du Fruit
Le Petit St-Benoît
Le Procope
La Rôtisserie d'en Face
Villa Medici Chez Napoli
Yugaraj
Ze Kitchen Galerie

Ternes
L'Auberge Dab
Le Bistrot d'à Coté
Brasserie La Lorraine
Hiramatsu
Le Stübli
Le Verre Bouteille

Trocadéro
Fakhr El Dine
Tse Yang

Outside the Périphérique
Chez Livio (Neuilly)
La Guinguette de Neuilly (Neuilly)
River Café (Issy-les-Moulineaux)

EATING

RESTAURANTS BY CUISINE

American
Coffee Parisien
Hard Rock Café
Joe Allen

Belgian
Bouillon Racine

Chinese
Tse Yang

French—Bistro
L'Accolade
L'Amaryllis

Goumard
La Grande Cascade
Les Grandes Marches
Guy Savoy
Hiramatsu
Jacques Cagna
Laurent
Maxim's
Muscade
Pierre Gagnaire
Le Procope
Relais Plaza
Taillevent
Toi

Japanese
Benkay

Latin American
Barrio Latino
Barroco

Lebanese
Fakhr El Dine

North African
404
L'Oriental
Palmiers du Sinaï

Au Pied du Sacré-Cœur
Le Bistro d'à Côté
Bistrot d'Hubert
Bistrot l'Oulette
Bistrot du Peintre
Les Bouchons de François Clerc
Café Cassette
Chez Paul
Chez Prune
Le Colimaçon
F&B
La Fontaine du Mars
La Guinguette de Neuilly
La Mère Lachaise
Le Petit St-Benoît
Le Pré Verre
Le Reminet
La Rôtisserie du Beaujolais
Le Verre Bouteille
Le Violon d'Ingres
Le Virage Lepic

French—Brasserie
L'Auberge Dab
Bofinger
Brasserie Flo
Brasserie La Lorraine
Café Marly
La Coupole
Fermette Marbeuf 1900
Le Grand Café
Grand Colbert
Marty
Nos Ancêtres Les Gaulois
La Rôtisserie d'en Face
Le Train Bleu

French—Elegant
Au Relais Louis XIII
Chiberta
Le Ciel de Paris
L'Envue

La Tour d'Argent
La Truffière

French—Regional
L'Alsace
Ambassade Auvergne
L'Ami Jean
L'Appart
Au Pied de Cochon
L'Auberge du Mouton Blanc
Chez Jenny
La Ferme St-Simon
Le Pamphlet
Le Pharamond
La Taverne
Thoumieux
Vin des Pyrénées

Fusion
6 New York
Buddha Bar
Market
Spoon Food and Wine
Ze Kitchen Galerie

Greek
Mavrommatis

Grill/Rotisserie
La Gare
Hippopotamus

Indian
Poona Lounge
Yugaraj

Italian
Bistro Romain
Chez Livio
Farnesina
Findi
Trésor
Villa Medici Chez Napoli

Pan-Asian
Asian
Chez Vong
Dragons Élysées
Spicy Restaurant
Tsé

Tea Rooms
Asian
Boulangerie Paul
Jean-Paul Hévin
Ladurée
Muscade
Le Stübli
Toraya

Thai
Blue Elephant
Khun Akorn

Trendy
Alcazar
L'Appart
L'Avenue
Chai Numéro 33
Le Comptoir
Georges
Man Ray
Market
Pomze
Poona Lounge
Spoon Food and Wine
Tanjia

Vegetarian
Le Bar à Soupes
Le Paradis du Fruit
Piccolo Teatro
Rose Bakery

EATING

Le Verre Bouteille
Guy Savoy
Le Bistrot d'à Côté, Brasserie La Lorraine, Le Stübli
L'Accolade

L'Auberge Dab, Chez Livio, La Guinguette de Neuilly

Taillevent
Chiberta
Pierre Gagnaire
Dragons Élysées

St-Philippe du Roule
ST-HONORÉ

Toi
L'Appart
Spicy Restaurant
L'Alsace
Market
Laurent
Bistro Romain

La Grande Cascade

Asian
Findi
Spoon Food and Wine
L'Avenue
Tse Yang
Fermette Marbeuf 1900
Relais Plaza
Les Bouchons de François Clerc

Fakhr El Dine
Hiramatsu
6 New York

INVALIDES
L'Ami Jean
Thoumieux
La Gare
Esplanade des Invalides
Place des Invalides

Le Violin d'Ingres
La Fontaine du Mars

Parc du Champ de Mars

INVALIDES

Benkay, L'Auberge du Mouton Blanc, River Café, Tsé

L'Amaryllis

Bistro d'Hubert

RESTAURANT LOCATOR

K · L · M

5 · 6 · 7 · 8 · 9

GARE ST-LAZARE

Hard Rock Café

La Taverne
Le Grand Café

L'Envue

Farnesina
Ladurée
Goumard
Maxim's
Toraya
Buddha Bar
Jean-Paul Hévin

Grand Colbert
Muscade
Palmiers du Sinai

Café Marly

Au Pied de Cochon
Joe Allen
Pharamond
Chez Vong

259

Seine

Le Ferme St-Simon

Le Petit St-Benoît

ST-GERMAIN-DES-PRÉS

Barroco
Alcazar

Yugaraj
Ze Kitchen Galerie
Jacques Cagna
Au Relais Louis XIII
Le Paradis du Fruit
La Rôtisserie d'en Face

Boulangerie Paul
Le Procope

Le Comptoir

Coffee Parisien

Café Cassette

Bouillon Racine
Le Pré Verre

258

QUARTIER LATIN

Villa Medici Chez Napoli

Jardin du Luxembourg

Le Ciel de Paris
La Coupole

La Truffière

9

GARE MONTPARNASSE

257

Restaurant Locator

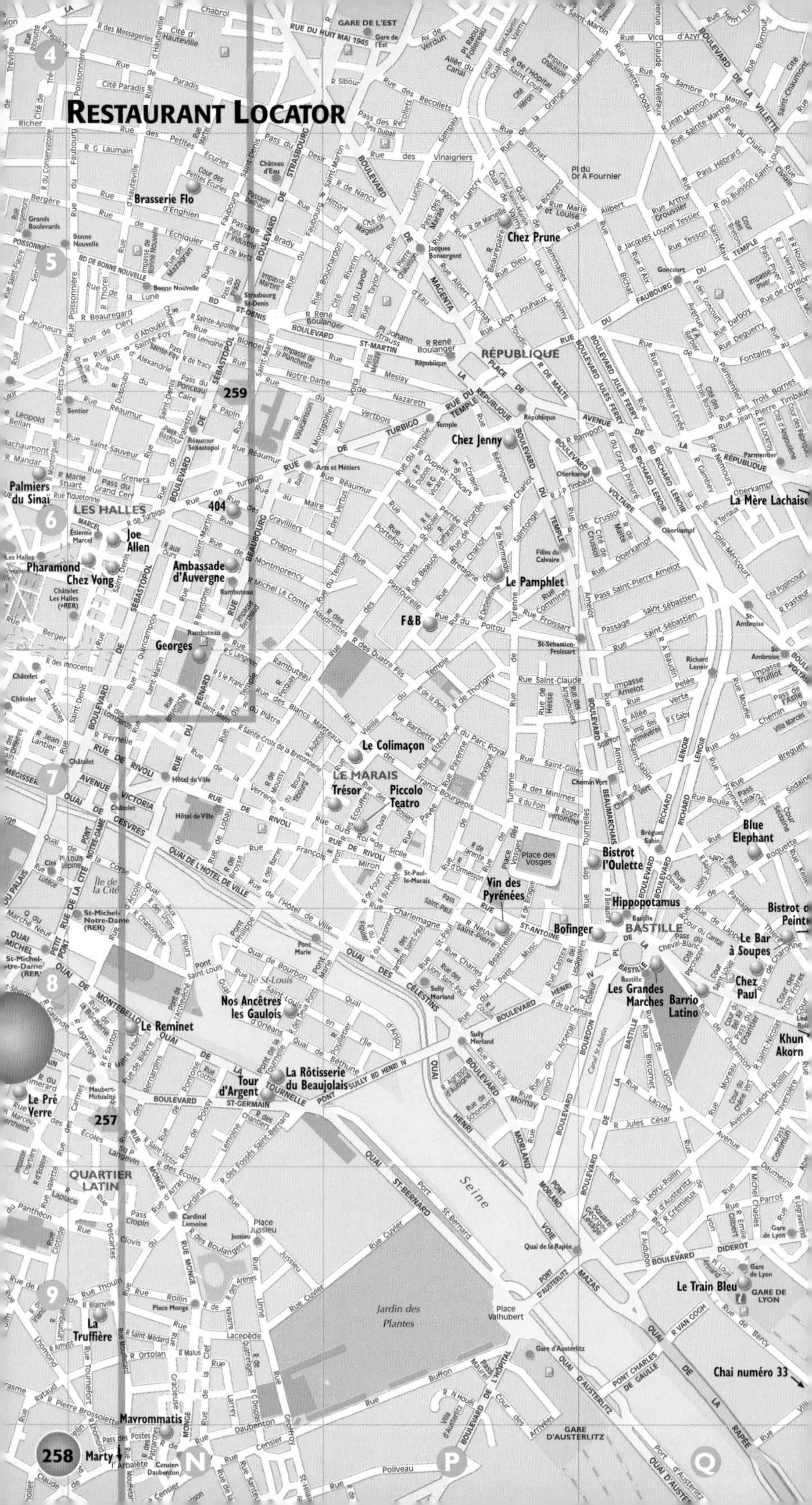

Brasserie Flo

Chez Prune

Palmiers du Sinaï

LES HALLES

404

Joe Allen

Pharamond

Chez Vong

Ambassade d'Auvergne

Georges

Chez Jenny

La Mère Lachaise

Le Pamphlet

F&B

Le Colimaçon

LE MARAIS

Trésor

Piccolo Teatro

Blue Elephant

Bistrot l'Oulette

Vin des Pyrénées

Hippopotamus

Bofinger

BASTILLE

Bistrot du Peintre

Le Bar à Soupes

Les Grandes Marches

Barrio Latino

Chez Paul

Khun Akorn

Nos Ancêtres les Gaulois

Le Reminet

La Rôtisserie du Beaujolais

Tour d'Argent

Le Pré Verre

QUARTIER LATIN

Le Train Bleu

GARE DE LYON

La Truffière

Chai numéro 33

Mavrommatis

Marty

257

Restaurants

The prices given are for a two-course lunch (L) for one person and a three-course dinner (D) for one person, without drinks. The wine price is the starting price for a bottle of wine.

404

Map 258 N6
69 rue des Gravilliers, 75003
Le Marais
Tel 01 42 74 57 81
This fashionable Moroccan restaurant is under the same ownership as Momo, off London's Regent Street. It serves excellent North African cuisine, including *tagines* and couscous, in chic Berber surroundings.
🕐 Daily 12–2.30, 8–12
🍴 L €23, D €40, Wine €20
🚇 Arts et Métiers

6 NEW YORK

Map 256 H6
6 avenue de New York, 75016
Champs-Élysées
Tel 01 40 70 03 30
This restaurant, named after its address, is reminiscent of an elegant Manhattan dining room. The striking contempo-

rary interior, with its sleek lines and light wood, is both stylish and peaceful, with subdued lighting from candle-shaped lamps. On the menu you'll find fusion dishes such as lobster and sun-dried tomato risotto, black and white chocolate millefeuilles, and traditional dishes such as pork and bean casserole. The menu changes every three months.
🕐 Mon–Fri 12.30–2, 7.30–10.30, Sat 7.30–11
🍴 L €35, D €60, Wine €23
🚇 Alma Marceau

L'ACCOLADE

Map 256 off H5
23 rue Guillaume Tell, 75017
Grands Boulevards
Tel 01 42 67 12 67
www.laccolade.com
Once a butcher's shop, this cosy and atmospheric bistro puts meat at the heart of the menu, and combines traditional items such as pigs' ears with modern styles and presentation, though the menu changes according to what's fresh in the market. Chef Sébastien Altazin trained under Michel Rostang, so the culinary skills are strong.
🕐 Tue–Fri 12–2.30, 7.30–10.30; Sat–Sun 7.30–10.30
🍴 L €30, D €40, Wine €18
🚇 Porte de Champerret

ALCAZAR

Map 257 M7
62 rue Mazarine, 75006
St-Germain-des-Prés
Tel 01 53 10 19 99
www.alcazar.fr

English designer Terence Conran's bar-restaurant is popular with a fashionable Parisian crowd. The key to its success? Some of the best fish in the capital, a vast and elegant dining room and impeccable service. The menu also includes sophisticated non-fish dishes such as grilled lamb. Upstairs there's a lounge-bar where international DJs take to the decks. Perfect for a pre-dinner drink, Alcazar is also worth a visit for its excellent Sunday brunch, which comes with the option of a head massage.
🕐 Sun–Thu 12–2.30, 7–1; Fri–Sat 12–2.30, 7–2
🍴 L €25, D €60, Wine €23
🚇 Odéon

L'ALSACE

Map 256 H5
39 avenue des Champs-Élysées, 75008
Champs-Élysées
Tel 01 53 93 97 00
www.restaurantalsace.com
This little piece of eastern France is an integral part of the Parisian landscape and is open round the clock. Brasserie-style cuisine forms the menu, with a choice of seafood platters, sauerkraut, apple strudel and iced *gugelhupf* (cake). The interior is equally regional, with comfortable wall seats, inlaid wood and large mirrors. There is a pleasant terrace for spring and summer days.
🕐 Daily 24 hours
🍴 L €30, D €50, Wine €17
🚇 Franklin D. Roosevelt

L'AMARYLLIS

Map 256 H9
13 boulevard Garibaldi, 75015
Champ du Mars
Tel 01 47 34 05 98
www.bistrotdelamaryllis.com
This 1950s-designed bistro takes you to the heart of French cuisine, concentrating on a limited menu of classic recipes, including *andouillette grillée* and *tartare de saumon*. All main courses cost the same. Every meal starts with a 'panier' of *charcuterie*, *crudité*, salads and seafood. This is good food without breaking the bank.
🕐 Tue, Wed, Sat 7.30–10pm; Thu–Fri 12–2, 7.30–10
🍴 L €16, D €21, Wine €20
🚇 Cambronne

AMBASSADE D'AUVERGNE

Map 258 N6
22 rue du Grenier St-Lazare, 75003
Les Halles
Tel 01 42 72 31 22
www.ambassade-auvergne.com
Ambassade d'Auvergne brings the finest regional cooking from the heart of the Auvergne, with ingredients such as foie-gras, mushrooms and lentils complementing meats including duck, guinea fowl and veal. Diners are seated in one of several cosy rooms so the atmosphere is intimate. The decor combines formal table settings with a

EATING

touch of mountain lodge on the walls. This is an excellent choice if you want to steer clear of the modern bistro-style eateries and try very hearty French dishes.

🕐 Daily noon–2, 7.30–last food orders at 10

🍽 L €28, D €35, Wine €16

Ⓜ Rambuteau

L'AMI JEAN

Map 256 H7
27 rue Malar, 75007
Grenelle
Tel 01 47 05 86 89

The well-established reputation of this bistro-style regional restaurant was enhanced by the arrival of Stéphane Jugo. The new chef's regularly renewed menu includes delicious classical French dishes as well as Basque specialities such as Axoa: thin slices of veal in a spicy tomato, onion and pimento sauce. The fixed-price menu is available for lunch and dinner.

🕐 Tue–Sat 12–2, 7–12

🍽 L €28, D €45 (à la carte), Wine €16

Ⓜ La Tour Maubourg

L'APPART

Map 256 H5
9–11 rue du Colisée, 75008
Champs-Élysées
Tel 01 53 75 42 00
www.appart.com

The unusual dining room in this two-floor house is like a comfortable library, lined with bookshelves and with beautiful Persian rugs covering the wooden floors. Expect inventive cuisine with a Mediterranean accent, such as pan-roasted veal in a creamy mustard and mushroom sauce. Before Sunday brunch, there's a children's brunch with a pastry workshop, the results of which you can take home.

🕐 Daily 12–2.30, 7–11.30, Sun brunch 12–3

🍽 L €30, D €50, Wine €20

Ⓜ Franklin D. Roosevelt

ASIAN

Map 256 H5
30 avenue George V, 75008
Champs-Élysées
Tel 01 56 89 11 00
www.asian.fr

This is a tea room by day and a bar-restaurant at lunch and dinner. The delightful interior uses pale wood columns,

Chinese wall lamps and a forest of bamboo. The oriental cuisine includes dishes such as the Dragons' Duel (finely cut

and marinated raw salmon and tuna with lemon) or *Chao Chao* (pork spare ribs marinated for three days and glazed with honey).

🕐 Tea room: daily 12–6. Restaurant: Sun–Fri 12–3, 7.30–1, Sat 7.30–1

🍽 L €40, D €75, Wine €25

Ⓜ George V

L'AUBERGE DAB

Map 256 off F4
161 avenue Malakoff, 75016
Ternes/Porte Maillot
Tel 01 45 00 32 22

This stylish brasserie is popular with the business crowd from the nearby Palais des Congrès, where trade shows are held. The menu focuses on traditional dishes, using seafood, fish and grilled meat. Wooden booths are perfect for those who want some privacy, and there's a lovely terrace for dining al fresco in spring and summer.

🕐 Daily noon–3, 9–2

🍽 L €40, D €55, Wine €17

Ⓜ Porte Maillot

L'AUBERGE DU MOUTON BLANC

Map 256 off F9
40 rue d'Auteuil, 75016
Auteuil
Tel 01 42 88 02 21

Molière, Jean Racine and Jean de La Fontaine were some of the famous writers who came here for discussions over a glass of wine. More than three centuries later, the place still has plenty of charm. Inside there are wooden panels, exposed bricks and elegantly laid tables. The menu is traditional, regional cuisine, including leg of lamb, calf's head and steak tartare.

🕐 Daily 12–3, 7–11

🍽 L €30, D €30, Wine €14

Ⓜ Michel-Ange Auteuil

AU PIED DE COCHON

Map 257 M6
6 rue Coquillère, 75001
Les Halles
Tel 04 40 13 77 00
www.pieddecochon.com

This Parisian institution is a blessing for hungry night owls. It has been open around the clock, every day of the week, since 1946. Take your place in the elegant dining room, feast your eyes on the fresco-covered walls and the

beautiful lighting, then your palate with one of France's regional special dishes. Vegetarians will want to avoid the pig's trotters, the house signature dish. Seafood is plentiful and the French onion soup a must.

🕐 Daily 24 hours

🍽 L €25, D €50, Wine €17

Ⓜ Les Halles

AU PIED DU SACRÉ-CŒUR

Map 259 L2
Square Caulaincourt, 75018
Montmartre
Tel 01 46 06 15 26
www.aupieddusacrecoeur.free.fr

As the name states, this restaurant is at the foot of Sacré-Cœur. Warm tones enhanced by indirect lighting and wooden furniture define the stylish, inviting interior. In fair weather you can eat out on the terrace. The cuisine ranges from traditional dishes such as pan-fried foie gras or grilled steak in pepper sauce to more innovative creations such as poultry stuffed with

EATING

prawns. The finest French ingredients are always used.

🕐 Tue–Sun 12–2.30, 7–12, Mon 7–12
🍴 L €20, D €35, Wine €15
🚇 Lamarck-Caulaincourt

AU RELAIS LOUIS XIII
Map 257 M7
8 rue des Grands-Augustins, 75006
St-Germain-des-Prés
Tel 01 43 26 75 96
www.relaislouis13.com

Manuel Martinez—previously chef at La Tour d'Argent (▷ 276)—set up his own restaurant in this 16th-century town house in 1996. There are exposed bricks in the vaulted cellar and beamed ceilings in the main dining room and in the upstairs salon. The rich menu includes lobster, foie gras, cep ravioli and vanilla and whisky millefeuilles.

🕐 Tue–Sat 12–2.30, 7.30–10.30
🍴 L €70, D €90, Wine €45
🚇 Odéon

L'AVENUE
Map 256 H6
41 avenue Montaigne, 75008
Champs-Élysées
Tel 01 40 70 14 91
www.avenue-restaurant.com

This restaurant is the haunt of film stars and models, and the cantina for designers from the nearby couture house, Dior. It is one of the hippest places in town and its stylish interior is both contemporary and elegant, with burgundy velvet armchairs and wall seats and handsome white candelabra. Although people-

watching is the main activity here, the food is also worth your attention. Seafood fans should enjoy the crab mille-feuille and tuna steak with balsamic vinegar sauce. The chocolate cake is delectable.

🕐 Daily 8am–2am
🍴 L €50, D €65, Wine €26
🚇 Alma-Marceau

LE BAR À SOUPES
Map 258 Q8
33 rue de Charonne, 75011
Bastille
Tel 01 43 57 53 79
www.lebarasoupes.com

At this brightly painted venue in the trendy Bastille district, you can choose from six varieties of fresh soup each day, with options including creamed tomato and red pepper, pumpkin and bacon,

chick peas Eastern style, and coconut milk and carrot. Inside it's like a simple but charming cantina, with plain tables and chairs and large paintings of vegetables.

🕐 Mon–Sat 12–3, 6.30–11
🍴 Bowl of soup €7
🚇 Bastille, Ledru Rollin

BARRIO LATINO
Map 258 Q8
46 rue du Faubourg St-Antoine, 75012
Bastille
Tel 01 55 78 84 75

A hit with the fashionable crowd, this bar-restaurant would like to take you to Cuba, or rather, to a funky, kitsch version of the real thing. Look out for the Che Guevara mosaic on the fourth floor. Try a Tequila Special or a Mojito at one of the cocktail bars, then sample some Mexican-style food, including guacamole, chicken *quesadillas* (folded tortillas filled with meat or vegetables) and more.

🕐 Daily 11am–2am
🍴 L €19, D €40, Wine €17
🚇 Bastille

BARROCO
Map 257 M7
23 rue Mazarine, 75006
St-Germain-des-Prés
Tel 01 43 26 40 24

This is chic Brasilia, in perfect harmony with its stylish district, and in contrast to some other Parisian venues with a South American theme, where kitsch and fun are de rigueur. The welcoming interior has comfortable striped velvet armchairs, wooden tables, elegant tableware and a library. The cuisine is equally good, combining Brazilian zest with French delicacy. The menu includes fish and seafood cooked in coconut milk, and lamb ribs and sweet potatoes. There is live South American music on Tuesdays and Fridays.

🕐 Daily 7.30pm–2am
🍴 D €50, Wine €21
🚇 Odéon

BENKAY
Map 256 off F9
61 quai de Grenelle, 75015
Grenelle
Tel 01 40 58 21 26

You can enjoy good *teppan-yaki* and panoramic views from this modern Japanese restaurant, on the fourth floor of the Novotel Paris Tour Eiffel. The set lunch menus are reasonably priced.

🕐 Daily 12–2, 7–10
🍴 L €35, D €60, Wine €21
🚇 Bir Hakeim

BISTRO D'HUBERT
Map 256 J9
41 boulevard Pasteur, 75015
Montparnasse
Tel 01 47 34 15 50
www.bistrodhubert.com

An excellent example of a 21st-century French bistro, the Hubert has two dining areas. The first, a Provençal-style, informal room decorated with

EATING

painted wooden dressers and pretty cotton table cloths; the second a more formal and contemporary area. The open kitchen shows the confidence of the staff, while the menu offers modern French cuisine touched by the latest food fashions.

⏱ Tue–Fri 12–2.30, 7–9.30, Sat, Mon 7–9.30. Closed Sun
🍽 L €35, D €50, Wine €20
Ⓜ Pasteur

BISTRO ROMAIN
Map 256 J5
26 avenue des Champs-Élysées, 75008
Champs-Élysées
Tel 01 53 75 17 84
www.bistroromain.fr
Drapes, classical-style paintings

and subdued lighting set the baroque tone here, which is reminiscent of an Italian opera house. The menu is not quite so refined, not venturing far from bowls of pasta, but those with big appetites will be delighted to learn that the carpaccio and chocolate mousse come on an all-you-can-eat basis. There are 18 Bistro Romains in the city.

⏱ Daily 11.30am–1am
🍽 L €25, D €35, Wine €15
Ⓜ Franklin D. Roosevelt

LE BISTROT D'À CÔTÉ
Map 256 off G4
10 rue Gustave Flaubert, 75017
Ternes
Tel 01 42 67 05 81
www.michelrostang.com
This is part of a small chain of bistros created by chef Michel Rostang, offering high-quality regional cooking. A large blackboard in the dining room displays the specials, which vary according to what's available in the market. Hearty dishes include pig's trotters or chicken with mashed potatoes. The interior is typical bistro-style and there is an interesting collection of curios.

⏱ Daily 12–3, 7–12
🍽 L €30, D €45, Wine €15
Ⓜ Courcelles

BISTROT L'OULETTE
Map 258 Q7
38 rue des Tournelles
Bastille
Tel: 01 42 71 43 33
A truly honest, no-frills but typically Parisian bistrot, serving good French dishes like Burgundian snails, *confit* and fresh apple tart, all made with the ingredients of south-west France. Owned by Marcel Baudis and his wife, Marie-Noëlle, who also run the upmarket l'Oulette in the 12th *arrondissement*, it has touches of the more expensive restaurant. It's popular with locals looking for good value, and those on a more limited budget won't be disappointed.

⏱ Mon–Fri 12–2.15, 7–midnight; Sat 7–midnight
🍽 L €30, D €40, Wine €13
Ⓜ Bastille

BISTROT DU PEINTRE
Map 258 off Q8
116 avenue Ledru-Rollin, 75011
Bastille
Tel 01 47 00 34 39
This beautiful art nouveau bistro, established in 1903, has wood panels, soft lighting and large mirrors. Not surprisingly, the 'painter's bistro' displays numerous paintings, including a beautiful oil of La Goulue, the celebrated cancan dancer. You can eat in the welcoming bar, which has a couple of tables in the first room, in the other dining room upstairs or on the small terrace in spring and summer. The high-quality traditional French cuisine includes chicory, diced bacon and poached egg salad, duck à l'orange and steak tartare.

⏱ Daily 12–12
🍽 L €25, D €40, Wine €11
Ⓜ Ledru Rollin

BLUE ELEPHANT
Map 258 Q7
43 rue de la Roquette, 75011
Bastille
Tel 01 47 00 42 00
www.blueelephant.com
This venue, in the fashionable Bastille district, is part of a small international chain of Blue Elephant restaurants.

Here, the beautifully laid wooden tables are set in the middle of a small jungle, surrounded by luxurious plants and cascading water. The menu offers the very best of Thai cuisine, prepared by a team of more than a dozen chefs. Typical dishes include chicken soufflé in banana leaves and *chiang rai* (minced pork with green peppers).

⏱ Mon–Fri 12–2.30, 7–12, Sat 7–12, Sun 12–2.30, 7–11
🍽 L €35, D €55, Wine €21
Ⓜ Bastille

BOFINGER
Map 258 Q8
5–7 rue de la Bastille, 75004
Bastille
Tel 01 42 72 87 82
www.flobrasseries.com
This elegant brasserie, which claims to be the oldest in Paris, has a lavish art nouveau interior with an impressive stained-glass ceiling, mirrors,

plenty of carved wood and lots of plants. The beautifully prepared French classic dishes include lobster, oysters, duck, steak tartare and *choucroute* (sauerkraut).

⏱ Mon–Fri 12–3, 6.30–1, Sat–Sun noon–1am
🍽 L €25, D €40, Wine €22
Ⓜ Bastille

LES BOUCHONS DE FRANÇOIS CLERC
Map 256 H6
7 rue Boccador, 75008
Latin Quarter
Tel 01 47 23 57 80
www.bouchonsdefrancoisclerc.com
Masterminded by chef François Clerc, this small chain of restaurants (there are three in Paris) boasts France's least expensive fine wine list, and probably also one of the most comprehensive, with about 400 vintages. Fine French cuisine is also on the menu: beef carpaccio, foie

EATING

gras, veal kidneys with garlic and parsley, and crème brûlée. Each branch of the chain has its own character.

🕐 Mon–Fri 12–2.30, 7–10.30, Sat 7–10.30
🍽 L €40, D €60, Wine €15
🚇 Alma-Marceau

BOUILLON RACINE
Map 257 M8
3 rue Racine, 75006
Latin Quarter
Tel 01 44 32 15 60
www.bouillon-racine.com
The bright and airy dining room is in a listed historic building, with a dazzling art

nouveau interior. There are wrought-iron chairs and candelabra, emerald green wall tiles and plenty of mirrors. The excellent Belgian food includes *waterzooi* (traditional Belgian soup) and shrimp croquettes. As you would expect in a Belgian restaurant, there is a comprehensive range of beers.
🕐 Daily noon–midnight (last orders 11)
🍽 L €25, D €35, Wine €25
🚇 Cluny La Sorbonne, Odéon

BOULANGERIE PAUL
Map 257 L8
77 rue de Seine, 75006
St-Germain-des-Prés
Tel 01 55 42 02 23
www.paul.fr
This bakery, on the same street as a lively fruit and vegetable market, sells a range of breads, including multi-grains, onion and even bacon bread. The pastries are just as appetizing and you can eat or have a tea, coffee or hot chocolate sitting on leather chairs at rustic wooden tables, enjoying the smell of freshly baked bread.
🕐 Daily 7.30am–8pm
🍽 Tea €4, slice of cake €5
🚇 Odéon, Mabillon

BRASSERIE FLO
Map 258 N5
7 cour des Petites Écuries, 75010
Grands Boulevards
Tel 01 47 70 13 59
www.flobrasseries.com
Brasserie Flo is a Parisian institution, established in 1886. It is housed in a listed building with a wonderful turn-of-the-century interior, with stained-glass panels, green leather booths and wooden panels on the ceiling. The actress Sarah Bernhardt was a regular here when she performed at the nearby Théâtre de la Renaissance. The menu includes steak, fresh seafood and Alsatian special dishes such as sauerkraut. For dessert, try the profiteroles or *vacherin* (ice cream and meringue).
🕐 Daily 12–3, 7–1.30
🍽 L €28, D €42, Wine €25
🚇 Château-d'Eau

BRASSERIE LA LORRAINE
Map 256 off G4
2 place des Ternes, 75008
Ternes
Tel 01 56 21 22 00
www.brasserielalorraine.com
This brasserie, a short distance from the Arc de Triomphe, explores regional French cuisine, with the menu including *choucroute* (sauerkraut) and Burgundy snails. The restaurant has been around for 70 years and its main attraction is seafood, with sea urchin and oysters on the menu.

There's even a take-out service at the seafood bar. The elegant dining room is bright and has a retro feel, with red padded seats and 1950s-style lighting fixtures. There are also plenty of tables outside for spring and summer dining.
🕐 Daily 7am–1am
🍽 L €40, D €65, Wine €17
🚇 Ternes

BUDDHA BAR
Map 257 K6
8 rue Boissy d'Anglas, 75008
Concorde
Tel 01 53 05 90 00
www.buddha-bar.com
Buddha Bar is just off the place de la Concorde. It is popular with the business and

fashion crowd and the strict door policy reflects this. Once inside, expect the exotic and the kitsch, but be aware that this is not a place for meditation. There is a bar upstairs and a restaurant downstairs, run by a Japanese-Californian chef who creates high-quality imaginative fusion food. The menu changes every four months and includes Peking-style duck, seared tuna in a sesame crust, and desserts such as chocolate cake and lemon pie.
🕐 Mon–Fri 12–3, 7–2, Sat–Sun 7–2
🍽 L €45, D €65, Wine €17
🚇 Concorde

CAFÉ CASSETTE
Map 257 L8
73 rue de Rennes, 75006
St-Germain-des-Prés
Tel 01 45 48 53 78
www.cafecassette.com
This modern venue is not far from the place St-Sulpice and is good for a meal in all weathers. It has a large terrace with bistro tables and chairs, a veranda with conical orange lighting fixtures, a bar and a comfortable salon. There are three menus: one for the

EATING

restaurant, with salmon tartare and grilled steak; one for the café, with lighter dishes such as salads and club sandwiches; and one for those who just want a drink or desserts.

🕐 Daily 7am–1am
🍴 L €23, D €30, Wine €15
🚇 St-Sulpice, Rennes

CAFÉ MARLY
Map 257 L6
93 rue de Rivoli, 75001
Louvre/Palais Royal
Tel 01 49 26 06 60

There are wonderful views of the Louvre pyramid from this elegant brasserie, whose interior covers contemporary

minimalism and Napoleon III style. There are sleek armchairs whose backs are adorned with gold rings and gilt-edged black wood panels. The menu has typical brasserie food with the occasional more modern offering such as rare tuna in a sesame crust or steak tartare.

🕐 Daily 7am–2am
🍴 L €40, D €55, Wine €22
🚇 Palais-Royal/Musée du Louvre

CHAI NUMÉRO 33
Map 258 off Q9
33 cour St-Emilion, 75012
Bercy
Tel 01 53 44 01 01
www.chai33.com

This former wine and spirit storehouse is in the middle of Bercy, a district once home to Paris's warehouses. It has been refurbished in contemporary style, with soft brown armchairs and water lily-shaped wooden

tables. Some original features have been retained, such as the exposed brick walls and the wine cellar. You'll be invited by the wine waiter to visit the cellar to choose the best accompaniment to your meal. The menu includes steamed fish served with potatoes, and steak tartare.

🕐 Daily 11.45–3, 7–12
🍴 L €20, D €35, Wine €15
🚇 Cour St-Emilion

CHEZ JENNY
Map 258 P6
39 boulevard du Temple, 75003
République
Tel 01 44 54 39 00
www.chez-jenny.com

Chez Jenny is named after

the Alsatian Robert Jenny, who established the restaurant in 1930, not far from place de la République. Several types of sauerkraut are on offer—including one with champagne—and you can also choose seafood and special dishes such as saveloy sausage salad. Desserts include iced *gugelhupf* (cake) with egg custard.

The decoration also pays tribute to the northeastern region of France, with frescos depicting its landscapes and marquetry by regional artist Charles Spindler.

🕐 Daily noon–midnight (until 1am Fri–Sat)
🍴 L €30, D €45, Wine €18
🚇 République

CHEZ LIVIO
Map 256 off F4
6 rue de Longchamp, 92200
Neuilly-sur-Seine
Neuilly
01 46 24 81 32

This little piece of Italy reflects the warmth and conviviality of its nation. The tables are on a terrace which is uncovered as soon as weather permits. It is a beautiful setting, with green, trellis-covered walls, black-and-white floor tiling, red woven osier chairs and matching tablecloths.

The traditional Italian cuisine includes mushroom risotto, fresh pasta and breaded veal escalope. Chez Livio is definitely one of the liveliest venues in this chic, residential district.

🕐 Daily 12–2.30, 7–10.45
🍴 L €20, D €35, Wine €14
🚇 Pont-de-Neuilly

CHEZ PAUL
Map 258 Q8
13 rue de Charonne, 75011
Bastille
Tel 01 47 00 34 57

This charming little bistro, not to be confused with the restaurant of the same name on rue de la Butte-aux-Cailles, was formerly an artisans' haunt, at the time when the Bastille area was famous for its furniture industry. It still looks authentic, although the clientele today is far more fashion-conscious. The menu includes good, French staples such as *gratin dauphinois* (sliced potatoes baked with cream) and grilled steak.

🕐 Daily noon–1am
🍴 L €20, D €35, Wine €15
🚇 Bastille

EATING

CHEZ PRUNE

Map 258 P5
36 rue Beaurepaire, 75010
République
Tel 01 42 41 30 47

The terrace at this bistro gives lovely views of the Canal St-Martin. The interior reflects the owner's enthusiasm for salvaging items from second-hand shops. The bistro is perfect for a drink or a light bite (try a cheese and cold meat platter) or for brunch, a feast of croissant, scrambled eggs, ham, salmon, orange juice and tea or coffee.

🕐 Daily 8am–2am
🍴 Cold meat or cheese plate €8, brunch €15
🚇 Jacques Bonsergent, République

CHEZ VONG

Map 259 N6
10 rue de la Grande Truanderie, 75001
Les Halles
Tel 01 40 26 09 36

This exotic, elegant Chinese restaurant is on a pedestrian-only street in the bustling Les Halles district. Inside there are lanterns and candles, dark wood, exposed brick walls and a profusion of tropical plants. Chef-proprietor Vai-Kuan Vong has created a

menu that includes both Cantonese and Vietnamese cuisine. The lobster with ginger and the pigeon are surprisingly good.

🕐 Mon–Sat 12–2.30, 7–11
🍴 L €30, D €55, Wine €23
🚇 Etienne-Marcel

CHIBERTA

Map 256 G5
3 rue Arsène Houssaye, 75008
Champs-Élysées
Tel 01 53 53 42 00
www.lechiberta.com

Chef Eric Coisel's cuisine follows the seasons, but you can expect the same high quality (and prices) all year round. Indulgent dishes include black truffle cooked in champagne and served on toast with a Madeira butter. The discreetly elegant interior has tawny hues, neatly dressed tables and abstract paintings on the walls.

🕐 Mon–Fri 12–2.30, 7–10.30, Sat 7–10.30
🍴 L €60, D €100, Wine €15
🚇 Charles de Gaulle–Étoile

LE CIEL DE PARIS

Map 257 K9
Tour Montparnasse, 33 avenue du Maine, 75015
Montparnasse
Tel 01 40 64 77 64
www.cieldeparis.com

This restaurant, on the 56th floor of the Tour Montparnasse, claims to be the highest restaurant in Europe and gives stunning views over the city. The sleek, contemporary dining room has dark tones and Tulip Knoll armchairs, and chef Jean-François Oyon's creations are rich and impressive. The menu changes with the season and examples include pan-sautéed fillet of beef with a truffle sauce, lobster risotto, crab with poached quails eggs, and fried scallops with a parsley purée.

🕐 Daily 12–2.30, 7–10.45
🍴 L €55, D €70, Wine €26
🚇 Montparnasse Bienvenüe

LA COUPOLE

Map 257 L9
102 boulevard du Montparnasse, 75014
Montparnasse
Tel 01 43 20 14 20

Dine in this Parisian institution, established in 1927, and you'll be following in the footsteps of Pablo Picasso, Ernest Hemingway and Man Ray. The elegant art deco brasserie is a symbol of Montparnasse's artistic heyday. The bright and airy dining room has fresco-adorned pillars, an imposing sculpture and Cubist floor tiles. You'll find all the brasserie classics on the menu, including seafood platters, sauerkraut and steak tartare, not forgetting the famous curried lamb.

🕐 Daily 8.30am–1am (Sat until 1.30)
🍴 L €25, D €40, Wine €20
🚇 Vavin

COFFEE PARISIEN

Map 257 L8
4 rue Princesse, 75006
St-Germain-des-Prés
Tel 01 43 54 18 18

As the name suggests, this is a hybrid of a place—a Parisian bistro serving American diner-style food. It's at the heart of St-Germain-des-Prés, in a picturesque pedestrian-only street. Inside you'll find square wooden tables and wall seats, and the occasional picture of John F. Kennedy. It's an excellent place for a lazy

Sunday brunch, with American classics such as eggs Benedict, chicken wings and one of the best cheeseburgers in Paris on the menu.

🕐 Daily 12–12
🍴 L €18, D €22, coffee €3
🚇 Mabillon, St-Germain-des-Prés

EATING

LE COLIMAÇON

Map 258 P7
44 rue Vieille du Temple, 75004
Le Marais
Tel 01 48 87 12 01

A small, old-style bistro run by a young and dynamic team. The menu concentrates on the archetypal staples, including *escargots*. It's no-frills, tasty food and it won't break the bank.

🕐 Daily 7pm–last order midnight
🍴 D €27.50, Wine €18
🚇 Rambuteau

LE COMPTOIR

Map 257 M8
Hôtel Relais St-Germain, 9 carrefour de l'Odéon, 75006
St-Germain-des-Prés
Tel 01 44 22 07 97
www.comptoirparis.com

Yves Cameborde is one of the city's most celebrated restaurateurs, and Le Comptoir, in the heart of the Left Bank, is one of a growing trend of gastro-bistros, championing simple food cooked well. This is modern French cuisine from one of the masters. There are no reservations for lunch (but try arriving after Parisians have finished eating, at around 2.30–3pm). You'll need to book well ahead to get a table for the gastronomic dinner.

🕐 Daily noon–midnight; bistro service noon–3
🍴 L €15, D €35, Wine €20
🚇 Odéon

DRAGONS ÉLYSÉES

Map 256 H5
11 rue de Berri, 75008
Champs-Élysées
Tel 01 42 89 85 10

The high standard of service and smart address, close to the Champs-Élysées, make this restaurant perfect for a business or more formal lunch. The menu includes Chinese and Thai dishes such as stuffed crab, spring rolls and Peking-

style pork. The unique selling point is the gigantic, underfoot aquarium, with more than 1,000 fish.

🕐 Daily 12–2.30, 7–11pm
🍴 L €25, D €40, Wine €14
🚇 George V

L'ENVUE

Map 257 K5
39 rue Boissy d'Anglas, 75008
Concorde
Tel 01 42 65 10 49

This restaurant, just off the Champs-Élysées, has an interior of grey tones peppered with splashes of pink and blue. The matching tableware, enhanced by fresh flowers, was designed by co-owner

Valérie Balard. Chef Gregory Shibeny's innovative French cuisine includes pear and strawberry duck, and chicken with coriander semolina.

🕐 Mon–Sat 8am–2am
🍴 L €35, D €50, Wine €15
🚇 Concorde, Madeleine

FAKHR EL DINE

Map 256 G6
30 rue de Longchamp, 75016
Trocadéro
Tel 01 47 27 90 00
www.fakhreldine.com

This restaurant has been popular with both Parisian and Lebanese diners for more than 25 years. The menu includes *warak enab* (stuffed vine leaves with rice and parsley) and *kharouf mehchi* (stuffed lamb with rice). Try the traditional *meze*, a selection of up to 20 hot and cold hors

d'oeuvres. The extra-sweet desserts are just as tempting, and the *baklava* (filo pastry with pistachio nuts and honey) is a must.

🕐 Daily 12–3, 7.30–11.30
🍴 L €25, D €32, Wine €15
🚇 Trocadéro

FARNESINA

Map 257 K5
9 rue Boissy d'Anglas, 75008
Concorde
Tel 01 42 66 65 57

Farnesina, in the pedestrian-only section of the rue Boissy d'Anglas, is close to

the luxury Hôtel Crillon. Inside, there are pale wooden tables and designer beige armchairs. A collection of teapots gives the place a welcoming feel. The menu is classic Italian, with dishes such as ravioli and beef *carpaccio* with rocket (arugula) and parmesan. Save room for the superb tiramisu.

🕐 Mon–Fri 12.30–3, 7.30–11.30, Sat 7.30–11.30
🍴 L €45, D €60, Wine €20
🚇 Concorde

F & B

Map 258 P6
14 rue Charlot, 75003
Le Marais
Tel 01 42 78 02 31
www.foodandbeverage.fr

This bar/restaurant is a great find. Three classically trained chefs, lately of Trianon Palace, Train Bleu and Bon, have blended their skills to produce an exciting modern menu with the lunch version representing excellent value. The decor is chic and contemporary, with burnt orange seats blending with dark wood furniture.

🕐 Mon–Fri noon–2.30, 7–11, Sat 7–11
🍴 L €18, D €32, Wine €17
🚇 Temple

LA FERME ST-SIMON

Map 257 K7
6 rue de St-Simon, 75007
Invalides
Tel 01 45 48 35 74
www.fermestsimon.com
Decorated like an elegant country house, with exposed beams, candelabra and flowery curtains, this 'farm' is in reality surrounded by embassies and government ministries. Chef Francis Vendehende's cuisine is refined-rustic, with dishes such as smoked salmon and calf's kidney pasta with foie gras, and roasted sea bass with wild mushrooms and polenta. The menu changes weekly and there's an excellent wine list.

🕐 Mon–Fri 12–4, 7.30–10, Sat 7.30–10
🍴 L €35, D €50, Wine €18
🚇 Rue-du-Bac

FERMETTE MARBEUF 1900

Map 256 H6
5 rue Marbeuf, 75008
Champs-Élysées
Tel 01 53 23 08 00
www.fermettemarbeuf.com

There is a profusion of stained glass, decorative wall tiles and beautiful lighting inside this restaurant. In such a splendid setting you could almost forget about the food, but chef Gilbert Isaac's wonderful creations ensure you don't. These include grilled seabass fillet with artichoke, braised veal sweetbreads, cold tomato soup with avocado mousse, sole fillets with basil and fresh pasta, and Grand Marnier soufflé.

🕐 Daily 12–3, 7–11.30
🍴 L €35, D €45, Wine €15
🚇 Alma-Marceau

FINDI

Map 256 H5
24 avenue George V, 75008
Champs-Élysées
Tel 01 47 20 14 78
www.findi.net

GEORGES

Map 258 N7
Centre Georges Pompidou,
Place Georges-Pompidou, 75004
Les Halles
Tel 01 44 78 47 99
www.centrepompidou.fr
You are on the top floor of the Centre Georges Pompidou, with a stunning view over Paris. The dining room could be a work of modern art itself, with its sleek lines and shells of metal and bright rubber. Nouvelle cuisine is served, including mushroom cappuccino (a light and foamy soup) and crab millefeuille (in puff pastry). Save room for dessert, as the melt-in-the-mouth chocolate cake is one of the restaurant's signature dishes.

🕐 Wed–Mon noon–2am
🍴 L €45, D €55, Wine €20
🚇 Rambuteau

Among the elegant clientele, you may recognize some celebrities staying at the nearby Four Seasons George V hotel. Rich red carpets, plush armchairs, subdued lighting and a library create an intimate atmosphere, although the interior is surprisingly modern. The food is Italian, with dishes

such as lasagne with truffle butter and vegetables, tagliatelle with prawns, and veal escalopes stuffed with scamorza cheese, sage and polenta. There is also a delicatessen selling salami, wine and cheese.

🕐 Daily 12–3, 7–12
🍴 L €30, D €45, Wine €25
🚇 George V

LA FONTAINE DU MARS

Map 256 H7
127 rue St-Dominique, 75007
Invalides
Tel 01 47 05 46 44
Excellent Parisian bistro with a host of local fans, and you'll love the country decor. The limited menu changes with the seasons, but favours regional classics from the southwest of france such as *escargots*, *cassoulet* and *boudin noir*.

🕐 Tue–Sun 12–2.30, 7.30–11. Closed late Jul–late Aug
🍴 L €30, D €50, Wine €18
🚇 École Militaire

LA GARE

Map 256 off F7
19 chaussée de la Muette, 75016
Auteuil
Tel 01 42 15 15 31
www.restaurantlagare.com
La Gare is popular with residents of this chic district and, as its name suggests, occupies an old railway station. The tables are set up on the railway platforms and diners are seated on old carriage benches. The menu includes grilled chicken, lamb and beef, and the rapid service is perfect for those who have another train to catch.

🕐 Daily noon–2am
🍴 L €31, D €38, Wine €17
🚇 La Muette

GOUMARD

Map 257 K5
9 rue Duphot, 75001
Concord
Tel 01 42 60 36 07
www.goumard.com
For exceptional cuisine in elegant surroundings, Goumard is worth a visit, especially because it opens on Sundays when many top-class restaurants in the heart of the city don't. Housed in an 1870s mansion, it concentrates on seafood, and everything is beautifully presented.

🕐 Daily 12.15–2.30, 7.15–11.30
🍴 L €46, D €90, Wine €21
🚇 Madeleine

LE GRAND CAFÉ

Map 259 L5
4 boulevard des Capucines, 75009
Grands Boulevards
Tel 01 43 12 19 00
www.legrandcafe.com
Theatregoers, seafood-lovers and an eclectic flock of night owls make up the clientele of

EATING

this restaurant (inaugurated in 1875 at the same time as the nearby Palais Garnier), which is open day and night, every day of the year. The interior is beautiful, art nouveau, with an impressive stained-glass

ceiling and fanciful furniture. Fish is king here and is served grilled, poached or *meunière* (in lemon and butter). The menu also includes some French meat dishes, such as fillet of Charolais beef with peppercorns or grilled with a Béarnaise sauce.

🕐 Daily 24 hours
🍴 L €30, D €45, Wine €18
Ⓜ Opéra

GRAND COLBERT

Map 257 M6
2 rue Vivienne, 75002
Louvre/Palais Royal
Tel 01 42 86 87 88
www.legrandcolbert.fr

There's something quintessentially Parisian about this chic brasserie, which dates from 1830. The listed building has high ceilings, black-and-white floor tiles, Café-de-Paris-style lamps and an army of highly professional waiters

wearing the traditional black-and-white *garçon* uniform. The menu includes seafood platters, sauerkraut and steaks.

🕐 Daily noon–3am (last orders 1am)
🍴 L €20, D €38, Wine €28
Ⓜ Bourse

GUY SAVOY

Map 256 G4
18 rue Troyon, 75017
Champs-Élysées
Tel 01 43 80 40 61
www.guysavoy.com

Guy Savoy's motto is that cooking is the art of taking foodstuffs and transforming them into pure happiness. Art is indeed on the menu

with delicacies such as poached-grilled pigeon and giblets in a beetroot and mushroom millefeuille, or the split langoustines with citrus fruit and peas.

Art is also on the walls, with many modern paintings. There are fine white linen tablecloths and black wooden chairs. This is a true culinary experience, just minutes away from the Champs-Élysées.

🕐 Mon–Fri noon–2, 7–10.30, Sat 7–10.30
🍴 L €200, D €300, Wine €90
Ⓜ Charles de Gaulle–Étoile

LA GRANDE CASCADE

Map 256 off F5
Allée de Longchamp, 75016
Auteuil (Bois de Boulogne)
Tel 01 45 27 33 51
www.lagrandecascade.fr

Napoleon III built this pavilion at the foot of La Grande Cascade (the Great Waterfall) for his visits to the Bois de Boulogne. It was converted

into a restaurant in 1900 and its belle-époque interior has a profusion of candelabra and red velvet drapes. The vast windows in the circular dining room give magical views of the woods. Chef Frédéric Robert creates fine French cuisine.

🕐 Daily 12.30–2.30, 7.30–10.30
🍴 L €80, D €140, Wine €25
Ⓜ Porte Maillot then bus 244

LES GRANDES MARCHES

Map 258 Q8
6 place de la Bastille, 75012
Bastille
Tel 01 43 42 90 32
www.groupe-bertrand.com

Les grandes marches (the big steps) refer to those of the Opéra Bastille, although this open two-floor house also has its own stylish staircase. Go to the upper floor for wonderful views of place de la Bastille. The modern decoration includes plenty of steel surfaces and subtle lighting.

Chef Jacky Ribault oversees the creation of innovative French dishes such as Loué chicken with pistachio and mustard juice, and caramel-coated monkfish with butter orange juices. The restaurant is also renowned for its superb seafood platters.

🕐 Daily noon–midnight
🍴 L €28, D €45, Wine €18
Ⓜ Bastille

LA GUINGUETTE DE NEUILLY

Map 256 off F4
12 boulevard Georges-Seurat, 92200 Neuilly-sur-Seine
Neuilly
01 46 24 25 04
www.laguinguette.net

Dine on the banks of the Seine at this restaurant, on the Île de la Grande Jatte. he tables have red-and-white tablecloths; on the walls, oars and pictures of fishing scenes evoke life by the river. The cuisine is equally traditional, simple but tasty, with choices such as grilled steak

EATING

JEAN-PAUL HÉVIN
Map 257 L6
231 rue St-Honoré, 75001
Right Bank
Tel 01 55 35 35 96
www.jphevin.com

Jean-Paul Hévin, winner of the international prize for chocolate-making and a member of the French chocolate and confectionery

academy, is behind this tea and chocolate house. The hot chocolate is delicious and provides the perfect excuse to sample other dishes, such as the orange or raspberry chocolate cake or the almond and chocolate macaroon. The design is equally evocative of the celebrated ingredient, with chocolate tones, wood panels and co-ordinating rattan furniture.
🕐 Mon–Sat 12–7
🍴 Hot chocolate €6, slice of chocolate cake €5
🚇 Tuileries

with fried potatoes, and roasted sea bass with mixed vegetables.
🕐 Daily 12–2.30, 8–11
🍴 L €30, D €38, Wine €17
🚇 Pont de Levallois or Porte de Champerret then bus 163 or 164

HARD ROCK CAFÉ
Map 259 M5
14 boulevard Montmartre, 75009
Grands Boulevards

Tel 01 53 24 60 00
www.hardrockcafe.com

You'll find rock music, beers on tap and American food (their hamburgers, grilled fajitas and Texas T-Bone steaks aren't at all bad) at this chain restaurant. Rock memorabilia include Eric Clapton's guitar and some of the Beatles' original scores. This is not the place for a romantic dinner, but a good spot to hang out with friends.
🕐 Sun–Thu 8.30am–1am, Fri–Sat 8.30am–2am
🍴 L €15, D €30, Wine €18
🚇 Grands-Boulevards

HIPPOPOTAMUS
Map 258 Q8
1 boulevard Beaumarchais, 75004
Bastille
Tel 01 44 61 90 40
www.hippopotamus.fr

This restaurant is part of a chain (there are about 20 in Paris) known for its grilled meat. Salads, steak tartare and carpaccio are also on the menu, and your dinner could start with some goat's cheese on toast or a terrine. It's worth a visit if you're looking for reasonable prices and a convivial, child-friendly atmosphere.
🕐 Daily 8am–3am
🍴 L €20, D €28, Wine €19.50
🚇 Bastille

HIRAMATSU
Map 256 F6
Address: 52 rue de Longchamp, 75016
Ternes
Tel: 01 56 81 08 80
www.hiramatsu.co.jp

When Hiramatsu opened its Paris branch in 2001, the chef became the first Japanese national to be awarded a Michelin star. The quality continues with an inventive menu based on French ingredients and dishes transformed by the lightness of touch of Japanese preparation of food. The restaurant is a suitably grand setting for the masterpieces on the plate.
🕐 Mon–Fri 12.30–2, 7.30–9.30
🍴 L €80, D €100, Wine €24
🚇 Trocadéro

JACQUES CAGNA
Map 257 M7
14 rue des Grands-Augustins, 75006
St-Germain-des-Prés
Tel 01 43 26 49 39

MARKET
Map 256 J5
15 avenue Matignon, 75008
Champs-Élysées
Tel 01 56 43 40 90
www.jean-georges.com

Interior designer Christian Liaigre has created a bare yet polished interior, with soft tones, pale wood furniture and panels punctuated by pieces of primitive art. There is the same pared-down approach to the menu, which offers the produce of a raw bar, notably a large choice of oysters, and fusion food by chef Jean-Georges Vongerichten. Try the black truffle pizza or the 'black plate', an hors d'oeuvre selection including shrimps on a skewer, ginger lobster roll, raw tuna and spiced quail. At the weekend you also have the option of brunch.
🕐 Daily noon–3, 7.30–12.30 (Sun–Mon until 11.30)
🍴 L €34, D €60, Wine €30
🚇 Franklin D. Roosevelt

www.jacques-cagna.com

For over 30 years, Jacques Cagna has been reinventing gourmet cuisine. Here you can expect true delicacies, such as veal rib in a ginger and lime sauce. and grilled langoustines. The restaurant is in a

17th-century town house, overseen by the chef's sister Annie. The beautiful interior has beamed ceilings, wood panels and Flemish paintings.
🕐 Tue–Fri noon–2, 7.30–10.15, Mon and Sat 7.30–10.15
🍴 L €60, D €110, Wine €30
🚇 St-Michel, Odéon

EATING

JOE ALLEN

Map 259 N6
30 rue Pierre Lescot, 75001

Les Halles
Tel 01 42 36 70 13

This relaxed American bar and restaurant is in a small street in the bustling Les Halles district. The brick walls are covered with pictures and you dine by candlelight in the evenings. The venue has been a hit with the show-business crowd since 1972, partly due to the professional barmen, but also because of the high quality of the all-American food.

🕐 Daily noon–1am
🍽 L €20, D €30, Wine €15
🚇 Etienne-Marcel

KHUN AKORN

Map 258 off Q8
8 avenue de Taillebourg, 75011
Nation
Tel 01 43 56 20 03

The Thai menu here offers a wide range of dishes, including *larb neua* (beef cooked in lemon and spices), duck in red curry sauce and crispy noodles. Each dish can be spiced according to how hot you want it to be. The interior design avoids kitsch although you'll still find some statues of dragons, carved wooden panels and chairbacks. There's also a pleasant terrace for spring and summer days.

🕐 Tue–Sun noon–2, 7.30–11
🍽 L €24, D €30, Wine €15
🚇 Nation

LADURÉE

Map 257 K5
16 rue Royale, 75008
Concorde
Tel 01 42 60 21 79
www.laduree.fr

This was the first tea room in Paris, established in 1862. It started life as a bakery but became a tea room as demand grew for its delicious pastries. The fin-de-siècle

---

MUSCADE

Map 257 L6
36 rue Montpensier, 75001
Louvre/Palais Royal
Tel 01 42 97 51 36
www.muscade-palais-royal.com

This high-class venue has an exceptional setting in the Palais Royal gardens and an elegant interior, with black-and-white floor tiles and Regency chairs. The lunch menu and one of the dinner menus have a Mediterranean accent and change every six months. At Muscade they are passionate about cakes, which you can enjoy as a dessert or as part of a traditional afternoon tea. This includes chocolate macaroons, fig and saffron caramel *pastilla* (a Middle Eastern filo-pastry dish) and ginger and lemon cake. Other

delicacies include muffins, chocolate gateaux and tarts.

🕐 Tea room: Tue–Sun 10–11.30, 3–6 (also 6–8pm Sep–end Apr)
🍽 Tea €4, slice of cake €6
🚇 Pyramides, Palais-Royal/Louvre

painter commissioned to decorate it used techniques employed in world-famous masterpieces such as the ceiling of the Sistine Chapel and the Opéra Palais Garnier. You can sample the very best teas and pastries in an elegant setting. Among the delicacies, the macaroon is an absolute

---

must. It comes in its original varieties—rose, Yunnan tea, apricot and ginger—but also some which change with the seasons. All are a treat.

🕐 Mon–Sat 8.30–7, Sun 10–7
🍽 Tea €7, 4 mini macaroons €6.90
🚇 Concorde, Madeleine

LAURENT

Map 256 J5
41 avenue Gabriel, 75008
Champs-Élysées
Tel 01 42 25 00 39
www.le-laurent.com

This grand French restaurant has been run by Edmond Ehrlich since the mid-1970s. Here you can be assured of the absolute highest standards of service and classic cuisine. The dining room is wonderfully formal, but many choose to eat in the sheltered gardens, a respite from the bustle of the Champs-Élysées a short walk away. The gastronomic menu changes with the seasons, but includes meat, fish and a mouth-watering range of desserts.

🕐 Mon–Fri 12.30–2, 7.30–10.30, Sat 7.30–10.30
🍽 L €100, D €130, Wine €25
🚇 Franklin D. Roosevelt

MARTY

Map 258 off N10
20 avenue des Gobelins, 75005
Mouffetard
Tel 01 43 31 39 51
www.marty-restaurant.com

This 1930s-style brasserie, on the first floor, offers delicious fresh shellfish, fish and meat dishes. There is a restaurant on the ground floor, although it is slightly more expensive. The venue is well-placed for a meal after a visit to the Gobelins factory (▷ 106–107).

🕐 Sun–Fri noon–3, 7–11, Sat noon–3, 7–midnight
🍽 L €30, D €40, Wine €17
🚇 Les Gobelins

MAVROMMATIS

Map 258 N10
42 rue Daubenton, 75005
Latin Quarter
Tel 01 43 31 17 17
www.mavrommatis.fr

This restaurant is round the corner from the lively rue Mouffetard, where cafés and restaurants are legion. It is run by two brothers, Andreas and Evagoras Mavrommatis, with Andreas in the kitchen.

EATING

The interior is elegant but unpretentious, with pale wood and woven osier chairbacks set off by fresh flowers. All the classics of Greek cuisine are here: preserved lamb and yoghurt with honey, vine leaves, moussaka and, of course, the syrup-soaked *baklava* (pastry with honey and pistachios) for dessert.

🕐 Tue–Sat noon–2.15, 7–11
🍴 L €65, D €95, Wine €23
🚇 Censier Daubenton

MAXIM'S
Map 257 K6
3 rue Royale, 75008
Concorde
Tel 01 42 65 27 94
www.maxims-de-paris.com
This belle-époque restaurant was established in 1893 by café waiter Maxime Gaillard and acquired in 1981 by designer Pierre Cardin. It is now a hub of Parisian

social life and has proved so successful that other Maxims have opened across the world, in New York, Beijing and Geneva. But it has managed to remain light years away from the atmosphere of some chain restaurants. Attentive service, refined French cuisine and a prestigious location all contribute to its touch of class.

🕐 Mon–Fri 12.30–2, 7.30–10, Sat 7.30–10
🍴 L €130, D €175, Wine €40
🚇 Concorde

LA MÈRE LACHAISE
Map 258 off Q6
78 boulevard de Ménilmontant, 75020
Belleville/Père Lachaise
Tel 01 47 97 61 60
This convivial bistro is as fashionable as it is authentic. It has a great terrace in summer, and two dining rooms, one with a retro feel (tiled floor, wrought iron and wooden tables) and the other with a contemporary atmosphere, with walls covered in silver fabric.

The menu has unpretentious high-quality food such as big salads, tartares and tarts, and a good brunch on Sundays. The name echoes the nearby Père Lachaise cemetery, where many celebrities, including Jim Morrison, are buried (▷ 88).

🕐 Daily 11am–2am
🍴 L €15, D €25, Wine €13
🚇 Père Lachaise

NOS ANCÊTRES LES GAULOIS
Map 258 N8
39 rue St-Louis en l'Ile, 75004
Île St-Louis
Tel 01 46 33 66 07
www.nosancetreslesgaulois.com
This fun Gallic-themed restaurant has been going strong since it opened in 1969. There's a rustic feel to the place, with exposed stone walls, beamed ceilings and decorative agricultural tools. The idea is simple—one fixed-price menu, including unlimited wine from the barrel, an all-you-can-eat buffet of starters (cold meats and salads) and a choice of freshly grilled kebabs, lamb chops, steaks and other meats from

the open fireplace. Vegetarians be warned.

🕐 Daily 7pm–2am
🍴 D €39 (including wine)
🚇 Pont-Marie

L'ORIENTAL
Map 259 M3
47 avenue Trudaine, 75009
Montmartre
Tel 01 42 64 39 80
www.loriental-restaurant.com
Although this restaurant is located close to touristy Montmartre not far from the famous Moulin Rouge, you could be in another world. Lanterns, mosaics, curtains and mirrors create a luxurious Moroccan palace feel. The cuisine is North African, with *pastillas* (dishes based on filo pastry), *tagines* (meat cooked in a cone-shaped terracotta dish) such as king's lamb with figs, almonds and dates, the essential couscous and a mint tea to conclude.

🕐 Daily noon–2.30, 7.30–10
🍴 L €25, D €35, Wine €19
🚇 Abbesses, Pigalle

PALMIERS DU SINAÏ
Map 257 M6
3 rue Mander, 75002
Les Halles
Tel 01 40 26 99 23
www.palmiersdusinai.com
This exciting Egyptian/Middle Eastern restaurant is a touch of Arabia in the middle of Paris. There's a vast choice of hot and cold starters that can make an early dinner by themselves. Main courses include *tagines*, savoury *galettes* and grilled meats. You can finish your evening relaxing with a hubble-bubble pipe, or hookah, in the *salon-du-thé*.

🕐 Daily 4pm–2am
🍴 D €30, Wine €15
🚇 Les Halles

LE PAMPHLET
Map 258 P6
38 rue Debelleyme, 75003
Le Marais
Tel 01 42 72 39 24
This is a reliable restaurant in the trendy Marais district. The excellent French cuisine, prepared by Chef Alain Carrère from southwest France, has a definite regional character, enhanced by the convivial surroundings. Try the braised sea bass with carrots, leeks and shrimp-flavoured sauce, followed by Carrère's take on *pot de chocolat Guanaja*, with a chocolate crust and rich chocolate cream. The good-value fixed-price menu changes every day.

EATING

Tue–Fri noon–2, 7–11.30, Sat,
Mon 7–11.30

L €30, D €45, Wine €18

Filles du Calvaire

LE PARADIS DU FRUIT
Map 257 M7
29 quai des Grands-Augustins, 75006
St-Germain-des-Prés
Tel 01 43 54 51 42
www.leparadisdufruit.fr

The concept of this chain
restaurant will delight
vegetarians and health food
fans alike, as you get to
compose your own meal and
drink from a large selection of

fresh fruit and vegetables. The
massive salads come with
taramasalata, guacamole,
cheese and other side dishes.
Carnivores needn't despair
as there are also some meat
side orders, such as spiced
chicken on a skewer. There
are nine Paradis du Fruit in
Paris, and at this branch
there is a small terrace
where you can enjoy views
of the Seine on spring and
summer days.

Daily noon–1am

L €15, D €25, Wine €12

St-Michel

LE PETIT ST-BENOÎT
Map 257 L7
4 rue St-Benoît, 75006
St-Germain-des-Prés
Tel 01 42 60 27 92

This popular bistro is a
St-Germain classic and the
look has barely changed
since the 1930s. Photos on
the walls show some of
the writers and intellectuals
who have visited. The menu
includes traditional soups,
terrines and dishes such as
rabbit with mustard. You can
sit outside in summer. Credit
cards are not accepted.

Sep–end Jul Mon–Sat noon–2.30,
7–10.30

L €25, D €35, Wine €18

St-Germain-des-Prés

LE PHARAMOND
Map 259 N6
24 rue de la Grande-Truanderie, 75001
Les Halles
Tel 01 40 28 45 18
www.le-pharamond.com

This restaurant, established in
1832, is in a listed historic
building. It has an extravagant
art nouveau interior with
ceramic murals, floor tiles,

huge mirrors, mosaics and
a dramatic spiral staircase.
There are two dining rooms
and a private salon on the
third floor. They serve
traditional food from the
Normandy region such as
Caen-style tripe with cider,
calvados (apple brandy) and
potatoes, and melt-in-the-
mouth chocolate cake.

This is a Parisian institution,
in keeping with the best
tradition of Les Halles, which
is the former home of Paris's
food market.

Mon–Sat noon–2.30, 7.30–10.30

L €25, D €60, Wine €18

Les Halles

PICCOLO TEATRO
Map 258 P7
6 rue des Ecouffes, 75004
Le Marais
Tel 01 42 72 17 79
www.piccolo-teatro.fr

This restaurant was a pioneer
of vegetarian cuisine at the
time of its launch in 1976 and
is now firmly established at
the heart of the picturesque
Marais district. The menu
includes dishes from all
over the world, using exotic

ingredients such as Indonesian
tempeh (fermented soya).
A wide range of *gratins*
(cheese-topped dishes),
soups and salads are on the
menu, some with evocative
names—*Calling the Sun*
is aubergine (eggplant),
mozzarella and basil gratin.

Daily noon–3, 7–11.30

L €15, D €25, Wine €12

St-Paul

PIERRE GAGNAIRE
Map 256 H5
6 rue Balzac, 75008
Champs-Élysées
Tel 01 58 36 12 50
www.pierre-gagnaire.fr

This three-star chef from the
Lyon region delights gourmets
with his boundless creativity.
He challenges all the senses
and turns the culinary art into
an ever-changing adventure in
which the simplest ingredients
appeal to the imagination and
the taste buds. Dishes include
mild-onion marmalade, veal
and foie gras with figs and
salted raw ham, bitter orange
and carrot paste and creamed
parsnip and chocolate.

Mon–Fri noon–1.30, 7.30–9.30,
Sun 7.30–9.30

L €80, D €110, Wine €60

George V

POMZE
Map 256 J4
109 boulevard Haussmann, 75008
Grands Boulevards
Tel 01 42 65 65 83
www.pomze.com

A boutique, a restaurant and a
bar all dedicated to…apples!
Stéphane Oliver's inventive
cooking is based on this
universal ingredient and the
shop offers a wide choice of
ciders, jams, chutneys as well
as six pure juices, each made
from a single variety of fruit.

Mon–Fri 8am–11pm, Sat
10am–11pm

L €30, D €45, Wine €21

St-Augustin

EATING

LE PRÉ VERRE
Map 257 M8
19 rue du Sommerard, 75005
Latin Quarter
Tel 01 43 54 59 47
www.lepreverre.com
Gourmets flock to this charming bistro, in the heart of the Latin Quarter, to taste Philippe Delacourcelle's reasonably priced inventive French/Asian fusion cuisine and enjoy the lively relaxed atmosphere. For a starter, try creamy lemon soup, served cold, and perhaps follow it with suckling pig in a spicy broth with crispy cabbage.
🕐 Tue–Sat noon–2, 7.30–10.30
🍽 L €13, D €25, Wine €17 (drink included in the fixed-price lunch menu)
🚇 Cluny-La-Sorbonne, Maubert-Mutualité

LE PROCOPE
Map 257 M8
13 rue de l'Ancienne-Comédie, 75006
St-Germain-des-Prés
Tel 01 40 46 79 00
www.procope.com
This former Parisian café, founded in 1686, now an elegant dining room, was once frequented by the philosophers Voltaire and Rousseau. Benjamin Franklin is said to have drafted part of the

EATING

American constitution here. The menu includes grilled beef fillet, coq au vin, and basil sorbet. Fish fans can choose from mackerel terrine with potatoes, fish soup or one of the rich seafood platters.
🕐 Daily noon–1am
🍽 L €30, D €50, Wine €17
🚇 Odéon

RELAIS PLAZA
Map 256 H6
21 avenue Montaigne, 75008
Champs-Élysées
Tel 01 53 67 64 00
The luxury hotel Plaza Athénée is home to this elegant restaurant, which was completely refurbished in

2002. The smart art deco dining room is filled with curios and there is a nightly piano accompaniment. Chef Philippe Marc is a disciple of maestro chef Alain Ducasse, and his gourmet menu of French dishes changes every two months.
🕐 Daily noon–2.45, 7–11.30
🍽 L €55, D €77, Wine €45
🚇 Alma-Marceau

LE REMINET
Map 258 N8
3 rue des Grands-Degrés, 75005
Latin Quarter
Tel 01 44 07 04 24
This tiny restaurant is ideally situated on the Left Bank in the picturesque old part of the Latin Quarter, a stone's throw from Notre-Dame. The inventive cuisine includes tasty modern-style dishes and traditional offerings such as snails. Note that Le Reminet is one of the rare bistros in Paris to be open on Sunday.
🕐 Thu–Mon 12–2.30, 7.30–11
🍽 L €25, D €35, Wine €15
🚇 Maubert-Mutualité

RIVER CAFÉ
Map 256 off F9
146 quai de Stalingrad, 92130
Issy-les-Moulineaux
01 40 93 50 20
www.lerivercafe.net
Dine in a big barge moored on the Seine and enjoy wonderful views of Île St-Germain. The interior is Parisian with an exotic touch: wooden floors, plants, café-de-Paris armchairs, and some rattan and neo-colonial furniture. The menu has the same influences, with subtly spiced fine French cuisine: duck with mushrooms in a honey and lemon sauce, bay prawns with pear and pineapple chutney, and chocolate macaroon with a guava and mango cream.
🕐 Daily noon–2.30, 8–11. Closed Sat lunch. Brunch on Sun

🍽 L €29, D €34, Wine €19
🚊 RER line C Issy-Val de Seine

ROSE BAKERY
Map 259 M4
46 rue des Martyrs, 75009
Montmartre
Tel 01 42 82 12 80
This English-style eatery has based its success on the quality of its organic products and on its healthy, delicious recipes. These include fresh soups, salads and, of course, pastries, to be eaten in the dining area or taken away. There is a weekend brunch menu and a grocery store (City Organic) in the nearby rue Milton.
🕐 Tue–Sun 9am–7pm (Sun until 6pm). Lunch served from noon
🍽 L €12.50, Wine €3.50 per glass
🚇 Notre-Dame-de-Lorette

LA RÔTISSERIE DU BEAUJOLAIS
Map 258 N8
19 quai de la Tournelle, 75005
Latin Quarter
Tel 01 43 54 17 47
www.latourargent.com
You'll get lovely views of Notre-Dame from the terrace of this quayside bistro. The restaurant is under the same ownership as La Tour d'Argent (▷ 276), across the road. The menu includes traditional dishes such as snails or pig's trotters, but the highlight is the roasted meat.
🕐 Tue–Sun noon–2.15, 7.30–10.15
🍽 L €35, D €45, Wine €21
🚇 Maubert–Mutualité

LA RÔTISSERIE D'EN FACE
Map 257 M8
2 rue Christine, 75006
St-Germain-des-Prés
Tel 01 43 26 40 98
www.jacques-cagna.com
This is the annexe of Jacques Cagna, the eponymous gastronomic restaurant across the street, where the celebrity chef himself rules the kitchen.

Expect the same perfection here, within the relaxed setting of an elegant brasserie, with leather wall seats and lines of small square wooden tables. On the menu, you'll find rotisserie dishes such as spit-roast chicken, suckling pig and veal kidney. Other options include meat and vegetable stew, Burgundy snails and frogs' legs in garlic and herbs.

🕐 Mon–Thu noon–2.30, 7–11, Fri noon–2.30, 7–11.30
🍽 L €30, D €45, Wine €20
🚇 St-Michel

SPICY RESTAURANT
Map 256 J5
8 avenue Franklin D. Roosevelt, 75008
Champs-Élysées
Tel 01 56 59 62 59
www.spicyrestaurant.com
Be prepared for inventive cuisine which explodes with taste and looks great. Try courgettes (zucchini) marinated in olive oil and served with tomato-infused goat's milk cheese; steamed salmon served with Chinese noodles, soy sauce and fresh mint; or gingerbread pudding with caramel butter sauce and vanilla ice cream. The interior is newly refurbished in the style of a classical Mediterranean villa.

🕐 Daily noon–midnight
🍽 L €30, D €45, Wine €19
🚇 Franklin D. Roosevelt

SPOON FOOD AND WINE
Map 256 H5
14 rue de Marignan, 75008
Champs-Élysées
Tel 01 40 76 34 44
www.spoon.tm.fr
The simply beautiful setting, signature of Boifils, mixes sleek lines and deep purple

walls, enhanced by the pastels of the chair cushions. There's just as much creativity in the kitchen, where celebrated chef Alain Ducasse dreams up highly

personalized menus—you choose the sauce and accompaniment to your meal. The menu combines French, American and Asian influences with plenty for vegetarians. Unusually, the wine list has mostly American and New World wines (California is particularly well represented), and some wines are available by the glass each day.

🕐 Mon–Fri noon–2, 7–11
🍽 L €50, D €70, Wine €24
🚇 Franklin D. Roosevelt

LE STÜBLI
Map 256 off G4
11 rue Poncelet, 75017
Ternes
Tel 01 42 27 81 86
This tea room has been an ambassador for Germany and Austria since it opened in 1956. Above the patisserie,

the tea room has a Viennese setting, with lots of wood, tones of beige and green and subdued lighting. The menu includes traditional cakes and pastries such as apple strudel and Black Forest gateau. The hot chocolate makes a perfect accompaniment. Le Stübli also runs a delicatessen across the street, which sells beer, cold meats and breads.

🕐 Tea room: Tue–Sat 9–5.30, Sun 9am–12.30pm
🍽 Viennese hot chocolate €4, slice of Black Forest gateau €4
🚇 Ternes

TAILLEVENT
Map 256 H4
15 rue Lamennais, 75008
Champs-Élysées
Tel 01 44 95 15 01
www.taillevent.com
This highly distinguished restaurant is named after a celebrated chef from the Middle Ages and is now the domain of master chef Alain Solivérès. The dining room is discreetly elegant, with wood

panels and candelabra. Expect the very best of French cuisine, with rich dishes such as foie gras, lobster and truffles. To sample the chef's latest creations, try his 'Menu Suggestions' (lunchtime only), which vary according to the availability of fresh produce. There is an exceptional wine cellar to match.

🕐 Mon–Fri 12.15–2, 7.15–2
🍽 L €70, D €140, Wine €28
🚇 Charles de Gaulle–Étoile, George V

LA TAVERNE
Map 259 L5
24 boulevard des Italiens, 75009
Grands Boulevards
Tel 01 55 33 10 00
www.taverne.com
The menu here has Alsatian influences, with dishes such as sauerkraut, monkfish in beer and tarte tatin (upside-down apple tart) with cream. The pale wood panels and candelabra give this restaurant

a touch of class, while curios such as a bull's head and a massive clock are more evocative of a tavern. Dinner-and-show deals are arranged with nearby theatres.

🕐 Daily 11.30am–2am
🍽 L €25, D €40, Wine €12
🚇 Richelieu-Drouot, Opéra

EATING

THOUMIEUX

Map 256 J7
79 rue St-Dominique, 75007
Invalides
Tel 01 47 05 49 75

Named after the Thoumieux family proprietors, this brasserie, which opened in 1923, is just minutes away from the Eiffel Tower. The elegant dining room has comfortable velvet wall seats and numerous mirrors. The present chef is Christian

Beguet, whose menu is a top-class excursion into the cuisine of southwest France. Expect quality, hearty dishes such as *cassoulet* (bean and sausage casserole) or one of the various duck dishes, including foie gras.

🕐 Mon–Sat noon–3, 7–11, Sun noon–11
🍴 L €30, D €40, Wine €15
Ⓜ Invalides

TOI

Map 256 J5
27 rue du Colisée, 75008
Champ-Élysées
Tel 01 42 56 56 58
www.restaurant-toi.com

The convivial atmosphere of this up-and-coming restaurant near the Champs-Élysées is created by the bright warm colours of the walls and contemporary furniture. Chef Hervé Nepple has worked with Pierre Gagnaire and Guy Savoy. Refreshing snacks are served daily until 6pm and there is a brunch menu on Sunday.

🕐 Daily noon–midnight
🍴 L €35, D €45, Wine €20
Ⓜ Franklin D. Roosevelt

TORAYA

Map 257 K5
10 rue St-Florentin, 75001
Concorde
Tel 01 42 60 13 00
www.toraya-group.co.jp/paris

This is a branch of Japan's oldest patisserie, founded in

SPECIAL

LA TOUR D'ARGENT

Map 258 N8
15–17 quai de la Tournelle, 75005
Latin Quarter
Tel 01 43 54 23 31
www.latourargent.com

A Parisian institution since 1582, this is one of the best restaurants in France, if not the world. It sits on the sixth floor of a beautiful building overlooking the Seine, offering panoramic views of the city.

This is exquisite French cuisine at its best, with lobster quenelles and duck being a couple of the signature dishes. The wine cellar is exceptional.

🕐 Tue–Sun noon–1.30, 8–9.30
🍴 L €120, D €150, Wine €59
Ⓜ Pont Marie

the 16th century and supplier to the Japanese Imperial family. Behind the stylish façade, adorned with a tiger, the company's logo, you'll find a chic tea room with a lot of dark brown wood and white and orange leather armchairs. The traditional pastries vary according to the seasons. An example is the leaf-shaped *Mayumi-No-Mochi*, served in autumn. Surprising in shape and taste (some use red beans), they resemble miniature works of art. The restaurant is entirely non-smoking.

🕐 Mon–Sat 10.30–7
🍵 Green tea €4.70, Japanese cake €4.70
Ⓜ Concorde

LE TRAIN BLEU

Map 258 Q9
Gare de Lyon, 75012
Bastille
Tel 01 44 75 76 76
www.le-train-bleu.com

To step inside this historic restaurant is to take a journey

back to 1900 when it was inaugurated as the new station buffet! It is indeed a splendid example of the flowery belle-époque style, with a profusion of gilt mouldings and frescoes. The classic French cuisine includes sole meunière, roast lamb with gratineed potatoes, and crème brûlée.

🕐 Daily 11.30–3, 7–11
🍴 L €45, D €80, Wine €28
Ⓜ Gare de Lyon

TRÉSOR

Map 258 P7
7–9 rue du Trésor, 75004
Le Marais
Tel 01 42 71 35 17

This restaurant is in a quiet no-through road in the picturesque Marais district and has one of Paris's finest terraces.

The interior is a sumptuous riot of neo-baroque design with luxurious period-style sofas, ornate mirrors and pea green and scarlet walls. Trésor's menu melds classical Italian dishes with French country cuisine.

EATING

Food served daily noon–3, 7.30–10, but drinks available all day until 2am

🍴 L €25, D €40, Wine €18

🚇 St-Paul, Hôtel de Ville

LA TRUFFIÈRE

Map 258 N9
4 rue Blainville, 75005
Latin Quarter
Tel 01 46 33 29 82
www.latruffiere.com

Here you can dine by candlelight in the picturesque 17th-century vaulted cellar or in the attractive dining room with exposed beams. The gourmet French cuisine

includes ingredients from southwest France, such as foie gras, duck and, above all, truffles. Start with duck foie gras with nuts, red wine and ginger jelly and baked apple, followed by 'confit' of duck with mashed potato cake and black truffles; and for dessert, you could try a hot black truffle soufflé or caramelized custard cream with truffle. The restaurant offers an unusual choice of small portions of certain dishes at lower prices for those with small appetites or those who would like to sample a wider range of dishes. There is a good selection of wines and brandies.

🕐 Tue–Sat noon–2, 7–10.30

🍴 L €70 (small portion menu €45), D €90 (à la carte), Wine €25

🚇 Place Monge

TSÉ

Map 256 off F9
78 rue d'Auteuil, 75016
Tel 01 40 71 11 90
Auteuil

This bar-restaurant has been a hit with this residential area's elegant night owls since it opened in 2001. It has an extravagant interior, with Chinese lanterns and wall lamps, exotic dark wooden furniture and even an antique Tibetan four-poster bed. There is a warm and welcoming bar

with a fireplace, a smoking room and a roof terrace.

The food is high-quality Asian cuisine, with Japanese, Thai and Chinese influences. You'll find sushi, duck fillet in a *teriyaki* sauce (soy sauce, sake and ginger) and sesame tuna on a skewer.

🕐 Sun–Thu 11.30am–1am, Fri–Sat 11.30am–3am

🍴 L €40, D €60, Wine €22

🚇 Porte d'Auteuil

TSE YANG

Map 256 G6
25 avenue Pierre 1er de Serbie, 75016
Trocadéro
Tel 01 47 20 70 22

Inside this elegant Chinese restaurant, in one of Paris's smartest districts, you'll find plenty of fresh flowers and some impressive murals.

Chef Yang Kui Fah brilliantly interprets the classics of Asian cuisine. Scallops in yellow rice wine and Peking-style duck are

among the house dishes. There is a comprehensive list of French wines and traditional Chinese beers.

🕐 Mon–Sat noon–2.30, 7.30–11.30, Sun noon–2.30

🍴 L €35, D €50, Wine €23

🚇 Iéna

LE VERRE BOUTEILLE

Map 256 off G4
85 avenue des Ternes, 75017
Ternes
Tel 01 45 74 01 02
www.leverrebouteille.com

This bistro, conveniently close to the place de l'Étoile, stays

open until the small hours. Chef Patrick Ameline's ambition is to satisfy with simple food cooked to perfection, and the warm goat's cheese, country-style *croque* and chocolate cake are all to die for. There's a good selection of wines, some available by the glass if you don't fancy a whole bottle.

The interior is traditional bistro in style, with a long bar and rectangular wooden tables with wrought-iron legs.

🕐 Daily noon–3, 7–5

🍴 L €24, D €30, Wine €16.80

🚇 Porte Maillot

VILLA MEDICI CHEZ NAPOLI

Map 257 K8
11 bis rue St-Placide, 75006
St-Germain-des-Prés
Tel 01 42 22 51 96
www.villa-medici.com

Moustachioed Michele Napoli (see the website for a photo) has been entertaining his guests here for more than 30 years. His regular clientele keeps coming back for the tasty Italian food (choose from pizza, pasta or risotto).

The interior is splendidly faux-Italian, with a Coliseum-style main room, with pillars and a circular table arrangement. There is another room at the back where groups are entertained by the performing *pizzaiolo* (pizza chef). There is one non-smoking room.

🕐 Mon–Sat 11.30–2.30, 7–11

🍴 L €20, D €30, Wine €18

🚇 St-Placide, Sèvres-Babylone

VIN DES PYRÉNÉES

Map 258 P8
25 rue Beautreillis, 75004
Le Marais
Tel 01 42 72 64 94

This restaurant takes you back to the 1930s. Gingham table-

cloths, old family pictures on the walls and antique dolls in a display cabinet mark the retro

EATING

look. The traditional menu includes salmon millefeuille, grilled meat (the house special dish), crème brûlée and chocolate cake. The wine list, as the restaurant's name suggests, includes a selection from the Pyrenees.

🕐 Sun–Fri noon–2.30, 8–11.30, Sat 8–11.30
🍽 L €20, D €35, Wine €19
Ⓜ St-Paul

LE VIOLON D'INGRES
Map 256 H7
135 rue Saint-Dominique, 75007
Champ du Mars
Tel 01 45 55 15 05
www.leviolondingres.com
This favourite locale has received a make-over, but the cuisine remains reassuringly top quality. The open kitchen concept is unusual in Paris, giving the restaurant a bustling atmosphere. Chef Christian Constant has worked at the Ritz and at the Michelin-starred Les Ambassadeurs, but has run the Violon since 1988 and added two more restaurants to his portfolio. The menu looks to market freshness with a few well chosen signature dishes, including woodpigeon in season.

🕐 Tue–Sat noon–2.30, 7–10.30
🍽 L €34, D €45, Wine €19
Ⓜ École Militaire

LE VIRAGE LEPIC
Map 259 L2
61 rue Lepic, 75018
Montmartre
Tel 01 42 52 46 79
Book ahead for this welcoming bistro, in Montmartre's windmill-crowned rue Lepic. You'll find meat-based main courses, tasty puddings and a good wine list. In summer you can sit outside.

🕐 Wed–Mon 7–11.30
🍽 D €25, Wine €15
Ⓜ Blanche/Abbesses

YUGARAJ
Map 257 M7
14 rue Dauphine, 75006
St-Germain-des-Prés
Tel 01 43 26 44 91
www.yugaraj.com
Yugaraj is one of Paris's best Indian restaurants. The French and Indian proprietors introduced Indian cuisine to the French with their previous restaurant, which opened in 1971.

The menu contains a few surprises, with options such as crab balls among more traditional dishes. The jumbo shrimps marinated in spices are a must.

🕐 Tue–Wed, Fri–Sun noon–2, 7–10.30, Thu noon–2
🍽 L €30, D €50, Wine €22
Ⓜ Odéon

ZE KITCHEN GALERIE
Map 257 M7
4 rue des Grands-Augustins, 75006
St-Germain-des-Prés
Tel 01 44 32 00 32
www.zekitchengalerie.fr
The deep-coloured wooden floor adds warmth to the contemporary, functional setting of this trendy restaurant located close to the river. Chef William Ledeuil, who trained with Guy Savoy, can be seen at work in his kitchen: His innovative fusion cuisine combines Mediterranean flavours with an Asian touch and his menu changes every month.

🕐 Mon–Fri noon–2.30, 7–11, Sat 7–11
🍽 L €27, D €50, Wine €21
Ⓜ St-Michel

Dining al fresco at a restaurant on the quai St-Michel

EATING

CHAIN RESTAURANTS

Although Paris is known for some of the best—and most expensive—restaurants in the world, you can also find reasonably priced, family-friendly chains if you want a more low-key meal. The chart below shows some of the chains with restaurants in the city.

NAME	Average in euros for 2 courses	Alcohol served	Children's menu	Take-out	Description
Bistro Romain	25	✔	✔	✗	Italian cuisine (▷ 263 for the Champs-Élysées branch).
Buffalo Grill	20	✔	✔	✗	Restaurant-grills serving chicken, steaks and salads.
Chez Clément	35	✔	✔	✗	Comfortable, family-friendly brasseries where oysters, seafood platters and rotisserie beef and pork are on the menu.
Courtepaille	18	✔	✔	✗	Steak-and-chips eateries that also have chicken dishes and salads.
El Rancho	18	✔	✔	✗	Tex-Mex food in a rural-Mexican interior.
Hippopotamus	20	✔	✔	✗	A leading chain of restaurant-grills, with 18 branches in the city (▷ 270 for the Bastille branch). Steak is the house dish.
Indiana Café	18	✔	✔	✗	Expect a Tex-Mex menu, plus burgers and salads.
Léon de Bruxelles	22	✔	✔	✗	Belgian-style brasseries where beer, waffles, mussels and chips are included on the menu.
Pizza Hut	18	✔	✔	✔	A well-known chain, with pizzas big enough to share.
La Taverne de Maître Kanter	27	✔	✗	✗	Twelve branches serve Alsatian dishes such as sauerkraut, chicken in Riesling and seafood platters.

CAFÉS AND FAST FOOD

NAME					
Columbus Café	N/A	✗	✗	✔	Espresso bars where you can grab a tea, coffee or cookie.
Flunch	10	✔	✔	✗	Snacks and meals, usually in hypermarkets.
McDonald's	8	✔	✔	✔	The world's most famous burger-and-fries chain.
Pat à Pain	8	✗	✔	✔	Fresh take-out sandwiches and pastries.
Quick	9	✔	✔	✔	Northern Europe's equivalent to McDonald's.

STAYING IN PARIS

Paris has the whole range of accommodation options, whether you're looking for luxury at the world-famous Ritz, a comfortable three-star hotel in the Latin Quarter or a low-cost hostel. The city's hotels have had a (sometimes deserved) reputation for being dated and pokey, but recent years have seen a complete overhaul. Small designer boutique-hotels have popped up in the once-inexpensive Marais district and up river to the west, and some of the classic hotels have added health spas for some post-sightseeing pampering.

LUXURY
At the top of the spectrum are the luxury hotels, some of them straight out of another era. Their prices on a one-off basis are high, but some give discounts through travel agents so it is worth asking back home before your trip.

ON A BUDGET
Paris is one of the rare European capitals where you can find a pleasant, affordable place to stay in a central part of the city. Prices often drop in July and August, when there are few business trips, and rise in May, June, September and October—the trade fair months.

Check whether the room price includes breakfast. It is often less expensive to buy your croissant and coffee in a local café rather than at the hotel. If you are bringing or renting a car, ask whether parking is available and how much it costs. Parking on the street can be expensive and frustrating.

Chain hotels on the outskirts can be less expensive, although they lack Parisian character. You'll also have to spend time taking the Métro or RER into the heart of the city. See page 294 for a selection of chain hotels.

WHICH DISTRICT?
Every district in Paris has its good and bad points and choosing which *quartier* to stay in depends on your priorities.

The 8th *arrondissement* (around the Champs-Élysées, avenue George V, avenue Montaigne and Faubourg St-Honoré) has a high concentration of luxury and four-star hotels and is handy if you want to shop for designer labels. You can also find luxury in the 1st *arrondissement* (Tuileries, Louvre, place Vendôme), although the side streets here have two- and three-star hotels.

Farther north, the 9th *arrondissement* (Opéra, *Grands Boulevards*, Faubourg Montmartre) is packed with hotels, many of them two-star. There are nightclubs and shops here.

Across the river, St-Germain-des-Prés and the Latin Quarter are less business-focused than their Right Bank counterparts and closer to the atmosphere of *vieux* Paris. There are plenty of two- and three-star hotels, as well as restaurants and cafés. Here, you are well placed for visiting the île de la Cité.

If you choose to stay in less central areas, check how close you are to a Métro or RER station.

The Staying by Area box on the opposite page lists the hotels according to area, to help you find a hotel in the part of the city where you want to be.

ALTERNATIVES TO HOTELS
Of course, you don't have to stay in a hotel. For tips on finding other types of accommodation, see the box on the opposite page.

PRICES
Prices given for the hotels on pages 286–293 are for two people sharing a double room for one night, unless otherwise stated.

STAYING

TIPS ON STAYING IN PARIS

● The Paris Tourist Office (tel 0892 683 000) has information on places to stay. You can reserve rooms if you visit in person.

● To rent an apartment, options include the UK-based Apartment Service (tel 020 8944 1444 from the UK; 011 44 20 8944 1444 from the US; www.apartment.co.uk); Home Rental Service at 120 avenue des Champs-Élysées, 75008 (tel 01 42 25 65 40; www.homerental.fr); and Paris Lodging at 25 rue Lacépède, 75005

(tel 01 43 36 71 69; www.parislodging.fr).

● For bed-and-breakfast accommodation with host families you could try France Lodge at 2 rue Meissonier, 75017 (tel 01 56 33 85 85; www.francelodge.fr).

● Some farms in the Île de France have converted barns into self-catering holiday homes, providing a base for taking the RER trains into the city and for exploring the countryside around Paris.

STAYING BY AREA

The hotels are listed alphabetically (excluding Le or La) on pages 286–293.
Here they are listed by area.

Bastille
Auberge Internationale des
    Jeunes
Corail Hôtel

Belleville/Père Lachaise
Le D'Artagnan

Champs Élysées
Hôtel Astrid
Hôtel du Bois
Hôtel Franklin Roosevelt
Hôtel Residence Foch
Hôtel Tilsitt

Île St-Louis
Hôtel des Deux Îles

Invalides
Best Western Eiffel Park Hôtel
Grand Hôtel Lévêque
Hôtel de L'Avre
Hôtel la Bourdonnais
Hôtel Duc de St-Simon
Hôtel Latour-Maubourg
Hôtel de Londres Eiffel
Relais Bosquet
Hôtel Valadon

Latin Quarter
Familia Hôtel
Hôtel Claude Bernard
Hôtel des Grandes Écoles
Hôtel du Levant

Hôtel du Panthéon
Minerve Hôtel
Relais St-Jacques
Les Rives de Notre-Dame

Louvre/Palais Royal
Hôtel Flor Rivoli
Hôtel Violet Louvre Rivoli
Hôtel Washington Opéra

Le Marais
Castex Hôtel
Hôtel St-Merry
Hôtel St-Paul Le Marais
Pavillon de la Reine

Montmartre
Hôtel Prima Lepic
Terrass Hotel

Montparnasse
L'Atelier Montparnasse
Hôtel Delambre

Mouffetard
Hôtel Sunny

Opéra
Hôtel Lautrec Opéra
Hôtel Queen Mary
Ritz

Passy
Hameau de Passy
Hôtel Square

République
Auberge de Jeunesse Jules Ferry

St-Germain-des-Prés
Grand Hôtel des Balcons
L'Hôtel
Hôtel de l'Abbaye St-Germain
Hôtel Atlantis St-Germain-des-
    Prés
Hôtel Delavigne
Hôtel du Globe
Hôtel Lenox St-Germain
Hôtel Madison
Hôtel La Perle
Hôtel de St-Germain

Ternes
Hôtel de Neuville

Outside the Périphérique
Auberge de Jeunesse Cité des
    Sciences (beyond Porte de
    Pantin to the northeast)
Auberge de Jeunesse Léo
    Lagrange (beyond Porte de
    Clichy to the north)

STAYING

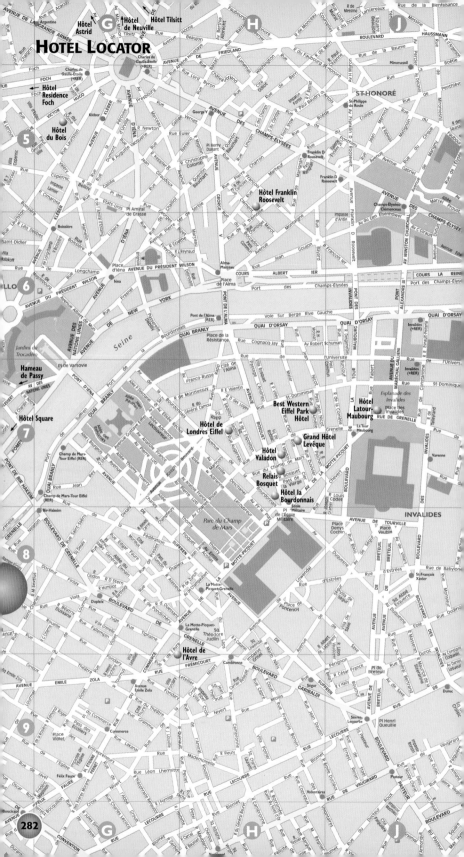

HOTEL LOCATOR

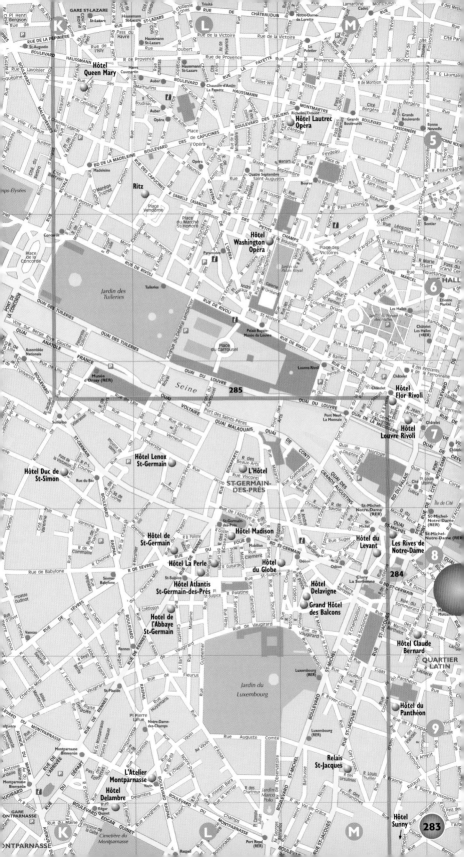

Hotels

LE D'ARTAGNAN

Map 284 off Q8
80 rue Vitruve, 75020
Ménilmontant
Tel 01 40 32 34 56
www.fuaj.org
France's largest youth hostel occupies a seven-floor building near Père Lachaise cemetery. It has a bar (open until 2am), souvenir shop, four internet booths, electronic lockers, a free cinema, TV lounge and a laundry. Rooms are for three to eight people.
🛏 €22 per person, including breakfast
ℹ 435 beds
Ⓜ Porte de Bagnolet

L'ATELIER MONTPARNASSE

Map 283 L9
49 rue Vavin, 75006
St-Germain-des-Prés
Tel 01 46 33 60 00
www.ateliermontparnasse.com
This three-star hotel pays tribute to 1930s Montparnasse,

with period furniture and mosaic reproductions of 1930s paintings in the bathrooms. Artists' haunts such as La Coupole (▷ 266) and Le Dôme brasseries are nearby. Facilities include a laundry service, room service, cable TV, hairdryer and mini-bar. Internet connection is available in some rooms.
🛏 €142–€167, excluding breakfast
ℹ 17
Ⓜ Vavin

AUBERGE INTERNATIONALE DES JEUNES

Map 284 off Q8
10 rue Trousseau, 75011
Bastille
Tel 01 47 00 62 00
www.aijparis.com
These lodgings, in the lively Bastille area, are at rock-bottom prices. Don't expect anything fancy, but the rooms are clean and the atmosphere friendly. Four-bed rooms have a separate bathroom and shower, while rooms for two or three people have a bathroom on each floor. A vending machine dispenses cold and hot drinks, and there is a safe at the front desk and internet access. Bed linen and blankets are provided.
🛏 Jul–end Aug €17 per person, including breakfast; Sep–end Oct, Mar–end Jan €15; Nov–end Feb €13
ℹ 200 beds
Ⓜ Ledru Rollin, Bastille

AUBERGE DE JEUNESSE CITÉ DES SCIENCES

Map 285 off N4
24 rue des Sept Arpents, 93310 Le Pré St-Gervais
La Villette
Tel 01 48 43 24 11
www.fuaj.org
This youth hostel is in a modern building near the Parc de la Villette (▷ 146–147). Dormitories have four or six beds and there are electronic lockers, internet terminals, a terrace, TV room, laundry, bicycle rental and a kitchen for guests to use.
🛏 €19.50 per person, including breakfast
ℹ 184 beds
Ⓜ Hoche

AUBERGE DE JEUNESSE JULES FERRY

Map 284 Q6
8 boulevard Jules Ferry, 75011
Canal St-Martin
Tel 01 43 57 55 60
www.fuaj.org
Ideally placed for strolls along the Canal St-Martin, this youth hostel has six-bed dormitories as well as some rooms for couples. Facilities include a laundry, electronic lockers and internet terminals. Breakfast is available but there are no other cooking facilities.
🛏 €19.50 per person, including breakfast
ℹ 99 beds
Ⓜ République

AUBERGE DE JEUNESSE LÉO LAGRANGE

Map 285 off K2
107 rue Martre, 92110
Clichy
Tel 01 41 27 26 90
www.fuaj.org
This youth hostel, on the northwestern outskirts, has rooms for two to six people, as well as a TV room, laundry, electronic lockers, internet terminals and a bar/restaurant (open in summer).
🛏 €20.50 per person, including breakfast
ℹ 338 beds
Ⓜ Mairie de Clichy

BEST WESTERN EIFFEL PARK HÔTEL

Map 282 H7
17 bis rue Amélie, 75007
Invalides
Tel 01 45 55 10 01
www.eiffelpark.com

The exotic decoration at this three-star hotel is thanks to the owner's trips to India and China. The bedrooms have a personal touch, such as an oriental rug or a Chinese chest of drawers, as well as minibar, modem connection, safe and hairdryer. There's a beautiful art deco bar downstairs and breakfast is served on the roof (weather permitting) or in the pleasant winter garden.
🛏 €80–€210, excluding breakfast
ℹ 36 rooms
♿
Ⓜ Latour-Maubourg

CASTEX HÔTEL

Map 284 P8
5 rue Castex, 75004
Marais
Tel 01 42 72 31 52
www.castexhotel.com
Situated on the border of the historic Marais and Bastille districts, this three-star hotel deliberately emphasizes its 17th-century features: period furniture in the reception areas and bedrooms, picturesque breakfast room with stone walls and vaulted ceiling. The stylish bedrooms are equipped with telephone, satellite TV and safe, and a fax service is available at the reception.
🛏 €100–€150, excluding breakfast
ℹ 30
♿
Ⓜ Bastille

STAYING

CORAIL HÔTEL

Map 284 Q9
23 rue de Lyon, 75012
Gare de Lyon
Tel 01 43 43 23 54
www.corail-hotel.fr

This three-star hotel is popular with the business crowd, being close to the Gare de Lyon, with its Métro, RER and mainline train services. The lively Bastille district is also nearby. Rooms may be slightly lacking in character, but come equipped with a hairdryer, private safe, telephone and satellite TV.

€78–€83, excluding breakfast
50
In the communal areas
Gare de Lyon

FAMILIA HÔTEL

Map 284 N9
11 rue des Écoles, 75005
Latin Quarter
Tel 01 43 54 55 27
www.hotel-paris-familia.com

This renovated mid-19th-century mansion makes a comfortable two-star base. There's pretty period-style furniture in the public areas, plus full-length wall frescoes. A Continental breakfast is served downstairs. Rooms, some with balconies, are decorated in French style and come with fridge and hairdryer. There is guarded parking close by at an extra cost.

€99–€129, including breakfast
30
Jussieu

GRAND HÔTEL DES BALCONS

Map 283 M8
3 rue Casimir-Delavigne, 75006
St-Germain-des-Prés
Tel 01 46 34 78 50
www.hotelgrandsbalcons.com

This two-star hotel is close to the Jardin du Luxembourg. Outside, there are flower-filled balconies; inside, the lobby and communal areas have an early 1900s feel, with period

furniture and stained-glass windows. The bright and airy bedrooms have modem connection, cable and satellite TV, a safe and a hairdryer. Breakfast is served in a bistro-style dining room.

€88–€110, excluding breakfast
50
Odéon

GRAND HÔTEL LÉVÊQUE

Map 282 H7
29 rue Cler, 75007
Eiffel Tower
Tel 01 47 05 49 15
www.hotel-leveque.com

The bedrooms at this two-star hotel have a direct line for internet access, satellite TV, safe, fan and hair dryer, and have been soundproofed to avoid disturbance from the lively fruit and vegetable market outside in the pedestrian-only street. Inside, the hotel is simple yet bright, with some nice pictures.

€90–€95, excluding breakfast
50
École-Militaire

HAMEAU DE PASSY

Map 282 off F7
48 rue Passy, 75016
Passy
Tel 01 42 88 47 55
www.paris-hotel-hameaudepassy.com

In a chic residential district, this two-star hotel offers peace and quiet in a leafy cul-de-sac. The modern interior is tasteful and the bedrooms face the garden. They have a direct dial phone with modem connection and cable TV. The hotel has a fax service, individual safes at the reception and a nearby garage.

€132–€193, including breakfast
32
Passy, La Muette

HÔTEL DE L'ABBAYE
ST-GERMAIN

Map 283 L8
10 rue Cassette, 75006
St-Germain-des-Prés
Tel 01 45 44 38 11
www.hotel-abbaye.com

Calm prevails at this three-star hotel, on the site of a former abbey. The salon and most of the rooms look out onto a terrace; four suites have private terraces. The elegant interior has fine furniture and there is an antique fireplace in

L'HÔTEL

Map 283 L7
13 rue des Beaux-Arts, 75006
St-Germain-des-Prés
Tel 01 44 41 99 00
www.l-hotel.com

This deluxe four-star hotel, in a 19th-century pavilion, was fully renovated at the turn of the millennium. The exuberantly elegant interior is by Jacques Garcia and the fully equipped rooms are named after famous

people, such as Marco Polo, Mistinguett and Oscar Wilde (who breathed his last at this hotel in 1900). The restaurant (closed Sunday, Monday and during August) has an impressive dome.

€255–€640, excluding breakfast
16 rooms, 4 suites
Indoor
St-Germain-des-Prés

the salon. The hotel is close to the Jardin du Luxembourg. Facilities include a bar, room service, car rental and laundry service. Bedrooms have hairdryers, WiFi connections, safes and satellite TV.

€232–€251, including breakfast
37 rooms, 7 suites

St-Sulpice, Sèvres-Babylone

HÔTEL ASTRID

Map 282 off G4
27 avenue Carnot, 75017
Champs-Élysées
Tel 01 44 09 26 00
www.hotel-astrid.com

This three-star hotel is in a peaceful side street close to the Champs-Élysées. No two bedrooms are the same—styles include romantic (think brass bedframe, chandelier and pink curtains) and country (pine

furniture contrasting with blue wallpaper). Facilities include a safe, hairdryer, internet connection and cable TV. There are parking spaces nearby.

€140–€154, excluding breakfast
40
Charles de Gaulle-Étoile

HÔTEL ATLANTIS ST-GERMAIN-DES-PRÉS

Map 283 L8
4 rue du Vieux-Colombier, 75006
St-Germain-des-Prés
Tel 01 45 48 31 81

Most of the bright and airy rooms in this two-star hotel

face onto pretty place St-Sulpice. All have been beautifully decorated with soft tones, fine furniture and quilted bedspreads, and have telephone, cable and satellite TV, internet connection and a hairdryer. The communal areas are elegant and there is a grandfather clock in the breakfast room.

€125–€180, excluding breakfast
27
St-Sulpice

HÔTEL DE L'AVRE

Map 282 G9
21 rue de l'Avre, 75015
Champ de Mars
Tel 01 45 75 31 03
www.hoteldelavre.com

Attention has been paid to every detail at this two-star hotel. Bedrooms have a floral design and satellite TV. In spring and summer you can have breakfast in the garden.

€77–€92, excluding breakfast
26
La-Motte-Picquet-Grenelle

HÔTEL DU BOIS

Map 282 G5
11 rue du Dôme, 75016
Champs-Élysées
Tel 01 45 00 31 96
www.hoteldubois.com

The interior of this three-star hotel is reminiscent of an elegant English mansion. There is Georgian furniture and crimson tones in the salon, where breakfast is served, and patterned fabrics in the bedrooms. Facilities include a hairdryer, cable TV, safe and minibar. The hotel is in an elegant district.

€145–€215, excluding breakfast
41
Kléber, Charles de Gaulle-Étoile

HÔTEL LA BOURDONNAIS

Map 282 H7
111–113 avenue de la Bourdonnais, 75007
Tour Eiffel
Tel 01 47 05 45 42
www.hotellabourdonnais.com

This three-star hotel is also home to the restaurant La Cantine des Gourmets, which serves exquisite French cuisine. Inside, the hotel resembles a comfortable bourgeois home, with elegant furniture and antiques. The suites and bedrooms with four beds are perfect for families; all bedrooms have satellite TV, a safe, telephone with modem connection and a hairdryer.

Breakfast is served in a pleasant winter garden.

€170, excluding breakfast
57 rooms, 3 suites
École-Militaire

HÔTEL CLAUDE BERNARD

Map 283 M8
43 rue des Écoles, 75005
Latin Quarter
Tel 01 43 26 32 52
www.paris-hotel-booking.com

This three-star hotel has a flamboyant, red lacquered façade and an elegant interior. Bright tones and flowers create a warm atmosphere and there are fine fabrics and furniture in the bedrooms, which have balconies and cable and

satellite TV. There is a bar, restaurant and internet booth.

€128–€188, excluding breakfast
34
Maubert-Mutualité

HÔTEL DELAMBRE

Map 283 K10
35 rue Delambre, 75014
Montparnasse
Tel 01 43 20 66 31
www.hoteldelambre.com

Close to Tour Montparnasse, this three-star hotel has a beautiful interior, with warm tones, wrought ironwork and period furniture covered in modern fabrics. Bedrooms have a telephone, satellite TV

and a modem connection, safe and laundry service. There are two parking areas nearby.

🛏 €85–€115, excluding breakfast
ⓘ 31
🚇 Vavin, Edgar-Quinet, Montparnasse

HÔTEL DELAVIGNE
Map 283 M8
1 rue Casimir-Delavigne, 75006
St-Germain-des-Prés
Tel 01 43 29 31 50
www.hoteldelavigne.com
The bedrooms in this three-star hotel are individually decorated, using, for example, rattan, antique furniture or floral or brocade wallpaper. They have a phone, satellite TV and safe. There is a babysitting service and WiFi connection. The salon is soberly classical, with period furniture. The hotel is in a great location, near the Jardin du Luxembourg.
🛏 €150–€165, excluding breakfast
ⓘ 34
🚇 Odéon, Cluny

HÔTEL DES DEUX ÎLES
Map 284 N8
59 rue St-Louis en l'Île, 75004
Île St-Louis
Tel 01 43 26 13 35
www.deuxiles-paris-hotel.com
A 17th-century mansion on the picturesque Île St-Louis is home to this three-star hotel. Provençal fabrics and painted rattan furniture enliven the comfortable bedrooms,

which have cable TV and a hairdryer. WiFi connection is available. Paris's most famous ice-cream store, Berthillon, is nearby.
🛏 €170, excluding breakfast
ⓘ 17
🅢
🚇 Pont-Marie, St-Michel

HÔTEL FLOR RIVOLI
Map 283 M7
13 rue des Deux Boules, 75001
Châtelet
Tel 01 42 33 49 60
www.hotel-flor-rivoli.com
This two-star hotel is close to the Musée du Louvre and one of Paris's longest shopping

streets, the rue de Rivoli, which may take your mind off the small size of the bedrooms. It is relatively comfortable and ideal for those on a budget, prepared to sacrifice character for convenience.
🛏 €85, excluding breakfast
ⓘ 20
🚇 Châtelet, Pont Neuf

HÔTEL FRANKLIN ROOSEVELT
Map 282 H5
18 rue Clément Marot, 75008
Champs-Élysées
Tel 01 53 57 49 50
www.hroosevelt.com
This hotel is close to the Champs-Elysées and avenue Montaigne, with its world-famous couture shops. Inside, there is subtle lighting, thick fitted carpets, rich red fabrics and dark wood. If you're looking for a bit of luxury, the suite on the sixth floor has a king-size bed and a Jacuzzi. Facilities include a bar, reading room and winter garden.
🛏 €260–€290, excluding breakfast
ⓘ 48
🅢
🚇 Franklin D. Roosevelt, Alma Marceau

HÔTEL DU GLOBE
Map 283 L8
15 rue des Quatre-Vents, 75006
St-Germain-des-Prés
Tel 01 43 26 35 50
www.hotel-du-globe.fr
A two-star hotel with this much character is hard to find in Paris. There are beamed ceilings and antique furniture in the bedrooms (some even have canopy beds) and 18th-century bergère armchairs and an 18th-century mirror in the salon. Facilities for the 21st century include TV, WiFi connection and phone. The hotel has the added bonus of being convenient for the Jardin du Luxembourg.

HÔTEL DUC DE ST-SIMON
Map 283 K7
14 rue de St-Simon, 75007
Invalides
Tel 01 44 39 20 20
www.hotelducdesaintsimon.com

Antiques and fine furniture decorate this beautiful three-star hotel, in an 18th-century mansion. Although close to the animated boulevard St-Germain, rue de St-Simon is very quiet. The hotel has a bar and terrace, and a garage on boulevard Raspail.
🛏 €220–€280, excluding breakfast
ⓘ 29 rooms, 5 suites
🅢 In some rooms
🚇 Rue-du-Bac

🛏 €150, excluding breakfast
ⓘ 14
🚇 Odéon

HÔTEL DES GRANDES ÉCOLES
Map 284 N9
75 rue du Cardinal Lemoine, 75005
Latin Quarter
Tel 01 43 26 79 23
www.hotel-grandes-ecoles.com
An oasis of peace in the lively Latin Quarter, this gem of a three-star hotel is at the end of a cul-de-sac, with its own garden. It is decorated in

elegant country-house style with wicker chairs and lace tablecloths in the breakfast room and floral wallpaper and quilted bedspreads in the bedrooms. Some rooms sleep up to four people. Hotel facilities include a babysitting

STAYING

service and 15 covered parking spaces. You can take your breakfast in the garden, under one of the trees.

💵 €110–€135, excluding breakfast
🛏 51
🚇 Cardinal-Lemoine, Place Monge

HÔTEL LATOUR-MAUBOURG
Map 282 J7
150 rue de Grenelle, 75007
Latin Quarter
Tel 01 47 05 16 16
www.latourmaubourg.com
Set in an elegant and beautifully renovated Napoleon III-era mansion, the Latour-Maubourg is named after the Marquis de la Tour Maubourg, who commissioned and lived in the building. The 2006 renovation brought 21st-century luxuries, yet the hotel still harks back to the historical heyday in its design features. All rooms are fitted out to a high standard with safe, mini-bar and WiFi access, though they do vary in size. There's a buffet breakfast every morning. The hotel has a garden.

💵 €140–€300, excluding breakfast.
🛏 16
🚫
🚇 Latour Maubourg

HÔTEL LAUTREC OPÉRA
Map 285 M5
8–10 rue d'Amboise, 75002
Opéra
Tel 01 42 96 67 90
www.paris-hotel-lautrec.com
This three-star hotel is named after the celebrated artist Henri Toulouse-Lautrec, who once lived here. It is classified as an historic monument and has a beautiful 18th-century façade. Inside, there's a more contemporary feel, with pale wood furniture and blue and yellow upholstery; some rooms have exposed bricks and beams and all have satellite TV.

💵 €151–€181, excluding breakfast
🛏 60
🚫
🚇 Richelieu-Drouot

HÔTEL LENOX ST-GERMAIN
Map 283 L7
9 rue de l'Université, 75007
St-Germain-des-Prés
Tel 01 42 96 10 95
www.lenoxsaintgermain.com
The Lenox Club Bar at this three-star hotel has comfortable armchairs and

a collection of jazz musical instruments on display. In the hotel itself, the elegant

bedrooms have beautiful wall lamps and pictures, as well as a safe, telephone, modem and satellite TV. There are also some duplex suites. Breakfast is served in a vaulted cellar.

💵 €130–€212, excluding breakfast
🛏 34
🚫
🚇 Rue-du-Bac, St-Germain-des-Prés

HÔTEL DU LEVANT
Map 283 M8
18 rue de la Harpe, 75005
Latin Quarter
Tel 01 46 34 11 00
www.hoteldulevant.com
In the heart of the Latin Quarter, this three-star hotel has been around for more than two hundred years and has been run by the same family for four generations. The decoration is bright and modern, though the salon contains some antiques, together with chessboards and newspapers. The bedrooms have cable TV and internet connections, and there is a laundry service.

💵 €118–€160, excluding breakfast
🛏 43 rooms, 4 suites
🚫
🚇 Cluny–La Sorbonne, St-Michel

HÔTEL DE LONDRES EIFFEL
Map 282 H7
1 rue Augereau, 75007
Eiffel Tower
Tel 01 45 51 63 02
www.londres-eiffel.com

Comfort is a priority at this three-star hotel, with soft armchairs in the salon and king-size beds in the bedrooms. Warm yellow and raspberry tones predominate in the classically decorated interior.

💵 €165–€185, excluding breakfast
🛏 30
🚫
🚇 École-Militaire

HÔTEL LOUVRE RIVOLI
Map 283 M7
7 rue Jean Lantier, 75001
Châtelet
Tel 01 42 33 45 38
www.paris-hotel-rivoli.com
This three-star hotel, within walking distance of the Louvre, Notre-Dame and Centre Georges Pompidou, has a welcoming salon, a winter

garden with a fountain, and a 16th-century vaulted breakfast room.

💵 €150–€180, excluding breakfast
🛏 30
🚇 Châtelet

HÔTEL MADISON
Map 283 L8
143 boulevard St-Germain, 75006
St-Germain-des-Prés
Tel 01 40 51 60 00
www.hotel-madison.com
Albert Camus finished writing his famous novel L'Étranger

(The Outsider; 1942) at this elegant three-star hotel. The celebrated café, Les Deux-Magots is opposite. The hotel has a beautiful 18th-century style salon with bergère armchairs, tapestries and wood panels, while the bedrooms have antique furniture, satellite TV, minibar, safe and hairdryer.

🛏 €203–€370, including breakfast
ⓘ 53 rooms, one suite
🅢
Ⓜ St-Germain-des-Prés

HÔTEL DE NEUVILLE
Map 282 off G4
3 rue Verniquet, 75017
Wagram
Tel 01 43 80 26 30
www.paris-hotel-neuville.com
This three-star hotel is in a 19th-century building with a pretty terrace. The bedrooms have been carefully decorated in a contemporary style, while retaining a romantic feel. Some have canopy beds and all have cable TV and internet connection. Try to get a room with a view of Sacré-Cœur. You can park your car in the hotel's garage, although check before you arrive that there is space.

🛏 €210, including breakfast
ⓘ 28
🅢
Ⓔ RER-metro Pereire

HÔTEL DU PANTHÉON
Map 283 M9
19 place du Panthéon, 75005
Latin Quarter
Tel 01 43 54 32 95
www.hoteldupantheon.com
The interior of this three-star hotel has an 18th-century feel, with gilded panels and fine fabrics. Most of the rooms look out onto the stately Panthéon, and have cable TV and a minibar. There is a laundry service and parking.

🛏 €90–€235, excluding breakfast
ⓘ 36
🅢
Ⓜ Cardinal Lemoine

HÔTEL LA PERLE
Map 283 L8
14 rue des Canettes, 75006
St-Germain-des-Prés
Tel 01 43 29 10 10
www.hotellaperle.com
This smart three-star hotel, in a picturesque street near place St-Sulpice, is in a 17th-century mansion with its own courtyard. Bright tones add a contemporary note to the otherwise classic interior, which has fleur de lys carpets and beamed ceilings. Facilities include internet connection, cable and satellite TV and a laundry service.

🛏 €160–€230 excluding breakfast
ⓘ 38
🅢
Ⓜ St-Germain-des-Prés, St-Sulpice, Mabillon

HÔTEL PRIMA LEPIC
Map 285 L3
29 rue Lepic, 75018
Montmartre
Tel 01 46 06 44 64
www.hotel-paris-lepic.com

This two-star hotel is close to Sacré-Cœur and place du Tertre and was renovated in 2001. The brightly painted bedrooms have been carefully furnished, five with canopy beds. Each has a TV, hairdryer and modem connection. The hotel has three suites that can each sleep up to four people.

🛏 €125–€150, excluding breakfast
ⓘ 35 rooms, 3 suites
Ⓜ Blanche, Abbesses

HÔTEL QUEEN MARY
Map 283 K5
9 rue Greffulhe, 75008
Opéra
Tel 01 42 66 40 50
www.hotelqueenmary.com
Elegance is the hallmark of this three-star hotel, near the Opéra Palais Garnier. The salon has moulded ceilings and printed fitted carpets, while the large dining room has a tromp-l'oeil painting. The spacious bedrooms are decorated with mahogany wood and burgundy fabrics. There's a small terrace and the usual facilities of cable TV, WiFi

connection, safe, hairdryer and minibar in the bedrooms.

🛏 €175–€217, excluding breakfast
ⓘ 35 rooms, 1 suite
🅢
Ⓜ Madeleine, Havre-Caumartin

HOTEL RESIDENCE FOCH
Map 282 off G5
10 rue Marbeau, 75116
Champs-Élysées
Tel 01 45 00 46 50
www.foch-paris-hotel.com
A charming three-star residence with well furnished rooms filled with good quality furniture and traditional French touches. There's a bright bar on the ground floor of this elegant town house and the hotel benefits from a private courtyard garden where you can relax over breakfast or a drink.

🛏 €150–€250, excluding breakfast
ⓘ 25
🅢
Ⓜ Porte Dauphine

HÔTEL DE ST-GERMAIN
Map 283 L8
50 rue du Four, 75006
St-Germain-des-Prés
Tel 01 45 48 91 64
www.hotel-de-saint-germain.fr
This two-star hotel's main selling point is its location, near the picturesque place St-Sulpice. The bedrooms are tiny but nicely decorated, with painted wooden furniture. Facilities include nearby parking and a laundry service.

🛏 €150, excluding breakfast
ⓘ 30
Ⓜ St-Sulpice, Sèvres-Babylone

HÔTEL ST-MERRY
Map 284 N7
78 rue de la Verrerie, 75004
Le Marais
Tel 01 42 78 14 15
www.hotelmarais.com
If you choose room nine of this three-star hotel you'll be sleeping under a flying buttress! The hotel was built during the Renaissance as the presbytery of the church of St-Merri. Its highly original interior also has many late-Gothic features, including sculptures, carved woodwork and beamed ceilings.

🛏 €160–€230, excluding breakfast
ⓘ 11 rooms, 1 suite
Ⓜ Hôtel-de-Ville, Châtelet

STAYING

HÔTEL ST-PAUL LE MARAIS

Map 284 P7
8 rue de Sévigné, 75004
Le Marais
Tel 01 48 04 97 27
www.hotel-paris-marais.com

A former 17th-century convent houses this three-star hotel, near the Musée Carnavalet. The bar and salon have burgundy carpets and plenty of mahogany. Bedrooms have cable TV, telephone and tea- and coffee-making facilities, and breakfast is served in a fine stone-vaulted room.

€165–€253, excluding breakfast
27
St-Paul

HÔTEL SUNNY

Map 283 off M10
48 boulevard du Port-Royal, 75005
Latin Quarter
Tel 01 43 31 79 86
www.hotelsunny.com

Pastel tones predominate in the neat bedrooms of this two-star hotel. Facilities include satellite TV, hairdryers and a laundry service.

€79–€85 excluding breakfast
37
Place Monge

HOTEL TILSITT

Map 282 off G4
23 rue Brey, 75017
Champs-Élysées
Tel 01 43 80 39 71
www.tilsitt.com

This three-star hotel is a great find in its price bracket. Set close to the Arc de Triomphe, the location is good and the decor is a melange of sleek minimalist Scandinavian style combined with a touch of classical Greek, set inside the Gallic structure. The furnishings have a luxurious feel, though the rooms can be compact. Each has a wide-screen TV, safe, mini-bar and wi-fi access. The lounge bar opens 24 hours and there's parking (extra cost).

€145–€185, excluding breakfast
38
Charles de Gaulle-Étoile; RER: Charles de Gaulle-Étoile

HÔTEL SQUARE

Map 282 off F7
3 rue de Boulainvilliers, 75016
Passy
Tel 01 44 14 91 90
www.hotelsquare.com

This four-star hotel close to the banks of the Seine is part of a larger complex including a conference room, a relaxing reading room and a restaurant, the Zebra Square. There's also a lounge bar with music most evenings and an art gallery with contemporary work. Sleek lines, subtle lighting, designer furniture and ethnic objets d'art create a warm, contemporary atmosphere.

€300–€380, excluding breakfast
22
Indoor
RER Kennedy-Radio-France

HOTEL VALADON

Map 282 H7
16 rue Valadon, 75007
Invalides
Tel 01 47 53 89 85
www.hotelvaladon.com

A family-owned small 2-star hotel close to the Eiffel Tower that offers simple but contemporarily furnished rooms at affordable prices. The Valadon has a communal fridge and dining room where guests can enjoy self-prepared picnic meals or take-outs. There's also a cosy conservatory.

€125–€155, including breakfast
12
École Militaire

HÔTEL WASHINGTON OPÉRA

Map 283 L6
50 rue de Richelieu, 75001
Palais Royal
Tel 01 42 96 68 06
www.hotelwashingtonopera.com

Madame de Pompadour, mistress of Louis XV, once lived here. Her home is now a lavish four-star hotel. The bedrooms have *Directoire*-style furniture and marble bathrooms; some have canopy beds.

€215–€275, excluding breakfast
35 rooms, 3 suites

Palais-Royal/Musée-du-Louvre

MINERVE HÔTEL

Map 284 N9
13 rue des Écoles, 75005
Latin Quarter
Tel 01 43 26 26 04
www.hotel-paris-minerve.com

Fine materials have been used throughout this three-star hotel to create an elegant but friendly atmosphere. Some of the bedrooms have balconies and all have satellite TV. Modern, sepia frescos depict various places in France. There is private supervised parking nearby (paying service.)

€102–€154, excluding breakfast
54 (in two buildings)

Cardinal Lemoine, Jussieu

RELAIS BOSQUET

Map 282 H7
19 rue du Champ de Mars, 75007
Eiffel Tower
Tel 01 47 05 25 45
www.relaisbosquet.com

Space, elegance and comfort characterize this three-star hotel, close to the Invalides and a 10-minute walk from the Eiffel Tower. Directoire-style furniture and soft hues set the tone. The bedrooms have cable TV, a phone, safe and minibar, as well as an iron and ironing board. The breakfast room looks out onto a pleasant terrace filled with flowers.

€160–€185, excluding breakfast
40

École-Militaire

STAYING

PAVILLON DE LA REINE
Map 284 P7
28 place des Vosges, 75003
Le Marais
Tel 01 40 29 19 19
www.pavillon-de-la-reine.com

It would be hard to find a more perfect setting for a four-star hotel than this 17th-century building on the historic place des Vosges. This was the residence of Anne of Austria, Louis XIII's wife, and the exquisite interior retains

much of its period furniture, with a particularly imposing fireplace in the salon. The vaulted cellar, where you can have breakfast, has tapestries on the walls. Bedrooms have cable TV, and some have canopy beds. A more recently constructed building houses some of the bedrooms.

💶 €360–€440, excluding breakfast
🛏 34 rooms, 14 suites, 10 duplex
🚭
🚇 Bastille, St-Paul

RELAIS ST-JACQUES
Map 283 M9
3 rue de l'Abbé-de-l'Epée, 75005
Latin Quarter
Tel 01 53 73 26 00
www.relais-saint-jacques.com

This building was a stopover for pilgrims on the route to Santiago de Compostela, in northwest Spain. It's now a stylish four-star hotel with a 1920s-style bar and a Louis XV-style salon. The bedrooms are bright, airy and

SPECIAL
RITZ
Map 283 L5
15 place Vendôme, 75001
Opéra
Tel 01 43 16 30 30
www.ritzparis.com

This world-famous hotel has been the epitome of elegance and luxury since it opened in 1898. Coco Chanel, Ernest Hemingway and Marcel Proust were regular guests here. The lavish interior is decorated with antiques and

chandeliers. The hotel has a club, several restaurants, bars and private salons, conference rooms and the gourmet cookery school, Ritz-Escoffier.

💶 €710–€810, excluding breakfast
🛏 135 rooms, 40 suites
🚭 💳 🎾
🚇 Tuileries, Pyramides, Madeleine, Concorde

comfortable with 18th-century furniture. Some have views of the nearby Panthéon, while others have a Jacuzzi in the bathroom. WiFi connection is available in the bedrooms and the lounge. Courtesy transportation to the airport is provided.

💶 €200–€255, excluding breakfast
🛏 21 rooms, 1 suite
🚭
🚆 RER Luxembourg

LES RIVES DE NOTRE-DAME
Map 283 M8
15 quai St-Michel, 75005
Latin Quarter
Tel 01 43 54 81 16
www.rivesdenotredame.com

This four-star hotel, housed in a small 16th-century building, overlooks the Seine and has wonderful views of the Île de la Cité. Beamed ceilings, marble tiling, tapestries and fine wrought-iron furniture are reminiscent of a Provençal or Tuscan villa. The bedrooms are large and

---

SPECIAL
TERRASS HOTEL
Map 285 L3
12 rue Joseph de Maistre, 75018
Montmartre
Tel 01 46 06 72 85
www.terrass-hotel.com

The terrace of this four-star hotel has wonderful views, as do bedrooms on the fourth floor and above. The classical decoration in the bedrooms is warmed up with blue and yellow Provençal fabrics. The hotel has its own bar and restaurant.

💶 €260–€325, excluding breakfast
🛏 88 rooms, 13 suites (2 non-smoking floors)
🚭
🚇 Place-de-Clichy, Blanche

two of them have sofas which can be converted into extra beds for children under 12 at no extra cost.

💶 €245–€290, excluding breakfast
🛏 9 rooms, 1 suite
🚭
🚇 St-Michel

STAYING

HOTEL CHAINS

Name of Hotel Chain	Description	Number of Hotels in Paris	Telephone Numbers and Websites
Best Western	The world's largest hotel group has hotels across the city. Each shares the branding but has its own individual style.	70	0800 393 130 (UK) 1-800/780-7234 (US) 0800 904 490 (France) www.bestwestern.com
Campanile	This chain of hotels with restaurants has nearly 500 establishments across France.	6	0825 003 003 (France) www.campanile.fr
Châteaux & Hotels de France	An affiliation of hotels and chateaux providing luxury places to stay.	21	0892 230 075 (France) www.chateauxhotels.com
Comfort Inn	This leading limited-service hotel chain claims 'luxury on a budget'.	21	0800 444 444 (UK) 1-877/424-6423 (US) 0800 912 424 (France) www.comfortinn.com
Ibis	Hotels in this budget chain usually have a restaurant, bar and 24-hour reception.	51	0870 609 0961 (UK) 0892 686 686 (France) www.ibishotel.com
Intercontinental/ Holiday Inn	The Intercontinental group includes Holiday Inn and Holiday Inn Express.	27	0800 405 060 (UK) 1-800/465-4329 (US) 0800 905 999 (France) www.ichotelsgroup.com
Kyriad	Comfortable, reasonably priced hotels.	12	0825 003 003 (France) www.kyriad.com
Marriott	The Marriotts in and around Paris include two four-star hotels, a five-star hotel and one near Roissy–Charles de Gaulle airport.	8	0800 221 222 (UK) 1-888/236-2427 (US) 0800 908 333 (France) www.marriott.com
Mercure	Choose from three grades—simple, enhanced comfort and refined.	44	0870 609 0965 (UK) 1-800/221-4542 (US) 0825 883 333 (France) www.mercure.com
Novotel	Comfortable hotels, usually with good-sized bedrooms.	15	0870 609 0962 (UK) 1-800/NOVOTEL (US) 0825 012 011 (France) www.novotel.com
Radisson	There is a Radisson at Roissy–Charles de Gaulle airport and another, with its classic Haussmann façade, on the Champs-Élysées.	4	0800 374 411 (UK) 1-888/201-1718 (US) 0800 916 060 (France) www.radisson.com
Relais & Châteaux	An affiliation of luxury hotels and chateaux.	2	0825 323 232 (France) www.relaischateaux.fr
Relais du Silence	This is an affiliation of peaceful hotels with character and good food.	1	01 44 49 90 00 (France) www.silencehotel.com
Sofitel	Comfortable hotels with restaurants.	12	0870 609 0964 (UK) 1-800/SOFITEL (US) 0825 012 011 (France) www.sofitel.com

STAYING

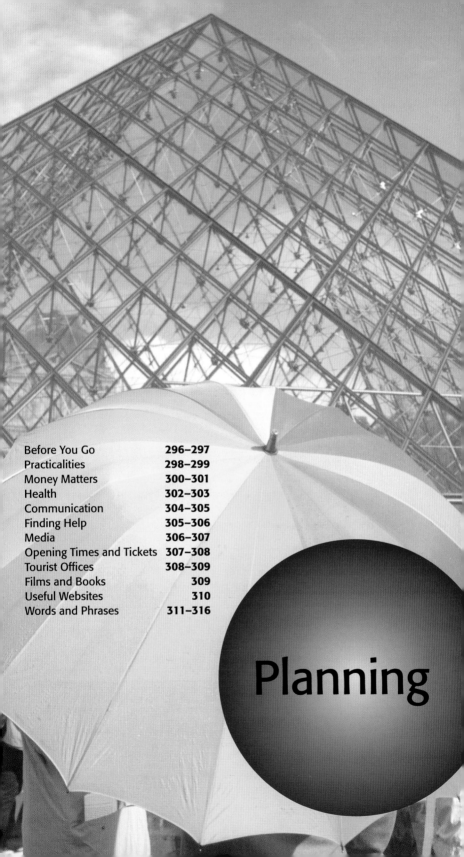

Planning

BEFORE YOU GO

CLIMATE

- Paris's climate is generally not subject to extremes. Winters are cool, but rarely bitterly cold, while summers are warm, but not rain-free. Although the city has a reasonably low rainfall overall, be prepared for showers.
- The cliché of 'Paris in the spring' does not usually apply until well into May, when the weather finally warms up.
- Summer (June to the end of August) can be glorious. The longest days are in June and July, when you're likely to enjoy the most sunshine and comfortable

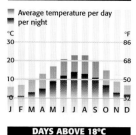

AVERAGE TEMPERATURES

Average temperature per day
per night

DAYS ABOVE 18°C

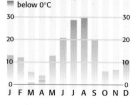

Average no. of days above 18°C
below 0°C

RAINFALL

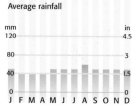

Average rainfall

temperatures. August can be hot, oppressive and stormy—Parisians who haven't fled the city tend to head down to the *quais* beside the Seine for a fresher breeze.
- If you are lucky, you'll have crisp, sunny days in autumn (September to November).
- Snow is rare in winter.

WHEN TO GO

- Spring is a pleasant time to visit Paris, when the chestnut trees are in blossom and the weather is warming up.
- If you choose hot and sunny July you'll be battling with many other visitors, but time it right and you'll experience the Bastille Day celebrations (14 July). August is quieter, as many Parisians flee to other parts of France to escape the oppressive heat. Some restaurants close for the whole month and there are fewer cultural activities.
- The weather can be pleasant in autumn but hotel rooms are harder to find as the trade fair season is in full swing. If you don't mind the cooler winter weather, December can be a magical time, with the streets sparkling with Christmas lights.
- Most monuments and museums close on 1 January, 1 May, 1 November, 11 November and 25 December. There are fewer buses, trains and Métro services on France's national holidays (▷ 305–306), so try to avoid arriving on those dates.

WHAT TO TAKE

- The key things to remember are your passport, travel documents, money, credit cards and any medication you need. You'll also need your driving licence if you plan to rent a car while in France, and car registration and insurance

TIME ZONES

CITY	TIME DIFFERENCE	TIME AT 12 NOON IN FRANCE
Amsterdam	0	12 noon
Berlin	0	12 noon
Brussels	0	12 noon
Chicago	-7	5am
Dublin	-1	11am
Johannesburg	+1*	1pm
London	-1	11am
Madrid	0	12 noon
Montréal	-6	6am
New York	-6	6am
Perth, Australia	+7*	7pm
Rome	0	12 noon
San Francisco	-9	3am
Sydney	+9*	9pm
Tokyo	+8*	8pm

Clocks in France go forward one hour on the last Sunday in March, until the last Sunday in October.
* One hour less during French Summer Time.

documents if you are taking your own car (▷ 60–61). Apart from these essentials, there are very few things you can't buy in Paris.
- Take clothing for a range of weather conditions, even in summer. Make sure you have suitable walking shoes, an umbrella, a raincoat and sunglasses (in spring/summer). In summer you'll also need sunscreen. You may like to take some smarter clothes for going out in the evening.
- A small rucksack or shoulder bag is useful for sightseeing. But bear in mind that these are potential goldmines to pickpockets, so keep your money tucked away safely and keep an eye on your bag when you're in restaurants and other crowded places (see Finding Help, ▷ 305–306).
- Take the addresses and phone numbers of emergency contacts,

PLANNING

WEATHER WEBSITES AND TELEPHONE NUMBERS			
ORGANIZATION	TELEPHONE	NOTES	WEBSITE
Météo France	0892 680 275, €0.34 per minute (within France)	Forecasts for Paris and the rest of France	www.meteofrance.com
The Met Office (UK)	0870 900 0100, £0.60 per minute (within UK)	Five-day forecasts for Paris, as well as information about the UV index	www.metoffice.gov.uk
Paris Tourist Office		Provides a link to the Météo France website, as well as information on air quality in Paris	www.parisinfo.com
Weather Channel (US)		Links to Paris forecasts from the website of the US-based Weather Channel	www.weather.com

including the numbers to call if your credit cards are stolen.
● It is wise to take photocopies of your passport, tickets and insurance documents and keep them separately from the originals, in case of loss. Keep a separate note of your credit card numbers.
● There is a language guide in this book (▷ 311–316), but if you are keen to communicate in French you may find a separate phrase book helpful.
● A first-aid kit is a good precaution. Useful items include antiseptic cream, sticking plasters, painkillers and diarrhoea medicine.
● If you wear glasses, take a spare pair, in case of any damage, or your prescription so you can buy a replacement pair.
● There are English-language bookshops in Paris but it is generally less expensive to bring your own books.
● Camera film is widely available, but it is easier to take at least one film with you.

PASSPORTS AND VISAS
● UK, US and Canadian visitors need a passport, but not a visa, for stays of up to three months. You should have at least six months' validity remaining on your passport. Citizens of other countries should check with their nearest French embassy or visit the official EU portel www. europa.eu.int for information on the documentation required.
● For more information about visa and passport requirements, look up the website of the **French tourist office** (www.franceguide.com) or the

CUSTOMS
From another EU country
Below are the guidelines for the quantity of goods you can bring to France from another EU country, for personal use:

• 800 cigarettes; or	• 110 litres of beer
• 400 cigarillos; or	• 10 litres of spirits
• 200 cigars; or	• 90 litres of wine
• 1kg of tobacco	(of which only 60 litres can be sparkling wine)
	• 20 litres of fortified wine (such as port or sherry)

From a country outside the EU
You are entitled to the allowances shown below only if you travel with the goods and do not plan to sell them.

• 200 cigarettes; or	• 2 litres of wine
• 100 cigarillos; or	• 1 litre of spirits or strong liqueurs over 22% volume; or
• 50 cigars; or	• 2 litres of fortified wine, sparkling wine or other liqueurs
• 250g of tobacco	
• 50g of perfume	
• 250cc/ml of eau de toilette	• Up to €175 of all other goods

French Embassy (www.ambafrance-uk.org or www.consulfrance-newyork.org).
● While in Paris, carry a photocopy of the relevant pages of your passport, so you can leave the actual passport in your hotel safe. Always keep a separate note of your passport number in case of loss or theft.
● Passport and visa rules can change at short notice so check before booking your visit.

LONGER STAYS
● UK and other EU citizens wishing to stay longer than three months should apply for a *Carte de Séjour* from the Préfecture de

Police. US and Canadian visitors need a *Carte de Séjour* and visa.
● For more information call the Immigration Department of the French Consulate in London (tel 020 7073 1248), in the US (tel 212/606 3600) or Canada (tel 514/878 4385).

TRAVEL INSURANCE
● Make sure you have full health and travel insurance.
● EU nationals receive reduced-cost health treatment with a European Health Insurance Card, but full insurance is still advised. For everyone else, full insurance is a necessity. Check your insurer has a 24-hour helpline.

FRENCH EMBASSIES AND CONSULATES ABROAD		
COUNTRY	**ADDRESS**	**WEBSITE**
Australia	31 Market Street, St. Martin's Tower, Level 26, Sydney, NSW 2000 Tel (02) 92 68 24 00	www.ambafrance-au.org
Canada	42 Sussex Drive, Ottawa, Ontario, K1M 2C9 Tel 613 789 1795	www.ambafrance-ca.org
Germany	Pariser Platz 5, 10117 Berlin. Tel 590 03 90 00	www.botschaft-frankreich.de
Ireland	36 Ailesbury Road, Ballsbridge, Dublin 4. Tel 01 277 5000	www.ambafrance-ie.org
Italy	Vía Giulia 251, 00186 Rome. Tel 06 68 60 11	www.ambafrance-it.org/consulat/rome
New Zealand	34–42 Manners Street, Wellington, 13th floor, PO BOX 11-343 Tel 644 384 25 55	www.ambafrance-nz.org
South Africa	3rd floor, Standard Bank Building, 191 Jan Smuts Avenue, 7th Avenue Parktown North 2196. Tel 011 778 56 00	www.consulfrance-jhb.org
Spain	Calle Marqués de la Ensenada 10, 28004 Madrid. Tel 91 700 78 00	www.ambafrance-es.org
UK	21 Cromwell Road, London, SW7 2EN. Tel: 020 7073 1200	www.frenchembassy.org.uk
USA (Los Angeles)	10390 Santa Monica Boulevard, Suite 410 & 115, Los Angeles, CA 90025. Tel 310/235-3200	www.consulfrance-losangeles.org
USA (New York)	934 Fifth Avenue, New York, NY 10021. Tel 212/606-3600	www.consulfrance-newyork.org

PLANNING

PRACTICALITIES

ELECTRICITY
- Voltage in France is 220 volts. Sockets take plugs with two round pins. UK equipment will need an adaptor plug, which you can buy at airports and the Eurostar terminal, as well as *droguerie* stores.
- American appliances using 110–120 volts will need an adaptor and a transformer. Dual voltage equipment should need only an adaptor.

LAUNDRY
- There are two options if you need a laundry service—a *laverie automatique* (laundrette) and a *pressing* (dry-cleaners).
- Dry-cleaners are more easily found but are also more expensive. Some have an economy service, but this is not recommended for your best silk jacket.

TOILETS
- Every café has toilets, although they are for customers only so you'll need to buy at least a drink. Some are coin-operated. Standards range from smelly to pristine, and you'll occasionally come across the old-fashioned squatter-style toilets.
- It's useful to have some tissues with you, in case there's no paper. In some stores and museums you'll need to tip the attendant before using the toilets so keep some change handy.
- Ask for *les toilettes* rather than *la toilette* (*la toilette* is what you do when you get washed and dressed in the morning). You can also use *WC*, pronounced *vay, say*.
- Coin-operated public toilets can be found all over Paris and are usually well maintained, with automatic flushing and disinfecting.

MEASUREMENTS
- France uses the metric system. Road distances are measured in kilometres, fuel is sold by the litre and food is weighed in grams and kilograms.

SMOKING
- Smoking is banned in all public places.
- By law restaurants and cafés

CONVERSION CHART		
FROM	TO	MULTIPLY BY
Inches	Centimetres	2.54
Centimetres	Inches	0.3937
Feet	Metres	0.3048
Metres	Feet	3.2810
Yards	Metres	0.9144
Metres	Yards	1.0940
Miles	Kilometres	1.6090
Kilometres	Miles	0.6214
Acres	Hectares	0.4047
Hectares	Acres	2.4710
Gallons	Litres	4.5460
Litres	Gallons	0.2200
Ounces	Grams	28.35
Grams	Ounces	0.0353
Pounds	Grams	453.6
Grams	Pounds	0.0022
Pounds	Kilograms	0.4536
Kilograms	Pounds	2.205
Tons	Tonnes	1.0160
Tonnes	Tons	0.9842

should provide a non-smoking section. Some taxis display a no-smoking sign.

CHILDREN
- At first glance, Paris is not a children's city, with its heavy emphasis on art and culture and its manic traffic. But there are plenty of attractions specifically aimed at younger visitors (▷ 221) and many adult-focused museums offer children's worksheets and workshops. Entrance to museums is often free to children.
- Squares and parks have slides and sandpits, and river trips are also a popular option. You can catch a puppet show in some of the larger parks (including the Jardin du Luxembourg) on Wednesday, Saturday and Sunday afternoons.
- Restaurants do not generally turn up their noses at the sight of a pushchair (stroller), although it is probably best to aim for family-style bistros where staff are usually more helpful. Chain restaurants (such as Bistro Romain and Hippopotamus) usually have a good-value children's menu, as do many other places.
- July and August are good times to try to get special family deals at hotels, as this is when they are less likely to be booked by people on business travel.

CLOTHING SIZES
The chart below indicates how European clothing sizes compare with those in the UK and US

UK	Metric	USA	
36	46	36	SUITS
38	48	38	
40	50	40	
42	52	42	
44	54	44	
46	56	46	
48	58	48	
7	41	8	SHOES
7.5	42	8.5	
8.5	43	9.5	
9.5	44	10.5	
10.5	45	11.5	
11	46	12	
14.5	37	14.5	SHIRTS
15	38	15	
15.5	39/40	15.5	
16	41	16	
16.5	42	16.5	
17	43	17	
8	36	6	DRESSES
10	38	8	
12	40	10	
14	42	12	
16	44	14	
18	46	16	
20	46	18	
4.5	37.5	6	SHOES
5	38	6.5	
5.5	38.5	7	
6	39	7.5	
6.5	40	8	
7	41	8.5	

If you need special facilities, reserve ahead.
- On the Métro and most buses, children under four travel free and children between the ages of four and nine can use half-price tickets. But bear in mind that the crowded trains can be unpleasant for children and that manoeuvring pushchairs (strollers) up and down the countless stairs en route to the platforms is not easy.
- Inter-Service Parents is a free telephone advisory service that provides information (in French only) on babysitting agencies and children's activities, among other things (tel 01 44 93 44 88; www.epe-idf.com; open 9.30–12.30, 1.30–5). Alternatively, you can try Baby

PLANNING

Sitting Services (tel 01 46 21 33 16; www.babysitting services.com).

● If you need baby-changing facilities, try the restrooms in department stores and the larger museums. You can buy baby food and other items in supermarkets and pharmacies.

VISITORS WITH DISABILITIES

● Although Paris is not an ideal city for people with special needs, modern or refurbished hotels (space providing) offer specially adapted facilities. Major museums and sights generally have good access and staff available to assist. Information is available on their websites.

● *Access in Paris* is a comprehensive guidebook. It covers accommodation and access to major sights. See www.accessinparis.org. A new edition is due to be published early in 2006. Another useful website is www.access-able.com.

● Mobile en Ville (tel 06 82 91 72 16; www.mobile-en-ville.asso.fr) provides information for wheelchair-users and organizes social events and rides through Paris.

CAR RENTAL

● Driving in Paris is not recommended (▷ 60–61), but you may like to rent a car if you are venturing farther afield. It is a good idea to book in advance, especially if you want an automatic transmission car. Make sure full insurance is included in the package. You can also arrange car rental through some travel

agents when you book your travel arrangements.

● Chauffeur-driven cars include Prestige Limousines (165 rue de la Procession, 75015; tel 01 40 43 92 92; www.prestige-limousines.fr).

LOCAL WAYS

● Greetings are often more formal in France, especially when they are written rather than spoken. Always offer to shake hands when you meet someone, and use *vous* rather than *tu* when addressing them.

● It is polite to use *Monsieur*, *Madame* or *Mademoiselle* when speaking to people you don't know, although think carefully about whether to choose *Madame* or *Mademoiselle* for a woman.

● The 'Continental kiss' may seem strange, but it is a common form of greeting among friends. Members of the opposite sex kiss each other once on each cheek, though suburbanites and people from the provinces go through this procedure two or three times.

● Communicating in French is always the best option, even if you can manage only *bonjour*, *s'il vous plaît* and *merci*. The French are very protective about their language and the visitor

Blue sky and a rainbow umbrella, at the Louvre Pyramid

who speaks loud English is much less welcome than the one who squeaks out *s'il vous plaît*, however poorly pronounced. If you can't understand the French reply, respond with *Parlez-vous anglais?* and hope the answer is *oui*.

● Churches require visitors to wear suitably modest clothes and some prefer you not to wander around during services. Don't take any photos inside without checking it is permitted.

● Waiters should be addressed as *Monsieur*, *Madame* or *Mademoiselle* when you are trying to attract their attention. Never use *garçon*.

CAR RENTAL COMPANIES INCLUDE:			
NAME	**ADDRESS**	**TELEPHONE**	**WEBSITE**
Ada	Central Booking	0825 169 600	www.ada.fr
Avis	5 rue Bixio, 75007	0820 05 05 05	www.avis.fr
Citer	42 cours de Vincennes, 75012	01 44 73 07 41	www.citer.fr
Europcar	Central booking	0825 358 358	www.europcar.fr
Hertz	Central booking	0825 86 18 61	www.hertz.fr
Rent-a-Car	79 rue de Bercy, 75012	01 43 45 98 99	www.rentacar.fr

PLACES OF WORSHIP

Whatever your religion, you should be able to find the appropriate church, temple, mosque or synagogue in Paris, although Catholics obviously get the biggest choice.

Catholic	Every *arrondissement* has at least four or five Catholic churches (▷ 161–163 for details of some). There are daily services at Notre-Dame (▷ 137–141) and Sacré-Cœur (▷ 154–157).
Jewish	Synagogue: 10 rue Pavée, 75004; tel 01 42 77 81 51. Métro: St-Paul.
Muslim	Mosquée: place du Puits-de-l'Ermite, 75005; tel 01 45 35 97 33. Métro: Jussieu, Place Monge, Censier-Daubenton.
Protestant	American Cathedral: 23 avenue George V, 75008; tel 01 53 23 84 00. Métro: Alma-Marceau.
	American Church: 65 quai d'Orsay, 75007; tel 01 40 62 05 00. Métro: Invalides.
	Church of Scotland: 17 rue Bayard, 75008; tel 01 48 78 47 94. Métro: Franklin D. Roosevelt.
	St-George's English Church: 7 rue Auguste Vacquerie, 75016; tel 01 47 20 22 51. Métro: Charles de Gaulle-Étoile.
	St-Michael's Church of England: 5 rue d'Aguesseau, 75008; tel 01 47 42 70 88. Métro: Madeleine.
Russian Orthodox	St-Alexandre de la Néva: 12 rue Daru, 75008; tel 01 42 27 37 34. Métro: Courcelles.

PLANNING

MONEY MATTERS

France is one of 15 European countries that have adopted the euro as their official currency. Euro notes and coins were introduced in January 2002, replacing the franc.

BEFORE YOU GO
● It is advisable to use a mixture of cash, traveller's cheques, ATM/debit cards and credit cards, rather than relying on one means of payment during your trip.
● Check that your credit or debit card can be used to withdraw cash from ATMs in France. Also check what fee will be charged.
● Traveller's cheques are a safer way of bringing in money as you can claim a refund if they are stolen—but commission can be high when you cash them.

CREDIT CARDS
Most restaurants, shops and hotels in Paris accept credit cards, but some have a minimum spending limit.

ATMS
The city has plenty of ATMs, with instructions often given in a choice of languages. Most accept MasterCard, Visa and Diners Club. You'll need a four-digit PIN.

BANKS
Most banks in Paris are open Monday to Friday 10–5, but close at noon the day before a public holiday. Only banks with *change* signs change traveller's cheques or foreign currency. You'll need to take your passport.

BUREAUX DE CHANGE
● Bureaux de change have longer opening hours than banks, but exchange rates can be worse.

● You'll find them across the city, including at train stations, airports and some department stores.
● Avoid changing large amounts of traveller's cheques at hotels, where the rates may not be competitive.

WIRING MONEY
● In an emergency money can be wired from your home country, but this can be time-consuming and expensive, as agents charge a fee.

BANKNOTES AND COINS

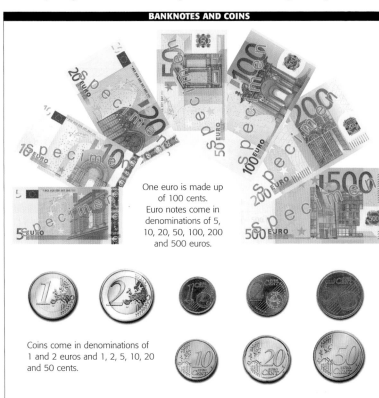

One euro is made up of 100 cents. Euro notes come in denominations of 5, 10, 20, 50, 100, 200 and 500 euros.

Coins come in denominations of 1 and 2 euros and 1, 2, 5, 10, 20 and 50 cents.

PLANNING

FOREIGN BANKS		
NAME	ADDRESS	TELEPHONE
American Express	11 rue Scribe, 75009	01 47 77 70 00
Bank of Scotland	21 rue Balzac, 75008	01 56 90 71 50
Barclays	21 boulevard de la Madeleine, 75001	01 44 58 32 32
Citibank	125 avenue des Champs-Élysées, 75008	01 53 23 33 60

ATMs often give instructions in a choice of languages

● Money can be wired from bank to bank, taking up to two working days. It is usually faster to use Travelex (www.travelex.fr) or Western Union (www.westernunion.com).
● Post offices also wire money (see Post Offices, right).

24-HOUR EXCHANGE SERVICES
● The Champs-Élysées has a 24-hour bureau de change: Bureau de change, Chèquepoint, 150 avenue des Champs-Elysées, 75008. Tel 01 42 56 48 63.
● Roissy-Charles de Gaulle and Orly airports also have exchange services, generally open between 7am and 11.30pm.

REDUCED-PRICE TICKETS
● Students and teachers should contact the International Student Travel Confederation (www.isic.org) in their own country for information about the benefits available.
● Senior citizens may get reductions on transportation and admission to museums by showing a passport.
● For more information about reductions on the entry price for museums and other attractions, see Tickets, ▷ 307.

TAXES
● Non-EU residents can claim a VAT refund (*détaxe*) of 12 per cent on certain purchases, although you must have spent more than €175 in one shop, at one time.

● Ask the store for the relevant forms, which should be completed and stamped by the trader.
● Present the forms to Customs when you leave France, along with the receipts, and they will be stamped.
● Remember that you may have to show the goods at Customs, so keep them within easy reach.
● Post the forms back to the shop and they will either refund your credit card account or send you a cheque.
● Exempt products include food and drink, medicine, tobacco, unset gems, works of art and antiques.
● Global Refund (tel 01 41 61 51 51; www.globalrefund.com) offers a reimbursement service.

POST OFFICES
● Most post offices have ATMs.
● Cards accepted are listed on each dispenser and instructions are available in English.
● Money can be wired, through Western Union, via most post offices and generally takes only a few minutes to receive.
● International Money Orders can be sent from all post offices (a charge is applied).
● Most post offices offer exchange services in various currencies, including American, Australian and Canadian dollars and the British pound.

TIPPING GUIDE	
Restaurants (service included)	Change *
Hotels (service included)	Change *
Cafés (service included)	Change *
Taxis	10 per cent
Tour guides	€2
Porters	€1
Hairdressers	€1–5
Cloakroom attendants	50c
Toilet attendants	Change
Usherettes	50c
* Or more if you are impressed with the level of service	

A French newspaper won't blow your budget (see chart below)

EVERYDAY ITEMS AND HOW MUCH THEY COST		
A sandwich (take-out)		€2.50–€3.50
Bottle of mineral water	(from a shop, 0.5 litres)	€0.40–€0.60
Cup of coffee	(from a café, espresso)	€1.30–€2
	(Crème, larger cup with milk)	€2.25–€3.50
Beer	(*Un demi*–half a litre)	€2.50–€3.50
Glass of house wine		€2.25–€3
French national newspaper		€1.20–€1.30
International newspaper		€2.30–€2.50
Litre of petrol	(98 unleaded)	€1.31
	(diesel)	€1.08
Métro ticket	(single)	€1.50
	(per ticket if you buy a carnet)	€1.10
Continental breakfast	(in bar or café)	€4–€5.50
20 cigarettes	(on average)	€5.50

PLANNING

HEALTH

USEFUL NUMBERS

General emergencies
112
Ambulance (emergencies)
15
Anti-Poison Centre
01 40 05 48 48
FACTS
(Aids advice in English.
Mon–Fri 11–2)
01 44 93 16 69
SOS Dentistes
(24-hour emergency
dental service)
01 43 37 51 00
SOS Help
(English crisis information
hotline. Daily 3–11)
01 46 21 46 46
SOS Médecins
(24-hour emergency house calls
by doctors)
01 47 07 77 77

BEFORE YOU GO

● EU citizens receive reduced-cost healthcare in France with the relevant documentation.
● For UK citizens this is the European Health Insurance Card (EHIC; formerly the E111 form). You'll find details of how to obtain one from your nearest post office.
● Even with the EHIC, full health insurance is still strongly advised.
● Full insurance is a must for citizens from non-EU countries.
● Make sure you are up to date with anti-tetanus boosters. Bring any medication you need and pack a first-aid kit. In summer, always bring sun-protection cream.

IF YOU NEED TREATMENT

● The French national health system is complex. Any salaried French citizen who receives treatment by a doctor or public hospital can be reimbursed by up to 70 per cent. The same is true if you are an EU citizen and have an EHIC. If you are relying on your EHIC, rather than travel insurance, make sure that the doctor you see is part of the French national health service (*a conventionné*), rather than the private system, otherwise you may face extra charges. In any case, you will have to pay up front for the consultation and treatment. To reclaim part of

HEALTHY FLYING

● If you are visiting France from the US, Australia or New Zealand you may be concerned about the effect of long-haul flights on your health. The most widely publicized concern is deep vein thrombosis, or DVT. Misleadingly named economy class syndrome, DVT is the forming of a blood clot in the body's deep veins, particularly in the legs. The clot can move around the bloodstream and could be fatal.
● Those most at risk include the elderly, pregnant women and those using the contraceptive pill, smokers and the overweight. If you are at increased risk of DVT see your doctor before departing. Flying increases the likelihood of DVT because passengers are often seated in a cramped position for long periods of time and may become dehydrated.

To minimize risk:
Drink water (not alcohol)
Don't stay immobile for hours at a time
Stretch and exercise your legs periodically
Do wear elastic flight socks, which support veins and reduce the chances of a clot forming

EXERCISES

1 ANKLE ROTATIONS   **2 CALF STRETCHES**   **3 KNEE LIFTS**

Lift feet off the floor. Draw a circle with the toes, moving one foot clockwise and the other counterclockwise

Start with heel on the floor and point foot upward as high as you can. Then lift heels high keeping balls of feet on the floor

Lift leg with knee bent while contracting your thigh muscle. Then straighten leg pressing foot flat to the floor

Other health hazards for flyers are airborne diseases and bugs spread by the plane's air-conditioning system. These are largely unavoidable but if you have a serious medical condition seek advice from a doctor before flying.

these costs, send the *feuille de soins* (a statement from the doctor) and the relevant EHIC documentation to the *Caisse Primaire d'Assurance-Maladie* (the state health insurance office) before you leave the country. Call 08 20 90 41 75 to find the nearest office. Attach the labels of any medicine you have to buy.
● If you have to stay overnight in a public hospital, you will have to pay 25 per cent of the treatment costs, as well as a daily charge (*forfait journalier*). These are not

refundable. It is far better to have full health insurance than to rely solely on the EHIC.
● If you are hospitalized while in Paris and have insurance, ask to see the *assistante sociale* to arrange reimbursement of the costs directly through your insurers.

FINDING A DOCTOR

● If you need to find a doctor (*médecin*) ask at the local *pharmacie* (pharmacy) or at your hotel. Appointments are usually made in advance, but very few

HOSPITALS WITH EMERGENCY DEPARTMENTS		
NAME	**ADDRESS**	**TELEPHONE**
Hôpital Pitié Salpêtrière	47 boulevard de l'Hôpital, 75013	01 42 16 00 00
Hôpital St-Antoine	184 rue du Faubourg-St-Antoine, 75012	01 49 28 20 00
Hôpital Hôtel Dieu	1 place du Parvis Notre-Dame, 75004	01 42 34 82 34
Hôpital Cochin	27 rue du Faubourg-St-Jacques, 75014	01 58 41 41 41
Hôpital Tenon	4 rue de Chine, 75020	01 56 01 70 00

These hospitals are all publicly owned and belong to the Hôpitaux de Paris group (the telephone numbers are those of the emergency departments).

doctors will refuse to see an emergency case. Emergency house calls (24-hours) can be arranged by calling SOS Médecins (tel 01 47 07 77 77).

FINDING A HOSPITAL
● There are plenty of hospitals in Paris—you'll find them listed in the phone book under *Hôpitaux*. Round-the-clock emergency services are called *urgences*.
● Private hospitals are a lot more expensive and treatment is not necessarily better. Check you are covered for the costs before receiving treatment.
● For ease of communication, English-speakers may prefer: The American Hospital (63 boulevard Victor Hugo, 92200 Neuilly; tel 01 46 41 25 25) or The Hertford British Hospital (3 rue Barbès, 92300 Levallois-Perret; tel 01 46 39 22 22). Both are private hospitals.

TAP WATER
● Tap water in Paris is drinkable, although you may prefer the taste of bottled water. In public places, you may see the sign *eau potable* (drinking water). Don't drink from anything marked *eau non potable*.

SUMMER HAZARDS
● The sun can be strong from May to September. High-factor sun block is recommended.
● There are few biting insects as such in Paris, but if you plan to visit the surrounding region take an insect repellent.

OPTICIANS
● Wearers of glasses and contact lenses should take their prescription in case of loss.

DENTAL TREATMENT
● EU citizens can receive reduced-cost emergency dental treatment with an EHIC, but insurance is still advised. The reclaim procedure is the same as general medical treatment.
● Other visitors should check their insurance.
● It's a good idea to have a dental check-up before you travel.

PHARMACIES
● A pharmacy (*pharmacie*) is identified by an illuminated green cross. Most are open Monday to Saturday 9–7 or 8, but they usually post details on their door of another pharmacy that is open later (called the *pharmacie de garde*).
● Pharmacists are highly qualified and provide first aid, as well as supplying medication.
● They are not able to dispense prescriptions from doctors outside the French health system, so bring sufficient supplies of any prescribed drugs you need.
● Some drugs are sold by prescription, or *ordonnance*, only.
● Pharmacists sell a range of health-related items, although it is sometimes less expensive to go to the supermarket.
● In France, some commonly used medicines, such as aspirins and cold remedies, can only be bought in pharmacies.

ALTERNATIVE MEDICAL TREATMENT
Alternative treatment is available, although certain types, such as chiropractics and reflexology, are not widespread.

OPTICIANS	
Opticiens Krys	40 rue St-Honoré, 75001; tel 01 44 88 98 98; **www.krys.com**
Optic 2000	92 avenue des Ternes, 75017; tel 01 45 74 47 56; **www.optic2000.fr**
Lissac Opticien	114 rue de Rivoli, 75001; tel 01 44 88 44 44; **www.lissac.com**
Alain Afflelou	62 boulevard du Montparnasse, 75006; tel 01 40 49 07 45; **www.alainafflelou.com**
Optical Center	123–125 rue du Faubourg-St-Martin, 75010; tel 01 42 05 40 40; **www.optical-center.com**

ALTERNATIVE MEDICAL TREATMENT	
Association Française de Chiropratique **www.chiropratique.org**	Centre de Santé Hahnemann *Homoeopathy, Acupuncture, Osteopathy and Herbal Treatment.* 1 rue Vergniaud, 75013 tel 01 45 80 15 03
Association Française d'Acupuncture **www.acupuncture-france.com**	
Association Europe Acupuncture **www.aea-org.com**	Naturosanté *Website about alternative medical treatments.* **www.naturosante.com**

LATE-NIGHT PHARMACIES			
NAME	**ADDRESS**	**TELEPHONE**	**HOURS**
Pharmacie les Champs	84 avenue des Champs-Élysées, 75008	01 45 62 02 41	24 hours
Drugstore Champs-Élysées	133 avenue des Champs-Élysées, 75008	01 47 20 39 25	Mon–Fri 8.30am–2am, Sat noon–2am, Sun 10am–2am
Pharmacie Centrale	52 rue du Commerce, 75015	01 45 79 75 01	Daily until midnight
Pharmacie des Arts	106 boulevard du Montparnasse, 75014	01 43 35 44 88	Daily until midnight
Pharmacie Européenne	6 place de Clichy, 75009	01 48 74 65 18	24 hours
Pharmacie British Villamayor	1 rue Auber, 75009	01 42 65 88 29	Mon–Fri 8.30–8.30, Sat 10–8

COMMUNICATION

TELEPHONES

French numbers All telephone numbers in France have 10 digits. The country is divided into five regional zones, indicated by the first two digits of the phone number (see chart, below). You must dial these two digits, even if you are calling from within the zone.

International Calls To call France from the UK dial 00 33, then drop the first zero from the 10 digit number. To call the UK from France, dial 00 44, then drop the first zero from the area code. To call France from the US, dial 011 33, then drop the first zero from the 10 digit number. To call the US from France, dial 00 1, followed by the number.

Call charges For calls within France, peak period is from Monday to Friday 8 to 7. You'll save money if you call outside of this time. Numbers beginning with 08 have special rates. 0800 or 0805 numbers are free. 0810 and 0811 numbers are charged at local rate. Other 08 numbers cost more than national calls—sometimes considerably more. Watch for the prefixes 0893, 0898 and 0899, which are particularly expensive.

COUNTRY CODES FROM FRANCE	
Australia	00 61
Belgium	00 32
Canada	00 1
Germany	00 49
Ireland	00 353
Italy	00 39
Netherlands	00 31
New Zealand	00 64
Spain	00 34
Sweden	00 46
UK	00 44
US	00 1

PREFIXES	
00	International
01	Île-de-France (including Paris)
02	Northwest France
03	Northeast France
04	Southeast France
05	Southwest France
06	Mobile telephone numbers
0800/0805	Toll-free
08	Special-rate numbers

USEFUL TELEPHONE NUMBERS
Directory Enquiries
(national)
118 008
(international)
118 700

TIP
● When reserving show tickets by telephone or calling for tourist information, bear in mind that you may be calling a higher-rate telephone number. This is usually indicated by the prefix 089.

GUIDE PRICES		
TYPE OF CALL	**INITIAL CHARGE**	**EACH FURTHER MINUTE**
Local, peak	€0.078 (1 min)	€0.028
Local, off-peak	€0.078 (1 min)	€0.014
National, peak	€0.105 (39 sec)	€0.078
National, off-peak	€0.105 (39 sec)	€0.053
Calling the UK, off-peak	€0.12 (15 sec)	€0.12
Calling the US, off-peak	€0.12 (27 sec)	€0.12

PAYPHONES

● Nearly all public payphones in Paris now use a phone card (télécarte) rather than coins. You can buy these (with 50 or 120 units) at post offices, tabacs, newsagents and France Telecom shops. Some phones also accept certain credit cards, although this may make the calls more expensive.

● You do not need to pay if you're calling an emergency number.

● The phones give instructions in various languages—press the flag button to select your choice. If the phone displays the blue bell sign, you can receive incoming calls.

● Public phones in cafés and restaurants use cards, coins or have to be switched on by staff, in which case you pay after the call. They tend to be more expensive than public payphones.

● Check the rates before you use a hotel phone, as calls can be substantially higher than from a public payphone.

MOBILE PHONES

You can usually use your own mobile, but there are a few points to check before leaving:

● Contact your Customer Service department to find out if you have any restrictions on making calls from France

● Check if you need an access code to listen to your voicemail.

● Make sure the numbers memorized in your directory are in the international format.

● Check the call charges, which can rise dramatically when you use your phone abroad.

● You can choose to rent a phone or SIM card on arrival in Paris but this can be rather an expensive solution. You could try Call'Phone (2 avenue de la Porte de St-Cloud, 75016; tel 01 40 71 72 54; www.callphone.com; also branches in Roissy-Charles de Gaulle and Orly airports).

SENDING A LETTER

● Stamps (timbres) are sold at post offices and tabacs. Letters are posted in yellow mail boxes. Some have two sections: one for mail to Paris and the suburbs (Paris—Banlieue) and the other for national and international mail (autres départements/étranger).

● A letter (lettre) sent abroad from France should take between two and five days to arrive, although it can take longer. Write par avion (by air) on the envelope or postcard.

● For registered post, ask at the post office for the letter to be sent recommandé.

● If you are sending a parcel

POSTAGE RATES FOR LETTERS	
Within France	€0.54
To Western Europe	€0.60
To Eastern Europe	€0.60
To America	€0.85
To Africa	€0.85
To Asia	€0.85
To Australia	€0.85

PLANNING

Mail boxes are yellow

CYBERCAFÉS	
La Baguenaude	30 rue Grande Truanderie, 75001
	tel 01 40 26 27 74; **www**.labaguenaude.com
Luxembourg Micro	81 boulevard St-Michel, 76005
	tel 01 46 33 27 98; **www**.luxembourg-micro.com
Milk	20 rue Faubourg St-Antoine, 75012
	tel 0820 00 10 00; **www**.milklub.com

INTERNET VENUES	
Cybersquare	1 place de la République, 75003
	tel 01 48 87 82 36; **www**.cybersquare-paris.com
Cyber Cube	5 rue Mignon, 75006
	tel 01 53 10 30 50; **www**.cybercube.fr
Le Meilleur des Mondes	4b rue Michel Chasles
	tel 01 43 46 01 64; **www**.lemeilleurdesmondes.com

(colis) abroad your options are *prioritaire* (priority) or the less costly, but slower, *économique* (economy).

POST OFFICES

● Post offices *(bureaux de poste)* are well signposted. The postal service is known as La Poste.

● Opening hours are generally Monday to Friday 8–7, Saturday 8–12, although some branches open later.

● Post offices tend to be busiest during lunch hours and in the late afternoon.

● Facilities usually include phones, photocopiers, fax *(télécopieur)* and access to the Minitel directory service. Poste restante services are available, although you will have to pay a fee.

● The post office at 52 rue du Louvre is open 24 hours. Other central post offices include:

● Paris Île de la Cité, 1 boulevard du Palais, 75004.

● Paris Archives, 67 rue des Archives, 75003.

● Paris Hôtel de Ville, 9 place de l'Hôtel de Ville, 75004.

● Paris Bastille, 12 rue Castex, 75004.

● Paris Sorbonne, 13 rue Cujas, 75005.

● Paris St-Germain-des-Prés, 53 rue de Rennes, 75006.

● Paris Pigalle, 47 boulevard de Clichy, 75009.

● Paris Champs-Elysées, 71 avenue des Champs-Élysées, 75008.

● Paris Gare de Lyon, 25 boulevard Diderot, 75012.

LAPTOPS

● Most hotels that are two stars and above provide modem points. Telephone charges apply. You may need a modem plug adaptor.

● TGV trains have a few electrical points where you can plug your laptop in if your battery needs recharging, but you'll need a two-pin continental plug or an adaptor.

INTERNET ACCESS

● Internet access is now fairly widespread in the capital.

● You can connect to the Net in trendy cybercafés.

● Some hotels and libraries have internet terminals.

FINDING HELP

Most visits to Paris are trouble-free, but make sure you have adequate insurance to cover any health emergencies, thefts or legal costs that may arise. If you do become victim of crime, it is likely to be at the hands of a pickpocket, so always keep your money and mobile phone safely tucked away.

PERSONAL SECURITY

● Take a note of your traveller's cheque numbers and keep it separately from the cheques themselves, as you will need it to make a claim in case of loss.

● Don't keep wallets, purses or mobile phones in the back pockets of trousers, or anywhere else that is easily accessible to thieves. Belt bags can be particular targets as thieves know you are likely to have valuables in them. Always keep

EMERGENCY NUMBERS
General emergency number
112
Ambulance
15
Police
17
Fire
18

an eye on your bags in restaurants, bars and on the Métro, and hold shoulder bags close to you, fastener inwards, when you are walking in the streets.

● Thieves are especially fond of crowded Métro trains, airports, the Gare du Nord station, flea markets and tourist hotspots. Be especially vigilant if someone bumps into you—it may be a ploy to distract you while

someone else snatches your money.

● If you are the victim of theft, you must report it at the local police station *(commissariat)* if you want to claim on your insurance. Keep the statement the police give you. You must also contact your credit card company as soon as possible to cancel any stolen cards.

● Paris is no more or less safe for women visitors than any other large western European city. Keep your wits about you and deal with any unwanted attention firmly and politely.

● Keep valuable items in your hotel safe.

● Outside the *périphérique*, some of Paris's suburbs can be rough. Unless you are with someone who knows the city well, it is best to stick to central areas.

PLANNING

LOSS OF PASSPORT

● Always keep a separate note of your passport number and a photocopy of the page that carries your details, in case of loss or theft. If you do lose your passport, report it to the police and then contact your embassy.

POLICE

● Each *arrondissement* has several police stations, including a main one that is open 24 hours. This is often part of the town hall. You can report crime to any of these stations. For information on driving licences and residency permits, go to the central Préfecture de Police, on the Île de la Cité.
● There are various types of police officer. The Paris police wear blue uniforms, with dark blue caps. The Seine is under the control of the river police. Demonstrations are watched over by the military-looking CRS.

FIRE

The French fire brigade deals with a range of emergencies. They are trained to give first aid.

HEALTH EMERGENCIES

See page 302.

LOST PROPERTY

The Bureau des Objets Trouvés is at 36 rue des Morillons, 75015 (tel 0821 002 525 or 01 55 76 20 00; Monday to Thursday 8.30–5, Friday 8.30–4.30).

EMBASSIES AND CONSULATES

COUNTRY	ADDRESS	WEBSITE
Australia	4 rue Jean-Rey, 75015; tel 01 40 59 33 00	www.france-embassy.gov.au
Canada	35 avenue Montaigne, 75008; tel 01 44 43 29 00	www.amb-canada.fr
Germany	13–15 avenue Franklin Roosevelt, 75008; tel 01 53 83 45 00	www.amb-allemagne.fr
Ireland	12 ave Foch, 75116; tel 01 44 17 67 00	www.embassyofirelandparis.com
Italy	51 rue de Varenne, 75007; tel 01 49 54 03 00	www.amb-italie.fr
Spain	22 avenue Marceau, 75008; tel 01 44 43 18 00	www.amb-espagne.fr
UK	35 rue du Faubourg-St-Honoré, 75008; tel 01 44 51 31 00	www.amb-grandebretagne.fr
US	2 avenue Gabriel, 75008; tel 01 43 12 22 22	www.amb-usa.fr

LOCAL POLICE STATIONS

ARRONDISSEMENT	ADDRESS	TELEPHONE
1	place du Marché St-Honoré	01 47 03 60 00
2	18 rue du Croissant	01 44 88 18 00
3	4 rue Ours	01 42 76 13 00
4	9 boulevard Palais	01 58 80 80 80
5	4 rue de la Montagne Ste-Geneviève	01 44 41 51 00
6	78 rue Bonaparte	01 40 46 38 30
7	9 rue Fabert	01 44 18 69 07
8	1 avenue du Général Eisenhower	01 53 76 60 00
9	14 bis rue Chauchat	01 44 83 80 80
10	72 rue du Faubourg St Martin	01 44 89 64 70
11	14 pass Charles Dallery	01 53 36 25 00
12	78 avenue Daumesnil	01 44 87 50 12
13	144 boulevard de l'Hôpital	01 40 79 05 05
14	112–116 avenue du Maine	01 53 74 14 06
15	250 rue de Vaugirard	01 53 68 81 00
16	58 avenue Mozart	01 55 74 50 00
17	19 rue Truffaut	01 44 90 37 17
18	79 rue Clignancourt	01 53 41 50 00
19	3 rue Erik Satie	01 55 56 58 00
20	6 place Gambetta	01 40 33 34 00

MEDIA

TELEVISION

● France has five non-cable television stations: the nationally owned and operated channels 2 and 3, the privately owned 1 and 6, and the Franco-German ARTE (channel 5). Almost all the shows are in French. There are adverts on all terrestrial channels except ARTE.
● TF1 has news, recent American and French films, soaps and shows.
● France 2 has news, recent French and foreign films, soaps, shows and documentaries.
● France 3, a regional and national channel, has regional and national news, regional shows, documentaries, mostly French films and, once a week, a film in its original language.
● ARTE is a Franco-German channel operating from 7pm every day with shows in French and German. International films are shown in their original language and there are also cultural documentaries.
● M6 shows a lot of low-budget films and past American sitcoms and soaps. There are also some interesting documentaries.
● Digital television has now taken off in France. More than 100 channels are on offer either through satellite or cable.
● If the TV listings mention *VO (version originale)*, the show or film will be in the language in which it was made, with French subtitles (Channel 3 usually screens a good film in *VO* every Sunday at around midnight).
● Note that French television channels do not always keep exactly to schedule.
● Most hotels have at least a basic cable service, which is likely to include BBC World and CNN. Cable channels now offer multilingual versions of some shows. Ask at your hotel how to use this option as the mechanics vary. The commercial-free ARTE usually offers a choice between French and German for its cultural shows.

Depending on what cable option your hotel has, you may have some of the following channels:

BBC Prime	With a mix of BBC shows, old and new
Canal+	Shows recent films (some in the original language)
MTV	Contemporary music channel
MCM	The French version of MTV
Eurosport or Infosport	For major sporting events
Planète	Nature and science documentaries
RAI Uno	Italian
TVE 1	Spanish
Euronews	A European all-news channel
LCI	All news in French
Canal Jimmy	Shows some British and American shows like *Friends* and *NYPD Blue* in English or multilingual versions
Paris Première	A cultural channel with some films in English
Canal J	With children's shows until 8pm
Téva	A women's channel that runs some English-language shows such as *Sex in the City*

RADIO

● French radio stations are available mainly on FM wavelengths with a few international stations on LW. Reception in Paris is very good. All FM stations are in French. Stations include:
● **Chérie FM:** 91.3 FM; French mainstream pop, news, reports.
● **France Infos:** 105.5 FM; news bulletins every 15 minutes.
● **France Musique:** 91.7 FM; classical and jazz music, concerts, operas, news.
● **NRJ:** 100.3 FM; French and international pop, techno, rap, R & B.
● **Radio Classique:** 101.1 FM; classical music.
● **Skyrock:** 96 FM; rap, hip-hop, R & B.
● **BBC Radio 4:** 198 kHz LW; news, current affairs, drama.
● **BBC Five Live:** 909 kHz MW; news and sport.

● **BBC World Service:** 648 kHz MW; international news.

NEWSPAPERS AND MAGAZINES

● British newspapers are available at large *kiosques* (news-stands) in tourist areas. *The International Herald Tribune* can be found at almost all news-stands, along with *The Economist*, *USA Today* and *The Wall Street Journal*.
● *Pariscope* is the most popular weekly listings magazine for events and films. Its competitors are *L'Officiel du Spectacle* and the hip (and slightly more expensive) *Zurban*. All three are published on Wednesday. *Time Out* also publishes a free quarterly Paris magazine available at English-language bookshops such as WH Smith, where you'll also find *Paris Voice*, a free city magazine in English.

French daily newspapers have clear political leanings.

Le Monde
This stately paper, left-of-centre, was until recently known for refusing to run photos.

Libération
A lively paper, more clearly leftist and youth-focused.

L'Humanité
Left wing.

Le Figaro
Mainstream conservative daily.

Le Parisien
This tabloid paper is written at a level of French that makes it fairly easy for non-native readers to understand.

Journal du Dimanche
Sunday newspaper.

● If you're looking for a housing exchange or holiday rental in Paris, pick up a free copy of *FUSAC*, a handy small-ads publication published twice a month.
● *Where*, an English-language listings magazine, is distributed free in hotels.
● Weekly news magazines include *Le Nouvel Observateur*, *Le Point* and *L'Express*.
● For women's fashions, options include *Elle*, *Vogue* or *Marie Claire*.
● For celebrity gossip and lots of photos, try *Paris Match*, *Voici* or *Gala*.

OPENING TIMES AND TICKETS

TICKETS

● If you want to see as many museums and other sights as possible, it may be worth buying a *Paris Museum Pass* (www.parismuseumpass.com). This gives free entry to around 60 museums and monuments in the city, and another 22 in the rest of the Île-de-France. A two-day pass costs €30, a four-day pass €45 and a six-day pass €60. You can buy them from participating museums, the Paris Tourist Office, major Métro

France has 11 national holidays (*jours fériés*), when Métro, bus and RER services are reduced and banks and many museums and shops close. The most steadfastly respected are 1 January, 1 May, 1 November, 11 November and 25 December. If you're in Paris during a national holiday, it's a good idea to ring ahead to see if the sight you want to visit is open.

1 Jan	New Year's Day
March/April	Easter Monday
1 May	Labour Day
8 May	VE Day
A Thursday in May	Ascension Day
May/June	Whit Monday
14 July	Bastille Day
15 August	Assumption Day
1 November	All Saints' Day
11 November	Remembrance Day
25 December	Christmas Day

PLANNING

Banks	Monday to Friday 10–5.	Smaller branches may close for lunch. Others are open on Saturday but closed Monday. Banks close at noon on the day before a national holiday, as well as on the holiday itself.
Shops	Monday to Saturday 9–7.	Some boutiques have a later start. Lunchtime closures are rare in the city, although small specialist traders may take a one- or two-hour break. Saturday is the busiest shopping day, while on Sunday most shops remain closed.
Museums	Most national museums close on Tuesday (the Musée d'Orsay is a notable exception, closing on Monday). Municipal museums (including the Musée Carnavalet and the Musée Cognacq-Jay) close on Monday.	Entrance is often free on the first Sunday of the month, although this can lead to uncomfortable crowds. The key museums usually have a late-night opening (*nocturne*), when there are fewer crowds. If you are trekking to the other side of the city to see one of the smaller museums, ring in advance–opening hours can be idiosyncratic and the renovation craze has not helped.
Restaurants	Lunch is generally served noon–2 or 2.30 and dinner 7.30–10 or 11.	Most Parisians wait until around 9pm to dine out. Brasseries usually serve food all day. Some restaurants close for the whole of August.
Nightclubs	Club action starts well after midnight and continues to around 5am.	
Post offices	Monday to Friday 8–7, Saturday 8–12.	Some branches open later.
Pharmacies	Monday–Saturday 9–7 or 8.	All display a list of local pharmacies that open later and on Sunday.

stations and FNAC ticket counters. Passes do not cover temporary exhibitions.
● Students with an International Student Identity Card and senior citizens receive reduced-price entry at some museums.
● For information on theatre and concert tickets, ▷ 193.
● For information on Métro, bus and RER tickets, ▷ 47–48.
● Most cinemas offer reduced-price tickets for all on Mondays. Reductions are available for students on certain days (with a valid International Student Identity Card) and for senior citizens (valid identity required).
● Theatres also offer special-priced tickets with varying conditions.
● Most museums are free for under-18s and offer reduced prices to young people aged between 18 and 25.
● Season tickets are available for people wishing to visit a particular sight or museum many times during a longer stay in Paris. Apply to each museum or sight.
● Most shows, including drama, opera, concerts and sporting events, can be booked through the FNAC shops (www.fnac.com) for a small fee.

TOURIST OFFICES

● Paris's main tourist office, which has now moved to rue des Pyramides, is a handy source of information on anything from sightseeing and accommodation to exhibitions and children's activities. You can also buy the *Paris Museum Pass* pass and the *Paris Visite* bus and Métro pass. There are other branches around the city.
● The regional tourist office, the Comité Régional du Tourisme—Paris Île-de-France, has offices at the Carrousel du Louvre and Disneyland Resort Paris. It covers the whole of the Île de France, including Versailles.
● In the summer there are also information kiosks at various sites around the city.

PLANNING

TOURIST OFFICES

**Paris Tourist Office
(Paris Convention and Visitors Bureau)**
25–27 rue des Pyramides, 75001
Tel 0892 683 000 (€0.34 per minute)
Open Apr–end Oct daily 9–7; rest of year
Mon–Sat 10–7, Sun and public holidays
11–7. Closed 1 May
Métro: Pyramides
www.parisinfo.com

Other branches are at the Eiffel Tower (Apr–end Oct), Gare de Lyon, Gare du Nord, Opéra (11 rue Scribe), Montmartre (21 place du Tertre), Anvers, Paris Expo and Carrousel du Louvre.

Maison de la France
The French Tourist Office.
(No public access to its Paris office.)
www.franceguide.com
Paris Île-de-France
Carrousel du Louvre (lower level)
Tel 0826 166 666
Open Wed–Mon 9–7
Métro: Tuileries
www.pidf.com

There is also an office at Disneyland Resort Paris (Place François Truffaut; tel 01 60 43 33 33).

FILMS AND BOOKS

FILMS

● The ultimate Paris atmosphere-steeped film is *Amelie* or *Le Fabuleux Destin d'Amélie Poulain* (2001), although it depicts an idealized vision of Montmartre's charm.

● *La Môme* (English: *La Vie en Rose*) (2007) is a harrowing biopic of Edith Piaf, filmed mostly in the heart of Montmartre.

● *The Da Vinci Code* (2006), starring Tom Hanks, has brought a new stream of visitors to the heart of the capital in search of answers to the mystery.

● For a more realistic view of everyday life today in another Paris district, the Bastille, see *When the Cat's Away* (1997).

● *Before Sunset* (2004) was Richard Linklater's sequel to *Before Sunrise* (1995), with Ethan Hawke and Julie Delpy exploring their feelings for each other in Paris.

● Other films set primarily in Paris include *French Kiss* (1995); Woody Allen's romantic musical *Everybody Says I Love You* (1996); *Prêt-à-Porter* (*Ready to Wear*; 1994), Robert Altman's acidic look at the city's fashion world; and *Jefferson in Paris* (1995), in which James Ivory depicts Paris just before the Revolution.

● No one has better expressed the romance of the City of Light than Audrey Hepburn in such delightful films as *Sabrina*

(1954; remade in 1995 with Julia Ormond) and *Funny Face* (1957). In *Love in the Afternoon* (1957) Hepburn cavorts illicitly with Gary Cooper at the Ritz Hotel; she is paired with Cary Grant in *Charade* (1963), a sophisticated crime comedy.

● For tap dances around Paris monuments, see *An American in Paris* (1951), starring Gene Kelly and Leslie Caron.

BOOKS

● For those who prefer to find their atmosphere on the page, Adam Gopnik's essays in *Paris to the Moon* (2000) provide one American's view of life in the French capital today.

● Ernest Hemingway's *A Moveable Feast* (published in 1964) and Gertrude Stein's *The Autobiography of Alice B. Toklas* (1933) describe a more romantic era in the early 20th century, when a young couple could live on $5 a day and an art collector could snap up works by Pablo Picasso and Henri Matisse for a song.

● A less flattering portrait of Paris can be found in *Down and Out in Paris and London* (1933), in which George Orwell describes the horrors of trying to survive in the city in the 1930s without a *sou*.

● The classics are always reliable for a vivid historic vision of Parisian life. Read Victor Hugo's *The Hunchback of Notre-Dame*

(1831) or *Les Miserables* (1862), or Charles Dickens' take on the French Revolution in *A Tale of Two Cities* (1859).

● Mystery lovers will get into the atmosphere of the City of Light from George Simenon's *Inspector Maigret* series.

● Dan Brown's *The Da Vinci Code* (2003) featured Paris at the centre of a 2,000-year-old religious cover-up, a story that has captured the popular imagination.

Why not try a show to give you a taste of Paris?

PLANNING

www.fodors.com
A comprehensive travel-planning site that lets you research prices, reserve air tickets and ask questions to fellow visitors. (English)

www.franceguide.com
You'll find practical advice on everything from arriving in France to buying a property on this site, belonging to the French Tourist Office. There are also features on holidays in other parts of France. (French, English, German, Italian, Spanish, Dutch, Portuguese)

www.parismuseumpass.com
The organization that runs the *Paris Museum Pass*. (French, English)

www.lemonde.fr
Catch up on current events on the site of *Le Monde* newspaper. (French)

www.meteofrance.com
Weather forecasts for Paris and the rest of France. (French only)

www.monuments-nationaux.fr
Learn more about some of Paris's most historic monuments, including the Arc de Triomphe, Panthéon and Notre-Dame, on the Centre des Monuments Nationaux' site. (French, English)

www.pagesjaunes.fr
France's phone directory, online. (French, English)

www.paris.fr
The information on the city council's website ranges from current events to exploring Paris's bicycle ways. There is also news about the running of the city, aimed at residents. (French, English)

www.parisdigest.com
An independent site that guides you to the best the city has to offer, whether you want to sightsee, shop or eat out. (English)

www.parisfranceguide.com
A site aimed at English-speakers living in or visiting Paris, with information ranging from fashion to visiting the dentist. (English)

www.paris-ile-de-france.com or www.pidf.com
Special offers, plus information on events, hotels, the Métro and the weather, on the site of the Île de France regional tourist office. (French, English, German, Spanish)

www.parisinfo.com
The website of the Paris Tourist Office is packed with information on sights, restaurants, shops, hotels, events and the Métro. It also has useful links to other sites. (French, English)

www.parisvoice.com
An insider's view of Paris, aimed at English-speaking Parisians. Includes book reviews, an entertainment calendar and even an agony aunt. (English)

www.ratp.fr
The site of Paris's Métro and bus operator, with information about getting around. (French, English, German)

www.rmn.fr
Site of the Réunion des Musées Nationaux. (French, English)

www.theAA.com
The Automobile Association website contains a helpful route planner if you are planning excursions farther afield. You can also buy maps of France. (English)

Other websites are listed alongside the relevant sights, or in the On the Move and Planning chapters.

Surf the Net to get the latest on events in Paris

KEY SIGHTS QUICK WEBSITE FINDER		
SIGHT	**WEBSITE**	**PAGE**
Arc de Triomphe	www.monuments-nationaux.fr	76–79
Centre Georges Pompidou	www.centrepompidou.fr	82–86
Conciergerie	www.monuments-nationaux.fr	89–91
Grande Arche	www.grandearche.com	94
Institute du Monde Arabe	www.imarabe.org	98
Invalides	www.invalides.org	99–101
Jardin du Luxembourg	www.senat.fr	102–103
Montmartre	www.montmartrenet.com	108–109
La Mosquée	www.la-mosquee.com	110
Musée des Arts Décoratif	www.ucad.fr	111
Musée Carnavalet	www.paris.fr/musees/musee_carnavalet	114–115
Musée du Louvre	www.louvre.fr	118–123
Musée Marmottan–Monet	www.marmottan.com	124–125
Muséum National d'Histoire Naturelle	www.mnhn.fr	127
Musée National du Moyen Âge–Thermes de Cluny	www.musee-moyenage.fr	128–129
Musée d'Orsay	www.musee-orsay.fr	130–134
Musée Picasso	www.musee-picasso.fr	135
Musée Rodin	www.musee-rodin.fr	136
Notre-Dame	www.monuments-nationaux.fr	137–141
Opéra Palais Garnier	www.operadeparis.fr	142
Panthéon	www.monuments-nationaux.fr	144
Parc de la Villette	www.cite-sciences.fr and www.cite-musique.fr	146–147
Sacré-Cœur	www.sacre-coeur-montmartre.com	154–157
Sainte-Chapelle	www.monuments-nationaux.fr	158–160
Tour Eiffel	www.tour-eiffel.fr	164–169
Tour Montparnasse	www.tourmontparnasse56.com	170

PLANNING

WORDS AND PHRASES

Even if you're far from fluent, it is always a good idea to try to speak a few words of French while in Paris. The words and phrases on the following pages should help you with the basics, from ordering a meal to dealing with emergencies.

CONVERSATION

What is the time?
Quelle heure est-il?

When do you open/close?
A quelle heure ouvrez/fermez-vous?

I don't speak French.
Je ne parle pas français.

Do you speak English?
Parlez-vous anglais?

I don't understand.
Je ne comprends pas.

Please repeat that.
Pouvez-vous répéter (s'il vous plaît)?

Please speak more slowly.
Pouvez-vous parler plus lentement?

What does this mean?
Qu'est-ce que ça veut dire?

Write that down for me please.
Pouvez-vous me l'écrire, s'il vous plaît?

Please spell that.
Pouvez-vous me l'épeler, s'il vous plaît?

I'll look that up (in the dictionary).
Je vais le chercher (dans le dictionnaire).

My name is…
Je m'appelle…

What's your name?
Comment vous appelez-vous?

This is my wife/husband.
Voici ma femme/mon mari.

This is my daughter/son.
Voici ma fille/mon fils.

This is my friend.
Voici mon ami(e).

Hello, pleased to meet you.
Bonjour, enchanté(e).

I'm from…
Je viens de…

I'm on holiday.
Je suis en vacances.

I live in…
J'habite à…

Where do you live?
Où habitez-vous?

Good morning.
Bonjour.

Good evening.
Bonsoir.

Goodnight.
Bonne nuit.

Goodbye.
Au revoir.

See you later.
A plus tard.

How much is that?
C'est combien?

May I/Can I?
Est-ce que je peux?

I don't know.
Je ne sais pas.

You're welcome.
Je vous en prie.

How are you?
Comment allez-vous?

I'm sorry.
Je suis désolé(e).

Excuse me.
Excusez-moi.

That's all right/no problem.
De rien.

USEFUL WORDS

Yes **Oui**	There **Là-bas**	Who **Qui**	How **Comment**	Open **Ouvert**	Please **S'il vous plaît**
No **Non**	Here **Ici**	When **Quand**	Later **Plus tard**	Closed **Fermé**	Thank you **Merci**
	Where **Où**	Why **Pourquoi**	Now **Maintenant**		

Could you help me, please?
(Est-ce que) vous pouvez m'aider, s'il vous plaît?

How much is this?
C'est combien?/Ça coûte combien?

I'm looking for…
Je cherche…

When does the shop open/close?
A quelle heure ouvre/ferme le magasin?

I'm just looking, thank you.
Je regarde, merci.

This isn't what I want.
Ce n'est pas ce que je veux.

This is the right size.
C'est la bonne taille.

Do you have anything less expensive/smaller/larger?
(Est-ce que) vous avez quelque chose de moins cher/plus petit/plus grand?

I'll take this.
Je prends ceci.

Do you have a bag for this, please?
(Est-ce que) je peux avoir un sac, s'il vous plaît?

Do you accept credit cards?
(Est-ce que) vous acceptez les cartes de crédit?

I'd like…grams please.
Je voudrais…grammes, s'il vous plaît.

I'd like a kilo of…
Je voudrais un kilo de…

What does this contain?
Quels sont les ingrédients?/ Qu'est-ce qu'il y a dedans?

I'd like…slices of that.
J'en voudrais…tranches.

Bakery
Boulangerie

Bookshop
Librairie

Chemist
Pharmacie

Supermarket
Supermarché

Market
Marché

Sale
Soldes

1 un	6 six	11 onze	16 seize	21 vingt et un	70 soixante-dix
2 deux	7 sept	12 douze	17 dix-sept	30 trente	80 quatre-vingts
3 trois	8 huit	13 treize	18 dix-huit	40 quarante	90 quatre-vingt-dix
4 quatre	9 neuf	14 quatorze	19 dix-neuf	50 cinquante	100 cent
5 cinq	10 dix	15 quinze	20 vingt	60 soixante	1000 mille

Where is the nearest post office/mail box?
Où se trouve la poste/la boîte aux lettres la plus proche?

How much is the postage to…?
A combien faut-il affranchir pour…?

I'd like to send this by air mail/ registered mail.
Je voudrais envoyer ceci par avion/en recommandé.

Can you direct me to a public phone?
Pouvez-vous m'indiquer la cabine téléphonique la plus proche?

What is the number for directory enquiries?
Quel est le numéro pour les renseignements?

Where can I find a telephone directory?
Où est-ce que je peux trouver un annuaire?

Where can I buy a phone card?
Où est-ce que je peux acheter une télécarte?

Please put me through to…
Pouvez-vous me passer…, s'il vous plaît?

Can I dial direct to…?
Est-ce que je peux appeler directement en…?

Do I need to dial 0 first?
Est-ce qu'il faut composer le zéro (d'abord)?

What is the charge per minute?
Quel est le tarif à la minute?

Have there been any calls for me?
Est-ce que j'ai eu des appels téléphoniques?

Hello, this is…
Allô, c'est… (à l'appareil)

Who is speaking please …?
Qui est à l'appareil, s'il vous plaît?

I would like to speak to…
Je voudrais parler à…

Monday **lundi**	January **janvier**	August **août**	spring **printemps**	morning **matin**	day **le jour**
Tuesday **mardi**	February **février**	September **septembre**	summer **été**	afternoon **après-midi**	month **le mois**
Wednesday **mercredi**	March **mars**	October **octobre**	autumn **automne**	evening **soir**	year **l'année**
Thursday **jeudi**	April **avril**	November **novembre**	winter **hiver**	night **nuit**	
Friday **vendredi**	May **mai**	December **décembre**	holiday **vacances**	today **aujourd'hui**	
Saturday **samedi**	June **juin**		Easter **Pâques**	yesterday **hier**	
Sunday **dimanche**	July **juillet**		Christmas **Noël**	tomorrow **demain**	

HOTELS

Do you have a room?
(Est-ce que) vous avez une chambre?

I have a reservation for… nights.
J'ai réservé pour…nuits.

How much each night?
C'est combien par nuit?

Double room.
Une chambre pour deux personnes/double.

Twin room.
Une chambre à deux lits/ avec lits jumeaux.

Single room.
Une chambre à un lit/pour une personne.

With bath/shower/lavatory.
Avec salle de bain/ douche/WC.

Is the room air-conditioned/ heated?
(Est-ce que) la chambre est climatisée/chauffée?

Is breakfast/lunch/dinner included in the cost?
(Est-ce que) le petit déjeuner/le déjeuner/le dîner est compris dans le prix?

Is there an elevator in the hotel?
(Est-ce qu')il y a un ascenseur à l'hôtel?

Is room service available?
(Est-ce qu')il y a le service en chambre?

When do you serve breakfast?
À quelle heure servez-vous le petit déjeuner?

May I have breakfast in my room?
(Est-ce que) je peux prendre le petit déjeuner dans ma chambre?

Do you serve evening meals?
(Est-ce que) vous servez le repas du soir/le dîner?

I need an alarm call at…
Je voudrais être réveillé(e) à…heures.

I'd like an extra blanket/pillow.
Je voudrais une couverture/ un oreiller supplémentaire, s'il vous plaît.

May I have my room key?
(Est-ce que) je peux avoir la clé de ma chambre?

Will you look after my luggage until I leave?
Pouvez-vous garder mes bagages jusqu'à mon départ?

Is there parking?
(Est-ce qu') il y a un parking?

Where can I park my car?
Où est-ce que je peux garer ma voiture?

Do you have babysitters?
(Est-ce que) vous avez un service de babysitting/garde d'enfants?

When are the sheets changed?
Quand changez-vous les draps?

The room is too hot/cold.
Il fait trop chaud/froid dans la chambre.

Could I have another room?
(Est-ce que) je pourrais avoir une autre chambre?

I am leaving this morning.
Je pars ce matin.

What time should we leave our room?
A quelle heure devons-nous libérer la chambre?

Can I pay my bill?
(Est-ce que) je peux régler ma note, s'il vous plaît?

May I see the room?
(Est-ce que) je peux voir la chambre?

Thank you for your hospitality.
Merci pour votre hospitalité.

Swimming pool.
Piscine.

No smoking.
Non fumeur.

GETTING AROUND

Where is the information desk?
Où est le bureau des renseignements?

Where is the timetable?
Où sont les horaires?

Does this train/bus go to…?
Ce train/bus va à…?

Do you have a Métro/bus map?
Avez-vous un plan du Métro/des lignes de bus?

Please can I have a single/return ticket to…?
Je voudrais un aller simple/un aller-retour pour…, s'il vous plaît.

I'd like to rent a car.
Je voudrais louer une voiture.

Where are we?
Où sommes-nous?

I'm lost.
Je me suis perdu(e).

Is this the way to…?
C'est bien par ici pour aller à…?

I am in a hurry.
Je suis pressé(e).

Where can I find a taxi?
Où est-ce que je peux trouver un taxi?

How much is the journey?
Combien coûte la course?

Go straight on.
Allez tout droit.

Turn left.
Tournez à gauche.

Turn right.
Tournez à droite.

Cross over.
Traversez.

Traffic lights.
Les feux.

Intersection.
Carrefour.

Corner.
Coin.

No parking.
Interdiction de stationner.

Train/bus/Métro station.
La gare SNCF/routière/la station de Métro.

Do you sell travel cards?
Avez-vous des cartes d'abonnement?

Do I need to get off here?
(Est-ce qu') il faut que je descende ici?

Where can I buy a ticket?
Où est-ce que je peux acheter un billet/ticket?

Where can I reserve a seat?
Où est-ce que je peux réserver une place?

Is this seat free?
(Est-ce que) cette place est libre?

Where can I find a taxi?
Où est-ce que je peux trouver un taxi?

MONEY

Is there a bank/currency exchange office nearby?
(Est-ce qu') il y a une banque/un bureau de change près d'ici?

Can I cash this here?
(Est-ce que) je peux encaisser ça ici?

I'd like to change sterling/dollars into euros.
Je voudrais changer des livres sterling/dollars en euros.

Can I use my credit card to withdraw cash?
(Est-ce que) je peux utiliser ma carte de crédit pour retirer de l'argent?

What is the exchange rate today?
Quel est le taux de change aujourd'hui?

COLOURS

brown	blue
marron/brun	**bleu(e)**
black	green
noir(e)	**vert(e)**
red	yellow
rouge	**jaune**

I'd like to reserve a table for … people at…
Je voudrais réserver une table pour…personnes à …heures, s'il vous plaît.

A table for…, please.
Une table pour…, s'il vous plaît.

We have/haven't booked.
Nous avons/n'avons pas réservé.

What time does the restaurant open?
A quelle heure ouvre le restaurant?

We'd like to wait for a table.
Nous aimerions attendre qu'une table se libère.

Could we sit there?
(Est-ce que) nous pouvons nous asseoir ici?

Is this table taken?
(Est-ce que) cette table est libre?

Are there tables outside?
(Est-ce qu') il y a des tables dehors/à la terrasse?

Where are the toilets?
Où sont les toilettes?

Could you warm this up for me?
(Est-ce que) vous pouvez me faire réchauffer ceci/ça, s'il vous plaît?

Do you have nappy-changing facilities?
(Est-ce qu') il y a une pièce pour changer les bébés?

We'd like something to drink.
Nous voudrions quelque chose à boire.

Could we see the menu/wine list?
(Est-ce que) nous pouvons voir le menu/la carte des vins, s'il vous plaît?

Is there a dish of the day?
(Est-ce qu') il y a un plat du jour?

What do you recommend?
Qu'est-ce que vous nous conseillez?

This is not what I ordered.
Ce n'est pas ce que j'ai commandé.

I can't eat wheat/sugar/salt/pork/beef/dairy.
Je ne peux pas manger de blé/sucre/sel/porc/bœuf/ produits laitiers.

I am a vegetarian.
Je suis végétarien(ne).

I'd like…
Je voudrais…

Could we have some more bread?
(Est-ce que) vous pouvez nous apporter un peu plus de pain, s'il vous plaît?

How much is this dish?
Combien coûte ce plat?

Is service included?
(Est-ce que) le service est compris?

Could we have some salt and pepper?
(Est-ce que) vous pouvez nous apporter du sel et du poivre, s'il vous plaît?

May I have an ashtray?
(Est-ce que) je peux avoir un cendrier, s'il vous plaît?

Could I have bottled still/sparkling water?
(Est-ce que) je peux avoir une bouteille d'eau minérale/gazeuse, s'il vous plaît?

The meat is too rare/overcooked.
La viande est trop saignante/trop cuite.

The food is cold.
La nourriture est froide.

Can I have the bill, please?
(Est-ce que) je peux avoir l'addition, s'il vous plaît?

The bill is not right.
Il y a une erreur sur l'addition.

We didn't order this.
Nous n'avons pas commandé ça.

I'd like to speak to the manager, please.
Je voudrais parler au directeur, s'il vous plaît.

The food was excellent.
La nourriture était excellente.

Breakfast **Petit déjeuner**	Sugar **Sucre**	Mushroom soup **Soupe aux champignons**	Casserole **Plat en cocotte**	Tomatoes **Tomates**
Lunch **Déjeuner**	Wine list **Carte/liste des vins**	Sandwiches **Sandwichs**	Roast lamb **Gigot**	Fruit **Les fruits**
Dinner **Dîner**	Main course **Le plat principal**	Ham sandwich **Sandwich au jambon**	Mixed cold meat **L'assiette de charcuterie**	Apples **Pommes**
Coffee **Café**	Dessert **Dessert**	Dish of the day **Plat du jour**	Potatoes **Pommes de terre**	Strawberries **Fraises**
Tea **Thé**	Salt/pepper **Sel/poivre**	Fish dishes **Les poissons**	Cauliflower **Chou-fleur**	Peaches **Pêches**
Orange juice **Jus d'orange**	Cheese **Fromage**	Prawns **Crevettes roses/bouquet**	Green beans **Haricots verts**	Pears **Poires**
Apple juice **Jus de pomme**	Knife/fork/spoon **Couteau/ fourchette/ cuillère**	Oysters **Huîtres**	Peas **Petits pois**	Fruit tart **Tarte aux fruits**
Milk **Lait**			Carrots **Carottes**	Pastry **Pâtisserie**
Beer **Bière**	Soups **Soupes/potages**	Salmon **Saumon**	Spinach **Épinards**	Chocolate cake **Gâteau au chocolat**
Red wine **Vin rouge**	Vegetable soup **Soupe de légumes**	Haddock **Églefin**	Onions **Oignons**	Cream **Crème**
White wine **Vin blanc**	Chicken soup **Soupe au poulet**	Squid **Calmar**	Lettuce **Laitue**	Ice cream **Glace**
Bread roll **Petit pain**	Lentil soup **Soupe aux lentilles**	Meat dishes **Viandes**	Cucumber **Concombre**	Chocolate mousse **Mousse au chocolat**
Bread **Pain**		Roast chicken **Poulet roti**		

TOURIST INFORMATION

Where is the tourist information office, please?
Où se trouve l'office de tourisme, s'il vous plaît?

Do you have a city map?
Avez-vous un plan de la ville?

Where is the museum?
Où est le musée?

Can you give me some information about…?
Pouvez-vous me donner des renseignements sur…?

What are the main places of interest here?
Quels sont les principaux sites touristiques ici?

Could you please point them out on the map?
Pouvez-vous me les indiquer sur la carte, s'il vous plaît?

What sights/hotels/restaurants can you recommend?
Quels sites/hôtels/restaurants nous recommandez-vous?

We are staying here for a day.
Nous sommes ici pour une journée.

I am interested in…
Je suis intéressé(e) par…

Does the guide speak English?
Est-ce qu'il y a un guide qui parle anglais?

Do you have any suggested walks?
Avez-vous des suggestions de promenades?

Are there guided tours?
Est-ce qu'il y a des visites guidées?

Are there organised excursions?
Est-ce qu'il y a des excursions organisées?

Can we make reservations here?
Est-ce que nous pouvons réserver ici?

What time does it open/close?
Ça ouvre/ferme à quelle heure?

What is the admission price?
Quel est le prix d'entrée?

Is there a discount for senior citizens/students?
Est-ce qu'il y a des réductions pour les personnes âgées/ les étudiants?

Do you have a brochure in English?
Avez-vous un dépliant en anglais?

What's on at the cinema?
Qu'est-ce qu'il y a au cinéma?

Where can I find a good nightclub?
Où est-ce que je peux trouver une bonne boîte de nuit?

Do you have a schedule for the theatre/opera?
Est-ce que vous avez un programme de théâtre/ d'opéra?

Should we dress smartly?
Est-ce qu'il faut mettre une tenue de soirée?

What time does the show start?
A quelle heure commence le spectacle?

How do I reserve a seat?
Comment fait-on pour réserver une place?

Could you reserve tickets for me?
Pouvez-vous me réserver des billets?

ILLNESS AND EMERGENCIES

I don't feel well.
Je ne me sens pas bien.

Could you call a doctor?
(Est-ce que) vous pouvez appeler un médecin/un docteur, s'il vous plaît?

Is there a doctor/pharmacist on duty?
(Est-ce qu') il y a un médecin/docteur/une pharmacie de garde?

I feel sick.
J'ai envie de vomir.

I need to see a doctor/dentist.
Il faut que je voie un médecin/docteur/ un dentiste.

Please direct me to the hospital.
(Est-ce que) vous pouvez m'indiquer le chemin pour aller à l'hôpital, s'il vous plaît?

I have a headache.
J'ai mal à la tête.

I've been stung by a wasp/bee.
J'ai été piqué(e) par une guêpe/abeille.

I have a heart condition.
J'ai un problème cardiaque.

I am diabetic.
Je suis diabétique.

I'm asthmatic.
Je suis asmathique.

I'm on a special diet.
Je suis un régime spécial.

I am on medication.
Je prends des médicaments.

I have left my medicine at home.
J'ai laissé mes médicaments chez moi.

I need to make an emergency appointment.
Je dois prendre rendez-vous d'urgence.

I have bad toothache.
J'ai mal aux dents.

I don't want an injection.
Je ne veux pas de piqûre.

Help!
Au secours!

I have lost my passport/ wallet/purse/handbag.
J'ai perdu mon passeport/ portefeuille/porte- monnaie/sac à main.

I have had an accident.
J'ai eu un accident.

My car has been stolen.
On m'a volé ma voiture.

I have been robbed.
J'ai été volé(e).

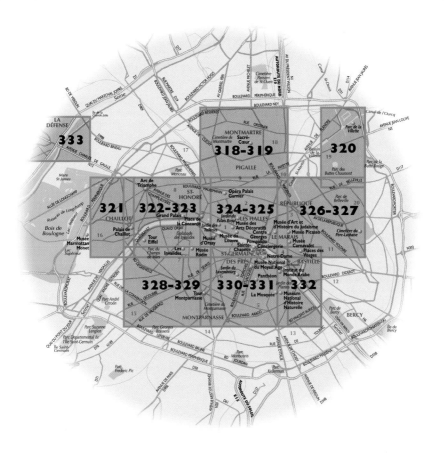

———	Main road
———	Other road
·········	Minor road/path
▬▬▬▬▬	Railway
▩	Park
■	Important building
●	Featured place of interest
🅸	Tourist information office
●	Métro station
▬	Railway station
🅿	Parking

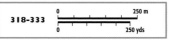

318-333

	0		250 m
	0		250 yds

Maps

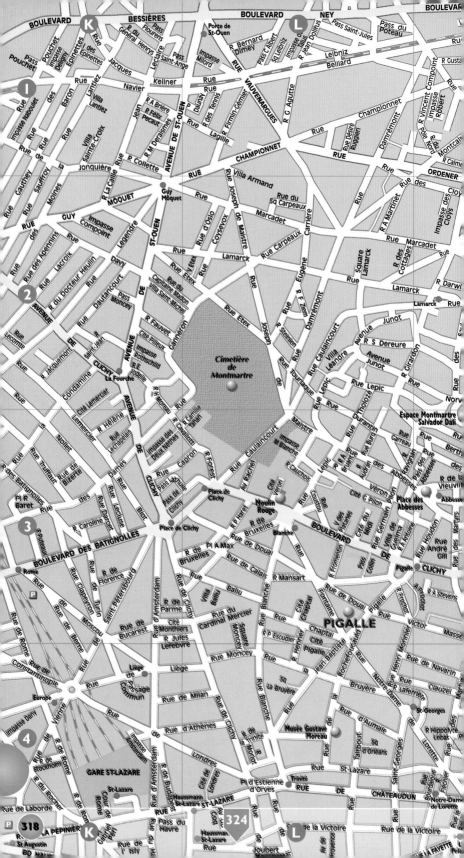

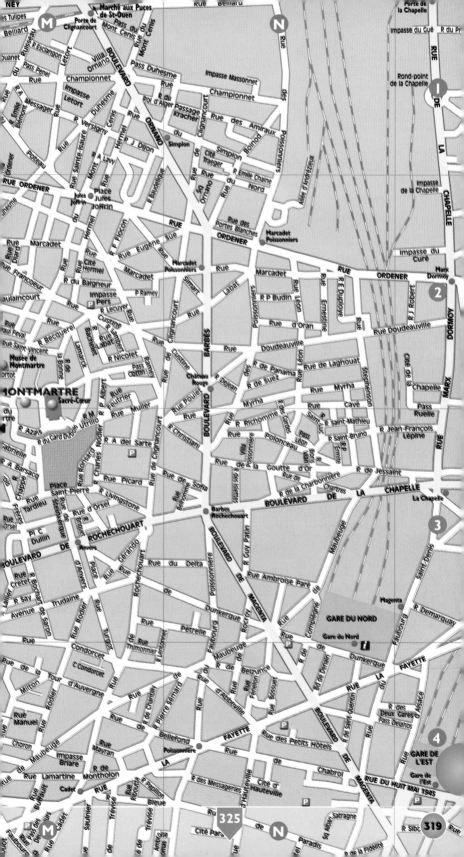

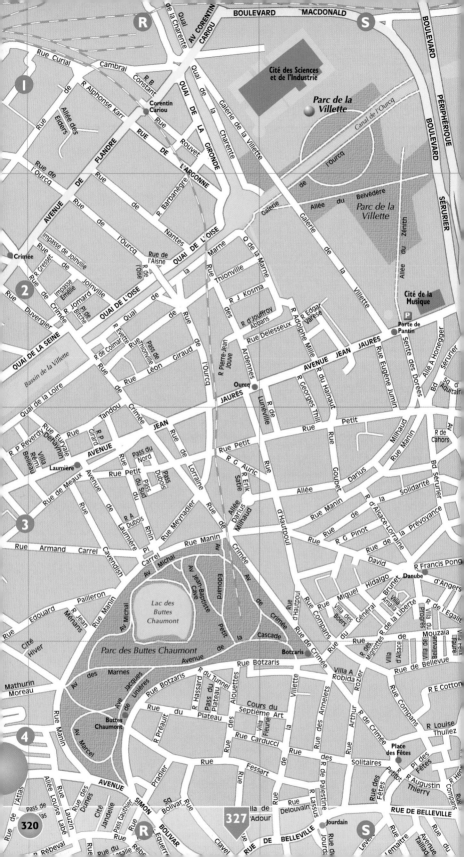

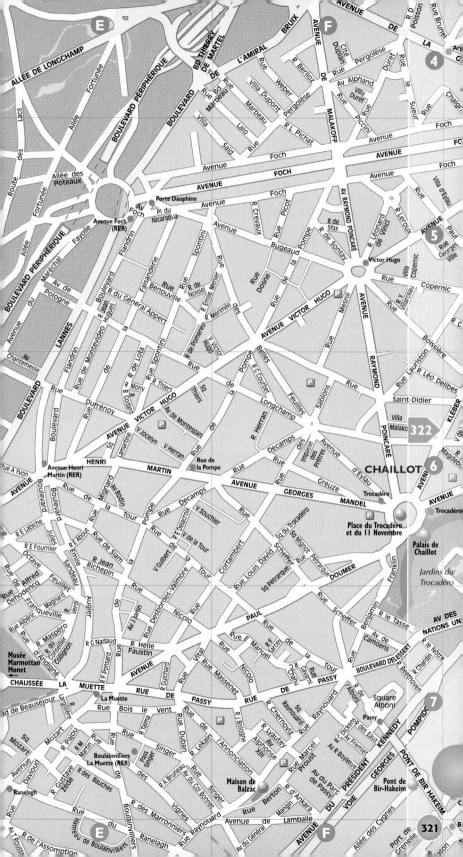

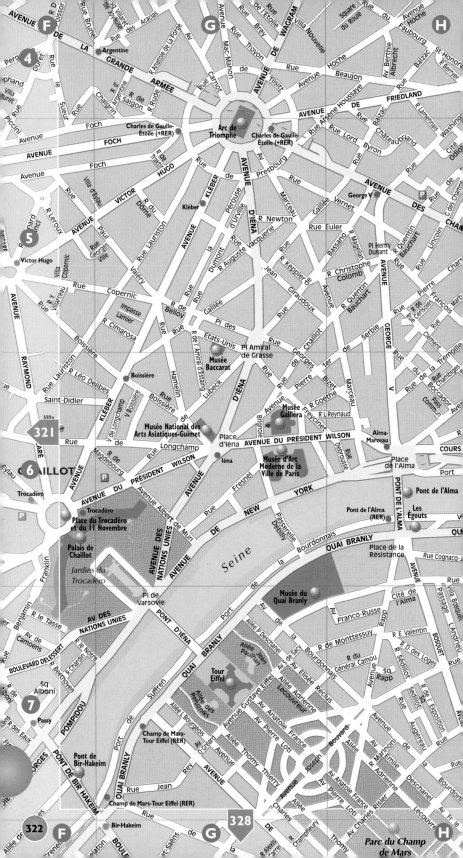

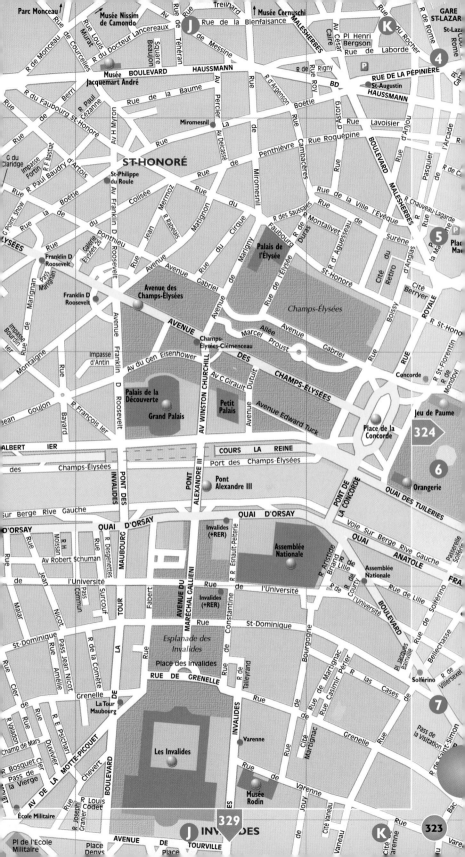

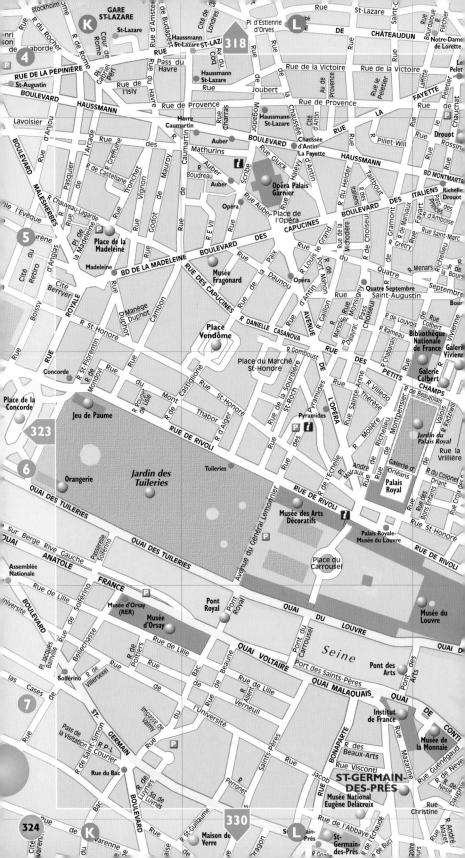

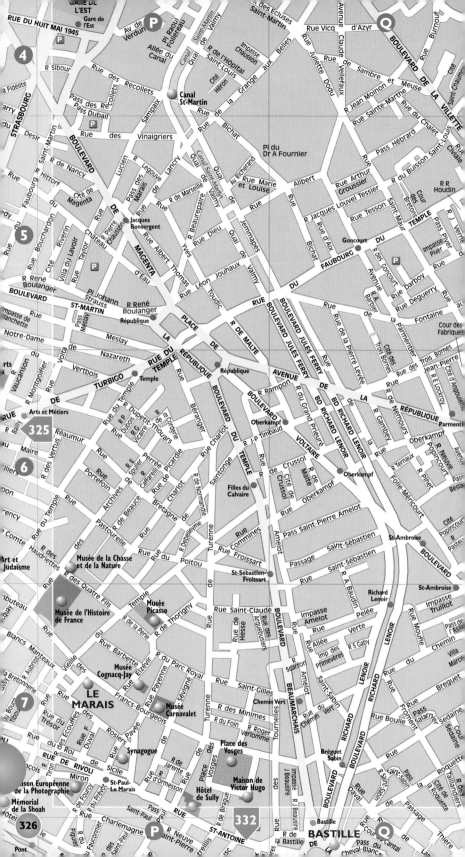

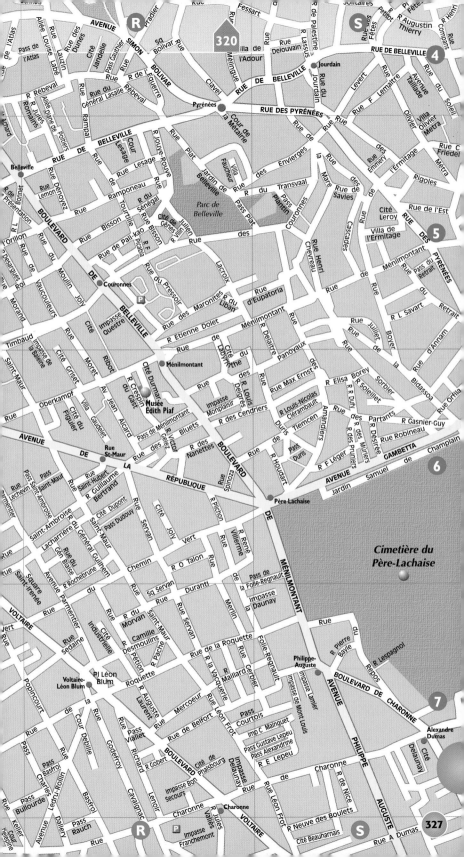

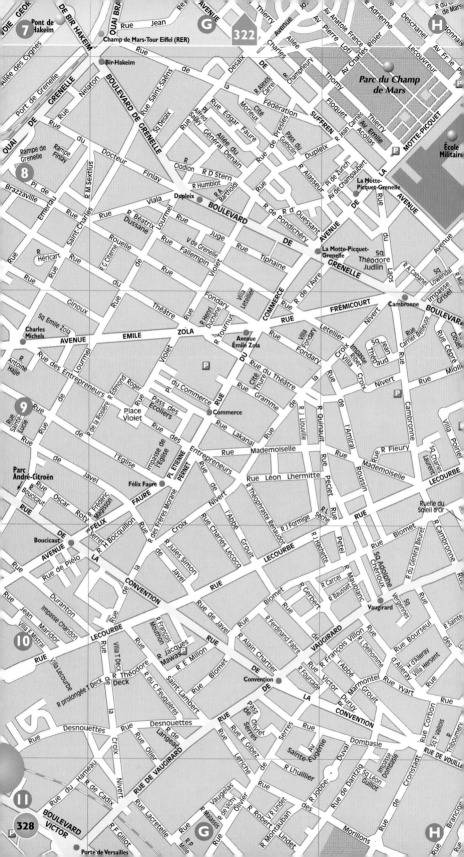

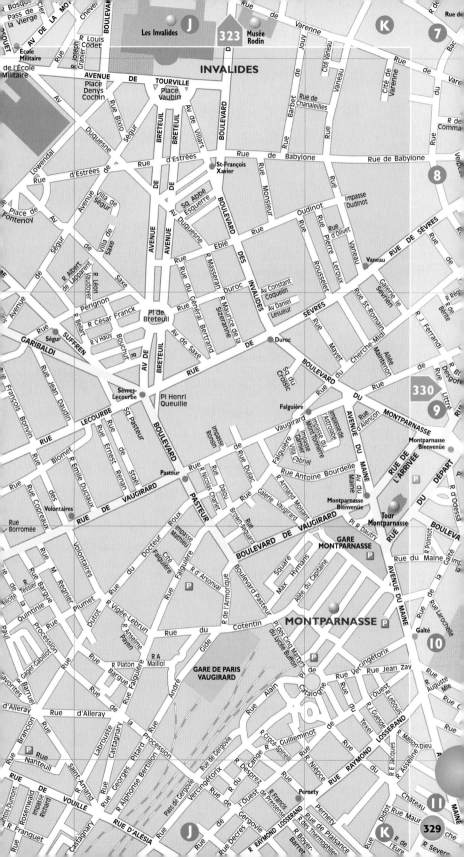

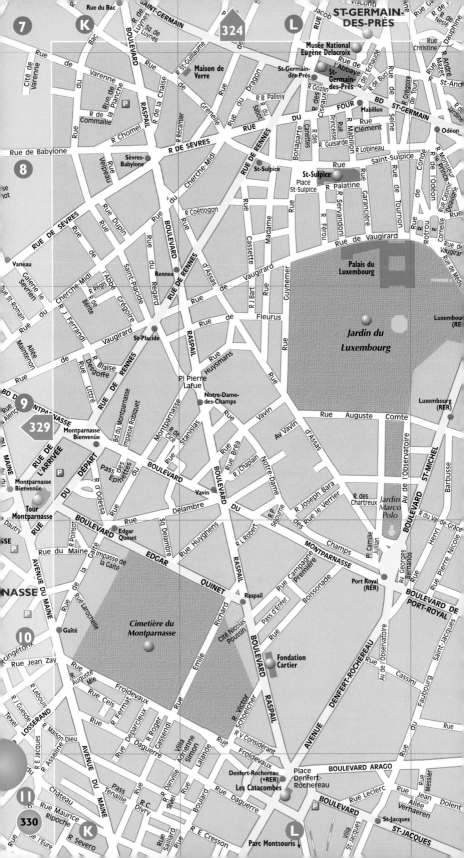

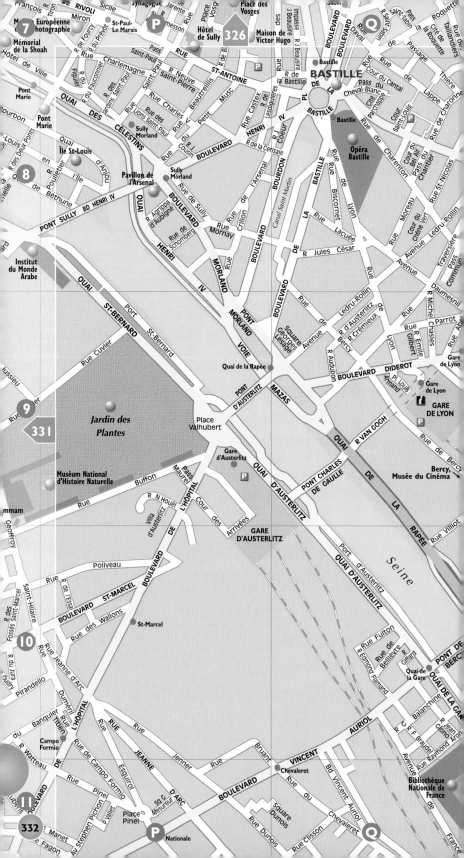

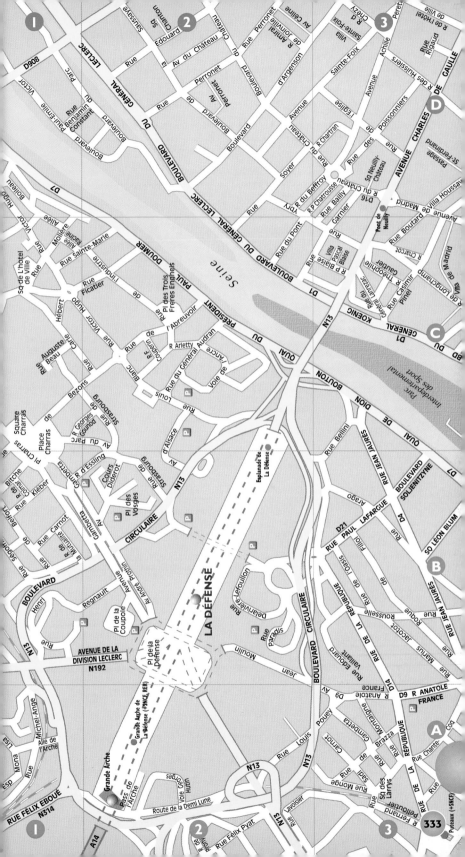

333

Acacias, Rue des 322 G4
Aguesseau, Rue d' 323 K5
Alger, Rue d' 324 L6
Abbaye, Rue de l' 330 L8
Abbé Esquerre, Square 329 J8
Abbé Grégoire, Rue de l' 330 K8
Abbesses, Passage des 318 M3
Abbesses, Rue des 318 L3
Abbeville, Rue d' 319 N4
Abel Hovelacque, Rue 331 N11
Abel, Rue 332 Q9
Adanson, Square 331 N10
Adrienne Lecouvreur, Allée 322
  H7
Agrippa d'Aubigné, Rue 332 P8
Alain, Rue 329 J10
Alasseur, Rue 328 G8
Alban Satragne, Square 325 N4
Albéric Magnard, Rue 321 E7
Albert 1er, Cours 323 H6
Albert de Lapparent, Rue 329 J8
Albert de Mun, Avenue de 322
  G6
Albert Thomas, Rue 326 P5
Albert, Rue P 319 M2
Alboni, Rue de l' 321 F7
Alboni, Square 321 F7
Alençon, Rue d' 329 K9
Alexandre III, Pont 323 J6
Alexandrie, Rue d' 325 N5
Alexandrine, Pass 327 S7
Alexis Carrel, Rue 328 G8
Alfred Dehodencq, Rue 321 E7
Alfred Sauvy, Place 328 G8
Allent, Rue 324 L7
Alma, Cité de l' 322 H7
Alma, Place de l' 322 H6
Alma, Pont de l' 322 H6
Alphonse XIII, Avenue 321 F7
Alsace, Rue d' 319 P4
Amandiers, Rue des 327 S6
Amboise, Rue d' 324 M5
Ambroise Paré, Rue 319 N3
Ambroise Thomas, Rue 325 M4
Amélie, Rue 323 H7
Amelot, Impasse 326 Q7
Amelot, Rue 326 Q7
Amiral d'Estaing, Rue de l' 322
  G5
Amiral de Grasse, Place 322 G5
Amsterdam, Impasse 318 K4
Amsterdam, Rue d' 318 K3
Amyot, Rue 331 M9
Anatole de la Forge, Rue 322 G4
Anatole France, Avenue 322 G7
Anatole France, Quai 323 K6
Andigné, Rue d' 321 E7
André Gide, Rue 329 J10
André Gill, Rue 318 M3
André Malraux, Place 324 L6
André Mazet, Rue 330 M8
André Prothin, Avenue 333 B2
Angoulême, Cité d' 326 Q6
Anjou, Quai d' 332 P8
Anjou, Rue d' 323 K5
Ankara, Rue d' 321 F7
Annam, Rue d' 327 S6

Annonciation, Rue de l' 321 F7
Anselme Payen, Rue 329 J10
Antin, Cité d' 324 L4
Antin, Impasse d' 323 J6
Antin, Rue d' 324 L5
Antoine Bourdelle, Rue 329 J9
Antoine Hajje, Rue 328 F9
Antoine, Rue A 318 L3
Anvers, Place d' 319 M3
Apennins, Rue des 318 K2
Arago, Boulevard 330 L11
Arcade, Rue de l' 324 K5
Arche, Pass de l' 333 A2
Archevêché, Pont de l' 331 N8
Archives, Rue des 326 P6
Arcole, Rue d' 331 N8
Arènes, Rue des 331 N9
Argenson, Rue d' 323 J4
Argentine, Rue d' 322 G4
Argout, Rue d' 325 M6
Aristide Briand, Rue 323 K6
Armand Moisant, Rue 329 J9
Armorique, Rue de l' 329 J10
Arquebusiers, Rue des 326 P7
Arras, Rue d' 331 N9
Arrivée, Rue de l' 329 K9
Arrivées, Cour des 332 P9
Arsenal, Rue de l' 332 P8
Arsène Houssaye, Rue 322 H4
Arsonval, Rue d' 329 J10
Artois, Rue d' 323 H5
Arts, Pont des 324 L7
Asile, Passage de l' 326 Q7
Assas, Rue d' 330 L9
Assomption, Rue de l' 321 E8
Astorg, Rue d' 323 K4
Astrolabe, Impasse de l' 329 K9
Athènes, Rue d' 318 L4
Atlas, Rue de l' 327 Q4
Auber, Rue 324 L5
Aubriot, Rue 325 N7
Audran, Rue 318 L3
Audubon, Rue 332 Q9
Augereau, Rue 322 H7
Auguste Comte, Rue 330 L9
Auguste Laurent, Rue 327 R7
Auguste Mie, Rue 330 K10
Auguste Vacquerie, Rue 322 G5
Aumale, Rue d' 318 L4
Austerlitz, Pont d' 332 P9
Austerlitz, Rue d' 332 Q9
Aux Ours, Rue 325 N6
Avenue Gabriel 323 K5
Azais, Rue 319 M3

Babylone, Rue de 329 J8
Bac, Rue du 330 K8
Bachaumont, Rue 325 M6
Bachelet, Rue 319 M2
Baigneur, Rue du 319 M2
Bailleul, Rue 325 M6
Bailly, Rue 325 N6
Baleine, Impasse de la 327 R5
Ballu, Rue 318 L3
Balzac, Rue 322 H4
Banque, Rue de la 325 M5
Banquier, Rue du 331 N10

Barbet de Jouy, Rue 329 J8
Barbette, Rue 326 P7
Baret, Place R 318 K3
Barres, Rue des 325 N7
Barsacq, Rue A 319 M3
Bart, Rue J 330 L9
Bartholdi, Rue A 328 G8
Basfour, Passage 325 N6
Basfroi, Pass 327 R7
Basfroi, Rue 327 R7
Bassano, Rue de 322 G5
Bastiat, Rue F 323 H5
Bastille, Boulevard de la 332 Q8
Bastille, Place de la 332 Q8
Bastille, Rue de la 332 Q8
Batignolles, Boulevard des 318
  K3
Batignolles, Rue des 318 K3
Bauches, Rue des 321 E7
Baudelique, Rue 319 M2
Baudin, Rue A 326 Q6
Bayard, Rue 323 H6
Béatrix Dussane, Rue 328 G8
Beaubourg, Rue 325 N6
Beauce, Rue de 326 P6
Beaujolais, Rue de 324 M6
Beaujon, Rue 322 H4
Beaumarchais, Boulevard 326
  Q7
Beaune, Rue de 324 L7
Beauregard, Rue 325 N5
Beaurepaire, Rue 326 P5
Beauséjour, Boulevard de 321
  E7
Beausire, Impasse J 326 Q7
Beausire, Rue J 326 Q7
Beautreillis, Rue 332 P8
Beaux-Arts, Rue des 324 L7
Becquerel, Rue 319 M2
Beethoven, Rue 322 F7
Bel Air, Cour du 332 Q8
Belfort, Rue de 327 R7
Belhomme, Rue 319 N3
Bellart, Rue 329 J9
Bellechasse, Rue de 324 K7
Bellefond, Rue de 319 N4
Belloy, Rue de 322 G5
Belzunce, Rue de 319 N4
Béranger, Rue 326 P6
Berbier du Mets, Rue 331 N10
Bercy, Rue de 332 Q9
Berger, Rue 325 M6
Bergère, Cité 325 M5
Bergère, Rue 325 M5
Bérite, Rue de 330 K9
Bernardins, Rue des 331 N8
Berne, Rue de 318 K3
Berri, Rue de 322 H5
Berryer, Cité 324 K5
Berryer, Rue 322 H4
Berthaud, Impasse 325 N6
Berthe, Rue 318 M3
Berthie Albrecht, Avenue 322 H4
Berthollet, Rue 331 M10
Berton, Rue 321 F7
Beslay, Passage 326 Q6
Béthune, Quai de 331 N8

Bidassoa, Rue de la 327 S6
Bienfaisance, Rue de la 323 J4
Bièvre, Rue de 331 N8
Biot, Rue 318 K3
Bir Hakeim, Pont de 322 F7
Birague, Rue de 326 P8
Biscornet, Rue 332 Q8
Bixio, Rue 329 J8
Bizerte, Rue de 318 K3
Blainville, Rue 331 N9
Blaise Desgoffe, Rue 330 K9
Blanche, Impasse M 318 L3
Blanche, Rue 318 L4
Blancs Manteaux, Rue des 325
  N7
Bleue, Rue 319 M4
Blondel, Rue 325 N5
Bluets, Rue des 327 R6
Boccador, Rue du 322 H6
Bochart de Saron, Rue 319 M3
Bois le Vent, Rue 321 E7
Boissonade, Rue 330 L10
Boissy d'Anglas, Rue 323 K5
Bologne, Rue J 321 F7
Bon Secours, Impasse 327 R7
Bonaparte, Rue 324 L7
Bonne Nouvelle, Boulevard de
  325 N5
Bonne Nouvelle, Impasse de
  325 N5
Bonne, Rue de la 319 M2
Bons Enfants, Rue des 324 M6
Boris Vian, Rue 319 N3
Bosquet, Avenue 322 H7
Bosquet, Rue 323 H7
Bossuet, Rue 319 N4
Bouchardon, Rue 325 N5
Bouchut, Rue 329 J9
Boucicaut, Rue 328 F9
Boudreau, Rue 324 L5
Boulainvilliers, Hameau de 321
  E8
Boulainvilliers, Rue de 321 E8
Boulangers, Rue des 331 N9
Boulard, Rue 330 L11
Boulle, Rue 326 Q7
Bouloi, Rue 325 M6
Bourbon, Quai de 331 N8
Bourdaloue, Rue 318 M4
Bourdin, Impasse 323 H5
Bourdon, Boulevard 332 P8
Bourdonnais, Avenue de la 322
  H7
Bourdonnais, Port de la 322 G6
Bourdonnais, Rue des 325 M7
Bourg Tibourg, Rue du 325 N7
Bourgeois, Allée L 322 G7
Bourgogne, Rue de 323 J7
Bourse, Place de la 325 M5
Bourse, Rue de la 324 M5
Boutebrie, Rue 331 M8
Boylesve, Avenue R 321 F7
Brady, Passage 325 N5
Branly, Quai 322 G7
Brantôme, Rue 325 N6
Brazzaville, Place de 328 F8
Bréa, Rue 330 L9

Ourcq, Galerie de l' 320 S1

Pache, Rue 327 R7
Paillet, Rue 331 M9
Paix, Rue de la 324 L5
Pajou, Rue 321 E7
Palais, Boulevard du 325 M7
Palatine, Rue 330 L8
Palestro, Rue de 325 N6
Palissy, Rue B 330 L8
Panoramas, Passage des 325 M5
Panoyaux, Rue des 327 R6
Panthéon, Place du 331 M9
Papillon, Rue 319 M4
Papin, Rue 325 N6
Paradis, Cité 325 N4
Paradis, Rue de 325 N4
Paradis, Rue 333 B2
Parc de Passy, Avenue du 321 F7
Parc Royal, Rue du 326 P7
Parchappe, Cité 332 Q8
Parme, Rue de 318 K3
Parrot, Rue 332 Q9
Partants, Rue des 327 S6
Pascal, Rue 331 N10
Pasquier, Rue 324 K5
Passy, Rue de 321 F7
Pasteur, Boulevard 329 J9
Pasteur, Rue 326 Q6
Pasteur, Square 329 J9
Pastourelle, Rue 326 P6
Patriarches, Rue des 331 N10
Paul Baudry, Rue 323 H5
Paul Cézanne, Rue 323 J4
Paul Feval, Rue 319 M2
Paul Lelong, Rue 325 M5
Paul Valéry, Rue 322 G5
Pavée, Rue 326 P7
Payenne, Rue 326 P7
Pecquay, Rue 325 N7
Pelée, Rue 326 Q7
Penthièvre, Rue de 323 J5
Pépinière, Rue de la 324 K4
Percier, Avenue 323 J4
Perle, Rue de la 326 P7
Pernelle, Rue 325 N7
Perrault, Rue 325 M7
Perrée, Rue 326 P6
Perronet, Rue 324 L7
Pers, Impasse 319 M2
Pétion, Rue 327 R7
Petit Musc, Rue du 332 P8
Petit Pont 331 M8
Petites Ecuries, Cour des 325 N5
Petites Ecuries, Rue des 325 N5
Petits Carreaux, Rue des 325 M5
Petits Champs, Rue des 324 L6
Petits Hôtels, Rue des 319 N4
Pétrelle, Rue 319 N3
Phalsbourg, Cité de 327 R7
Philippe Auguste, Avenue 327 S7
Philippe, Pont L 331 N8
Picard, Rue 319 M3
Picardie, Rue de 326 P6
Pierre 1er de Serbie, Avenue 322 G6
Pierre Bayle, Rue 327 S7

Pierre Brossolette, Rue 331 M9
Pierre Charron, Rue 322 H5
Pierre Chausson, Rue 326 P5
Pierre Lafue, Place 330 L9
Pierre Leroux, Rue 329 K8
Pierre Loti, Avenue 322 G7
Pierre Nicole, Rue 330 M10
Pierre Sarrazin, Rue 331 M8
Pierre Sémard, Rue 319 N4
Pigalle, Cité 318 L4
Pihet, Rue 326 Q6
Pirandello, Rue 331 N10
Planche, Rue de la 330 K8
Planchette, Impasse de la 325 N5
Platon, Rue 329 J10
Plâtre, Rue du 325 N7
Plélo, Rue de 328 F10
Plichon, Rue 327 R6
Poinsot, Rue 330 K10
Point Show, Galerie 323 H5
Poirée, Rue B 325 M7
Poissonnière, Boulevard 325 M5
Poissonnière, Rue 325 N5
Poissy, Rue de 331 N8
Poitiers, Rue de 324 K7
Poitou, Rue du 326 P6
Polonceau, Rue 319 N3
Ponceau, Passage du 325 N5
Pondichéry, Rue de 328 G8
Ponsard, Rue F 321 E7
Pont Neuf, Rue du 325 M7
Pont, Rue du 333 C2
Ponthieu, Rue de 323 J5
Pontoise, Rue de 331 N8
Popincourt, Cité 326 Q6
Popincourt, Rue 327 Q7
Port Mahon, Rue de 324 L5
Port Royal, Square de 331 M10
Portefoin, Rue 326 P6
Port-Royal, Boulevard de 331 M10
Postes, Pass des 331 N10
Poulletier, Rue 332 P8
Prado, Passage du 325 N5
Pré, Rue du 319 P1
Presbourg, Rue de 322 G5
Président Kennedy, Avenue du 321 F7
Président Paul Doumer, Quai du 333 C2
Président Wilson, Avenue du 322 G6
Presles, Rue de 328 G8
Prévôt, Rue du 326 P7
Primatice, Rue 331 N11
Primevères, Impasse des 326 Q7
Princes, Passage des 324 M5
Princesse, Rue 330 L8
Prony, Rue de 333 A2
Provence, Avenue de 324 L4
Provence, Rue de 324 L4
Pruniers, Rue des 327 S6
Psichari, Rue E 323 H7
Puteaux, Rue 318 K3
Pyramides, Rue des 324 L6

Quatre Fils, Rue des 326 P6

Quatre Septembre, Rue du 324 L5
Quatrefages, Rue de 331 N9
Quentin Bauchart, Rue 322 H5
Quincampoix, Rue 325 N7

Rabelais, Rue 323 J5
Rachel, Avenue 318 L3
Racine, Rue 331 M8
Radziwill, Rue 324 M6
Rambuteau, Rue 325 N6
Rameau, Rue 324 L5
Ramey, Passage 319 M2
Ramey, Rue 319 M2
Rampon, Rue 326 P6
Ranelagh, Rue du 321 E8
Raoul Follereau, Place 326 P4
Rapée, Quai de la 332 Q9
Rapp, Avenue 322 H7
Rapp, Square 322 H7
Raspail, Boulevard 324 K7
Raspail, Boulevard 330 K8
Rataud, Rue 331 M9
Rauch, Passage 327 R8
Ravignan, Rue 318 L3
Raynouard, Rue 321 F7
Raynouard, Square 321 F7
Réaumur, Rue 326 P6
Récamier, Rue 330 L8
Recollets, Passage des 326 P4
Recollets, Rue des 326 P4
Refuzniks, Allée des 322 G7
Regard, Rue du 330 K8
Régis, Rue 330 K9
Reilhac, Passage 325 N5
Reine Blanche, Rue de la 331 N10
Reine, Cours la 323 J6
Renard, Rue du 325 N7
René Boulanger, Rue 325 N5
René Villerme, Rue 327 R6
Rennes, Rue de 330 L8
Repos, Rue du 327 S7
République, Avenue de la 326 Q6
République, Place de la 326 P6
Résistance, Place de la 322 H6
Retiro, Cité du 323 K5
Reynaud, Rue L 322 H6
Riboutte, Rue 319 M4
Richard Lenoir, Boulevard 326 Q7
Richard Lenoir, Rue 327 R7
Richelieu, Rue de 324 L6
Richer, Rue 325 M4
Richerand, Avenue 326 P5
Richomme, Rue R 319 N3
Rigny, Rue de 323 K4
Rive Gauche, Voie Sur Berge 323 H6
Riverin, Cité 326 P5
Rivoli, Rue de 325 M7
Robert Schuman, Avenue 323 H6
Robert, Rue J 319 P2
Robert, Rue L 330 L10
Robineau, Rue 327 S6
Rochebrune, Rue 327 R6

Rochechouart, Boulevard de 319 M3
Rochechouart, Rue de 319 M3
Rocher, Rue du 318 K4
Rocroy, Rue de 319 N3
Rodier, Rue 319 M4
Roger Verlomme, Rue 326 P7
Roger, Rue 330 K10
Roi de Sicile, Rue du 326 P7
Rollin, Rue 331 N9
Rome, Cour de 318 K4
Rome, Rue de 318 K4
Ronsard, Rue 319 M3
Ronsin, Impasse 329 J9
Roquépine, Rue 323 K5
Roquette, Cité de la 326 Q7
Roquette, Rue de la 327 R7
Rosiers, Rue des 326 P7
Rossini, Rue 324 M5
Rothschild, Impasse 318 K2
Rotrou, Rue 330 M8
Rouelle, Rue 328 F8
Rougemont, Rue 325 M5
Rouget de Lisle, Rue 324 K6
Roulé, Rue du 325 M6
Roulé, Square du 322 H4
Rousseau, Avenue T 321 E8
Rousselet, Rue 329 K8
Roy, Rue 323 K4
Royal, Pont 324 L7
Royale, Rue 324 K5
Royer-Collard, Rue 331 M9
Rubens, Rue 331 N11
Rude, Rue 322 G4
Rue De Sèvres 329 J9
Rue Larochelle 330 K10
Ruelle, Passage 319 P2

Sabot, Rue du 330 L8
Sacy, Avenue S de 322 G7
Saigon, Rue de 322 G4
St-André des Arts, Rue 330 M8
St-Antoine, Rue 332 P8
St-Bernard, Port 332 P9
St-Bernard, Quai 332 P9
St-Denis, Boulevard 325 N5
St-Dominique, Rue 323 J7
St-Florentin, Rue 324 K5
St-Germain, Boulevard 330 L8
St-Germain-L'auxerrois, Rue 325 M7
St-Guillaume, Rue 330 L8
St-Honoré, Rue 324 M6
St-Jacques, Boulevard 330 L11
St-Jacques, Rue 331 M9
St-Lazare, Rue 318 L4
St-Martin, Boulevard 326 P5
St-Médard, Rue 331 N9
St-Michel, Boulevard 330 M9
St-Michel, Quai 331 M8
St-Nicolas, Rue 332 Q8
St-Ouen, Avenue de 318 K2
St-Roch, Rue 324 L6
St-Romain, Rue 329 K9
St-Sulpice, Place 330 L8
St-Ambroise, Passage 327 R6
St-Ambroise, Rue 327 R6
St-Augustin, Rue 324 L5
St-Bruno, Rue 319 N3

STREET INDEX 339

ACKNOWLEDGMENTS

Abbreviations for the picture credits are as follows:
AA = AA World Travel Library, t (top), b (bottom), c (centre), l (left), r (right)

UNDERSTANDING PARIS

5l AA/C Sawyer; 5c AA/M Jourdan; 5r AA/M Jourdan; 8l AA/W Voysey; 8tr AA/C Sawyer; 8ctr AA/W Voysey; 8cbr AA/C Sawyer; 8br AA/C Sawyer; 9t AA/C Sawyer; 9lt AA/C Sawyer; 9ct AA/C Sawyer; 9cb Brasserie Lorraine; 9ub AA/M Jourdan; 9b Brand X Pictures; 9r AA/M Jourdan; 10tl AA/M Jourdan; 10tc AA/J Tims; 10tr AA/M Jourdan; 10cl AA/M Jourdan; 10bl AA/T Souter; 10ltr AA/M Chaplow; 10ucr AA/C Sawyer; 10lcr AA/P Kenward; 10ubr AA/T Souter; 10br AA/M Jourdan.

LIVING PARIS

11 AA/K Paterson; 12/13b/g AA/M Jourdan; 12tl AA/M Jourdan; 12tc AA/M Jourdan; 12tr AA/C Sawyer; 12ctl AA/M Jourdan; 12c AA/B Rieger; 12cr © "BE", Boulangepicier/Alain Ducasse. Photo: M de L'Ecotais; 12cl AA/B Smith; 12bl AA/C Sawyer; 13tl AA/M Jourdan; 13tc AA/M Jourdan; 13tr AA/C Sawyer; 13cl AA/T Souter; 13cr Courtesy Le Train Bleu; 13bl Rex Features Ltd; 14/15 AA/K Paterson; 14tl AA/M Jourdan; 14tc AA/M Jourdan; 14tr AA/B Rieger; 14ctl AA/M Jourdan; 14c AA/C Sawyer; 14cr AA/M Jourdan; 14l AA/B Rieger; 15tl AA/M Jourdan; 15tr AA/M Jourdan; 15cl AA/P Kenward; 15c AA/M Jourdan; 15cr AA/M Jourdan; 15bl AA/M Jourdan; 15r Rex Features Ltd; 15b Rex Features Ltd; 16/17b/g AA/K Paterson; 16t AA/J Tims; 16cl AA/C Sawyer; 16c AA/M Jourdan; 16cr AA/J Tims; 16r Rex Features Ltd; 16cl AA/M Jourdan; 16bl AA/M Jourdan; 17tl AA/T Souter; 17tc AA/B Rieger; 17tr AA/M Jourdan; 16/17 AA/J Tims; 17c Courtesy Modus Publicity; 17cr AA/M Jourdan; 18/19b/g AA/M Jourdan; 18tl Paramount/Kobal; 18tc AA/K Paterson; 18tr AA/T Souter; 18cl Rex Features Ltd; 18cr AA; 18b AA; 19t Courtesy Club Med; 19c AA/T Souter; 19tr AA/K Paterson; 19cr AA/M Jourdan; 20/1b/g AA/M Jourdan; 20tl AA/M Jourdan; 20tr AA/M Jourdan; 20cl AA/K Paterson; 20cl AA/K Paterson; 20cr Courtesy Club Med; 21tl AA/M Jourdan; 21tr AA/C Sawyer; 21cl AA/T Souter; 21ctr AA/M Jourdan; 21cr AA/T. Souter; 21b AA/M Jourdan; 22b/g AA/C Sawyer; 22tl AA; 22tr AA/T. Souter; 22c AA/M Jourdan; 22ctr AA/M Jourdan; 22cr AA/M Jourdan.

THE STORY OF PARIS

23 AA; 24/5 AA; 24cl AA/K Paterson; 24cr AA; 24bl AA; 25cl AA/B Rieger; 25cr AA; 25bl Mary Evans Picture Library; 25br AA; 26/7 AA/P Enticknap; 26cl AA; 26cr AA/P Enticknap; 26bl AA; 26br AA/J Tims; 27cl Mary Evans Picture Library; 27cr AA; 27bl AA; 27bc M Jourdan; 27br AA; 28cl AA/D Noble; 28cr Mary Evans Picture Library; 28bl AA/D Noble; 28/9 Mary Evans Picture Library; 28/9b/g AA/R Moore; 29cl AA; 29cr AA; 29bl AA; 29c AA; 29br AA; 30/1 AA/D Noble; 30cl AA/P Kenward; 30bl AA/M Jourdan; 31cl AA; 31c AA; 31cr AA; 31bc AA; 31br AA/M Jourdan; 32/3 AA; 32c AA; 32bl AA/P Kenward; 32/3 Mary Evans Picture Library; 33cl AA; 33c AA; 33cl AA; 33bc AA/K Paterson; 33br Mary Evans Picture Library; 34/5 AA/M Jourdan; 34cl AA; 34c AA/J Tims; 34bl AA; 35cl AA; 35c Mary Evans Picture Library; 35cr AA; 35b Mary Evans Picture Library; 36/7 AA; 36cl AA/M Jourdan; 36bl Illustrated London News; 36bc AA/M Short; 36br AA; 37cl AA; 37c Illustrated London News; 37cr Illustrated London News; 37bl AA; 37bc AA/C Sawyer; 37br Mary Evans Picture Library; 38/9 AA/C Sawyer; 38cl AA; 38cr Rex Features Ltd; 38bl Illustrated London News; 38br Hulton Archive/Getty Images; 38bc L'Apres Midi d'un Faune by Debussy, Nijinsky's Faune costume, 1912 by Leon Bakst, Bibliotheque Nationale/Bridgeman Art Library; 39cl Illustrated London News; 39c Rex Features Ltd; 39tr Rex Features Ltd; 39b AA/C Sawyer; 39br AA/K Paterson; 40b/g AA/M Jourdan; 40cl AA; 40cr Rex Features Ltd;; 40bl Getty Images; 40br Jean-Louis Margoche for www.parisrama.com, the Paris-lover's website.

ON THE MOVE

41 AA/K Paterson; 42/3 Digital Vision; 43 AA/C Sawyer; 44/45 Digital Vision; 44 AA/C Sawyer; 45tl AA/C Sawyer; 45b AA/C Sawyer; 46t Digital Vision; 46b Digital Vision; 47t AA/B Rieger; 47c AA/C Sawyer; 48t AA/B Rieger; 48b AA/C Sawyer; 49t AA/C Sawyer; 49r AA/T Souter; 50/1t AA/C Sawyer; 51 AA/C Sawyer; 52/3 AA/C Sawyer; 54/5 AA/M Jourdan; 54 AA/M Jourdan; 55 AA/M Jourdan; 56/7 Digital Vision; 56 AA/C Sawyer; 57cl AA/C Sawyer; 57br AA/C Sawyer; 58t Digital Vision; 58cr AA/K Paterson; 58br AA; 59t AA/M Jourdan; 59r AA/M Jourdan; 60/1 Digital Vision; 60 AA/T Souter; 61 AA; 62 AA/S McBride; 63t Digital Vision; 63b AA/M Adelman; 64t Digital Vision; 64r AA/C Sawyer.

THE SIGHTS

65 AA/J A Tims; 70l AA/C Sawyer; 70r AA/C Sawyer; 71l AA/C Sawyer; 71r AA/C Sawyer; 72l AA/M Jourdan; 72r AA/J Tims; 73l AA/C Sawyer; 73r AA/M Jourdan; 74l AA/C Sawyer; 74r AA/M Jourdan; 75l AA/B Rieger; 75r AA/C Sawyer; 76 AA/M Jourdan; 77t AA/J Tims; 77cl AA/K Paterson; 77cr AA/M Jourdan; 77b AA/P Kenward; 78cl AA/K Glendenning; 78c AA/M Jourdan; 78cr AA/J Tims; 78b AA/M Jourdan; 79l AA/M Jourdan; 79r AA/M Jourdan; 80t AA/M Jourdan; 80b AA/P Kenward; 81tl AA/M Jourdan; 81tr AA/J Tims; 82t AA/M Jourdan; 82cl AA/M Jourdan; 82c AA/M Jourdan; 82cr AA/M Jourdan; 82b AA/J Tims; 83 AA/T Souter; 84/5 AA/M Jourdan; 86 AA/M Jourdan; 87tl AA/T Souter; 87tr AA/C Sawyer; 87b AA/C Sawyer; 88tr AA/M Jourdan; 88l AA/J Tims; 89t AA/J Tims; 89c AA/T Souter; 90/1 AA/T Souter; 90 AA/M Jourdan; 92l AA/J Tims; 92c AA/C Sawyer; 92r AA/C Sawyer; 93l AA/C Hatley with kind permission of the Fondation Cartier; 93r AA/J Tims; 94t AA/J Tims; 94l AA/J Tims; 95t AA; 95b AA/M Jourdan; 96t AA/B Rieger; 96c AA/K Paterson; 96b AA/M Jourdan; 97 AA/C Sawyer; 98t AA/M Jourdan; 98b AA/M Jourdan; 99t AA/K Paterson; 99cl AA/K Paterson; 99cr AA/M Jourdan; 100l AA; 100r AA/B Rieger; 101t AA/B Rieger; 102t AA/P Enticknap; 102cl AA/C Sawyer; 102c AA/C Sawyer; 102cr AA/M Jourdan; 102b AA/M Jourdan; 103 AA/M Jourdan; 104t AA/K Glendenning; 104l AA/T Souter; 104b AA/M Jourdan; 105t AA/C Sawyer; 105r AA/M Jourdan; 106l AA/K Paterson; 106c Gobelins tapestry, Fin de Siecle de cinq a sept, after Eduardo Arroyo (GOBT1336), Courtesy Collection du Mobilier National, cliché Mobilier National. Photo: Mobilier National – Isabelle Bideau; 106r AA/J Tims; 107l AA/K Paterson; 107r AA/K Glendenning; 108t AA/M Jourdan; 108l AA/M Jourdan; 108r AA/M Jourdan; 109l AA/M Jourdan; 109r AA/J Tims; 110t AA/C Sawyer; 110b AA/C Hatley; 111l AA/P Enticknap; 111r Courtesy Union Central des Arts Decoratifs. Photo: L Sully Jaulmes; 112t AA/M Jourdan; 112b AA/M Jourdan; 113l AA/K Glendenning; 113r View of the Canal of Santa Chiara, Venice (oil on canvas) by Canaletto, Musee Cognacq-Jay, Paris/Bridgeman Art Library; 114t AA/K Paterson; 114l AA/M Jourdan; 114l AA/J Tims; 115l AA/M Jourdan; 115r AA/K Paterson; 116l AA/J Tims; 116r Courtesy GREVIN Paris Wax Museum; 117l AA/K Glendenning; 117r AA/B Rieger; 117b AA/P Kenward; 118 AA/M Jourdan; 119t Mona Lisa, c.1503-6 (oil on panel) by Leonardo da Vinci, Louvre, Paris/Bridgeman Art Library; 119c Egyptian papyrus, Louvre, Paris/Bridgeman Art Library; 119l AA/T. Souter; 119r AA/M Jourdan; 120 AA/J Tims; 121 AA/M Jourdan; 122/3t AA/M Jourdan; 124t Promenade near Argenteuil, 1873 (oil on canvas) by Claude Monet, Musee Marmottan, Paris, Bridgeman Art Library/ADAGP, Paris & DACS, London 2004; 124c Impression: Sunrise, Le Havre, 1872 (oil on canvas) by Claude Monet, Musee Marmottan, Paris, Bridgeman Art Library/ADAGP, Paris & DACS, London, 2004; 124b Illuminated initial 'R', depicting St Catherine of Alexandria, c. 15th century by Luchino

Belbello, Musee Marmottan, Paris, Giraudon/Bridgeman Art Library; 125 AA/J Tims, 126r AA/J Tims, 126l *Two Cranes on the edge of a Pond*, 17th century (w/c on paper) by Indian School, Musee Guimet, Paris/Bridgeman Art Library; 127l AA/C Hatley; 127r AA/J Tims; 127b AA/C Hatley; 128t AA/J Tims; 128l *The Lady and the Unicorn: "Sight"*, 15th century (tapestry) by French School, Musee National du Moyen Age et des Thermes de Cluny, Paris/Bridgeman Art Library; 128c Scene from the Old Testament, mid-13th century (stained glass) by French School, Musee National du Moyen Age et des Thermes de Cluny, Paris/J. P. Zenobel/Bridgeman Art Library; 128r AA/M Jourdan; 129 AA/K Paterson; 130t *Ball at the Moulin de la Galette*, 1876 (oil on canvas) by Pierre Auguste Renoir, Musee d'Orsay, Paris/Giraudon/Bridgeman Art Library; 130l AA/P Enticknap; 130c *End of an Arabesque*, 1877 (oil & pastel on canvas) by Edgar Degas, Musee d'Orsay, Paris/Bridgeman Art Library; 130r AA/J Tims; 132t AA/M Jourdan; 132b AA/T Souter; 132/3 AA/M Jourdan; 133r AA/M Jourdan; 133b AA/M Jourdan; 133c Dining room belonging to Adrien Benard at Champrosay, 1900-01 (photo) by Alexandre Charpentier, Musee d'Orsay, Paris/Bridgeman Art Library; 134b AA/J A Tims; 135l AA/M Jourdan; 135r AA/M Jourdan/© Succession Picasso/DACS 2004; 136 AA/M Jourdan; 137t AA/K Paterson; 137l AA/C Hatley; 137c AA/M Jourdan; 137r AA/P Enticknap; 138 AA/C Sawyer; 139l AA/P Enticknap; 139c AA/C Sawyer; 139r AA/C Sawyer; 140/1 AA/C Sawyer; 141tr AA/P Enticknap; 142t AA; 142b AA/M Jourdan; 143 AA/K Paterson; 144tl AA/M Jourdan; 144tr AA/J Tims; 144b AA/M Jourdan; 145l AA/K Paterson; 145r AA/C Sawyer; 146 AA/M Jourdan; 147l AA/T Souter; 147c AA/K Paterson; 147r AA/M Jourdan; 148t AA/M Jourdan; 148cl AA/M Jourdan; 149tl AA/M Jourdan; 149tc AA/B Rieger; 149tr AA/M Jourdan; 149b AA/M Jourdan; 150t AA/M Jourdan; 150cl AA/B Rieger; 151tl AA/M Jourdan; 151c AA/M Jourdan; 151r AA/T Souter; 152t AA/C Sawyer; 152cl AA/M Jourdan; 152c AA/C Sawyer; 152cr AA/C Sawyer; 153l AA/M Jourdan; 153r AA/M Jourdan; 154 Courtesy Sacre-Coeur de Montmartre; 155t AA/B Rieger; 155cl AA/K Paterson; 155c AA/K Paterson; 155cr AA/J Tims; 155b AA/K Glendenning; 156/7 AA/K Paterson; 158 AA/J Tims; 159cl AA/J Tims; 159t Courtesy Centre des Monuments Nationaux; 159c Courtesy Centre des Monuments Nationaux; 159cr Courtesy Centre des Monuments Nationaux; 161l AA/M Jourdan; 161r AA/K Paterson; 162l AA/K Glendenning; 162c AA/K Glendenning; 162r AA/C Sawyer; 163l AA/C Sawyer; 163c AA/M Jourdan; 163r AA/T Souter; 164t AA/M Jourdan; 164l AA/M Jourdan; 164c AA/B Rieger; 164r AA/J Tims; 165 AA/J Tims; 166/7 AA/K Paterson; 168 AA/T Souter; 169 AA/M Jourdan; 170t AA/C Sawyer; 170cl AA/C Sawyer.

WHAT TO DO

171 AA M Jourdan; 176t AA/C Sawyer; 176l AA/C Sawyer; 176r AA/C Sawyer; 177l AA/C Sawyer; 177r AA/C Sawyer; 178l AA/T Souter; 178r AA/C Sawyer; 179l AA/K Paterson; 179r AA/ M Jourdan; 180l AA/C Sawyer; 180r AA/M Jourdan; 181l AA/C Sawyer; 181r AA/T Souter; 182/3t AA/C Sawyer; 182c AA/C Sawyer; 183c AA/C Sawyer; 184/5t AA/C Sawyer; 184c Galeries Lafayette; 185c AA/C Sawyer; 186/7t AA/C Sawyer; 186c AA/C Sawyer; 187c AA/B Rieger; 188/9t AA/C Sawyer; 188c AA/C Sawyer; 189c AA/C Sawyer; 190/1t AA/C Sawyer; 192t AA/C Sawyer; 192c AA/C Sawyer; 193t AA/K Paterson; 193cl Digital Vision; 193cr AA/M Jourdan; 198/9t AA/P Enticknap; 199c AA/M Jourdan; 200/1t Opera Comique; 200c AA/C Sawyer; 201c AA/B Rieger; 202/3t Opera Comique; 202c Opera Comique; 203c La Balle Au Bond; 204/5t Elysee Monmartre; 204c Elysee Monmartre; 205c AA/W Voysey; 206/7t AA/K Paterson; 206c AA/B Rieger; 207c AA/B Rieger; 208t AA/K Paterson; 208c AA/T Souter; 209t AA/T Souter; 209cl AA/C Sawyer; 209cr AA/C Sawyer; 210/1t AA/T Souter; 210c AA/C Sawyer; 211c AA/K Paterson; 212/3t AA/T Souter; 212c Lizard Lounge; 213c AA/B Rieger; 214/5t Brand X Pics; 214c Brand X Pics; 215c Le Nouveau Casino/Luc Boegly; 216/7t AA/K Paterson; 216cl AA/K Paterson; 216cr AA/M Jourdan; 217c France

Montgolfières/R Short; 218/9t AA/K Paterson; 218c Photodisc; 219c Photodisc; 220t Digital Vision; 220cl Digital Vision; 220cr Lancôme Faubourg Saint-Honoré; 221t AA/K Paterson; 221cl AA/M Jourdan; 221cr Parc Astérix; 22t AA/M Lynch; 222cl Photodisc; 222cr AA/M Lynch.

OUT AND ABOUT

223 AA M Jourdan; 224 AA/J Tims; 225t AA/M Jourdan; 225bl AA/B Rieger; 225br AA/M Jourdan; 227t AA/M Jourdan; 227bl AA/M Jourdan; 227br M Jourdan; 228/9 AA/C Sawyer; 229tl AA/C Sawyer; 229tr AA/C Sawyer; 229br AA/M Jourdan; 230b AA/M Jourdan; 231tl AA/K Paterson; 231tr AA; 231bl AA/M Jourdan; 231br AA/M Jourdan; 233tl AA/M Jourdan; 233tr AA/M Jourdan; 233bl AA/M Jourdan; 233cr AA/M Jourdan; 234c AA/M Jourdan; 234b AA/B Rieger; 235 AA/M Jourdan; 236 AA/K Paterson; 237 AA/K Paterson; 238 AA/D Noble; 239 AA/C Hatley; 240c © Disney; 240cb © Disney; 240/1 © Disney; 241 © Disney; 242 AA/M Jourdan; 243t AA/M Jourdan; 243b AA/M Jourdan; 244/5 AA/M Jourdan; 245 AA/M Jourdan; 246 AA/M Jourdan; 247 AA/M Jourdan; 248tl AA/M Jourdan; 248tc AA/M Jourdan; 248tr AA/M Jourdan.

EATING AND STAYING

249 AA/C Sawyer; 250cl AA/C Sawyer; 250c AA; 250cr AA/C Sawyer; 251t AA/E Meacher; 251b AA/B Smith; 252cl AA/T Souter; 252cc AA/M Jourdan; 252cr AA/M Jourdan; 253cl AA/M Jourdan; 253cc AA/ B Rieger; 253cr AA/B Smith; 253br Rex Features Ltd; 255cl AA/E Meacher; 255cc AA/C Sawyer; 255cr AA/B Smith; 256cl AA/C Sawyer; 256cc AA/T Souter; 256cr AA/B Rieger; 260cl AA/C Sawyer; 261tc AA/C Sawyer; 261bc AA/C Sawyer; 261r AA/C Sawyer; 262l AA/C Sawyer; 262br AA/C Sawyer; 263c AA/C Sawyer; 264bl AA/C Sawyer; 264tr AA/C Sawyer; 264br AA/C Sawyer; 265tl AA/C Sawyer; 265c AA/C Sawyer; 265r AA/C Sawyer; 266cl AA/C Sawyer; 266bl AA/C Sawyer; 266c AA/C Sawyer; 266br AA/C Sawyer; 267l AA/C Sawyer; 267tr AA/C Sawyer; 268tl AA/C Sawyer; 268tr AA/C Sawyer; 269bl AA/C Sawyer; 269r AA/C Sawyer; 270tl AA/C Sawyer; 270bl AA/C Sawyer; 270c AA/C Sawyer; 270br AA/C Sawyer; 271c AA/C Sawyer; 271cb AA/C Sawyer; 271r AA/C Sawyer; 272ct AA/C Sawyer; 272bc AA; 273cl AA/C Sawyer; 273r AA/C Sawyer; 274tr AA/C Sawyer; 275bl AA/C Sawyer; 275c AA/C Sawyer; 275tr AA/C Sawyer; 276tl AA/C Sawyer; 276cl AA/C Sawyer; 276c AA/C Sawyer; 276tr AA/C Sawyer; 277tl AA/C Sawyer; 277cb AA/C Sawyer; 277r AA/C Sawyer; 278c AA/C Sawyer; 278b AA/T Souter; 279cr AA/C Sawyer; 279bl AA/B Rieger; 279cbt AA/C Sawyer; 279cbb AA/C Sawyer; 279br AA/T Souter; 280cl AA/C Sawyer; 280c AA; 280cr AA/C Sawyer; 281cl AA/C Sawyer; 281c AA/C Sawyer; 281cr AA/C Sawyer; 286l AA/C Sawyer; 286r AA/C Sawyer; 287l AA/C Sawyer; 287c AA/C Sawyer; 287r AA/C Sawyer; 288bl AA/C Sawyer; 288tc AA/C Sawyer; 288bc AA/C Sawyer; 288r AA/C Sawyer; 289bl AA/C Sawyer; 289c AA/C Sawyer; 289tr AA/C Sawyer; 289br AA/C Sawyer; 290tl AA/C Sawyer; 290c AA/C Sawyer; 290r AA/C Sawyer; 291tl AA/C Sawyer; 291cl AA/C Sawyer; 291tc AA/C Sawyer; 291tr AA/C Sawyer; 291bl AA/C Sawyer; 292r AA/C Sawyer; 293cl AA/C Sawyer 293c AA/C Sawyer; 293bl AA/C Sawyer; 293bc AA/C Sawyer.

PLANNING

295 AA/C Sawyer; 299 AA/C Sawyer; 300 European Central Bank; 301l AA/C Sawyer; 301r AA/B Rieger; 305 AA/C Sawyer; 309 AA/M Jourdan; 310 AA M Jourdan.

Project editors
Kathryn Glendenning, Cathy Hatley

Interior design
David Austin, Glyn Barlow, Alan Gooch, Kate Harling, Bob Johnson,
Nick Otway, Carole Philp, Keith Russell

Additional interior design work
Nautilus Design, Jo Tapper

Picture research
Kathy Lockley, Carol Walker

Cover design
Tigist Getachew

Internal repro work
Susan Crowhurst, Ian Little, Michael Moody

Production
Helen Brown, Lyn Kirby

Mapping
Maps produced by the Mapping Services Department of AA Publishing

Main contributors
Lindsay Bennett, Heidi Ellison, Colin Follett, Kathryn Glendenning, Cathy Hatley, Elisabeth Morris,
Michael Nation, Josephine Perry, Laurence Phillips, Andrew Sanger, The Content Works

Copy editor
Philippa Richmond

Updater
Lindsay Bennett

Revision management
Bookwork Creative Associates Ltd

See It Paris
ISBN 978-1-4000-0692-2
Third Edition

Published in the United States by Fodor's Travel and simultaneously
in Canada by Random House of Canada Limited, Toronto.
Published in the United Kingdom by AA Publishing.

Fodor's is a registered trademark of Random House Inc, and Fodor's See It
is a trademark of Random House, Inc.
Fodor's Travel is a division of Random House, Inc.

Color separation by Keenes, UK
Printed and bound by Leo, China
10 9 8 7 6 5 4 3 2 1

Special Sales: This book is available for special discounts for bulk purchases for sales promotions or
premiums. Special editions, including personalized covers, excerpts of existing books, and corporate
imprints, can be created in large quantities for special needs. For more information, write to
Special Markets/Premium Sales, 1745 Broadway, MD 6-2, New York, NY 10019
or e-mail specialmarkets@randomhouse.com.

A03306
Mapping in this title produced from Paris data © Tele Atlas N.V. 2003
& mapping © ISTITUTO GEOGRAFICO DE AGOSTINI, Novara
Relief map images supplied by Mountain High Maps ® Copyright © 1993 Digital Wisdom, Inc
Weather chart statistics supplied by Weatherbase © Copyright 2003 Canty and Associates, LLC
Transport map © Communicarta Ltd, UK

Important Note: Time inevitably brings changes, so always confirm prices, travel facts,
and other perishable information when it matters. Although Fodor's cannot accept
responsibility for errors, you can use this guide in the confidence that
we have taken every care to ensure its accuracy.